FIFTH EDITION

# International Marketing

**Vern Terpstra**
**University of Michigan**

**Ravi Sarathy**
**Northeastern University**

The Dryden Press
**Harcourt Brace Jovanovich College Publishers**
Fort Worth   Philadelphia   San Diego
New York   Orlando   Austin   San Antonio
Toronto   Montreal   London   Sydney   Tokyo

Acquisitions Editor: Rob Zwettler
Project Editor: Karen Shaw
Art & Design Director: Jeanne Calabrese
Production Manager: Robert Lange
Permissions Editor: Doris Milligan
Director of Editing, Design, and Production: Jane Perkins


Interior and Cover Design: Shriver/Waterhouse Design, Inc.
Copy Editor and Indexer: Margaret Jarpey
Compositor: Impressions, Inc.
Text Type: 10/12 Times Roman

**Library of Congress Cataloging-in-Publication Data**
Terpstra, Vern.
      International marketing / Vern Terpstra, Ravi Sarathy. — 5th ed.
         p.    cm.
      Includes bibliographies and indexes.
      ISBN 0-03-032767-9
        1. Export marketing—Management.  I. Sarathy, Ravi.  II. Title
HF1416.T48    1991
658.8′48—dc20                                  90-3403

Printed in the United States of America
  2-032-9876543
Copyright © 1991, 1987, 1983, 1978, 1972 by The Dryden Press

Address orders:
The Dryden Press
Orlando, FL 32887




Harcourt Brace Jovanovich, Inc.
The Dryden Press
Saunders College Publishing


Map Insert: Copyright John Bartholomew & Son Limited.


Cover Illustration: © 1990 Curtis Parker.

# The Dryden Press Series in Marketing

# Preface

Our evening news constantly reminds us that we are, indeed, living in a global village. We hear about our "neighbors" in China, South Africa, eastern Europe, and other formerly remote places. This global village also has become a global marketplace in which the products of the world become available almost everywhere. Such international competition makes international marketing one of the most critical skills for business survival in today's world economy.

When this book was first published, international business was a subject occasionally taught in business schools. With each succeeding edition, business schools' coverage of international subjects has grown stronger and more sophisticated. This text has evolved accordingly. This fifth edition has been extensively revised to meet students' and practitioners' needs to know about the contemporary environment, problems, and practices in international marketing. It continues to address the challenges facing both small exporters and large multinationals. It is relevant not only for U.S. firms but for firms anywhere that want to market internationally. (Previous editions have been translated into Chinese — both in China and Taiwan.)

This edition emphasizes the importance of linking international marketing with the overall strategy of the firm. Integration of marketing with other functional areas, such as new product R&D and manufacturing, is essential to successful marketing worldwide. The growing strength and sophistication of global competitors are also emphasized in this edition. International marketing is about successfully meeting customer needs worldwide and doing so better than the competition — be it local companies or foreign multinationals.

## Changes to This Edition

This fifth edition introduces a new co-author, Ravi Sarathy, who has broad international experience. Together the authors have lived and worked professionally on every continent except Australia.

All chapters have been revised, plus there are three completely new chapters. Chapter 6, "Global Marketing Strategy," links international marketing strategy to overall corporate strategy. Chapter 16, "International Marketing of Services," covers this newly important and dynamic area. The third new chapter is "The Future of International Marketing," Chapter 18. Another new feature in this edition is the increased emphasis on Japanese international marketing and company experience.

Other major changes to the book include a revised introductory Chapter 1 with a wealth of recent examples to help convey the variety and excitement of international marketing. Chapters 7, 8, and 9 have additional new content summarizing recent developments and adding new examples. Pricing is covered in two chapters, 14 and 15, with additional treatment of topics such as hedging and countertrade. Chapter 17 integrates two chapters from the previous edition into one and covers planning, organizational structure, and control issues. A special feature of the book is the discussion of the single European market in 1992 in an Appendix to Chapter 2. Later chapters highlight other aspects of this major development, and the *Instructor's Manual* suggests how a teaching module on this topic can be developed by using the Appendix to Chapter 2 with additional elements such as readings and cases. Although the authors read and commented on each other's chapters, Professor Terpstra had primary responsibility for Chapters 2–5 and 10–13, while Professor Sarathy was responsible for Chapters 1, 6–9, and 14–18.

This edition includes 37 cases, half of which are new. This mixture of shorter and longer cases draws from the current experiences of companies in the United States, Europe, and Japan, as well as newly industrializing countries. These contemporary cases and examples about companies such as Boeing, Saatchi & Saatchi, and Pall Corporation help link theory to corporate practice and seek to stimulate and maintain student interest while demonstrating practical applications of international marketing concepts. Some cases from the previous edition have been included in the *Instructor's Manual.*

The *Instructor's Manual* also has been substantially revised. Over half the questions are new, with a greater emphasis on multiple choice questions. Detailed lecture notes have been added, and additional lecture illustrations and transparencies are provided to help instructors use the book. All new cases have detailed teaching notes to help the instructor use them effectively in the teaching process. We hope that this results in an enriched manual.

Finally, we have added a brand new pedagogical item to every chapter of the fifth edition. Entitled "Global Marketing," this new boxed feature highlights a specific international firm or situation that serves to provide the student with interesting, up-to-date examples of international marketing in action.

## Acknowledgments

This edition, like earlier ones, has benefited from the contributions of many people. We thank the hundreds of American, Asian, European, and Latin American executives we have worked with over the years in consulting, research, and seminars. They have given us many practical insights and examples. Our students, both in the United States and abroad, also have challenged and stimulated us to sharpen our analyses.

Many faculty colleagues have given us cases, materials, and constructive suggestions. We want to acknowledge some of them: Andrew C. Gross, Cleveland State University; Donald G. Halper, University of the Pacific; Basil Janavaras, Mankato State University; A.H. Kizilbash, Northern Illinois University; J. Alex Murray, Wilfred Laurier University; Philip J. Rosson, Dalhousie University; John K. Ryans, Jr., Kent State University; Dharma de Silva, Wichita State University; John A. Weber, University of Notre Dame; and Attila Yaprak, Wayne State University.

We want to thank those who reviewed this edition for their many helpful insights that contributed to the revision: Sanjeev Agarwal, University of Wisconsin–LaCrosse; Dharma de Silva, Wichita State University; Philip Dover, Babson College; Thomas Griffin, Pace University; Hale Newcomer, North Texas State University; Zahir Quraeshi,Western Michigan University; Daniel Rountree, Middle Tennessee State University; John Ryans, Kent State University; S. Samiee, University of South Carolina; and Joseph Yu, University of Illinois.

We would like to thank Professor Farok Contractor of Rutgers University for permission to include the Metro Corporation case in this edition. Special thanks are due to our research assistants Betsy Petrick and Bob Norberg in helping us gather material for this edition. We would also like to thank our families for their support and tolerance of the many hours spent in researching and writing this text. Our thanks also to our institutions and colleagues who have contributed with their comments and suggestions during the writing of this edition.

We wish to thank our editors at The Dryden Press — Rob Zwettler, Karen Shaw, and Maggie Jarpey — for their commitment to excellence. Finally, we always welcome comments and suggestions from users of this edition, as it is through such feedback that we can continue to provide an up-to-date and useful product.

Vern Terpstra
Ravi Sarathy
*September 1990*

# About the Authors

**Vern Terpstra** (Ph.D., M.B.A., University of Michigan) is Professor of International Business at the University of Michigan. He has taught at the Wharton School, Cranfield School of Management in Britain, Erasmus University in Rotterdam, Dalian Institute of Technology in China, and National Cheng Chi University in Taiwan. He has written numerous books and articles on international business. His books have been used around the world and two of them have been translated into Chinese. He is a past President of the Academy of International Business and is a Fellow of the Academy. He has consulted with corporations here and abroad and with government agencies.

**Ravi Sarathy** (Ph.D., University of Michigan) is Associate Professor of International Business at Northeastern University in Boston, Massachusetts. He has also taught in Brazil, Italy, and France. His articles have appeared in the *Journal of International Business Studies, California Management Review, International Marketing Review,* and others. He has served as an expert witness in tax court and has consulted in Brazil, Cameroon, India, and Europe.

# Brief Contents

# Contents

## Chapter 9      301
## International Product Policy: New-Product Development and Product-Line Policies

## Chapter 10      361
## Distribution: Entering Foreign Markets

## Part 3
## Coordinating International Marketing

637

PART 1

# The International Environment

In Part 1 we look at the world environment in which the international marketer must operate. The economic, political, and cultural dimensions of the world's markets form a complex mosaic that constrains the practice of international marketing.

CHAPTER 1

# Introduction
## The Concept of Global Marketing

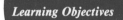

International marketing has become more important to the United States for three reasons: foreign markets constitute an increasing portion of the total world market; foreign competitors are increasing their market share in the United States; and foreign markets can be essential sources of low-cost products, technology, and capital. In a word, the U.S. economy is now more interdependent with world markets.

The main goals of this chapter are to:

1. Show how the United States is more interdependent with the world economy.
2. Distinguish between international marketing and marketing in the domestic context.
3. Through the examples of firms such as Nintendo and Walt Disney, show the varieties of ways in which a firm may practice international marketing.
4. Describe how large U.S. multinationals increasingly market overseas through foreign subsidiaries as well as through exports.
5. Emphasize that global marketing is a matter of perspective, in which firms consider the whole world as their market.

"The world is too much with us," said Wordsworth. In a different sense, that could be the complaint of many American businesses that see themselves threatened by imported goods. The threat has been growing. Imports were only 1 percent of United States gross national product (GNP) in 1954; they were 6 percent of GNP in 1964 and 10 percent of GNP in 1984! In any case, the interdependence suggested by such terms as *Global Village, Spaceship Earth*, and *World Economy* is being recognized by business managers as much as by politicians and ecologists. This book deals with the significance of this international interdependence for the business firm.

As can be seen in Table 1–1, U.S. imports have been steadily growing, contributing to a worsening balance of trade. Though U.S. interdependence with the world economy is still less than that of many of the other nations

3

**Table 1-1**                    **International Trade Profiles, Selected Countries**

|  | Exports | U.S. Imports $ Billions | GDP | Exports | Japan Imports $ Billions | GDP |
|---|---|---|---|---|---|---|
| 1988 | 508 | 629 | 4600* | 371 | 288 | 2806 |
| 1987 | 425 | 565 | 4484 | 304 | 214 | 2780 |
| 1986 | 375 | 499 | 4185 | 259 | 171 | 1956 |
| 1985 | 361 | 461 | 3947 | 220 | 169 | 1328 |
| 1984 | 361 | 455 | 3635 | 210 | 174 | 1255 |
| 1983 | 334 | 371 | 3276 | 183 | 161 | 1063 |
| 1982 | 349 | 350 | 3010 | 179 | 171 | 1062 |

*Estimate

n.a.–not available

Note that exports and imports are the total of merchandise exports and imports, together with other goods, services and income.

portrayed in Table 1–1, it is likely to increase. Many more U.S. firms, whether they like it or not, will be forced to become part of world markets and global competition.

International marketing is best explained by first briefly reviewing marketing in a domestic context. Although *marketing* can be defined in several ways, in this book, we define it broadly as the collection of activities undertaken by the firm to relate profitably to its market. Whereas the firm is, in some sense, master in its own house, its ultimate success depends primarily on how well it performs outside, in the marketplace. This requires knowledge of the market. Therefore, the first task of the firm is to study its prospective buyers. Who are they? Where are they? What factors are important in their purchase (or nonpurchase) of our product? The second task of the firm is to develop the products or services that satisfy customer needs and wants. The third is to set prices and terms on these products that appear reasonable to buyers, while at the same time returning a fair profit. The fourth task is distribution, making the products conveniently available to buyers. As its fifth task, the firm must inform the market about its wares; it will probably have to use some persuasion to get buyers interested. Furthermore, although the firm's marketing responsibility is thought to end with the sale, this is not always true. There is an implied warranty of satisfaction with the product; thus, the firm must often reassure the buyer, and, in many cases, perform after-sale service.

In addition, firms must monitor the marketing activity of their domestic and international competitors and develop appropriate long-term marketing strategies and competitive responses. Marketing management, therefore, is the planning and coordination of all of these activities in order to achieve a successful integrated marketing program.

| W. Germany | | | S. Korea | | | Brazil | | |
| Exports | Imports $ Billions | GDP | Exports | Imports $ Billions | GDP | Exports | Imports $ Billions | GDP |
|---|---|---|---|---|---|---|---|---|
| 395 | 328 | 1350* | 71 | 58 | 171 | 34 | n.a. | 354 |
| 360 | 298 | 1271 | 56 | 48 | 126 | 29 | 30 | 326 |
| 298 | 245 | 892 | 42 | 38 | 98 | 25 | 30 | 207 |
| 224 | 197 | 625 | 33 | 35 | 86 | 29 | 30 | 188 |
| 209 | 189 | 613 | 33 | 35 | 83 | 30 | 30 | 187 |
| 208 | 193 | 653 | 30 | 33 | 77 | 24 | 31 | 255 |
| 216 | 200 | 663 | 28 | 31 | 68 | 23 | 39 | 248 |

Source: Exports & Imports, International Financial Statistics, July 1988; GDP, 1987, Business International Indicators; GDP, 1982–86, World Bank Development Report, various years.

## Characteristics of International Marketing

The activities just described—market intelligence, product development, pricing, distribution, and promotion—together constitute the essence of marketing. What then is *international marketing?* It is finding out what customers want around the world and then satisfying these wants better than other competitors, both domestic and international. At its simplest, it is the practice of all of these activities at home, plus the effort to export products to a few countries. The same firm becomes more of an international marketer as it increases its direct involvement in these markets by participating in pricing, promotion, after-sale service, and ultimately, manufacturing.

The company may begin manufacturing overseas to lower its costs, in order to be able to match the lower prices of strong international competition. Sometimes, it might be manufacturing and selling in the same market. However, a firm may not find it feasible to go alone into foreign markets. In this case, its international-marketing endeavor becomes more complex as it joins with a partner who has specialized knowledge of a specific foreign market and its customers, or, perhaps, good contacts in the local government. The partner may be needed to share risk and contribute capital or products or a distribution channel. Sometimes the local government may prohibit the foreign company from operating in its country unless it has a local partner.

Companies unwilling to commit capital and management time to marketing in foreign countries might be happy to settle for less risk, less involvement, and lower returns by licensing their product or technology to a foreign company. The goal is still to earn profits from foreign demand, but the approach is indirect. Management is saying: We'll take fewer headaches in return for lower profits.

Some firms find that the only way to match foreign competition in their home market is to import their products, either from factories established and operated overseas or from independent manufacturers overseas who make products according to designs and specifications provided by the home company.

Overseas customers can also force a company to change the ways it does business. A foreign buyer may insist that the selling firm accept payment in kind: orange juice or wine or chickens in return for machinery. The firm might accept the offer, and then find itself peddling orange juice and chickens around the world, a consequence of the growing trend toward countertrade in international marketing.

Thus, international marketing can include activities such as

- Overseas manufacturing.
- Working with local partners (joint ventures).
- Licensing.
- Importing, sometimes from overseas subcontractors.
- Countertrade.

The complexity of international marketing is largely due to two factors: global competition and the global environment. Competitors now come from all over the world, with a myriad of different strengths. Likewise, the global environment presents a bewildering variation in national governments, culture, and income levels. Domestic marketing management is often portrayed as the task of responding to the uncontrollable factors in the firm's environment while manipulating the controllable factors. International marketing management has the same task, but with the critical distinction that both the "uncontrollables" and the "controllables" are different internationally. Thus, price, product, channels of distribution, and promotion will vary across, say, France, Brazil, India, and the United States.

An added dimension of international marketing management is the coordination and integration of the firm's many national marketing programs into an effective multinational program. Indeed, a principal rationale of multinational business operations, as opposed to the alternative of independent national companies, is that the division of labor and the transfer of know-how in international operations enable the whole to be greater than the sum of its parts.

A practical result of these differences is that an *international* marketing manager requires a competence broader than that of domestic marketing managers or managers of marketing in a specific foreign country. Failure to recognize this may account for the fact that a majority of the blunders committed by American firms abroad are in the field of marketing.

In other words, the international marketing manager has a dual responsibility: *foreign marketing* (marketing within foreign countries) and *global marketing* (coordinating marketing in multiple markets, in the face of global competition). These two aspects of global marketing management are further discussed in Chapter 6 and illustrated throughout Part 2.

# The Global Marketplace

Let us consider some examples of companies operating in the global marketplace to get a sense of the range of activities that constitute international marketing. It is helpful to see how different companies make decisions regarding their products, prices charged, distribution channels, countries sold to, and partners chosen, all in order to increase sales and profits.

**Nintendo in America**

Is there a teenager in America who has not played a *Nintendo* game? This 100-year-old Japanese company of the same name originally sold playing cards and began marketing the Nintendo game machine as a "Famicom," a family computer, in Japan in 1983. The company test-marketed its computer in New York in 1984. By 1988 it had achieved a greater penetration with it than had any other home computer or personal computer (PC): 28 million Nintendo machines had been sold to Japanese and U.S. consumers, and 17 percent of American homes had the machine.

The Nintendo is simple, designed to be hooked up to the home TV set, and the company calls it a "game" rather than a "computer" so as not to intimidate families. The first Nintendo machines did not have a keyboard, had no functions other than to play games, and were sold through toy stores, priced at just under $100 retail.

But the United States had been through one video game craze with the Atari just a few years earlier, with the market peaking at $3.2 billion in 1983. Therefore, Nintendo carefully controlled the availability of games for its machines. It designed the Nintendo machine with a proprietary chip, so that cartridges containing the game software would play on the Nintendo only if they had a complementary compatible chip—one that only Nintendo could insert. Therefore, anyone who wanted to sell a game for Nintendo had to license the game software to Nintendo and allow that company to manufacture the cartridge.

Nintendo's licensing agreements also required that the software developers not sell the same game to other video game manufacturers. Such control enabled Nintendo to keep the games scarce and relatively high-priced at $40 a cartridge. It prevented a proliferation of shallow and repetitive games, which it saw as the cause of the fading of the Atari-led video game boom in 1983.

The result: U.S. sales of $800 million in 1987 and $1.7 billion in 1988, and a U.S. market share of nearly 80 percent. Nintendo was able to capture one of every five dollars spent on toys in the United States. Its preeminent position in the American home has led AT&T to join it in developing home shopping and information services accessible by means of the Nintendo game machine. Previous attempts at delivering videotext services to U.S. homes have failed because relatively few households owned computers.

Nintendo has been developing a 16-bit "Super Family Computer" as its next-generation product. Naturally, companies are challenging Nintendo's monopoly. In court, Atari is suing Nintendo's use of the proprietary cartridge on antitrust grounds, claiming that it unfairly excludes competition. In the marketplace, NEC, the giant Japanese electronics company, is attempting to introduce a family entertainment computer into the United States, NEC's TurboGrafx 16, priced at $199 and expandable to include a compact disk player and an audio/video enhancer. NEC has been selling this system in Japan since October 1987 and was able to obtain a 28 percent unit share of the market. The company hopes for similar success in the United States, seeking to break Nintendo's hold on the market. Nintendo's success is due to its vision in seeing that middle-class families in the advanced nations worldwide were ready for an unintimidating family computer.[1]

**Disney with a French Accent**

With characters such as Mickey Mouse that are known all over the world from movies and cartoons shown for 50 years, Tokyo Disneyland was a logical creation. It was started in 1983 as a joint venture between Mitsui Real Estate Development Co. and Keisei Railway Co. Walt Disney Co. has no ownership share; it designed the amusement park and supplies its managerial expertise, receiving in return royalties of 10 percent of gate and 5 percent of concessions. As Table 1–2 shows, the Japanese have welcomed Disney and his characters with open hearts and purses. Within five years of opening, they were spending about $39 per person.

Disney then began expanding into Europe. Construction of Euro Disneyland, begun in the summer of 1989, 20 miles east of Paris, will cost $2.8 billion for its first phase. Disney will own 49 percent, the maximum permitted by the French government. Disney has already begun promoting the Disney characters with corporate partners. Renault saluted Mickey Mouse in its Champs-Élysées showrooms, and Banque Nationale de Paris is featuring Mickey in promotions. Disney has started a Disney Channel on European television in a joint venture with media entrepreneur Rupert Murdoch and plans to air a new Disney entertainment special in Europe in 1990.

**Table 1-2**                           **Attendance and Spending at Disney Parks**

|  | Walt Disney World | | Tokyo Disneyland | |
|---|---|---|---|---|
| Year | Attendance (Thousands) | Spending per Person ($) | Attendance (Thousands) | Spending per Person ($) |
| 1983 | 22,714 | 35.21 | 5,683 | 25.00 |
| 1984 | 21,121 | 39.76 | 10,151 | 25.52 |
| 1985 | 21,760 | 43.08 | 10,450 | 25.34 |
| 1986 | 24,155 | 47.91 | 10,700 | 30.00 |
| 1987 | 26,740 | 52.06 | 10,950 | 39.13 |
| 1988[a] | 25,830 | 57.71 | 11,100 | 41.74 |

[a]Estimate.

Source: Lee Isgur, "Walt Disney Co. Report," Paine Webber, August 24, 1988.

Disney's theme parks are the core of its business, accounting for 60 percent of sales and 64 percent of profits in 1988. As the U.S. market matures, Euro Disneyland is expected to be the major thrust of the company's growth through the year 2000, with a goal of 11 million European visitors in the first year of operation in 1992. A high-speed train connection will enable visitors to reach the park in 30 minutes. The Paris location was chosen in part because of a population of 109 million people within a six-hour drive.

Disney will adapt the park to European tastes. "Fantasyland" will focus on the Grimms Brothers fairy tales and Lewis Carroll's *Alice in Wonderland*. A "Discoveryland" exhibit will draw attention to European thinkers such as Jules Verne, Leonardo da Vinci, and H. G. Wells. Signs will be in multiple languages, and employees will be expected to speak at least two languages. And the world will watch Disney rake in the cash as it sells quintessentially American tastes with a European accent.[2]

## You See the Nicest People on Japanese Motorbikes

The Japanese have long appreciated that international marketing can be profitable. In 1960 Japanese motorcycles were almost unknown in the United States, but Japan was already the biggest producer of motorcycles in the world. Its small bikes, 125cc, were made for narrow and crowded streets and were affordable given Japan's low purchasing power. In the United States, motorcycles meant Harley Davidson hogs, ridden by the "Wild Ones" made famous by Marlon Brando—definitely not what the boy next door would ride. Japan set out to convince Americans to buy small 125cc motorcycles instead.

Beginning in 1960, first Honda, and then Yamaha and Suzuki, began marketing motorcycles in California. Their ad, "You meet the nicest people on a Honda," was designed to change the image of motorcycles in general. Producing about 90 percent of the world's motorcycles, Japan enjoyed economies of scale that allowed it to price bikes at around $250, low enough to attract many new buyers who had never owned a motorcycle before. In addition, California was relatively close to Japan, and its citizens had a reputation for being willing to try new ideas and fads.

As sales mounted, the Japanese expanded distribution gradually across the United States, ploughing back profits into distribution and advertising. They also began producing and marketing larger motorcycles, convincing many of their customers to trade up to more powerful models. By 1966 Japanese manufacturers had about 85 percent of the U.S. market and were beginning to go after Harley Davidson, with large bikes of 750cc and up. They also introduced new models of motorcycles, off-road bikes, and combination bikes for touring. In 1983 Harley Davidson had to ask the U.S. government for protection as it tried to recover from years of losses and loss of market share brought on by the inexorable march of Japanese motorcycles. What is astonishing is that Japan began marketing these bikes to the United States in 1960, at a time when few American companies took Japan seriously as a competitor.[3] Large numbers of Americans were converted into buyers of small motorcycles, a market segment that had not previously existed.

**Profiting from
the Newly Rich**

Succeeding in international marketing has much to do with forming and understanding consumer tastes in different countries. Dickson Poon of Hong Kong has made himself a fortune estimated at $180 million by selling luxury brand-name goods to the newly rich from Japan and the fast-growing countries of Southeast Asia, namely, Hong Kong, Malaysia, Singapore, South Korea, and Taiwan. While working as an apprentice in Geneva at Chopard, a jeweler and maker of fine watches, he absorbed the ambience of high-fashion, high-price retailing. Stores were understated, refined, luxurious, and there was no hard sell. He took this style back to Hong Kong, opening a European-type store with fine interiors in Hong Kong's most upscale shopping center. He emphasized attentive service and carefully selected merchandise, concentrating on brands such as Chopard, Rolex, Hermes, and Audemars Piguet. The concept worked, and he next obtained the Charles Jourdan fashion franchise, adding similar names such as Polo/Ralph Lauren and Guy Laroche, and obtaining, in some cases, licensing rights to manufacture and distribute franchise products in the Far East or even, occasionally, worldwide. His watchword is elegant shops in prime locations; he now operates over 70 stores. But his winning insight is the appeal of famous brand names to newly rich customers. He claims, "The Japanese today are the single most brand-name-conscious consumers in the world." It helps that prices within Japan are high, and that the Japanese feel that they are getting bargains by buying in Hong Kong. About one-third of Dickson's sales are to traveling Japanese businessmen and tourists.

Dickson Poon also manufactures and wholesales mid-range merchandise, and he is expanding rapidly into neighboring countries, such as Taiwan, with plans to add stores in key European cities in the next few years. In November 1987, he purchased S. T. Dupont, which makes luxury lighters and pens. His aim is to use the Dupont name to introduce new lines of menswear, luggage, and watches. His business is vanity, making a profit from it wherever it can be found.[4]

**Korean Furs
(For Less)**

Similar thinking drives the world's largest fur manufacturer, Jindo Fur Company of South Korea. Jindo's goal is to develop a chain of stores selling furs worldwide. It targets the low end of the market—furs selling under $2,000. This figure was chosen because approximately 60 percent of all fur sales are at or below this price. In order to sell profitably at this price Jindo uses Korean labor and vertical integration. It buys pelts at auctions in North America, Scandinavia and Russia. Jindo then treats and assembles the pelts in its Seoul factories before selling them in its worldwide outlets. There are 45 Jindo Fur Salons, located in South Korea, Hong Kong, Europe, North America, Hawaii and Guam. Although tropical islands might seem like odd locations, Jindo markets furs to tourists on vacation.

Jindo began its worldwide marketing by selling in duty-free shops to Japanese tourists and advertising in in-flight magazines. Its discounted prices were appealing to Japanese tourists when compared with the high prices charged at home. Recently a joint venture, Jindorus, was established with Interlink of Russia. The first store is planned for the Intourist Hotel in Moscow, with 10 more to be opened in two years. Jindo sees a huge untapped market potential for furs, but attention to both costs and global marketing expansion is essential to its long-term success.

**Where the
Buyers Are**

Sometimes foreign markets may be the only markets into which a company's products can be sold. MRS Technology, in Chelmsford, Massachusetts, makes equipment used to manufacture large liquid crystal displays (LCDs) that can be used as screens on high-quality televisions and computer terminals. All of MRS's customers are Japanese.

The company's flat-panel LCDs are made by machines costing $1.2 million each. They are used heavily for small color televisions with 4-inch screens, about 2 million of which were sold in Japan in 1988, though only 150,000 were imported into the United States; such flat-panel screens are compact, light, able to run on batteries, and provide color quality and sharpness equal to that of the best photographs made with 35mm cameras.

The trend in Japan is to make larger flat-panel screens (12 to 14 inches), hoping to benefit from projected worldwide demand for larger LCD-screen TV sets of about 10 million units by 1995. But Japanese equipment produces only 10 glass substrates per hour, while MRS can produce 35.

MRS's problem is that there are no American TV manufacturers left except for Zenith. Therefore, MRS must sell to the Japanese (though there are also sales possibilities with Dutch and French manufacturers), so MRS has acquired a Japanese partner, Dainippon Screen Mfg. Co., itself partially owned by Sony. The danger is that Canon and Nikon will quickly copy MRS technology and take over the market. But without the Japanese market, MRS would have no market at all.[5]

While MRS's situation is extreme, foreign demand may represent the majority of demand for a product. Take water desalination, for instance. About two-thirds of the world's water desalination plants used to convert salt water into fresh water are in Saudi Arabia. These plants use considerable energy and are expensive to run. Saudi Arabia has plentiful energy and high incomes, and it is a country where salt water is plentiful while fresh water is scarce. Ionics Inc. of Watertown, Massachusetts, has built its business around water desalination, with considerable sales coming from North Africa and the Middle East.

**Where the
Ideas Are**

Overseas markets can also be a source of new product ideas. Takasago International of Japan has introduced a line of "mood-enhancing" fragrances—those that influence people to eat less or work harder or sleep better. In one experiment, it found that a soothing lemon fragrance sent through an office reduced terminal operators' error rate by half. Takasago has collaborated with a construction company, Shimizu, to envelop entire buildings with its fragrances. One application is at a highway rest stop, where cedar smells waft out of the central air conditioning system, to relax drivers. Shimizu plans to install a similar prototype system in a hotel that it owns in the United States. Some of the fragrances created by Takasago have been licensed by Avon Products for use in the United States in a floral bath line meant to relax bathers.

## Global Marketing

### Exporting Lumber to Japan

In the depths of the recession in 1981, Webco Lumber of Oregon watched its sales drop 80 percent from the 1979 peak, and over half of its employees were laid off or had left. Webco decided to look for some Japanese business. Participating in a two-week trade mission to Japan, led by Oregon's Department for Economic Development, it met with 60 Japanese companies. The trip cost $5,000. Barbara Webb, president, told the treasurer, Ronald Webb, "I don't think we can afford not to go."

Within six weeks of the trip to Japan, several Japanese companies sent representatives to the Webco sawmill. They were careful buyers, with exacting standards. They wanted hemlock, white fir, and Douglas fir grown in the Cascade range, harvested from the western slopes between altitudes of 2,000 and 4,500 feet. Such trees grow more slowly, leading to a tighter ring count and a more attractive grain. Twenty rings an inch is considered ideal by Japanese buyers, and eight rings are the minimum accepted. The Japanese use a traditional post-and-beam method of construction, slower and perhaps less strong than the interlocking frame of hidden two-by-fours that the United States uses, but requiring 20 percent less wood. More wood is thus left exposed, in accordance with the Japanese appreciation for attractive wood grain. Hence, Webco had to be more careful in harvesting lumber meant for sale to the Japanese.

The Japanese use different sizes of wood, too. The American mill would have to change its sawmill setup and also its woodcutting process in the forest, where trees are "bucked" to the appropriate length. The Japanese buyer is also insistent on exact sizes whereas in the United States sawmills cut large volumes that produce minor variations in standard sizes.

When Webco began cutting its first major Japanese order, a Japanese representative was on hand, and he would periodically stop the cutting to measure the dimensions. An order that would normally be cut in one and a half days took twice as long. Webco found that all of its Japanese customers insisted on watching their orders being cut, so it actually converted one of its buildings into a guesthouse for these buyers. The unfamiliar sizes took longer to cut, too. But the volume of Japanese orders enabled the mill to grow again and begin rehiring workers.

The Japanese buyers wanted high quality and a long-term relationship, extending even after the U.S. industry recovered and sales could be diverted back to U.S. buyers. In the past U.S. mills had used export orders as a way of sopping up excess capacity, dropping them as soon as U.S. business became available again. Webco will not follow that pattern. The company's export business from Japan, says Barbara Webb, "is the only reason we are alive."

Source: "Small Sawmill Survives by Setting Its Blades for Exports to Japan," *The Wall Street Journal*, May 7, 1982.

---

Similarly, Traffic Monitoring Technologies of Texas has been leasing a European device called the *photoradar* to U.S. police districts. The device, which has been used in Europe for over a decade, consists of a high-speed camera linked to a radar gun that shoots a beam across the highway to detect speeding cars, evading radar detectors in cars. Pictures of the speeding vehicle allow police to send a ticket by mail to the owner of the offending car. They need not risk the potential danger of approaching the car.

## Learning from the Examples

As our examples show, there are several reasons for a company to market internationally:

1. The most obvious reason is the market potential of world markets. Firms such as Nintendo, Disney, the Japanese motorcycle industry, and Jindo Furs have all benefited from exploiting foreign market potential.

2. Geographic diversification is another reason. Webco Lumber is a firm whose long-run prospects are brighter for having diversified internationally.
3. Using up excess production capacity and taking advantage of a low-cost position due to experience-curve economies and economies of scale is another reason. The Japanese motorcycle industry's thrust into the United States was aided greatly by its superior low-cost position.
4. A product can be near the end of its life cycle in the domestic market while beginning to generate growth abroad. Dickson Poon's export of brand-name luxury goods marketing to the Far East is an example of taking advantage of the general rise in conspicuous consumption that accompanies prosperity.
5. Sometimes overseas markets can be the source of new products and ideas. Companies in foreign markets can become joint-venture partners, providing capital and market access, as in the case of MRS Technology.

## The U.S. Firm in the Global Marketplace

While the global market is attractive, U.S. firms have been slow to take advantage of it. The United States has always been one of the world's largest markets itself. It is also a self-contained, continent-sized market. For about 20 years after World War II, there was little foreign competition, but now foreign firms from all over the world vie for a piece of the United States market. At the same time, other countries have grown so fast and become so prosperous that their markets are sometimes larger and more attractive than the U.S. market. Examples include the fax machine, which initially grew rapidly in Japan, and only subsequently became popular in the United States, as the Japanese market was reaching saturation. And the market for railroad cars is small in the United States, as compared to Europe, where train transportation is more popular. Also, the United States has legislated the building of nuclear power plants out of existence, even though foreign countries still accept them as a source of energy.

Ignoring foreign markets and foreign competition has two dangers for U.S. companies: losing market share at home and not profiting from higher growth in overseas markets.

**Export Sales and Sales from Foreign Subsidiaries**

Larger U.S. firms have generally been more able to participate in global marketing due to their superior financial and managerial resources. Table 1–3 lists U.S. companies with the largest export sales that also have foreign sales, that is, from their foreign sales subsidiaries. Note that some of the largest U.S. exporters, such as Boeing Co. (exports of $7.85 billion, 46 percent of 1988 sales), McDonnell Douglas ($3.47 billion, 23 percent) and Raytheon ($1.31 billion, 16 percent) are not included in this list as they have no significant foreign revenues. Also missing are firms such as Mobil (foreign revenues of $33 billion), Texaco ($16.3 billion), IT&T ($10.4 billion), Procter & Gamble ($7.3 billion) and Xerox ($5.7 billion), all of which have insignificant exports compared to revenues obtained through subsidiaries located overseas.

**Table 1-3**                **Export Sales, Foreign Sales, and Total Sales of U.S. Multinationals, 1988 (Billions of Dollars)**

| Company | Export Sales | Foreign Sales[a] | Total Sales |
|---|---|---|---|
| General Motors | 9.4 | 29.1 | 121.1 |
| Ford Motor | 8.8 | 41.8 | 92.4 |
| General Electric | 5.7 | 4.6 | 49.4 |
| Int'l Business Machines | 4.95 | 34.4 | 59.7 |
| Chrysler | 4.3 | 4.1 | 35.5 |
| E. I. DuPont de Nemours | 4.2 | 12.9 | 32.5 |
| Caterpillar | 2.9 | 3.1 | 10.4 |
| United Technologies | 2.8 | 5.3 | 18.1 |
| Eastman Kodak | 2.3 | 7.1 | 17.0 |
| Digital Equipment | 2.1 | 5.7 | 11.5 |
| Hewlett-Packard | 2.1 | 5.1 | 9.8 |
| Unisys | 2.0 | 4.5 | 9.9 |
| Philip Morris | 1.9 | 5.5 | 25.9 |
| Motorola | 1.7 | 3.96 | 8.3 |
| Occidental Petroleum | 1.7 | 1.5 | 19.4 |
| Allied-Signal | 1.5 | 2.7 | 11.9 |
| Union Carbide | 1.4 | 2.6 | 8.3 |
| Westinghouse Electric | 1.1 | 1.3 | 12.5 |
| Dow Chemical | 1.1 | 9.2 | 16.7 |
| Monsanto | 1.1 | 3.1 | 8.3 |
| Exxon | .9 | 48.2 | 79.6 |
| Intel | .9 | 1.2 | 2.9 |
| Minnesota Mining & Mfg. | .8 | 4.2 | 10.6 |
| Phillips Petroleum | .7 | 1.6 | 11.3 |
| Deere | .6 | 1.7 | 5.4 |
| Rockwell Int'l | .6 | 1.96 | 11.95 |
| Merck | .6 | 2.9 | 5.9 |
| Honeywell | .6 | 1.6 | 7.1 |
| Aluminum Co. of America | .6 | 3.5 | 9.8 |
| Dresser Industries | .6 | 1.7 | 3.9 |
| Amoco | .6 | 4.8 | 21.2 |
| Baxter International | .5 | 1.6 | 6.9 |

[a]Foreign sales are sales by a company's overseas operations. Export sales are made by the U.S.–based company. Thus, total foreign revenues would be the total of export sales plus foreign sales.

Source: Derived from "America's 50 Biggest Exporters," *Fortune*, July 17, 1989; and "The 100 Largest U.S. Multinationals," *Forbes*, July 24, 1989.

For almost every company on the list, foreign revenues exceed export sales. The reason is that it is more efficient for them to sell from their foreign manufacturing subsidiaries than through exports. It may even be that exports have no chance, either being too high-priced in relation to local competition, or being kept out by government barriers. Most of the firms on the list could not maintain their market share in foreign markets without establishing a foreign subsidiary.

The question of how much a firm should obtain from foreign revenues and how much it should export is unresolved. Is it better to be a Ford, with foreign revenues five times that of exports, or an IBM, with foreign revenues nine times that of exports, than to be a Boeing, which gets most of its overseas sales through exports from the United States? As we shall see later in this book, as market conditions and the product life cycle change, companies may find that effective selling overseas requires foreign subsidiaries, and that such foreign subsidiary sales may replace exports.

**International Marketing: The Trade Barrier of The Mind**

As the trade deficit shows, the United States lags behind other nations in the general level of international trade activity. Then how does a U.S. firm approach overseas markets? In most cases, reluctantly.

As Kenneth Butterworth, chairman of Loctite Corp., puts it, "The problem really lies in the mind. That is the greatest trade barrier in America."[6] In other words, long insularity and overdependence on the American market has made American firms unsure about their ability to capture markets overseas. Culture, language, and environmental differences are sometimes intimidating. Firms from other countries, however, have certainly overcome such differences in entering U.S. markets. And many U.S. companies are following suit. Loctite Corp., for example, insists on looking like a local firm, rarely posting an American executive overseas permanently. Over half its employees are not American, and most of its top managers have overseas executive experience. Such overseas assignments have taught them the value of persistence and patience in approaching foreign markets.

Due to continued U.S. trade deficits, small and medium-sized businesses are being urged, both at the federal and state level, to export. They can get help by signing up on trade missions sponsored by the U.S. Department of Commerce and other organizations. Export finance is available to carry export receivables for longer periods, and to offer favorable interest-rate financing. The greater number of foreigners and immigrants hired by these companies helps them learn about opportunities in foreign markets, as well as efficient ways to approach these markets. A weaker dollar has also made exporting easier. From its peak in 1985, the dollar had declined by half in 1989, against currencies such as the yen, the German mark, and the Swiss franc. This makes U.S. products more competitive and allows U.S. firms to raise dollar prices while staying lower priced than foreign competitors.

Ultimately, international marketing is a matter of perspective. The term *global marketing*[7] best captures this perspective of the world as the market, with individual countries being submarkets. For those who hold such a view, the distinction between domestic and international marketing disappears, and the focus is on market opportunities, *wherever they may be.*

## Many Roads to Foreign Markets

When the firm chooses to become an international marketer, its degree of commitment to foreign markets can vary widely. The following sections give an overview of the range of possible ways of engaging in international marketing.

**Casual or Accidental Exporting.**   At this passive level of involvement, the firm may be selling abroad without even knowing it. Resident buyers for foreign companies may buy the firm's goods and send them overseas while the firm considers these typical domestic sales. Regular American customers of industrial goods producers may export the firm's goods as part of their supplies for their own foreign operations. Opportunistic firms may see such occasional exporting as a way to unload an unexpected surplus or some obsolete inventory.

**Active Exporting.**   Because of the number of unsolicited orders from abroad, an overseas move by a competitor, a company officer's hearing a speech or success story about exporting, or for any of several other reasons, the firm may decide to seek export sales actively. The company may either set up its own in-house export operation or hire some outside organization to handle its export marketing. The key point here is that the firm is making a commitment to seek export business.

**Foreign Licensing.**   The firm may license foreign manufacturers to produce its products in the foreign market instead of exporting. The company's products are now being produced in foreign markets, even though by proxy.

**Overseas Marketing by the Firm.**   Establishment of a sales office or marketing subsidiary abroad represents a further commitment to international business. Foreign marketing is controlled more directly by the firm through its physical presence in the market.

**Foreign Production and Foreign Marketing.**   A firm reaches the utmost degree of international involvement when it engages in its own foreign manufacturing operations. Significant financial and managerial resources probably will be needed for foreign production, though a joint venture will mean a sharing of costs and risks with the partner, who is usually a national.

Thus, there is a wide range of possibilities for involvement in international marketing. Even the small firm can be a successful international marketer through a type of involvement appropriate to its own situation and resources. The billion-dollar corporations have a wider range of choices, but even for them the alternatives vary on the basis of division, product line, and country.

Moreover, there is no necessary progression from casual exporting to foreign production and marketing, although there are many examples of this. A large, diversified company is apt to be participating at all these levels of involvement for different products or in different countries. For example, General Electric owns several manufacturing plants abroad. It has joint ventures in some countries, licensing in others, and a large export operation from the United States. The company even used an export agent for foreign sales of its line of aircraft lamps. GE's variety of international marketing activities accounted for 1988 sales of $10.3 billion: $5.7 billion of exports to unaffiliated companies and $4.6 billion from foreign operations and licensing.

Marketing strategies, of course, will depend in large part on the method of foreign-market involvement a firm chooses. For example, the pricing problems facing the exporter will differ from those facing a foreign subsidiary or joint venture. The promotional options available to a licensor will be more restricted than those open to a firm that is the sole owner of an operation. These important managerial implications will be examined in Part 2.

## The Approach of This Book

The sources of the differences between international and domestic marketing are to be found not in the functions themselves but in the parameters that determine how the functions are performed. Therefore, students of international marketing should be able to identify the relevant parameters and understand how they affect the marketing program. This book assumes that readers have that ability from their background in other marketing courses. Part 1 discusses the world environment in which international marketing is practiced, whereas Part 2 analyzes the management of marketing in this multinational context. Part 3 deals with planning and coordinating the international marketing program.

**Part 1: International Environment (Chapters 1-5).**  In domestic business studies, consideration of the environment plays a critical though somewhat unrecognized role in the behavior of the firm. A number of "environmental" courses in the curriculum deal with topics such as business and society, business and government, business conditions, and business law. In the functional courses, too, much attention is paid to the external environment of the firm. In marketing, for example, there will be discussions of buyer behavior, demographic trends, competition, laws regulating pricing or promotion, developments in retailing, and the like. Part 1 of this text attempts to cover the same ground for international marketing.

An illustration from another business function, accounting, might help to highlight further the influence of environment. If we ask what determines the practice of accounting in the United States today, we would answer with a number of factors, including the following:

1. The Internal Revenue Service
2. The Securities and Exchange Commission
3. Requirements of state and local governments
4. Requirements of other organizations such as the New York Stock Exchange or the Interstate Commerce Commission
5. The role of business schools in teaching accounting and conducting research
6. Certification examinations, such as for the CPA
7. The role of professional organizations, such as the American Accounting Association and the American Institute of Certified Public Accountants

8. The influence of the "Big Eight" accounting firms
9. The complex structure of American business enterprise and the separation of ownership from management
10. The historical influence of English accounting practice

If we then ask what determines the practice of accounting in France or Brazil, we see immediately that there is a nearly complete lack of identity or uniformity of parameters in the different countries. There are important similarities, of course, but the differences are more striking. Asking the same questions about other business functions, such as marketing, gives a similar result.

**Part 2: International Marketing Management (Chapters 6-16).**   The various functions of marketing as they are performed in the international environment are discussed in Part 2. An examination of the problems peculiar to international marketing should help to broaden the student's understanding of marketing in general as well. The foreign environment dealt with in Part 1 will then be seen to be the key variable in international marketing. In addition, Part 2 stresses the importance of an overall marketing strategy to shape and guide the formulation and implementation of specific international marketing tasks.

**Part 3: Coordinating International Marketing (Chapters 17, 18).**   A second critical international aspect of marketing management, considered in Part 3, is the task of integrating and coordinating many individual national marketing programs into an effective multinational operation. For purposes of this text, the principal actors in the international marketing drama are the practitioners, that is, the firms and managers who actually market internationally. This does not mean that consumers, governments, advertising agencies, and other participants are not involved. It merely means that our major focus will be on the problems and decisions facing management in international marketing.

A large part of our discussion will center on international marketing by manufacturers. However, the specific international marketing problems of service industries are covered in Chapter 16. We will discuss and illustrate with many examples the large multinational firms' marketing practices. By this we do not mean to exclude the smaller firms. Much of the discussion will apply equally as well to small firms as to large ones. Many of the problems peculiar to small firms in international marketing will be covered in the discussion of exporting throughout the chapters in Part 2.

# Summary

As foreign economies continue to grow and account for a larger portion of the total world market, and as foreign competitors actively seek market share in the United States, many U.S. firms are being forced into some degree of international marketing. This may extend to foreign manufacturing, carrying out joint ventures with local partners, licensing, importing, and taking part in countertrade transactions. The varied strengths of foreign competitors and the ramifications of dealing with different national governments and economic and cultural differences in foreign markets contribute to the complexity of international marketing.

Companies compete globally because (1) strong market potential exists overseas, (2) selling internationally allows them to enhance their long-run profitability, (3) low-cost production and quality are critical to successfully competing in global markets, and (4) they can achieve success by carefully choosing certain market segments, as witnessed by Dickson Poon's success in profitably marketing luxury goods to the growing numbers of newly rich in the Far East.

Large U.S. multinationals are more likely to get more of their foreign revenues from sales of their foreign subsidiaries than through exports. This can be a key element of strategic success in international marketing. More important, though, is a global-marketing perspective of the world as one market, with individual countries treated as submarkets and the focus on exploiting market opportunities wherever they may occur.

## Questions

1.1    What is international marketing, and how does it differ from domestic marketing?

1.2    Why is international marketing important to most U.S. firms?

1.3    Consider the examples described in the section, "The Global Marketplace." Compare and contrast the international marketing actions of these firms. Focus on their choices in the areas of products, market segments, the sequential choice of countries to sell to, pricing, and the use of licensing and joint ventures.

1.4    Why did Webco decide to export lumber to Japan? How were Japanese buyers different from their U.S. customers?

1.5    How do large U.S. multinationals compete in the global marketplace? Why do most of them sell more from their foreign subsidiaries than through exports?

1.6    "The greatest trade barrier to exporting lies in the mind." Explain.

1.7    "Global marketing is a shift in perspective." Explain.

1.8    Choose a prominent publicly held company in your city and find out what its total foreign revenues have been for the past five years. Also, study the comments about international markets made by the chairman of the company in its annual report. How important is international marketing to this firm?

## Endnotes

[1]"Just Like the Computer Games It Sells, Nintendo Defies Persistent Challengers," *The Wall Street Journal*, June 27, 1989. "Atari Tests Technology's Antitrust Aspect," *The Wall Street Journal*, December 14, 1988.

[2]"Disney's Magic PR Job in Europe," *Boston Globe*, April 2, 1989.

[3]See *Strategy Alternatives for the British Motorcycle Industry*, Her Majesty's Stationery Office 1975, and *Note on the Motorcycle—1975*, Harvard Business School, Case #578–210.

[4]Andrew Tanzer, "Keep the Calculators out of Sight," *Forbes*, March 20, 1989.

[5]"Selling the Future—to Japan," *Boston Globe*, January 31, 1989.

[6]"You Don't Have to Be a Giant to Score Overseas," *Business Week*, April 13, 1987.

[7]Gerald Hampton and E. Buske, "The Global Marketing Perspective" in *Advances in International Marketing*, vol. 2, ed. by Tamer S. Cavusgil (Greenwich, CT: JAI Press, 1987).

# Further Readings

Boddewyn, Jean. "Comparative Marketing: The First Twenty-five Years." *Journal of International Business Studies* 12 (Spring-Summer 1981).

Hampton, Gerald, and E. Buske. "The Global Marketing Perspective" in *Advances in International Marketing*, vol. 2, ed. Tamer S. Cavusgil. Greenwich, CT: JAI Press, 1987.

Kaynak, Erdener, ed. *Global Perspectives in Marketing.* New York: Praeger, 1985.

Ricks, David. *Big Business Blunders: Mistakes in Multinational Marketing.* Homewood, IL: Irwin, 1983.

Terpstra, Vern. "The Evolution of International Marketing," *International Marketing Review* 4 (Summer 1987).

*Other useful international marketing textbooks:*

Cateora, Philip. *International Marketing.* 7th ed. Homewood, IL: Irwin, 1990.

Jain, Subhash. *International Marketing Management.* Boston, MA: PWS-Kent Publishing, 1987.

Jeannet, Jean-Pierre, and Hubert Hennessey. *International Marketing Management.* Boston, MA: Houghton Mifflin, 1988.

CHAPTER 2

# Economic Environment
## The World Economy

*Learning Objectives*

When a firm leaves its home market to market internationally, it must deal with the challenges of the larger, more complex world economy. Here we introduce the various dimensions of that environment.

The main goals of this chapter are to

1. Present an overview of world trade — the economic linkages between nations.
2. Explain the usefulness of data on the balance of payments, the record of international economic transactions.
3. Discuss commercial policy, that is, how nations regulate their trade, and how it constrains the international marketer.
4. Describe how GATT and UNCTAD influence trade, offering both promise and threat to a firm.
5. Explore the political divisions between so-called Eastern and Western nations that present both challenges and opportunities to Western firms and the attempts at regional economic integration.
6. Discuss the international financial system, floating dollar and the factors affecting the pricing and financial side of international marketing.
7. Discuss the role of the United States in the world economy and how the home country affects a firm's international marketing.

Marketing is an economic activity affected by the economic environment in which it is conducted. International marketing has a twofold economic environment: (1) the global, or world, economy, and (2) the individual economies of countries. This chapter will discuss the international economy, and Chapter 3 will consider the relevant dimensions of foreign economies.

It is reasonable to speak of the "world economy" because the nations of the world do relate to each other economically. Nations, of course, also relate to each other politically, diplomatically, militarily, and culturally. Many of these other elements of international relations are intertwined with economic considerations. For example, Marco Polo's travels and the Cru-

21

sades had significant economic impact. The great voyages of discovery and the building of colonial empires were motivated by economic as well as political aspirations. More recently, economic considerations have played a role in regional cooperative movements such as the *European Community (EC)*. International economic concerns are also frequent items on the agenda of the United Nations and its affiliated agencies.

The existence of this world economy is critical for the business firm. Because nations do relate to each other economically, international business operations are possible. Today, in fact, international marketers are major participants in international economic relations. For that reason, it is necessary to examine the world economy to see how it aids and constrains international marketing. We begin by considering international trade, a major element in international economic relations. Figure 2–1 illustrates how the international environment influences the firm's international marketing.

## Nation Trades with Nation

Although our primary concern is international marketing rather than international trade, a brief survey of international trade will prove useful. Trading between groups has been going on for thousands of years, at least since the beginning of recorded history. Much early trade was economically motivated, carried on through barter or commercial transactions. However, a large part of the exchange of goods historically occurred through military conquest: "To the victor belong the spoils." The predominant pattern of international trade today is the voluntary exchange of goods and services.

**Figure 2–1**         **The International Environment of Marketing**

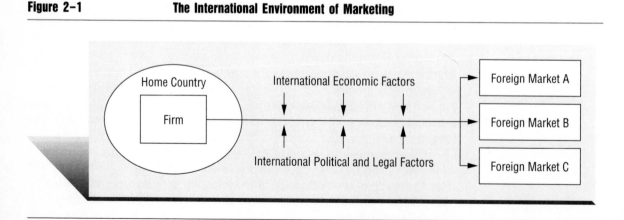

# A Picture of World Trade

**Global Volume.** The volume of world trade (world exports) in 1988 was over $2.8 trillion, a figure larger than the gross national product (GNP) of every nation in the world except the United States and over three times the GNP of Latin America. This is one indication of international trade's importance as part of world economic activity. Not only is it large in volume, it is also one of the fastest-growing areas of economic activity. Since World War II, the volume of world trade has risen faster than most other indicators of economic activity. In fact, it has increased over 25 times whereas world GNP has increased only about 13 times.

This trend suggests that internationalism is increasing as a way of life. Both nations and firms must consider its significance for their own well-being. Nations moving in the direction of trade expansion can raise their standard of living. Nations moving in the direction of trade restriction may enhance their political separation and isolation, but at the expense of economic progress. Firms, like nations, must recognize that they are in the world marketplace in considering opportunities for growth and facing new competition. The isolationist position today is difficult to maintain for firms as well as for nations.

**Foreign Trade of Individual Nations.** Let us consider the importance of international trade to individual nations. In the United States, exports and imports of goods and services in 1988 amounted to about $900 billion or over 20 percent of GNP. This percentage is twice as high as it was 20 years earlier. Yet, even these figures do not adequately measure the importance of international trade to the American economy. For one thing, exports in some lines represent much higher percentages of output, up to 50 percent in some cases. Some major U.S. exports in 1988 were as follows: machinery, $65 billion; transport equipment, $40 billion; chemicals, $25 billion; raw materials, $20 billion.

Conversely, imports account for a large part of American supplies in many products — 100 percent for coffee, crude rubber, diamonds and some other minerals, and bananas, for example. Major import categories in 1988 were as follows: machinery, $90 billion; petroleum, $40 billion; transport equipment, $75 billion; food, $20 billion; and clothing, $20 billion. Thus, some industries are more dependent on international trade than others.

Some nations are also much more dependent on trade than others. Although the United States is the world's leading exporter and importer, such trade is only a modest percent of its GNP — about 10 percent. The figures are much higher for most other developed countries — for example, 26 percent for Germany, 43 percent for the Netherlands, and 56 percent for Belgium. Put another way, Sweden imports goods each year to the value of about $5,000 per capita. The United States imports about $1,700 per capita. For the communist economies, the figures are low because these countries have desired self-sufficiency and independence from the outside world. In general, the figures for developing countries are low because many lack the wherewithal to trade. Their needs are great, but they have little to sell, except for the oil exporters.

# Global Marketing

### The International Automobile inside the 1989 Pontiac Le Mans

| | |
|---|---|
| Designed | West Germany |
| Final Assembly | South Korea |
| 1.6 Liter Engine | South Korea |
| 2.0 Liter Engine | Australia |
| Transmission and Automatic Transaxle | Canada and U.S. |
| Manual Transaxle | South Korea |
| Brake Components | France, U.S., and South Korea |
| Tires | South Korea |
| Electrical Wiring Harness | South Korea |
| Sheet Metal | Japan |
| Fuel Injection | U.S. |
| Fuel Pump | U.S. |
| Radio | Singapore |
| Steering Components | U.S. |
| Windshield Glass | South Korea |
| Battery | South Korea |
| Rear Axle Components | U.S. and South Korea |
| Stamping of Exterior Body | South Korea |

The export involvement of the nation influences that of the firm. It is not surprising, therefore, that firms from heavy exporting countries tend to be more internationally oriented than those from other countries. For example, the average American manufacturer is less apt to be an exporter than is the average Belgian or Dutch firm, and there are more exporting firms in Taiwan than in the whole United States.

**Foreign Trade of Individual Firms.**   Foreign trade is just as important to the international marketing firm as it is to the nation that wants to increase its income and raise its standard of living. In fact, much of international marketing involves international trade — the cross-border movement of goods and services — as we shall see when we discuss the management of international marketing in Part 2. In relation to this subject, "Global Marketing" shows how one company, General Motors, tied together eight different countries around the world to present the 1989 Pontiac Le Mans.

| Table 2-1 | **Commodity Shares in World Trade** | | |
| --- | --- | --- | --- |
| | | **1965** | **1987** |
| | Food | 18% | 10% |
| | Fuel | 10 | 11 |
| | Other Primary Commodities | 18 | 8 |
| | Manufactures | 54 | 73 |
| | Total | 100% | 100% |

Source: *World Development Report 1989*, (Washington, D.C.: World Bank, 1989), 192, 193.

## Composition of World Trade

A study of the commodity composition of world trade gives further insight into international economic relations. Considering just four commodity categories — food, fuel, other primary commodities, and manufactured goods — we see long-run shifts in market share. Table 2-1 shows that the shares of both food products and other primary commodities have been cut in half from 1965 to 1987. Fuel increased its share slightly over the same period. The share of fuel was much higher in the late 1970s, but as the power of OPEC waned, fuel returned about to its original share of world trade. That left manufactures as the only growth market in world trade, with manufactured exports increasing market share from 54 percent in 1965 to 73 percent in 1987.

The developing countries are very unhappy about this situation. The drop in their share of international trade roughly parallels the drop in the proportion of primary materials exported to total exports. There are several reasons for these changing market shares. One is the development of synthetics and other substitutes for primary products. Another is growing agricultural self-sufficiency in the industrialized countries. A third reason is the growth of manufacturing as compared to primary production in total world output. Countries with falling market shares consequently need to change their product line, that is, industrialize. This does not mean dropping existing primary exports but rather adding manufactured exports, which is just what most less developed countries, of course, are trying to do.

An important omission in our discussion of the composition of world trade has been services (advertising, banking, communications, insurance, transportation, etc.). This is a growth area of world trade and one of special interest to American firms, who often have a comparative advantage in those businesses. Trade in services is over one-fourth the size of merchandise trade, or over $700 billion a year. Unfortunately, data on trade in services are much harder to come by than data on merchandise trade, but we do know that as of the late 1980s, the United States was the leading exporter and importer of services, just as it was for merchandise trade.

For international firms, a detailed study of the composition of world trade reveals what is being traded as well as who is buying and selling at the national level. Trend analysis shows which products are growing and which are fading, indicating opportunities available to the firm. The interest of less developed countries in changing their international trade position through industrialization may also create investment opportunities for the firm in manufacturing or processing. Ventures such as these could help the less developed countries increase their manufactured exports by adding new items to their export line, or by refining or processing their primary commodities.

**Patterns of World Trade**

Who are the major players — and winners — in the great game of international trade? Table 2–2 identifies them, using UN statistics. It shows that the industrial countries supply 70 percent of all world exports, thus finding large external markets for their factories. They also buy 70 percent of all world imports, thus raising their standard of living.

Though large in numbers and population, the developing countries supply only one-fifth of the world's exports and take about one-fifth of the world's imports. (Over 60 percent of their trade is with the industrial countries.) Because of their small share of exports and imports, the developing countries receive a significantly smaller contribution of international trade to their income and standard of living than do the industrial countries. The exceptions to this gloomy Third World picture are the *newly industrializing countries (NICs)*, which have gained significant shares of trade in recent years. Major members of this group include Hong Kong, Singapore, South Korea, and Taiwan.

The centrally planned, or communist, countries play a small role in international trade, accounting for only about 10 percent of exports and imports — over half of that among themselves. They limit their economic relations with non-communist countries, especially the industrial countries.

**Table 2–2**            **Origin and Destination of Merchandise Exports as a Percentage of World Exports**

| | Exports to: | | | |
|---|---|---|---|---|
| **Exports from:** | **Industrial Countries** | **Developing Countries** | **Centrally Planned Countries** | **World** |
| Industrial Countries[a] | 54.7 | 12.4 | 2.4 | 69.7 |
| Developing Countries[b] | 12.5 | 5.8 | 1.6 | 20.0 |
| Centrally Planned Countries[c] | 2.4 | 1.7 | 5.4 | 9.9 |
| World[d] | 69.7 | 19.9 | 9.4 | 100.0 |

[a] United States, Canada, Western Europe, Japan, Australia, New Zealand, and South Africa.

[b] Asia, Africa, the Middle East, and Latin America excluding the countries in footnote "a" above and the communist countries.

[c] Communist countries. The world and regional totals exclude the intertrade of the communist countries of Asia.

[d] Regional totals may not add to world totals because it is not possible to distribute all trade by direction.

Source: *Monthly Bulletin of Statistics*, United Nations, December 1987, New York.

They do this for reasons of ideology, central planning, and national self-sufficiency. The result of their choice, of course, is to limit their income and standard of living. The upheavals in Eastern Europe in 1989 and 1990 will undoubtedly change this.

The overall picture of word-trade patterns provides necessary background for understanding world trade. However, it is often more important to the individual firm to identify the trading patterns of the *particular* nations it is dealing with. Table 2–3 shows the major trading partners of the United States. To complement this information, a firm might use a *product* breakdown by country to provide a more complete profile of a nation's trade.

Similar tables can be prepared for most countries, and are useful where the firm is considering operations. In these facts of international trade are some clues to the reasons for a particular country's trade patterns. The general statement that most trade is with industrial countries is borne out by the figures for the United States, of course, but the importance of other factors becomes evident as well. For example, the role of Canada and Mexico as trading partners of the United States cannot be explained very well in terms of their size or degree of industrialization. *Geographic proximity* is an important consideration in this case. Countries that are neighbors are going to be better trading partners, other things being equal, than those distant from each other. The lower transport costs are accompanied by greater familiarity and ease of communication and control.

The *political influences* on trade can also be revealed in such a table. For example, although Cuba is also a close neighbor of the United States, there is practically no trade between the two countries. The East-West trade split among European neighbors shows similar patterns. The point here is that an analysis of trade patterns both on an aggregate and on a national basis can be useful to the firm in planning its global marketing and logistics systems. Examination of the causes of trade patterns will suggest possible

| Table 2–3 | **Major Trading Partners of the United States, 1987** | | |
|---|---|---|---|
| **Major Customers** | **Billions of Dollars** | **Major Suppliers** | **Billions of Dollars** |
| Canada | $59.8 | Japan | $84.6 |
| Japan | 28.2 | Canada | 71.1 |
| Mexico | 14.6 | Germany | 27.1 |
| United Kingdom | 14.1 | Taiwan | 24.6 |
| Germany | 11.7 | Mexico | 20.3 |
| Netherlands | 8.2 | United Kingdom | 17.3 |
| South Korea | 8.1 | South Korea | 17.0 |
| France | 7.9 | Italy | 11.0 |
| Taiwan | 7.4 | France | 10.7 |
| Belgium | 6.2 | Hong Kong | 9.9 |

Source: *Statistical Abstract of the United States* (Washington, D.C.: Bureau of the Census, 1989), 774–775.

approaches either to adapting to the patterns or to modifying them where
feasible.

**International Trade Theory**

In domestic marketing, much emphasis is laid on the analysis of buyer
behavior and motivation. For the international marketer, a knowledge of
the basic causes and nature of international trade is important. It is easier
for a firm to work with the underlying economic forces than against them.
But to work with them, the firm must understand them.

Essentially, international trade theory seeks the answers to a few basic
questions: Why do nations trade? What goods do they trade? Nations trade
for economic, political and cultural reasons, but the principal economic basis
for international trade is differences in price; that is, a nation can buy some
goods more cheaply from other nations than it can make them itself. In a
sense, the nation faces the same "make-or-buy" decision as does the firm.
Just as most firms do not go for complete vertical integration but buy many
materials and supplies from outside firms, so most nations decide against
complete self-sufficiency (or *autarky*) in favor of buying cheaper goods from
other countries.

An example given by Adam Smith helps illustrate this: In discussing
the advantages to England in trading manufactured goods for Portugal's
wine, he noted that grapes could be grown "under glass" (in greenhouses)
in England but that to do so would lead to England's having both less wine
and fewer manufactures than if it specialized in manufactures. In fact,
Smith's major conclusion was that the wealth of nations derived from the
division of labor and specialization. Applied to the international picture,
this means trade rather than self-sufficiency.

**Comparative Advantage.**   It has been said that price differences are the
immediate basis of international trade. The firm that decides whether to
make or buy also considers price as a principal variable. But why do nations
have different prices on goods? Prices differ because countries producing
these goods have different *cost* structures. And why do countries have different costs? The Swedish economist Bertil Ohlin came up with an explanation generally held to be valid: Different countries have dissimilar prices
and costs on goods because different goods require a different mix of factors
in their production, and because countries differ in their supply of these
factors. Thus, in reference to Smith's example, Portugal's wine would be
cheaper than wine made in England because Portugal has a relatively better
endowment of wine-making factors (for example, land and climate) than
does England.

What we have been discussing is the principle of *comparative advantage*,
namely: a country will tend to produce and export those goods in which it
has the greater comparative advantage (or the least comparative disadvantage) and import those goods in which it has the least comparative advantage
(or the greatest comparative disadvantage). On this basis it is possible to
predict what goods a nation will trade, both its exports and imports. As
Smith suggested, the nation maximizes its supply of goods by concentrating

production in those areas where it is most efficient and trading some of these products for imported products where it is least efficient. An examination of the exports and imports of most trading nations tends to support this theory.

**Product Life Cycle.** A recent refinement in trade theory is related to the *product life cycle*, which in marketing refers to the consumption pattern for a product. When applied to international trade theory, it refers primarily to international trade and production patterns. According to this concept, many products go through a trade cycle wherein one nation is initially an exporter, then loses its export markets, and finally may become an importer of the product. Empirical studies have demonstrated the validity of the model for some kinds of manufactured goods.[1]

There are four phases in the production and trade cycle, which is outlined below with the United States as an example. We'll assume an American firm has come up with a high-tech product.

Phase 1.  U.S. export strength is evident
Phase 2.  Foreign production starts
Phase 3.  Foreign production becomes competitive in export markets
Phase 4.  Import competition begins

In Phase 1, product innovation and development are likely to be related to the needs of the home market. The firm usually serves its home market first. The new product will be produced in the home market because, as the firm moves down the production learning curve of this product, it will need to communicate with both suppliers and customers. As it begins to fill home-market needs, the firm begins to export the new product, seizing on its first-mover advantages. (We will assume the American firm is exporting to Europe.)

In Phase 2, importing countries gradually gain familiarity with the new product. As foreign markets expand, producers in wealthy countries begin producing the product for their own markets. (Most new product innovations begin in one rich country and then move to other rich countries.) Foreign production will reduce the exports of the innovating firm. (We will assume the American firm's exports to Europe are replaced by production within Europe.)

In Phase 3, foreign firms gain production experience and move down the cost curve. If they have lower costs than the innovating firm, which is frequently the case, they will begin to export to third-country markets, replacing the innovator's exports there. (We will assume that European firms are now exporting to Latin America and taking away the American firm's export markets there.)

In Phase 4, the foreign producers now have sufficient production experience and economies of scale to allow them to export back to the innovator's home country. (We will assume the European producers have now taken away the home market of the original U.S. innovator.)

In Phase 1 the product is "new." In Phase 2 it is "maturing." In Phases 3 and 4 it is "standardized." The product may become so standardized by Phase 4 that it almost becomes a commodity. Textiles in general are an example of a product in Phase 4, whereas large computers have moved into Phase 2. Products in Phase 4 may be produced in less developed countries for export to the developed countries. This modification of the theory of comparative advantage provides further insight into patterns of international trade and production and helps the international company plan logistics, such as when it will need to produce — or source — abroad.

## Balance of Payments

In the study of international trade, the principal source of information is the *balance-of-payments* statements of the trading nations. These are summary statements of all the economic transactions between one country and all other countries over a period of time, usually one year.

In governmental reporting, the balance of payments is often broken down into a current account and one or more capital accounts. The current account is a record of all the *goods and services* the nation exchanged with other nations. The capital account includes international *financial transactions*, such as private foreign investment and government borrowing, lending, or payments. The international marketer usually is more interested in the details of current account transactions, that is, the nature of the goods being traded and their origin and destination. The *World Trade Annual* contains an international summary based on United Nations data.

**Marketing Decisions.**   The balance of payments is an indicator of the international economic health of a country. Its data help government policy makers plan monetary, fiscal, foreign-exchange, and commercial policies. Besides fulfilling a government requirement, such data have marketing applications. They can provide information for decisions in international marketing. In our discussion of international trade thus far, we have presented tables useful in making international marketing decisions, and these tables are drawn from balance-of-payments data. Two important decisions are the choice of location of supply for foreign markets and the selection of markets to sell to. Balance-of-payments analysis can show which nations are importers and exporters of the products in question. The firm can thus identify its own best import and export targets, that is, countries to sell to and countries to supply from. Longitudinal analysis of the balance of payments can help to track the international product life cycle.

When the firm is considering foreign market opportunities, it will find a country's import statistics for its products to be a preliminary indicator of market potential. Furthermore, the firm can get an indication of the kind of competition in these countries by noting the major supplying nations for the products in question. The statistics sometimes even permit identification of low-price supplying nations and high-price (high-quality?) suppliers. Please note, though, that in use of balance-of-payments data it is necessary to consider a period of several years to get an idea of trends.

Figure 2–2 is drawn from the United Nations World Trade Annual, a comprehensive five-volume publication detailing exports and imports by SITC category (Standard International Trade Classification). Only very partial data are given for illustrative purposes. Column 1 shows some of the major importing countries for satchels and briefcases, and the countries who supplied them. Column 2 shows some of the major exporters of satchels and briefcases and their export markets. Study of this kind of data, drawn from countries' balance of payments, can allow helpful competitive analysis.

**Financial Considerations.**   Up to now, we have considered primarily the current account in the balance of payments, and especially the movement of goods. A look at the capital account is also useful. A nation's international solvency can be evaluated by checking its capital account over several years. If the nation is steadily losing its gold and foreign exchange reserves, there is a strong likelihood of a currency devaluation or some kind of *exchange control*, meaning that the government restricts the amount of money sent out of the country as well as the uses to which it can be put. With exchange control, the firm may have difficulty getting foreign exchange to repatriate profits or even to import its products. If the firm is importing products that are not considered necessary to the nation's development, the scarce foreign exchange will go instead to goods on which the nation places a higher priority.

The firm's pricing policies, too, will be affected by the balance-of-payments problems of the host country. If the firm cannot repatriate profits from a country, it will try to use its transfer pricing to minimize the profits earned in that country, gaining its profits elsewhere where it can repatriate them. If the exporting firm fears devaluation of a currency, it will hesitate to quote prices in that currency, preferring to give terms in its home currency or another "safe" currency. Thus, for both international marketing and international finance, the balance of payments is an important information source.

**Commercial Policy**

One of the reasons international trade is different from domestic trade is that it is carried on between different political units, each one a sovereign nation exercising control over its own trade. Although all nations control their foreign trade, they vary in the degree of such control. Each nation invariably establishes trade laws that favor its nationals and discriminate against traders from other countries. This means, for example, that a U.S. firm trying to sell in the French market will face certain handicaps deriving from the French government's control over its trade. These handicaps to the U.S. firm are in addition to any disadvantages resulting from distance or cultural differences. By the same token, the French firm trying to sell in the United States will face similar restrictions when competing with U.S. firms selling in their home market.

*Commercial policy* is the term used to refer to government regulations bearing on foreign trade. The principal tools of commercial policy are tariffs, quotas, exchange control, and administrative regulation or the "invisible

## Figure 2–2       Example of Import/Export Statistics from Balance of Payments Data

### Importer and Source

| SITC NUMBER Importer Provenance | QUANTITY Unit | VALUE Thousands of U.S. Dollars |
|---|---|---|
| **831.03 SATCHELS AND BRIEF-CASES** | | |
| BELGIUM-LUX.... TOT | W 819 | 4336 |
| OTH ASIA NES | W 72 | 356 |
| DENMARK | W 12 | 92 |
| FRANCE | W 120 | 831 |
| GERMANY, FR | W 28 | 377 |
| ITALY | W 44 | 665 |
| NETHERLANDS | W 24 | 239 |
| YUGOSLAVIA | W 25 | 99 |
| CZECHOSLOVAK | W 101 | 415 |
| GERMAN DM RP | W 294 | 833 |
| POLAND | W 45 | 84 |
| ROMANIA | W 18 | 97 |
| | | |
| DENMARK........... TOT | W 223 | 2054 |
| HONG KONG | W 6 | 90 |
| KOREA REP. | W 17 | 285 |
| THAILAND | W 5 | 60 |
| OTH ASIA NES | W 56 | 271 |
| CHINA | W 21 | 73 |
| BELGIUM-LUX | W 3 | 72 |
| FRANCE | W 5 | 59 |
| GERMANY, FR | W 26 | 586 |
| ITALY | W 22 | 165 |
| GERMAN DM RP | W 37 | 179 |
| | | |
| FRANCE ............... TOT | W 2841 | 14239 |
| MOROCCO | W 59 | 448 |
| TUNISIA | W 117 | 1144 |
| HONG KONG | W 18 | 210 |
| INDIA | W 5 | 62 |
| KOREA REP. | W 85 | 583 |
| OTH ASIA NES | W 377 | 1917 |
| CHINA | W 130 | 667 |
| BELGIUM-LUX | W 11 | 92 |
| GERMANY, FR | W 28 | 413 |
| ITALY | W 156 | 2197 |
| NETHERLANDS | W 12 | 55 |
| UK | W 2 | 55 |
| AUSTRIA | W 6 | 60 |
| SWEDEN | W 30 | 69 |
| SPAIN | W 10 | 155 |
| YUGOSLAVIA | W 12 | 63 |
| BULGARIA | W 244 | 491 |
| CZECHOSLOVAK | W 444 | 1757 |
| GERMAN DM RP | W 1015 | 3112 |
| POLAND | W 66 | 493 |
| ROMANIA | W 6 | 65 |
| | | |
| GERMANY, FR.... TOT | W 1626 | 11043 |
| BRAZIL | W 21 | 381 |
| TURKEY | W 7 | 182 |

### Importer and Source

| SITC NUMBER Importer Provenance | QUANTITY Unit | VALUE Thousands of U.S. Dollars |
|---|---|---|
| **831.03 SATCHELS AND BRIEF-CASES** | | |
| GERMANY, FR..... TOT .....CONTINUED | | |
| HONG KONG | W 138 | 832 |
| INDIA | W 12 | 263 |
| KOREA REP. | W 13 | 208 |
| OTH ASIA NES | W 706 | 3199 |
| CHINA | W 77 | 414 |
| DENMARK | W 6 | 64 |
| FRANCE | W 20 | 149 |
| ITALY | W 176 | 1040 |
| NETHERLANDS | W 81 | 1105 |
| AUSTRIA | W 20 | 173 |
| YUGOSLAVIA | W 44 | 585 |
| BULGARIA | W 47 | 137 |
| CZECHOSLOVAK | W 162 | 1017 |
| HUNGARY | W 6 | 207 |
| POLAND | W 50 | 728 |
| ROMANIA | W 17 | 116 |
| | | |
| GREECE................. TOT | W 27 | 223 |
| | | |
| IRELAND ............. TOT | W 103 | 712 |
| OTH ASIA NES | W 19 | 200 |
| UK | W 23 | 203 |
| GERMAN DM REP | W 36 | 120 |
| | | |
| ITALY ................... TOT | W 943 | 5726 |
| USA | W 4 | 65 |
| JAPAN | W 10 | 57 |
| HONG KONG | W 9 | 81 |
| KOREA REP. | W 218 | 1513 |
| OTH ASIA NES | W 466 | 2594 |
| CHINA | W 96 | 470 |
| FRANCE | W 5 | 96 |
| GERMANY, FR | W 25 | 261 |
| UK | W 4 | 66 |
| AUSTRIA | W 6 | 70 |
| SPAIN | W 16 | 82 |
| YUGOSLAVIA | W 15 | 66 |
| POLAND | W 8 | 85 |
| | | |
| NETHERLANDS .. TOT | W 449 | 2220 |
| HONG KONG | W 24 | 145 |
| INDONESIA | W 14 | 140 |
| KOREA REP. | W 6 | 60 |
| OTH ASIA NES | W 42 | 216 |
| BELGIUM-LUX | W 6 | 66 |
| DENMARK | W 7 | 70 |
| GERMANY, FR | W 24 | 253 |
| CZECHOSLOVAK | W 110 | 398 |
| GERMAN DM RP | W 176 | 622 |
| POLAND | W 14 | 71 |

*(continued)*

| Exporter and Destination | | | | Exporter and Destination | | |
|---|---|---|---|---|---|---|

| SITC NUMBER<br>Exporter<br>Provenance | QUANTITY<br>Unit | | VALUE<br>Thousands<br>of U.S.<br>Dollars | SITC NUMBER<br>Exporter<br>Provenance | QUANTITY<br>Unit | VALUE<br>Thousands<br>of U.S.<br>Dollars |
|---|---|---|---|---|---|---|
| **831.03 SATCHELS AND BRIEF-CASES** | | | | **831.03 SATCHELS AND BRIEF-CASES** | | |
| GERMANY, FR..... TOT .....CONTINUED | | | | ITALY..... TOT .....CONTINUED | | |
| CANADA | W | 3 | 51 | GREECE | W | 4 | 71 |
| USA | W | 16 | 833 | NETHERLANDS | W | 11 | 140 |
| JAPAN | W | 9 | 533 | UK | W | 101 | 1120 |
| SAUDI ARABIA | W | 6 | 88 | AUSTRIA | W | 84 | 602 |
| HONG KONG | W | 4 | 212 | NORWAY | W | 14 | 102 |
| SINGAPORE | W | 3 | 155 | SWEDEN | W | 4 | 66 |
| BELGIUM-LUX | W | 35 | 443 | SWITZERLAND | W | 95 | 2137 |
| DENMARK | W | 7 | 154 | SPAIN | W | 11 | 238 |
| FRANCE | W | 29 | 403 | USSR | W | 5 | 77 |
| ITALY | W | 40 | 369 | AUSTRALIA | W | 16 | 488 |
| NETHERLANDS | W | 21 | 252 | | | |
| UK | W | 10 | 235 | NETHERLANDS .. TOT | W | 158 | 1741 |
| AUSTRIA | W | 58 | 686 | BELGIUM-LUX | W | 29 | 263 |
| FINLAND | W | 6 | 59 | GERMANY, FR | W | 82 | 1185 |
| ICELAND | W | 5 | 65 | SWITZERLAND | W | 6 | 78 |
| NORWAY | W | 7 | 82 | | | |
| SWEDEN | W | 6 | 85 | UK ..........................TOT | W | 98 | 1047 |
| SWITZERLAND | W | 129 | 1716 | USA | W | 5 | 177 |
| | | | | JAPAN | W | 2 | 58 |
| GREECE.................TOT | W | 14 | 152 | FRANCE | W | 5 | 61 |
| KUWAIT | W | 8 | 58 | IRELAND | W | 15 | 108 |
| SAUDI ARABIA | W | 5 | 69 | NETHERLANDS | W | 23 | 93 |
| | | | | NORWAY | W | 8 | 76 |
| IRELAND ..............TOT | W | 24 | 187 | | | |
| UK | W | 24 | 186 | FINLAND .............TOT | W | 7 | 81 |
| | | | | NORWAY ..............TOT | W | 47 | 63 |
| ITALY ....................TOT | W | 2168 | 25269 | | | |
| CANADA | W | 26 | 512 | PORTUGAL ..........TOT | W | 10 | 75 |
| USA | W | 202 | 7750 | | | |
| NETH. ANTILLES | W | 1 | 114 | SWEDEN...............TOT | W | 52 | 653 |
| ISRAEL | W | 3 | 54 | FINLAND | W | 10 | 109 |
| JAPAN | W | 57 | 2714 | NORWAY | W | 34 | 422 |
| KUWAIT | W | 3 | 69 | | | |
| LEBANON | W | 3 | 64 | SPAIN.....................TOT | W | 84 | 2077 |
| SAUDI ARABIA | W | 34 | 345 | CANADA | W | 3 | 82 |
| UNTD ARAB EM | W | 2 | 69 | USA | W | 54 | 1370 |
| HONG KONG | W | 11 | 491 | JAPAN | W | 1 | 50 |
| KOREA REP. | W | 1 | 71 | GERMANY, FR | W | 2 | 53 |
| PHILIPPINES | W | 1 | 50 | UK | W | 9 | 162 |
| SINGAPORE | W | 3 | 132 | SWEDEN | W | 4 | 87 |
| BELGIUM-LUX | W | 94 | 1226 | SWITZERLAND | W | 1 | 54 |
| DENMARK | W | 10 | 88 | | | |
| FRANCE | W | 1013 | 3531 | NEW ZEALAND... TOT | | 61 |
| GERMANY, FR | W | 314 | 2372 | AUSTRALIA | | 60 |
| | | | | **831.09 OTHER TRAVEL BAGS, CASES** | | |

W = weight in metric tons

Source: *World Trade Annual 1985*, (New York: United Nations, 1988), vol. IV, 29, 328.

tariff." Each of these will be discussed in turn as it relates to the task of the international marketer.

**Tariffs.**   A *tariff* is a tax on products imported from other countries. The tax may be levied on the quantity — such as 10 cents per pound, gallon, or yard — or on the value of the imported goods — such as 10 or 20 percent *ad valorem*. The former tax is called a *specific duty* and is used especially for primary commodities. Ad valorem duties are generally used on manufactured products.

Governments may have two purposes in imposing tariffs: They may wish to earn revenue and/or make foreign goods more expensive in order to protect national producers. When the United States was a new nation, most of the government revenues came from tariffs. Many less developed countries today earn a large amount of their revenue from tariffs because they are one of the easiest taxes for them to collect. Today, however, the protective purpose generally prevails. One could argue that with a tariff a country penalizes its consumers by making them pay higher prices, and its producers in the case of raw materials or components imported. The rationale is that if the nation is too liberal with imports, it may hurt employment in its own industries.

Tariffs affect pricing, product, and distribution policies of the international marketer as well as foreign investment decisions. If the firm is supplying a market by exports, the tariff increases the price of its product and reduces competitiveness in that market. This necessitates the design of a price structure that will tend to minimize the tariff barrier. A greater emphasis on marginal cost pricing could result. This examination of price will be accompanied by a review of other aspects of the firm's approach to the market. The product may be modified or stripped down to lower the price or perhaps to get a more favorable tariff classification. For example, watches going into a country could be taxed as timepieces at one rate, or as jewelry at a higher rate. The manufacturer might be able to adapt its product to meet requirements for the lower tariff.

Another way the manufacturer can minimize the tariff burden is to ship products CKD (completely knocked down) for assembly in the local market. The tariff on unassembled products or ingredients is usually lower than that on completely finished goods. The country employs a differential tariff to promote local employment. This establishment of local assembly operations is a mild form of the phenomenon known as a *tariff factory*, the term used when the primary reason for the local plant is to get behind the tariff wall to protect markets that the firm can no longer serve by exports. In its strongest form, this would mean complete local production rather than just assembly.

In some circumstances, the firm may seek to turn the tariff to its own advantage. Assume that the host country is exerting pressure for local manufacture that will be noncompetitive with existing sources. The firm might acquiesce on the condition that the plant it sets up be protected by tariffs imposed against more efficient outside suppliers. It would seek this protection as an "infant industry" against mature companies abroad. Thus, if the firm becomes a local company by establishing a subsidiary there, it may benefit from the tariff protection.

**Quotas.**    Quantitative restrictions, or *quotas*, are a barrier to imports. They set absolute limits on the amount of goods that may enter the country. An import quota can be a more serious restriction than a tariff because the firm has less flexibility in responding to it. Price or product modifications will not get around quotas the way they might get around tariffs. The government's goal in establishing quotas on imports is obviously not revenue. It will get none. Its goal is rather the conservation of scarce foreign exchange and/or the protection of local production in the product lines affected. About the only response the firm can make to a quota is to assure itself a share of the quota or to set up local production if the market size warrants it. Since the latter is in accord with the wishes of government, the firm might be regarded favorably for taking such action.

The case of the Japanese auto companies in the United States illustrates some of the problems firms can have with tariffs and quotas. For many years, the United States had a "voluntary" quota on Japanese car imports. Japanese producers responded in two ways: (1) They exported more expensive cars with higher margins, thereby earning high profits (along with their U.S. dealers). (2) They also began to build assembly plants in the United States as the long-run answer to quota constraints.

In 1989, the U.S. Customs Service ruled that the Suzuki Samurai and most small vans would be classified as "trucks" subject to a 25 percent tariff rather than as "cars," subject to a 2.5 percent duty. The positive side of the ruling was that this would allow more "car" imports by the Japanese. American auto firms applauded the decision but the Japanese (and European) producers complained.

**Exchange Control.**    The most complete tool for regulation of foreign trade, except for comprehensive state trading as practiced in the communist economies, is *exchange control*, a government monopoly of all dealings in foreign exchange. A national company earning foreign exchange from its exports must sell this foreign exchange to the control agency, usually the central bank. A company wishing to buy goods from abroad must buy its foreign exchange from the control agency. Exchange control means that foreign exchange is scarce, and the government is rationing it out according to its own priorities. It is practiced especially by communist countries and the developing countries without oil.

Firms in the country have to be on the government's favored list to get exchange for imported supplies. Alternatively, they may try to develop local suppliers, running the risk of higher costs and indifferent quality control. The firms exporting to that nation must also be on the government's favored list. Otherwise they will lose their market if importers can get no foreign exchange to pay them. Generally, exchange control countries favor the import of capital goods and necessary consumer goods but avoid luxuries. The definition of "luxuries" will vary from country to country, but it usually includes cars, appliances, and cosmetics. If the exporter does lose its market through exchange control, about the only option is to produce within the country, if the market is large enough for this to be profitable.

Another implication for the firm when foreign exchange is limited is that the government is unlikely to give priority to a company's profit remittances as a way of using the country's scarce foreign earnings. In this situation, the firm will try to use transfer-pricing to get earnings out or to avoid accumulating earnings there. It accomplishes this by charging high transfer prices on supplies sold to the subsidiary and low transfer prices on goods sold by that subsidiary to affiliates of the company in markets. The firm's ability to do this depends on the plan's acceptance by tax officials of the country with exchange control.

For international executives in exchange-control countries, dealing with the government exchange authorities is a major preoccupation and problem — and never more so than in Venezuela, where in 1989 the government issued arrest warrants for 47 executives of multinational companies for abuses in dealing with the government foreign exchange office. All professed innocence, and many left the country.

**Invisible Tariff and Other Government Barriers.**   There are other government barriers to international trade that are hard to classify — for example, administrative protection, the invisible tariff, or *nontariff barriers (NTBs)*. As traditional trade barriers have declined since World War II, the NTBs have taken on added significance. They include such things as customs documentation requirements, marks of origin, food and drug laws, labeling laws, "buy national" policies, and so on. Because these barriers are so diverse, their international marketing impact cannot be covered in a brief discussion. Their implications will be discussed in Part 2. For the present, it is sufficient to note that they can affect many elements of marketing strategy.

## Other Dimensions and Institutions in the World Economy

GATT

Since each nation is sovereign in determining its own commercial policy, the danger is that arbitrary national actions will minimize international trade. This was the situation in the 1930s when international trade was at a low ebb and each nation tried to maintain domestic employment while restricting imports that might help foreign rather than domestic employment. The bankruptcy of these "beggar my neighbor" policies was evident in the worldwide depression to which they contributed. This unhappy experience led the major trading nations to seek better solutions after World War II. One outcome of their efforts was the *General Agreement on Tariffs and Trade (GATT)*.

Though GATT's initial membership consisted of only 23 countries, these included the major trading nations of the Western world. Today GATT is more than ever the world's trading club; it counts over 120 members and associates. The member countries account for well over 80 percent of total world trade. There are about 20 members from the industrialized nations of the West, including Japan, and over 90 members or associates from the less developed countries. The communist countries are represented by six members. GATT has undoubtedly contributed to the expansion of world trade. Since 1947, GATT has sponsored eight major tariff negotiations, the latest being the Uruguay Round that started in 1986. As a result of these conferences, the tariff rates for tens of thousands of items have been reduced, and a high proportion of world trade has seen an easing of restrictions.

To provide a framework for multilateral trade negotiations is a primary reason for GATT's existence, but there are other GATT principles that further trade expansion. One is the principle of *nondiscrimination*. Each contracting party must grant all others the same rate of import duty; that is, a tariff concession granted to one trading partner must be extended to all GATT members under the most-favored-nation clause. The U.S.S.R., not a member, sought most-favored-nation treatment to help its trade with the United States.

Another GATT principle is the concept of *consultation*. When trade disagreements arise, GATT provides a forum for consultation. In such an atmosphere, disagreeing members are more likely to compromise than to resort to arbitrary trade-restricting actions. All in all, world-trade cooperation since World War II has led to a much better trading policy than the world might have expected. GATT has been a major contributor to this. Economic troubles, however, are making further contributions from GATT very difficult to come by. Unemployment in the industrialized nations, large trade deficits in the United States, and heavy debts in many developing countries are causing nations to give more attention to national concerns than to international cooperation. This made for very difficult negotiations in the Uruguay Round.

## UNCTAD

Although GATT has been an important force in world-trade expansion, benefits have not been distributed equally. The less developed countries have been dissatisfied with trade arrangements because their share of world trade has been declining, and the prices of their raw material exports compare unfavorably with the prices of their manufactured goods imports. Though many of these countries are members of GATT, they felt that GATT did more to further trade in goods of industrialized nations than it did to promote their own primary products. It is true that tariff reductions have been far more important to manufactured goods than to primary products. The result of these countries' dissatisfaction was the formation of the *United Nations Conference on Trade and Development (UNCTAD)* in 1964. UNCTAD is a permanent organ of the United Nations General Assembly and counts over 160 member countries.

The goal of UNCTAD is to further the development of emerging nations — by trade as well as by other means. Under GATT, trade expanded especially in manufactured goods, creating a growing trade gap between industrial and developing countries. UNCTAD seeks to improve the prices of primary goods exports through commodity agreements. If the commodity-producing countries could get together to control supply, this would mean higher prices and higher returns.

UNCTAD also worked to establish a tariff preference system favoring the export of manufactured goods from less developed countries. Since these countries have not been able to export commodities in a quantity sufficient to maintain their share of trade, they want to expand in the growth area of world trade; industrial exports. They feel they might achieve this if manufactured goods coming from developing countries faced lower tariffs than the same goods coming from developed countries.

UNCTAD has made some modest progress. One achievement is its own formation, a new club for world trade matters. It is a lobbying group for developing-country interests. Indeed, Julius Nyerere called it "the labor union of the developing countries." Developing countries have also received preferential tariff treatment from the EC, Japan, and the United States, as they asked for in UNCTAD. This can be significant, as we will see soon. Overall, UNCTAD has focused world attention on the trade needs of developing countries and given them a more coherent voice. UNCTAD's committees and studies have also made for a more informed dialog.

## GATT, UNCTAD, and the Firm

GATT's success in reducing barriers to international trade has meant that a firm's global logistics can be more efficient than in a world of trade restrictions. Further, the firm, through its national subsidiaries in various markets, can help protect its interest in trade matters through discussions with governments in advance of trade negotiations. In the United States, for example, a committee holds hearings at which business representatives can present their international trading problems. These problems are noted for consideration in GATT negotiations. Firms in the EC usually work with trade associations that channel industry views to the EC negotiators. Brazil also looks to trade associations for industry views.

UNCTAD can have a more direct impact on the firm than GATT. International firms can play a major role relating to the tariff preferences on developing-country manufactures granted by the industrialized nations. Developing countries have limited experience and success in exporting manufactured goods. Elimination of tariffs by itself is not sufficient to help them. Here the multinational can be a decisive factor. If the firm combines its know-how and resources with those of the host country, competitive exports could result. Included in the firm's resources is its global distribution network, which could be the critical factor in gaining foreign market access. Also, it supplies the foreign marketing know-how lacked by most developing-country producers. For example, if Ford had the choice of importing engines from its plant in Britain or its plant in Brazil, it might choose Brazil as the supplier if engines from Brazil had a zero tariff and engines from Europe faced a 15 percent duty.

There can be a complementarity of interest between the less developed countries and international firms in the question of preferences. On the one hand, the marriage of these interests could help nations achieve their industrialization and balance-of-payments goals; on the other, multinational companies could expand their international markets and participate more actively in the growth of the less developed nations, which have a majority of the world's population.

## East-West Trade

We have been discussing the trading problems between developed and less developed nations, or what could be called the problems of North-South trade. Another division in the world economy that also has a geographic designation is between the communist economies and the so-called Western nations, that is, East-West trade. In this section we discuss the economic problems arising from this ideological split.

*East* means primarily the Soviet Union, the socialist economies of Eastern Europe, plus China. However, other countries have joined that group, such as North Korea, Vietnam, and Cuba. Furthermore, there are degrees of "Eastern-ness," or separation from the West, in this group of nations. From the U.S. viewpoint, for example, the most Eastern of these countries are Cuba, Albania, North Korea, and Vietnam. For many years, all trade was absolutely prohibited with this subgroup. At the other extreme, the most Western of these nations were Yugoslavia and Poland, with whom much more trade and business was permitted. After the liberalization in the fall of 1989, most of Eastern Europe became an open market.

There are degrees of "Western-ness" also. Though the term *West* is often used to describe all noncommunist nations, for trade purposes it is more accurate to restrict it to NATO (North Atlantic Treaty Organization) members and/or OECD (Organization for Economic Cooperation and Development) members. This includes primarily the nations of Western Europe, the United States, Canada, and Japan. Australia and New Zealand might also be included.

What is significant for the international firm is that there are wide differences among Western nations in their controls on trade with the East. When the East-West Cold War was very cold, most nations agreed on rather severe restrictions on exports to the East. Since the thaw of the 1960s, there has been a steady easing up on trade restrictions (interrupted by the invasion of Afghanistan). Western Europe, however, has been much more liberal on such trade than the Americans. Firms may find themselves with subsidiaries in countries with differing controls on trade with the East. This presents both problems and opportunities, as in the pipeline squabble of 1982.

**Market Big, Business Small.**  The volume of East-West trade has always been small in terms of the size of the two groups. In 1988 each group exported about $60 billion to the other. That was less than 4 percent of the West's exports but about 30 percent of communist-country exports. U.S. exports to the East bloc (including China) were about $6 billion in 1988. That represents, however, about a billion-dollar surplus for the United States.

There are several reasons for this low volume of trade between East and West. One, already mentioned, is the Cold War. To some extent, NATO countries consider communist countries to be the enemy. Though this attitude has been weakening steadily in the past decade or two, such incidents as the Russian invasion of Afghanistan tend to revive it. On the other hand, after the Reagan-Gorbachev summit in November 1985, a group of 350 business people and officials went to Moscow on a trade mission, and by 1989 over 500 joint ventures between Western and Soviet firms were registered in Moscow.

Another reason for the low volume of trade is ideological. The centrally planned economies lean toward autarky rather than interdependence. The more an economy is opened to the outside world through trade, the more difficult it is to control that economy. Therefore, much of the international trading that the communist countries do is within the framework of the *Council for Mutual Economic Assistance (CMEA)*, the Soviet counterpart of the European Community. CMEA includes most of the communist countries as members.

A further reason for limited East-West trade is lack of marketing skills within the communist economies. These economies are designed to meet the desires of the planners rather than the needs of the market. The purpose of exports is to pay for imports, not to fulfill market demand. Because they deal within a command economy at home, they generally lack the marketing skills necessary for selling in the market economies of the West. Related to this problem is their difficulty in earning hard currencies to pay for their imports from the West. This financing problem causes them to try to barter goods for goods, an approach unwelcome to most Western traders.

**The Firm Looks East.**   The Russian withdrawal from Afghanistan, Gorbachev's policies of *glasnost* and *perestroika*, and democratic liberalization in Poland and some other Eastern countries have created the greatest relaxing of tensions between East and West since the Cold War began thawing in the 1960s. China was an early leader in liberalization and by 1988 was the most popular Eastern bloc target of American firms. The tragic events of June 4, 1989, in Tiananmen Square put a damper on foreign interest in China with the long-run results yet to be determined. East-West trade is always subject to the political relations between the two sides. These political relations fluctuate, but the volume of trade grows. The desire for trade exists on both sides. The East wants the goods and technology of the West. Western business looks longingly on the market potential of the East.

In this variable trading climate, the firm must evaluate its own strategy. Since most Western European governments have a liberal attitude toward East-West trade, the problem for the American firm is acute. The United States has the most restrictions on such trade and the American public is also sometimes cool to it. In spite of the constraints, the potential market is so great that it demands American executive attention; all the more so because the entry of European firms could preempt this market. As an executive of a farm equipment producer said enviously, "They (the CMEA countries) have twice the population and three times the land area of the United States."

As consumer interests receive more attention in the Eastern economies, market opportunities may appear for consumer-oriented Western firms. Industrial goods firms already have market opportunities. Their problem is to find ways to finance their sales or to learn to use barter effectively.

In 1989 a consortium of U.S. firms (RJR Nabisco, Kodak, Archer Daniels Midland, Johnson & Johnson, and Chevron-Ford dropped out at the last minute) agreed in Moscow to develop up to 25 joint ventures with Soviet enterprises.

The American negotiators received red carpet treatment (no pun intended) including personal intervention by Gorbachev. What clinched the deal, however, was the promise that the hard currency earnings of Chevron (exporting oil from Russia) could be shared among consortium members so that they could repatriate their earnings.

Perhaps the key to expanded sales to Eastern countries lies in helping them overcome their marketing weaknesses. Western firms could do this by integrating these countries into their international operations. There are two possible methods: One is to incorporate Eastern suppliers into the firm's operations; their supplies would pay for the firm's sales to the supplying country. Another is for the Western firm to include some Eastern country's related products in its own multinational marketing program. Again, these related products would pay for the firm's sales to the supplying country. After liberalization in Eastern Europe in 1989, many Japanese and Western firms began exploring such ventures there. The most publicized opening was the giant McDonald's restaurant in Moscow. Pepsi-Cola scored a coup by being the first Western firm permitted to sell cola drinks in the U.S.S.R. The coup was a personal victory for Pepsi president Donald Kendall, who took advantage of his previous contacts with Russian leaders. As a means of payment, Pepsi is distributing Russian vodka in the United States.

## Regional Economic Integration

One of the major developments in the world economy since World War II is the growth of regional groupings. The European Community (EC) is the most famous and successful of these, but it is only one of many. Regional groupings are agreements between nations in the same region to cooperate in various economic matters. There may also be political ties between these same nations, but it is the economic aspect that concerns us here. *Regionalism*, or the tendency toward economic cooperation within regions, is an attempt by nations to attain goals they cannot achieve in isolation. NATO is a counterpart in the military field. The major regional groupings are shown in Table 2–4.

There are costs to a nation in joining regional groupings, the chief one being that it must give up some of its sovereignty in economic matters. Nations do this only because they hope the benefits will be greater than the costs. The major benefit sought through economic integration is faster economic growth. By joining together, member nations get larger resources, larger markets, and economies of scale for their industries. Another objective of regional groupings is countervailing power. For example, the EC seeks a stronger position against the economic power of the United States and Japan.

**Table 2–4**                    **Some Principal Regional Economic Associations**

| Name | Membership |
|---|---|
| ANCOM: Andean Common Market | Bolivia, Colombia, Ecuador, Peru, Venezuela (Chile withdrew in 1977) |
| ASEAN: Association of Southeast Asian Nations | Brunei, Indonesia, Malaysia, Philippines, Singapore, Thailand |
| CACM: Central American Common Market | Costa Rica, El Salvador, Guatemala, Honduras, Nicaragua |
| CMEA: Council for Mutual Economic Assistance | Bulgaria, Cuba, Czechoslovakia, Germany-D.R., Hungary, Mongolia, Poland, Romania, USSR, Vietnam |
| ECOWAS: Economic Community of West African States | Benin, Burkina Faso, Cape Verde, Ivory Coast, Gambia, Ghana, Guinea-Bissau, Liberia, Mali, Mauritania, Niger, Nigeria, Senegal, Sierra Leone, Togo |
| EC: European Community | Belgium, Denmark, France, Germany-F.R., Greece, Ireland, Italy, Luxembourg, Netherlands, Portugal, Spain, United Kingdom |
| EFTA: European Free Trade Association | Austria, Iceland, Norway, Sweden, Switzerland, Finland (associate) |
| LAIA: Latin American Integration Association (Replaced LAFTA) | Argentina, Bolivia, Brazil, Chile, Colombia, Ecuador, Mexico, Paraguay, Peru, Uruguay, Venezuela |

The European Free Trade Association was formed largely to gain bargaining strength with the EC.

The reduction of trade barriers in the group provides dynamism to the member economies by increasing competition. Sluggish national firms or monopolies lose their protective walls and are forced to change in a more competitive direction. Furthermore, the group of countries together may be able to afford an industry too large for any individual member country to support. Thus, industrialization can be aided by regional integration. All this could mean greater wealth, progress, and self-sufficiency for the region. Various forms and degrees of economic integration are possible.

**Free-Trade Areas.**   Although all regional groupings have economic goals, the various groups differ in organization and motivation. There are three basic kinds of organization for economic integration. The simplest is a *free-trade area*, in which the member countries agree to have *free movement of goods among themselves*; that is, no tariffs or quotas are imposed against goods coming from other members. EFTA is a major example. EFTA achieved an industrial free-trade area in 1967, only seven years after its founding. However, it lost some of its membership when Britain and Denmark joined the EC in 1973. The remaining members continue EFTA as a free-trade area in industrial goods. Agricultural products are still subject to restrictions between members. As of July 1, 1977, EFTA and the EC formed

# WORLD MAPS

**Trade and Travel Networks**

**Gross National Product and Working Populations**

**Economic Groups**

# Trade and Travel Networks

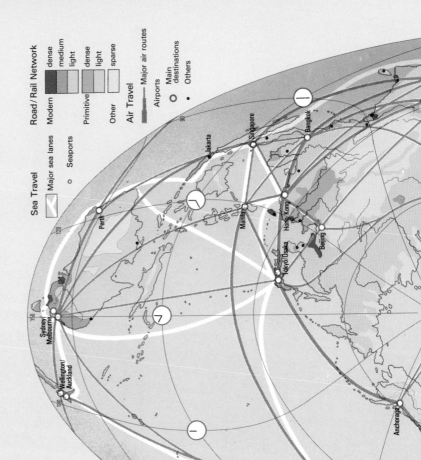

## Road and Rail

Integrated road and rail networks are the basis of industrialised society. Containerisation and the extension of modern highway systems have increased flexibility and reduced the emphasis on railways transporting freight.

**Roads – comparative lengths (Log scale)**

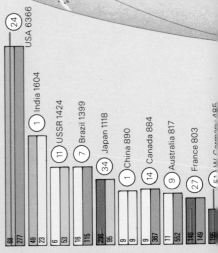

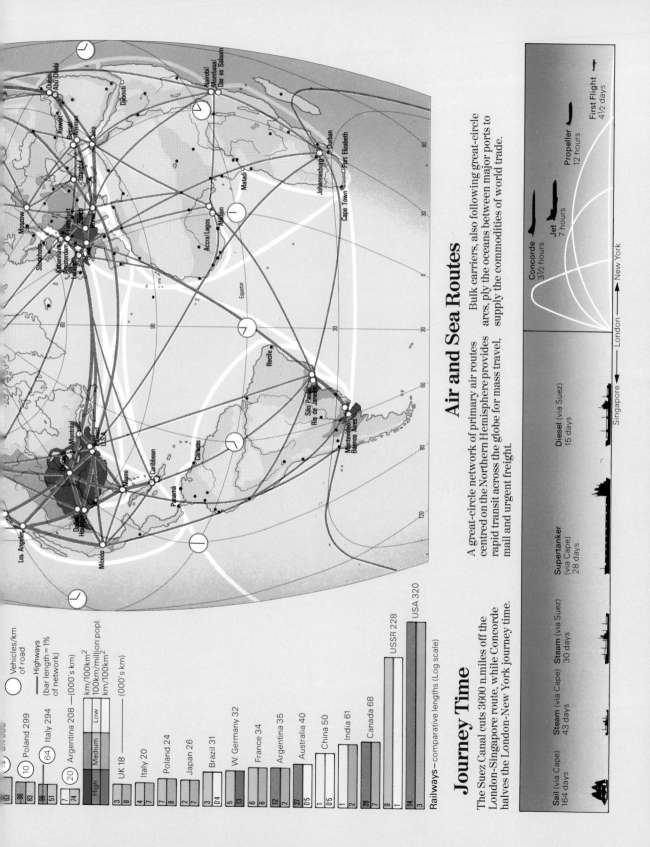

## Air and Sea Routes

A great-circle network of primary air routes centred on the Northern Hemisphere provides rapid transit across the globe for mass travel, mail and urgent freight.

Bulk carriers, also following great-circle arcs, ply the oceans between major ports to supply the commodities of world trade.

## Journey Time

The Suez Canal cuts 3600 n.miles off the London-Singapore route, while Concorde halves the London-New York journey time.

Concorde
3½ hours

Jet
7 hours

Propeller
12 hours

First Flight
4½ days

London — New York

Singapore — London — New York

Sail (via Cape)
164 days

Steam (via Cape)
43 days

Steam (via Suez)
30 days

Supertanker
(via Cape)
28 days

Diesel (via Suez)
15 days

Railways—comparative lengths (Log scale)

USA 320

USSR 228

Canada 68

India 61

China 50

Australia 40

Argentina 35

France 34

W. Germany 32

Brazil 31

Japan 26

Poland 24

Italy 20

UK 18

Vehicles/km of road

Highways
(bar length = 1% of network)

km/100km² — (000's km)
100km/million popl.
km/100km²

High   Medium   Low

Poland 299
Italy 294
64
Argentina 208 — (000's km)
10
20

# Gross National Product and
# Working Populations

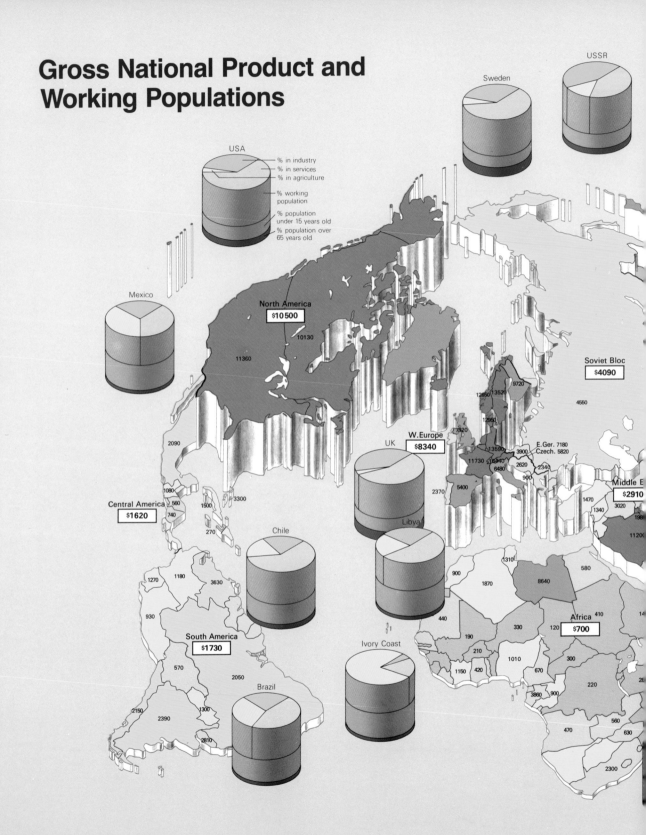

Sweden

USSR

USA

% in industry
% in services
% in agriculture

% working
population

% population
under 15 years old

% population over
65 years old

Mexico

North America
**$10 500**

10130

11360

Soviet Bloc
**$4090**

9720

12650 13520

4550

12950

UK

W.Europe
**$8340**

7920

13590

E.Ger. 7180
Czech. 5820

Middle E
**$2910**

2090

11730 15910 3900
6480 2620 2340

900

1080

560
740

Central America
**$1620**

1500 3300

2370 5400

1470

1340 3020

270

1980

11200

Chile

Libya

1310

580

1270 1180

3630

900

1870

8640

930

440

Africa 410
**$700**

14

South America
**$1730**

Ivory Coast

330 120

570

190

300

2050

Brazil

210

1010

670

220

2

1150 420

2150

1300

3860 900

560

2390

2810

470

630

2300

China

Japan
$8730

Japan

780

690

290

S. & E. Asia
$310

Oceania
$7000

Australia

11890

9820

130   170   670

300   300   240

350

270

Israel   India

Indonesia

7090

350

S. Africa

1620

# Economic Groups

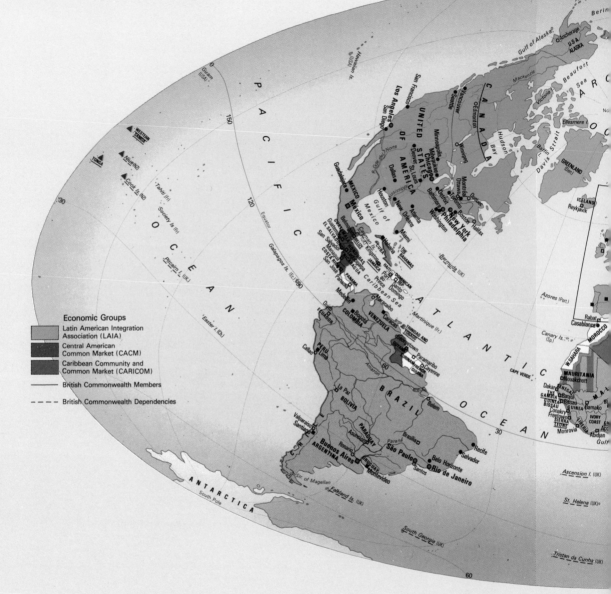

**Economic Groups**

Latin American Integration
Association (LAIA)

Central American
Common Market (CACM)

Caribbean Community and
Common Market (CARICOM)

—— British Commonwealth Members

---- British Commonwealth Dependencies

## Economic Groups

| | Organisation for Economic Co-operation and Development (OECD) | | Arab League |
| | Council for Mutual Economic Assistance (COMECON) | | Economic Community of West African States (ECOWAS) |
| | Colombo Plan (also ASEAN) | | Southern African Development Co-ordination Conference |
| | Association of Southeast Asian Nations (ASEAN) | | Central African Customs and Economic Union (UDEAC) |
| ▲ | South Pacific Forum | ◯ | Organisation of African Unity (OAU) |

## European Economic Groups

European Economic Community (EEC)

European Free Trade Association (EFTA)

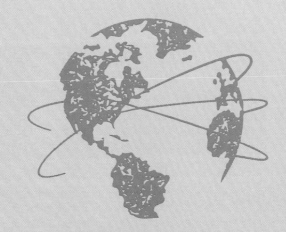

# Global Marketing
NCR's Eurostrategy for 1992

NCR established its first sales agency in England in 1885, one year after the company was founded in Dayton, Ohio. Soon thereafter it allied itself with other agencies all over Europe and eventually converted these operations into wholly owned subsidiaries. Today NCR has a presence in all of the European countries and employs around 13,000 people in the region. NCR Europe, which covers both EC and EFTA countries, accounted for one third, or $2 billion, of NCR's total revenues of $6 billion in 1988.

In 1987, shortly after the EC's ratification of its 1992 program, management decided that to cope with the EC's plans for full integration, it would need more information and guidance than the standard system was set up to supply. So it designed and initiated a multi-year, four-phase project called, simply, "Project 1992."

**Phase I.** For the introductory phase, which was completed in October 1988, NCR retained Hill & Knowlton, a European consulting firm, to carry out a very broad investigation of the issues associated with the EC's full integration in 1992. The consultants were asked to analyze the effect of 1992 not only on the IT (Information Technology) industry but also on a half-dozen target industries that are heavy users of NCR products.

**Phase II.** In this phase, two parallel activities take place. First, about a dozen issues, or areas, have been assigned to NCR experts (known as issue "owners"). These issues include manufac-

turing, law, marketing, distribution, services, software consulting, hardware maintenance, finance and treasury, telecommunications, standards and issues related to suppliers. The issue owners have been asked to define the scope of each issue and make preliminary recommendations about how NCR should position itself on each issue. Second, company executives have commissioned the development of a set of scenarios for the Europe of the 1990s, within which the specific issue recommendations can be evaluated. Late last year NCR signed an agreement with Battelle in Columbus, Ohio, to prepare jointly a series of scenarios for the European IT industry through the 1990s.

**Phase III.** The third element of Project 1992, which should begin in the fall of 1989, is implementation and monitoring of the issue owners' recommendations.

**Phase IV.** This part of the project will be introduced several months after Phase III is under way and will also continue for several years. During Phase IV the company will form 1992 partnerships with leading companies in the targeted industries by saying, essentially, that "1992 is a complex issue. We know you've been looking at it very carefully. We've been looking at it very carefully from the perspective of our business, and we'd like to share with you the approach that we've taken and work closely with you to understand the impact of 1992 on your industry."

Source: *Business International*, July 24, 1989, 217, 218, 224.

---

a giant industrial free-trade area, joining most of Western Europe together for trade in manufactured goods.

The *Latin American Integration Association (LAIA)* is also aiming at a free-trade area. LAIA was born in August 1980 as the successor to the Latin American Free Trade Association (LAFTA), which started in 1960 and sought free trade among members by 1973. That target was later advanced to 1980, but continued lack of progress led to the formation of LAIA, which has basically the same goals and unfortunately also retains the same problems, primarily that (1) some governments feel that the gains from integration will go primarily to other members, and (2) national producers are afraid of the competition from other member countries. In 1967 these and other problems led six of its members to form a new group — the *Andean Common Market (ANCOM)*.

The United States is a member of two free-trade areas, one with Israel and one with Canada. The U.S.–Canadian agreement is very important because it ties even more closely two of the world's richest economies, which already have bilateral trade of $200 billion a year. For American and Canadian firms it means new opportunities and new patterns of competition as the markets become even more integrated.

**Customs Union.**   Though similar to a free-trade area in that it has no tariffs on trade among members, a *customs union* has the more ambitious requirement that members also have a uniform tariff on trade with nonmembers. Thus a customs union is like a single nation, not only in internal trade, but also in presenting a united front to the rest of the world with its common external tariff. A customs union is more difficult to achieve than a free-trade area because each member must yield its sovereignty in commercial policy matters, not just with member nations but with the whole world. Its advantage lies in making the economic integration stronger and avoiding the administrative problems of a free-trade area. For example, in a free-trade area, imports of a particular good would always enter the member country with the lowest tariff on that good, regardless of the country of destination. To avoid this perversion of trade patterns, special regulations are necessary.

The leading example of a customs union is the EC. Although the EC is often referred to as the *Common Market*, it is more accurately described as a customs union. In July 1968, the EC achieved a full customs union, a goal toward which member nations had been working since January 1, 1958. Though this is a slower timetable than that of EFTA, it represents a much more ambitious endeavor, because it includes not only a free-trade area among members but also a common external tariff. In addition, it covers agricultural products, which are omitted by EFTA.

**Common Markets.**   A true *common market* includes a customs union but goes significantly beyond it, since it seeks to standardize or harmonize all government regulations affecting trade. These include all aspects of government policy that pertain to business — for example, corporation and excise taxes, labor laws, fringe benefits and social security programs, incorporation laws, and antitrust laws. In such an economic union, business and trade decisions would be unaffected by the national laws of different members because they would be uniform. The United States is the closest example of a common market. Even here, however, the example is not perfect, because different states do have different laws and taxes pertaining to business. American business decisions therefore are somewhat influenced by differing state laws.

The EC is the best contemporary example of a common market in formation. It always had the goal of achieving such, but what it achieved earlier was actually a customs union with a few extra dimensions. What is exciting about 1992 is the 300 new directives undertaken by the member states to reach a true common market by 1992, by harmonizing the different national regulations in 12 member countries. Even if this goal is not reached fully by 1992, great strides toward market integration will have been made. The fact that 300 directives were still necessary 30 years after forming the EC shows how difficult and complex it is to form a true common market.

While the member states must implement the 300 directives, the major marketing organizations in the EC are making their own preparations for the new "single market." Ad agencies, manufacturers, wholesalers, and retailers are reorganizing and forming alliances to become European-scale companies. (See the chapter appendix on "Europe, 1992.")

**Other Groupings.**   There are a number of examples of looser forms of economic cooperation. Many of these are of interest because they can affect the operations of the firm. Many nations of Africa are associated with the EC and enjoy preferential entry of their goods into EC countries. EC producers in turn have an advantage over non-EC producers in selling to the associated states. Turkey is also an associate member of EC. Israel signed an agreement in 1970.

In Asia, there have been various halting steps toward regional cooperation. The biggest is the *Association of Southeast Asian Nations (ASEAN)*. Though the agreement makes no mention of a common market or free-trade area, it does mention more effective collaboration in industry and agriculture. ASEAN has made some progress in allocating automotive production among member countries; and in 1988, it agreed to accelerate tariff reductions on intra-ASEAN trade.

The appearance of regional economic groupings is a promising development both for the regions and for multinational firms. The unfortunate reality is that apart from Europe, these groupings have made very little progress. Because the organizational framework remains in place for these groupings, there is always the hope that there will be further progress in the future. Firms should monitor their development.

**Regionalism and the Multinational Company.**   The rise of regional groupings is a change in the environment. It means that fewer but larger economic entities are gradually replacing the multitude of national markets. When the firm is considering an investment decision, the relevant market area may include six or seven countries rather than just one national market. Much of the large American investment in Western Europe in the 1960s, and again in the 1980s, was a result of the attraction of the larger market offered by the EC. The "United States of Europe" was one expression used to describe the new Europe. In the 1980s the Japanese were matching U.S. investments in the EC.

The firm's logistics will be modified by regional groupings. There will be pressures to supply from within a region rather than to export to it. The firm will have the added incentive of the larger market, but it will be pressured to get behind the external tariff to compete with local producers. At the same time, these local producers will become stronger competitors because of the economies of scale they realize in the larger market, the alliances they are forming, and because of the stronger competition in the free-trade area. A firm's operations within a regional group will tend to be more uniform and self-contained than they would be in ungrouped national markets.

The firm's marketing program will be modified in common market areas. As the differences in markets diminish, there will be greater uniformity in the marketing approach to the member countries. The firm will gain economies of scale in product development, pricing, distribution, and promotion. For example, as member nations harmonize their food, drug, and labeling laws, the firm can eliminate product and packaging differences which were required solely by the differences in national laws. Similar modifications would occur in the other functional areas. Some examples will illustrate how firms have adapted to take advantage of the new market realities created by regional groupings.

A manufacturer of home-care products closed down eight national production sources in Europe soon after the common market was formed. The firm concentrated its continental European production in the Netherlands to gain economies of scale possible within the free-trade area. To further facilitate and benefit from centralized production, the firm standardized its package sizes and designs, including color, even though copy was continued in different national languages.

As another example, Eversharp was challenging Gillette's strong position in razor blades in Latin America. Gillette had plants in Argentina, Brazil, Mexico, and Colombia. Eversharp chose to begin production in Venezuela, where it could purchase a local blade manufacturer. Here it could protect the local market while gaining entry into third markets in LAFTA where Gillette had already obtained concessions under the Montevideo Treaty. One of Eversharp's managers in Venezuela acted as LAFTA coordinator to search out opportunities for further concessions in LAFTA markets. With the help of the Venezuelan government, happy to see its exports expand, this effort has paid off. Two of Gillette's protected markets, Mexico and Colombia, were opened to Eversharp through the LAFTA negotiation process.

## International Financial System

A major goal of business is to make a profit, so firms pay close attention to financial matters. International companies must be even more concerned with financial matters than national firms are, because they must deal with many currencies and many national financial markets where conditions differ from one to the other. Marketing across national boundaries involves financial considerations which we will discuss here.

**Exchange Rate Instability.**   The international payments system is the financial side of international trade. A special dimension in international payments is the fact that transactions occur in many different currencies. Dealing with multiple currencies is not a serious problem in itself. The difficulty arises because currencies frequently change in value vis-à-vis each other, and in unpredictable ways. Since 1973 the major currencies have been floating, often in a volatile manner.

The exchange rate is the domestic price of a foreign currency. For the United States, this means that there is a dollar rate, or price, for the British pound, the Swiss franc, the Brazilian cruziero, as well as every other currency. If one country changes the value of its currency, firms selling to or from that country may find that the altered exchange rate is sufficient to wipe out their profit, or, on the brighter side, give them a windfall gain. In any case, they must be alert for currency variations in order to optimize their financial performance.

For 22 years Mexico maintained the value of its peso at 12.5 to the U.S. dollar. On August 31, 1976, the government abruptly let the peso float, and it immediately fell to about 20 pesos to the U.S. dollar — an effective devaluation of almost 40 percent! Suddenly imports into Mexico became very expensive, while exports from Mexico were much more competitive. International companies had to rethink their logistics patterns involving Mexico. While the initial change to floating and the 40 percent drop was a shock, firms then had to get used to a long-run depreciating peso. By 1989 the exchange rate was more than 2,500 pesos to the dollar. In the days of the gold standard, exchange rates did not change in value. The stability and certainty of the international gold standard came to an end, however, with the advent of World War I. The international financial system of the 1930s had no certainty, stability, or accepted rules. Instead there were frequent and arbitrary changes in exchange rates. This chaotic and uncertain situation contributed to the decline in international trade during that period. The worldwide depression of the thirties was reinforced by the added risks in international finance.

In 1944 some of the allied nations met at Bretton Woods to design a better international economic system for the postwar world. One element of this system dealt with international trade, and left us with GATT. Another element concerned with the need for international capital led to the formation of the International Bank for Reconstruction and Development (IBRD), commonly called the *World Bank*. A third aspect involving the international monetary system resulted in the establishment of the *International Monetary Fund (IMF)*.

**International Monetary Fund (IMF).**   The Bretton Woods international monetary system was an attempt to avoid the uncertainty of the 1930s and to regain some of the stability of exchange rates that existed under the gold standard. Countries who joined the International Monetary Fund (IMF) were required to establish a par value for their currency (in terms of the U.S. dollar) and maintain it within plus or minus 1 percent of that value. Up to 1970, the Bretton Woods system of stable "pegged" rates worked reasonably well, although there were numerous devaluations during that period. The increased confidence in the international monetary system contributed to the great surge in international trade since World War II.

In the late 1960s and early 1970s there existed very large funds in the hands of corporations, banks, and others with international dealings. This made it increasingly difficult for central banks to defend the par value of their currency. For example, the holders of funds tended to move them out of currencies they considered weak, and therefore candidates for devaluation, and into currencies they considered strong.

Those who were moving funds called it prudent management because they were protecting their assets. Others called the same activity speculation. In any case the results were the same. Central banks had fewer resources than those who were moving funds and had to give up the struggle to maintain the par value of their currencies. As a result, since 1973 the major industrialized countries have let their currencies "float," that is, fluctuate daily according to the forces of supply and demand. Thus, the international marketer today must contend with exchange rates which are continually moving targets, a complication for international pricing and logistics. (These implications will be covered in Chapters 14 and 15.)

The Bretton Woods system of pegged exchange rates is dead. However, like an old soldier, the IMF did not die. It did not even fade away. But it now has a more nebulous role in a world of floating exchange rates. Even so, the IMF is a help to international marketing. It still lends money to countries with balance-of-payments problems, enabling them to continue their international trade — and making them better customers. The IMF also continues to provide a forum for international monetary cooperation that lessens the chances of nations taking arbitrary actions against others, as occurred in the 1930s.

**World Bank.**   The International Bank for Reconstruction and Development (IBRD, or World Bank) is another institution conceived at Bretton Woods. It also has an impact on the world economy in which international business operates. Whereas the IMF is concerned with the provision of short-term liquidity, the World Bank supplies long-term capital to aid economic development. It provides over $10 billion a year for this purpose. IDA (International Development Association) is a daughter organization of the World Bank, created for the purpose of giving "soft" loans to developing countries, that is, long-term loans at very low interest rates. Lending done by these two groups is for all aspects of development, for example, providing infrastructure, industrial projects, agriculture, education, tourism, and population control.

World Bank activities have improved the international economic environment and aided international business. The supply of capital has meant a higher level of economic activity and therefore better markets for firms. For example, many firms are suppliers to projects in developing countries for which the World Bank and IDA are lending billions of dollars. This often opens up new import markets that might have been impossible to enter if the World Bank had not given financial assistance to the country. Many firms find profitable contracts in projects financed by the World Bank.

**The United
States in the
World Economy**

Although the international environment in which the firm operates is important, the global influence of the country in which the international firm has its home base cannot be ignored. In ways varying from country to country, the home government affects the international operations of the firm, both positively and negatively. A Swedish or Dutch multinational company operates under a set of advantages and constraints different from those that affect an American firm or a Japanese firm or a firm from one of the former colonial powers, England or France. Since most of the readers of this book will be Americans, we will examine the advantages and constraints peculiar to an American multinational company. The pattern can be applied to international firms domiciled in other nations.

One obvious impact on the firm's international operations is its home government's policies toward such business. Most governments encourage exports. U.S. government assistance is given through the information and promotional services of the Department of Commerce. Furthermore, the Export-Import Bank helps finance many American exports, and there is a government assisted program of export credit insurance and political-risk insurance.

The United States foreign aid program has helped American companies export to markets that otherwise would have been closed because of their lack of foreign exchange. If the foreign aid programs have a favorable effect on recipient nations' attitudes toward Americans, this will improve the environment for American firms. A critical determinant of the firm's ability to export is, of course, the resource endowment of its home country. Furthermore, the business environment at home may have taught the firm skills that aid its performance abroad.

There are other U.S. policies that relate to international business. The government has encouraged investment in less developed countries by its investment-guarantee program. Government tax policy is favorable to foreign business. Firms do not pay United States tax on foreign earnings until remitted back to America. In effect, while this money is being used abroad, it is an interest-free loan from the U.S. Treasury.

The government's commercial policy can help or hinder the firm in selling internationally. A national free-trading posture will make it easier for the firm than a protectionist policy because the latter will stimulate retaliation in foreign markets. For example, U.S. protectionism in the 1980s (against Japan) had an influence on Japanese reaction to U.S. firms. The firm is often able to influence its nation's commercial policy through trade association representation to the appropriate government bodies.

One direct restriction on the firm's foreign sales is the U.S. government's policy on trading with communist countries. If the British or French government wanted to sell equipment to Cuba or North Korea, the American subsidiaries in Britain and France could not supply components for this equipment. France did, in fact, lose aircraft sales for this reason. This caused trouble for American firms in France.

Other government actions and national achievements can affect the firm internationally. U.S. antitrust policy has constrained American companies abroad. American technological and space achievements aid American companies in sales of high-technology products. In part, these technological advances are supported by government funds for research and development. On the other hand, foreign dissatisfaction with America's role in the world can threaten foreign operations of American firms. Dissatisfaction over Nicaragua or some other American action may lead to a march on the United States Embassy — or the local Goodyear plant or Coca-Cola bottler.

The size and wealth of the U.S. economy is a source of both envy and resentment. It affects the image of American companies abroad — they are often considered to have an unfair advantage over local companies. The United States is the world's leading exporter and also the largest importer. This lends weight to American commercial policy negotiations, which is favorable to the foreign sales of American firms. Since the American market is so attractive, other countries must open up their markets a bit if they wish to sell to the United States. In all these ways, a company's nationality affects its international marketing.

## Summary

International trade, the economic link between nations, is one of the largest and fastest-growing markets in the world economy. A study of the subject should include the composition of trade — that is, the shifting shares of manufactured goods versus various other commodities — and the patterns of trade, both globally and for individual countries, to help a firm's international logistics planning.

The theory of international trade helps in understanding a nation's comparative advantage and is useful for locating supply or production sources. The international product life cycle theory can help the firm know when to source, or produce abroad.

The balance of payments is a summary statement of a nation's imports and exports that can be analyzed to determine market potential and competition in a country.

All countries have regulations on their international trade (commercial policy), usually to protect employment in home industries. Tariffs and quotas are the major tools used by industrial countries to control their trade. These affect the firm's pricing, product, and logistics decisions. Exchange control, a more comprehensive and rigid form of trade control, is used primarily by developing countries and communist countries.

GATT, as the world trade club, works to liberalize the exchange of goods and services between countries. To the degree it is successful, it facilitates the firm's international marketing. UNCTAD is the lobby for developing country interests in trade. It, too, can affect the firm's international marketing, such as when preferences are available to influence the firm's logistics.

Economic relations between the Eastern and Western blocs are much more restricted than trade among the industrial countries. Thus, the volume of East-West trade is small though the potential is large. Liberalizing trends in China, the Soviet Union, and other East bloc countries could mean great market opportunities in the future.

In the growing interdependence of the world economy, nations are finding it desirable to have some kind of economic integration with their neighbors. This offers larger resources, larger markets, and economies of scale to help them compete and prosper in the competitive world economy. Unfortunately, the EC is the only major successful integration story, with EFTA doing reasonably well. Efforts elsewhere, such as ASEAN in Asia or LAIA in Latin America, have made very little progress. Where integration is successful, it offers great opportunities for those firms who can operate inside the integrated group, and great challenges for those who are on the outside.

The major world currencies have been floating since 1973. The instability and uncertainty this causes disrupts the sourcing patterns and the pricing of the international firm. The IMF, though no longer able to maintain stable currencies, is still a force for moderation and stability in international finance. IMF lending to deficit countries helps to keep their markets viable and open to the international marketer. The World Bank, through its development loans, provides resources to help poorer countries strengthen their economies and become more prosperous, and thus more attractive markets for the international firm. And World Bank projects themselves can provide attractive marketing opportunities.

A firm's home country is an important determinant of its international marketing success. U.S. regulations, for example, can limit the scope of a firm's international marketing, but the government also supports international business by making available information, insurance, financing and other kinds of assistance. Moreover, the large, competitive U.S. domestic market is a good training group for international marketing. The U.S. image in the world, however, can be a plus or a minus for the firm's international marketing.

## Questions

2.1   What can be learned from studying the composition and patterns of world trade?

2.2   How can an understanding of international trade theory help the international marketer?

2.3   What is a balance of payments? Of what use is it to international marketing?

2.4   How can an exporter respond to a new tariff imposed on its product? To a quota?

2.5   What are the implications of exchange control to the international marketer?

2.6   What is GATT, and what does it do for the environment of international marketing?

2.7   Under UNCTAD pressure, preferential tariff treatment has been granted to many developing countries. What might this mean for the multinational firm?

2.8   What problems/opportunities are posed for the firm by the East-West trade split?

2.9   Why might an American exporter feel threatened by the formation of regional economic groupings? How might the firm react?

2.10   What might 1992 mean for American firms already operating in the EC?

2.11   How can the IMF be considered a friend of the international marketer?

2.12   What are the potential benefits of World Bank activity for international marketing?

## Endnotes

[1]Louis T. Wells, Jr., "A Product Life Cycle for International Trade?" *Journal of Marketing* (July 1968): 1–6.

## Further Readings

*For further discussion of international economic questions and institutions, see standard texts in the field, such as the following:*

Peter H. Lindert. *International Economics.* 8th ed. Homewood, Ill.: Irwin, 1988.

Root, Franklin R. *International Trade and Investment.* 6th ed. Cincinnati: Southwestern, 1990.

## Data Sources

*International Financial Statistics.* Washington, D.C.: International Monetary Fund monthly.

International Monetary Fund. *Annual Reports.* Washington, D.C.

IBRD. *Annual Reports.* Washington, D.C.

*Survey of Current Business.* Washington, D.C.: U.S. Department of Commerce monthly.

United Nations. *Statistical Yearbook.* New York: United Nations annual.

United Nations. *Yearbook of International Trade Statistics.* New York: United Nations annual.

*World Trade Annual.* New York: United Nations annual.

# CASE 2.1 Foreign Exchange Rates

### Currency per U.S. Dollar September 30, 1989

| Country | Currency | Rate |
|---------|----------|------|
| Argentina | Austral | 615.0 |
| Brazil | New cruzado | 3.69 |
| Britain | Pound | .620 |
| Canada | Dollar | 1.18 |
| Colombia | Peso | 412.0 |
| France | Franc | 6.37 |
| Israel | Shekel | 2.00 |
| Italy | Lira | 1,369.0 |
| Japan | Yen | 140.0 |
| Mexico | Peso | 2,565.0 |
| Singapore | Dollar | 1.96 |
| South Korea | Won | 667.0 |
| Taiwan | Dollar | 25.38 |
| West Germany | Deutsche mark | 1.88 |

## Questions

1. Find the latest quotations for these currencies. (*The Wall Street Journal* is a convenient source.)
2. Calculate the approximate changes in the value of these currencies. Show the increase or decrease vis a vis the U.S. dollar.
3. Why have these changes occurred? (Give a general explanation.)
4. What are some of the implications for international marketing of changing exchange rates?

# CASE 2.2 U.S. Pharmaceuticals, Inc. (A)

U.S. Pharmaceuticals (USP) is an American firm with about 30 percent of its sales outside the United States. USP concentrates on the ethical drug business but has diversified into animal health products, cosmetics, and some patent medicines. These other lines account for about one-fourth of USP's $800 million sales.

USP's international business is conducted in some 70 countries, mostly through distributors in those markets. In six countries, however, it has manufacturing or compounding operations. (*Compounding* refers to the local mixing, assembling, and packaging of critical ingredients shipped from the United States.) USP's only Latin American manufacturing/compounding operations are in Latinia, a country with a population of about 30 million. Some products are shipped from Latinia to other Latin American markets.

USP's Latinian plant is operated by the pharmaceutical division. It is engaged in the production and especially the compounding of USP's ethical drug line. It does no work for other USP divisions (cosmetics, proprietary medicines, and animal health). All the other divisions, which also sell in Latinia, export their finished products

53

from plants in the United States. The Latinian plant employs 330 people, of whom only two are North Americans — the general manager, Tom Hawley, and the director of quality control, Frixos Massialas.

USP's cosmetics and toiletries business accounts for $150 million in sales and is handled by a separate division — Cosmetics and Toiletries. The division sells in only 38 of USP's 70 foreign markets. One of the divisions' better foreign markets is Latinia, where it has sales of over $8 million and an acceptable market position. Cosmetics and Toiletries has a marketing subsidiary in Latinia to handle its business there. Jim Richardson, an American, heads the subsidiary. The rest of the staff are Latinians.

Jim Richardson was very disturbed by the latest news received from the Latinian Ministry of International Trade. Tariffs were being increased on many "nonessential products" because of the balance-of-payments pressures the country had been undergoing for the past year and a half. For USP's Cosmetics and Toiletries, specifically, this meant a rise in the tariffs it pays from 20 percent to 50 percent ad valorem. The 20 percent duty had posed no particular problem for Cosmetics and Toiletries because of the prestige of the imported product and the consumer franchise it had established, Richardson explained. He felt, however, that the 50 percent duty was probably an insurmountable barrier.

Cosmetics and Toiletries competition in Latinia was about evenly divided between local firms and other international companies from Europe and North America. Jim felt that local firms, which had about 40 percent of the market, stood to benefit greatly from the tariff increase unless the international firms could find a satisfactory response. When Jim received the news of the tariff increase, which was to be imposed the first of October — one week away — he called a meeting to consider what Cosmetics and Toiletries could do. Deborah Neale, Manager, Cosmetics Marketing, and Emilio Illanes, Manager, Toiletries Marketing, met with Jim to discuss the situation.

Several different courses of action were proposed at the hastily called meeting. Deborah suggested, "We could continue importing, pay the high duty, and change the positioning strategy to appeal to a high-price, quality market." Another idea was to import the primary ingredients and assemble (compound) and package them in Latinia. (Duties on the imported ingredients ranged between 10 percent and 35 percent ad valorem.) Emilio suggested asking Cosmetics and Toiletries in the United States for a lower price on the products shipped to Latinia so that the duty would have a lesser impact on the final price in the local market. Jim mentioned the alternative that none of them wanted to think about. "If we can't compete at those high prices, we may have to give up the market."

## Questions

1. Evaluate the alternatives that were brought up at the meeting.
2. Are there any other possible courses of action?
3. Propose and defend a course of action.
4. How would your response differ if, instead of a tariff increase, Latinia had imposed a quota cutting the imports of these products by 75 percent?

# Europe, 1992
## Background and Summary

World War II was the latest and most damaging chapter of centuries of conflict on the European continent. After that war there developed a strong revulsion against these national rivalries and the European civil wars to which they led. European statesmen such as Jean Monnet and Robert Schuman of France and Paul Henri Spaak of Belgium looked ahead to a united Europe as the necessary basis for European strength and security, and the best way of preventing another, and even worse, European holocaust. They were active in laying plans for what was to become the European Community.

Support for European reconstruction and plans for unity came from the United States in the Marshall Plan. From 1948 to 1952 the United States gave about $200 billion to help Europe get reestablished. This aid was administered by a new organization formed for that purpose—the Organization for European Economic Cooperation (OEEC). In the 1950s, restrictions on intra-OEEC trade were being dismantled, and the European countries grew accustomed to cooperation on trade and economic matters.

Many Europeans felt, however, that even closer cooperation and integration was necessary. The first step in this direction was the establishment of the European Coal and Steel Community (ECSC) in 1952, creating a common market in coal, steel, and iron ore among Belgium, France, Germany, Italy, the Netherlands, and Luxembourg. The next great step was the signing of the Treaty of Rome in 1957 by the same six nations of the ECSC. The Rome Treaty set up the European Community (EC), often called the Common Market, in 1958. The third member of the European Community, the European Atomic Energy Community (Euratom), was also formed in 1958. Its six members pledged common development of their nuclear energy resources by coordinating their nuclear R&D programs.

The EC, or Common Market, was and is the major integration effort in Europe. We shall review briefly its goals and achievements leading up to the final drive for a "single market" by 1992.

1. *Customs union.* The customs union part of the Rome Treaty envisaged the removal of all restrictions on trade among the six member countries, and the establishment of a common system of tariffs and quotas against all third countries. The customs union was achieved in 1968.

2. *Common agricultural policy.* Agricultural trade always receives strong protection from national governments, so it was a major achievement for the EC to reach a common agricultural policy among the six member states. Thus, the customs union, by 1968, included both agriculture and industrial goods, making the common market much stronger, albeit with strong barriers to agricultural products coming in from outside the EC.

3. *Common market.* A common market is more than a customs union. It requires the free movement of labor, capital, and enterprise as well as the free movement of goods. The EC has achieved quite a degree of freedom for factor movement among member states, though it is far from having complete freedom.

4. *Expansion of the EC.* The EC had only the original six members from 1958 till 1973 when Britain, Denmark, and Ireland were admitted. Greece joined in 1981 and Spain and Portugal in 1986 bringing the total membership to twelve nations.

A different kind of expansion occurred with the Lomé Convention of 1975. At this time, the EC eliminated most trade barriers on imports from 46 developing nations in Africa, the Caribbean, and the Pacific region that were former colonies of EC countries. These 46 countries became "associated states" of the EC, enjoying preferential access to its large market. Later Lomé conventions raised the number of associated states to 66, expanding even further the economic influence of the EC.

The economic influence of the EC expanded with the other developed countries of Western Europe also. In 1972, when European Free Trade Association (EFTA) members Britain, Denmark, and Ireland were joining the EC, it agreed to establish a free-trade area with the remaining EFTA members (Iceland, Norway, Sweden, Finland, Austria, and Switzerland). This free-trade agreement covers only industrial goods and not agricultural products, so it is a much looser tie than that existing between the 12 EC-member states.

5. *European Monetary System (EMS).* In 1979 the EC took another strong step toward greater economic union when it created the European Monetary System (EMS) in order to foster "closer monetary cooperation leading to a zone of monetary stability in Europe." The method of operation was very similar to the Bretton Woods monetary system that operated on the global scene till 1971. Although Britain did not join the EMS, the system worked reasonably well in reducing inflation and exchange rate volatility among the other member nations. It represented a further degree of cooperation and integration in the EC.

6. *Institutional development.* The EC operates through four main institutions: (1) The *Council of Ministers* is its ultimate decision-making body. Its 12 members are the foreign ministers of each country. With the exception of the budget, the Council makes all the final decisions. (2) The *Commission* has 17 members representing, not their home country, but, rather, special aspects of the EC economy. The Council of Ministers drafts legislation for proposal to the Commission and oversees implementation of EC policies. It has a staff of over 10,000 in Brussels. (3) The *European Parliament* is

| Table 2A-1 | Economic Overview of the European Community, 1987 | | | | |

| | GNP | Population | Per Capita GNP | Extra-EC Imports[a] | Imports from the U.S. |
|---|---|---|---|---|---|
| | Billions of U.S. Dollars | Millions | U.S. Dollars | Billions of U.S. Dollars | |
| EC | $4,120.2 | 323.62 | $12,732 | $391.6 | $65.7 |
| Belgium-Luxembourg | 144.7 | 10.27 | 14,090 | 23.0 | 3.9 |
| Denmark | 97.5 | 5.12 | 19,041 | 12.0 | 1.2 |
| France | 846.9 | 55.61 | 15,229 | 53.5 | 11.3 |
| Germany | 1,129.9 | 60.99 | 18,526 | 103.1 | 14.2 |
| Greece | 45.9 | 10.01 | 4,584 | 5.5 | 0.3 |
| Ireland | 25.6 | 3.56 | 7,180 | 3.8 | 2.3 |
| Italy | 632.1 | 57.36 | 11,021 | 53.9 | 6.7 |
| Netherlands | 213.5 | 14.64 | 14,581 | 36.7 | 6.6 |
| Portugal | 33.4 | 10.35 | 3,229 | 4.9 | 0.7 |
| Spain | 284.0 | 38.84 | 7,312 | 20.8 | 4.0 |
| U.K. | 666.7 | 56.87 | 11,723 | 74.3 | 15.1 |
| U.S. | 4,486.2 | 243.77 | 18,403 | 405.9[b] | None |

[a]Imports from non-EC countries.

[b]Total U.S. imports

Source: *Business America,* August 1, 1988

directly elected by voters in the 12 countries. It serves as a watchdog on EC expenditures and evaluates other decisions of the Council. (4) The *European Court of Justice* is the official interpreter of EC law. Most of its cases are related to interpretation or application of the Treaty of Rome, the constitution of the EC. As more EC law develops, the European Court serves frequently as a court of appeals for national courts on EC issues. Its role is increasing with greater integration.

7. *The EC as an economic entity.* Table 2A–1 summarizes and compares key economic data for EC-member countries and the United States. The 12-nation EC forms a market almost as large as the United States, but with a population one-third larger. As in any economic union, EC-member countries benefit by the large volume of trade among themselves. Table 2A–2 summarizes intra-EC exports, imports, and unemployment data.

## Toward a Single European Market in 1992

A pressing need for EC nations is to increase future economic growth so as to reduce unemployment. Certain economic barriers have prevented the realization of a truly integrated and efficient common market. The barriers are *physical, technical,* and *fiscal,* namely,

- Border controls.
- Divergent standards, testing, and certification procedures.
- Differing technical regulations.
- Conflicting business laws.

**Intra-EC Trade and Unemployment in the EC, 1987**

|  |  | Intra-EC Trade (Percent of Total Going to EC) | |
| --- | --- | --- | --- |
|  | Unemployment | Exports | Imports |
| Belgium | 15.9% | 74% | 72% |
| Denmark | 8.0 | 49 | 52 |
| France | 10.6 | 60 | 61 |
| Germany | 8.9 | 53 | 53 |
| Greece | n.a. | 67 | 62 |
| Ireland | 19.0 | 74 | 66 |
| Italy | 12.0 | 56 | 57 |
| Netherlands | 14.1 | 75 | 64 |
| Portugal (March 1988) | 6.8 | 68 | 63 |
| Spain | 20.9 | 64 | 55 |
| U.K. | 10.3 | 59 | 53 |

Source: EC statistics.

- Protected public procurement.
- Differences in taxation: VAT and excise taxes.

While these barriers hurt different industries in different ways, they affect small business the most. Removing border controls alone could increase profit margins by 25 percent. Such controls, for example, require 56 hours for a London-Italy truck route (excluding the channel crossing), while a route of similar length within England requires only 36 hours.

The EC estimated "the costs of non-Europe" at $250 billion in a major 1988 study known as the Cecchini report. This means that creating a more efficient EC would increase its gross domestic product by 5 percent, while reducing unemployment and inflation. Figure 2A-1 outlines how such gains would be made. Moreover, larger and more efficient European companies would emerge, who would be better able to withstand U.S. and Japanese competition. The EC also issued a report (the Lord Cockfield report) outlining 300 measures that would have to be passed by 1992 to create an efficient *single Europe.* These measures focus on removing the barriers to intra-EC trade and establishing a common Europe-wide approach to mergers and acquisitions, patent law, broadcasting standards, product-labeling rules, vocational training, and other issues.

How will the physical barriers within the EC be eliminated? Borders cannot be eliminated; however, the EC advocates using a *single administrative document (SAD)* to reduce red tape in goods crossing borders. Further, a new, single EC-wide tariff would be applied to goods, with a harmonized EC-wide system for description and coding of traded goods, so as to reduce delays. Restrictions on the trucking industry, such as provisions preventing trucks from one country from picking up goods on their return leg of a journey, would be removed. Such a measure would immediately increase truck capacity in the EC.

**Figure 2A–1**          **Market Integration**

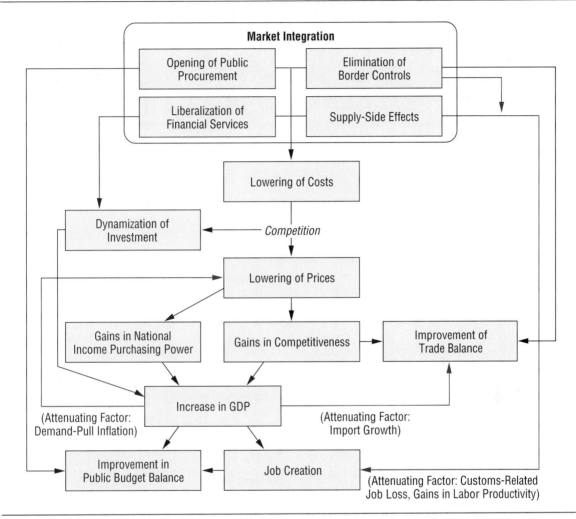

Source: P. Cecchini, *The European Challenge: 1992, the Benefits of a Single Market.* Gower Publishing Co., Brookfield, VT., Chart 10.1.

A second major problem is posed by the differences in technical regulations and standards of EC nations. Such differences prevent firms from achieving economies of scale, as they must approach each market with different products, manufactured in suboptimal small plants, sometimes resulting in narrow product lines and reduced technological spending. Such regulations are burdensome in competing with global firms. To overcome these problems, the EC recommends the following:

1. *Mutual recognition.* A provision in force in a member-state must be recognized as being equivalent to those applied by another, with exceptions for health, safety, and certain national objectives.

2. *Selective harmonization.* Nations should reconcile their differences wherever possible in order to adopt similar national standards.

3. *Mutual information.* When national standards must differ, companies should be provided with adequate information to comply with these differences.

A third major problem area is government protectionism in public procurement. Public procurement within the EC was estimated at 530 billion *European Currency Units (ECUs)* in 1986, about 15 percent of GDP; between 240 and 340 billion ECUs were tradable, that is, could be supplied by non-national firms. (An ECU was worth about $1.20 in 1989.)

An example comes from European telecommunications, where there are seven different competing digital switching systems, of which five were developed by national telephone companies. As a result, 1987 estimated cost per telephone line in the EC was $225 to $500, compared with $100 in the United States. EC recommendations include

- Ease of market entry by non-nationals.
- Transparency, and better rights of redress.
- Removal of exemptions for industries such as energy, transportation, telecommunications, utilities, so that they are open to competition to firms from other countries.

Service industries also can gain from a single Europe. Currently, financial services, banking, insurance, and the securities industries are all affected by different national regulations such as

- Controls on capital movements.
- Restrictions on foreign banks.
- Prohibition on non-national insurers seeking local business.
- Restrictions on licensing foreign brokers.
- Discriminatory taxation.
- Disproportionately higher prices on international telecommunications services, such as international long-distance dialing.

EC measures promoting competition and deregulation are intended to bring down prices. For example, an EC study showed that the cost of buying annual commercial fire and theft insurance in Italy, for property valued at about $500,000, was 245 percent of the average cost of such insurance in the four countries with the lowest prices. Open competition will result in prices coming down in Italy because of competition from the more efficient foreign insurance companies. As part of such liberalization, there will be a single banking license valid for all EC countries, and freedom of capital movement.

The move to a single Europe will also affect tax policy in EC-member nations. Nations use taxes to achieve different national objectives, and they have different ideas on whether to tax income or expenditure, and at what level. Countries also adopt different approaches to taxing capital gains. Higher taxes are often accompanied by higher levels of social services, such as national health care systems in West Germany and the United Kingdom.

**Table 2A-3**　　　　　　　　**VAT Rates in the EC, 1988**

|  | Reduced Rate | Standard Rate | High Rate |
|---|---|---|---|
| Belgium | 1 and 6% | 19% | 25 and 33% |
| Britain | 0 | 15 | None |
| Denmark | None | 22 | None |
| France | 2.1 to 7 | 18.6 | 33⅓ |
| Greece | 6 | 18 | 36 |
| Holland | 6 | 20 | None |
| Ireland | 2.4 and 10 | 25 | None |
| Italy | 2 and 9 | 18 | 38 |
| Luxembourg | 3 and 6 | 12 | None |
| Portugal | 8 | 16 | 30 |
| Spain | 6 | 12 | 33 |
| West Germany | 7 | 14 | None |
| Commission Proposal | 4 to 9 | 14 to 20 | None |

Source: The Economist, July 9, 1988.

EC nations in general also make heavy use of *value-added taxes (VAT),* which are taxes on consumption. The free movement of goods will make differential taxation of consumption (VAT or sales tax) by each country difficult. As Table 2A–3 shows, most EC countries have two rates of VAT tax, with a higher rate on "luxury" goods, while some categories of products (such as food) are exempt or are taxed at low rates for social reasons. Based on the data in this table, one might conclude that a mail-order sales firm could prosper by locating in Luxembourg and selling to all of the EC countries, taking advantage of the lowering of barriers to trade. This means that over time, countries with higher tax rates will be forced to lower their taxes or lose businesses to lower tax locations.

The move to a single market raises several other important issues, including the following:

1. *Competition policy.* The enlarged market and enhanced competition will lead to a wave of restructuring and mergers, with the need to derive economies of scale leading to the acquisition of smaller firms. If a merger involves two EC countries, and if combined sales are expected to exceed 1 billion ECU, EC rules governing mergers would be enforced and EC approval would be required. Such a policy would have affected 100 of the 300 mergers that took place in 1987.

2. *Political realities.* EC countries follow different political ideologies, especially regarding the role of the state in the economy. For this reason, the United Kingdom under Prime Minister Thatcher is opposed to granting wide powers to the EC, for fear of "socialism coming in through the back door." One result is that EC nations have been slow in adopting pan-European measures passed in Brussels.

**Table 2A–4**          **Is a Single Europe Possible?**

|  | United States | European Community |
|---|---|---|
| *Language* | One. | Many. |
| *Currency* | One. | Many; volatile. |
| *Culture* | Relatively homogeneous. | Diverse, historical differences. |
| *Ideology* | Free market. | Conflicting; free market versus socialistic. |
| *Government* | Strong; federal. | National sovereignty versus Brussels; but the achievement of the Single Europe Act. |
| *Mobility of People* | Unrestricted, active. | Theoretically possible. |
| *Legislation* | Federal takes precedence. | Conflicting national laws; attempts at harmonization. |
| *Regional Disparities* | A nationwide fiscal policy to ameliorate poorer regions. | Only 2.5% of European spending to combat regional differences; large disparities. |

3.   *Unions.* A single Europe could lead to firms from the higher-wage countries such as Germany moving their plants and expanding operations into poorer EC countries such as Portugal, Spain, Ireland, and Greece. Unions in the richer countries of France and Germany will obviously oppose such moves.

4.   *Regional disparities.* Within the EC, there are several depressed economic regions, such as the south of Italy, parts of the United Kingdom, Spain, and Portugal. If Turkey's application to enter the EC is ultimately approved, the poorer parts of Turkey would also require special treatment. The fear is that such regions will be ignored and become even poorer with the formation of a single market. How can the economic development of such regions be encouraged in a single Europe striving for greater efficiency?

5.   *Changes in Eastern Europe.* The pace of economic and political liberalization in Eastern Europe has taken the EC by surprise. As these countries seek to become members of the EC, the large economic and political differences will make achieving European unity even more difficult. At the same time, the availability of low-cost labor and the large market potential of Eastern Europe make a future enlarged EC even more powerful relative to the United States and Japan.

A natural reaction to the creation of a single European market is to ask, what about outsiders? There is fear that a single Europe will become a so-called *Fortress Europe,* keeping out foreign goods and foreign firms. Such fears seem overblown, as the EC accounts for about 20 percent of world trade, and would lose from the retaliation that would ensue if it raised trade barriers to outsiders. However, the EC has announced that it will seek *reciprocity.* This means that it will not discriminate against foreign firms in

EC countries, provided that the foreign firm's country will provide reciprocal, nondiscriminatory treatment to firms from EC countries located overseas.

Another difficult area is *local content,* which refers to the degree of value-added production within the EC countries. EC nations are not yet in agreement over whether a product with, say, 70 percent local content can be considered as a European product or as an import. U.S. interests are affected, since the specific local-content regulations adopted may keep out products manufactured in the United States and then exported to the EC.

European *industrial policy* also matters to U.S. companies, since EC-wide subsidized programs such as Esprit have helped EC companies carry out subsidized research and product development in areas such as consumer electronics, semiconductors, high-definition television, and commercial aircraft.

In summary, if the ambitious goals of a single Europe are fully realized, a major growth market will be available for global firms. At the same time, EC companies will emerge stronger and mount a challenge to dominant American and Japanese firms. The real gains of 1992 may lie in the removal of barriers that stop entrepreneurs in one European country from entering the same business in other European countries. However, there are some obstacles to the realization of a single Europe, and firms must consider them, though they are more likely to postpone rather than prevent that event. Table 2A–4 summarizes these difficulties.

# Further Readings

"A Survey of Europe's Internal Market." *The Economist,* July 9, 1988, and July 8, 1989. (A similar survey will be published in a July 1990 issue.)

P. Cecchini, *The European Challenge: 1992, the Benefits of a Single Market.* (Often referred to as the Cecchini Report.) Available from Gower Publishing Co., Old Post Road, Brookfield, VT., (802) 276-3162.

*Research on the Costs of 1992: Vol. 1, Basic Studies: Executive Summaries.* From European Community Information Service, 2100 M. St., N.W., 7th Floor, Washington, D.C. 20037.

*Harvard Business Review* (May–June 1989). Articles on 1992 include:

    Magee, "1992: Moves Americans Must Make."
    Friberg, "1992: Moves Europeans are Making."
    Stone, "Globalization of Europe, Interview with Wisse Dekker."

    Vernon, "Can U.S. Negotiate for Trade Equality?"

D. Swann, *The Economics of the Common Market.* New York, Pelican, 6th edition, 1988.

*European Trends,* a quarterly published by the Economist Intelligence Unit, 10 Rockefeller Plaza, 12th Floor, New York, NY 10020. (212) 541-5730.

*Journal of Common Market Studies* (March 1987). Special issue on making the common market work. Useful material on patents, trademarks, and standardization.

"Reshaping Europe, 1992 and Beyond." *Business Week,* December 12, 1988.

*Business International Europe* and its special studies on the 1992 question.

CHAPTER 3

# Economic Environment
## The Foreign Economies

**Learning Objectives**

A firm wishing to market abroad must select target markets from the 200 or so countries in the world economy. Toward that end, the firm wants some idea about the *size* of the market in various countries to help it establish its potential markets and priorities abroad. It also wants to know about the *nature* of these markets to determine the kind of marketing task it will face there.

The main goals of this chapter are to

1. Explore how information on population size, density, and distribution help give an initial idea of market size.
2. Explore how information on income, both national income and per capita income, can further identify potential markets.
3. Describe what constitutes the nation's physical endowment, and explain how it gives clues as to the nature of a firm's market and marketing task.
4. Explain how the nature of economic activity in a country can suggest how a firm's marketing will fit in.
5. Examine the effects of the infrastructure of a country (transportation, communication, etc.) on a firm's marketing there.
6. Demonstrate why the degree of urbanization is a useful indicator both of market potential and the marketing task in a country.

The second dimension of the economic environment of international marketing includes the *domestic* economy of every nation in which the firm is selling. Thus the international marketer faces the traditional task of economic analysis, but in a context that may include 100 countries or more. This chapter addresses the economic dimensions of individual world markets. The investigation will be directed toward answering two broad questions: (1) How big is the market? (2) What is the market like? Answers to the first question help determine the firm's market potential and priorities abroad. Answers to the second question help to determine the nature of the marketing task.

65

## Size of the Market

The firm's concern in examining world markets is the potential they offer for its products. The international marketer must determine market size not only for present markets but also for potential markets. This helps allocate effort among present markets and determine which markets to enter next. *Market size* for any given product is a function of particular variables, and its determination requires an ad hoc analysis. However, certain general indicators are relevant for many goods. We will see how world markets are described by the following general indicators: (1) population — growth rates and distribution; and (2) income — distribution, income per capita, and gross national product.

Possible markets are numerous. The *United Nations Statistical Yearbook* lists data for over 200 political entities. Of course, many of these are very small. United Nations membership itself counts about 155 countries. On a more practical level, the World Bank counts 131 countries with a population of over 1 million. The number of these nations that are worthwhile markets will vary from firm to firm. However, many companies sell in over 100 markets. Singer and Komatsu, for example, sell in over 150 countries.

**Population**

It takes people to make a market and, other things being equal, the greater the population in a country, the better the market. Of course, other things are never equal, so population figures in themselves are not usually a sufficient guide to market size. Nevertheless, the consumption of many products is correlated with population figures. For many "necessary" goods, such as ethical drugs, health care items, some food products, and educational supplies, population figures may be a very good first indicator of market potential. For other products that are low in price or meet particular needs population again may be a useful market indicator. Products in these latter categories include soft drinks, ballpoint pens, bicycles, and sewing machines.

Population figures are one of the first considerations in analyzing foreign economies. One striking fact is the tremendous differences in size of the nations of the world. The largest nation in the world has about 10,000 times the population of some of the smallest countries. Well over half the people of the world live in the ten countries that have populations of more than 100 million. On the other hand, two-thirds of the countries have populations of less than 10 million, and about 55 have fewer than 1 million people.

The marketer is concerned primarily with individual markets, but regional patterns can also be important for regional logistics. For example, Asia contains six of the ten most populous markets. By contrast, Africa, the Middle East, and Latin America are rather thinly populated. Nigeria is the only populous African nation, with 107 million people. Turkey is the largest market in the Mideast with 53 million people. Latin America has only two relatively populous countries: Brazil with 141 million and Mexico with 82 million. Europe, much smaller in land area but more densely populated than any other region, has four countries with populations over 56 million, plus the Soviet Union, which straddles Europe and Asia. These facts and others can be noted in Table 3–1.

**Table 3–1**                    **The World's Most Populous Nations**

| Nation | Population (Millions) | Nation | Population (Millions) |
|---|---|---|---|
| 1. China | 1,009 | 28. Zaire | 33 |
| 2. India | 798 | 29. Argentina | 31 |
| 3. USSR | 279 | 30. Colombia | 30 |
| 4. United States | 244 | 31. Canada | 26 |
| 5. Indonesia | 171 | 32. Tanzania | 24 |
| 6. Brazil | 141 | 33. Yugoslavia | 23 |
| 7. Japan | 122 | 34. Romania | 23 |
| 8. Nigeria | 107 | 35. Morocco | 23 |
| 9. Bangladesh | 106 | 36. Sudan | 23 |
| 10. Pakistan | 103 | 37. Algeria | 23 |
| 11. Mexico | 82 | 38. Kenya | 22 |
| 12. Vietnam | 65 | 39. North Korea | 21 |
| 13. Germany, FR | 61 | 40. Taiwan | 20 |
| 14. Philippines | 58 | 41. Peru | 20 |
| 15. Italy | 57 | 42. Afghanistan | 18 |
| 16. United Kingdom | 57 | 43. Germany, DR | 18 |
| 17. France | 56 | 44. Venezuela | 18 |
| 18. Thailand | 54 | 45. Nepal | 18 |
| 19. Turkey | 53 | 46. Iraq | 17 |
| 20. Egypt | 50 | 47. Czechoslovakia | 16 |
| 21. Iran | 47 | 48. Sri Lanka | 16 |
| 22. Ethiopia | 45 | 49. Australia | 16 |
| 23. South Korea | 42 | 50. Malaysia | 16 |
| 24. Spain | 39 | 51. Uganda | 16 |
| 25. Burma | 39 | 52. Netherlands | 15 |
| 26. Poland | 38 | 53. Mozambique | 15 |
| 27. South Africa | 33 | 54. Ghana | 14 |

Source: *World Development Report 1989* (New York: Oxford University Press, 1989), 164, 165.

**Population Growth Rates.**    The international marketer must be concerned with population trends as well as the current population in a market. This is because many marketing decisions have future effects. While most countries experience some population growth, many countries in Western Europe have reached a stationary population already. The World Bank projects 14 Western European countries to have no population increase from 1987 to 2025 (Austria, Belgium, Denmark, Finland, Germany, Greece, Ireland, Italy, Netherlands, Norway, Portugal, Sweden, Switzerland, and United Kingdom).[1] At the other extreme, 26 countries, mainly in Africa and the Mideast, are projected to triple their population between 1987 and 2025. Some of these countries are Ethiopia, Ivory Coast, Kenya, Tanzania, and Zaire in Africa, and Iraq, Libya, and Saudi Arabia on the Mideast side.

These differential population growth rates can affect the firm's long-run evaluation of markets. Markets must be evaluated on an individual basis, but an overview is useful and is given in Table 3–2. It shows the strong

**Table 3-2**                       **Population Growth Rate, 1980–1987**

|                | Number of Countries | GNP (Millions of U.S. Dollars) 1987 | Population (Millions) 1987 | GNP per Capita (U.S. Dollars) 1987 |
|----------------|---------------------|--------------------------------------|----------------------------|-------------------------------------|
| Less than 1%   | 36                  | $6,084,000                           | 561                        | $10,850                             |
| 1.0%–1.5%      | 16                  | 5,561,000                            | 1,412                      | 3,940                               |
| 1.5%–2.2%      | 23                  | 556,000                              | 986                        | 560                                 |
| 2.2%–3.0%      | 40                  | 922,000                              | 976                        | 950                                 |
| 3.0% or more   | 42                  | 342,000                              | 467                        | 730                                 |
| No data        | 29                  | –                                    | 612                        | –                                   |

Source: *World Bank Atlas 1988*, (Washington, D.C.: The World Bank, 1988), 12.

correlation between level of economic development and population growth. The rich countries have stable populations, while the poorer countries are growing rapidly. It illustrates another World Bank finding: affluence is the most powerful contraceptive.

The population growth in the foreign economy has contrary implications for the international marketer. On the favorable side, it often lends buoyancy to the economy. It can mean the formation of new households and increased demand for goods. On the negative side, however, it can hinder development of the economy by keeping down per capita income. This can make a market less attractive rather than more attractive. But it is an ill wind that blows good for no one, and some firms could market profitably even to countries with population problems. Examples are producers of birth control supplies, medicines, certain foods, or educational materials.

**Distribution of Population.** Understanding population figures involves more than counting heads. It makes a difference what kind of heads one is counting. The population figures for a foreign economy should be classified — by age group, sex, education, or occupation, for example — in ways that show the relevant segments of the market. Religious, tribal, educational, and other sociocultural attributes will be discussed in Chapter 4. Here we will consider such population characteristics as age and density.

*Age.* People in different stages of life have different needs and present different marketing opportunities. In the U.S. market, for example, many firms recognize different market segments related to age groupings. Each country will have a somewhat different profile as to age groupings. Generally, however, there are two major patterns, one for the developing countries and one for the affluent industrialized countries. The developing countries are experiencing population growth and have relatively short life expectancies. That means they have about 40 percent of their population in the inactive, dependent 0–14 age group and just over half in the productive 15–64 age group. Contrast that with the rich industrialized countries, which have only 20 percent in the dependent 0–14 group versus two-thirds in the 15–64 group and about one-eighth in the over-65 category. Figure 3–1 illustrates these patterns.

***Density.***   The concentration of population is important to the marketer in evaluating distribution and communication problems. The United States, for example, had a population density of 67 persons per square mile in 1987. This is only about one-fourteenth of the population density of the Netherlands. Even with a modern transportation network, distribution costs in the United States are likely to be higher than in the Netherlands. Promotion is also facilitated where population is concentrated.

Other things being equal, the marketer prefers to operate in markets with concentrated populations. There is a great difference in population density among nations and regions of the world. On a regional basis, the population densities range as follows: Oceania, 8 persons per square mile; North America and the U.S.S.R., 33; South America, 44; Africa, 56; Europe, 265; and Asia, 290.[2]

Regional figures on population density give generally good clues as to the densities of countries within the region. Occasionally, however, there are some extremes around the regional average. For example, in Southeast Asia the range is from 44 persons per square mile in Laos to 2,082 in Bangladesh. In Europe, the average is 265 persons per square mile, but the range is from 34 in Norway to 943 in the Netherlands. Nevertheless, in evaluating a particular country, a firm will be interested in the figures not only for that

**Figure 3–1**                    **How the Proportion of People in Different Age Groups Differs**

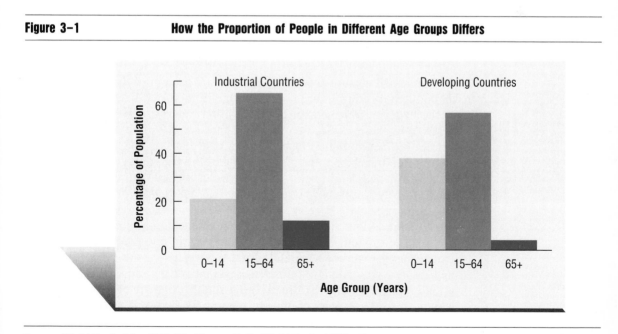

Source: *World Bank Atlas 1985* (Washington D.C.: World Bank, 1985), 12.

country, but for a potential regional market that could be served by common production facilities.

Even when using the density figure for a given country, careful interpretation is necessary. For example, Egypt in 1989 was listed as having about 145 persons per square mile. That is very misleading, because Egypt's population is among the world's most concentrated, almost entirely located along the Nile River. The rest of the country is desert. Canada provides a similar example with a density of 7 persons per square mile but with most of the population concentrated in a narrow band along the United States border and the major portion of the landmass unoccupied. In such cases, the population is very much more concentrated and reachable than the statistics indicate.

## Income

Markets require not only people, but people with money. Therefore, it is necessary to examine various income measures in a country to go along with a population analysis. We will look at three aspects of income in foreign markets: the distribution of income among the population, the usefulness of per capita income figures, and gross national product.

**Distribution of Income.**   One way of understanding the size of a market is to look at the distribution of income within it. *Per capita income figures* are averages and are meaningful, especially if most people of the country are near the average. Frequently, however, this is not the case. Among world nations, the United States has a rather equal distribution of income among people. Even in the United States, however, marketers are very attentive to differences in income levels when studying potential for their product, if the product is at all income-sensitive.

Many countries have a relatively uneven distribution of income. Extreme examples are Brazil, Kenya, and Mexico where the lowest 20 percent of the population receives less than 3 percent of the national income whereas the highest 20 percent receives from 58 to 67 percent of that income. Even the industrial countries are not egalitarian in this regard. The income share of the highest 20 percent of the population ranges from 36 percent to 46 percent. In these rich-nation markets, the income share of the lowest 20 percent of the population ranges from 5 to 8 percent. The more skewed the distribution of income, the less meaningful the per capita income figure is. When most people are below the per capita income figure, and there is a small wealthy group above it, the country has a *bimodal* income distribution and no middle class.[3]

A bimodal income distribution means that the marketer must analyze not a single economy but a dual economy within one country. The poorer group must be studied separately from the wealthy group. One might find that the two groups are not different segments of the same market, but are actually different markets. Brazil, India, and Mexico are examples of countries with sizable groups of affluent consumers alongside a majority of the population living in poverty. Italy is an example of a European country with a dual economy, that is, the impoverished south versus the affluent north. For many products, the affluent groups in these countries can be considered as strong a potential market as similar groups in North America.

**Per Capita Income.**   The statistic most frequently used to describe a country economically is its *per capita income*. This figure is used as a shorthand expression, not only for a country's level of economic development, but also for its degree of modernization and progress in health, education, and welfare. Partial justification for using this figure in evaluating a foreign economy lies in the fact that it is commonly available and widely accepted. A more pertinent justification is that it is, in fact, a good indicator of the size or quality of a market.

There is a very wide range of per capita income figures among the countries of the world. Figures for 1987 show Ethiopia at $130 per capita and Switzerland at $21,330 as the extreme cases. The World Bank found over half of the world's population living in 45 countries with an average per capita income of only $300. That figure is only 2 percent of the $14,970 average for the 38 richest countries, which, however, have only one-seventh of the world's population. If markets are people with money, these figures show a rather grim picture of many of the world's markets. Table 3–3 gives a more detailed breakdown of per capita GNP and the share of the world's income going to the various groups.

Table 3–3 is a summary of the data for all of the countries tracked by the World Bank. Many of those countries, however, are "nonreporting" for various reasons, especially several communist countries. The table in "Global Marketing" shows the actual economic groupings used by the World Bank in its analyses, based on 120 countries providing relatively complete data. Even here, however, several omissions can be noted in the low- and middle-income groups, such as Afghanistan, Kampuchea, Lebanon, and Iran — mostly countries suffering military strife during the reporting period. The bank reports provide a good starting point for foreign market studies.

**Table 3–3**                    **GNP per Capita, 1987**

|  | Number of Countries | GNP (Millions of U.S. Dollars) 1987 | Population (Millions) 1987 | GNP per Capita (U.S. Dollars) 1987 |
|---|---|---|---|---|
| Less than $500 | 45 | $    810,000 | 2,683 | $    300 |
| $500–$1,500 | 36 | 369,000 | 416 | 890 |
| $1,500–$3,000 | 22 | 999,000 | 478 | 2,090 |
| $3,000–$6,000 | 16 | 493,000 | 103 | 4,790 |
| $6,000 or more | 38 | 10,793,000 | 721 | 14,970 |
| No data | 29 | — | 612 | — |

Source: *World Bank Atlas 1988*, (Washington, D.C.: World Bank, 1988), 10.

# Global Marketing

## The World Bank Economic Groupings

| Low-Income Economies (42) | GNP/Capita Dollars 1987 (Average 290) | Lower-Middle-Income Economies (35) | GNP/Capita Dollars 1987 (Average 1,200) | Upper-Middle-Income Economies (18) | GNP/Capita Dollars 1987 (Average 2,710) |
|---|---|---|---|---|---|
| 1 Ethiopia | 130 | 45 Zimbabwe | 580 | 83 Yugoslavia | 2,480 |
| 2 Bhutan | 150 | 46 Philippines | 590 | 84 Algeria | 2,680 |
| 3 Chad | 150 | 47 Yemen Arab Rep. | 590 | 85 Korea, Rep. | 2,690 |
| 4 Zaire | 150 | 48 Morocco | 610 | 86 Gabon | 2,700 |
| 5 Bangladesh | 160 | 49 Egypt, Arab Rep. | 680 | 87 Portugal | 2,830 |
| 6 Malawi | 160 | 50 Papua New Guinea | 700 | 88 Venezuela | 3,230 |
| 7 Nepal | 160 | 51 Dominican Rep. | 730 | 89 Greece | 4,020 |
| 8 Lao PDR | 170 | 52 Côte d'Ivoire | 740 | 90 Trinidad and Tobago | 4,210 |
| 9 Mozambique | 170 | 53 Honduras | 810 | 91 Libya | 5,460 |
| 10 Tanzania | 180 | 54 Nicaragua | 830 | 92 Oman | 5,810 |
| 11 Burkina Faso | 190 | 55 Thailand | 850 | 93 *Iran, Islamic Rep.* | — |
| 12 Madagascar | 210 | 56 El Salvador | 860 | 94 *Iraq* | — |
| 13 Mali | 210 | 57 Congo, People's Rep. | 870 | 95 *Romania* | — |
| 14 Burundi | 250 | 58 Jamaica | 940 | | |
| 15 Zambia | 250 | 59 Guatemala | 950 | | |
| 16 Niger | 260 | 60 Cameroon | 970 | High-Income Economies (25) | GNP/Capita Dollars 1987 (Average 14,430) |
| 17 Uganda | 260 | 61 Paraguay | 990 | | |
| 18 China | 290 | 62 Ecuador | 1,040 | | |
| 19 Somalia | 290 | 63 Botswana | 1,050 | 96 Spain | 6,010 |
| 20 Togo | 290 | 64 Tunisia | 1,180 | 97 Ireland | 6,120 |
| 21 India | 300 | 65 Turkey | 1,210 | 98 Saudi Arabia[a] | 6,200 |
| 22 Rwanda | 300 | 66 Colombia | 1,240 | 99 Israel[a] | 6,800 |
| 23 Sierra Leone | 300 | 67 Chile | 1,310 | 100 New Zealand | 7,750 |
| 24 Benin | 310 | 68 Peru | 1,470 | 101 Singapore[a] | 7,940 |
| 25 Central African Rep. | 330 | 69 Mauritius | 1,490 | 102 Hong Kong[a] | 8,070 |
| 26 Kenya | 330 | 70 Jordan | 1,560 | 103 Italy | 10,350 |
| 27 Sudan | 330 | 71 Costa Rica | 1,610 | 104 United Kingdom | 10,420 |
| 28 Pakistan | 350 | 72 Syrian Arab Rep. | 1,640 | 105 Australia | 11,100 |
| 29 Haiti | 360 | 73 Malaysia | 1,810 | 106 Belgium | 11,480 |
| 30 Lesotho | 370 | 74 Mexico | 1,830 | 107 Netherlands | 11,860 |
| 31 Nigeria | 370 | 75 South Africa | 1,890 | 108 Austria | 11,980 |
| 32 Ghana | 390 | 76 Poland | 1,930 | 109 France | 12,790 |
| 33 Sri Lanka | 400 | 77 *Lebanon* | — | 110 Germany, Fed. Rep. | 14,400 |
| 34 Yemen, PDR | 420 | | | 111 Finland | 14,470 |
| 35 Mauritania | 440 | | | 112 Kuwait[a] | 14,610 |
| 36 Indonesia | 450 | Upper-Middle-Income Economies (18) | GNP/Capita Dollars 1987 (Average 2,710) | 113 Denmark | 14,930 |
| 37 Liberia | 450 | | | 114 Canada | 15,160 |
| 38 *Afghanistan* | — | | | 115 Sweden | 15,550 |
| 39 *Burma* | — | 78 Brazil | 2,020 | 116 Japan | 15,760 |
| 40 *Guinea* | — | 79 Uruguay | 2,190 | 117 United Arab Emirates[a] | 15,830 |
| 41 *Kampuchea, Dem.* | — | 80 Hungary | 2,240 | 118 Norway | 17,190 |
| 42 *Viet Nam* | — | 81 Panama | 2,240 | 119 United States | 18,530 |
| 43 Senegal | 520 | 82 Argentina | 2,390 | 120 Switzerland | 21,330 |
| 44 Bolivia | 580 | | | | |

[a]Non-OECD

Source: *World Development Report 1989* (New York: Oxford University Press, 1989), 164, 165.

**Table 3-4**

### Gross Domestic Product Per Capita as Percentage of U.S. Gross Domestic Product Per Capita 1985

| Country | According to Actual Purchasing Power[a] | According to Exchange Rate Conversion[b] | Multiplier[c] |
|---|---|---|---|
| India | 4.7 | 1.6 | 2.9 |
| Kenya | 5.3 | 1.8 | 3.0 |
| Nigeria | 7.2 | 2.0 | 3.6 |
| Zimbabwe | 9.9 | 3.1 | 3.2 |
| Egypt | 15.8 | 3.7 | 4.3 |
| Thailand | 17.0 | 4.6 | 3.7 |
| Turkey | 21.8 | 6.6 | 3.3 |

[a] *World Development Report 1989*, (New York: Oxford University Press, 1989), 222, 223.

[b] Calculated by the author, same source, 164, 165.

[c] To obtain first column's results from second column's; calculated by author, same source, 164, 165.

Because per capita income figures are relied on so extensively, however, the following words of caution are in order.

***Purchasing Power Not Reflected.*** Per capita income comparisons are expressed in a common currency — usually U.S. dollars — through an exchange rate conversion. The dollar figure for a country is derived by dividing its per capita income figure in national currency by its rate of exchange against the dollar. The resulting dollar statistic for a country's per capita income is accurate only if the exchange rate reflects the relative domestic purchasing power of the two currencies. There is often reason for doubting that it does.

The *exchange rate* is the price of one currency in terms of another. The supply and demand determinants of that price are the demand for and supply of foreign exchange, or a country's imports and exports — plus speculative demand. A country's external supply and demand have quite a different character from supply and demand within the country. Thus, it is not surprising that the external value of a currency (the exchange rate) may be different from the domestic value of that currency. Furthermore, the impact of speculation can further pull a currency away from its "true" value. Table 3-4 gives some data from studies made of the differences between the exchange rate value of a currency and its real purchasing power. In almost every case the real purchasing power is estimated at more than three times the exchange rate value.

The limitations of an exchange rate in indicating relative purchasing power can be illustrated further. Take the experience of tourists, who soon learn that their own currency does not have an "average" value in terms of their consumption in any given foreign country. Instead, they observe that some prices appear high, others low. In other words, the value of their own currency there depends on what they buy with it.

If they wish to live in the same style abroad as at home, their expenses probably will be considerably higher than if they live like the residents of the host country. For example, the price of white bread in Germany is over twice as much as it is in France. Of course, the Germans do not consume as much white bread as the French. This indicates another aspect of prices and purchasing power — that is, people tend to consume more of the things that are inexpensive in their country. However, the exchange rate reflects the *international* goods and services of a country, not its *domestic* consumption.

A further example is the case of exchange rate changes, as with a devaluation or currency appreciation. Britain devalued its currency by 14.3 percent in November 1967. This certainly did not mean that the British market for any given product was down 14 percent the day after the devaluation. Yet this is what is implied with the use of per capita income figures derived from an exchange rate conversion. A more extreme example involves Japan. In 1985 the Japanese yen was 240 to the U.S. dollar. In 1988 the yen was 120 to the dollar. This meant that, in *dollar* terms, the Japanese market was twice as large in 1988 as in 1985. This was obviously not true in *real* terms, as American marketers to Japan learned. Their sales to Japan rose only modestly. It is precisely because of the inadequacies of per capita income figures expressed in U.S. dollars that the World Bank has worked so hard to determine true purchasing power.

***Lack of Comparability.***   Another limitation to the use of per capita income figures is that there is a twofold lack of comparability in the income figures themselves. First, many goods entering into the national income totals of the developed economies are only partially in the money economy in less developed countries. A large part of an American's budget, for example, goes for food, clothing, and shelter. In many less developed nations, these items may be largely self-provided and therefore not reflected in national income totals.

Second, many goods that figure in the national income of developed nations do not figure in the national incomes of poorer countries. For example, a significant amount of United States national income is derived from such items as snow removal, heating of buildings and homes, pollution control, military and space expenditures, agricultural support programs, and winter vacations in Florida or other warmer states. Many less developed nations are in tropical areas, and their citizens are not necessarily poorer for not having the above-mentioned items of consumption. However, their national income figure is lower because of the absence of these items. The author spent eight years in a rural area of Zaire. Although not living entirely in the African manner, he found his food, clothing, and housing expenses to be a fraction of those he incurred living in the northern part of the United States. This meant that a given income went much further for consumption of these basic items.

***Sales Not Related to Per Capita Income.***   A third limitation to using per capita income figures to indicate market potential is that the sales of many goods show little correlation with per capita income. Many consumer goods sales correlate more closely with population or household figures than with per capita income. Some examples might be Coca-Cola, ballpoint pens, bicycles, sewing machines, and transistor radios. Industrial goods and capital equipment sales generally correlate better with the industrial structure or total national income than with per capita income. For example, the airport and office buildings in Kinshasa, Zaire, are equipped in much the same way similar places in New York City are. Extractive or manufacturing industries tend to use similar equipment wherever they are located. Where governments run health and education programs, per capita income is not necessarily a useful guide to the national potential in goods supplied to the health and education industries.

*Uneven Income Distribution.*   Finally, per capita figures are less meaningful if there is great unevenness of income distribution in the country. This has already been discussed.

**Gross National Product (GNP).**   Another useful way to evaluate foreign markets is to compare their *gross national products*, or *GNP*. As already discussed, for certain goods, total GNP is a better indicator of market potential than per capita income. Where this is true, a ranking of countries by GNP is a useful starting point. Table 3–5 gives a listing of the economies with a GNP of $50 billion or more in 1987. The fact that only 30 nations can qualify for this list provides another insight into the poverty in the world and the limitations of most economies.

**Table 3-5**                       **Countries with GDP Over $50 Billion, 1987**

| Country | Billions of U.S. Dollars | Country | Billions of U.S. Dollars |
|---|---|---|---|
| 1. United States | $4,497 | 16. Belgium | $142 |
| 2. Japan | 2,376 | 17. Sweden | 138 |
| 3. Germany, FR | 873 | 18. South Korea | 121 |
| 4. France | 873 | 19. Austria | 117 |
| 5. Italy | 749 | 20. Denmark | 85 |
| 6. United Kingdom | 576 | 21. Norway | 83 |
| 7. Canada | 374 | 22. Finland | 78 |
| 8. Brazil | 299 | 23. South Africa | 74 |
| 9. China | 294 | 24. Argentina | 71 |
| 10. Spain | 288 | 25. Saudi Arabia | 71 |
| 11. India | 221 | 26. Taiwan | 71 |
| 12. Netherlands | 214 | 27. Indonesia | 70 |
| 13. Australia | 183 | 28. Algeria | 65 |
| 14. Switzerland | 170 | 29. Turkey | 61 |
| 15. Mexico | 142 | 30. Yugoslavia | 60 |

Note: Iran and most communist countries are "nonreporting" to the World Bank.

Source: *World Development Report 1989* (New York: Oxford University Press, 1989).

It is helpful to contrast the GNP approach to measuring market potential with the per capita income approach. For example, Kuwait's per capita income in 1987 was $14,610 and India's was $300. Judging from these figures, Kuwait is about 50 times as attractive as India. However, India's GNP in 1987 was over 12 times that of Kuwait and its population 420 times as large. This is an extreme example, but it illustrates the need for proper comparisons.

At this point, we should balance our criticism of the per capita income approach. For goods that require high consumer income, it may be true that a small country like Belgium (about 10 million people) is a better market than India, even though Belgium's GNP is less than two-thirds that of India. For example, in 1987 Belgium had more telephones than India and almost three times as many cars. On the other hand, India had twice as many computers, and its consumption of cement, steel, trucks and buses was three to four times that of Belgium. Obviously, the relevant income figure for evaluating a market depends largely on the product.

## Nature of the Economy

In addition to their size and market potential, foreign economies have other characteristics that affect a marketing program, including those produced by the nation's physical endowment, the nature of its economic activity, its infrastructure, and its degree of urbanization.

**Physical Endowment of Nation**

**Natural Resources.** A nation's *natural resources* include its actual and potential forms of wealth supplied by nature — for example, minerals and waterpower — as well as its land area, topography, and climate. The international marketer needs to understand the economic geography of a nation in relation to the marketing task there. Land area as such is not very important, except where it figures in population density and potential distribution problems. However, knowledge of local natural resources can be important to the international marketer in evaluating a country, since they may provide raw materials for local production.

Merck, for example, built a compounding plant in India and received the Indian government's permission to ship key ingredients from the United States. This permission was later withdrawn, and Merck had to locate a new raw-material source in India to keep the plant operating.

Another reason for exploring the country's resource base is to evaluate its future economic prospects. Some countries that today have relatively weak markets might develop more rapidly than others because of their richer resource endowment. New technologies or discoveries can revolutionize a nation's economic prospects. Oil changed the outlook for Libya and Nigeria, for example. In Australia it was the discovery of other minerals that started a boom in the late 1960s.

By the same token, technological change can also impoverish an economy that is largely dependent on just one export commodity. For example, the development of rayon, nylon, and synthetic rubber did great damage to the countries exporting silk and natural rubber. What would be the impact on Brazil if a good synthetic coffee were developed? A glance through the maps in any good atlas will give a picture of how the various natural resources — animal, vegetable, and mineral — are distributed among the nations of the world. A nation's human resources must be identified in other ways.

**Topography.**   The surface features of a country's land, including rivers, lakes, forests, deserts, and mountains are its *topography*. These are features that interest the international marketer as well as the tourist, for they indicate possible physical distribution problems.

Flat country generally means easy transportation by road or rail. Mountains are always a barrier that raises transportation costs. Mountains also may divide a nation into two or more distinct markets. For example, in many South American nations, the Andes Mountains divide the country into entirely separate areas. Although these areas are united politically, the marketer will often find that culturally and economically they are separate markets. Deserts and tropical forests also separate markets and make transportation difficult. The international marketer analyzes the topography, population, and transportation situation to anticipate marketing and logistical problems.

Navigable rivers are desirable features because they usually enable economical transportation. The Mississippi and the St. Lawrence Seaway are North American examples. In Europe, river and canal transportation are more important than anywhere else in the world. Even landlocked Switzerland can ship by river barge to Atlantic ports. The accessibility of a market will also be determined by its ports and harbors, its contact with sea transportation.

Landlocked countries such as Bolivia, Zambia, and Zimbabwe are more costly to reach than neighboring countries with seaports. These countries have transportation problems other than cost if there are political differences with the neighbors whose seaports and railroads they must use. Both Zimbabwe and Zambia are cases in point. Finally, the existence of lakes, seashores, rivers, and mountains can indicate particular marketing opportunities. Suppliers to the tourist, recreation, and sporting industries will find markets in countries endowed with places for boating, skiing, and similar recreational activities.

**Climate.**   Another dimension of a nation's physical endowment is its *climate,* which includes not only the temperature range, but also wind, rain, snow, and dryness and humidity. The United States is a very large country and thus has great climate variation within its borders. Most nations are smaller and have more uniform climatic patterns. Climate is an important determinant of the firm's product offerings. An obvious example is the heater or air conditioner in an automobile. However, it also affects a whole range of consumer goods from food to clothing and from housing to recreational

## Global Marketing
### Adjusting to the Local Economy

Ford opened a state-of-the art assembly plant in Hermosillo, Mexico, in 1987. It is one of the most technologically advanced plants in the world. The challenge was to build a Mexican workforce capable of operating the plant, which was to export to the United States as well as supplying the Mexican market.

Ford began its recruiting and training program two years before the plant opened. Recruiting efforts focused on students approaching the end of secondary school. Among 1,600 candidates, 300 were finally selected for an intensive training program.

Initially, the 300 were given a six-month course in Mexico on basic skills and English. They received a salary above the Mexican minimum wage during this time. After this program, the workers were divided into specialized groups and sent abroad for training. One group went to Ford's Spanish plant for assembly training. Another went to its Belgian plant for paint applications. A third went to U.S. plants for quality control and equipment maintenance. And a fourth went to Mazda's plant in Japan to study robotics. Training abroad ranged from two to nine months depending on the specialization.

---

supplies. Even medical needs in the tropics are different from those in temperate zones.

Extremes of climate may dictate modifications in product, packaging, or distribution. For example, electric equipment and many consumer packaged goods need special protection in hot, humid climates. There is great international variation on this score; for example, India has 13 inches of rainfall in the month of July, Guinea has 51 inches, New York City has 4 inches. By contrast, the American military in Vietnam found that their transport vehicles required extra attention because of the very dry, dusty conditions in some parts of Vietnam at certain times of the year.

Climate may have another, more subtle effect on the nature of the market. Although there is insufficient scientific evidence to prove cause and effect, almost all of the less developed countries are tropical or subtropical. Tropical countries generally have low per capita incomes and a high percentage of the population in agriculture. Gunnar Myrdal's gloomy conclusions as to Asia's prospects for development[4] were based in part on his evaluation of the adverse effects of climate. The marketing manager needs to be aware of climate to the extent that it affects people as consumers or workers.

## Nature of Economic Activity

**Rostow's View.**   The stages of economic growth described by economist Walt Rostow provide a useful description of foreign economies.[5] According to Rostow, all the nations of the world are in one of the following levels of economic development: (1) the traditional society; (2) the preconditions for takeoff; (3) the takeoff; (4) the drive to maturity; (5) the age of high mass consumption. Each level represents a different type of economy, that is, differing production and marketing systems. The marketing opportunities and problems encountered by the international firm will vary according to the host country's state of economic growth.

Although Rostow's classification was developed from the viewpoint of the economist, a similar type of analysis may be useful to the international marketer. In Chapter 7 we suggest how international marketers might develop a classification system to meet their own needs. Here we will look at various aspects within foreign economies that affect the marketing task.

**Farm or Factory?**   One way to determine the kind of market a country offers is to look at the origin of its national product. Is the economy agricultural or industrial? What is the nature of its agricultural, manufacturing, and service industries? Such an analysis is especially useful to industrial marketers. However, even consumer goods marketers will find that consumer demands and mentality are related to the nature of economic activities in the country. For example, there are invariably differences in the consumption patterns of the farmer compared with those of a factory worker.

Table 3–6 shows some of the international variation in patterns of economic activity. The World Bank groups the countries of the world according to the share of agriculture in GDP (gross domestic product). There is a very strong inverse correlation between the size of a nation's agricultural sector and its level of development and income. The poorer the country, the more it depends on agriculture — and the less income it generates in manufacturing industry. It is understandable why the poorer countries are striving to industrialize. This kind of data is useful for marketing because the nature of the market and the marketing task follow the nature of the economy.

**Input-Output Tables.**   Although it is useful to analyze an economy in terms of its agricultural and industrial sectors, frequently it is desirable to make a more detailed examination. Such sources as the *United Nations Statistical Yearbook* show national production in a wide range of products and commodities. Industrial marketers are especially concerned with the industrial structure of an economy. A firm that sells to particular industries must know which economies contain those industries as well as the industries' sizes.

| Table 3–6 | **Share of Agriculture in GDP, 1987** | | | |
|---|---|---|---|---|
| | Number of Countries | GNP (Millions of U.S. Dollars) 1987 | Population (Millions) 1987 | GNP per Capita (U.S. Dollars) 1987 |
| Less than 6% | 37 | 10,892,000 | 777 | 14,010 |
| 6%–10% | 16 | 596,000 | 199 | 3,000 |
| 10%–20% | 30 | 974,000 | 521 | 1,870 |
| 20%–30% | 30 | 309,000 | 536 | 580 |
| 30% or more | 44 | 694,000 | 2,369 | 290 |
| No data | 29 | — | 612 | — |

Source: *World Bank Atlas 1988*, (Washington, D.C.: World Bank, 1988), 16.

Even beyond this, the firm would like to know the technology used in its client industries. For example, many nations have textile industries, but not all use the same combinations of materials, labor, and equipment. The economist would say they do not all have the same production function.

If the firm can construct *input-output tables* for its industry for relevant markets, it can gain a better idea of how its supplies or equipment fit in with the industrial structure in given markets. Such tables are often used in American marketing, and their use is increasing in international marketing. Although their construction, even for one industry, can be difficult, the technique is worth mastering. As our data improve, economic analysis through input-output tables is becoming more common.[6]

## Infrastructure

A manufacturing firm generally divides its activities into two major categories: production and marketing. Domestic management is not required to consider the extent to which its operations depend on supporting facilities and services outside the firm. These external facilities and services collectively are called the *infrastructure* of an economy. They include paved roads, railroads, energy supplies, and other communication and transport services. The commercial and financial infrastructure includes such things as advertising agencies and media, distributive organizations, marketing research companies, and credit and banking facilities. The more adequate these services in a country, the better the firm can perform its own production and marketing tasks there. Where these facilities and services are not adequate, the firm must adapt its operations, or perhaps avoid the market altogether.

When considering the potential profitability of operations in a given country, the international marketer must evaluate the infrastructure constraints as well as the market potential. As might be expected, there is great international variation. Generally, the higher the level of economic development, the better the infrastructure. Table 3–7 gives some indication of the variation in transportation and energy services available. The United States figures are given as a basis for comparison. Although to yield the most accurate information the figures should be related to population size and land area, even the absolute figures are revealing. (Energy consumption is on a per capita basis.)

**Transportation.**   The importance of transportation for business operations needs no elaboration. In Table 3–7, transportation facilities are suggested by trucks and buses in use and rail freight. Air freight and river freight are important for some countries, but comparable data are not available. The two indicators that are given, however, can tell a lot about internal transport capability in foreign markets. Some interesting international comparisons can be made on the basis of both of these statistics.

The table shows a country's relative dependence on trucks versus rail for moving freight. It also shows something of the absolute level of transport capability of a country compared to its neighbors in the region. In Asia, for example, the Philippines has twice as many trucks as much larger, more populous Pakistan. However, it has less than 1 percent as much rail freight

**Table 3-7**                    **Transportation and Energy Consumption**

|  | Trucks and Buses (Thousands)[a] | Rail Traffic Freight (Ton Kilometers)[b] | Energy Consumption per Capita (Kilograms Oil Equivalent)[a] |
|---|---|---|---|
| United States | 39,583 | 1,377,264 | 6,694 |
| Western Europe |  |  |  |
| France | 3,426 | 60,120 | 2,809 |
| Germany | 1,723 | 61,471 | 4,024 |
| Italy | 1,824 | 17,457 | 2,303 |
| Spain | 1,610 | 11,239 | 1,528 |
| Sweden | 231 | 18,040 | 3,472 |
| United Kingdom | 2,753 | 12,456 | 3,439 |
| Latin America |  |  |  |
| Argentina | 1,427 | 11,244 | 1,192 |
| Brazil | 2,214 | 74,792 | 484 |
| Chile | 241 | 2,315 | 623 |
| Colombia | 599 | 726 | 588 |
| Peru | 209 | 1,014 | 414 |
| Venezuela | 916 | 22 | 2,205 |
| Asia |  |  |  |
| India | 1,189 | 168,849 | 178 |
| Japan | 18,313 | 23,191 | 2,600 |
| Pakistan | 270 | 7,385 | 175 |
| Philippines | 521 | 17 | 203 |
| Sri Lanka | 132 | 240 | 77 |
| Thailand | 702 | 2,618 | 292 |
| Africa |  |  |  |
| Egypt | 244 | 2,303 | 463 |
| Ghana | 46 | 61 | 63 |
| Ivory Coast | 89 | 469 | — |
| Kenya | 133 | 2,246 | 58 |
| Mozambique | 24 | 536 | 63 |
| South Africa | 1,216 | 82,026 | 2,147 |

[a] "Indicators of Market Size," *Business International*, June 1988.

[b] *UNESCO Statistical Yearbook 1983/84* (New York: United Nations, 1986), 1006–1010.

as Pakistan. In Europe, Sweden, with 8 million people, moves much more total freight by rail than much larger Italy, Spain, or the United Kingdom. At the same time, Sweden, even though it manufactures large trucks, moves only a small fraction of its freight by truck compared to these other countries.

The level of a country's transport capability can also be seen by international comparisons. In Africa, for example, Ghana, the Ivory Coast, and Kenya are not widely different either in population size or land area. Yet Ghana has only half of the trucks and buses of its neighbor, the Ivory Coast, and only about one-eighth of the rail freight. Comparing the Ivory Coast to Kenya suggests Kenya has an even stronger transportation infrastructure, with 50 percent more trucks and buses, and six times as much rail freight. Making comparisons between geographic regions suggests the relative ease of arranging logistics in Europe and the potential difficulties in logistics in African markets, and even in much of Asia and Latin America.

**Energy.**   The statistics on energy consumption per capita serve both as a guide to market potential and as a guide to the adequacy of the local infrastructure. Marketers of electrical machinery and equipment and consumer durables are concerned about the extent of electrification throughout the market. In countries with low figures for energy consumption, the marketer will find that power is available only in the cities and not in the villages or countryside where most of the population may live. Energy consumption is also closely related to the overall industrialization of an economy and thus is correlated to the market for industrial goods there. Finally, energy consumption per capita is probably the best single indicator as to the adequacy of a country's overall infrastructure. Table 3–8, third column, gives an idea of the great international differences in energy consumption, with a ratio of 100 to 1 from top to bottom.

**Communications.**   In addition to being able to move its goods, a firm must be able to communicate with its various audiences, especially workers, suppliers, and customers. Communication with those outside the firm will depend on the communications infrastructure of the country. Intracompany communications between subsidiaries or with headquarters will be equally dependent on local facilities. Table 3–8 shows the distribution and availability of several communications media in the major regions of the world. Again, United States figures are given as a basis for comparison.

In general, variations in communications infrastructure follow variations in the level of economic development. Thus, Japan and the countries of Western Europe are well supplied with all kinds of media, whereas the developing countries in Africa, Asia, and Latin America are weak in all the media, except perhaps for radio. The table also illustrates the problems of trying to gather international comparative data. The developing countries are less effective at gathering statistics. One can reasonably assume, however, that the newspaper figures would be low for the countries without data, because literacy rates and per capita income are also low in most of these countries.

A more complete and detailed listing of countries in the manner of Table 3–8 would benefit the international manager in two ways. First, it would aid analysis of the communication and promotional possibilities in foreign markets. Second, it would help to locate marketing subsidiaries or regional headquarters where there are good internal and international communication facilities. One can see even from Table 3–8 the extensive international variability in communications infrastructure, with ratios of 100 to 1 for the first three columns.

**Commercial Infrastructure.**   Equally important to the firm as the transportation, communication, and energy capabilities of a nation is its commercial infrastructure. By this is meant the availability and quality of such

**Table 3–8**                                    **Distribution of Communications Media**

| | Telephones per 100 Population | Newspapers Copies per 1,000 Population | TVs per 1,000 Population | Radios per 1,000 Population |
|---|---|---|---|---|
| United States | 76 | 268 | 798 | 2,101 |
| Western Europe | | | | |
| France | 61 | 212 | 394 | 879 |
| Germany | 62 | 350 | 373 | 430 |
| Italy | 45 | 96 | 253 | 259 |
| Spain | 36 | 80 | 270 | 298 |
| Sweden | 89 | 521 | 390 | 868 |
| United Kingdom | 52 | 414 | 437 | 1,016 |
| Latin America | | | | |
| Argentina | 10.4 | NA | 213 | 654 |
| Brazil | 8.4 | 57 | 184 | 391 |
| Colombia | 7.0 | NA | 96 | 139 |
| Ecuador | 3.6 | 64 | 64 | 293 |
| Mexico | 9.1 | 120 | 108 | 190 |
| Venezuela | 8.3 | 186 | 130 | 422 |
| Asia | | | | |
| India | 0.5 | 21 | 5 | 66 |
| Indonesia | 0.3 | 18 | 39 | 117 |
| Japan | 55.5 | 562 | 580 | 787 |
| Pakistan | 0.6 | NA | 13 | 90 |
| Philippines | 1.5 | NA | 28 | 65 |
| Thailand | 1.5 | NA | 97 | 175 |
| Africa | | | | |
| Egypt | 2.4 | 42 | 82 | 256 |
| Ghana | 0.6 | 35 | 10 | 184 |
| Madagascar | 0.4 | 5 | 8 | 213 |
| Nigeria | 0.3 | 6 | 5 | 85 |
| South Africa | 14.3 | NA | 93 | 309 |
| Sudan | 0.4 | 5 | 51 | 251 |

NA = Not available

Source: *Statistical Abstract of the United States* (Washington, D.C.: Bureau of the Census, 1989), 809.

supporting services as banks and financial institutions, advertising agencies, distribution channels, and marketing research organizations. Firms accustomed to strong supporting services at home will often find great differences in foreign markets. Wherever the commercial infrastructure is weak, the firm must make adjustments in its operations that will affect costs and effectiveness.

No comparable table on commercial infrastructure is available, and data are more difficult to find in this area. Nevertheless, a firm can get reasonably good information on the commercial infrastructure of a country. The best sources are commercial attachés in embassies and domestic service organizations with foreign operations, for example, banks, accounting firms, and advertising agencies.

## Urbanization

One of the most significant characteristics of an economy is the extent to which it is urbanized. There are numerous cultural and economic differences between people in cities and those in villages or rural areas. These differences are reflected in the vocabulary and attitudes of the people. For example, *urbane* and *urbanity* derive from *urban* and signify a sophistication of outlook. By contrast, the words *peasant* and *farmer* are often used to describe not just a vocation but a way of life and thought. Modern transportation and communication have greatly reduced the differences between urban and rural populations in the United States, but in much of the world the urban-rural differences persist. Because these differences are important determinants of consumer behavior, the international marketer needs to be aware of the situation particular to each market.

**Farm versus City.**   There are several reasons for the contrasting behavior of urban and rural populations. Urbanites tend to be dependent for all their material needs, whereas rural dwellers often supply much of their food, clothing, and shelter through their own efforts. The city dweller must meet his needs through money payments to others. Cities are centers of industry and commerce. Because city dwellers deal constantly in money within a commercial-industrial framework, they become more sophisticated consumers than rural dwellers, who are often unaware of the technical and economic complexities of modern society. Hill and Still found that products aimed at rural markets in developing countries required more adaptation than products sold in urban markets.[7]

Cities are the places in an economy where communications media are most developed; information contributes to the city dweller's sophistication. Cities also offer more possibilities for formal and informal education, which affect the literacy, skills, and attitudes of their inhabitants. Urbanites therefore tend to be less conservative and tradition-oriented than rural dwellers. There is a stronger demonstration effect of new products and consumption patterns in urban areas, which leads to stronger markets there. All in all, there are many attitudinal and behavioral differences related to the urban-rural dichotomy in a given economy.

The international marketer must study the relation of urbanization to the consumption of the firm's product. For some products in some countries, urban and rural populations will be distinct segments; in other cases, there will be no difference; in yet others, the firm may decide that urban areas provide the only feasible market. There could be several factors favoring the urban markets: income and consumption patterns, distribution facilities, and communications possibilities.

Table 3–9 shows the degree of urbanization for the World Bank economic groupings. Looking at the averages for the four groupings, we see a strong correlation between degree of urbanization and the level of economic de-

| Table 3–9 | **Urbanization** |
|---|---|

| | Urban Population (as a Percent of Total Population) | |
|---|---|---|
| | Country | Average for Economic Group |
| Low-Income Economies (40) | | 24 |
|   Indonesia | 27 | |
|   Uganda | 10 | |
| Lower-Middle-Income Economies (35) | | 51 |
|   Mexico | 71 | |
|   Thailand | 21 | |
| Upper-Middle-Income Economies (18) | | 66 |
|   Argentina | 85 | |
|   Portugal | 32 | |
| High-Income Economies (25) | | 77 |
|   Austria | 57 | |
|   Netherlands | 88 | |

Source: *World Development Report 1989*, (New York: Oxford University Press, 1989), 224, 225.

velopment. Looking at some of the country figures within each economic group, we see some wide deviations from the group average. Urbanization is an important indicator of the attractiveness of a market. For example, the United States has a very large land area with a low population density. Because three-fourths of the population is urban, however, distribution and communications are relatively easy and efficient. The other highly urbanized nations provide similarly attractive markets from this point of view.

The developing countries are generally much less urbanized, especially the low-income nations. Combined with low incomes in these regions, the lack of urbanization makes these markets unattractive to many consumer goods marketers. Not only are these poor markets small, they are also difficult to reach when most of the population is rural. Thus the degree of urbanization is an indicator of both the size of the market and the nature of the marketing task. Though this kind of data is especially significant for consumer goods marketers, even industrial goods firms will find a correlation between their market potential and urbanization. Because urbanization is increasing in all categories of countries, the marketer will need up-to-date figures.

**Other Characteristics of Foreign Economies**

Our survey of foreign economies has been introductory rather than exhaustive. It should be helpful, however, in giving the market analyst a feel for the relevant dimensions of national economies. Before concluding this chapter, we look briefly at a few other characteristics of foreign economies that can be important in operations there.

**Inflation.**   Each country has its own monetary system and an independent monetary policy. The result is differing kinds of financial environment and differing rates of inflation among nations. Inflation is a concern in all countries but not all are equally afflicted. Of the 120 countries in the World Bank economic groupings, 60 had single-digit inflation rates for the 1980–1987 period. (Japan had a 1.4 percent annual rate, Germany, 2.9, and the United States, 4.3.) That means the other 60 countries had double-digit inflation and reason for much more serious concern, especially such extreme cases as the following: Mexico, 69 percent annual rate for the period of 1980–1987; Uganda, 95 percent; Peru, 102 percent; Israel, 159 percent; Brazil, 166 percent; Argentina, 299 percent; and Bolivia, 601 percent.

It might be noted that inflation tends to be much more common in the developing countries, which means a further complication for operating in those markets. High rates of inflation complicate cost control and pricing. Differential rates of inflation also influence how the firm moves funds and goods among its various markets. The marketing implications of inflation are discussed in Chapter 15.

**Role of Government.**   The business environment and the nature of business operations in an economy are very dependent on the role government plays in that economy. If government has strong socialist leanings, it may restrict the sectors of the economy where private companies may be engaged. Where international companies are allowed to operate, governments will have regulations restricting their operations.

In a number of countries, international companies may have the government as a partner in a joint venture. This is especially true in less developed countries that want local partnership but lack a strong private sector to provide the capital. Such a partnership provides constraints of its own on the international company.

**Foreign Investment in the Economy.**   When contemplating operations in a foreign economy, the international marketer will be interested to know what other international firms are operating there. This information will give clues as to the government's attitude toward foreign companies. It will help determine something about the competitive environment the firm will encounter.

That a country has few or no international companies operating in it could indicate a good opportunity for one to enter — or it could indicate that the environment is inhospitable. Conversely, an economy that has many international companies operating in it indicates an open market, but one that may be very competitive. A distinction must be made, of course, between extractive industries and manufacturing or marketing subsidiaries. Extractive industries go into a country for raw-material supply rather than for marketing reasons.

In Table 3–10, we see the number of U.S. companies with investments in selected markets. (Unfortunately data are not available for other investing countries.) The figures are for two base years, 1975 and 1987, so trends can

Table 3–10

**Number of American Firms with Operations in Selected Foreign Countries, 1975 and 1987**

|  | Number of Firms 1975 (Approximate) | Number of Firms 1987 (Approximate) |
|---|---|---|
| Canada | 1,560 | 1,295 |
| Africa |  |  |
| Egypt | 56 | 114 |
| Ghana | 19 | 23 |
| Kenya | 72 | 79 |
| Nigeria | 51 | 115 |
| South Africa | 314 | 311 |
| Zambia | 11 | 35 |
| Asia |  |  |
| India | 261 | 259 |
| Indonesia | 73 | 143 |
| Philippines | 193 | 223 |
| Sri Lanka | 15 | 27 |
| Taiwan | 130 | 176 |
| Thailand | 150 | 150 |
| Latin America |  |  |
| Argentina | 233 | 267 |
| Brazil | 478 | 605 |
| Chile | 116 | 143 |
| Colombia | 233 | 201 |
| Mexico | 876 | 682 |
| Peru | 221 | 159 |
| Western Europe |  |  |
| France | 726 | 743 |
| Germany | 1,100 | 924 |
| Italy | 541 | 506 |
| Netherlands | 707 | 577 |
| Norway | 77 | 132 |
| Spain | 349 | 399 |

Source: *Directory of American Firms Operating in Foreign Countries*, 8th, 11th eds. (New York: Uniworld Business Publications, 1975, 1987).

be identified. Canada is given as a basis for comparison. The companies include extractive and service industries as well as manufacturing. Though the data do not reveal the size of the investment in each country, they do indicate generally how American firms evaluated the different markets. Canada and Western Europe remain the most popular markets but there has been a leveling off or even retrenchment in many places.

Latin America is the next most attractive area for U.S. investments with Brazil and Mexico the most popular host countries. Asia is more distant but should prove a growth area as we approach the "Pacific Century." Africa is still relatively an unknown continent for American firms, except for South Africa. Political developments there will cause a further decline in the number of American firms in that country.

The reader can go through Table 3–10 and evaluate personally the role of geography, politics, and economics in determining the patterns of American foreign investment. The international marketer must be alert for trends. In some nations there may be a leveling off, or even a decrease, in foreign investment. Iran is an extreme example. It is also possible to identify growing economies with relatively stable political environments and an absence of strongly negative attitudes toward foreign investors. Such a table needs to be kept up to date, because changes in the investment climate can occur rapidly. For example, the 1987 figures for South Africa are very much out of date, as there has been a big exodus of American firms from South Africa since that time. On the other hand, Gorbachev was encouraging foreign firms to come to the U.S.S.R., and liberalization in other Eastern European countries in 1989 may greatly change the figures there.

## Summary

The two main areas of investigation for a company evaluating a foreign market are (1) the size of the market and (2) the nature of the economy. Population is one of the primary indicators of market size. Two-thirds of the countries have less than 10 million people and represent small markets, especially compared to the United States. Growth rates vary widely and are generally inversely correlated with the attractiveness of a market, being highest in the poor countries. The marketer is concerned about the distribution of the population among different age groups that have different purchasing power and consumption patterns. Population density is important for evaluating distribution and communication problems.

Markets are "people with money," so income figures on a country are necessary for market evaluation. One dimension is the distribution of income among the members of a society. Countries with a bimodal distribution of income represent dual economies with two major market segments, generally one rich and one poor. Countries with a more even distribution of income or a large middle class represent more of a mass market for the international firm.

Per capita income is the most widely used indicator of market potential. Figures vary widely, with the poorest countries reporting less than 1 percent of the per capita income of the richest countries. World Bank studies show that these figures are often inaccurate, however. Actual purchasing power in many poor countries is three or four times as high as that indicated by the per capita income figure expressed in dollars. Per capita income figures are a useful indicator of potential for some consumer goods, but misleading for others and for industrial goods.

Total GNP gives an idea of the total size of a country market and is a helpful indicator of potential for some kinds of products. The range of GNP figures between the largest and smallest economies is over 10,000 to 1.

A country's physical endowment affects the nature of its economy. Its natural resources are one indicator of its economic potential and raw-material availability. Its topography will help determine physical distribution problems and market accessibility. Its climate will influence the kind of products offered and the kind of packaging needed.

Countries can be grouped according to the nature of their economies or level of economic development, as Rostow has done. Such groupings can be a useful form of segmentation for international marketers. Also, their economies can be divided into agricultural, manufacturing, and service sectors for better analysis. Input-output analysis can be a powerful tool for industrial marketers.

A firm's ability to operate in a country will depend on the supporting facilities and services available, collectively called its infrastructure. The transportation and communication facilities in a country will affect its ability to get its goods to consumers and to communicate with customers, suppliers, and the home office. Energy availability will affect the kinds of products that can be sold to consumer and industrial markets. The country's commercial infrastructure (ad agencies, wholesalers, etc.) will constrain the firm's marketing task and capability there.

Generally, there are major differences between urban consumers and rural consumers. Countries differ greatly in their degree of urbanization, with the number of city dwellers declining with the level of economic development. The marketing task varies between the city and the countryside.

Inflation complicates the marketing task, and its incidence varies, generally being much higher in developing countries. The role of government as regulator, customer, partner is another variable affecting the firm's marketing in a country.

## Questions

3.1 Discuss the use of population size as an indicator of market potential.

3.2 What is the significance of a nation's population growth rate for the international marketer?

3.3 Why is the international marketer interested in the age distribution of the population in a market?

3.4 What is the dual economy phenomenon, and what does it mean for international marketing?

3.5 Discuss the limitations of per capita income figures in evaluating market potential.

3.6 In evaluating markets, what kind of firms might prefer per capita income figures? GNP figures?

3.7 What is the value of knowing about a country's natural resource base?

3.8 What can a study of topography tell the international marketer about a foreign market?

3.9 Discuss the role of climate in international market analysis.

3.10 Marketing opportunities and problems in a country will vary according to its level of economic development. Discuss.

3.11 What marketing differences might be encountered in an agricultural versus an industrialized country?

3.12 Discuss a nation's infrastructure as a constraint on marketing there.

3.13 How does the degree of urbanization in a country affect a firm's marketing?

# Endnotes

[1] *World Development Report 1989* (Washington, D.C.: World Bank, 1989), 214, 215.

[2] All figures from *Statistical Abstract of the United States* (Washington, D.C.: Bureau of the Census, 1989), 795–797.

[3] All figures from *World Development Report 1989* (Washington, D.C.: World Bank, 1989), 222, 223.

[4] Gunnar Myrdal, *Asian Drama* (New York: The Twentieth Century Fund, 1968).

[5] W. W. Rostow, *The Stages of Economic Growth* (New York: Cambridge University Press, 1960).

[6] Input-output tables give a detailed picture of the industrial structure of an economy, showing the interconnections between the various sectors. The input-output matrix shows what each industry bought from every other industry in a given year. For a discussion of input-output analysis, see Wassily Leontief, *Input-Output Economics* (New York: Oxford University Press, 1966).

[7] John S. Hill and Richard R. Still, "Effects of Urbanization on Multinational Product Planning," *Columbia Journal of World Business*, Summer, 1984, 62–67.

# Further Readings

Leontief, Wassily. *Input-Output Economics*. New York: Oxford University Press, 1966.

Rostow, W. W. *The Stages of Economic Growth*. 2d ed. Cambridge: The University Press, 1971.

# Data Sources

*Commercial Atlas and Marketing Guide*. New York: Rand McNally, annual.

*Europa Yearbook*. London: Europa Publications, Ltd., annual.

U.S. Bureau of the Census. *Statistical Abstract of the United States*. Washington, D.C.: U.S. Government Printing Office, annual.

United Nations. *United Nations Demographic Yearbook*. New York: United Nations, annual.

United Nations. *United Nations Statistical Yearbook*. New York: United Nations, annual.

*World Bank Atlas*. Washington, D.C.: World Bank, biannual.

*World Development Report*. Washington, D.C.: World Bank, annual.

# 3.1 American Mining Machinery, Inc.

American Mining Machinery (AMM) is a specialized producer of equipment for the extractive industries. Its machines tend to be large and expensive, each averaging over $150,000. AMM was founded in 1902 by Edward Bednar, an inventive mining engineer, with backing from a few wealthy investors. Bednar ran the company quite successfully, and quite autocratically, till his retirement at age 75 in 1948. His son, Harry Bednar, succeeded him as president and continued his father's management style, which could be described as antiunion paternalism.

Both Bednars were skilled engineers and designers with an intuitive rather than professional approach to the actual administration of the business. They were rather casual about such matters as financial controls and market planning. Nevertheless, AMM sales had risen to $190 million by the time Harry Bednar retired in 1981. At this time, the board of directors succeeded in getting a nonfamily professional manager appointed as president. With the help of an executive search firm, they chose Michael Luce, 41,

Pertinent data source: *United Nations Statistical Yearbook.*

who had been division manager with a capital equipment firm in Cleveland. Luce had an engineering degree but also an M.B.A. and was much more oriented to management than to technical questions.

At the end of 1986, the board of directors reviewed the five years of Michael Luce's presidency. Though sales had risen only to $208 million, this was attributed to conditions in the industry during this period. On the other hand, the board was very pleased with the increased profitability of AMM. The controls and procedures initiated by Luce had caused net profits to rise from 3 percent to 6 percent of sales, which meant a handsome return on investment.

The board was now considering Luce's proposal to expand AMM's operations outside the United States. The strong feelings and prejudices of the Bednar family had confined AMM's operations to the United States. Mike Luce argued that there was a bigger potential market for AMM in the mining industries outside the United States than inside, and that the company could no longer let personal political feelings hinder its growth.

## Questions

1. Rank the 20 countries with the largest employment in the extractive industry.
2. Rank the 20 largest iron-ore-producing countries outside the United States.
3. Do the same for gold producers.
4. Choose the 10 countries that you would recommend to AMM for further investigation as target markets. Explain and defend your choices.

CASE
# 3.2   Medical Specialties, Inc.

Medical Specialties, Inc. (MSI) is an American firm founded in 1955 by a small group of medical and scientific research professionals. The firm is unusual in that its product line is aimed at two specific but unrelated markets: prenatal and post-natal care and geriatric medicine. The firm has grown steadily, and sales now are almost $200 million.

James R. Becker, M.D., president of MSI, recently has been thinking about foreign markets for the firm's products. The question was on the agenda at the last meeting of the board of directors (none of whom has had international ex-

Pertinent data sources: *United Nations Demographic Yearbook* and *World Development Report* (annual).

perience save for some overseas military service). The board was interested but cautious. They suggested Dr. Becker begin to investigate possible markets in Western Europe as being closest to MSI's U.S. experience. They were also influenced by all the talk they had heard about "Europe 1992." (The firm was already selling in Canada).

Becker met with Ben Markowitz, MSI's marketing vice-president. After some discussion, they agreed on a list of factors they felt would be useful as a preliminary screening device for the non-communist European markets. These variables were population, per capita income, birth rates, infant mortality rates, female life expectancy, and ratio of physicians to population.

## Questions

1. Prepare a table showing the scoring of the non-communist Western European countries on the six variables. Your list should have about fourteen countries.

2. Choose the seven countries that represent what you believe are the best initial target markets. Explain and defend your choices.
3. What other information would you like on these countries?

CASE
# 3.3   Unicola

Unicola is a medium-size beverage and snack food company based in the United States. Annual sales are $450 million. The firm has developed some special enriched beverage and snack foods that offer high nutrition value as well as convenience and refreshment. Unicola is interested in

Data source: *United Nations Statistical Yearbook.*

foreign markets for these new products. (Its present business is confined to the United States and Canada.) The company feels that these products should not be promoted as "health foods" but as traditional soft drinks and snacks, because consumers do not like to buy products just because "they are good for you."

In view of the importance of promotion to the successful introduction of these products, George Horton, Unicola advertising manager, has been looking at promotional possibilities in various foreign markets of interest. One of these areas is Southeast Asia. His preliminary screening includes four variables: (1) newsprint consumption or newspaper circulation per capita, (2) radio receivers per capita, (3) television receivers per capita, (4) population. The markets being investigated have already been screened on the basis of political criteria. After the political screening, the following Southeast Asian nations remain on the list for a further screening on the basis of promotional possibilities: Bangladesh, Hong Kong, India, Indonesia, Malaysia, Pakistan, Philippines, Singapore, Sri Lanka, Taiwan, Thailand.

## Questions

1. Prepare a table showing the scoring for these eleven countries on the four criteria suggested.
2. Which five countries would you choose as offering the best possibilities for promoting Unicola's products? Explain and defend your choices.
3. What other information would you need on these countries? How would you get it?

# CHAPTER 4

# Cultural Environment
## The People of the World

Economic factors are important in determining a consumer's ability to purchase a product. Whether a purchase will actually occur, however, depends largely on cultural factors. Therefore, to understand markets abroad, the marketer must have an appreciation for the cultural environment of buyer behavior. Here we shall look at the major ingredients of that cultural environment.

The main goals of this chapter are to

1. Show how a country's material culture determines whether a firm's products fit in with the local way of life and what adaptation may be necessary.
2. Explain the role of a culture's language in shaping the marketing task.
3. Explore the subject of a society's aesthetics, its sense of beauty, proportion, and appropriateness, in connection with a firm's products and communications.
4. Describe the way that the local educational system can help or hinder a firm's marketing and staffing situation.
5. Discuss the effect of the religious situation in a foreign market on consumer behavior there.
6. Distinguish among different values and attitudes that influence purchasing decisions.
7. Explain how the social organization in a given country (family influences, reference groups, etc.) will affect consumer behavior.

Marketing has always been recognized as an economic activity involving the exchange of goods and services. Only in recent years, however, have sociocultural influences been identified as critical determinants of marketing behavior, revealing marketing as a cultural as well as economic phenomenon. Because our understanding of marketing is culture-bound, we must acquire a knowledge of diverse cultural environments in order to achieve successful international marketing. We must, so to speak, remove our culturally tinted glasses to study foreign markets.

Two major developments in marketing in recent decades have been the use of quantitative methods and the application of behavioral science. The growing use of anthropology, sociology, and psychology in marketing is explicit recognition of the noneconomic bases of marketing behavior. We now know that it is not enough to say that consumption is a function of income. Consumption is a function of many other cultural influences as well. Furthermore, only noneconomic factors can explain the different patterns of consumption of two individuals with identical incomes—or, by analogy, of two different countries with similar per capita incomes.

Showing the importance of non-income factors in determining consumption behavior is a survey of consumer durables ownership in Western European countries with similar per capita incomes.[1] For telephones the range was 42 percent in Belgium to 89 percent in Sweden; for televisions, 24 percent in Italy to 48 percent in Britain; for automatic washers, 70 percent in Sweden to 91 percent in Italy; for dishwashers, 12 percent in the Netherlands to 26 percent in Britain; and for freezers, 31 percent in warm Italy to 71 percent in colder Sweden.

These figures show a dramatic difference in consumption behavior among presumably similar countries. And the variations are obviously not attributable to differences in income. They can be explained only by differences in culture and lifestyle. The differences must be great—note that on almost every item, the degree of market saturation in the highest country is two or more times that in the lowest country! In Europe's Common Market, cultural differences continue to be important variables in consumer behavior.

## What Is Culture?

Culture is too complex to define in simple terms. It seems that each anthropologist has a definition. Certain agreed upon fundamentals, however, appear in this definition by Hoebel: "Culture is the integrated sum total of learned behavioral traits that are shared by members of a society."[2] One fundamental is that culture is a total pattern of behavior that is consistent and compatible in its components. It is not a collection of random behaviors but behaviors that are internally related and integrated. A second fundamental is that culture is learned behavior. It is not biologically transmitted. It depends on environment, not heredity. Thus, it can be called the man-made part of our environment. The third fundamental is that culture is behavior that is shared by a group of people, a society. It can be considered as the distinctive way of life of a people. We will look at the major dimensions of culture after we consider the role of cultural analysis in American marketing.

## Cultural Analysis in American Marketing

In approaching the cultural environment of international marketing, it is revealing to see how cultural analysis is used in American marketing. If we scan textbooks in marketing, for instance, we are struck by the fact that no text is without one or more chapters on the contributions of the behavioral sciences to marketing. In addition to chapters on consumer behavior, there are concepts from the behavioral sciences in chapters on marketing research, promotion, and pricing. Even the product is likely to be defined in terms of psychic as well as physical utility. For example, the marketing manager is supposed to be familiar with the following concepts: (1) reference groups, (2) social class, (3) consumption systems, (4) family structure and decision making, (5) adoption-diffusion, (6) market segmentation, and (7) consumer behavior.

Another evidence of the role of cultural analysis in American marketing is the number of persons trained in anthropology or sociology who are working in marketing. Major companies employ such people on their staffs. Others are employed in advertising agencies or consulting firms. University consultants to industry today come not only from schools of business and engineering but also from departments of anthropology and sociology. Considering that most American marketers are born and bred in the American culture, such attention to cultural analysis is notable. How much more important is such analysis in foreign markets, where the international marketer generally knows little about the local culture.

## Elements of Culture

There are varying definitions of the elements of culture, including one that counts 73 "cultural universals." For our purpose, we will use a simpler list covering eight major areas: (1) material culture, (2) language, (3) aesthetics, (4) education, (5) religion, (6) attitudes and values, (7) social organization, and (8) political life. We reserve the political aspect of culture for Chapter 5. Our discussion of the other aspects of culture will not be definitive and perhaps would not satisfy the anthropologist. Nonetheless, it should contribute to an understanding of some dimensions of the cultural environment and how they affect the firm's foreign marketing. A broad definition of culture would include economics as well, however, the subjects are often treated separately, as we have done here.

## Technology and Material Culture

*Material culture* includes the tools and artifacts — the material, or physical, things — in a society, excluding those physical things found in nature unless they undergo some technological (man-made) procedure. For example, a tree per se is not part of a culture, but the Christmas tree is, and so is an orchard. Technology refers to the techniques or methods of making and using those things. Technology and material culture are related to the way a society organizes its economic activities. The term *technology gap* refers to differences in two societies' ability to create, design, and use things.

When we refer to industrialized nations, developing nations, the nuclear age or the space age, we're referring to different technologies and material cultures. We can also speak of societies being in the age of the automobile, the bicycle, or foot transportation. Or societies may be in the age of the computer, the abacus, or pencil and paper calculation. The relationships between technology, material culture, and the other aspects of life are profound but not easily recognized because we are so much the products of our own culture. It is primarily as we travel abroad that we perceive such relationships.

When discussing this topic, Karl Marx went so far as to say that the economic organization of a society shapes and determines its political, legal, and social organization. That is the essence of his economic determinism, his materialistic interpretation of history. Few today would take such a strong position, but we can recognize many examples of the impact of our tools, techniques, and economic organization on the nature of life in our society. For example, our behavior as workers and consumers is greatly influenced by our technology and material culture.

The way we work, and how effectively we work, is determined in large part by our technology and material culture. When Henry Ford created the assembly line, it revolutionized American productivity and ultimately our standard of living. The American farmers' use of equipment and technology has made them the world's most productive agriculturalists. Ironically, agriculture is one of America's most capital-intensive and technology-intensive industries. The R&D is not done by the farmer, however, but by land-grant universities, equipment manufacturers, seed and chemical companies. The computer, as one of our newest artifacts, affects the way we work, the kind of work we can do, and even where we work. If after these examples, we consider the nature of the factory, agricultural methods, and the role of the computer in an African nation (see "Global Marketing"), we can see the impact of technology and material culture as a constraint on the nature of work and productivity in a culture.

The way we consume and what we consume are also heavily influenced by our technology and material culture. For example, the car has helped to create the suburbs with their accompanying lifestyle and consumption patterns. The car has also shaped dating behavior. Television has a wide-ranging impact on consumer and voter behavior. The microwave oven influences not only the preparation of food but the nature of the food consumed. Considering newer artifacts such as the Sony Walkman or the cellular telephone, one can imagine further ramifications of each new product on the life of the consumer. Knowing the impact of these products in the American culture, one can conjecture how consumer behavior might be different in countries with much lighter penetration of such products. For example, the number of persons per car ranges from 1.8 in the United States to 15 in Mexico, 554 in India and 1,374 in China.

## Material Culture as a Constraint

Managers need insight into how material culture in foreign markets affects their operations there. In manufacturing, foreign production by the firm may represent an attempt to introduce a new material culture into the host economy. This will usually be the case when the firm builds a plant in a less developed country. The firm generally checks carefully on the necessary economic prerequisites for such a plant, for example, raw-material supply, power, transportation and financing. Frequently overlooked are the other cultural preconditions for the plant.

## Global Marketing
### Marketing in Malaysia

Marketing efforts must be sensitive to the cultural and religious traditions of the Malays, the Chinese, and the Indians — and what's appealing to one ethnic group may be off-putting or offensive to another. Expatriates based in Kuala Lumpur offer the following pointers for marketing to this increasingly wealthy society:

✓ *Leave your cultural baggage at home.* Executives pinpoint Western thinking as the main stumbling block for firms trying to sell into Malaysia. Expats should make an effort to familiarize themselves with local values: Concepts like fatalism, "face" and filial duty could affect attitudes toward life insurance, the marketability of high-status brand names, and teenage spending power.

✓ *Acknowledge a wide spectrum of tastes.* The great differences between the three groups' preferences affect everything from product development to advertising. Colgate-Palmolive commercial director Dorset Sutton says the company develops its products to meet Malays' specific tastes in laundry detergent. An example? "They like floral perfume, they like lots of suds — we give it to them." In advertising, firms should keep in mind that colors are important to the Chinese (red and gold are positive; white, blue and black, negative).

✓ *Compile a thorough laundry list of all relevant taboos:* Muslim no-no's include alcoholic products, so it's a bad idea to advertise them in Malay. Foods not labeled "halal" also are turned down by the Malays (but Chinese and Indian Malaysians eat them, as are chemical-based products applied to the body (most Malays use talcum powder instead of deodorant).

✓ *Take advantage of the urban-rural split.* Many Malays are rural and most Chinese are urban, which makes it easier to target each group in packaging and point-of-sale advertising.

✓ *Keep the message clear, simple — and multilingual.* Packaging should be labeled in at least Chinese and Malay, and sometimes also in English or Jawi, the traditional Malay script.

✓ *Forget Western and generic Asian advertising.* Information Minister Mohamed Rahmat banned the many TV ads portraying so-called hedonistic Western lifestyles and/or using white and "pan-Asian" (indistinguishable Asian ethnicity) models or actors.

✓ *When marketing, emphasize domestic cultural themes.* To achieve its most successful product launch in 20 years, Colgate surveyed consumers before naming a new dishwashing paste — and used local folklore to advertise the newly named product.

Source: From *Business Asia*, October 23, 1989, 352.

---

Prior to making foreign production decisions, the firm must evaluate the material culture in the host country. One aspect is the economic infrastructure, that is, transportation, power, communications. Other questions are as follows: Do production processes need to be adapted to fit the local economy? Will the plant be more labor-intensive than plants at home? The manager in the international company realizes what the economist long overlooked, namely, that production of the same goods may require a different production function in different countries. A study of both the material and the nonmaterial culture is necessary to determine appropriate plant and production organization.

**Material Culture and Marketing.**  For marketing as well as for manufacturing, it is equally important to understand the material culture in foreign markets. For example, the industrial marketer will find it useful to obtain input-output tables for these markets. Where tables can be even partially designed, the firm has a better idea of how its products relate to the material culture and industrial structure of the country. Such information helps identify customers and usage patterns.

In the giant, diversified economy of the United States, almost any industrial good can find a market. Going down the scale of development, however, industrial goods marketers will find increasingly limited markets, where they can sell only part of their product line, or perhaps not any of it. The better the picture of the material culture in world markets, the better able the firm will be to identify the best prospects. The prospects in countries where the principal agricultural implement is the machete will differ from those in which it is the tractor, or where the abacus is used instead of the computer.

In the early 1970s, General Motors created a "basic transportation vehicle" (BTV) for Third World markets. It was an innovative attempt to respond to markets with a very different technology and material culture. Ford developed a similar vehicle, called the "Model T for Asia." After being marketed in a number of Third World countries for several years, both products eventually failed.

In 1988 Toyota introduced its version, the "Toyota utility vehicle" (TUV). By 1989 the Kijang version, a 62-horsepower model, had 20 percent of the market in Indonesia. Offered as either pickup or van, the Kijang starts at $5,700, compared to $18,000 for a Toyota Corolla.

Consumer goods marketers are also concerned with the material culture in foreign markets; such simple considerations as electrical voltages and use of the metric system of measurement must be taken into account. Product adaptations may also be necessitated by the material culture of the family. Does the family have a car to transport purchases? Does the family have a stove to prepare foods, or a refrigerator to store them? If electrical power is not widely available, electrical appliances will not be marketable unless they can be battery-powered. To women who wash clothes by a stream or lake, detergents or packaged soaps are not useful; there will be a market only for bar soaps. Such examples show how material culture affects the product policy of consumer goods marketers.

Parts of the marketing program other than product policy are also influenced by the material culture. The promotional program, for example, will be constrained by the kinds of media available. The advertiser wants to know the relative availability of television, radio, magazines, and newspapers. Is color TV available? How good is the reproduction process in newspapers and magazines? Are there advertising and research agencies to support the advertising program? The size of retail outlets will affect the use of point-of-purchase displays. The nature of travel and the highway system will affect the use of outdoor advertising.

Modifications in methods of distribution may be necessary. These changes must be made on the basis of the alternatives offered by the country's commercial infrastructure. What kind of wholesale and retail patterns exist? What warehouse or storage facilities are available? Is refrigerated storage possible? What is the nature of the transport system—road, rail, river, or air—and what area does it cover? Firms that use direct channels in the United States, with large-scale retailers and chain store operations, may have to use indirect channels where there is a multitude of small independent retailers. These small retailers may be relatively inaccessible if they are widely dispersed and transportation is inadequate.

If local storage facilities are insufficient, the firm may have to supply its own or provide special bulk packaging to offer extra protection. Whereas highways and railroads are most important in moving goods in the United States, river transport is a major means in some countries. And in others, such as some African nations, air is the principal means. Thus, in numerous ways, international management is concerned with the material culture in foreign markets.

**Imperialism?**   Perhaps the most subtle role of international marketing is that of agent of cultural change. When the firm introduces its new products into the market, it is, in effect, seeking to change the country's material culture. The change may be fairly modest — a new food product — or it may be more dramatic — a machine that revolutionizes agricultural or industrial technology in the host country. The product of the international firm is alien in the sense that it did not originate in the host country. The firm must consider carefully the legitimacy of its role as an agent of change. It must be sure that changes it introduces are in accordance with the interests of the host country. The people may resent the firm's market penetration as a form of "Americanization" or "imperialism"; along this line, someone coined the term *Cocacolanization* in regard to American business abroad.

When Nestle introduced infant formula in developing countries, it had a mature product well proven in the affluent industrialized countries. In the very different technology and material culture of some Third World markets, the way the product was used, or misused, led to a number of infant deaths. It was not a question of product quality — rather, the misapplication of the product by customers in a very different cultural setting.

# Language

Language is the most obvious difference between cultures. Inextricably linked with all other aspects of a culture, *language* reflects the nature and values of that culture. For example, the English language has a rich vocabulary for commercial and industrial activities, reflecting the nature of the English and American societies. Many less industrialized societies have only limited vocabularies for those activities but richer vocabularies for matters important to their culture.

An Indian civil servant, Nabagopal Das, commented on the important role of the English language in India's development. He said it would be a serious error for India to replace English with Hindi or other Indian languages because none of them gives adequate expression to the modern commercial or technical activities necessary for India's development. On the other hand, these other languages are more than adequate, indeed rich, for describing the traditional culture. To use another example, Eskimo has many words to describe snow, whereas English has one general term. This is reasonable, because the difference in forms of snow plays a vital role in the lives of Eskimos. The kinds of activities they can engage in depend on the specific snow conditions. Of course, in America the subculture of skiers has a richer vocabulary for snow than the nonskiers.

Because language is such an obvious cultural difference, everyone recognizes that it must be dealt with. It is said that anyone planning a career in international business should learn a foreign language. Certainly, if a career is going to be importantly or exclusively involved with a particular country, learning that language will be very useful. However, learning German or Japanese is not a great help to those whose career does not involve Germany or Japan. Because it is usually impossible to predict to which countries a career will lead, it is best to study a language with large international coverage. Americans are fortunate in having English as their mother tongue, for English comes close to being a world language for international dealings. French and Spanish follow English as the languages most frequently used in conducting international business.

## Language as a Cultural Mirror

A country's language is the key to its culture. Thus, if one is to work extensively with any one culture, it is imperative to learn the language.

Learning a language well means learning the culture, because the words of the language are merely concepts reflecting the culture from which it derives. For the firm's representatives to communicate well with political leaders, employees, suppliers, and customers, they must assimilate this one aspect of culture more than any other.

Study of the language situation within foreign markets can yield useful information about them. The number of languages in a country is a case in point. In a real sense, a language defines a culture; thus, if a country has several spoken languages, it has several cultures. Belgium has two national languages, French in the South and Flemish in the North. This linguistic division goes back to the days of Julius Caesar, but even today there are political and social differences — and hostilities — between the two language groups.

Canada's situation is similar to Belgium's, with both French and English languages and cultural groups. Many African and Asian nations (and the Soviet Union) have a far greater number of languages and cultural groups. To communicate in this diversity, *lingua francas* have been chosen for communication between the groups. These are language bridges, usually the language spoken by the largest or most powerful group. In the U.S.S.R. it is Russian; in India, it is Hindi; in many countries it is the colonial language.

Zaire serves as an example of this situation in many Third World countries. Separate tribal languages are spoken by the numerous tribes living there. Four African lingua francas partially link four regions of Zaire, but the only national language is again a European one — French. Such situations present real obstacles to learning the "language of the people." The usual approach in these situations is to rely on the European language and the lingua francas for business and marketing communications. Unfortunately, these are not the first language for the nationals.

**Diversity: Linguistic and Social.**   There are other problems with language diversity within a nation. Many tribal languages are not written; for some that are, there are very low literacy rates. All intertribal communications are in the lingua franca, which is a written language. However, because the lingua franca is not everyone's native tongue, it does not communicate as well as the parties' native languages. The European languages used as lingua francas in former colonies have the virtue of covering a wide territory. However, they have the disadvantage of being foreign to the culture and spoken by only a small part of the population.

Language differences within a country may indicate social as well as communication problems. In both Canada and Belgium, the two linguistic groups have occasionally clashed to the point of violence. Zaire, Nigeria, and India are examples of less developed countries where linguistic groups have also engaged in violent hostilities.

When Belgium's Sabena Airline discussed an alliance with KLM Royal Dutch Airlines, the talks were grounded by protests from Belgium's French-speaking Socialist Party who were worried about increasing the influence of the Dutch (Flemish) language in Belgium. Observers ruled out an alliance with Air France because of similar concerns by the Flemish-speaking parties.

Many former colonies have some linguistic unity in the language of the former colonial power, but even this is threatened in some countries. For example, in India, Hindi is an official language along with English. Hindi has the advantage of being an Indian language but the drawback of belonging to just one segment of India's population. Thus when it was declared an official language, there were riots by the other language groups in India.

It is said that a language defines a cultural group—that nothing distinguishes one culture from another more than language. But what does it mean when the same language is used in different countries? French, for example, is the mother tongue not only for the French but also for many Belgians and Swiss. Spanish plays a similar role in Latin America. The anthropologist, however, stresses the *spoken* language as the cultural distinction. The spoken language changes much more quickly than the written and reflects the culture more directly. Although England, the United States, and Ireland use the same written English, they speak somewhat different "dialects." These three cultures are separate yet related, just as are the Spanish-speaking cultures of Latin America.

Even where a common language is spoken, different words are occasionally used as well as different pronunciations. In Latin America, for example, the word for tire is not the same in all the Spanish-speaking countries. In England, they say "lorry," "petrol," and biscuits," but in America, we say "truck," "gasoline," and "cookies." It should be noted, incidentally, that even within one country — for example, the United States, where almost all speak "American" — there are different cultural groups, or subcultures, among which the spoken language varies. Parents continually have problems understanding their teenage offspring.

## Language as a Problem

In advertising, branding, packaging, personal selling, and marketing research, marketing is highly dependent on communication. If management is not speaking the same language as its various audiences, it is not going to enjoy much success. In each of its foreign markets the company must communicate with several audiences: its workers, managers, customers, suppliers, and the government. Each of these audiences may have a distinctive communication style within the native language common to all. The number of language areas the firm operates in approximates the number of countries it is selling in. Any advantage gained by the fact that one language may be used in more than one country is partly offset by the fact that in many countries, more than one language is necessary.

When Lotus was planning to introduce Lotus 1-2-3 into Japan, it formed a development team. The team expected to work three months in Japan modifying the input and output routines. The job lasted 18 months! The Japanese write in four alphabets, and Kanji, used for business correspondence, is almost incompatible with keyboard entry. Lotus 1-2-3 had to speak Kanji. The solution was to work with a leading-edge Japanese software company.

Language diversity in world markets could be an insuperable problem if it meant that managers had to master the languages of all their markets. Fortunately, that is not the case. It is true that, to be effective, any person assigned to a foreign operation for a period of a year or more should learn the local language. However, cultural bridges are available in many markets. For example, in countries where the firm is operating through a distributor, the distributor may act as the bridge between the firm and its local market. In advertising, the firm can rely on a local advertising agency. The international advertising manager must communicate with the agency, but agency personnel, like the distributor, probably speak the advertising manager's language — especially if the international firm communicates principally in English. For example, the Dutch firm Philips uses English as the official company language, even though it is domiciled in the Netherlands. Because of its widespread operations, it finds English the most useful language for contact with all its markets. When Swedish ASEA merged with Swiss Brown Boveri, they made English the corporate language.

In countries where the firm has subsidiaries, the language requirement becomes greater. The firm then has more extensive communication with its audiences. Even here, however, the language burden is lessened because, among its national managers, the firm can usually count people of the "third culture." This expression is used to describe nationals who have become so familiar with another culture that they become a bridge between the two. The firm that has such people has one of the best solutions to both the language gap and the culture gap. Developing such people is a key task of international management.

We have suggested that there are ways to circumvent the language problem in international marketing. However, we hasten to add that language *is* a critical factor. It is the key to understanding and communicating with the local cultures around the world. The international firm does need language capabilities, not only among its distributors and other collaborators, but also among its own personnel. Furthermore, the individual who hopes for international management responsibilities had better get some foreign language facility also.

Canada provides an illustration of a situation requiring linguistic sensitivity on the part of the international firm. In labor negotiations in the province of Quebec, General Motors helped underwrite the cost of an interpreter to provide documentation in both French and English. GM agreed to recognize the French language version of the contract as official. Other guidelines recommended to alleviate tension between the two groups were (1) bilingual labeling and advertising; (2) bilingual annual reports and press releases (French in Quebec); (3) bilingual executives for operations in Quebec.

## Aesthetics

*Aesthetics* refers to the ideas in a culture concerning beauty and good taste, as expressed in the fine arts — music, art, drama, and dancing — and the particular appreciation of color and form. There are important international differences in aesthetics, but they tend to be regional rather than national. For example, Kabuki theater is exclusively Japanese, but Western theater includes at least all of Western Europe plus the United States and Canada in its audience.

Musical tastes, too, tend to be regional rather than national. In the West, many countries enjoy the same classical and popular music. In fact, with modern communications and performers with worldwide appeal, popular music has become truly international. Nevertheless, there are obvious differences between Western music and that of the Middle East, black Africa, or India. Likewise, the dance styles of African tribal groups or the Balinese are quite removed from Western dance styles. The beauty of India's Taj Mahal is different from that of Notre Dame in Paris or the Lever Building on Park Avenue in New York.

**Design**

The aesthetics of a culture probably do not have a major impact on economic activity. In aesthetics, however, lie some significant implications for international business operations. For example, in the design of its plant, product, or package, the firm should be sensitive to local aesthetic preferences. This requirement may run counter to the firm's desire for international uniformity, but the firm at least must be aware of the positive and negative aspects of its designs.

A historical example of lack of cultural sensitivity is illustrated by the early Christian missionaries from Western nations who were often guilty of architectural "imperialism." The Christian churches built in many non-

Western nations almost always reflected Western rather than indigenous architectural ideas. This was not usually done deliberately or with malicious intent but because the missionaries were culture-bound in their aesthetics; that is, they had their own ideas as to what a church should look like, ideas that reflected the aesthetics of Western culture.

The United States government faces a similar problem in designing its embassies. The American Embassy in India received praise both for its beauty as a building and for the way it blended in with Indian architectural ideas. The American Embassy in London, however, has received more than its share of criticism for various things, including the size of the sculptured American eagle on top of the building. Some Britons also took exception to the architecture of the London Hilton. For the firm, the best policy is to design and decorate its buildings and commercial vehicles to reflect local aesthetic preferences. In its thousands of outlets abroad, McDonald's has learned to adapt its facilities to local tastes.

## Color

The significance of different colors can vary from culture to culture. In the United States, for instance, we use colors to identify emotional reactions; we "see red," we are "green with envy," or we "feel blue." Black signifies mourning in Western countries, whereas white is often the color of mourning in Eastern nations. Certain colors have particular meanings because of religious, patriotic, or aesthetic reasons. For example, green is popular in Muslim countries; while red and black are negative in several African countries. The marketer needs to know these patterns in planning products, packages, and advertising. Advertising especially must be culturally sensitive. For any market, the right choice of colors, illustrations, and appeals will be related to the aesthetic sense of the *buyer's* culture rather than that of the *marketer's* culture. Generally, the colors of the country's flag are safe colors.

## Music

As noted earlier, there are cultural differences in music. An understanding of these differences is critical to the firm in creating advertising messages that use music. The music of nonliterate cultures is generally *functional*, or has significance in the people's daily lives, whereas the music of literate cultures tends to be separate from the people's other concerns. For example, a Western student has to learn to "understand" a Beethoven symphony, but aborigines assimilate musical culture as an integral part of their existence. Malm says that to understand the symbolism in different kinds of music requires considerable cultural conditioning. Therefore, aesthetic homogeneity in music throughout world cultures is not possible.[3] One implication for the firm is that wherever it can use music in its operations, generally it had best use that of the culture in which it wishes to function. A contrary example is Pepsi's use of a Michael Jackson commercial in many countries abroad, including Japan and the U.S.S.R.

Paul Anka provides an example of the value of "going native" in music and language. Anka has recorded 10 albums that have sold, collectively, 10 million copies, none of which have been heard in the United States. The secret is the albums were sung in Japanese, German, French, Spanish and Italian — songs that Anka composed strictly for those countries in a style indigenous to their musical cultures.

Anka naturally isn't fluent in all those languages. He worked months in each country with local musicians on music and lyrics that would appeal to each nation. He sings in the local language phonetically. Anka said, "As far as my income is concerned, I could live off the rest of the world and never play the U.S. again." He earns up to $70,000 a night in concert abroad. "They love you over there when you record in their language," he said.[4]

**Brand Names**

The choice of brand names is affected by aesthetics. Frequently, the best brand name is one that is in the local language and pleasing to the local taste. This necessarily leads to a multiplicity of brand names, which some firms try to avoid by searching out a nonsense word that is pronounceable everywhere but has no specific meaning anywhere: *Kodak* is a famous example. In other cases, local identification is important enough that firms will seek local brand names. For example, Procter & Gamble has 20 different brand names for its detergents in foreign markets.

We may conclude that the aesthetics of a culture do influence a firm's marketing there, and often in ways that marketers are unaware of until they have made mistakes. The firm needs local inputs to avoid ineffective or damaging use of aesthetics. These inputs may be from local marketing research, local nationals working for the firm, and a local advertising agency or distributor.

## Education

To an American, education usually means formal training in school. In this formal sense, the aborigines in Australia or the Pygmies in Africa are not educated; that is, they have never been to school. However, this formal definition is too restrictive. *Education* includes the process of transmitting skills, ideas, and attitudes, as well as training in particular disciplines. Even primitive peoples have been educated in this broader sense. For example, the Bushmen of South Africa are well educated for the culture in which they live.

One function of education is the transmission of the existing culture and traditions to the new generation. This is as true among the people of America as among the aborigines of Australia. However, education can also be used for cultural change. The Soviet Union and the People's Republic of China are notable examples, but this, too, is an aspect of education in most nations of the world. For example, in India educational campaigns are carried on to improve agriculture and to quell the population explosion. In Britain, business schools were established to improve the performance of the economy.

## International Differences in Education

In looking at education in foreign markets, the observer is limited primarily to information about the formal process, that is, education in schools. This is the only area where UNESCO (United Nations Educational and Social Council) and others have been able to gather data. Literacy rates are used to describe educational achievement.

The education information available on world markets refers primarily to national enrollments in the various levels of education — primary, secondary, and college or university (see Table 4–1). This kind of information can give the international marketer insight into the sophistication of consumers in different countries. One can also observe a rather good correlation between educational attainment and economic development.

Because only quantitative data are available, there is a danger that the qualitative aspects of education might be overlooked. Furthermore, in addition to the limitations of international statistics, there is the problem of interpreting them in terms of business needs. For example, the firm's needs

**Table 4–1**                 **Educational Participation: Selected Nations**

| Countries | Percentage of Age Group Enrolled in Education | | |
|---|---|---|---|
| | Primary | Secondary | Tertiary |
| *Low-Income Countries* | | | |
| China | 129 | 42 | 2 |
| India | 92 | 35 | 3 |
| Kenya | 94 | 20 | 1 |
| Pakistan | 44 | 18 | 5 |
| Sudan | 50 | 20 | 2 |
| Zambia | 104 | 19 | 2 |
| *Lower-Middle-Income Countries* | | | |
| Bolivia | 87 | 37 | 19 |
| Malaysia | 101 | 54 | 6 |
| Mexico | 114 | 55 | 16 |
| Philippines | 106 | 68 | 38 |
| Turkey | 117 | 44 | 10 |
| *Upper-Middle-Income Countries* | | | |
| Algeria | 95 | 54 | 7 |
| Argentina | 109 | 74 | 39 |
| Hungary | 98 | 70 | 15 |
| Portugal | 117 | 52 | 13 |
| *High-Income Countries* | | | |
| Italy | 97 | 76 | 25 |
| Japan | 102 | 96 | 29 |
| Sweden | 99 | 83 | 37 |
| United States | 102 | 100 | 59 |
| West Germany | 97 | 72 | 30 |

Source: *World Development Report 1989,* (New York: Oxford University Press, 1989), 220, 221.

for technicians, marketing personnel, managers, distributors and salesforces will have to be met largely from the educated manpower in the local economy. In looking for people, the firm is concerned not only with the level but also with the nature of their education. Table 4–1 does not give any indication as to the kind of education available at the different levels.

Training in law, literature, music, or political science is probably not the most suitable education for business needs. Yet in many nations such studies are emphasized almost to the exclusion of others more relevant to commercial and economic growth. Too often, primary education is preparation for secondary, secondary education is preparation for university, and university education is not designed to meet the needs of the economy. University education in many nations is largely preparation for the traditional prestige occupations. Although a nation needs lawyers and philosophers, it also needs agricultural experts, engineers, business managers, and technicians. The degree to which the educational system provides for these needs will be a critical determinant of the nation's ability to develop economically. Similarly, observers comparing the performance of the U.S. and Japanese economies in recent years have noted the role of the educational systems in the two countries as a critical factor in Japan's catch-up performance.

## Education and International Marketing

The international marketer must be something of an educator also. The products and techniques the international firm brings into a market are generally new to that market. The firm must educate consumers about their uses and benefits. Although the firm does not use the formal educational system to accomplish its own educational goals, its success will be constrained by that system, since the firm's ability to communicate will depend in part on the educational level of its market.

The international marketer is further concerned about the educational situation in foreign markets because it is a key determinant of the nature of the consumer market and the kinds of marketing personnel available. Some implications are the following:

1.  If consumers are largely illiterate, advertising programs and package labels will need to be adapted.
2.  If girls and women are largely excluded from formal education, marketing programs will differ greatly from those aimed at the American housewife.
3.  Conducting marketing research can be difficult, both in communicating with consumers and in getting qualified researchers.
4.  Products that are complex or need written instructions may need to be modified to meet the educational and skill levels of the market.
5.  Cooperation from the distribution channel will depend partly on the educational attainments of members in the channel.
6.  The nature and quality of marketing support services, such as advertising agencies, will depend on how well the educational system prepares people for such occupations.

# Religion

In this chapter we are concerned with the cultural or human environment of business. We have already seen several aspects of this environment. The material culture, language, and aesthetics are, in effect, outward manifestations of a culture. If we are to get a full understanding of a culture, however, we must gain a familiarity with the internal or mental behavior that gives rise to the external manifestations. Generally, it is the *religion* of a culture that provides the best insights into this behavior. Therefore, although the international company is primarily interested in knowing *how* people behave as consumers or workers, management's task will be aided by an understanding of *why* people behave as they do. Even in the domestic market, studies of worker and consumer motivation are used extensively.

There are numerous religions and religious groups in the world; here we will discuss briefly animism, Buddhism, Christianity, Hinduism, Islam, and the Japanese situation. We selected these on the basis of their importance in terms of numbers of adherents and their impact on the economic behavior of their followers. These religions account for over three-fourths of the world's population. A massive survey completed in the 1980s gives us the best estimate of the numbers for each religion: animism, 300 million; Buddhism, 310 million; Christianity, 1,900 million; Hinduism, 700 million; and Islam, about 900 million.[5]

**Animism or Nonliterate Religion**

*Animism* is the term used to describe the religion of primitive peoples. It is often defined as spirit worship, as distinguished from the worship of God or gods. Animistic beliefs have been found in all parts of the world. With the exception of revealed religion, some form of animism has preceded all historical religions. As Frazer put it in *The Golden Bough*, "An Age of Religion has everywhere been preceded by an Age of Magic."[6] In many less developed parts of the world today, animistic ideas affect the behavior of the people.

Magic, the key element of animism, is the attempt to achieve results through the manipulation of the spirit word. It represents an unscientific approach to the physical world. When cause-and-effect relationships are not known, magic is given credit for results. The same attitude prevails toward many modern-day products and techniques.

For example, during the author's years in Zaire, he had an opportunity to see reactions to European products and practices that were often based on a magical interpretation. As one instance, a number of Africans affected the wearing of glasses, believing the glasses would enhance the intelligence of the wearer. Some consumer goods marketers in Africa have not hesitated to imply that possession of their products gives magical qualities to the owners. Of course, the same is occasionally true of marketers on American TV.

Other aspects of animism include casting spells, ancestor worship, taboos, and fatalism. All of these tend to promote a traditionalist, status quo, backward-looking society. Because such societies are more interested in pro-

# Global Marketing

## Shinto in Japan

The hold of tradition in Japan is vividly apparent in religion. Most shops have, tucked away somewhere, a shrine to a deity whose customary symbol is a pair of foxes. Japanese companies generally choose a patron god or goddess. These deities are part of Japan's own primitive folk religion, Shinto.

Jan Swyngedouw, a Belgian professor of Japanese culture and religion at Nanzan University in Japan, points out that Japan is the only industrialized country in the world with its own primitive religion still intact. As a national religion unique to Japan, Shinto helps knit the nation together and separate Japanese from outsiders.

Unlike Western religions, Shinto has no scriptures or commandments. It does have customary practices, including ancestor worship adopted from Confucianism. And it has a body of traditional myths, passed on from one generation to the next. The priests do not preach. They tend their shrines and offer quiet places for reflection and prayer, as well as for weddings and elaborate baby-blessing ceremonies.

Shinto coexists with Buddhism, and a Japanese can embrace both. Many a Japanese has been married at a Shinto shrine and buried with a Buddhist ceremony. But despite this tolerance of diverse religious traditions, Christianity has never taken hold in Japan. Swyngedouw has an explanation. "The Japanese," he says, "are already saved. They are a sacred race. It is understood, in the traditions of Shinto, that they descend from God."

These beliefs, he adds, do involve a danger of ultranationalism. On the positive side, they contribute to a sense of unity of purpose. This spills into the workplace. Over the past several decades, the Japanese have extended their religious feelings to the company, according to Swyngedouw. The transfer can take place because of the sense of sacredness the Japanese feel toward their country, its development, and its place in the world. This devotion, he says, is sometimes called the religion of

Source: Carla Rapoport, "Understanding How Japan Works," *Fortune* 120, no. 13 (Fall 1989):18. © 1989 The Time Inc. Magazine Company. All rights reserved.

---

tecting their traditions than in accepting change, marketers face problems when working with them. Their success in bringing change depends on how well they understand and relate to the culture and its animistic foundation.

## Hinduism

There are over 700 million Hindus, almost all of them living in India. In a broad sense, about 90 percent of India's population is Hindu, but in the sense of strict adherence to the tenets of Hinduism, the number of followers would be smaller. It is a common dictum that Hinduism is not a religion but a way of life. Its origins go back to about 1500 B.C. It is an ethnic, noncreedal religion. A Hindu is born, not made, so Americans cannot become Hindus, although they can become Buddhists, for example. Modern Hinduism is a combination of ancient philosophies and customs, animistic beliefs, legends, and more recently, Western influences, including Christianity. One of the strengths of Hinduism over the centuries has been its ability to absorb ideas from outside; Hinduism tends to assimilate rather than to exclude.

Because Hinduism is an ethnic religion, many of its doctrines apply only to the Indian situation. However, they are key factors in understanding

India. One important Hindu practice is the caste system. Each member of a particular caste in Hindu society has a specific occupational and social role, which is hereditary. Marriage is forbidden outside of the caste. Although efforts have been made to weaken this system, it still has a rather strong hold. Discrimination based on caste is forbidden by the Indian constitution, but such deep-rooted customs do not disappear with the passage of a new law. The caste system is aimed at conserving the status quo in society at large.

Another element, and one of the strengths of Hinduism, is *baradari*, or the "joint family." After marriage, the bride goes to the groom's home. After a series of marriages, there is a large joint family where the father or grandfather is chief authority. In turn, the older women have power over the younger. The elders advise and consent in family council. The Indian grows up thinking and acting in terms of the joint family. If he goes abroad to a university, the joint family may raise the funds. In turn, he is expected to remember the family if he is successful. *Baradari* is aimed at preserving the family.

Veneration of the cow is perhaps the best-known Hindu custom; Gandhi himself called this the distinguishing mark of the Hindu. Hindu worship of the cow involves not only protecting it; eating the products of the cow is also considered a means for purification. Another element of traditional Hinduism is the restriction of women, following the occasional belief that to be born a woman is a sign of sin in a former life. Marriages are arranged by relatives; although a man may remarry if widowed, a woman may not. This attitude toward women makes it all the more remarkable that India placed a woman in its highest office, Prime Minister Indira Gandhi.

Nirvana is another important concept, one that Hinduism shares with Buddhism. It will be discussed in the following section. The marketing implications of Hindu thought will be considered in the section, "Religion and the Economy," later in the chapter.

## Buddhism

Buddhism springs from Hinduism and dates from about 600 B.C. Buddhism has approximately 300 million followers, mostly in South and East Asia from India to Japan. There are, however, small Buddhist societies in Europe and America. Buddhism is, to some extent, a reformation of Hinduism. It did not abolish caste but declared that Buddhists were released from caste restrictions. This openness to all classes and both sexes was one reason for Buddhism's growth. While accepting the philosophical insights of Hinduism, Buddhism tried to avoid its dogma and ceremony, stressing tolerance and spiritual equality.

At the heart of Buddhism are the Four Noble Truths:

1.  The Noble Truth of Suffering states that suffering is omnipresent and part of the very nature of life.
2.  The Noble Truth of the Cause of Suffering cites the cause to be desire, that is, desire for possession and selfish enjoyment of any kind.
3.  The Noble Truth of the Cessation of Suffering states that suffering ceases when desire ceases.

4. The Noble Truth of the Eight-fold Path which leads to the Cessation of Suffering offers the means to achieve cessation of desire. This is also known as the Middle Way because it avoids the two extremes of self-indulgence and self-mortification. The eight-fold path includes (1) the right views, (2) the right desires, (3) the right speech, (4) the right conduct, (5) the right occupation, (6) the right effort, (7) the right awareness, and (8) the right contemplation. This path, though simple to state, is a complicated and demanding ethical system. Nirvana is the reward for those who are able to stay on the path throughout their lifetime or, more probably, lifetimes.

Nirvana is the ultimate goal of the Hindu and Buddhist. It represents the extinction of all cravings and the final release from suffering. To the extent that such an ideal reflects the thinking of the mass of the people, the society would be considered antithetical to such goals as acquisition, achievement, or affluence. This is an obvious constraint on marketing.

## Islam

Islam dates from the seventh century A.D. It has some 900 million adherents, mostly in Africa and Asia. The bulk of the world of Islam is found from the Atlantic across the northern half of Africa, the Middle East, and across Asia to the Philippines. Although there are two major groups in Islam (Sunni, 90 percent, and Shia, 10 percent), there is enough similarity between them on economic issues to permit identification of the following elements of interest to us.

Muslim theology, *Tawhid*, defines all that a man should believe, whereas the law, *Shari'a*, prescribes everything he should do. The Koran (*Qur'an*) is accepted as the ultimate guide. Anything not mentioned in the Koran is quite likely to be rejected by the faithful. Introducing new products and techniques can be difficult in such an environment. An important element of Muslim belief is that everything that happens, good or evil, proceeds directly from the Divine Will, and is already irrevocably recorded on the Preserved Tablet. This fatalistic belief tends to restrict attempts to bring about change in Muslim countries; to attempt change may be a rejection of what Allah has ordained. The name Islam is the infinitive of the Arabic verb *to submit.* Muslim is the present participle of the same verb, that is, a Muslim is one who is submitting to the will of Allah.

The Five Pillars of Islam, or the duties of a Muslim, include (1) the recital of the creed, (2) prayer, (3) fasting, (4) almsgiving, and (5) the pilgrimage. The creed is brief: There is no God but God, and Mohammed is the Prophet of God. The Muslim must pray five times daily at stated hours. During the month of Ramadan, Muslims are required to fast from dawn to sunset—no food, no drink, no smoking. As the Muslim year is lunar, Ramadan sometimes falls in midsummer when the long days and intense heat make abstinence a severe test. The fast is meant to develop both self-control and sympathy for the poor. During Ramadan, work output falls off markedly, which is probably attributable as much to the Muslim's loss of sleep as to the rigors of fasting, because the average family spends much more on the food consumed at night during Ramadan than on the food consumed by day in the other months. Other spending rises also. One Egyptian writer claimed that spending during Ramadan equalled six months of normal spending.[7]

By almsgiving the Muslim shares with the poor. It is an individual responsibility, and there are both legal alms (*zakat*) and freewill gifts. The pilgrimage to Mecca is a well-known aspect of Islam. The thousands who gather in Mecca each year return home with a greater sense of the international solidarity of Islam. Spending for the pilgrimage is a special form of consumption and affects other consumption also.

Muslims are not allowed to consume pork or alcohol. There is also a prohibition against usury, although this is often ignored in modern business practice. The role of women is quite restricted in Muslim nations, but very conservative Pakistan elected a woman as prime minister, Benazir Bhutto. Some marketing implications of Islam are noted in Table 4–2.

**Japan: Shinto, Buddhist, and Confucianist**

Japan is a homogeneous culture with a composite religious tradition. The original national religion is Shinto, "the way of the gods." In the seventh century, however, Japan fell heavily under the influence of China and imported an eclectic Buddhism mingled with Confucianism. In 604, Prince Shotoku issued a moral code based on the teachings of both Confucius and Gautama Buddha. Its 17 articles still form the basis of Japanese behavior. The adoption of the religions from China was only after the authorities decided they would not conflict with Shinto. Traditional Shinto contains elements of ancestor and nature worship. State or modern Shinto added political and patriotic elements to traditional Shinto. Government figures count 107 million followers of Shinto and 93 million Buddhists, obviously a tremendous overlap.[8]

Among the more important aspects of modern Shinto are (1) reverence for the special or divine origin of the Japanese people and (2) reverence for

---

**Table 4–2**    **Islam and Marketing**

| Islamic Element | Marketing Implication |
|---|---|
| 1. Daily Prayers | Consider when planning sales calls, work schedules, customer traffic, and so forth. |
| 2. Prohibition against Usury (Charging Interest) | Avoid direct use of credit as marketing tool. |
| 3. Zakat (Compulsory Almsgiving) | Use "excessive" profits for charitable purposes. |
| 4. Religious Holidays (Example — End of Ramadan) | A major selling time for food, clothing, and gifts. |
| 5. Public Separation of Sexes | Access female consumers by saleswomen, catalogs, home demonstrations, and women's shops. |

Source: Mushtaq Luqmani, Zahir A. Quraeshi and Linda Deline, "Marketing in Islamic Countries," *MSU Business Topics* (Summer 1980): 20, 21.

the Japanese nation and the imperial family as the head of that nation. We use the term *modern* Shinto because when the imperial powers were restored in 1868, state Shinto became a patriotic cult, whereas sectarian Shinto was purely religious. Of course, sectarian Shinto, through ancestor worship, also affects Japanese attitudes. In many houses, there is a god-shelf (*Kamidana*) in which the spirits of the family ancestors are thought to dwell and watch over the affairs of the family. Reverence is paid to them, and the sense of the ancestors' spirit is a bulwark of the family's authority over the individual.

The impact of modern Shinto on Japanese life is reflected in an aggressive patriotism. The mobilization of the Japanese of World War II and their behavior during the war are examples of that patriotism. One longtime observer said, "Nationalism is the Japanese religion."[9] More recently, the economic performance of Japan is due, in part at least, to the patriotic attitude of all those working in the economic enterprise. The family spirit has largely carried over to the firm, which has meant greater cooperation and productivity. Some oriental religions seek virtue through passivity. Shinto, by contrast, stresses the search for progress through creative activity. Japan's economic performance clearly seems to follow the Shinto path. The aggressive Japanese attitude is reflected in the company song of Kyoto Ceramics, a Japanese firm.

*As the sun rises brilliantly in the sky,*
*Revealing the size of the mountain, the market,*
*Oh this is our goal*

*With the highest degree of mission in our heart, we serve our industry*
*Meeting the strictest degree of customer requirement.*
*We are the leader in this industry and our future path*
*Is ever so bright and satisfying.*

## Christianity

Since most readers of this book will be from countries where Christianity is the dominant religion, little time need be spent describing it. What concerns us here is the impact of the different Christian religious groups (Roman Catholic and Protestant) on economic attitudes and behavior. Two well-known studies have dealt with this subject: Max Weber's *The Protestant Ethic and the Spirit of Capitalism* and R. H. Tawney's *Religion and the Rise of Capitalism*. The Eastern Orthodox churches are not discussed here, but in their impact on economic attitudes they are similar to Catholicism.

Roman Catholic Christianity traditionally has emphasized the Roman Catholic Church and the sacraments as the principal elements of religion and the way to God. The church and its priests are the intermediaries between God and man, and apart from the church there is no salvation. Another element in Roman Catholicism is the strong distinction between the religious orders and the laity, with different standards of conduct applied to each. Along with this distinction there is an implicit difference between the secular and the religious life.

The Protestant Reformation, and especially Calvinism, made some critical changes in emphasis but retained agreement with Catholicism on most of traditional Christian doctrine. The Protestants stressed that the church, its sacraments, and its clergy were not essential to salvation: "Salvation is by faith alone." The result of this was a downgrading of the role of the church and a consequent upgrading of the role of the individual. Salvation became more of an individual matter.

Another change in emphasis by the reformers was the elimination of the distinction between secular and religious life. Luther said all of life was a *Beruf*, a "calling," and even the performance of tasks considered to be secular was a religious obligation. Calvin carried this further and emphasized the need to glorify God through one's calling. Whereas works were necessary to salvation in Catholicism, works were evidence of salvation in Calvinism.

Hard work was enjoined to glorify God; achievement was the evidence of hard work; and thrift was necessary because the produced wealth was not to be used selfishly. Accumulation of wealth, capital formation, and the desire for greater production became Christian duty. The Protestant Reformation thus led to greater emphasis on individualism and action (hard work) as contrasted with the more ritualistic and contemplative approach of Catholicism.

Although it is useful to recognize the separate thrust of Roman Catholic and Protestant Christianity, it is also important to note the various roles Christianity in general plays in different nations. Some nations are varying mixtures of Catholic and Protestant, and the resulting ethic may be some combination of both doctrines. The impact of Catholicism in these countries will obviously differ from that in the overwhelmingly Catholic countries such as Italy, Spain, or Brazil.

## Religion and the Economy

In our discussion of the various religions, we suggested some economic implications that we will elaborate on here. Religion has a major impact on attitudes toward economic matters. Under the section, "Attitudes and Values," we will discuss the different attitudes religion may inspire. Besides attitudes, however, religion may affect the economy more directly.

1.   Religious holidays vary greatly among countries, not only from Christian to Muslim, but even from one Christian country to another. Italy, for example, has approximately 13 religious holidays, depending on how Sundays fall. In general, Sundays are a religious holiday in all nations where Christianity is an important religion. In the Muslim world, however, the entire month of Ramadan is a religious holiday for all practical purposes. The international firm must see that local work schedules and marketing programs are related to local holidays, just as American firms plan for a big marketing season at Christmas.

2.   Consumption patterns may be affected by religious requirements or taboos. Fish on Friday for Catholics used to be a classic example. Taboos against beef for Hindus or pork for Muslims and Jews are other examples. The Muslim prohibition against alcohol has been a boon to companies like Coca-Cola. Stroh's and some other brewers sell a nonalcoholic beer in Saudi Arabia. On the other hand, dairy products find favor among Hindus, many of whom are also vegetarian.

3.   The economic role of women varies from culture to culture, and religious beliefs are an important cause. Women may be restricted in their capacity as consumers or consumption influencers, as workers, or as respondents in a marketing study. These differences can require major adjustments in the approach of a management conditioned in the American market.

Procter & Gamble's products are mainly used by women. When the company wanted to conduct a focus group in Saudi Arabia, however, it could not induce women to participate. Instead, it used the husbands and brothers of the women for the focus group.

4.   The caste system restricts participation in the economy. The company will feel the effects not only in its staffing practices (especially the salesforce) but also in its distribution and promotional programs, because it must deal with the market segments set up by the caste system.

5.   The Hindu joint family has economic effects. A particular form of nepotism is characteristic of the family business. Staffing will be based on considerations of family rank more than on other criteria. Furthermore, consumer decision making and consumption in the joint family may differ from those in the American family, requiring an adapted marketing strategy. Pooled income in the joint family may lead to different purchase patterns.

6.   Religious institutions themselves can play a role in economic matters. The church, or any organized religious group, can often block the introduction of new products or techniques if it sees the innovation as a threat. On the other hand, the same product or technique can be more effectively introduced if the religious organization sees it as a benefit to itself and its followers. Even Nasser, the Muslim ruler of a Muslim nation, had to get the support of Islamic leaders to further his program for modernizing Egypt. The theologians had to be persuaded that Nasser's modern reforms were not contrary to the spirit of the Koran. More recently, the Ayatollah Khomeini and the Islamic leaders had a strong impact on consumption in Iran.

7.   Finally, religious divisions in a country can pose problems for management. The firm may find that it is in effect dealing with different markets. In Northern Ireland there has been strong Catholic-Protestant hostility. In India, Muslim-Hindu clashes led to the formation of the separate Muslim state of Pakistan, but the problem is not settled yet. In Lebanon it is Christians versus Muslims. In the Netherlands there are major Catholic and Protestant groups that have their own political parties and newspapers. Such religious divisions can cause difficulty in staffing an operation or in distributing and promoting a product. Religious differences may indicate market segments that require separate marketing strategies and media.

Clearly, the international firm must be sensitive to religious differences in its foreign markets and willing to make adaptations where called for. To cite one example, the firm that is building a plant abroad might plan the date and method of opening and dedicating the plant to reflect the local religious situation. A firm's advertising, packaging, and personal-selling practices especially need to take local religious sensitivities into account.

## Attitudes and Values

Our values and attitudes help determine what we think is right or appropriate, what is important, and what is desirable. Some relate to marketing, and these are the ones we will look at here. We must consider values and attitudes because, as someone said, "People act on them."

**Marketing Activities**

Ever since Aristotle, activities related to selling have failed to gain high social approval. The degree of disapproval, however, varies from country to country. In countries where marketing is rated very low, marketing activities are likely to be neglected and underdeveloped. Capable, talented people will not be drawn into business. Often marketing activities will be left to a special class, or perhaps to expatriates. One is reminded of the role of medieval bankers played by the Jews, or the merchant role of the Chinese in Southeast Asia. In any case, the international firm can have problems with personnel, distribution channels, and other aspects of its marketing program, depending on a country's attitude toward business. There is a brighter side to this picture, however. Because marketing is well accepted and developed in the United States, the American firm abroad may have a comparative advantage in marketing.

**Wealth, Material Gain, and Acquisition**

The United States has been called the "affluent society," the "achieving society," and the "acquisitive society." These somewhat synonymous expressions reflect motivating values in our society. In America, wealth and acquisition are often considered the signs of success and achievement and are given social approval. In a Buddhist or Hindu society where nirvana or "wantlessness" is an ideal, people are not so motivated to produce and consume. Marketers obviously prefer to operate in an acquisitive society. However, as a result of the revolution of rising expectations around the world, national differences in attitudes toward acquisition seem to be lessening.

**Change**

When a company enters a foreign market, it brings change by introducing new ways of doing things and new products. Americans in general accept change. The word *new* has a favorable connotation in the United States and facilitates change when used to describe techniques and products. Many societies are more tradition-oriented, revering their ancestors and their traditional ways of consuming.

The marketer as an agent of change has a different task in such traditional societies. Rather than emphasizing what is new and different about the product, it might be better to relate it to traditional values, perhaps noting that it is similar but better. In seeking to gain acceptance of its new product, the firm might try to get at least a negative clearance — that is, no objection — from local religious leaders or other opinion leaders. Any product must first meet a market need. Beyond that, however, the product must also fit in with the overall value system if it is to be accepted.

Campbell's, for example, met this kind of obstacle when it was introducing its canned soups into the Italian market. In conducting marketing research, it received an overwhelmingly negative response to the question "Would you marry a user of prepared soups?" Campbell's had to adjust its marketing accordingly.

**Risk Taking**

Risk taking is usually associated with entrepreneurial activity. However, consumers also take risks when they try a new product. Will it do what they expect it to do? Will it prejudice their standing or image with their peers? Middlemen handling the untried product may also face risks beyond those associated with their regular line. In a conservative society, there is a greater reluctance to take such risks. Therefore, the marketer must seek to reduce the risk involved in trying a new product as perceived by customers or distributors. In part, this can be accomplished through education; guarantees, consignment selling, or other marketing techniques can also be used.

**Consumer Behavior**

The attitudes we have been discussing are relevant to understanding consumer behavior in the markets of the world. International managers must have such an understanding to develop effective marketing programs. Because of the impossibility of gaining intimate knowledge of a great number of markets, they must rely on help from others in addition to company research. Those who may assist in understanding local attitudes and behavior include personnel in the firm's subsidiary, the distributor, and the advertising agency. Although the firm is interested in changing attitudes, most generally it will have to adapt to them. As Confucius said, "It is easier to move mountains than to change the minds of men."

## Social Organization

**Kinship**

*Social organization* refers to the way people relate to other people. This differs somewhat from society to society. The primary kind of social organization is based on *kinship*. In America, the key unit is the family, which includes only the father and mother and the unmarried children in the household. Of course, the definition is changing with every decennial census. The family unit elsewhere is often larger, including more relatives. The large joint family of Hinduism was discussed previously. In many other less developed nations there is also a large *extended family*. Those who call themselves brothers in Zaire, for example, include those whom we call cousins and uncles.

The extended family in developing countries fulfills several important social and economic roles. It does not necessarily depend on a specific religious sanction, as does the *baradari* of Hinduism. The extended family provides mutual protection, psychological support, and a kind of economic insurance or social security for its members. In a world of tribal warfare and primitive agriculture, this support was invaluable. The extended family, still significant in many parts of the world, means to the international marketer that consumption decision making takes place in a larger unit and in different ways. Pooled resources, for instance, may allow larger purchases. (Singer, for example, finds per capita income a misleading guide to market potential.) The marketer may find it difficult to determine the relevant consuming unit for some goods. Is it a household or family? How many members are there?

## Common Territory

In America, *common territory* can be the neighborhood, the suburb, or the city. In many countries of Asia and Africa, it is the tribal grouping. The tribe is often the largest effective unit in many countries, because the various tribes do not voluntarily recognize the central government. Gradually, diverse tribes are being formed into single nations; that is, nationalism is replacing tribalism. However, the transition is often slow and bloody, as the examples of Angola, Biafra, and Pakistan show; even in Europe, the Scots and the Welsh are not happy about being under British rule. For the marketer, these groupings based on common territory might be a clue to market segmentation in many countries.

## Special Interest Group

A third kind of social grouping, the *special interest group* or association, may be religious, occupational, recreational, or political. Special interest groups can also be useful in identifying different market segments. For example, in America, the Sierra Club or the National Organization for Women (NOW) represent market segments for some firms.

## Other Kinds of Social Organizations

Some kinds of social organizations cut across the three categories above. One is *caste or class groupings*. These may be detailed and rigid, as in the Hindu caste system, or they may be more loose and flexible, as in American social classes. Americans have a democratic, relatively open society, but there is still much concern about social standing and status symbols. Social class is more important and more rigid in many other countries. The marketer must be aware of this in planning strategy in different markets. Different social classes will require different marketing programs.

A kind of grouping based on *age* occurs, especially in the United States and some of the other affluent industrialized nations. We recognize both the "senior citizen" and the teenage subcultures. Senior citizens usually live as separate economic units with their own needs and motivations. They are a major market segment in the United States and other industrialized countries. And although teenagers do not commonly live apart from their families, they are nonetheless a separate economic force to be reckoned with in marketing. Indeed, in American advertising, the youth appeal often appears dominant. As noted in our discussion of the extended family, there is much less separation between age groups in less developed areas. There is generally strong family integration at all age levels and a preponderant influence of age and seniority, in contrast to the youth motif prevalent in the United States.

A final aspect of social organization concerns the *role of women* in the economy. Women seldom enjoy parity with men as participants in the economy, and their participation declines as one goes down the scale of economic development. The extent to which they participate in the money economy affects their role as consumers and consumption influencers. Even developed

**Table 4-3**                              **Cultural Variables and Marketing**

| Cultural Variables | Marketing Functions | | | | | |
| --- | --- | --- | --- | --- | --- | --- |
| | Product | Promotion | Price | Distribution | Marketing Research | Strategy Formulation |
| Material Culture | | | | | | |
| Language | | | | | | |
| Education | | | | | | |
| Aesthetics | | | | | | |
| Values, Attitudes | | | | | | |
| Social Organization | | | | | | |
| Political-Legal | | | | | | |

countries exhibit differences in attitude toward female employment. For example, of active women in the United States, 65 percent are employed; in Japan, 60 percent; Germany, 52 percent; Great Britain, 50 percent; and Italy, 43 percent. ("Active women" excludes schoolgirls and retired or disabled women.)[10] These differences will be reflected both in household income levels and consumption patterns.

In spite of the constraints we have noted, the economic role of women is undergoing notable change in many countries. One evidence is that American and European multinationals (but not Japanese) have successfully employed women managers on assignments to such unlikely places as Brazil and Saudi Arabia. Other evidence is provided by the Women in Management program at the American University in Cairo. Egyptian companies have more female middle-level managers than many Western firms. The affluence of many Muslim OPEC nations is leading to more education and power for Arab women who have been among the most restricted. In Kuwait, for example, women not only own boutiques, but also serve as presidents of companies and even as corporate chairwomen.

**Cultural Variables and Marketing Management**

Culture is an integrated pattern of behavior shared by people in a society. We have looked at several dimensions of culture. The importance of these cultural variables to firms marketing internationally is that what they are *able* to do in marketing to a particular society (market) and what they will *want* to do will be shaped by them. In other words, international marketing management is a function of the culture. Table 4–3 is a matrix representing pictorially the interrelationships between cultural variables and international marketing.

## Summary

Culture is an integrated pattern of behavior and the distinctive way of life of a people. The various dimensions of culture influence a firm's marketing.

Worker behavior and consumer behavior in a country are shaped by its technology and material culture. The kinds of products a firm can sell and its distribution and promotional programs are constrained by the country's infrastructure. This includes not only the country's transportation and communications systems but also such things as the availability of media and advertising agencies.

Communications are a major part of the marketing task so the firm must communicate in the languages of its markets. This may require adaptation by the firm in its packaging and labeling, advertising and personal selling, and marketing research. Fortunately for the international marketer, national employees, distributors and advertising agencies help with the language problem.

Each society has its own ideas about beauty and good taste — its own aesthetics. In the design and color of its products and packaging, its advertising and selection of music and brand names, the firm must try to appeal to those tastes.

Differences in literacy and consumer skills, as a result of a country's educational system, will determine what kinds of adjustments in products and in marketing communications are necessary. The quality of marketing support services (advertising, marketing research) in a country will also be affected by the output of the educational system there.

Religion is a major determinant of attitudes and behavior in a society. Each country has its own religious profile but such major world religions as animism, Buddhism, Hinduism, Christianity and Islam cover eighty percent of the world's population. Each of these religions has its own particular impact on the attitudes and behavior of consumers who follow the religion. For example, the traditional animist might be reluctant to accept new products. The devout Buddhist who is seeking an absence of desire, or a state of wantlessness, is not a strong potential consumer. Other religious impacts on marketing include religious holidays and product taboos, and social dimensions such as the role of women in the economy and society or the caste system. Finally, religious divisions in a country may indicate market segments that require different marketing programs and salesforces. Japan's composite religious tradition has also affected the economy of that country.

Attitudes and values greatly affect consumer behavior. Attitudes toward wealth and acquisition, toward change, and toward risk taking are especially important for the international marketer who may be introducing innovation to a society in the form of new products — and even new lifestyles.

Social organization refers to the way people relate to each other, and to the various groups and divisions in a society. The size and nature of the family, tribalism and ethnic divisions, and different roles for women or age groups (such as senior citizens) all may influence a marketing program.

## Questions

4.1   What is culture?

4.2   Give examples of cultural concepts used in American marketing.

4.3   How can a nation's technology and material culture affect a firm's marketing in that country?

4.4   Discuss the role of the international marketer as an agent of cultural change. Is this role legitimate?

4.5   Why is the international marketer interested in the linguistic situation in its markets?

4.6   How can the international firm deal with the language challenges in its foreign markets?

4.7   How can the aesthetic ideas and values of a society influence the firm's marketing there?

4.8   How is international marketing constrained by the educational level in a market?

4.9   What, if anything, does a country's religious situation have to do with a firm's marketing there?

4.10   Discuss the marketing implications of the following religious phenomena: (a) religious holidays, (b) taboos, (c) religious institutions (church and clergy), (d) nirvana.

4.11   Identify some constraints in marketing to a traditional Muslim society.

4.12   What is the marketing significance of these aspects of social organization: (a) the extended family, (b) tribalism, (c) the role of women in the economy?

4.13   Convenience Foods Corp. has asked you to do a cultural analysis of a South American country where it is considering operations. How would you go about this task?

## Endnotes

[1]*Europa Yearbook 1986* (London: Europa Publications 1986).

[2]Adamson Hoebel, *Man, Culture and Society* (New York: Oxford University Press, 1960), 168.

[3]Interview at the University of Michigan.

[4]Hollywood, UPI, May 18, 1981.

[5]*World Christian Encyclopedia* (New York: Oxford University Press, 1983).

[6]James G. Frazer, *The Golden Bough*, abridged ed. (London: Macmillan, 1922), 56.

[7]*International Herald Tribune*, May 8, 1989, 1.

[8]*The Wall Street Journal*, February 23, 1989, 1.

[9]Ibid.

[10]*International Advertiser*, January–February, 1989, 16.

## Further Readings

Graham, John L. "The Influence of Culture on Business Negotiations." *Journal of International Business Studies* Vol. 16, No. 1, (Spring, 1985):81–96.

Hofstede, Geert. "National Cultures Revisited." *Asia Pacific Journal of Management* Vol. 2, No. 1, (September 1984):22–29.

Morris, Cynthia T., and Irma Adelman. "The Religious Factor in Economic Development." *World Development* Vol. 8, No. 1, (Fall 1980):491–501.

Rosenberg, Larry J., and Gregory J. Thompson. "Deciphering the Japanese Cultural Code." *International Marketing Review* Vol. 3, No. 3, (Autumn 1986):47–57.

Sheth, Jagdish N. "Cross Cultural Influences on the Buyer-Seller Interaction." *Asia Pacific Journal of Management* Vol. 1, No. 1, (September 1983):46–55.

Terpstra, Vern, and Kenneth David. *The Cultural Environment of International Business*, 3d ed. Cincinnati: Southwestern, 1990.

# 4.1 Bottled Spirits

The Hopi are the westernmost tribe of Pueblo Indians, located in Northeastern Arizona. There are less than 10,000 of them. They live in typically terraced pueblo structures of stone and adobe and are clustered into a number of small, independent towns. Like all Pueblo Indians, the Hopi are peaceful, monogamous, diligent, self-controlled, and very religious.

The most conservative tribe in the Southwest, the Hopi want no tourists to photograph, sketch, or record their dances. They do, however, allow visitors to observe their ceremonies, where they may watch masked Kachina dancers impersonate Hopi gods. The Hopi also invite tourists into their homes to buy Kachina dolls or Hopi pottery.

Kachinas are the Hopi Indians' holy spirits. They are sometimes personified by masked dancers and sometimes represented by wooden dolls. There are roughly 250 different Kachinas. While the Hopi will sell Kachina dolls to tourists, they are sensitive to how others may use the Kachina costume or idea. For example, in 1987 Miss New Mexico won the costume competition in the Miss USA competition wearing a Kachina costume. Hopi religious leaders complained that that use was sacrilegious.

In another incident, the Hopi protested when Kentucky's Ezra Brooks distillery began marketing its bourbon in bottles shaped like Kachina dolls. The Brooks distillery had planned as a Christmas promotion to distribute 5,000 of the Kachina doll bottles in Arizona and the Southwest. It had already shipped 2,000 bottles when the Hopi complaint reached it.

Reflecting the Hopis' anger, tribal chairman Clarence Hamilton asked, "How would a Catholic feel about putting whiskey in a statue of Mary?" The Hopi not only complained, they asked for the help of Senator Barry Goldwater of Arizona. Goldwater is a noted collector of Kachina dolls—but not the whiskey-bottle variety.

## Questions

1. What should the distillery do? What courses of action are open to it?
2. Propose and defend your solution to this problem.
3. Could this problem have been avoided? How?

# 4.2 Foremost Dairy in Thailand

Foremost Foods Company is the world's largest processor of whey-based products, including lactose and high-protein items. Foremost International, the international arm of Foremost Foods, has operations in 16 countries, including Guam, Indonesia, Taiwan, El Salvador, Guatemala, Saudi Arabia, and Iran.

Foremost Foods produces and markets several proprietary grocery-shelf items and is a leading processor and distributor of dairy products, principally in the western United States. According to the annual report, the company's long-term objective in the food industry is to be an aggressive, profitable, multinational marketer of a broad line of nutritious food products to the consumer. In keeping with these goals, it entered Thailand in 1956. By 1985, Foremost sales in Thailand were over $20 million.

When Foremost and three local partners set up their first dairy products processing plant in Thailand in 1956, they were starting from scratch in a market where milk and ice cream were virtually unknown commodities. Hence, the first problem was how to make people aware of dairy products, their many uses, and the sanitary measures necessary to keep them fresh. In cooperation with the Thai government, company representatives were sent into schools to give talks on sanitation and nutrition, at the same time supplying the schools with dairy products for the students. The program was a huge success, and a demand was created.

Next came the tricky question of refrigeration. How was the corner grocer to keep milk from souring and ice cream from melting? The answer was to supply every one of the tiny retail outlets—"Mom and Pop" groceries and restaurants—with a freezer, either through leasing, or more often, under the terms of a conditional sales contract. If the contracts were met, the freezers were sold to the stores for one U.S. dollar. The initial capital outlay was sizeable, running into hundreds of thousands of dollars, and the accompanying headaches were multitudinous (e.g., keeping stores from unplugging the freezers at night to save electricity and preventing their use for other products), but the effort eventually worked.

From the beginning, Foremost has tailored operations to the local Thai scene. Products find their way to market via crude water transportation and brightly colored company trucks. They are sold either from pushcarts, from company retail outlets, or through traditional channels (e.g., wholesalers).

The pushcarts, also brightly decorated in the local style with dragons and brilliant umbrellas, are supplied by the company and manned by independent retailers. These sidewalk salesmen come to a company-owned depot every morning to pick up their pushcarts and their day's supply of milk and ice cream. At the end of the day they return and pay for the amount sold, with a profit margin for themselves, of course. That margin approximates 20 percent, but the sidewalk salesmen can, and do, set their own retail price.

The company-owned retail outlets are modern soda fountains dispensing such American favorites as the chocolate sundae and vanilla milkshake. The company builds the store, supplies the equipment, and hires and trains local people to manage the operation, to cook, and to wait on customers.

The category accounting for the biggest chunk of total sales (almost 80 percent of which are in the Bangkok area) is composed of wholesalers, small stores, restaurants, hotels and schools. A Thai salesman (Foremost normally has only one expatriate in Bangkok, the general manager) usually is assigned a territory and given responsibility for one category of outlet, such as all corner grocery stores, while another salesman will handle all the schools.

To train its salesforce, Foremost first taught trainees basic English, while expatriate instructors learned basic Thai. With such a minimal bilingual communications channel established, the salesforce-to-be was taught about dairy products. The last part of the program consisted of sales techniques, for which key Thai staff were sent to the United States for training, while several Americans went to Thailand to instruct the local salesforce.

The patient cultural bridge building has paid off well. Foremost already has replaced the original plant with a larger, more modern one. More meaningful still for the long pull, a very strong brand identification was created. Today *Foremost* and *milk* are all but synonymous in Thailand.

## Question

Identify and outline in detail the marketing program of Foremost Dairy in Thailand as depicted here. For each element in that marketing program, identify the particular factor in the Thailand environment that gave rise to the marketing approach used.

CASE
# 4.3  An American Firm Wins Big in Japan

The American Family Life Assurance Company entered the Japanese market in 1975. It soon became one of the most successful foreign companies in any industry operating in Japan. By 1982 one in twenty Japanese households was a policyholder. By 1988 one in six Japanese households was covered by an American Family Life policy, and the firm had become the fifth-largest seller of new life insurance policies in the country. Its Japanese revenues in 1988 were almost $2 billion.

Founded in the United States in 1955, American Family Life Assurance Company specializes in cancer insurance (about 90 percent of its policies are in this field). Although American Family was the second foreign insurance company to enter the Japanese market, it was the first company, either Japanese or foreign, to introduce a policy for cancer protection in Japan. Two Japanese firms also issued independent health insurance coverage, but they had a much smaller number of policies outstanding.

Cancer insurance is a controversial product in the United States (it is banned in four states), because consumer advocates argue that disease-specific policies are an inefficient, costly form of coverage. Attitudes in Japan are somewhat different. When American Family hired Nomura Research to see what its customers wanted, the answer was "Higher coverage." On the government side, company president, John Amos, had developed very good relations with the powerful Japanese bureaucracy. Indeed, in 1988 John Amos was named by *Forbes* magazine as the insurance industry's most innovative executive for his success in penetrating the Japanese market. Because of differences between the U.S. and Japanese markets, American Family is in the unusual position of obtaining almost three-quarters of its total revenue from Japan versus only about one-quarter from the United States.

Japan is one of the largest insurance markets in the world. About 90 percent of Japanese households carry life insurance with a relative contract value much higher than in either Europe or the United States. Japan also has rather comprehensive national health insurance, so private company plans supplement the government program in such areas as private rooms, costly major disease, and lost income. American Family's cancer insurance sales grew rapidly, in part because cancer is the major cause of death in Japan and it is usually associated with very costly treatment and long stays in the hospital. Thus, the Japanese perceive cancer as the most threatening and the most expensive disease they can encounter, and they want to provide for it as best they can.

Most Japanese insurance companies use housewives as a part-time salesforce for door-to-door sales. John Amos came up with another idea—use retired Japanese workers to sell to their former colleagues. "Their retirement benefits weren't good enough to last them forever, so American Family became a little like their social security," he recalled. As of 1988, American Family employed about 10,500 sales agents. Sales were made to companies as well as to individuals. Sales to companies were paid by a payroll deduction plan. Over 17,000 payroll groups had been established. Over three-fourths of the corporations listed on the Tokyo Stock Exchange use American Family's payroll deduction plan, although less than half of their employees subscribe to the plan. Nevertheless, such payroll groups are an important part of American Family's business in Japan.

Another part of American Family's approach is "bank set sales." This is a program whereby a bank automatically deducts the annual premium from the accumulated interest on a policyholder's savings account and transfers it to American Family's account. Some 250 banks were participating in this program, serving about 500,000 policyholders. The Japanese have a very favor-able attitude toward saving, and this program appeals to their orientation toward saving plus their strong desire for insurance coverage. Because the banks enjoy a strong reputation, American Family's insurance program gains further credibility by this association with them.

American Family has not relied on advertising in Japan, depending instead on its strong sales network and full-time salesforce. Because the company innovated cancer insurance and because of its different marketing approach, however, it received a lot of publicity in the various media.

One indicator of the company's success is a first year renewal rate of 90 percent—and 94 percent after the second year. Both of these figures are higher than in either the Japanese or American life insurance industries. The company also has become one of the largest life insurance companies in Japan. American Family views these figures as corroboration of its product and marketing program.

## Question

Describe American Family's marketing program in Japan—product policy, pricing, promotion, and distribution. Explain how this marketing program re-lates to the Japanese culture and economy and why it is so successful.

CASE

# 4.4 Marketing Sea Urchins to Japan

Sea urchins are prickly, greenish, disk-shaped spiny creatures, and local lobstermen dislike them. They carpet the ocean floor and feast on

Case prepared by Ravi Sarathy for use in classroom discussion. All rights reserved. Source: "Miracle in Maine: Sea Urchin is turned into the Golden Uni," *The Wall Street Journal*, March 18, 1988; and "How Slimy Things Saved Harrington," *New England Monthly*, February 1989.

shallow-water seaweed beds, competing with and driving away the lobster that share the same food.

But sea urchins, *uni* to the Japanese, have become the salvation of Harrington, in Washington County, Maine. Washington County, in the northeast corner of Maine, is its poorest county. Winter work is scarce, and one in five residents is below the federal poverty line. Unemployment is 9 percent. But uni, the orange-yellow roe and reproductive organs of the sea urchin, is a delicacy in Japan. Raw uni is used to garnish seaweed-wrapped sushi. Sea urchins are also eaten in France, as "chataigne de mer," eaten raw with a lemon or vinegar and shallot dressing. Uni is expensive: a wooden tray of uni sells for 8,000 yen at Tokyo's Tsukiji market, about $100 a pound, about the price of silver.

California used to supply sea urchins to Japan during the period of October to February, when it was out of season in Japan. But dwindling California supplies and environmental regulations led the Japanese to consider the East Coast. One difficulty was transportation costs. But a rising yen made the extra freight cost bearable. So Mitake Trading Co., which supplies the Daiei chain of stores in Japan, sent Shiro Nakagawa to prospect the Maine coast. Fishing was better nearer the Canadian border, but the fragile and perishable uni had to be shipped immediately to Japan if they were to be served fresh. Harrington became the ideal location, with good fishing at hand, and within one day's drive of Boston's Logan Airport. And Mr. Nakagawa became resigned to the subzero weather and 18-hour workdays. California it was not.

Harrington residents are only too glad of employment, especially during the winter months; $4.00 an hour for scooping uni from the shells, to $5.75 an hour for sorting and arranging them on trays. And the local fishermen can earn over $1,000 a week for dragging the seabed for sea urchins, better than what they can get for scallops or mussels. Mr. Nakagawa set up factory in an abandoned garage. Others imitated him, shipping urchins to Europe, and even to Japan, for further processing and removal of roe.

Mr. Nakagawa now has a new factory, 10,000 square feet, employing 85 workers and 13 fishermen. Even in the summer, when uni will be scarce, he expects to operate with at least 30 people. The workers need to be reminded of the importance of quality control. For example, a shipment of polystyrene plastic trays used to package the uni may be defective, with crumbling edges, so that bits of plastic get mixed up with the uni. The custom-made trays are grooved to keep the uni in place, and it must be carefully placed on the trays. The product is so delicate that the heat of an employee's fingers could dissolve it. Quality control is a must.

Not that the residents of Maine are going to acquire a taste for uni. When a visitor to the plant samples the roe, employees comment to one another: "He's eating the stuff." And now Maine fishermen have begun harvesting sea cucumber at the behest of the same businessmen. Sea cucumbers are glistening, slimy, mud-colored, mucus-covered animals; but Chinese around the world eat them. So Maine will sell them, and make money at it.

Maine's Fishery Technology Service has set up a sea urchin study project, as the urchin appears to be in danger of being overharvested. In Frenchmen Bay, fewer urchins of the acceptable size of 2.5 to 4 inches were being harvested in March when compared to the previous September. At the same time, reducing the numbers of sea urchins could increase the lobster catch, as overgrazing of seaweed beds by sea urchins in shallow water might be reduced. Sea urchin exports exceeded $1 million by year-end 1988.

## Questions

1. Why did Maine not exploit its sea urchin resources earlier?
2. Is the market for sea urchins a fad? Or are there long-term prospects for the sea urchin industry in Maine?
3. What are the dangers and competitive pressures facing Maine's newfound sea urchin industry? What are your recommendations to maintain a healthy and viable sea urchin industry in Maine for the long term?
4. What broad lessons can you draw from Maine's experience with uni?

CHAPTER 5

# The Political-Legal Environment

*Learning Objectives*

The political environment of international marketing has three dimensions, that of the host country, that of the home country, and the international environment. The many laws affecting international marketing fall into three categories: U.S. law, international law, and foreign law.

The main goals of this chapter are to

1. Identify the areas of the host-country environment that a firm must understand, including that country's national interests, such as sovereignty, security, and prestige, as well as the controls it uses to achieve those goals, in order to assess political risk.
2. Describe how a firm engages in international relationships, and discuss the consequences.
3. Identify the areas of the home-country environment that affect a firm's international marketing.
4. Explain how U.S. export controls, antitrust law, and tax law affect the feasibility and profitability of a U.S. firm's international marketing.
5. Discuss the effect of international organizations such as the IMF and the GATT, and regional groups such as the European Community, on the international legal environment.
6. Describe how treaties between the United States and other countries can ease American firms' marketing in those countries.
7. Describe the international conventions on patents and trademarks that help a firm protect itself against piracy.
8. Identify the types of foreign laws that affect the four Ps of marketing.

The politics and the laws of a nation obviously influence the practice of international marketing. This chapter will examine the nature of the political-legal environment and its impact on international marketing management.

# Political Environment

The *political environment* of international marketing includes any national or international political factor that can affect its operations. A factor is political when it derives from the government sector. Three dimensions are involved: the host-country environment, the international environment, and the home-country environment. Surveys have shown that dealing with the problems in the political arena is the number one challenge facing international managers and occupies more of their time than any other management function. Yet international managers' concerns are somewhat different from those of the political scientist. Managers are concerned primarily about just one thing, political risk — the possibility of any government action adversely (or favorably) affecting their operations.

## Host-Country Political Environment

By definition, the international firm is a guest, a foreigner in all of its markets abroad. Therefore, international managers are especially concerned with nationalism and dealings with governments in host countries.

**Host-Country National Interests.**   One way to get a feeling for the local situation in a foreign market is to see how compatible the firm's activities are with the interests of the host country. While each country has its own set of national goals, most countries also share many common objectives. *Nationalism* and *patriotism* are terms referring to citizens' feelings about their country and its interests. Such feelings exist in every country.

For example, all countries wish to maintain and enhance their *national sovereignty*. Every country has a major holiday when the people celebrate their national birthday and recall their achievement of independence or nationhood. These holidays reinforce the sense of national identity and nationalism. Foreign firms, individually or collectively, may be perceived as a threat to that sovereignty. The larger and more numerous the foreign firms, the more likely they are to be perceived as a threat — or at least an irritant. The perceived threat may also apply to an individual industry or firm. For example, IBM might be viewed as having too large a share of the critical computer industry.

Countries wish to protect their *national security*. Although the foreign firm does not represent a military threat as such, it may be considered as potentially prejudicial to national security. Governments generally prohibit foreign firms from "sensitive" industries, such as defense, communications, and perhaps energy and natural resources. For example, when Libya nationalized the service stations of foreign oil companies, the minister said, "This commodity is very important to the nation and shouldn't be left in the hands of foreigners." If the foreign firm is from a country deemed unfriendly to the host country, it may have difficulty operating or even be denied admission. In Castro's Cuba and Khomeini's Iran, American firms were persona non grata.

Countries are concerned about their *national prestige*. They establish national airlines and try to win at the Olympics as ways of gaining international recognition. On the economic side, they may foster certain industries or certain firms for the same reason. Foreign firms may be prevented from entering those industries, or from acquiring a national firm. For example, Britain was reluctant to allow foreigners to acquire Jaguar, a famous British name. A number of countries have sought "national solutions" for troubled companies to retain what they perceive to be national champions. International firms need to be sensitive to these issues and be careful not to be too "foreign" in their operations. This would relate to advertising and branding policies as well as ownership and staffing. Establishing local R&D would be perceived favorably in this context.

All countries want to enhance *national welfare*. Generally this means raising employment and income in the country. Foreign firms contribute to this by the employment they generate locally. They can contribute further by using local suppliers and having a high degree of local content in their products. They can contribute further still by exporting from the host country, generating new employment and foreign exchange. They can contribute in a different way by supplying products, services, and/or training that enhances productivity in the host country.

**Host-Country Controls.**   Host countries don't depend entirely on the goodwill of the foreign firm to help them achieve their national goals. To try to assure desirable behavior by foreign firms — and prevent undesirable behavior — governments have a variety of tools to control foreign firms in their country. We note some of these controls here.

1. *Entry restrictions.* If allowed to enter the country, the firm may be restricted as to the industries it may enter. It may be prohibited from acquiring a national firm. It may not be allowed to have 100 percent ownership but be required to enter a joint venture with a national firm. It may be restricted as to the products it sells. The Indian government decided that soap and matches could be made by cottage industry. This naturally affected Unilever and Swedish Match in India.

2. *Price controls.* Once in the country, the foreign firm may encounter a variety of operating restrictions. One of the most common is price controls, and in inflationary economies, they can severely limit profitability. Gerber's left Venezuela because a decade of price controls prevented a profitable operation. Other regulations may affect advertising or other marketing practices of the firm.

3. *Quotas and tariffs.* The country's use of quotas and tariffs may limit the firm's ability to import equipment, components and products, forcing a higher level of local procurement than the firm may want.

4. *Exchange control.* Many countries run chronic deficits in their balance of payments and are short of foreign exchange. They ration its use according to their priorities. Foreign firms may be low on that priority list and have great difficulty getting foreign exchange for needed imports or profit repatriation.

5.  *Expropriation*. This is defined as official seizure of foreign property and is the ultimate government tool for controlling foreign firms. This most definitive and drastic action against foreign firms is fortunately occurring less often as developing countries begin to see foreign direct investment as an attractive alternative to debt. From a peak of 83 cases in 1975, the number of expropriations declined as the 1980s progressed, with only one case in 1985.[1]

An earlier United Nations' study evaluated the situation up to 1975 and found that two-thirds of all takeovers were accounted for by just 10 countries, including Argentina, Chile, Cuba, Peru, Algeria, Libya, and Iraq. On the other hand, 50 countries had no expropriations at all.

Venezuela has generally been considered as a low-risk political environment. The situation changed dramatically in 1989, when the country was investigating corruption in an official foreign exchange institution called Recadi. Its government said foreign firms were involved and issued arrest warrants for 47 foreign executives. Companies under scrutiny included General Motors, Toyota, Johnson & Johnson, Bristol Myers, and Goodyear. Dozens of executives left the country. Cornelius Koreman, president of Ford Venezuela, said, "It is the first time in my career I've had someone try to arrest me for doing nothing." He had to operate out of company headquarters in Dearborn, Michigan. In an unrelated case, a Caracas judge ordered the arrest of the Venezuelan presidents of Procter & Gamble and Colgate-Palmolive for alleged misleading advertising of their products.[2]

**Political-Risk Assessment.**   The Venezuelan example shows the importance of continuous monitoring of host-country political environments, as they can change rapidly. Besides Venezuela, China, Panama, Eastern Europe and the U.S.S.R. are other countries whose environment has changed rapidly in recent years. The firm must develop political and diplomatic skills in-house, but will probably also use consultants with expertise on particular countries. There are commercial services available as well that are useful as a continuing input. Three major ones are (1) Business International's service, Country Assessment Service, which surveys 75 countries twice a year; (2) BERI S.A. (Business Environment Risk Information), which has a Political Risk Index that reviews 48 countries three times a year; and (3) Frost & Sullivan, which publishes *Political Risk Country Reports* that review 120 countries quarterly. These services are moderate in cost — up to a few thousand dollars a year, depending on coverage. They use different methods and come up with somewhat different country scorings, though the rankings are generally quite comparable. Table 5–1 gives some idea of the kinds of criteria used to evaluate political risk.

In its own study of the political environment the firm can include a preliminary analysis of its own political vulnerability in a particular host country. Some of the ingredients in such an analysis are the following.

| Table 5-1 | **Political-Risk Indicators** |
|---|---|

*Economics*
  Falling GDP
  Inflation
  Capital flight
  Foreign debt
  Low food output
  Commodity dependence

*Politics*
  Bad neighbors
  How authoritarian
  Staleness
  Illegitimacy
  Generals in power
  War

*Society*
  Urbanization
  Islamic fundamentalism
  Corruption
  Ethnic tension

Source: *The Economist,* December 20, 1986, 70.

## External Factors

1. *The firm's home country.* Other things being equal, a firm will have a better reception in a country that has good relations with its own.
2. *Product or industry.* Some industries are more sensitive than others. Generally, raw materials, public utilities, communications, pharmaceuticals and defense-related products are most sensitive.
3. *Size and location of operations.* The larger the foreign firm, the more threatening it is perceived to be. This is especially true if the firm has large facilities and is located in a prominent urban area, such as the capital. This serves as a constant reminder of the foreign presence.
4. *Visibility of the firm.* The greater the visibility of the firm as a foreign business, the greater its vulnerability is. Visibility is a function of several things. One is the size and location of the firm's operations in the country. Another is the nature of its products. Consumer goods are more visible than industrial goods. Finished goods are more visible than components or inputs that are hidden in the final product. Heavy advertisers are more visible than nonadvertisers. International brands are more provocative than localized brands.
5. *Host-country political situation.* Each host country will have some rating as to its political attractiveness and stability.

## Company Factors

1. *Company behavior.* Each firm develops some record of corporate citizenship based on its policies and practices. Some firms are more sensitive and responsive than others. Goodwill in this area is a valuable asset.

2. *Contributions of the firm to the host country.* Many of these are quite objective and quantifiable. How much employment has been generated? How much tax has been paid? How many exports by the firm? What new resources or skills has the firm brought in?

3. *Localization of operations.* Generally, the more localized the firm's operations, the more acceptable it is to the host country. There are several dimensions to localization, including having local equity, local managers and technical staff, local content in the products, use of local suppliers of goods and services, local product development and local brand names.

4. *Subsidiary dependence.* This factor is somewhat in contradiction to those above. The more the firm's local operation is dependent on the parent company, the less vulnerable it is. If the local operation cannot function as a separate, self-contained unit, but is dependent on the parent for critical resources and/or for markets, it is a less rewarding takeover target.

Political monitoring and political-risk assessment are continuing tasks for the international marketer. The information these analyses provide must be used to manage the firm's political relations. Table 5–2 suggests some approaches to managing host-country relations, both before and after entering the country.

## International Political Environment

The international political environment involves political relations between two or more countries. This is in contrast to our previous concern for what happens only *within* a given foreign country. The international firm almost inevitably becomes somewhat involved with the host country's international relations, no matter how neutral it may try to be. It does so, first, because it is a foreigner from a specific home country; and second, because its operations in a country are frequently related to operations in other countries, either on the supply or demand side or both. East-West relations are a good example of a situation in the international political environment, and one that is continually evolving.

One important aspect of a country's international relations is its relationship with the firm's home country. American firms abroad will be affected by the nation's attitude toward American foreign policy. Where the host nation dislikes any aspect of American policy, it may be the American firm that is bombed or boycotted along with the U.S. Information Service office. English or French firms operating in the former colonies of those countries will be affected by that relationship, sometimes favorably, sometimes otherwise.

A second critical element is the host country's relations with other nations. If a country is a member of a regional grouping, such as EC or ASEAN, that fact will influence the firm's evaluation of the country. If a nation has particular friends or enemies among other nations, the firm will have to modify its international logistics to comply with how that market is supplied and to whom it can sell. For example, the United States limits trade with communist countries. Black African nations restrict trade with South Africa. Arab nations may boycott companies having any dealings with Israel.

**Table 5–2**                                 **Managing Host-Country Relations**

*Pre-Entry Planning*
1. Avoid threatening countries.
2. Negotiate with host government.
3. Buy insurance — OPIC, MIGA.
4. Adjust entry method.

*Post-Entry Operations*
1. Have a monitoring system.
2. Develop corporate communications program.
3. Develop local stakeholders (employees, suppliers, customers).
4. Have appropriate national executives and advisory board.
5. Change operations over time as perceived host-country cost-benefit ratio changes. Examples: new products and processes, more local equity and management, new exports, local R&D.
6. Have contingency plans.

The expansion of Japanese firms into the European Common Market provides a case example of the tensions that can arise for companies in the international political arena. (See "Global Marketing.") Another clue to a nation's international behavior is its membership in international organizations. We have mentioned regional groupings, but there are other kinds of international organizations that affect a member's behavior. One is military agreements such as NATO, which may restrict unilateral military or political action. Membership in GATT reduces the likelihood that a country will impose new trade barriers. Membership in the IMF or the World Bank aids a country's financial situation but it also puts constraints on the country's behavior. Many other international organizations or agreements impose rules on their membership. These agreements cover patents, communication, transportation, and other items of interest to the international marketer. As a rule, the more international organizations a country belongs to, the more regulations it accepts, and the more dependable is its behavior.

**Home-Country Political Environment**

The firm's home-country political environment can constrain its international operations as well as its domestic operations. As a first step, it can limit the countries the international firm may enter. The United States, for example, prohibits U.S. firms from dealing with Cambodia, Cuba, Libya, North Korea, and Vietnam. It has special restrictions on trade with Iran, Nicaragua, and South Africa. The United States also can limit the products its firms can sell abroad under its strategic technology controls. That power is even occasionally exercised against foreign firms, as when Toshiba was penalized for selling technology to the Russians that allowed their submarines to move more quietly.

The best-known example of the home-country environment affecting international operations is, of course, South Africa. Home-country political pressures have induced, as of 1989, over 175 American firms to leave that

# Global Marketing
## The Rising Sun Over Europe

Ryuzaburo Kaku, president of Canon, says his aim is *dochakuka*, the "localization" of operations in Europe. "Our goal is to be a truly global enterprise contributing to worldwide prosperity. We aim to be a premier corporate citizen *welcomed by local residents everywhere*." This is a noble goal but one that, for the following reasons, will not be easy to achieve for Japanese companies in Europe.

1. Canon and many other Japanese companies have been found guilty of dumping by EC officials.
2. Many prominent European executives such as the head of Philips, FIAT, and CGE in France have expressed concern about the unfettered rise in Japanese investment.
3. Edith Cresson, French minister for European Affairs, argues that there is a great danger for Europe because "the Japanese have applied their militarist and corrupt system in countries where they dominate."

4. The growing European investment by the Japanese is welcomed on one hand, but causes complaints on the other hand. Europeans say Japanese investment
   a. leads to overcapacity in some industries.
   b. has insufficient local content — "Screwdriver plants."
   c. is not integrated into Europe.
   d. lacks R&D facilities.
   e. leads to domination in specific industries. (Almost one-third of Japanese plants are in the electronics industry.)
5. The Europeans complain that the Japanese play one country against another on incentives for plant location.
6. They also complain that new Japanese entrants get subsidies at the expense of old, established competing European firms.

Source: Jane Sasseen, "The Rising Sun Over Europe," *International Management* (July–August 1989):14–20.

---

country altogether, while about 130 remain. Among the departed are Coca-Cola, Exxon, Ford, General Electric, General Motors, and Chase Manhattan. Remaining are such firms as Caltex, Goodyear, International Paper, and Johnson & Johnson, under the conviction that, "Walking away is not the best way to fight apartheid."[3]

When the American companies were leaving South Africa, the Germans and the Japanese remained as the major foreign presence. German firms did not face the same political pressures at home that American firms had. However, the Japanese government was embarrassed when Japan became South Africa's leading trading partner. As a result, some Japanese companies did reduce their South African activity. Matsushita closed an office there; Sanyo and Nissan reduced their exports to South Africa; NEC and Pioneer Electronics agreed to suspend exports, and Mitsubishi pulled out of the bidding to build an industrial plant.

One challenge facing multinationals is that they truly have a triple-threat political environment. Even if the home country and the host country give them no problems, they can face threats in third markets. Firms that do not have problems with their home government or the South African government, for example, can be bothered or boycotted about their South African operations in third countries, like the United States. Nestlé's problems

| Table 5–3 | **U.S. Exports: Foreign Policy Controls** |
|---|---|

1. Terrorism equipment controls
2. Crime equipment controls
3. Regional stability controls — arms sales that might destabilize a region
4. Antiapartheid controls
5. Missile technology controls
6. Chemical/biological weapons precursors controls — ingredients
7. Nuclear controls
8. Short-supply controls
9. Supercomputer controls
10. Treasury Department controls — trade with specific countries such as Cuba, Iran, North Korea, and Vietnam

Source: Bureau of Public Affairs, Department of State, April, 1989.

with its infant formula controversy were most serious, for example, not at home, in Switzerland, or in African host countries, but in a third market — the United States. Table 5–3 gives an indication of American political concerns as they apply to U.S. exports.

## The Legal Environment

The political environment in a nation includes the prevalent attitudes toward business enterprise. From this political climate is generated the *legal environment* for business, that is, the nation's laws and regulations pertaining to business. A firm must know the legal environment in each market because these laws constitute the "rules of the game." At the same time, the firm must know the political environment because it determines how the laws are enforced and indicates the direction of new legislation. The legal environment of international marketing is complicated, having three dimensions. For an American firm these are (1) U.S. laws, (2) international law, and (3) domestic laws in each of the firm's foreign markets.

**U.S. Law and International Marketing**

American marketers are familiar with domestic regulations affecting marketing, such as the Pure Food and Drug Act and the Robinson-Patman Act. These are not the American laws that affect international marketing, however. A variety of other laws are relevant for international marketing and relate to exporting, antitrust, and organization and ownership arrangements.

**Export Controls.**   Like other countries, the United States has a variety of controls on export trade, but the United States has more than most countries. Since these are continually evolving with the political climate, we will not give precise details, but merely an indication of the kinds of controls used. One kind of control pertains to *country destinations*. As of 1989, there were prohibitions on exports to Cambodia, Cuba, Libya, North Korea and Vietnam and severe restrictions for several other countries. A few years earlier, China was on that list but Libya was not. The ban also prohibits the sale of components that go into a foreign firm's products that are destined for one of the prohibited markets.

For example, one time before the United States was trading with China, the French wanted to sell planes to that country. However, the inertial guidance system for this aircraft was supplied by General Electric. The U.S. government forbade GE from selling this key component to the French for this purpose. This type of conflict can be avoided only if the American firm has less than 50 percent ownership of the firm supplying the parts.

Another U.S. export control relates to the *nature of the products* exported. Many products are exported without restriction, though under the monitoring eye of the Department of Commerce. These are usually goods easily obtainable elsewhere and not considered significant for national security. For products having national security or foreign policy significance, there are tighter controls, or even prohibitions. Examples are terrorism equipment, missile technology, and nuclear technology. Others relate to foreign policy concerns such as antiapartheid or regional stability. (See Table 5–3.) These controls can hurt the firm in two ways. One is administrative time and expense. In 1987, 104,000 export licenses were issued by the United States. Another is lost sales. The National Academy of Sciences estimates that these controls cost U.S. companies over $11 billion in lost sales a year.[4] Foreign buyers may switch suppliers because of them.

These controls are imposed to protect American security and foreign policy interests. Violation can bring severe punishment. One U.S. manufacturer and his executive secretary were fined $10,000 each and imprisoned for five years for illegal export of missile firing devices. These controls can be a serious constraint on both product line and market selection for some international marketers. The long arm of U.S. law reaches even to operations and firms outside the United States, as the following examples show.

The West Germany subsidiary of Digital Equipment Corp. was fined $1.5 million for allowing sophisticated computers to be shipped to the U.S.S.R. ASEA, the Swedish firm, was fined $440,000 for allowing the illegal transfer of U.S.–made computers to Russia. And L. M. Ericson, another Swedish firm, was assessed a $3.1 million criminal fine for allowing the shipment of a sensitive air traffic control device to Russia.

Another restriction on the freedom to export is in the *pricing* area. Although the international marketer would like to base export prices on supply and demand and internal company considerations, the Internal Revenue Service (IRS) can also have a voice in the price. In other words, the IRS has a say in international transfer prices on exports to foreign affiliates of American companies. On such exports the exporter might wish to charge a low transfer price as a way of aiding the subsidiary, of gaining income in a lower tax jurisdiction, or for some other reason. However, the IRS will not allow such transfer prices if they are unduly low, because they would lower the firm's profits in America and therefore lower income taxes paid by the firm in the United States.

**Antitrust.**   It might seem strange that U.S. antitrust laws would affect the *foreign* business activities of American companies. However, that is a fact of life for international management. The opinion of the U.S. Justice Department is that even if an act is committed abroad, it falls within the jurisdiction of American courts *if the act produces consequences within the United States.* Many activities of American business abroad will have some repercussions on the American domestic market. The question arises primarily in three kinds of situations: (1) when an American firm *acquires* a foreign firm; (2) when it engages in a *joint venture* with a foreign firm; or (3) when it makes some overseas marketing *agreement* with another firm.

When an American firm expands abroad by acquiring a foreign company, the Justice Department will be concerned about the possible impact on competition in the United States. It may take action under Section 7 of the Clayton Act, which prohibits certain corporate amalgamations that could lessen competition. Action would be more probable if the acquisition were in the same product line as the company.

Remington Arms Company tried to acquire Sweden's AB Norma Projektilfabrik. Sweden had a free-trade agreement with the EC on industrial products so Remington hoped to use Norma to get a foothold in the EC, where high tariffs on third-country ammunition were nearly pricing Remington out of the market. The Justice Department, however, said that acquiring Norma would allow Remington to increase its U.S. market share, as Norma was selling 10 percent of its output in the United States already. Remington gave up its efforts in the face of the challenge by the Justice Department.

Joint venturing with foreign firms either in the United States or abroad can lead to government intervention similar to that in the example just considered. The reasoning by the government is the same — competition in the U.S. market will be reduced by a particular marriage of a U.S. and foreign firm.

General Electric and Hitachi wanted a joint venture in the United States to produce televisions. GE wanted to bolster its relatively weak position and Hitachi wanted to increase its very small, 2 percent market share. The Justice Department wrote to GE, "Our investigation has led us to conclude that this venture would eliminate significant existing and potential competition between GE and Hitachi in the manufacture and sale of television sets. It would create the third or fourth largest producer in an already concentrated industry. We are not persuaded that the venture is needed to maintain the viability of either party."

There are no sure guidelines to possible Justice Department actions regarding joint ventures or acquisitions of American firms abroad. But any such moves by a large company certainly will be investigated and probably challenged. Smaller companies have greater freedom to expand overseas without challenge.

We have seen how U.S. laws can reach abroad and touch the international marketing of American – and foreign — firms. Obviously, these laws will also cover the international marketing of foreign firms in the United States. Panasonic Co., the U.S. subsidiary of Matsushita in Japan, illustrates this as it was charged under U.S. antitrust laws.

In what New York Attorney General Robert Abrams called "the largest vertical price-fixing scheme in the nation's history," Panasonic agreed to pay $16 million. Over 700,000 consumers would receive rebates of $17 to $45. Abrams said Panasonic threatened to cut supplies to retailers if they didn't raise prices 5 to 10 percent. Panasonic president Imura allegedly personally pressured retailers. According to Abrams, among the many retailers who complied, at least partly, were Circuit City Stores, Dayton Hudson Corp. and K Mart.[5]

**Organization and Ownership Arrangements.**   The organization of a firm can be influenced by specific laws that are designed to promote foreign trade. These laws may make exceptions from general, more restrictive laws, for firms that meet certain standards.

*Webb-Pomerene Associations.*   The Webb-Pomerene, or Export Trade Act, deliberately permits the cooperation of competing firms in export trade. This 1918 act specifically excludes from antitrust prosecution the cooperation of competitive firms in the development of foreign markets; that is, firms that compete domestically can collaborate in exporting. The law was passed following study by the Federal Trade Commission, which noted, "If Americans are to enter the markets of the world on more nearly equal terms with their organized competitors and their organized customers, and if small American producers and manufacturers are to engage in trade on profitable terms, they must be free to unite their efforts."[6]

The commission's intent was that American exporters be given countervailing power to enable them to compete against foreign oligopolies or cartels and to prevent foreign monopsonists from playing off one exporter against another. It was expected that this would be especially helpful to smaller firms that could combine and gain economies of scale in setting up export operations. Actually, some very large American firms have also set up Webb-Pomerene associations, such as the major film producers, cigarette makers, and chemical companies. Further discussion of Webb-Pomerene associations as a method of reaching foreign markets is given in Chapter 10, along with a list of current members.

*Foreign Sales Corporation (FSC).*   Most governments use the power of taxation to encourage or discourage different kinds of activity. Members of the EC remit value-added taxes on exports, permitting lower costs and encouraging exports. The United States does not have value-added taxes, so it has sought other tax devices to encourage exports. The effort in operation today is the *foreign sales corporation*, or *FSC* (pronounced Fisc), invented by Congress in 1984. An FSC is a sales company set up in a foreign country or U.S. possession that can obtain a tax exemption on a portion of export earnings. Because the costs of establishing an FSC might discourage smaller firms, the law allows an FSC to be shared by up to 25 exporters. Several states (Delaware, Illinois, Michigan, New York, and Virginia) were promoting or organizing shared FSCs to spur their medium and small-sized firms into exporting. Export volume of firms in some of the early shared FSCs ranged from $500,000 to $16 million.

The details of these arrangements for gaining tax benefits in exporting are not important here. What is significant is the potential impact of home-country tax law on the firm's method of organizing for exports. Countries want to expand exports, and tax incentives seem to offer the strongest motivation to firms. If the firm's goal is profits, management must consider tax laws in organizing its international marketing activity. The firm's choice of a country to supply international markets will depend in part on the export incentives offered by different countries.

***Export Trading Company (ETC) Act.***   In 1982 President Reagan signed the Export Trading Company Act. This was another effort by the United States to aid exports. An *export trading company (ETC)* is supposed to emulate some of the export success of the Japanese trading companies. To get the size and sophistication needed for this, the legislation permitted banks to invest in ETCs and eased antitrust restrictions on export activities. It was felt that this freer environment would encourage the participation of large U.S. banks and corporations with international experience and contacts. This would aid smaller firms who could collaborate in the ETC and enjoy financial strength and economies of scale.

Though ETCs may offer promise for the future, progress has been very slow. As of 1989, the Department of Commerce had registered 119 certificates for corporate ETCs but these were mostly smaller companies, including many export management companies who converted to ETC status. Sears started an ETC but discontinued it after a few years as an unprofitable venture: a bad omen for ETCs. The Federal Reserve had applications for bank ETCs. Though some were from giant banks like Chase Manhattan and Bank of America, the performance has been very modest. The volume of export business of American ETCs is limited, only a pale shadow of a Japanese trading company.

**Other Controls.**   Examples of other controls include the U.S. laws against bribery by U.S. firms and against support of Arab boycotts.

***Foreign Corrupt Practices Act.***   In the 1970s there was a lot of publicity about the practice of bribery by American firms abroad. Though bribery has been a longstanding practice by many firms in all countries — indeed, payoffs to high government officials have often been the most effective promotional tool in international business — the publicity created a scandal in the United States. The most sensational cases involved United Brands and the president of Honduras, and Lockheed and the Japanese prime minister. As a result of the public outcry in 1977, the U.S. government passed the Foreign Corrupt Practices Act to prohibit U.S. firms from engaging in such payoffs abroad.

Elimination of such practices is certainly a desirable goal. The only problem for U.S.–based international marketers is that their competitors from Japan and Western Europe are not forbidden to bribe in their foreign markets. Because bribery is often the most effective kind of persuasion, American firms complain of being put at a competitive disadvantage. Bribery as a form of promotion is discussed further in Chapter 13.

***Anti-Arab Boycott Rules.***   The conflict between Israel and the Arab states has extended its influence into U.S. control over the international marketing of U.S. firms. The oil wealth of the Arab states has given them power that they use in several ways. One way is to try to force companies that sell to their now-rich markets not to have any dealings with Israel. In other words, the Arabs will boycott firms which do not boycott Israel. Because the Arab markets are collectively much larger than Israel, many firms would be tempted to drop the Israeli market and sell to the Arabs. That is counter to U.S. foreign policy interests, however, so the government has legislated rules to prevent U.S. firms from cooperating with the Arab boycott. These include provisions requiring U.S. exporters to forego Arab contracts that bar Israeli ingredients. One estimate suggested this legislation would reduce U.S. sales to Saudi Arabia by 25 percent. As OPEC power declines, this could become less of a problem.

The application of the U.S. antiboycott provisions can be rather extensive and rigorous, as the Sara Lee example shows: In 1988 the Commerce Department's Office of Antiboycott Compliance announced a fine of $2.35 million against Sara Lee for violating the antiboycott provisions. In attempting to protect its L'eggs trademark in Kuwait, Sara Lee provided information about the company, its subsidiaries, and directors. The U.S. government prohibits supplying of certain business information to countries that boycott Israel. Sara Lee is active in Israel and does not sell in the Arab countries because it is blacklisted by the Arab League. The company was appealing the charges.

## International Law and International Marketing

It is difficult to learn international laws, since there is no international law-making body that corresponds to the legislatures of sovereign nations. What then is *international law*? For our present discussion we will define it as the collection of treaties, conventions, and agreements between nations which have, more or less, the force of law. International law in this sense is quite different from national laws that have international implications, such as the American antitrust laws. The international extension of American law is on a unilateral basis. International law involves some mutuality, with two or more countries participating in the drafting and execution.

What is the impact of international law on international marketing? Many treaties and conventions have an impact. We begin our discussion with those international agreements having a general effect on international business and go on to those dealing with more specific marketing questions. Then we look at the legal implications of regional groupings.

**FCN and Tax Treaties.**   The United States has signed *treaties of friendship, commerce, and navigation (FCN)* with many countries. FCN treaties cover commercial relations between the two signing nations. They commonly identify the nature of the right of American companies to do business in those nations with which the United States has such a treaty, and vice versa. FCN treaties usually guarantee "national treatment" to the foreign subsidiary; that is, it will not be discriminated against by the nation's laws and judiciary. This nondiscrimination may not always be realized, but it is more likely in an FCN-treaty nation than elsewhere.

Of a similar type are the *tax treaties* that the United States has signed with a number of nations. The purpose of the tax treaty is to avoid double taxation; that is, if a company has paid income tax on its operations in a treaty nation, the United States will tax that income only to the extent that the foreign tax rate is less than the American rate. Thus, if the corporate income tax rates are equal in the two countries, there is no tax to pay in the United States on income earned in the other country. Obviously, tax-treaty nations are, other things being equal, better places for a subsidiary than countries that do not have such a treaty. Most Western industrialized nations have treaties similar to these of the United States.

**IMF and GATT.**   The International Monetary Fund (IMF) and the General Agreement on Tariffs and Trade (GATT) were both discussed in Chapter 2. Here we want merely to note that both agreements are part of the limited body of effective international law. Both agreements identify acceptable and nonacceptable behavior for the member nations. Their effectiveness lies in their power to apply sanctions. The IMF can withhold its services from members who act "illegally," that is, contrary to the agreement. GATT allows injured nations to retaliate against members who have broken its rules. In IMF and GATT we come reasonably close to finding international bodies with legislative, executive, and judicial powers — prerequisites for true international law.

The international marketer is interested in both IMF and GATT because of a shared concern in the maintenance of a stable environment conducive to international trade. The firm is concerned about the IMF's ability to reduce restrictions on international finance. The firm supports GATT's efforts to free the international movement of goods.

The legal implications of GATT and the IMF do not apply to the international marketer's behavior, but rather to the behavior of the nations within which the firm is marketing. The environment for international marketing is more dependable and less capricious because of these two organizations.

**UNCITRAL: A Step Ahead.**   The United Nations established a Commission on International Trade Law (UNCITRAL) with a goal to promote a uniform commercial code for the whole world. It works with government and private groups, such as the International Chamber of Commerce. Its first output (in 1983) was the Convention on Contracts for the International Sale of Goods. The convention is somewhat similar to Article 2 of the Uniform Commercial Code of the United States. It should bridge the communications gap between countries having different legal systems. It should minimize contract disputes and facilitate the task of selling goods between countries.

**ISO.** Numerous other international organizations have a semi-legal influence on international marketing. One group of special interest is the International Standards Organization (ISO). Industry groups in most of the major industrial countries participate in the work of ISO, but the United States has been a laggard here. The ISO has no fewer than 114 technical committees through which it is working toward the development of uniform international standards.

Differing national standards are a major hindrance to international trade. But standardizing is a very slow task because the changing of national standards often hurts vested interests. In this area multinational companies and their subsidiaries can have a voice in determining what will be the standards for tomorrow. Each national subsidiary of the company can present its views, perhaps joining forces with its national trade association, to the relevant body in that country. Thus, when international negotiations are held, the company can be sure that its viewpoint is presented through the voice of each of its subsidiaries. Perhaps because the export market is relatively small compared to the domestic market, American industry has been less active in ISO than other exporting nations. This lack of interest may be costly in the long run; the United States may find itself closed out of many markets. For example, Western Hemisphere standards for television sets are different from those set by the International Telecommunications Union (ITU). This difference has cost some American manufacturers millions of dollars in lost sales to areas with other standards, namely, Africa, Asia, and Europe.

**Patents.** Many firms have patented products to sell. When selling outside their home market, they want to protect their patent right. Generally, patents must be registered separately in each country where the firm wants protection. This can be a time-consuming and expensive process. For example, it is estimated that 10 percent of the development costs of Hovercraft was spent on securing patents around the world. Individual national registration is also expensive for nations, as each goes through a similar search and evaluation procedure, duplicating the efforts of other countries.

In one two-year period three American drug companies — Squibb, Merck and Upjohn — filed 349 international patents at a cost of $30 million or about $85,000 per patent.

Borg-Warner, an industrial marketer, had 15 patent attorneys who at any time were considering up to 400 "disclosures." B-W typically applies for between 100 and 150 patents each year and 80 percent of its applications are approved. The company holds over 1,500 patents in the United States and over 3,000 abroad.

Because of the expense and inconvenience of individual national approaches to patenting, various multilateral efforts have been made. The largest is the Paris Union (officially, the International Convention for the

Protection of Industrial Property). This 90-year-old organization includes 94 countries. The Inter-American Convention includes most of Latin America plus the United States. There are other multi-country efforts in Europe that should become important with greater integration in 1992. The main feature of these is the simplified application system, which can be a major convenience for firms wanting coverage in many countries. Generally, individual national filing fees will still have to be paid. For nations, the benefit will be the elimination of duplicative procedures. Developing countries particularly will tend to accept the preliminary search and evaluation findings of the industrialized countries.

The advantage of patent protection is that the holder can prevent others from selling the patented product wherever the patent is registered. This element of monopoly protection allows somewhat higher prices and encourages R&D activity by the firm. Because the vast majority of patents originate in the industrialized countries, the less developed nations argue that, for them, patents mean high prices for products, import monopolies rather than local manufacturing, and high royalty payments for the use of patents. The development to watch for is the effort of these nations in UNCTAD and elsewhere to change the patent system to give them cheaper access to technology.

The World Intellectual Property Organization (WIPO), a UN agency, was given centralized administration over various unions (Paris, Madrid, etc.). The Paris Union is a private organization of about 90 countries whose voting procedures require unanimity. The developing countries in WIPO are trying to move to decisions by majority, which would give them effective control over future developments — and less protection to patent holders.

**Trademarks.**   Trademarks are another form of intellectual property of significance to the international marketer. Like patents, trademarks or brands must go through a national registration process to be protected; registration is less time-consuming and costly, though. There are two major international trademark conventions. One is the Paris Union, which, as mentioned, also covers patents. The Paris Union allows a six-month protection period in the case of trademarks, as contrasted with a one-year period for patents. That is, registration of a trademark in one member country gives the firm six months in which to register in any other member countries before it loses its protection in those countries.

The second major convention is the Madrid Arrangement for International Registration of Trademarks, which has 26 members, mostly in Europe, though China has also joined. The United States is not a member, although an American firm's subsidiary in a member country can qualify for its benefits. The principal advantage offered by the Madrid Arrangement is that it permits a registration in just one member country to qualify as registration in all other member countries, with appropriate payments. This is the direction the new patent arrangements are taking. The convenience and economies of scale are evident — a form of international one-stop shopping. A new single European trademark law is also on the way.

The former French colonies have their own multinational arrangement, and an Inter-American Convention for Trademark Protection gives coverage for the Western Hemisphere similar to that given by the Paris Union. The most interesting question in brand and trademark protection concerns the countries that are *not* members of one of these arrangements. It is in these markets that the question of brand piracy occurs. (See the U.S. Pharmaceutical case, Case 5.2, at the end of this chapter.)

Conflict over trademark or brand-name protection can lead to costly, acrimonious legal battles. One case that was neither costly nor acrimonious, however, involved General Motors' choice of a strong name for a sporty new Chevrolet — the Beretta. The 463-year-old Italian weapons maker with the same name brought suit in a New York court. Rather quickly a settlement was reached. GM gave $500,000 to the Beretta Foundation for Cancer Research and got the right to use the name. Roger Smith also gave Pier Giuseppe Beretta a Beretta GTU coupe and received from Beretta a rifle and a shotgun.

**Regional Groupings and International Law.**   As we saw in Chapter 2, many nations have felt the need for larger market groupings to accelerate their economic growth. Such multinational regional groupings have developed on all continents. What each regional grouping has found, however, is that economic integration alone is not sufficient without some international legal agreement. Initially, this takes the form of the treaty that establishes the regional grouping. Inevitably, however, as integration proceeds, further legal agreements are necessary. In this way, the body of international (regional) law grows. Because these groupings are primarily *economic* alliances, the international law that develops relates primarily to economic and business questions. Therefore, regional groupings provide a development of international law of interest to multinational companies.

*The EC Example.*   The basic law of the EC is the Rome Treaty. Under this international law the 12 member countries succeeded in forming a customs union and harmonizing certain economic regulations. By 1985, however, the attainment of a true common internal market was still a long way off. Under Jacques Delors' presidency of the European Commission, a new initiative was launched. The Single European Act identified 300 further measures needed to create a common market (the number later reduced to 279). It was adopted by the member governments at the end of 1985 and specified 1992 as the target date.

These 300 measures, or directives, will become European laws effective in all 12 member nations. Business and marketing in the EC will largely be governed by these new international laws rather than by national laws of the 12 member countries. The prospects for successful achievement of these directives and goals is much higher than for the original Rome Treaty because most of the directives are to be adopted by a form of majority voting, rather than by unanimity. Reinforcing the strength of international law in the EC is the European Court of Justice, which is much more effective in dealing with supranational legal questions than the famous World Court in The Hague. Because a European common market now appears to be a real possibility, European, American, and Japanese firms have been actively positioning themselves for this great new reality.

***Experience Elsewhere.***    The EC has made by far the most progress of all the regional groupings. This is true especially in the area of regional law. The Central American Common Market made great strides in its early years but has been rather stagnant since 1969 because of disagreements between members. The Andean Common Market also started off reasonably well in its early years but then slowed down. Advances seem to come slowly after an initial burst of activity. ASEAN also moves at a glacial pace.

The Latin American Free Trade Association also had made only halting progress before its reorganization into the Latin American Integration Association (LAIA). A partial offset to the failure of the free-trade area, however, is a unique phenomenon called the *complementation agreement*, which, initiated by industry, establishes free trade on a narrow list of products for specific countries. Since the LAIA-wide free-trade area is so slow in coming, manufacturers have proposed narrower agreements covering their product line in LAIA countries where they have plants. The governments concerned have been glad to sign these, giving them the force of law, because they avoid the problems of a free-trade area while conferring some of its benefits.

The problem of a free-trade area lies in each nation's fear that its industry will be hurt by imports from other member countries. To avoid economic injury, a nation can choose to trade in those industries where it has some strength as well as select other member countries that do not pose a competitive threat. The benefits of a free-trade area are economies of scale in a larger market and cheaper imports. It can be seen that a multinational company with plants in several LAIA countries could be the major element in such a complementation agreement. The firm could rationalize production among its LAIA plants, gain economies of scale, and assure to its host nations the benefits of free trade in that product.

**The World of International Law.**    The body of international law is small compared to domestic law. Nevertheless, we have seen a number of examples of international law. Our survey illustrates the ways international law can impinge on international marketing. Furthermore, international law, whether regional or global, is the growth area in the legal environment of international marketing.

Because agreement is easier to obtain the smaller the number of countries involved, regional law will grow faster than other international law. The company will find that international law generally facilitates international trade. But even if the firm considers a change unfavorable, it will want to be informed so as to optimize corporate performance within the new constraints.

Two other areas of international law will need scrutiny by international marketers. One is the growth of *codes of conduct* by international groups

# Global Marketing
Copying in Korea

Seoul, South Korea — It may look like Juicy Fruit gum, with its bright yellow wrapper, bold black lettering, and a small red design on one end. But it isn't. More than likely, it's Juicy & Fresh gum from Lotte Confectionery Co. Or it could be Tong Yang Confectionery Corp.'s Juicy Green gum, which has a package that resembles Lotte's. Then again, it could be Heart Juicy, made by Haitai Confectionery Co., which mimics all three.

Copycat goods and trademarks are epidemic in South Korea. Going well beyond pirated computer software and fake designer goods from struggling mom-and-pop factories and backstreet markets, copycat products are solidly in the Korean mainstream: Even the biggest companies mimic some of the world's best-known products, and they sell their wares in the best department stores and supermarkets.

In the soap section, Tie laundry detergent bears the orange box and whirlpool design of Procter & Gamble Co.'s stalwart Tide brand. Except P&G doesn't make Tie, or license it. A subsidiary of the giant Lucky Goldstar Group produces it.

Nearby is white bar soap packaged much like P&G's Ivory. But it's either White soap, also from Lucky, or Bory, from Dong San Fat & Oil Industry Co. Dong San, which makes Dial deodorant soap under license from a subsidiary of Greyhound Corp. of the U.S., faces competition from a brand called Date, which apes Dial's logo and gold package design.

The American products being copied are rarely available in Korean stores. But the U.S. products are widely known — largely through the presence of American troops here — and sometimes can be found on the black market.

The copying in Korea reflects problems that businesses face in protecting intellectual property worldwide. In a survey of 245 big U.S. companies, the U.S. trade representative found that they estimated their 1986 losses from inadequate protection of such intellectual property at more than $23.8 billion. Korea accounted for $496.1 million of the total, ranking third, behind Taiwan ($752.5 million) and Mexico ($533.4 million). Trade specialists say the survey only caught a fraction of the total costs because it excluded smaller and non–U.S. companies.

Source: Quoted from Damon Darlin, *The Wall Street Journal*, December 5, 1989, B1.

---

such as UNCTAD and the OECD. While these codes for multinational firms are technically not true international law, in a practical sense they become the norms by which nations, labor unions and other critics judge the multinational. As an illustration, the World Health Organization (WHO) passed a code of conduct for the marketing of infant formula that for all intents and purposes serves as international law on the subject.

The second development affecting the internationalization of law is the increasing *cooperation between countries in legal matters*. As one example, Britain and the United States signed a treaty in 1977 spelling out legal situations in which judgments of the courts of one country will be enforced in those of the other. Most commercial disputes will be covered. Broader than that treaty is the informal cooperation between regulators in different countries. There are visits and exchanges of information in formulating new regulations concerning business. In the antitrust area there have even been exchanges of key enforcement personnel between the United States and the EC.

The industrialized countries are one area where legal cooperation exists. A second area is the developing countries who work together not only in UNCTAD and WIPO but also in the United Nations Centre for the Transnational Corporation, where mechanisms exist for the exchange of information on the multinationals. The rapid transplantation of regulatory initiatives from one country to another means that companies can no longer deal with regulations on an individual country basis but will have to devise coordinated strategies.

## Foreign Laws and International Marketing

American laws play a ubiquitous role in American business practice. The laws of other nations play a similar role in the activities of business within their boundaries. The importance of foreign laws to the marketer lies primarily in domestic marketing in each foreign market. The problem arises from the fact that the laws in each market tend to be somewhat different from those in every other market.

**Differing Legal Systems.**   Before considering national peculiarities in marketing law, we will look briefly at the basic legal systems that underlie individual national law. Most countries derive their legal system from either the common-law or the civil- or code-law traditions. *Common law* is tradition-oriented; that is, the interpretation of what the law means on a given subject is heavily influenced by previous court decisions as well as by usage and custom. If there is no specific legal precedent or statute, common law requires a court decision. To understand the law in a common-law country, one must study the previous court decisions in matters of similar circumstance, as well as the statutes. Common law is English in origin and is found in the United States and other countries that have had a strong English influence, usually a previous colonial tie (about 26 countries).

*Civil* or *code law* is based on an extensive and, presumably, comprehensive set of laws organized by subject matter into a code. The intention in civil-law countries is to spell out the law on all possible legal questions, rather than to rely on precedent or court interpretation. The "letter of the law" is very important in code-law countries. However, this need to be all-inclusive may lead to some rather general and elastic provisions, permitting an application to many facts and circumstances. Because code-law countries do not rely on previous court decisions, various applications of the same law may yield different interpretations. This can lead to some uncertainty for the marketer.

Code law is a legacy of Roman law. It is predominant in Europe and in nations of the world that have not had close ties with England. Thus code-law nations are more numerous than common-law nations. Many civil-code systems are influenced by the French, German, or Spanish systems because of previous colonial or other relationships. For example, the German code has had influence on the Teutonic and Scandinavian countries. There are about 70 civil-law countries.

*Islamic law* represents the third major legal system in the world. About 27 countries follow Islamic law in varying degrees, usually mixed with civil, common, and/or indigenous law. The Islamic resurgence in recent years has led many countries to give Islamic law, Shari'a, a more prominent role in their legal systems. Shari'a law governs all aspects of life where it is the dominant legal system, as in Saudi Arabia. Rules not defined by Shari'a are left to decision by government regulations and Islamic judges. Although it has harsh penalties for adultery and theft, Islamic law is not dramatically different from other legal systems insofar as business is concerned. In Saudi Arabia, for example, the Committee for Settlement of Commercial Disputes operates in a manner that would not be uncongenial to a Westerner.

The differences among national legal systems are important to the international marketer. Because the legal systems of no two countries are exactly the same, each foreign market must be studied individually and appropriate local legal talent hired where necessary. All we can do here is alert the marketer to some of the variations in legal systems abroad.

**Foreign Laws and the Marketing Mix.**   One familiar with marketing regulation in the United States will not be surprised at the range of laws affecting marketing in other nations, although one may be surprised at the lack of such regulation in some less developed countries. We will not catalog foreign laws but rather show how they influence marketing — that is, product, price, place (distribution) and promotion. The treatment will be brief and suggestive of the problem areas. A more extensive study is in order only when considering a specific market.

*Product.*   If we consider *product* as everything the consumer receives when making a purchase, the international marketer will find many regulations affecting the product. The physical and chemical aspects of the product will be affected by laws designed to protect national consumers with respect to its purity, safety, or performance. As the thalidomide tragedy showed, nations differ as to the strictness of their controls. The Food and Drug Administration had not cleared the drug for sale in America, but many deformed babies were born in Europe from its legal use there.

In a similar vein, European manufacturers were disturbed by the American safety requirements for automobiles, because this meant that they had to modify their products to meet the needs of one particular market. Because the American market is large, the adaptation was not so serious as meeting the peculiar requirements of a small market would have been. Nevertheless, Jaguar temporarily stopped selling Jaguar sedans in America in 1968 because of U.S. safety requirements. This highlights what frequently appears to be the protectionist use of these laws. Although consumers should be protected, different safety requirements are not necessary for the consumers of every country. By maintaining different standards, nations seem to be saying that consumers in other countries are not being adequately protected. One reason nations often persist in particular legal requirements is that they protect their own producers. For example, Britain kept French milk out of its stores by requiring it to be sold in pints rather than metric measures. German noise standards kept British lawnmowers off German lawns.

Local laws also constrain the marketer's freedom as to other product features, such as package, label, and warranty. For example, in Belgium the containers in which pharmaceuticals for *external* application are put up for sale must be manufactured of yellow-brown glass and have a regular octagonal shape. In addition, the words "Usage Externe — Uitwendig Gebruik" must be molded in relief on the containers themselves. (Belgium is bilingual.)

Labeling is subject to more legal requirements than the package. Labeling items covered include (1) the name of the product, (2) the name of the producer or distributor, (3) a description of the ingredients or use of the product, (4) the weight, either net or gross, and (5) the country of origin. As to warranty, the marketer has relative freedom to formulate a warranty in all countries.

Brand names and trademarks are product attributes that also face different national requirements. Most of the larger nations are members of the Paris Union or some other trademark convention. That assures a measure of international uniformity. However, there are differences between code-law countries (ownership by *priority in registration* of a brand) and common-law countries (ownership by *priority in use*), in their treatment of the brand or trademark. The law in each country is reviewed periodically in *Business America*, a publication of the Department of Commerce. One important thing to know is the countries where brand piracy is a problem.

Foreign tobacco companies faced a challenge along this line in Japan. Japan Tobacco, Inc. (JTI), a government monopoly, had 98 percent of cigarette sales, and foreign firms faced many restrictions. Negotiations between the U.S. and Japanese governments in 1985 liberalized the cigarette market somewhat. Then the foreign companies were disturbed to find that JTI had applied for trademark rights for 50 foreign brand names of cigarettes not yet sold in Japan. In Japan, brand ownership is by priority in registration. Kinya Kitsukawa, marketing manager of JTI, said, "This isn't cheating. Anyone can apply for trademarks. Maybe the foreign companies were idle or lazy in not protecting their brands."[7]

***Pricing.*** There is no foreign counterpart to the American Robinson-Patman Act, but price controls are pervasive in the world economy. *Resale-price maintenance* (RPM) is a common law relating to pricing. Many nations have some legal provisions for RPM, but there are many variations. Another variable is the fact that some countries allow price agreements among competitors.

Some form of government price control is another law of a majority of nations. The price controls may be economy-wide or limited to certain sectors. For example, France has had a number of economy-wide price freezes. At the other extreme, Japan controlled the price on only one commodity — rice. Generally, price controls are limited to "essential" goods, such as foodstuffs. The pharmaceutical industry is one of the most frequently controlled. The control mechanism here sometimes takes the form of controlling margins.

For example, at one time Ghana set manufacturers' margins at between 25 and 40 percent, depending on the industry. Argentina allowed a standard

11 percent "profit" on pharmaceuticals, whereas Belgium fixed maximum prices and both wholesale and retail margins on pharmaceuticals (12.5 and 30 percent, respectively). Germany does not set margins but has an obligatory price register that details both prices and margins for public scrutiny.

**Distribution.**    This is an area with relatively few laws to constrain the international marketer. The firm has a high degree of freedom in choosing distribution channels from among those available in the market. Of course, one cannot choose channels that are not available in a market. For example, France had a specific prohibition against door-to-door selling, but the Singer Company in France received a special exemption from this law. One major question in distribution is the legality of exclusive distribution. Fortunately for the marketer, this option is allowed in most markets of the world. In fact, the strongest legal constraint does not apply to firms managing their own distribution in foreign markets, but rather to exporters who are selling through distributors or agents there.

Careful selection of an agent or distributor is critical in two ways. First, the quality of the distributor will help determine the firm's success in the market. Second, the contract with the distributor may commit the exporter to a marriage that is difficult and costly to terminate. The problem for the exporter is to be aware of national laws concerning distributor contracts in order to avoid the potential problems associated with them. It is much easier to enter an agency agreement than to end one.

**Promotion.**    Advertising is one of the more controversial elements of marketing and is subject to more control than some of the others. Most nations have some law regulating advertising, and advertising groups in many nations have self-regulatory codes. New Zealand has no fewer than 33 laws relating to advertising. Advertising regulation takes several forms. One pertains to the *message* and its truthfulness. In Germany, for example, it is difficult to use comparative advertising and the words "better" or "best." In Argentina, advertising for pharmaceuticals must have the prior approval of the Ministry of Public Health.

Another form of restriction relates to control over the advertising of certain products. For example, Britain allows no cigarette or liquor advertising on television. Finland is more restrictive and allows no newspaper or television advertising of political organizations, religious messages, alcohol, undertakers, slimming drugs, immoral literature, or intimate preparations. A more indirect restriction is the prohibition of advertising in certain media. A number of nations allow no commercials on radio or TV. Another restriction is the growing popularity of taxes on advertising. For example, Peru had an 8 percent tax on all outdoor advertising, whereas Spain taxed cinema advertising in particular.

Sales promotion techniques encounter greater restriction in some markets than in America. In the United States, there is often no constraint on contests, deals, premiums, and other sales promotion gimmicks. The situation is quite different elsewhere. For contests, it is a general rule that participation must not be predicated on purchase of the product. Premiums may be restricted as to size, value, and nature. A premium may be limited to a certain fraction of the value of the purchase and its use might have to relate to that product; that is, steak knives could not be used as a premium with soap, or a towel with a food product. Free introductory samples may be restricted to one-time usage of the product, rather than a week's supply. In the infant formula controversy, sampling was completely forbidden. National variations are great, but in most cases the American marketer will be limited in comparison to the practice at home.

**Enforcement of the Laws.**   The firm wants to know how foreign laws will affect its operations in a market. For this purpose it is not sufficient to know only the laws. One must also have some idea how the laws are enforced. Most nations have a number of laws that have been forgotten and are not enforced. Others may be enforced haphazardly, whereas still others may be strictly enforced.

An important aspect of enforcement is the degree of impartiality of justice. Does a foreign subsidiary have as good a standing before the law as a strictly national company? Courts have been known to favor national firms over foreign subsidiaries. In such cases, biased enforcement makes it one law for the foreigner and another for the national. Knowledge of this discrimination is helpful in evaluating the legal climate.

## The Firm in the International Legal Environment

**Whose Law? Whose Courts?**   Domestic laws govern marketing within a country. Questions of the appropriate law and the appropriate courts may arise, however, if the transaction involves international marketing. We have seen that there is little international law that can apply to international marketing disputes. Moreover, there is no international court in which to try them, except the European Court of Justice for the EC.

When commercial disputes arise between principals of two different nations, each would probably prefer to have the matter judged in its own national courts under its own nation's laws. By the time the dispute has arisen, however, the question of jurisdiction has usually already been settled by one means or another. One way parties can decide the issue beforehand is by inserting a *jurisdictional clause* into the contract. Then when the contract is signed, each party agrees that the laws of a particular nation, or state of the United States, will govern.

If the parties did not have prior agreement as to jurisdiction, the courts where the appeal is brought will decide the issue. One alternative they have is to apply the laws of the nation *where the contract was entered into*. Another is on the basis of *where contract performance occurs*. In one of these ways, then, the issue of which nation's laws shall govern is already out of the company's hands when a dispute arises. Most companies prefer to make that decision themselves and therefore insert a jurisdictional clause into the contract, making possible the choice of the more favorable jurisdiction. Of course, the choice of jurisdiction has to be acceptable to both parties.

The decision as to which nation's courts will try the case will depend on who is suing whom. The issue of which courts have jurisdiction is separate from the issue of which nation's laws are applied. Suits are brought in the courts of the country of the person being sued. For example, an American company might sue a French firm in France. This kind of event leads not infrequently to the situation where a court in one country may try a case according to the laws of another country; that is, a French court may apply the laws of New York State. This could happen if the parties had included a jurisdictional clause stating that the laws of New York State would govern; it could also happen if the French court decided that the laws of New York State were applicable for one of the other reasons mentioned in the preceding paragraph.

Some American courts have a particularly long international reach. The California Supreme Court ruled that a Taiwanese tire maker, Cheng Shin, could sue a Japanese tire valve maker, Asahi, in a California court, even though Asahi does no business in California. In a motorcycle accident, the driver was killed when his tire burst. The family sued Cheng Shin, who settled out of court. He decided Asahi should share the cost and brought suit in California with the jurisdictional approval of the California Supreme Court. The implications of this global reach were so threatening to foreign firms that when Asahi appealed to the U.S. Supreme Court, it was joined in its appeal by the Confederation of British Industry and even the American Chamber of Commerce in London.

**Arbitration or Litigation?**   The international marketer is interested in laws and contracts. Contracts provide for two things: (1) they spell out the responsibilities of each party, and (2) they provide for legal recourse to obtain satisfaction. Actually, however, international marketers consider litigation a last resort and prefer to settle disputes in some other way. For several reasons litigation is disliked as a way of settling disputes with foreign parties. Litigation usually involves long delays, during which inventories may be tied up and trade halted. Further, it is costly, not only in money but also in customer goodwill and public relations. Firms also frequently fear discrimination in the foreign court. Litigation is thus seen as an unattractive alternative, to be used only if all else fails.

More peaceful ways to settle international commercial disputes are offered by conciliation, mediation, and arbitration. Conciliation and mediation are informal attempts to bring the parties to an agreement. They are attractive, voluntary approaches to the settlement of disputes. If they fail, however, stronger measures such as arbitration or litigation are needed. Because of the drawbacks of litigation, arbitration is used extensively in international commerce.

Arbitration generally overcomes the weak points of litigation. Decisions tend to be faster and cheaper. Arbitration is less damaging to goodwill because of the secrecy of the proceedings and their less hostile nature. This means that the climate for conciliation is better so that almost one-third of the cases are settled in direct talks before the judgment stage is reached. Decisions are more equitable and informed because of the expertise of the arbitrators, who are not judges but people with more practical experience.

Arbitration allows business to continue while the dispute is being settled. It neutralizes the differences between different legal systems because decisions are not based on points of law but rather on practical considerations of equity. Each party also has the satisfaction of avoiding the courts of the adversary's country. There is now even an arbitration office in Stockholm to settle disagreements in East-West trade.

In a growing number of countries, arbitration awards have the status and enforceability of court decisions. This was assured for the United States when the Supreme Court in 1974 upheld the primacy of arbitration. Deciding against Alberto-Culver, the Court said that the parties *must* submit to the agreed upon arbitration and may not bring suit in U.S. courts. This was reaffirmed strongly in 1981 when the Court upheld President Carter's deal with Iran whereby private U.S. claims against Iran were to be settled by international arbitration rather than by American courts. The fact that such foes as Iran and the United States agreed to this was significant. One lawyer called this "the most important thing that's happened in international law in this century," in strengthening the growing role of arbitration in international disputes.

The arbitration procedure is relatively simple and straightforward. If the firms wish to settle disputes by arbitration, they include an arbitration clause in the contract. A common form is the one suggested by the American Arbitration Association:

*Any controversy or claim arising out of or relating to this contract, or the breach thereof, shall be settled by arbitration in accordance with the Rules of the American Arbitration Association, and judgment upon the award rendered by the Arbitrator(s) may be entered in any Court having jurisdiction thereof.*

Because of its advantages, arbitration is increasingly popular for settlement of commercial disputes. Supporting this trend are two developments of the 1980s. One is from UNCITRAL, which has formulated a model law on arbitration. This law, because of its multinational source, could lead to a leveling of national arbitration rules into a single global standard. The second development is the increase in the number of centers for hearing arbitration. The International Chamber of Commerce (ICC) in Paris is the leading center but in recent years New York, London, Geneva, Stockholm, and other European cities are becoming more important, as well as such nontraditional locations as Bermuda, Hong Kong, and Kuala Lumpur. The World Bank's International Center for the Settlement of Investment Disputes (ICSID) is also involved. ICSID is especially useful when a government is a party in a commercial dispute.

We've stressed the advantages of arbitration over litigation. While they are very important, arbitration should not be considered a panacea. It does cost time and money. Cases often run up to two years, and the average cost is over $100,000. (Rates vary according to the sum in dispute.) Nevertheless, if disagreements do arise, it is a much preferred alternative. The ICC says that only 8 percent of its decisions have been challenged.

The following landmark case illustrates the usefulness of arbitration: In 1983 IBM sued Fujitsu for stealing software used in its mainframe computers. After four years of very expensive legal battles, the issue was still unresolved. In December 1986 the two companies gave the case to two arbitrators from the American Arbitration Association and agreed to dispense with all the legal machinery. In September 1987 the arbitrators came up with a solution acceptable to both parties.

This landmark case showed the inability of the traditional legal system to handle complex disputes over new technology. The two arbitrators even received powers over future software relations between IBM and Fujitsu. It was said that they will "constitute the intellectual property law between these two companies."[8]

## The Marketer Is Not a Lawyer

What are the implications for the international marketer of all of the legal parameters discussed in this chapter? The marketing manager is not a lawyer. Even a lawyer could not cover all the domestic, international, and foreign legal aspects involved. Although the international marketer cannot know all the relevant laws, it is essential to know which decisions are affected by the laws. With a knowledge of which decisions are affected by the law, the firm can call in legal counsel when special expertise is needed. Legal counsel in this case includes not only the domestic legal staff, but representation for the firm's foreign markets as well.

The firm's need of legal expertise will be related to its international involvement. If the firm is involved only through exporting or licensing, its legal needs are fewer than if it has foreign subsidiaries and joint ventures. Where it operates through licensees or distributors, these parties relieve the firm of some of its legal burden. Where it has subsidiaries, however, it will need local legal counsel.

A study by Business International (BI) throws further light on the problems of managing international legal affairs. BI interviewed 12 multinationals in four industries which had at least one-fourth of their sales abroad. The findings:[9]

1.  The international legal function is growing and getting more complex because of the proliferation of local and international regulation.
2.  The international legal staff at headquarters ranged from 4 to 25 lawyers, with 10 to 15 most common.
3.  In foreign subsidiaries, the number of local lawyers ranged from 1 to 10, depending on the size of the local operation.
4.  Local lawyers were hired abroad, and the function was largely decentralized because of local peculiarities. Some control from headquarters was maintained, however, through such mechanisms as prior approval for certain kinds of work, regular reporting systems, and visits by corporate attorneys. Some companies even had annual meetings for the general counsels of all foreign affiliates to foster coordination and exchange of learning.

# Summary

The host country's behavior will be guided by its national interests, such as security, sovereignty, prestige, and economic welfare. To achieve its goals, it will use a variety of controls over the firm, such as entry restrictions, price controls, quotas and tariffs, exchange control, and even expropriation. These national interests and controls constitute the political environment of an international firm.

The firm will need to evaluate the host-country environment and assess its own political risk there. Then it needs a plan for managing host-country relations, both before and after entering the country.

The international firm often gets involved in international relations, usually against its will. It needs to know how a given host country relates to its own country and to other nations as well. Also, the firm's home country may restrict its international marketing activities. The United States, for example, is especially attentive to these issues.

The U.S. government has many laws affecting American firms' international marketing, relating to regulation of exports and the antitrust implications of overseas ventures as well as special organizational formats to help American firms market abroad, such as Webb-Pomerene Associations, foreign sales corporations (FSCs), and export trading companies (ETCs).

Still other U.S. laws are concerned about the behavior of American firms abroad. The Foreign Corrupt Practices Act attacks bribery, while antiboycott provisions are meant to hinder the Arab boycott of Israel.

Treaties of friendship, commerce, and navigation (FCNs) help give the firm better treatment in foreign markets. UNCITRAL's Convention for the International Sale of Goods smooths the international selling task. IMF and GATT, each in its own way, help to create an environment more favorable to international marketing. And ISO is creating standards for international products that the firm must incorporate into its product planning.

International patent conventions help international firms protect their most valuable intellectual property.

Regional economic groupings, and especially the EC, are writing new multi-country laws covering many aspects of business. These facilitate international marketing in the region.

Each foreign country has its own legal system, but it usually is part of the common-law, code-law, or Muslim law tradition that shapes the laws and their application. These foreign laws affect all aspects of product policy, including the physical product itself, the package and label, the brand name, and the use of warranty.

Pricing and promotion programs are generally more strictly regulated in foreign markets than in the United States.

In cases of legal disagreements, each party usually prefers its own country's courts. A jurisdictional clause should be included in the contract to settle the issue. However, rather than litigate in anyone's court, many international firms prefer to settle differences by arbitration. This is often more efficient and equitable and less damaging to continuing relations.

## Questions

5.1   Explain the threefold political environment of international marketing.

5.2   Discuss the various kinds of host-country controls over the international firm.

5.3   In the table of political-risk indicators, discuss how some of these variables might affect political risk.

5.4   How might a firm analyze its own political vulnerability in a particular host country?

5.5   What can a firm do to help manage its host-country relations?

5.6   Identify the elements of the international political environment.

5.7   Explain the foreign policy concerns in U.S. export controls.

5.8   Discuss the various aspects of international marketing that can be affected by U.S. laws.

5.9   Discuss the ambivalent attitude of the U.S. government toward antitrust in international business.

5.10  Give examples of the kinds of international laws that can influence the firm's international marketing.

5.11  Explain the firm's concerns relating to international patent and trademark law.

5.12  Discuss the influence of regional groupings — especially the European Community — on the development of international law.

5.13  Show how foreign laws can affect the four Ps of marketing.

5.14  Why is arbitration preferred to litigation?

## Endnotes

[1]*Business International*, November 28, 1988, 374.

[2]*Business Week*, July 31, 1989, 46.

[3]*Fortune*, June 5, 1989, 17.

[4]*The Wall Street Journal*, January 29, 1988, 4.

[5]*The Wall Street Journal*, January 19, 1989, B1.

[6]FTC, *Report on Cooperation in American Export Trade*, Part 1 (1916), 8.

[7]*The Wall Street Journal*, March 7, 1986, 20.

[8]*The Wall Street Journal*, September 18, 1987, 1.

[9]*Business International*, December 22, 1978, 406–407.

## Further Readings

*Antitrust Guide to International Operations*. Washington, D.C.: U.S. Government Printing Office, 1988.

Graham, John L. "The Foreign Corrupt Practices Act." *Journal of International Business Studies* Vol. 15, No. 3 (Winter 1984):107–121.

Kaikati, Jack G. "The Export Trading Company Act." *California Management Review* Vol. 27, No. 4, (Fall 1984):59–69.

Kennedy, Charles. *Political Risk Management*. Westport, Conn.: Quorum Books, 1987.

"Legal Aspects of Doing Business Abroad." *Business America*, November 11, 1988, 2–18.

Maronick, Thomas J. "European Patent Laws: Implications for International Marketing." *International Marketing Review* Vol. 5, No. 2, (Summer 1988):31–40.

Sun, Xiao Hong and Peter D. Bennett. "The Effect of Political Events on Foreign Investment in Marketing." *Journal of Global Marketing* Vol. 1, No. 3, (Spring 1988):7–28.

Yoffie, David B. "How an Industry Builds Political Advantage." *Harvard Business Review* Vol. 66, No. 3, (May–June 1988):82–89.

# CASE 5.1 Ford Motor Company Facing the Arab Boycott

In April 1975 a team of ten executives of the Ford Motor Company visited Egypt to explore the possibilities of reestablishing full operation at the Ford auto assembly plant in Alexandria, which became idle in 1966 when Ford was placed on the Arab boycott list. Ford had sold cars in the Arab countries until 1966. In that year Ford started shipping completely knocked-down (CKD) automobiles to Israel for assembling there. While this assembly operation was handled by independent Israeli dealers with no Ford equity, the boycott office of the 20 Arab countries put Ford on the boycott list. The effect of the boycott was not so damaging until 1973, when the Middle-East oil cartel decided to quadruple oil prices and raise its oil income. As the income of the Arab countries increased, Ford decided to examine its stand on the relationships with the Arab countries. As an initial step, Ford wanted to resume operation of its Alexandria plant.

If Ford would stop shipping CKD to Israel, it could be removed from the blacklist by the boycott office located in Damascus, Syria. Ford could then resume its marketing operations in all other Arab countries as well as in Egypt (see Table 1). But the decision was not so simple because the company had to consider the other side of the coin: possible adverse effects resulting not only from the loss of the Israeli market itself, but also from the influential Jewish community in the United States, with a population of more than six million.

In August 1975 Ford offered to launch $230 million worth of industrial projects in Egypt, including the manufacture of diesel engines and the assembly of tractors and trucks. This included the eventual building of a new factory to manufacture trucks and tractors. The Arab press said that Ford was trying to get itself lifted from the blacklist by offering to set up these industrial projects.

In making its decision about operations in Israel, Ford also had to consider the possibility of antiboycott legislation by the U.S. Congress. Such legislation could penalize companies for cooperating with the Arab boycott by refusing business with Israel.

## Ford-Egypt

Ford began its operation in Egypt in 1926 when it established an assembly plant in Alexandria. It was incorporated as Ford Motor Company Egypt SAE in 1932. In 1950 Ford-Egypt moved to a new assembly plant on the outskirts of Alexandria on 8.5 acres of land. The plant consisted of an assembly operation, a parts and accessories depot, an engine reconditioning shop, and general offices. When fully operated, the plant assembled passenger cars shipped in CKD from the United Kingdom and West Germany, CKD trucks from the United States and the United Kingdom, and tractor kits from the United Kingdom. When the Arab boycott was invoked, Ford Egypt was assembling 2,500 trucks and 3,500 tractors annually. At present, the facilities are limited to repair and reconditioning operations.

## Blacklist by Arab Countries

In 1948 when Israel was created, the Arab countries in the Middle East established the boycott office to punish companies that were helping Israel. The Arab countries have ignored direct trade with Israel, but any permanent investment in that country or any long-term agreements, such as licensing arrangements or technical assistance, earned a company a place on the blacklist. For example, Coca-Cola could have exported all the Cokes it wanted to Israel without being blacklisted. But when it licensed a bottler in Israel, it was blacklisted.

**Table 1   Motor Vehicle Registrations for Arab League Countries and Israel, 1975**

|  | Cars | Trucks and Buses | Total |
|---|---|---|---|
| Algeria | 270,000 | 30,000 | 300,000 |
| Bahrain | 19,338 | 6,314 | 25,652 |
| Egypt | 170,000 | 50,000 | 220,000 |
| Iraq | 83,437 | 58,998 | 142,435 |
| Jordan | 23,050 | 6,999 | 30,049 |
| Kuwait | 172,272 | 53,594 | 225,866 |
| Lebanon | 220,205 | 23,380 | 243,585 |
| Libyan Arab Republic | 227,533 | 104,920 | 332,453 |
| Mauritania | 7,755 | 7,343 | 15,098 |
| Morocco | 287,866 | 100,419 | 388,285 |
| Oman | — | — | — |
| Qatar | — | — | — |
| Saudi Arabia | 133,000 | 145,000 | 278,000 |
| Somalia | 7,000 | 10,000 | 17,000 |
| Sudan | 44,184 | 22,687 | 66,871 |
| Syria | 37,278 | 23,068 | 60,346 |
| Tunisia | 113,864 | 37,081 | 150,954 |
| The United Arab Emirates | — | — | — |
| Yemen | — | — | — |
| The People's Democratic Republic of Yemen | — | — | — |
| Totals (rounded) | 1,817,000 | 680,000 | 2,497,000 |
| Israel | 272,000 | 95,000 | 367,000 |

Source: *World Motor Vehicle Data* (Detroit: Motor Vehicle Manufacturer's Association, 1976).

Twice a year, boycott representatives of the Arab nations meet to revise the blacklist and boycott regulations. Between meetings, however, the boycott office often polls national representatives by mail on the proposed changes in the list. Because of the boycott, British Leyland Motor Company withdrew from a joint venture in Israel and was rewarded with new business in Arab markets. General Motors cars are also sold throughout the Arab world because GM has no special contracts in Israel.

## Questions

1. Identify and evaluate the alternatives open to the Ford Motor Company in its business in the Middle East.
2. What course of action do you recommend?
3. Prepare a brief statement on the degree to which firms engaged in international marketing should let political considerations affect their economic and business decisions.

C A S E
# 5.2 U.S. Pharmaceuticals, Inc.(B)

U.S. Pharmaceuticals (USP) is an American firm with about 30 percent of its sales outside the United States. USP concentrates on the ethical drug business but has diversified into animal health products, cosmetics, and some patent medicines. These other lines account for about one-fourth of USP's $800 million sales.

USP's international business is conducted in some 70 countries, mostly through distributors in those markets. In six countries, however, USP has manufacturing or compounding operations. (Compounding refers to the local mixing, assembling, and packaging of critical ingredients shipped from the United States.) USP's only Latin American manufacturing/compounding operations are in Latinia, a country with a population of about 30 million. Some products are shipped from Latinia to other Latin American markets.

USP has run into a problem in Latinia recently with its newest drug, Corolane 2. This drug is effective in treating certain intestinal diseases and infections. The drug has been under development for several years. Three years ago, when the drug showed considerable promise in the extensive testing process, USP registered the name Corolane 2 in the United States and several other major world markets. Last year, USP introduced Corolane 2 in the United States and several large foreign markets. Its early promise was confirmed by its quick acceptance by the medical profession in these countries.

Because of Corolane 2's initial success, USP plans to introduce it in all of its foreign markets. It planned both to manufacture and to market the drug in Latinia. The problem arose because Jorge Rodriguez, a Latinian citizen, had already

registered local rights to the name Corolane 2. Though a questionable procedure, this is perfectly legal, for Latinia is a code-law country that gives exclusive rights to trade names according to priority in registration rather than to priority in use, the basis for exclusive rights in the United States. Furthermore, Latinia is one of several countries around the world that is not a member of the international patent and trademark agreements.

The problem for USP was that it could not sell Corolane 2 under that name in Latinia because Rodriguez owned the rights to the name. Of course, Rodriguez was quite willing to sell his rights to the Corolane 2 name for $20,000.

Registering foreign brand names was Rodriguez's way of supporting himself. He made a good living by subscribing to foreign trade and technical publications (especially in the medical field) and registering all the new names he found. Not all of these names would be exploited in Latinia, but enough of them were to make it profitable for him. Corolane 2 was a typical case. Early in its development process there were journal articles telling of successful tests and applications. As soon as the name Corolane 2 was mentioned in one of these articles, Rodriguez registered it in Latinia. It turned out that he beat USP lawyers to the registration by just two weeks.

USP had encountered problems like this before in Latinia and some other countries. USP conducted research and development on very many projects, most of which did not reach the market. Some company officials felt it was not profitable to register every new product name in every market.

## Questions

1. Identify and evaluate the alternatives open to USP in Latinia.

2. What variables are important in this decision?
3. How could this kind of problem be avoided?

# International Marketing Management

In Part 1 we examined the environment variables that shape the management of international marketing. In Part 2 we consider the strategies and tactics that can lead to successful international marketing given those environmental constraints. We discuss the typical management decisions and problems faced, highlighting those peculiar to the international arena. A chapter on the international marketing of services is included.

CHAPTER 6

# Global Marketing Strategy

**Learning Objectives**

This chapter explains how a company can formulate international marketing strategy. Once a carefully thought-out strategy is in place, effective and consistent actions can be taken in the various areas of the marketing mix.

The goals of this chapter are to

1. Describe the process of formulating global marketing strategy that is consistent with and integrated with the firm's overall global strategy.
2. Delineate the steps involved in arriving at a global strategy.
3. Explain how global strategy relates to the product line and to individual country markets. We discuss the basic question of adaptation versus standardization of the marketing mix for the various country markets, pointing out why some adaptation may be necessary.
4. Describe how firms compete in the global marketplace. We show how firms configure and coordinate the value-added chain to obtain a global competitive advantage.
5. Detail the effects of corporate goals such as a short-term orientation or seeking market share on strategy formulation. We highlight basic strategies based on being a low-cost producer or competing with differentiated products, and show how this influences the choice of strategies for international marketing.
6. Discuss government influences and the impact of major trends such as European integration in 1992 and the emergence of the triad economies of Europe, Japan and the United States. Throughout the chapter, we use company examples to illustrate the concepts being discussed.

The existence of global markets for a firm, and competitors who think and act globally, must be considered in formulating marketing strategy. Worldwide competition is intense enough that firms must plan on obtaining significant market positions in *all* major developed-country markets, where technology has become so widely diffused that "all developed countries are equally capable of doing everything, doing it equally well and doing it equally fast."[1] Widespread availability of information and volatile currencies pose additional challenges to the firm seeking leadership in a global industry.

A *global industry* can be defined as an industry in which a firm's competitive position in one country is affected by its position in other countries, and vice versa. And, "If no one challenges a global competitor in its home market, the competitor faces a reduced level of rivalry, its profitability rises and the day when it can attack the home markets of its rivals is hastened."[2]

**Marketing and Its Links to Global Strategy**

Marketing does not take place in isolation but is inextricably linked to a firm's overall strategy. International marketing is likewise linked to its global strategy. Takeuchi and Porter use the term *linkage* to describe how technology development and manufacturing can make global marketing more effective and further enhance global competitive advantage.[3]

Table 6–1 summarizes the linkages between global marketing strategy and overall corporate strategy in the areas of technology, global logistics, manufacturing, finance, organization structure, competitive response, personnel, and government relations. Thus, a firm cannot cut prices to match its global competitors unless its global manufacturing policies allow it to manufacture at low cost. Similarly, a global hedging policy is needed if a company wants to prevent local prices from going up or down because of currency fluctuations. And unless the company has a policy of transferring experienced personnel to new markets, it cannot expect to benefit from their accumulated expertise.

As in the case of marketing in a domestic context, *international marketing is about creating and keeping customers in global markets*. The customers may themselves be global in character, or they may be limited to individual national markets. The added complexity is that the firm faces global competitors.

## Global Strategy: A Framework

Firm-level global strategies will cut across product lines. For example, global management of international financial flows can match cash inflows and outflows in a specific currency and integrate cash needs for specific currencies across product lines. If a company has several product lines in Japan, it can aggregate the surplus or deficit cash flow produced by each product line; it will thus have a total deficit or surplus position in yen that would have to be financed and hedged. This procedure can reduce spending on hedging and reduce the firm's overall exchange rate risk. But if the firm has organizationally distinct product-line divisions, deliberate planning is needed to achieve such integration of foreign exchange management.

Similarly, a multinational firm selling several distinct product lines within a country can gain economies of scale by performing a basic analysis

**Table 6-1**      **Linkages between Global Corporate Strategy and Global Marketing Strategy**

| Strategy Area | Examples of Linkage |
|---|---|
| *Technology* | Worldwide patents allow foreign marketing from a protected position; the firm does not have to fear price-based competition. |
| *Global Logistics* | Developing a worldwide logistics network allows the firm to promise speedy delivery, attracting clients with just-in-time inventory systems. |
| *Manufacturing* | Multiple geographically dispersed manufacturing sites allow the firm to effect least-cost sourcing and to cut prices in order to gain market share. |
| *Finance* | Centralized global hedging and swaps permit production-line management to set prices in terms of local currencies without having to worry about exchange rate fluctuations. |
| *Organization Structure* | A decentralized or matrix organization supervised by headquarters executives with extensive international-line experience allows for balancing of local responsiveness and global integration. |
| *Competitive Response* | Forming strategic alliances to respond to market forces such as a "single Europe" in 1992; and retaliating against competitor's encroachment into one's domestic market by price-cutting and new product introductions so as to dent competitor's cash flow in its critical home market. |
| *Personnel* | Transfer of experienced personnel into new markets so as to transfer know-how and help achieve standardization and expertise in implementation. |
| *Government Relations* | Pooling country-risk analysis and expertise across product lines and across countries, and transferring government relations know-how to critical markets. |

of that country market's cultural, political, and economic structure before considering competition and demand profiles for individual product lines.

Another major firm-wide influence that cuts across product lines is management attitude. Management attitudes that lead to focusing on the domestic market and/or on a few foreign markets without regard to global markets and competition will hinder the formulation of global actions. Global vision or a lack thereof is one reason why a firm's global strategies may be inadequate, and even why it has not formulated a global strategy.

The consequences of management attitudes can be seen in the attempts of family-led European corporations to adjust to the single European market planned for 1992. Many such family corporations are led by CEOs who grew up during World War II and conceive of Europe as a series of nations that had once been at war. It is difficult for such executives to abandon nationalistic thinking and formulate pan-European strategies, while the younger generation, their sons and daughters, have less difficulty in this regard.

**Global
Strategy
and the
Product Line**

Figure 6–1 sets out the framework for developing product-line global strategy. The three basic influences are the global environment, the industry, and the firm itself. In analyzing the firm, we evaluate its *competitive advantage:* that is, why the firm should be able to make a profit in its chosen line of activity in the face of competition and why customers should buy its product or service, preferring it to that of competition. Competitive advantage can come from many sources: a firm's proprietary technology, its superior manufacturing, its skills in marketing or in managing global financial flows, and in its overall management talent and organizational capabilities. These sources of competitive advantage comprise the firm's *value-added chain.* It is through carrying out these activities that the firm provides value to the customer. And it is able to attract customers because of its superiority over its competitors in one or more elements of the value-added chain. That is, the firm attracts customers because of its superior technology, or manufacturing or marketing.

In attempting to formulate a strategy for competitive advantage, several *environmental influences* must be taken into account. Most important is the *global competition* that the firm faces. Then, *host-government* actions, which vary from country to country, and can affect the firm's freedom to carry out its strategy, must be considered. Also important are the firm's *customers*, the reason for its being. Careful customer analysis is absolutely critical to developing competitive advantage. Lastly, *suppliers* and their influence over the firm are relevant to strategy formulation.

The third major influence is the industry to which the product line belongs. Basic industry analysis is necessary to establish its stage of growth, future prospects, and barriers to entry. A fundamental tool is the international product life cycle, which may be at different stages in different national markets. This is useful in forecasting demand and selecting potential markets for future entry.

Hercules Inc., for example, began exporting cigarette filters made from polypropylene fiber—a substitute for the scarce cellulose acetate that is normally used in filters—at a pilot plant in Georgia. But anti-smoking campaigns have led to a decline in smoking in the United States; hence, cigarette consumption is more likely to grow in countries such as China, where anti-smoking campaigns are not widespread. Leaving aside the ethical question of promoting a product in foreign markets that is deemed harmful in the parent country, Hercules will have to decide whether to locate new filter factories in the United States or Asia. This is one example of how the basic assessment of an industry's attractiveness can vary across countries.

**Product-Line
Strategy for
Individual
Country Markets**

After the firm has developed an initial strategy, it must begin to consider individual markets. While global marketing involves considering all of a firm's markets with regard to their interdependence, there is still the question of whether strategy will be the same in all of its markets, or whether aspects of strategy, including global marketing strategy, will be adapted to fit individual countries. In part, this depends on the goals set for a product line within a particular country market. In some markets, the firm may seek

**Figure 6-1**                        **Global Strategy at the Firm**

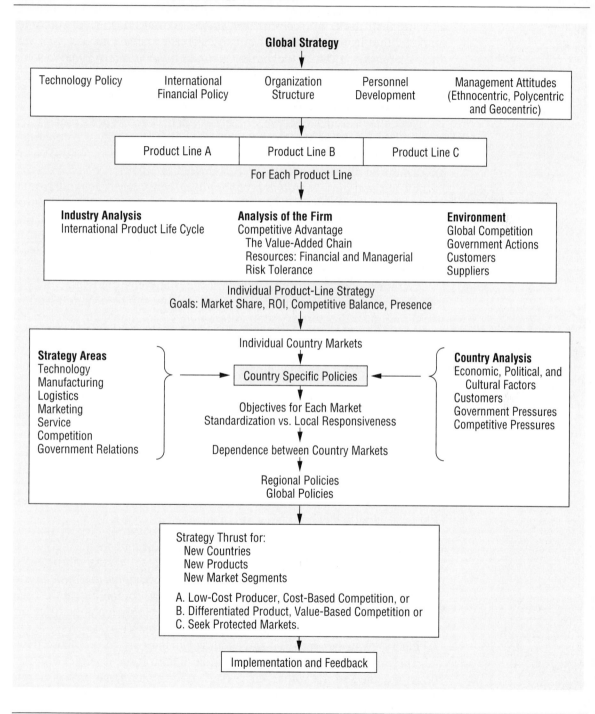

*market share*, planning to obtain profits after market share has been established. In other cases, the goal may be to challenge strong global competitors as a means of preserving *competitive balance* across countries. In still other markets, the firm may simply want to establish a small *market presence*, and wait for the day when the market becomes more attractive. And in some more mature markets, the firm may actively seek *profits* and set up *return-on-investment targets*. The goals set for each country and for the product line as a whole determine which strategies are selected.

Next, the firm must analyze whether it will have to change its marketing polices in a specific market because of government restrictions, competitive pressures, or because of differences in customer needs that may arise partly out of cultural differences. This choice, between *standardizing policies across markets, or adapting them and becoming locally responsive* is fundamental to international marketing. Not all aspects of global strategy need to be adapted for each market. Local responsiveness can vary across the marketing mix, with perhaps promotion and distribution tailored to individual national markets, while the same basic product and price strategies are used for all markets.

The interaction between product-line goals and environmental analysis leads to strategies in a variety of areas, including technology, manufacturing, marketing, customer service, competition policy, and managing government relations. As described in Table 6–1 there are linkages between marketing strategy and strategy in other areas. Explicit consideration of these linkages will lead to a more integrated strategy and thus more successful international marketing.

In addition, the interdependence of many national markets must be considered—when do changes in one market dictate changes in marketing strategy in other markets? A firm may develop standardized global policies for a product line in some aspects of strategy—say, in the area of technology—while in other areas, it may adopt a regional policy covering a group of countries, such as a common brand policy for countries of the European Community. And in other areas, such as advertising and promotion, it may adopt national policies.

While it is difficult to categorize strategies, in essence they all purport to find out what customers around the world want and then satisfy these desires better than the competition. The basic strategy thrust will be either (1) becoming the lowest-cost producer, and competing on the basis of low prices; or (2) providing a differentiated product, and competing on the basis of providing unique value to the customer; or (3) avoiding competition and seeking government help to operate in protected markets.

Lastly, strategies must be implemented if they are to be of use. How well they are implemented will depend on organization structure and personnel assigned to a given country. And once implementation has begun, feedback of results is essential to monitor the plan and decide when and how it should be changed.

**Table 6-2**                         **The Firm and the Global Value-Added Chain**

| Countries/ Markets | Technology | Purchasing | Manufacturing | Logistics | Marketing | Service |
|---|---|---|---|---|---|---|
| U.S. | X | | X | X | X | X |
| Europe | | | X | X | X | X |
| Japan | X | | | X | X | X |
| S.E. Asia | | X | X | | X | X |
| LDCs | | | | | X | X |
| E. Europe | | | | | X | |
| Others | | | | | | |

LDCs = less developed countries

X = firm carries out the value-added activity in that country

Note: The above represents a hypothetical firm's choices about countries and value-added activities: i.e., configuration and coordination.

## Competitive Advantage

As Figure 6–1 shows, competitive advantage provides the basis for choosing a strategy. Competitive advantage arises through matching a firm's capabilities with the chain of value-added activities. That is, a product line or service emerges through carrying out a series of activities such as technology development, manufacturing, logistics, marketing, and after-sales service. A firm with a competitive advantage in one or more activities that constitute the value-added chain would be able to make a long-run profit by specializing in those activities. Table 6–2 illustrates the application of the value-added chain to a hypothetical global firm.

## The Basic Question: Which Activities, and Where?

In a global industry, the firm must decide not only which value-added activities it will carry out itself, but also where (in which countries) such activities will be carried out. Thus, two decisions are being made:

1.   The firm decides which activities it will specialize in and which activities it will farm out, thus adopting a make-or-buy decision on each of the activities that constitute the value-added chain; for example, a firm in the running-shoe business might decide to develop a new type of running shoe in-house, in its own laboratories, using its own equipment and scientists; then it might provide product specifications and ask another company to manufacture the product; after receiving delivery of the shoes, the firm might carry out its own marketing campaign in major markets around the world, thus controlling the technology and marketing activities while subcontracting the manufacturing value-added activity.

2.   The firm must also decide where it will carry out the value-added activities it has chosen; here, principles of comparative advantage come into play in deciding which activities are most appropriately carried out in which countries. A country will typically have a comparative advantage in activities

**Figure 6–2**                    **Value-Added Analysis for Consumer Electronic Products**

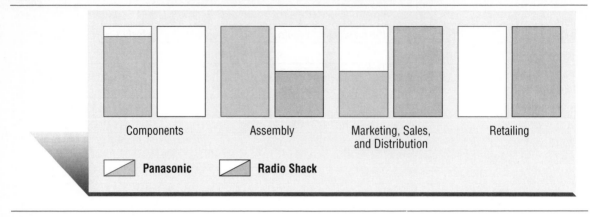

Note: Shaded area represents portion kept in-house.
Source: Bruce Kogut, "Designing Global Strategies: Comparative and Competitive Value-Added Chains," *Sloan Management Review.*

that use large amounts of its abundant factor of production. For example, a country with large quantities of abundant unskilled labor might be an appropriate site for manufacture of products that use unskilled labor, such as garments or shoes.

Going back to our example of the running-shoe company, suppose the company had previously decided to let another independent company manufacture running shoes based on its technology and design. With the addition of the country factor, the company could decide not to subcontract the manufacturing of shoes but instead manufacture the shoes itself in another (low-wage) country, by making an investment and managing a running-shoe factory. The company could add manufacturing to its value-added chain, by carrying out the activity in a different country. Moreover, if it decides to continue to subcontract the manufacturing, it now has to decide which country's manufacturers to use as a source of supply. In choosing between competing subcontractors in different countries, low delivery cost, quality, timely delivery, and low risk of interruptions of supply are all relevant factors.

Companies within the same industry can take different approaches to the value-added chain. Kogut[4] cites the examples of Panasonic and Radio Shack in the consumer electronics industry. As Figure 6–2 shows, Panasonic has chosen to emphasize component manufacture, assembly, and some marketing and distribution activities, while Radio Shack concentrates on marketing and retailing, assembling its products from purchased components. Panasonic will then choose manufacturing locations based on comparative advantage, while Radio Shack, by subcontracting manufacturing of components, will source from manufacturers in those countries that have a comparative advantage in manufacturing. The implications of these choices are that Panasonic can profit from the U.S. market mainly by selling its equipment to independent electronics retailers in the United States, whereas Radio Shack, by selling consumer electronics products to the end-user, will profit from the mark-up on inventory purchased from suppliers such as Panasonic.

## Environmental Change and Value-Added Choices

Comparative advantage can shift over time as economies grow and acquire technology, capital, and skilled labor. Companies must change their value-added configuration to accommodate such shifts. If wage costs are important to the firm's competitive advantage, and wages rise in its present manufacturing location, it must consider whether to shift manufacturing to another, lower-cost location, as the following example shows.

Micromotors are used in products such as cameras, hair dryers, cordless tools, and in cars to run adjustable mirrors, central door locks, and fuel injection systems. Hong Kong's Johnson Electric Ltd. is the world's second largest producer of micromotors. As wages in Hong Kong rise at a rate of 15 to 20 percent a year, Johnson has subcontracted its labor-intensive processes to factories in China, where wages are a fifth of Hong Kong levels. Johnson sends equipment, technology, and components, while Chinese partners provide land, labor, and the factory building. Johnson sends components by truck in the morning and receives subassemblies back by evening, with final assembly and quality control taking place in Hong Kong. Such subcontracting has allowed Johnson to raise output by 60 percent while reducing the number of employees in Hong Kong. In Hong Kong, Johnson carries out R&D and has invested in automated equipment. It works closely with customers such as Black & Decker, Kodak, and Sunbeam to design specialized value-added motors. As Johnson grows, it continues to stress quality, while the China connection also allows it to use low costs in competing with Mabuchi Motor, the Japanese company that is the global industry leader.[5]

## Configuration and Coordination of the Value-Added Chain

Combining value-added chain analysis with the complexities of global markets leads to firms having to make decisions about both configuration and coordination.[6] *Configuration* refers to the decision about where a firm's value-added activities are carried out. Once the activities have been spread out (configured) in different countries, the firm must *coordinate* them so as to manage them effectively. Configuration decisions can result in a company having a presence in more than one national market. We can distinguish between a global perspective, a multi-domestic perspective and a (domestic) market-extension perspective.[7]

The *market-extension* idea, which is typically the way in which a small firm becomes involved in international marketing, represents an unplanned and short-term exploitation of foreign markets while the domestic market remains the focus of the company. Products developed for the home market are sold in one or more overseas markets to obtain incremental revenue, with little planning of the role of foreign markets in the firm's overall strategy.

A *multi-domestic* orientation represents a more careful consideration of foreign markets but with a clear separation of each country market. That is, the firm approaches each market on its own terms, and little effort is made to capitalize on interdependencies between various markets. Such an approach may be consistent with the nature of consumers and line of business.

For example, Nomura Securities feels that the retail brokerage business, involving the sale of securities to individual customers, must be carried out differently from country to country.[8] Selling securities to the retail customer in Japan is quite different from the same transaction in the United States. Yet, Nomura can justify higher levels of spending on investment analysis because it can spread the additional overhead cost over the retail customer base in both countries. Detailed research on Japanese industries allows it to develop a recommended list of Japanese-company securities that can then be marketed to both U.S. and Japanese customers, albeit using different retail-selling methods.

Nomura thus obtains economies of scale by realizing that its research on Japanese companies can be sold to both American and Japanese customers. Scale economies could also be obtained, for example, by combining product development for several markets, or by developing a regional or global brand, or by running common advertising themes, or by centralized manufacturing for sale to several markets. *A multi-domestic approach is generally appropriate for industries with low economies of scale and major differences in customer profiles across national markets.* Sometimes governments may force a company to adopt a narrow single-country approach, deliberately encouraging such local responsiveness, particularly in critical industries such as telecommunications and software. In such cases, corporate strategy might accommodate government pressures. In return, it might negotiate for favors such as protection against foreign competition, and fiscal incentives. However, if competitors are acting globally, a fragmented nationally responsive strategy will be less successful in the long run.

A *global perspective* is one where the firm directs special attention to the interdependence among national markets and competitors' actions in those markets when formulating its own strategic plans. Such an approach can lead to economies of scale in technology development, manufacturing, and marketing, and in making the appropriate competitive responses.

In the early 1960s, Komatsu was a small manufacturer of a narrow line of earth-moving equipment, of indifferent quality, selling mainly in a protected Japanese market. When Caterpillar sought to enter the Japanese market through a joint venture with Mitsubishi, Komatsu quickly signed technology-licensing agreements with U.S. firms to upgrade its products. Then Komatsu launched an internal program, first to match Caterpillar in quality, and then to reduce costs. Komatsu's corporate slogan became, "Encircle Caterpillar."

Komatsu began to sell its products extensively in the neighboring Asian countries, and to the Middle East and Third World countries, where much infrastructure development was taking place. It next embarked on a factory-automation program and a new-product development program. It also set up dealer networks in Europe and the United States. By 1980 it had begun to capture market share in the United States. When the dollar began gaining value, Komatsu cut prices and was able to increase its U.S. market share to about 25 percent by 1984 while Caterpillar experienced losses. In 20 years, Komatsu had become number two in the world in earth-moving equipment, the result of a carefully balanced global strategy with equal attention given to (1) configuration of value-added activities across global markets and (2) coordination of these growing and far-flung activities.[9]

But Komatsu is a multibillion-dollar company, and a legitimate question is whether small companies should be adopting global strategies.

## Why Should Firms Think Globally?

Reasons to plan for global markets and to compete on a global basis can be summarized as follows:

- Markets.
- Customers.
- Production resources.
- Governments.
- Technology, especially patents.
- Competition.
- The time factor: speed of response.

**Global Markets**
Markets are one reason a firm should think globally. There are major markets around the world that a global orientation could exploit. Post–World War II economic development brought about three areas of roughly equal economic size: United States–Canada, Europe, and Japan with its neighboring countries. Each of these blocs represents roughly one-third of the world market, so a company that sells only in the United States is ignoring roughly two-thirds of the potential world market.[10] Further, as markets grow more alike, especially in the developed countries, additional sales in Europe and Japan can be gained with a product that may have been initially designed for the U.S. market. What we are really saying is that there is a convergence of national markets, with European, Japanese and U.S. markets for certain products displaying similar profiles. Hence, selling simultaneously to all of these markets could maximize sales, especially if the company has introduced its products ahead of competition. Overhead costs can be spread out over a larger volume base, allowing a lower price to be charged. If sales volume in the United States has already exceeded the breakeven point, R&D and other fixed costs have been amortized. In this case, the firm can capture larger market share in overseas markets by charging lower prices, since product-development costs have been recovered.

Most multinationals that market globally depend on certain critical markets for a stable source of profits and cash flow, usually their home market and some other markets in which they have been long established. A global orientation means looking beyond these familiar markets and recognizing the need for a market presence in all major national markets in order to protect their position in the critical markets.

Certain markets are highly innovative *"lead" markets*,[11] and a presence in these markets helps firms refine their products and services and learn lessons that can be transferred to other markets. Innovative ideas are not all that abundant, so being able to leverage new ideas across markets gives the global company an advantage over its national or regional competitors. As an example of the use of lead markets, large Japanese manufacturers and trading companies have made sizable equity investments in start-up high-technology U.S. companies in California's Silicon Valley. Aside from an ownership share, they generally obtain exclusive product-distribution rights for Japan and access to advanced technology. While the small U.S. company benefits from the possibility of selling to the large but difficult Japanese market, the Japanese firm can license the technology and begin manufacturing in Japan, thus readying itself for the product-cycle stage when low-cost competitors can gain a competitive edge. An example of such an approach is Mitsubishi Corp., which purchased a 5 percent stake in Micro-rim, a manufacturer of R-Base, a powerful database software package. Mitsubishi modified the package with the help of a Japanese software company and then began selling the Japanese version in Japan. What the Japanese are after is technology, not quick profits, when they invest in Silicon Valley companies.[12]

The United States is also a lead market for the film industry. Though saturated with cinemas at a time when U.S. movie-going is declining, it produces a large number of new movies every year for which there is an avid audience in Europe. Thus, Albert Bert visits the United States often to pick up new films to exhibit in Europe, at the Show West convention in Las Vegas, and at the American Film Market. More importantly, he also picks up new ideas and new technology. The Bert family owns a cinema complex outside Brussels, the Kinepolis, with 7,500 seats and 25 screens, equipped with Showscan.[13] This process, which has just become available in the United States, shows 70 mm films at 60 frames per second, producing very sharp and clear images. He plans to build cinemas all over Europe, following one simple rule: "Always worry about service to the customer before profits."[14] Accordingly, he is willing to commit to Showscan even though it costs about $300,000 additional to so equip a theater.

## Global Technology Markets

One characteristic of lead markets is their function as a showcase for new technologies. Technology is a critical element of the value-added chain, and a resource, just as much as raw materials or skilled labor. Certainly technology is an essential factor for firms seeking to compete in world markets using a differentiated-product strategy thrust. It is expensive to develop, but patents can protect the firm's investment, allowing it to recoup development costs and make a profit.

Symbol Technologies learned the importance of patent protection when Opticon of Japan entered the U.S. market with a competing product. Long the leading U.S. source of hand-held portable laser scanners used to read bar codes on products, Symbol had about a 90 percent U.S. market share in 1987. Its product, which can read a code at distances between two to twelve feet, is used by clients such as Toys R' Us, and can be used for inventory tracking and control, with growing applications in the military, medical and movie markets. Symbol has filed a suit against Opticon alleging patent infringement.[15]

## Global Production Resources

Production resources are another reason to think globally. Global sourcing of raw materials and scarce commodities can result in timely delivery and reduced cost. A global strategy also allows firms to plan manufacturing configuration across countries to take advantage of the availability of another resource—labor, whether it be cheap unskilled labor, or high-quality technically skilled and expensive labor (such as large pools of trained scientists).

## Global Competition

A global competitor who is strong and unchallenged in its home market can undercut its competitors in their strong markets by deliberately channeling resources into these markets. Such a competitor will buy market share by price cuts and accepting low profits or even losses for a while. Such threats can be countered only by similar tactics from a similar global position. Such an exchange of threats, or *cross-patrolling*, helps maintain the balance of power while firms go about further strengthening their competitive advantages. A global presence helps firms plan for both offensive and defensive strategic responses, as circumstances warrant.

**Time-based Global Competition.**    Time is also becoming an important factor in global competition. Speedy introduction of new products, and speedy response to competitive actions are essential to maintain competitive strength. Such speed of response is heightened when a firm has a global presence, as it can draw on resources, ideas, and personnel from a variety of national markets.

Honda exemplifies such behavior: when faced with stiff competition from Yamaha in motorcycles, it responded by introducing 113 new models in just 18 months, equal to changing its entire product line twice over.[16] These rapid model changes had several consequences:

- Motorcycles came to be judged on fashion, with consumers expecting newness and freshness.
- At the same time, Honda brought technology to the forefront, with four-valve engines, composite materials, direct drive, and other features.
- While the number of new-product introductions forced Honda's sales and service networks to work overtime, its bewildering variety of models left Yamaha in the dust, with over 12 months' inventory at one point. As Stalk puts it, "Variety had won the war."[17]

How was Honda able to introduce over 100 models in 18 months? By managing time well, using flexible manufacturing and rapid-response systems, stepping up the pace of innovation. Why does time-based competition

work? Customers are willing to pay higher prices for new products introduced in a timely fashion. Even small innovations introduced frequently
can be appealing to consumers and aid in sharpening product differentiation.
If the customers are themselves using just-in-time techniques, they are willing to pay more for timely delivery. Another reason is that a firm capable
of speedy product development, manufacturing, and delivery can reduce
costs by saving on inventory (particularly work-in-progress) and working
capital. Time-based competition asks the question, how quickly can the
product be made for a given quality and price? Stalk believes that Japanese
companies compete on the basis of time: the firm that can implement new-
product introductions faster, manufacture a variety of products efficiently,
move swiftly to sales and distribution and do all this faster than competition
gains competitive advantage.[18]

**Global
Customers**

Customers also play a role in influencing the firm's global orientation. As
customers themselves become global, their first impulse is to continue to
do business with established suppliers. Banking on this tendency, Recruit
Co., a Tokyo computer-service company that found that U.S. computer-
service firms did not offer extra capabilities to handle Japanese-language
computing, set up an office in New York City. Large Japanese banks such
as Dai-Ichi Kangyo that were expanding into the United States had to have
this capability, so Recruit moved into the United States to retain such clients.

Similarly, Hitachi Ltd. had sold few of its large mainframe computers
in the United States; but when its Japanese customers started building factories and opening offices here, Hitachi expanded its U.S. presence to maintain its relationships with those clients. Hitachi plans to use its U.S. operations to win business from new Japanese clients such as the Japanese auto-
parts makers who themselves followed the Japanese auto firms and firms
such as Nomura Securities, which has been expanding its U.S. brokerage
operations. To serve a potentially larger market, Hitachi plans to expand
product development and marketing in the United States, creating new software, and augmenting consulting operations for Japanese clients.

Even IBM Japan moved Japanese marketing and system engineers to
the United States once it realized that its Japanese clients wanted IBM
Japanese-made equipment and familiar faces.[19] Such relationship-building
is particularly important in industrial marketing. But similar motivations
can be found in consumer-oriented companies; for example, *The Wall Street
Journal* began marketing a European edition partly because of the growing
numbers of American managers in Europe (though at the same time, European demand for American business news and stock quotes was growing,
which was another factor).

**Government
Actions**

Government actions can be a very important influence on global strategy.
For example, governments can strengthen competitive advantage by subsidizing national firms. Such support can be most helpful in the early stages
of the development of an industry, reducing risk and augmenting scarce
resources.

Subsidies estimated at about $14 billion since the inception of Airbus in 1972 have allowed it to offer a family of new commercial jet aircraft.[20] Without them, Airbus would have been unable to fund the development of its three new models, the A320, the A330 and the A340. Internal cash flow would have been inadequate, as Airbus has not made a profit in all its years of existence.

Governments may also participate directly in competition through *state-owned enterprises (SOEs)*. Such enterprises do not have to worry about profits, backed as they are by the deep pockets of the national treasury. SOEs often have objectives such as maintaining employment and earning foreign exchange, which may lead to behavior quite at odds with profit-maximizing behavior. Private firms competing against such government-owned enterprises have to worry about maintaining long-run profitability. In competing with Airbus, for instance, Boeing must maintain profits high enough so that it can set aside the $3 billion needed to develop its latest new aircraft, the 767-X.

Government influence can be felt in other ways. France has obtained a dominant position in electronic information services (*videotext*) for consumers through its Minitel network, consisting of a small terminal with a keyboard that is hooked up to telephone lines. Using the Minitel, subscribers can look up telephone numbers, stock market prices, order products and services, and use the Minitel as an electronic mail service. The French Telecommunications authorities wanted Minitel to be a low-cost public-access service, so the terminals were provided free, and the customers were charged only for usage, about 6¢ a minute to look up telephone numbers, and between 20¢ and $2 a minute for using commercial services. As a result, over 4.5 million homes use Minitel, and France's videotext service has become the largest in the world.

The early experience gained with videotext services in France can be a competitive and comparative advantage (low-cost production of the terminals themselves, along with marketing know-how gained from marketing a new technology service to French users unfamiliar with computers). Not surprisingly, France has sold the Minitel approach to Spain and Switzerland, and has begun marketing in the United States.[21] Since personal computers are more widespread here, Minitel has adapted by providing terminal emulation software that allows PCs to function as Minitel terminals, and has formed a joint venture with Infonet to make Minitel available in over 150 American cities.

## Corporate Goals and Global Strategy

Global strategy differs among multinational firms according to whether

- The dominant orientation is short-term or long-term.
- Profits and return on investment are willingly sacrificed in return for higher market share.
- Global or national competitive position is more important in determining competitive strategy and response.

Time, as mentioned earlier, may also be a key goal, with corporations giving strategic priority to the timely formulation and implementation of strategy.

## Dangers of a Portfolio Approach to International Markets

Given differences in strategic thinking, it is also debatable whether a portfolio approach to country markets and products is useful. Under a portfolio approach, national markets and product lines are analyzed based on expected profitability and level of competition. Future profitability is used to judge the attractiveness of a particular country and product line, and country-market positions are nurtured or culled depending on the forecasted returns. But competition may deliberately take actions to lower returns in a particular market in the hope that its competitors would conduct portfolio analysis and decide on a strategy of segment and country retreat. Over time, a global competitor who gives less attention to portfolio analysis and financial return will gain market share and customer loyalty.

An MIT study on the declining market share of U.S. industry in several sectors including semiconductors, machine tools, automobiles, VCRs and others blames objectives chosen by U.S. firms for the decline.[22] Typically, U.S. firms evaluate a market, say, consumer electronics, with a return-on-investment target in mind. Foreign firms in the same industry might aim for market share by lowering prices, resulting in less than target returns for the U.S. firm. The firm's financial analysts and accountants then recommend withdrawal from that industry segment. Of course, the high(er) cost of capital in the United States makes returns further out in time less attractive, which may account for the shorter-term planning horizon. But if U.S. industry is to retain market share, global strategic response dictates that U.S. firms must match foreign competition and cut prices if necessary, sacrificing short-term profits while assessing alternatives for the long run.

## Modes of Global Competition

Are there some standard approaches to global competition? In a broad sense, yes: (1) competing based on low costs, (2) competing with differentiated products, and (3) competing by seeking protected markets.

## Competing as a Low-Cost Producer

If a firm can produce its product or service at a lower cost then competitors can, yet achieve comparable quality, it can lower its prices and still make an adequate profit. Or it can charge similar prices compared to its competitors but make higher profits because its costs are lower.

Low-cost production is typically linked to high-volume production. Economies of scale reduce costs, and learning- and experience-curve factors also lead to cost reduction. *Learning-curve economies* result from workers becoming more productive as they work at a job longer and learn from mistakes. Similarly, *experience-curve economies* result from the company learning to manage a line of business better. As accumulated production grows, the company learns to manage its machines better, reduces overhead, and typically finds that average cost per unit declines with each doubling of accumulated volume of production. Low cost and high market share are closely linked, since it is the large market share that allows for large-volume production.

## Competing with Differentiated Products

Some firms rely on attracting customers with products that their competitors do not have. Such *differentiated products* may have superior design or better performance, or better quality and reliability, more durability, or may be backed up by better service, or may simply appeal more to the consumer for aesthetic and psychological reasons. Examples abound: Caterpillar Co., when initially faced with competition from Komatsu said that its prices, which were 10 to 15 percent higher than Komatsu's, reflected the higher quality and value offered. When a luxury automobile such as BMW or Mercedes-Benz sells for over $60,000, the price reflects superior engineering, performance, and also a certain cachet. The buyers are willing to pay extra for the prestige a luxury automobile seems to confer.

Firms who compete on this basis must monitor world markets to ensure that the features differentiating their product have not been copied by competitors. They must be constantly working on new features, since what is a differentiated product today will soon become a commodity. The global competitor must constantly stay ahead of the pack at its heels, else the basis of its competitive advantage disappears. Once the product has become a commodity, the lowest-cost competitor will win out.

## Competing by Seeking Protected Markets

We mentioned earlier that governments are a key factor affecting global competition. One mode of competition, therefore, is to rely on government protection against foreign competition. Such protection buys time by holding the efficient competitor at bay until the firm can lower its costs or develop a differentiated product. If it fails in these attempts, it can at least make profits until the foreign competitor figures out a way to evade the protectionist barrier, perhaps by setting up manufacturing and sales facilities within the protected sales market. Once that happens, of course, the inefficient protected firm will disappear.

We mentioned Airbus earlier as a firm receiving government subsidies and protection. After being in operation for eighteen years, Airbus has finally launched a commercially successful product, the A320, which has received enough orders to go beyond the breakeven point. Airbus seems to have used protection wisely and may now be capable of competing with Boeing without the benefit of subsidies.

## Where Do Global Competitors Come From?

New firms are constantly augmenting the pool of potential competitors. Competitors often emerge from their domestic markets to begin challenging established firms in major foreign markets. Komatsu began emerging as a global competitor in just such a fashion. Firms from countries like South Korea have begun competing in industries such as consumer electronics, where such companies as Samsung, Gold Star, and the Lucky Group have gained market share in color televisions, VCRs, and personal computers, as well as semiconductors. In this case, *market extension* forms the basis for the entry of new competitors. The South Korean companies have extended their reach to global markets after solidifying their position at home.

Firms may also *diversify into new product markets* to emerge as potent competitors. This is particularly true for large multinationals seeking to diversify out of mature industries. An example is the graphics supercomputer industry, which consists of computers with enormous abilities in displaying three-dimensional graphics and handling vast amounts of data. Such computers have applications in areas such as weather forecasting, analysis of astronomical data, and in design applications such as in visualizing stress on an aircraft wing.

Kubota, a Japanese manufacturer of tractors and industrial equipment, purchased a 44 percent share in an American supercomputer firm, Ardent Computer Inc. Kubota will thus be entering an industry composed of firms such as Silicon Graphics, Apollo Computer, Sun Microsystems, and Digital Equipment Corp. Kubota/Ardent plan to introduce a new computer for about $25,000, as against existent selling prices for competing products of $79,000. Kubota will build and market Ardent computers in Japan with a goal of gaining a commanding market share early on, just when the supercomputer graphics industry is entering a fast-growth stage. Kubota's entry poses questions of how to respond to its threatened price-cut and market-share strategy, particularly for the smaller U.S. start-up firms such as Stellar, Convex, and Alliant.[23]

Existing competitors may also *extend their product lines to enter new market segments*. Japanese auto firms in the United States have followed such a policy. Honda was the first, with the higher-priced Acura being a product for the luxury-car segment in the United States. They were promptly imitated by Nissan and Toyota, with their Infiniti and Lexus lines. Such product-extension moves by the Japanese auto industry will affect the market share of Cadillac and Lincoln, as well as Mercedes, Volvo, Saab, and BMW.

Finally, competition can also arise through *forward or backward integration by suppliers*. This is happening in semiconductors, with manufacturers of memories and microprocessors deciding to incorporate their semiconductor components into board-level and systems products, thus selling complete systems as opposed to components. Such moves not only create competition for the firm but also affect its logistics position by creating uncertainty of supply. When shortages of critical components develop, will the supplier prefer to feed its own manufacturing lines?

## Assessing Global Competition

Global strategy must include careful study of sources of competition and the likely responses of individual competitors in global markets. Such an analysis usually begins with an assessment of a competitor's strengths and weaknesses, its goals, and how it will respond to the firm's actions. Much depends on the balance of competitive power, that is, whether the competitor is a leader in a particular product/market area. The same firm may hold a dominant market position in one national market and be playing catch-up in another. And within the same country-market, the firm may be a leader in one product line and hold a minor market share in another product line. Thus, how a firm reacts depends on its market position, whether it is a market leader, whether it seeks to challenge the market leader, or whether it is a follower, holding a small market position and using niche strategies to hold on to its market share.

A special place is held in global competition by *national champions*—firms that have dominant positions in their national markets and often receive government support. In the European auto industry, Fiat in Italy and Peugeot and Renault in France enjoy such a position, with their dominant market share in their home markets partly attributable to regulations that restrict Japanese auto imports. While Japanese cars accounted for 15 percent of total auto sales in West Germany in 1988, they were only 3 percent of French sales and only .7 percent of Italian auto sales. Similar national champions can be found in the computer industry, where firms such as Olivetti in Italy and France's Bull dominate their home markets but have low market share across Europe when compared to U.S. computer firms with a pan-European presence. As the "single market" of 1992 looms, the position of these nationally dominant firms seems shaky.

## Impact of Government Actions on Strategy

Sometimes national governments come to the aid of their national-champion firms, especially in industries where a national presence is deemed important. Thomson, the French state-owned electronics company, is in such a position. Its 1988 sales of about $12.6 billion were about equally divided between defense products and consumer electronics—it is the world's fourth-largest manufacturer of television sets and VCRs. As defense spending declines, it has pursued diversification into semiconductor manufacturing, an industry dominated by Japanese and U.S. industry. It has merged its semiconductor operations with SGS of Italy, and is working on an EEC-funded microchip research program in collaboration with Siemens and Philips. French government support is an essential element of the strategy to challenge Japanese firms in semiconductors, televisions and VCRs.[24]

Much of what we have said about global strategy formulation assumes free markets. But government intervention in international business is quite common, and firms must temper their global strategies to accommodate government actions that serve to fragment a global outlook. Doz and Prahalad describe the juggling act that corporations must engage in to handle the conflicting demands of global integration and national responsiveness.[25] Changes in product and process technology, economies of scale, national factor cost advantages and global distribution all require a global stance. Yet, political processes and the interventionist policies of governments require firms to modify their global integration policies and accommodate government demands. That is, the underlying thrust is still global strategy; but temporary and shifting local accommodations are necessary to continue to do business.

An example is the problems facing Nissan in Europe due to protectionist pressures from European governments. Japanese auto makers voluntarily agreed to restrict their European exports, with an import ceiling in the United Kingdom of about 11 percent of the total market, and an even lower 3 percent share of the French market. In response, Nissan opened a small factory in Northern England, producing about 50,000 cars a year, with some of the output being exported to other European countries. Local content is about 70 percent; that is, the value-added chain in Britain accounts for about

70 percent of the car's value. But France will not accept exports of these cars from Britain as European products, classifying them instead as Japanese autos subject to the 3 percent ceiling. An industry association headed by Mr. Umberto Agnelli of Fiat suggested that autos should have at least 80 percent local content to be classified as European.

France's two manufacturers, Renault and Peugeot, account for 23 percent of the market, and about one job in ten in France still relies, either directly or indirectly, on the auto industry. This may explain French opposition to the Nissan imports from Britain. Nissan hopes to achieve 80 percent local content by 1992 when its planned output will exceed 200,000 cars. Imported Japanese parts used in engine assembly in Britain would be replaced with British-made parts. Nissan would obtain higher economies of scale if complete engines were imported from Japan, as volume in a Japanese plant would be higher. But the sacrifice of cost economies is the price in terms of national responsiveness that Nissan is paying for freedom of access to the European market.[26]

## Global Marketing Strategies

It is clear that we cannot separate global marketing strategy from overall corporate strategy. Decisions about technology, new-product development, and manufacturing inevitably affect marketing decisions and marketing success. Thus, a corporate strategy focused on time-based competition and speedy innovation requires that marketing plan for continued new-product introduction and relay feedback on customer information to the product-development department so as to help speed the innovation process. If a firm decides to focus on being the lowest-cost producer, low selling price becomes an essential element of the global marketing mix.

**Impact of Differences among National Markets**

Keeping in mind the linkages between a firm's overall global strategy and global marketing strategy, a decision must be made between *standardization* versus *adaptation* to local markets. Management complexity is reduced with a completely standardized marketing mix applied without change to all national markets. But usually some local adaptations are necessary to accommodate differences in consumer tastes, income levels, government regulations, and differences in distribution channels and structure of competition.

In trying to decide what degree of adaptation is appropriate, the firm must consider the factors that distinguish different national markets:

- Buyer profiles differ across countries; their tastes, income, culture, and buying-decision processes are different.
- The marketing infrastructure differs from country to country; different kinds of media are available in different countries, and there are differences in what products and messages are acceptable in advertising.
- Variations in countries' transportation and communications systems affect marketing approaches such as the use of mail-order. Different legal provisions may govern conditions of sale.

- Distribution systems are different, in the number of layers and in ease of access, while differences in the physical environment of various national markets may dictate changes in product design and sale.

## Some Adaptation Will Be Necessary

The real question is not whether to adapt, but how much to adapt. Some elements of the marketing mix are more likely to be standardized than others. The basic product itself probably needs to be standardized in order to permit economies of scale in manufacture. Firms are also likely to standardize brand names and the basic advertising message. Adaptation is more likely in areas such as packaging, pricing, sales promotion and media decisions, distribution channels, and after-sales service. Although management will be motivated to standardize in order to reduce costs and management complexity, satisfying consumers in different markets and responding to competition should be the main criteria. Further, government restrictions could circumscribe the degree of standardization possible.

## The Global Marketing System

Doz and Prahalad stress the importance of managing the *global marketing system*.[27] They focus on managing net prices in the various markets so as to control global cash flow. The global marketing system, in their view, has three components:

1. Presence in multiple markets so as to take advantage of their differences—that is, use high prices and cash flow in markets where the firm is dominant and competition weak in order to subsidize market penetration by charging lower prices in other markets. (Of course, this assumes that leakage of low-priced products back into the high priced markets is not a danger.)
2. Global brand presence and strong distribution to help achieve target prices in various markets.
3. Deployment of extended product lines and product families across countries to gain economies of scope and greater competitive strength and allow opportunities for cross-subsidization across businesses and across national markets.

## Coordinating the Global Marketing System

As mentioned earlier, coordination of global marketing activities is as essential as configuring marketing activities across national markets. Table 6–3 summarizes some of the coordination issues, highlighting the adaptation-standardization dichotomy for various elements that enter into formulating a global marketing strategy. Such coordination can take place in the following ways:[28]

1. *Using similar methods to carry out marketing activities across countries.* Avon Products' use of door-to-door selling of cosmetics in different markets or some companies' use of similar standards for warranty and after-sales service across countries are examples of such an approach.
2. *Transferring marketing know-how and experience from one country to another.* This is particularly true in transferring information gained in lead markets to other countries.

**Table 6–3**                     **Global Marketing Strategy Choices**

|  | Total Standardization |  | Complete Adaptation |
|---|:---:|:---:|:---:|
| ***New-Product Development/ Product Line*** | X | | |
| ***Marketing Mix:*** | | | |
| Product Positioning | | | X |
| Market Segmentation | | X | |
| Brand Policy | X | | |
| Packaging | | | X |
| Advertising and Promotion | | X | |
| Distribution Channels | | | X |
| Pricing | | | X (Pricing) |
| Customer Service | | X | |
| ***Country Markets:*** | | | |
| Market 1 | X | | |
| Market 2 | | X | |
| . | | | |
| . | | | |
| . | | | |
| Market *n* | | | X |

X = a hypothetical firm's choice

Source: Adapted from John Quelch and E. Hoff, "Customizing Global Marketing," *Harvard Business Review* (May–June 1986).

3. *Sequencing marketing programs*, so that successful elements are gradually introduced into different markets, often in conjunction with evolution of the product life cycle there.

4. *Integrating efforts across countries*, so that international clients with operations in many countries can be offered the same service in each country. For example, a client may wish to use the same computer equipment or software at all of its international subsidiaries. Closing such a sale might require coordination of the sales effort in key markets where the largest subsidiaries are located; a clincher might be offering worldwide service with a response time of 48 hours maximum.

## Targeting Individual Country Markets

Since management must determine the sequence in which various global markets should be entered, an essential ingredient of global marketing is assessing their attractiveness. Criteria include current size and growth prospects, the product life cycle stage in that market, level of competition, similarity to existing markets, and the extent of government restrictions.

**Corporate Goals and Choice of Markets**

The firm's objectives will help decide which markets are attractive, as shown in Table 6–4. Three kinds of objectives are apparent:

- Short-term and long-term returns on investment in the form of profits and cash flow.

**Table 6-4**                          **Market Characteristics and Corporate Objectives**

|  | Goal | | | |
|---|---|---|---|---|
|  | Competitive Response/ Retaliation | Cash-Flow/ Profits | Market Share | Lead Market Entry |
| Market Characteristics Size/Market Potential Growth Prospects Margins Product Life Cycle Stage Similarity to Existing   Markets Level of Competition Basis of Competition:   Value-added Chain   Emphasis Government Attitudes |  |  |  |  |

- Market-share objectives, partly aimed at maintaining competitive balance and serving to provide credibility in exchanging threats with key global competitors.
- Entry into lead markets, with learning objectives paramount, at least initially. (A special case might be that of protected markets, but even here, entry is based on either attractive economic returns or the impact on a global competitor of gaining market share in the protected market.)

Firms primarily interested in profits will seek high-growth markets where less competition will be encountered and higher margins are offered, and may consider early entry into protected markets.

Firms that are aggressively challenging their competitors will prioritize markets based on growth characteristics and market share held by key competitors. They will enter markets that offer a chance of achieving reasonable market share, which can then be used as a deterrent in cross-patrolling (exchange of threat) with key global competitors.

Firms seeking to establish a presence in lead markets will choose markets based on the growth prospects and product life cycle stage, with little attention given to competitors' market share or their own profit and market-share prospects.

Lastly, firms seeking to enter protected markets will first evaluate the likelihood of establishing cordial relations and favorable treatment from local government.

A firm may have different objectives for different markets. Typically, it will seek strong profits and cash flow from one or two critical markets, including its home market. It might adopt market-share and competitive-balance objectives for emerging markets where the competition is strong. Simultaneously, it might seek protected markets in large developing countries. But firms will find it easier to develop an integrated global strategy by consciously tailoring objectives to country-market characteristics.

## Market Positioning in the Triad Economies

In considering which national markets to enter, most firms seek to balance their market position in three major regional markets: *North America*, consisting of the U.S.–Canada market; *Europe*, especially important as a single unified market after 1992; and the *Japan/Southeast Asia* market, consisting of the rich high-income Japanese market and the fast-growing neighboring countries of Taiwan, Hong Kong, South Korea, Singapore, Thailand, and Malaysia. These market regions are sometimes referred to as the *triad economies*. When oil prices recover, the OPEC countries will constitute another significant block of markets. The communist nations of East Europe represent another group of markets with possible future potential if they adopt free-market approaches to economic growth. Then there are the developing countries of the world, including those large self-contained markets of India, Brazil, and China, and the smaller nations ranging from low-income to poor to extremely poor.

Certain nations and industries manifest a pattern in their expansion into foreign markets. For example, U.S. companies typically begin overseas expansion by branching into Canada, the United Kingdom, and then Europe. Studies of Japanese companies show some distinct patterns of overseas market expansion.[29] Japanese typically begin with establishing themselves in the domestic Japanese market. Then one pattern of expansion is to refine international strategies in the developing countries neighboring on Japan before moving into advanced developed-country markets such as the United States; such a pattern has marked Japanese expansion in steel, petrochemicals, autos, watches, consumer electronics, and cameras. A slightly different pattern emerges in high-technology industries, such as computers, where Japan expanded into markets similar to the United States, such as Australia, before entering U.S. and European markets.

Equally significant was the manner in which Japanese companies built up a marketing network in foreign markets. Initially, they used independent distributors, such as regional wholesale jewelers in the United States to sell watches. Next, after sales had reached a reasonable level, they began establishing their own branches and sales companies, taking control of local advertising, promotion and after-sales service. Subsequent steps included local production in developing and developed countries and eventual establishment of a global integrated manufacturing and sales network.

## Responding to Regional Integration

Changing economic and political circumstances within a country can affect a firm's global strategies. The creation of a single European market in 1992, and the U.S.–Canada Free Trade Agreement, represent two examples. Both are attempts at regional integration that reduce barriers between markets within the region, leading to market growth.

**The EC in 1992.**   Companies have responded to European plans for a single market by taking over other companies with significant market share and brand presence in major European markets. Nestle's takeover of Britain's

Rowntree PLC is an example. Nestle held about 4 percent of the world's confectionery market when its Swiss rival, Jacobs Suchard AG, attempted to acquire Rowntree (having previously acquired Chicago based candymaker E. J. Brach and Sons). Nestle reacted by buying Rowntree for $4.3 billion. Rowntree's strength is in the fast-growing segment of chocolate-coated candies containing caramel, cookies or nuts (brands such as Kit Kat, Rollo and After Eight). Earlier, Nestle had acquired the Italian food firm Buitoni, whose brands include Perugina chocolates, increasing its global market share to 11 percent. The possibility of pushing more established brands through existing distribution channels and acquiring new channels in other European markets are the two reasons driving the consolidation.[30]

There was a similar rush to buy established food brands put on sale by RJR Nabisco. RJR was selling five major food companies in Europe. Their attractions were[31]

- Walkers, a potato chip and snack food company, with a number one market share in the United Kingdom.
- Smiths, a British snack food company, with a number one market share.
- Belin, a French firm selling premium cookie products and snacks, with a number one market share position in snacks and number two in biscuits.
- Saiwa of Italy, the third-ranked biscuit company in Italy.
- U.K. Biscuits, a maker of cookies and crackers, with a number two market share.

Each of these firms had a dominant market position in a national market, and the acquiring company could seek to expand sales into neighboring countries, capitalizing on and extending brand presence across national borders. It takes time to develop such brand presence and to develop distribution channels in the various European countries. Saving time while preempting the competition is perhaps the most significant reason for such acquisitions. The single market planned for Europe in 1992 adds pressure to establish a significant pan-European brand presence before the competition does so. Sometimes this requires developing Europe-wide manufacturing facilities, or striking strategic alliances, or acquiring key firms in European nations where the firm has a weak market presence.

Reactions to the U.S.–Canada free-trade agreement have been similar, with the lowering of tariffs leading to a reshuffling of manufacturing activities. Large-volume manufacturing is being concentrated in the United States, with more specialized low-to-medium-volume production being shifted to Canadian factories; again, firms hope to achieve cost reductions that could be used to lower prices and increase sales in both the United States and Canada.[32]

## Marketing to Japan

The Japanese market is considered difficult to break into. It is a highly competitive one, usually requiring considerable adaptation, which is easier with well-informed local operations handling Japanese market research and advertising. Japanese distribution can be Byzantine. But, although it takes time to establish adequate control of distribution channels, the effort is well worthwhile.[33]

As Japan's wealth grows, the large-car segment is the fastest-growing part of the automobile market. In 1987 imported cars accounted for over one-third of the large-car segment (over 2-liter engines). And West German manufacturers accounted for over 70 percent of all Japanese car imports. How West German car manufacturers have gone about winning sales in Japan is instructive:[34]

- Both BMW and Mercedes Benz have set up their own independent dealer network in Japan, replacing the former reliance on Japanese importers.
- They have used financing as a marketing tool, offering low interest rates and long repayment periods. One result is that monthly payments on the costly imports are about the same as on domestic cars.
- Targeted and heavy advertising is used. Mercedes advertises mainly in the economic daily newspaper, *Nihon Keizai*, thus reaching about 50 percent of its customers. BMW advertises weekly with 60-second spots in prime-time television. Advertising stresses the BMW corporate image, since Japanese buyers seem swayed more by the reputation of the company than by product-specific features.
- Price stability is also used. Both BMW and Mercedes have kept yen prices constant, aided by the rising yen.

Of course, neither German auto manufacturer faced Japanese competition. Now that Toyota, Nissan, and Honda have all introduced upscale models such as the Lexus, Infiniti, and Acura, maintaining market share may be more difficult for them.

Why have the Japanese been unable to dominate the PC industry worldwide with a low-cost strategy (see "Global Marketing")? How have IBM, Compaq, Zenith, and Apple been able to stay on top? Japanese market share in the United States has increased marginally, from 13 percent in 1984 to 16 percent by 1988, while U.S. share has dropped only slightly, from 68 percent to 62 percent. The relative Japanese failure might be due to the following factors:[35]

1. The small domestic market in Japan means that Japanese manufacturers cannot obtain large-volume manufacturing and sales at home.
2. While the U.S. PC market has coalesced around a common operating system, MS-DOS, Japan has several competing standards.
3. The PC components industry is global, with U.S. manufacturers buying lowest-cost components wherever they might be available, be it the United States, Taiwan, or wherever.
4. The price-sensitive end of the business is dominated by mail-order companies such as Dell Computer, offering little competitive space for a solely price-based Japanese strategy.
5. The major U.S. firms use a variety of actions to get higher margins: a strong brand image, nationwide after-sales service, control of distribution channels, particularly retail dealer space, with discounts between 40 to 50 percent off list price, "soft dollars," and subsidies to support advertising, promotion, and customer training by dealers. Compaq assures dealers that they will never have to compete against Compaq salespeople, in selling to large Fortune 500 firms, for example.[36]

## Global Marketing
### Global Strategy in the Personal Computer Industry

The product cycle seems to be playing out in the personal computer industry. While the United States has long been the biggest market, the European market is growing faster. IBM's PC unit in Europe had a 48 percent growth in units in 1988, while Apple doubled sales. Consumption is forecasted to reach $30 billion and 9 million PCs a year in 1992, matching U.S. market size. This amounts to a 20 percent annual growth and about twice the expected U.S. growth rate. Compaq Computer expects that Europe will account for half of its revenues by 1992.

If the expected growth materializes, prices should fall, because of greater volumes and scale economies. Local content will rise as U.S. manufacturers try to save on freight and import duties of about $160 per unit by building larger plants in Europe. Locations such as Scotland's Silicon Glen become attractive as European volumes rise. Apple has expanded its plant in Cork, Ireland to stop importing Macs from the United States, has a new R&D center in Paris to develop network software for Macs, and has begun developing Mac software in local languages.

European computer dealers have typically been small and limited their operation to one country. The House of Computers is representative, with 20 outlets in West Germany in 1988. Apple prefers such small dealers, as they can be persuaded to sell only Macs. However, mergers among European dealers from different nations are likely, and could create continent-wide dealer networks, changing marketing strategies.

European competitors such as Olivetti, Siemens, and Philips will attempt to take advantage of European growth, and could become stronger, even as opportunities abound for the major U.S. suppliers. Olivetti had the number two market share in Europe, and had developed a partnership with AT&T. But its market share dropped from 10 percent to 8.5 percent, and it fell to a number four position, behind IBM, Compaq, and Apple, due to quality problems and slowness in adding new products. In an effort to recover, it has begun supplying PCs to Digital Equipment Corp. and was the first to introduce an advanced PC based on Intel's 80386 chip, as well as a clone of the IBM PS/2. Though based in Italy, it has considered moving its entire marketing organization to Paris to provide a more European outlook.

Sources: "Apple Takes a Bigger Bite Out of the Continent," *Business Week*, December 19, 1988; "Europe's Appetite for PCs May Surpass U.S.'s After 1992 Market Unification," *The Wall Street Journal*, March 31, 1989; "Can Cassoni Get Olivetti off the Slippery Slope," *Business Week*, June 12, 1989.

6.   The major U.S. firms are effectively listening to the customer and thus avoiding mistakes that would give the Japanese an advantage. For example, Compaq uses focus groups and carefully monitors customer responses to decide what mix of features to incorporate in new products. It consequently knew to delay introduction of laptop computers until display and battery technology were improved.

7.   The major U.S. firms have been innovating rapidly: 90 percent of Compaq's sales come from products introduced within the last two years. Such innovation includes the use of the latest microprocessor chips from Intel and Motorola, and IBM's new MicroChannel bus and Compaq's EISA standard (though it is not clear how well these have been accepted). U.S. manufacturers may get advance notice of innovations from their U.S. source suppliers. In software, both Unix and OS/2 are possible candidates to dominate the next generation of PCs. The point is, PC design has not been stable long enough for Japanese firms to begin to derive competitive advantage from lowering costs.

Japanese response has been interesting—an attempt to maintain a presence in various emerging segments of the personal computer industry, including the engineering workstation and the NEXT computer. While Canon has invested $100 million for a 16 percent share of NEXT, Fujitsu has licensed the SPARC microprocessor, which is the heart of powerful engineering workstations. On another slant, NEC has been developing its own microprocessors. Thus, the Japanese are staying in the game, waiting to see what shape the industry takes without closing off any of the major options.

## Summary

Most companies are being forced into marketing their products or services globally because (1) demand for their products is global and (2) they face global competition.

Global marketing strategy must form part of and be consistent with a firm's overall global strategy. There are linkages between the two in areas such as technology, manufacturing, organization structure and finance.

Formulating global strategy begins with corporate strategies that cut across product lines. Then product-line strategies are formed, influenced by the industry, the firm's competitive advantage and its value-added chain. Other important influences are the environment, competition, government actions, and the firm's customers and suppliers.

Next, the firm sets product-line strategy for individual markets. It will also consider whether to standardize policies across markets or adapt them to individual markets.

Basic strategies are to become the lowest-cost producer, provide a differentiated product, or seek government protection against foreign competition. Configuration and coordination decisions follow. In configuring value-added activities, companies typically choose between market extension, a multi-domestic perspective, and a global perspective.

Some of the variables to be considered in adopting a global orientation include differences in global markets, customers, and competition; different host-government policies, technology, production resources, and the time factor.

The government's policies can influence strategy, by keeping foreign competition out and by subsidizing the global strategies of "national champion" firms.

A company may be willing to sacrifice short-term profits for higher market share, or it may place priority on its competitive position worldwide rather than in specific national markets. This suggests that a portfolio approach to individual national markets may be shortsighted, causing a firm to cede competitive position to German and Japanese multinationals with longer-term orientations.

Global competitors emerge by (1) diversifying out of national markets that they dominate, (2) diversifying into new products, or (3) extending their product lines into new-product segments. Suppliers are another source of competition.

Factors leading to adaptation in global marketing strategy include differences in: customers; marketing infrastructure; legal, transportation and communication systems; and distribution channels. In general, national markets are sufficiently different that adaptation in some elements of the marketing mix will be necessary.

Another component of a global marketing system is market position: should the company aim to sell the same product to different segments in the various country markets or sell to the same segment in each country with some product adaptation?

Coordinating the global marketing system is a complex task. Some common methods include using similar marketing approaches across countries, transferring marketing know-how and experience, sequencing marketing programs across countries, and integrating approaches to multinational clients.

Management must decide which countries to target. Factors relevant to this decision include market size and growth, the product life cycle stage in that market, the level of competition, similarity to markets already served, and the influence of government restrictions. In general, multinationals will seek market position in all three of the triad economy regions: United States, Europe and Japan.

Another challenge is to respond to regional integration, such as the creation of a single European market in 1992. Alliances and acquisitions are two common approaches. The key goals are to obtain distribution and brand presence in a timely manner across Europe.

Another marketing challenge is selling to Japan. The critical issues are providing quality, overcoming the Japanese preference for domestic products, and working with complex distribution systems.

## Questions

6.1   Why must companies think globally?

6.2   What is a global industry?

6.3   How is marketing strategy linked to global strategy?

6.4   What are some factors that affect global strategy at the level of the firm?

6.5   How can management attitudes affect global strategy?

6.6   What are some factors that influence global strategy at the product-line level?

6.7   What is the value-added chain? How is it relevant to a firm in formulating a global strategy?

6.8   What are some goals that a firm might set for itself in individual country markets?

6.9   What are the basic strategies open to a firm in the global marketplace?

6.10   What does "configuring the value-added chain" mean? How do firms differ in their perspective on configuring the value-added chain in different countries?

6.11   What are some factors that lead a firm to think globally?

6.12   What is a "lead" market? Why is it important?

6.13   Give an example of how time and speed of response affect global competition.

6.14   Why is it dangerous to adopt a portfolio approach in international marketing?

6.15   How can government policies affect a firm's ability to compete globally?

6.16   Explain why standardization versus adaptation is a fundamental issue in international marketing.

6.17   Highlight the key issues in coordinating the global marketing system.

6.18   How would a firm target individual country markets?

6.19   How do the predictions for Europe in 1992 affect a firm's *global marketing strategy* in Europe? Why have firms reacted by acquiring and merging with other European firms?

6.20   Discuss global competition and marketing strategy in the personal computer industry worldwide.

# Endnotes

[1]Peter Drucker, "The Transnational Economy," *The Wall Street Journal*, August 25, 1987.

[2]Gary Hamel and C. K. Prahalad, "Do You Really Have a Global Strategy," *Harvard Business Review* (July–August 1985).

[3]Hirotaka Takeuchi and M. Porter, "Three Roles of International Marketing in Global Strategy," chap. 4 in *Competition in Global Industries*, ed. M. Porter (Boston: Harvard Business School Press 1986).

[4]Kogut, Bruce, "Designing Global Strategies: Comparative and Competitive Value-Added Chains," *Sloan Management Review* (Summer 1985):15–27.

[5]"Small Motors, Big Profits," *Forbes*, July 11, 1988.

[6]M. Porter, "Competing in Global Industries: A Conceptual Framework," chap. 1 in *Competition in Global Industries*, ed. M. Porter (Boston, Mass.: Harvard Business School Press, 1986).

[7]See Thomas Hout, M. E. Porter, and E. Rudden, "How Global Companies Win Out," *Harvard Business Review* (September–October 1982).

[8]Michael Schrage, "A Japanese Giant Rethinks Globalization," *Harvard Business Review* Vol. 67, No. 4 (July–August 1989): 71.

[9]*Komatsu Ltd.*, Harvard Business School Case Services #9-385-277.

[10]Kenichi Ohmae, *Triad Power: The Coming Shape of Global Competition* (New York: Free Press, 1985).

[11]Jean-Pierre Jeannet and H. Hennessey, *International Marketing Management* (Boston: Houghton-Mifflin, 1988), chap. 8, 259.

[12]"The Silicon Valley Greater Co-Prosperity Sphere," *Forbes*, December 17, 1984.

[13]"The Hottest Thing Since Cinerama," *Forbes*, September 4, 1989.

[14]"Belgian Cinema Leads World," *The Wall Street Journal*, September 11, 1989.

[15]"Producers of Scanners That Read Prices Tries Patent Suit to Fend Off Japanese," *The Wall Street Journal*, April 24, 1989.

[16]George Stalk, "Time—The Next Source of Competitive Advantage," *Harvard Business Review* Vol. 66, No. 4, (July–August 1988).

[17]Ibid., 45.

[18]See also Joseph L. Bower and Thomas Hout, "Fast-Cycle Capability for Competitive Power," *Harvard Business Review* Vol. 66, No. 6, (November–December 1988).

[19]"Japanese Computer Firms See a Market in Domestic Customers' U.S. Operations," *The Wall Street Journal*, May 4, 1988.

[20]"All Shapes and Sizes: A Survey of the Civil Aerospace Industry," *The Economist*, September 3, 1988.

[21]"Videotex in France: High-Wired Society," *The Economist*, August 19, 1989.

[22]Michael Dertouzos, Richard Lester, Robert Solow, et al., *Made in America* (Cambridge, Mass.: MIT Press, 1989).

[23]"Ardent's Daddy Warbucks," *Business Week*, June 12, 1989.

[24]"Thomson: Battling on," *The Economist*, July 15, 1989.

[25]Yves Doz and C. K. Prahalad. *The Multinational Mission* (New York: The Free Press, 1987).

[26]"When Made-in-Europe Isn't," *The Economist*, October 8, 1988.

[27]Yves Doz and C. K. Prahalad, "The Dynamics of Global Competition" in *The Multinational Mission* (New York: The Free Press, 1987), 47–48.

[28]Hirotaka Takeuchi and M. Porter, "Three Roles of International Marketing in Global Strategy," chap. 4 in *Competition in Global Industries*, ed. M. Porter (Boston: Harvard Business School Press, 1986).

[29]Somkid Jatuspritak, Liam Fahey, and Philip Kotler, "Strategic Global Marketing: Lessons from the Japanese," *Columbia Journal of World Business* Vol. 2, No. 1, (Spring 1985): 47–53.

[30]See "Swiss Go On a European Shopping Spree" *The Wall Street Journal*, August 31, 1988; and "How Much Chocolate Can the Swiss Devour," *Business Week*, May 9, 1988.

[31]"RJR Puts 5 European Units on Block, Sparking Scramble by Global Food Firms," *The Wall Street Journal*, May 10, 1989.

[32]"Getting Ready for the Great North American Shakeout," *Business Week*, April 4, 1988.

[33]"Ways into Fortress Japan," *The Economist*, October 22, 1988.

[34]"Foreign Business in Japan: Drive on, Fritz," *The Economist*, October 22, 1988.

[35]"Personal Computers: Staying American," *The Economist*, August 19, 1989.

[36]"Soft Dollars, Hard Choices," *Forbes*, September 4, 1989.

# Further Readings

Dertouzos, Michael, Richard Lester, Robert Solow, et al. *Made in America*. Cambridge, Mass.: MIT Press, 1989.

Doz, Yves, and C. K. Prahalad. *The Multinational Mission*. New York: The Free Press, 1987.

Ghoshal, Sumantra. "Global Strategy: An Organizing Framework." *Strategic Management Journal* (October 1987).

Hamel, Gary and C. K. Prahalad. "Do You Really Have a Global Strategy." *Harvard Business Review* (July–August 1985).

Hampton, Gerald M. and Erwin Buske. "The Global Marketing Perspective" in *Advances in International Marketing*, vol. 2, ed. S. Tamer Cavusgil. Greenwich, Conn.: JAI Press, 1987.

Hout, Thomas, M. E. Porter, and E. Rudden. "How Global Companies Win Out." *Harvard Business Review* (September–October 1982).

Kogut, Bruce. "Designing Global Strategies: Comparative and Competitive Value-Added Chains." *Sloan Management Review* (Summer 1985): 15–27.

Ohmae, Kenichi. *Triad Power: The Coming Shape of Global Competition*. New York: Free Press, 1985.

Porter, M., ed. *Competition in Global Industries*. Boston, Mass.: Harvard Business School Press, 1986, especially chap. 1, "Competing in Global Industries: A Conceptual Framework."

Quelch, John A., and Edward J. Hoff. "Customizing Global Marketing." *Harvard Business Review* (May–June 1986).

Stalk, George. "Time—The Next Source of Competitive Advantage." *Harvard Business Review* (July–August 1988).

Takeuchi, Hirotaka, and M. Porter. "Three Roles of International Marketing in Global Strategy" in *Competition in Global Industries*, ed. M. Porter. Boston: Harvard Business School Press, 1986.

# 6.1   Windmere Corporation

Windmere Corporation, headquartered in Miami Lakes, Florida, sells a variety of hair, beauty and personal-care products to consumers and professionals (barber shops and beauty salons). It celebrated its twenty-fifth year in business in 1988. Although it was originally a wholesale cash-and-carry barber and beauty supply store, over time, emphasis has shifted toward consumer products.

Windmere is one of the largest U.S. suppliers of curling irons and curling brushes, and a leading seller of hand-held hair dryers, instant hair setters, and lighted cosmetic mirrors. It introduced its first 1,000-watt hair dryer in 1973. Today it sells such items as the Crimper, a curling iron that adds texture and volume to hair with a permanent-wave effect; kitchen appliances such as toasters and fans; and a product called the Clothes Shaver that is designed to remove lint and fuzz from woolen, linen, and other garments. Table 1 summarizes Windmere's product-line performance.

Case prepared by Associate Professor Ravi Sarathy, for use in classroom discussion. All rights reserved. Source: Windmere Corporation Annual Reports; "Windmere Tries to Comb Out the Kinks," *Business Week,* July 24, 1989; and "U.S. Importers Aren't Jumping Ship—Yet," *Business Week,* June 26, 1989.

## Windmere Production Policies

Most of these products are manufactured in Hong Kong and China, through the Durable Electrical Metal Factory Ltd., a joint-venture manufacturing operation. Windmere first subcontracted with Durable in 1972 and acquired a 50 percent joint interest in the late 1970s. In 1981 Durable expanded capacity by setting up a factory in mainland China. Windmere faced production constraints in Hong Kong with labor shortages and rising wage rates. It chose Durable as its local joint-venture partner because Durable had the contacts and expertise to begin discussions with the People's Republic of China concerning the establishment of a factory in China.

The factory is vertically integrated, manufacturing its own tool and dies and injection molding equipment. Besides manufacturing components, it also carries out quality testing and assembly. Advantages to owning its production facilities in China include

- Maintaining a continuous flow of new products, with innovative designs that lower costs of production.
- Providing tooling for new products at low cost.
- Reducing the lag between product innovation and market launch.

**Table 1   Windmere Product Line Performance**

| | Percent of Sales [a] | |
| | Consumer Products | Professional Products |
|---|---|---|
| 1988 | 60% | 33% |
| 1987 | 59 | 38 |
| 1986 | 65 | 33 |
| 1985 | 68 | 28 |
| 1984 | 65 | 32 |

[a]Remainder of sales from foreign markets

- Allowing flexibility in production scheduling according to sales performance of product items, so that inventory build-up and risk of inventory obsolescence can be reduced.
- Providing control over quality during every phase of manufacturing so that the rigorous standards of the U.S. marketplace can be met.

Durable is one of the largest low-cost producers of small appliances in the Far East. Of a total of 1.7 million square feet of factory space, 1.5 million is located in the People's Republic of China, where about 80 percent of Windmere's products are manufactured. The rest of the factory space is in Hong Kong. Of 12,000 employees, 10,000 are in China, which makes Windmere one of the largest foreign employers.

The Durable factory facilities are expanded and upgraded constantly. For example, Durable has recently begun to manufacture motors and handle electroplating, anodizing, spray painting, and powder coating. These abilities allow it to take on the manufacture of new products for third parties with clients such as Sunbeam, Waring, Krupps, Bausch & Lomb, and Trion—products such as toasters, blenders, hand mixers, air cleaners, soft contact lens cleaners, waffle irons, heaters, and other home appliances. These third-party sales increased to $50 million in 1988, from $16 million in 1987, $6 million in 1986, and only $500,000 in 1985. Such incremental sales allow existing capacity to be utilized more fully, leading to greater recovery of fixed costs and, consequently, higher profits.

Of course, the bulk of Durable's sales still go to Windmere (see Table 2). The decision to seek third-party business was made in 1984 as excess capacity developed, and Windmere reduced its purchases from Durable in 1985.

Windmere's share of profit in 1988 from its Durable manufacturing plant was about $5.7 million. Over the years, it has accumulated earnings of $67 million from its foreign operations, on which no taxes have been paid, as the profits have not been repatriated to the United States but instead used to reinvest in expanding foreign operations.

## Implications of Manufacturing in the People's Republic of China

Building on its expertise in China, Windmere has begun helping other companies who want to develop manufacturing operations there. For instance, it helped an embroidery manufacturer set up a factory in Hong Kong and China in return for a percentage of profits.

Investing in expanding manufacturing operations in the Far East may be risky. Capacity must be utilized, which means that Windmere must continue to sell its share of the output of the Durable factory. As Table 2 shows, Durable's sales fell in 1985 because Windmere reduced its purchases. Because the Chinese and Hong Kong factories are distant from the principal market, the United States, Windmere must cope with inventory shortages in the United States by shipping products by air freight, which adds to total delivered costs. The additional time needed to move goods from the Far East factories to the United States means that additional inventories must be maintained, resulting in higher working capital and carrying costs. At the end of December 1988, the combined inventories of Windmere and Durable totaled $84.5 million, compared to a total combined sales of $222.5 million (after deducting inter-company transactions between Durable and Windmere).

Because of the fixed costs of the facility in China, Windmere must continue to expand its U.S. sales to ensure efficient factory operation. It has concentrated on developing its Windmere and Belson brand names, developing a national TV campaign around the theme, "It doesn't cost a fortune to look like a million." So far it has gained large national retail clients such as K Mart, Target Stores, Caldor, and Lechmere.

## Efforts at Expanding Sales

Windmere's new-product introductions have been successful, with strong sales for the Clothes Shaver and the Crimper. It has also branched out into selling fans, humidifiers, heaters and other seasonal products through a 50 percent owned

**Table 2   Durable Company Profile**

|      | (Millions of Dollars) | | Percent Manufactured in PRC | Number of Employees |
|      | Total Sales[a] | Sales to Windmere | | |
|------|------|------|------|------|
| 1988 | $181.1 | $100 | 83% | 12,000 |
| 1987 | 71.5 | 55 | 80 | 7,500 |
| 1986 | 35.3 | 28 | 50 | 6,000 |
| 1985 | 26.4 | 17 | — | — |
| 1984 | 46.2 | 33 | — | — |

[a]Includes inter-company sales to Windmere

PRC = People's Republic of China

joint venture with Paragon Sales, now one of the three largest distributors of electric oscillating fans in the United States. (Earlier in its history, Windmere had distributed Australian-made Mistral fans on an exclusive basis.) The company has acquired additional products such as the Comare line of brushes and combs from Comair, and a line of skin- and nail-care treatments under the brand name of European Secrets. It has also sought new market segments. It combined its lighted make-up mirror with a wall-mounted hair dryer and began direct marketing the "appliance amenity" to hotel chains such as Sheraton and Radisson.

Expanding the number of Save-Way beauty-supply stores, which sell to professional barber and beauty trade (though open to the public at retail prices), it added 60 stores in 1987 alone, to reach a total of 151 stores concentrated principally in the Southeast United States—Florida to Virginia, and west to Alabama. Windmere is one of the largest operators of professional beauty-supply stores in the country.

## Windmere's International Marketing Focus

Windmere has begun emphasizing international sales, particularly in Canada (see Table 3). Foreign markets, principally Britain and Canada, have been supplied with products through a company-owned trading company based in Hong Kong. A new Canadian subsidiary was created in

1985 to take control of sales that were previously handled by distributors.

This move led to Canadian sales of $10.6 million in 1987, up from $2.6 million in 1986. At the same time, Windmere decided to close down Hairflayre, its joint-venture subsidiary in the United Kingdom, due to poor results, choosing to use established independent distributors instead. It adapted products for the U.K. and European markets, including a European-style variable-temperature hair dryer, and a mini dual-voltage hair dryer for worldwide travel.

Not all of its international business forays have been successful. At one point, Windmere licensed the Ronson brand name, and began selling rotary-head electric shavers purchased from a Japanese supplier. The market leader was Norelco, which sells products manufactured by Philips of the Netherlands. Norelco promptly accused Windmere of patent violations and won the case on grounds of unintentional patent infringement. As a result, Windmere had to write off $1.4 million in inventory and tooling and decided to abandon that market.

## Recent Windmere Actions

Earnings in 1988 after taxes were $32.6 million, up from $11.9 million in 1987. Windmere decided to acquire control of the Durable joint venture by raising its ownership to 80 percent in exchange for 750,000 shares, valued at about $13 million. Windmere also sold the Save-Way

**Table 3    Windmere Corp. Revenue Breakdown by Geographic Region**

| | (Millions of Dollars) | | | |
| --- | --- | --- | --- | --- |
| | **Total Sales** | **U.S. Sales** | **International Sales** | **Gross Margins** |
| 1988 | $193.3 | $145.0 | $48.3 | 41.1% |
| 1987 | 145.2 | 113.3 | 32.0 | 40.0 |
| 1986 | 95.3 | 79.1 | 16.2 | 39.6 |
| 1985 | 91.0 | 74.9 | 16.1 | 38.4 |
| 1984 | 91.0 | 76.3 | 12.4 | 39.6 |
| 1983 | 73.6 | 66.1 | 6.5 | 41.6 |

beauty-supply line of business for approximately $24 million. It began marketing air cleaners, which it had formerly sold only to Sears, through a 50 percent joint venture with Trion. Another new product was PlakTrac, a counter-rotational plaque-removal device. And Windmere began using independent distributors to penetrate new markets in Japan and Australia.

But 1989 saw a reduction in the rate of sales growth, and inventories began increasing. Earnings declined 11 percent. Then, on June 4, 1989, the Chinese army moved against students in Tiananmen Square. Investors began to worry about the safety of investments in mainland China. Production declined in its Chinese factories, and its stock price fell from a high of $27 a share to below $10. Is Windmere, in relying on 30¢ an hour Chinese labor, on shaky ground?

## Questions

1. Has Windmere been successful? What are the elements of its international strategy?
2. What choices has it made with regard to the value-added chain? And how has it been configured? Why?
3. Analyze Windmere's strategy in terms of comparative and competitive advantage. Do you see any weaknesses in its strategy choices?
4. What are the risks to Windmere of manufacturing in China? What other risks does Windmere face?
5. Analyze Windmere's product line; are these differentiated products? What is your estimate of the demand for such products over the next three to five years in the United States, Europe, and Japan? Could competition easily arise in these product lines?
6. What do you recommend that Windmere do over the next two to three years? And for the longer term?

CASE

# 6.2 A. L. Labs, Inc.

A. L. Labs manufactures and distributes generic pharmaceuticals and animal feed. The U.S. unit is majority-owned and controlled by its Norwegian parent, A. L. Oslo; 1988 was the first year that U.S. sales accounted for more than 50 percent of total (worldwide) sales.

## Animal-Feed Segment

A. L. Labs began operating in the United States by selling animal-feed additives. Patent protection on bacitracin had expired, and the Norwegian parent company developed a biologically stable and effective product branded as BMD, sold as an antibiotic mixed into feed to aid in animal growth and to prevent disease. Major U.S. markets were the broiler and swine industries. Since it left no residue in animal tissue, and thus could not be ingested by humans, BMD easily met the human-safety standards of the U.S Food and Drug Administration (FDA) and was able to boast an advantage over the penicillin, tetracycline, and sulfa products already on the market. Another advantage of BMD is that bacteria do not build up resistance to it as they do to penicillin and tetracycline. Sales of BMD and other bacitracin antibiotic products accounted for 16, 21, 24, and 25 percent of total company sales in 1988, 1987, 1986, and 1985, respectively.

New manufacturing processes helped raise quality and reduce production costs. In the United States, enhanced technical service marketing focused on educating potential users of the product's advantages. The company carried out a constant round of controlled animal tests to establish the optimal relationship between amounts of BMD used, in its various formula-

Case prepared by Associate Professor Ravi Sarathy, for use in classroom discussion. All rights reserved. Source: A. L. Labs Prospectus, June 30, 1988; Annual Reports 1987 and 1988.

tions, and animal weight gain. Such studies helped convince farmers that BMD in the most economic doses would work with a variety of modern animal-feed rations. Promotion of new potential applications led to rapid acceptance of BMD in the United States. It has achieved considerable penetration in the poultry market, and promotional efforts gradually raised penetration in the swine industry from 20 percent a few years ago to around 35 percent in 1988. (It has not been introduced in the cattle market yet.)

In 1982 A. L. Labs began manufacturing BMD in a U.S. plant in Chicago Heights, purchasing fermentation cultures from A. L. Oslo as well as paying annual royalties (of 2.5 percent on sales) in return for the license from the parent company to produce BMD in the United States; capacity had been expanded several times. By 1987, capacity limits had once again been reached at the Chicago plant, and additional purchases of BMD from Norway were being made while plant expansion was being considered. As the Danish kroner had appreciated against the U.S. dollar, this also increased production costs, for imported BMD was more expensive than that produced in U.S. plants. In the years 1985 through 1988, A. L. Labs' purchases from its parent totaled $7 million, $9.3 million, $8 million, and $9 million, respectively, while license fees paid to the parent for the same period were $.6 million, $.8 million, $1 million, and $1.1 million, respectively. But such foreign sourcing is partly due to having a foreign parent company with a global manufacturing capability including factories in Copenhagen and Jakarta, Indonesia, as well as in the United States (in Chicago Heights, Baltimore, and Niagara Falls).

Subsequent to the success of BMD, new products introduced for the animal-feed market included Vitamin D3, a life-essential nutrient required by livestock and poultry for proper growth

**Table 1  A. L. Labs Revenues**

|  | 1988 | 1987 | 1986 | 1985 |
|---|---|---|---|---|
| **Sales by Segment (Millions of Dollars)** | | | | |
| Animal Health | $ 51 | $46 | $39 | $32 |
| Pharmaceuticals | 149 | 85 | 58 | 40 |
| Human Nutrition | 36 | 27 | 26 | 25 |
| **Sales by Geographic Region (Millions of Dollars)** | | | | |
| U.S. Sales | $132 | $73 | $47 | $29 |
| Percent of Total Sales: | 55 | 46 | 38 | 30 |
| Foreign Sales | 108 | 87 | 78 | 69 |
| Percent of Total Sales: | 45 | 54 | 62 | 70 |
| **Foreign Sales by Geographic Region (Percent of Total Sales)** | | | | |
| Europe (primarily Scandinavia) | 21% | 30% | 26% | |
| Far East | 17 | 16 | 26 | |
| Other | 6 | 8 | 10 | |
| U.S. | 56 | 46 | 38 | |
| **Assets by Geographic Region (Millions of Dollars)** | | | | |
| U.S. Assets | $155.3 | $40.1 | $20.6 | |
| Foreign Assets | 95.5 | 79.4 | 71.7 | |

and health. Animals normally produce D3 when in contact with direct sunlight. But as commercial farming of livestock and poultry is done indoors in artificial light, D3 must be provided as a micronutrient feed additive. A. L. Labs' premium brand called "Color-Guard Vitamin D3" is a brilliant blue, permitting visual verification that it has been mixed in the feed. Another new product is a water-soluble concentrated form of BMD called Solutracin for treatment of poultry diseases. Plans are to extend the use of BMD to the cattle market and to improve the efficiency of marketing to animal-feed markets so as to take advantage of the growing consolidation of farms and the trend to larger farms.

Table 1 provides information on the proportion of revenues derived at A. L. Labs from each of its three major product segments, as well as from overseas sales. As can be seen, the company has gradually increased the proportion of its business derived from the United States; at the same time, it has diversified away from animal feed so that its principal product line now is pharmaceuticals, specifically, generic pharmaceuticals.

## Generic Pharmaceutical Segment

By 1985, A. L. Labs had begun focusing on the distribution of generic pharmaceuticals and increasing its presence in U.S. markets. This shift was based on the satisfactory results from acquiring Dumex Ltd., headquartered in Copenhagen, Denmark. Dumex functions partly as a European development division, building on known pharmaceuticals and formulating and shepherding new drug applications through the approval process in Europe. Dumex also can obtain Danish government funding for new drug projects.

For example, Dumex obtained a grant to work with physicians in developing a treatment for a skin disorder, acne rosacea, that is generally treated with antibiotics, which may lead to undesirable side effects and resistance problems. Metronizadole, a generic antibacterial, was combined with Decubal, an existing Dumex skin cream. The result was a new drug, Elyzol, which has already received approval in Sweden and Denmark and captured a dominant market share. The drug is now being registered in other European countries and will soon be in the United States; clearly, there are opportunities for cross-fertilization of new drug discoveries between Europe and the United States. Dumex relied on sales reps to sell in Europe; but as new branded products are created, it has taken more control of its sales, creating three new sales organizations alone in 1988 in West Germany, Switzerland, and Portugal.

Hence, in 1986 A. L. Labs acquired ParMed, a distributor of generic pharmaceuticals. Along with telemarketing to pharmacies, the company used an in-house magazine, *The Prescription*, to provide information about new generic pharmaceuticals and their profit potential (equal, the company claims, to that of branded drugs). ParMed helps independent pharmacists cope with the mandate to prescribe generics for Medicare-paid prescriptions. A side benefit for A. L. Labs is that telemarketing selling techniques perfected at ParMed can be tried out in foreign markets.

## Diversification Into Liquid Pharmaceuticals

In 1987, in A. L. Labs' biggest move, Barre Labs was acquired for almost $100 million. Barre began operations in 1923 and, concentrating on liquid generic pharmaceuticals, has attained a strong position in cough and cold remedies, which typically have higher sales in the winter months. Taste, texture, appearance, and fragrance are all important in manufacturing liquid versions of drugs. The total market in 1988 was $150 million, with only about 12 percent of all approved liquid drugs having a generic counterpart, compared to 24 percent of generic capsules and tablets. Of course, profit margins on generic drugs are lower, and fall as more manufacturers begin making a particular one, and as the major drug companies cut prices on their branded products once the period of patent protection expires.

Liquid pharmaceuticals are particularly important in the over-65 (geriatric) market, and in pediatric markets (particularly children under 6).

Senior citizens, who use two to three times the pharmaceuticals that other segments of the population do, prefer liquid pharmaceuticals. And the senior citizen group is a growing segment.

The increased concentration on generic pharmaceuticals also seems appropriate given passage of the Medicare Catastrophe Coverage Act of 1988, which mandated that U.S. pharmacies must dispense generic drugs when filling Medicare patients' prescriptions unless a physician specifies otherwise. A. L. Labs expects generics to capture 22 percent of a $1.8 billion total liquid pharmaceutical market in the United States in 1995. Barre's current 40 percent market share should therefore increase.

The effects of the Barre acquisition were to (1) give A. L. Labs a strong position in selling to the geriatric market, the largest consumer of liquid pharmaceuticals, (2) increase its presence in the U.S. market, and (3) reduce the preponderance of foreign sales, and thus the volatility resulting from rapidly changing exchange rates of European currencies vis-a-vis the dollar.

Barre's position in liquid pharmaceuticals has been described by I. Roy Cohen, CEO, as the "wings of the business"; he says that A. L. Labs deliberately chose the liquid drug market over pills and capsules to avoid competition. Barre plans to diversify into ointments, aerosols, and injectables. A part of its strategy is to concentrate on "unit-of-use," that is, exact quantities of liquid drugs in prescription-sized tamper-resistant containers. Many pharmacists use gallon jugs of liquid pharmaceuticals, pouring out quantities needed for each prescription. Barre plans to stress the potential liability problems that this might create.

Barre was purchased from Revco Labs, which had gone private in a leveraged buyout and was raising capital by shedding what it thought were peripheral business lines. A. L. Labs plans to sell more Barre products to large drugstore chains, a plan that Revco as a major chain could not as easily carry out. Barre Labs also provides products that can be introduced into Europe, complementing new products supplied by Dumex and A. L. Oslo.

**Table 2   A. L. Labs: Sales and Profits (Millions of Dollars)**

|  | Total Sales | Net Income |
|---|---|---|
| 1988 | $236.5 | $8.75 |
| 1987 | 159.0 | 6.60 |
| 1986 | 123.6 | 5.50 |
| 1985 | 96.8 | 5.50 |
| 1984 | 88.4 | 4.31 |
| 1983 | 47.6 | 1.61 |

## Human Nutrition:
## A Candidate for Divestment?

The third major line of business is human nutrition. A. L. Labs' human-nutrition products consist principally of formulated powdered-milk products developed by Dumex and sold mainly in the Far East, in Malaysia, Singapore, and Thailand, and in the Middle East, as well as through the P. T. Dumex subsidiary in Indonesia and its licensees. Dumex receives royalties from a license granted to two subsidiaries of the East Asiatic Company of Denmark (EAC), located in Malaysia and Thailand. Dumex sales of human-nutrition milk products in 1988, 1987, 1986, and 1985 to the two subsidiaries of EAC totaled $29.7 million, $22.7 million, $23.2 million, and $18 million, respectively.

Dumex recently granted an option to EAC to acquire the Dumex trademark in 1995, while preserving the flow of royalties from Dumex sales in the Far East for the next ten years. While competition is heavy in this line of business, Dumex has the advantage of an established brand name. It obtains raw materials by buying bulk powdered-milk supplies from the New Zealand Dairy Board for processing and sale as formulated milk products in the Far East. This line of business has exhibited slow growth, with demand fluctuating, as in Nigeria, where oil-related recession reduced demand considerably.

Overall, A. L. Labs has managed to achieve sales growth without sacrificing profits. Table 2 summarizes sales and net income after taxes at A. L. Labs during the period of 1983 through 1988. Of course, past sales and profit success is no guarantee of continued prosperity, and A. L. Labs is constantly reassessing its plans for the future.

## Questions

1. What are the benefits to A. L. Labs of having a foreign parent? How has this affected its choice of strategy in international marketing?
2. Trace the evolution of A. L. Labs' product and geographic-area strategy. What are the strengths of the approach adopted? And what, in your opinion, are the flaws in its approach to global markets?
3. Most U.S. companies attempt to increase their foreign sales. A. L. Labs has been successful in decreasing foreign sales as a percent of total sales to the point where U.S. sales now account for over 55 percent of total sales. Why has A. L. Labs chosen to implement such a strategy?
4. Why has A. L. Labs positioned itself so that generic pharmaceuticals have become its largest product line?

# CHAPTER 7

# International Marketing Intelligence

*Learning Objectives*

When a firm initially considers marketing to the world, it finds world markets to be "foreign" in several senses. They are located outside the firm's home country; they have different languages, currencies, and customs; and they are unknown to management. Lack of knowledge of world markets is thus the first barrier to overcome in marketing internationally. Marketing decisions cannot be made intelligently without knowing the environment. For this reason, our study of international marketing management will begin with the nature and scope of international marketing intelligence.

The goals of this chapter are to

1. Review the range of tasks involved in international marketing research. We outline typical problems encountered in conducting research overseas and ways to solve such problems.
2. Present techniques for conducting research, including analysis of demand, regression analysis, and cluster analysis.
3. Discuss the screening of international markets and give an example showing the typical steps involved.
4. Explain how to evaluate information collected through international marketing research. We also address how a company should be organized to carry out research effectively.
5. Discuss the role of models in market research, and present a detailed model for deciding the mode of market entry.

## Breadth of the Task

*International marketing intelligence* is more comprehensive than domestic marketing research. Although all the firm's domestic marketing research studies are potential candidates for international application, they are not sufficient to provide all the information necessary to make sound international marketing decisions. The firm needs an *information system* to not only identify and measure market potential in foreign markets, but also take into account the many cultural, political, and macroeconomic variables that are ignored or assumed to be constant in domestic studies.

One group of specifically international parameters affecting marketing decisions are the economic factors considered in Chapter 2. A second group are the political-legal aspects of international relations as discussed in Chapter 5. A third element is the analysis of competition. Although the firm must analyze the competitive situation in each market, this kind of analysis alone is not sufficient. Because competition in many industries is now international, the study of the competitive situation must also be multinational. It cannot be limited to studies of individual markets.

Finally, international comparative studies are a further dimension of analysis. As can be seen, the distinctiveness of international marketing intelligence arises from the fact that the firm is operating within a *number of foreign environments*. These differences necessitate not only the adaptation of domestic techniques but also the development of new methods of analysis. The scope of the international researcher's task is apparent in the following notice:

> The International Division is seeking a research analyst to work on broad scope individual projects relating to . . . international economic and marketing research. . . . *The general subjects which will be researched are economic statistics, sales and marketing forecasts, distribution methodology, market planning on existing and new products, and* related subjects which would have an impact on aggregate marketing plans for given geographical areas. . . . Because of the scope of the projects, it is necessary to have a much broader familiarity with economic and marketing subjects than may be normally required for a marketing research professional. [Emphasis added.]

The smaller firm in international marketing will have information needs similar to those of the large firm. However, it must rely more on others for its international information needs — its distributors, licensees, or joint-venture partners, for example. Or it may choose to market through another firm that has superior knowledge of foreign markets.

**What Information?**

An enormous amount of information is available on the countries of the world, but there are also information gaps in certain matters of interest to business. To economize on research funds and to facilitate storage of the data, the researcher wants only relevant information. Table 7–1 identifies the major decision areas requiring information.

In a broad sense, *marketing* involves all the decisions a firm makes in relating to its markets. For this text, we assume that the firm has already decided to go international, so we shall look primarily at the other decisions. The next decision, then, is which world markets to enter. Since the firm cannot usually sell to all world markets, it must find a way of ranking them according to their attractiveness. This will require an investigation of their market potential and the local competitive situation. Once the firm has identified desirable target markets, it must decide how to serve those mar-

| Table 7-1 | **The Task of International Marketing Research** |
|---|---|

| Marketing Decision | Intelligence Needed |
|---|---|
| 1. Go international or remain a domestic marketer? | 1. Assessment of global market demand and firm's potential share in it, in view of local and international competition and compared to domestic opportunities. |
| 2. Which markets to enter? | 2. A ranking of world markets according to market potential, local competition and the political situation. |
| 3. How to enter target markets? | 3. Size of market, international trade barriers, transport costs, local competition, government requirements, and political stability. |
| 4. How to market in target markets? | 4. For each market: buyer behavior, competitive practice, distribution channels, promotional media and practice, company experience there and in other markets. |

kets — by exporting, licensing or local production, for example. For these decisions on market selection and market entry, Richard Holton, using game-theory language, suggests three questions to ask:[1]

1. Who are the players? Who are the competitors, customers, suppliers, government officials and others who can affect our operations?
2. What strategic alternatives or actions is each player likely to consider?
3. What are the probabilities attached to each strategic alternative?

Once a decision has been made to market in a particular country, the conventional marketing questions will arise. These are usually classified into functional areas such as product decisions, pricing decisions, or channel decisions. These decisions can be further broken down until eventually a very specific local issue is reached — the kind of package and label that should be used for the firm's floor wax in the Philippines, for example.

Each firm needs to identify the people making international marketing decisions. The next step is to find out what marketing decisions these people make. The final step is to determine the information necessary for these marketing decisions.

As a starting point, each person making the marketing decisions would probably have a checklist of data necessary for his or her own decisions. For example, in planning the annual advertising campaign in country $X$, the subsidiary advertising manager would have a list including the following items: budget allowance; competitors' activity; distributors' promotion; media costs, availability and coverage. As experience and sophistication in-

Figure 7–1                                    **The Problematic Task of International Marketing Research**

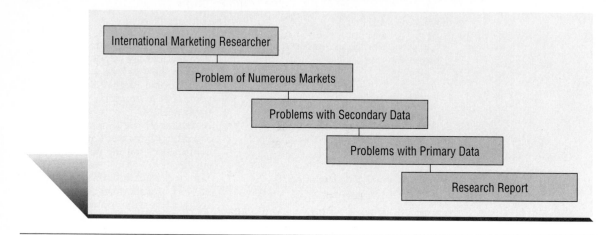

crease, the checklist becomes a model, which not only includes the data but shows their interrelationships. As Andrew Gross notes "It is vital to have a conceptual framework, an idea of how markets function for a given product."[2]

For the firm new to international marketing, no tested model may be available for reference. The researcher is not without guidelines, however. The checklist that the firm has developed for domestic operations can be a useful starting point. Insights into the changes required for a foreign market could be obtained in part from potential foreign collaborators such as distributors, advertising agencies, licensees, or joint-venture partners. If the firm already has foreign experience but is new to a particular market, it can draw on all its other foreign experience in approaching the new market. Comparative analysis can be very useful in reducing the firm's ignorance about the new market.

## Problems in International Marketing Research

Because of its complexity, the task of international marketing research gives rise to more and different problems than are encountered in domestic marketing research (Figure 7–1). One problem is that intelligence must be gathered for *many markets* — over 100 countries in some cases — and each country poses a unique challenge. A second problem is the frequent absence of *secondary data.* Most research begins with a study of secondary data, and there is a wealth of such data in some industrialized countries. For most world markets, however, there are serious lacks. A third problem is the frequent difficulty in gathering *primary data.*

**Problem of
Numerous
Markets**

Multiplying the number of countries in a research project multiplies the costs and problems involved, though not in a linear manner. There are some economies in designing multinational studies. Offsetting these economies are the unique nature and requirements of each national market. Because the firm's markets are not identical from one country to another, the research manager must be alert to the various errors that can arise in replicating a study multinationally. Mayer identifies the following kinds of errors to look for in multinational research:[3]

1.   *Definition error.* From the way the problem is defined in each country.
2.   *Instrument error.* Those arising from the questionnaire and the interviewer.
3.   *Frame error.* Sampling frames are available from different sources in different countries.
4.   *Selection error.* The way the actual sample is selected from the frame.
5.   *Nonresponse error.* Different cultural patterns of nonresponse. Example: in one five-country study, the response rate ranged from 17 percent to 41 percent. Furthermore, in one country women were 64 percent of the respondents while in another country men were 80 percent of the respondents.

Marketing research entails large expenditures in the U.S. economy. These sums can be effectively used here, however, because of the size of the market and the expertise available. In foreign markets, the cost may be the same to design and implement a marketing study as it is in the United States, but the potential market is smaller, usually involving a much smaller population as well as a lower per capita income. For example, even though India has a population three times as large as the United States, its total GNP is much less than one-tenth the American GNP. In considering the smaller size of the foreign market added to the other problems, the researcher must ask: *How much* research can I afford to do abroad?

It is not easy to answer this question. Less reliable figures on the cost of research in foreign markets make a cost-benefit analysis difficult. Calculating the benefits is also difficult because less is known about the foreign market. Comparative analysis of foreign markets can shed some light on cost-benefit parameters.

**Problems with
Secondary Data**

Secondary data for market analysis are less available and less reliable in many foreign markets. The lower the per capita income in a country, the weaker the statistical sources.

The use of probability sampling is necessarily limited where the nature of the relevant universe cannot be reliably determined. Quota sampling is limited for the same reason, so the most frequently employed technique is the *convenience sample.* This is defensible primarily because of a lack of alternatives. Trade associations are often important data sources for particular industries. Unfortunately, trade associations do not even exist in some countries, whereas in a number of others, their data are neither complete nor reliable.

**Comparing Several Markets.**   We have been considering the data problems in individual markets, but another difficulty arises when comparing several markets. When the researcher makes a list of the kinds of data needed from the several markets, there will be many gaps when the data are compiled. On some items, data may be available in only half the countries. This is not the extent of the difficulty, however. Even the analyst who has data from all the countries on certain items will often find that the data are hardly comparable.

The lack of comparability may result from varied causes. Different base years may have been used in different countries, or the underlying definitions may not have been the same. The terms *commercial vehicle, wholesaler,* or *family dwelling* may mean something a bit different in each country. An example comes from a youth market survey done for a soft drink firm. The data available on the "youth market" came in the following categories from different countries: the 10–14 age group, the 13–20 group, the 14–18 group, and the 15–24 group. Differing degrees of accuracy in data gathering can be another cause of lack of comparability.

Finally, the private data and information-gathering agencies so valuable in American marketing research are often missing in foreign markets. *Ward's Automotive Reports,* the Dodge reports on the construction industry, and the Audit Bureau of Circulation are examples of widely used data services. In addition to these are the information services or studies available from magazines and newspapers, universities, banks, advertising agencies, and so on. No other country has the wealth of information services available to the American marketing researcher; and some countries have practically no services at all. Table 7–2 shows the international availability of the largest research services. Most cover only a few countries.

**Problems with Primary Data**

Much of marketing research involves getting information from people about their attitudes concerning a company's products, brands, prices, or promotion. This reliance on human subjects as the primary source of marketing intelligence gives rise to what we might call "people problems." Whereas production inputs generally behave the same way in all countries, people generally do not. The tourist may find such diversity glorious, but it is a complication for the researcher, for whom a tidy uniformity would be more manageable and efficient.

**Languages.**   Language is the initial cultural difference that comes to mind when one thinks of foreign markets, and it was discussed at length in Chapter 4. At the minimum, language difference poses problems of expense and communication. For the American firm, there is probably the expense of double translation. First, the research design and specifications must be translated from English into the language of each country where a study is to be conducted. Then, on completion of the study, the results must be

| Table 7–2 | **The Top Ten Research Companies Worldwide** |
| --- | --- |

| Company | Research Revenues (Millions of Dollars) | Countries with Office | Headquarters |
| --- | --- | --- | --- |
| A. C. Nielsen | 765 | 27 | New York |
| IMS International | 298 | 64 | New York |
| Pergamon/AGB | 195 | 21 | London |
| SAMI/Burke | 170 | 2 | Minneapolis |
| Arbitron | 155 | 1 | Minneapolis |
| Information Resources | 106 | 1 | Chicago |
| GfK Group | 102 | 11 | W. Germany |
| Research International | 93 | 14 | New York |
| Infratest | 67 | 6 | W. Germany |
| Video Research | 66 | 1 | Tokyo |

Source: *Advertising Age,* December 5, 1988.

translated back into English. Of course, marketing research used exclusively by a national subsidiary does not need to go through these steps.

More important than translation expense is the communication problem, which, as mentioned, is discussed in Chapter 4.

**Social Organization.**   Much of marketing research is concerned with gaining insights into the buyer's decision process. Such research is predicated on the assumption that the decision makers and influencers have been identified. In foreign markets, the researcher usually finds that the social organization is different enough that it is necessary to identify anew the decision makers and influencers. This subject, including the varying roles of women, is discussed in Chapter 4. Adaptation can affect the efficiencies otherwise attainable in international marketing research; the more the research has to be adapted to each market, the fewer economies of scale.

Differences in social organization affect the industrial market as well as the consumer market. The nature of the decision-making structure in foreign companies is likely to be quite different from that in American companies. One reason is the greater importance of family business in other countries. When family business is combined with an extended family structure, it means that the family relationships must be identified. Organization charts or titles are much less meaningful than family ties in influencing decisions.

**Obtaining Responses.**   Marketing activities and the marketing profession are not held in high esteem in most countries. Manufacturers have a production orientation and little interest in the market. Where the respondents are business people, their reluctance to participate may stem from various motives. Where tax evasion is common practice, respondents may suspect the questioner of being a government tax representative rather than a legitimate market researcher, or they may be reluctant to respond for fear of giving up information to competitors. The idea of business people giving information to anyone, government or private person, is not well accepted in many countries. One of the researcher's greatest problems is trying to demonstrate the value of the research to the respondent personally. Unless this can be done, little will be accomplished with business respondents.

Consumers, too, may be reluctant to respond to marketing research inquiries. This may be in part the result of a general unwillingness to talk to strangers. Respondents are more reluctant to discuss personal consumption habits and preferences than are Americans. In contrast to the reluctant respondent is the cooperative respondent who feels obliged to give responses that will please the interviewer rather than state true opinions or feelings. In some cultures this is a form of politeness, but it obviously does not contribute to effective research.

Reluctant or polite responses are not the only barriers. Occasionally, the respondent is not able to answer meaningfully. For example, illiteracy is a barrier when written material is used. This problem can be avoided by using purely oral communications. Even when the interview is oral, however, a communication problem that could be called "technical illiteracy" may arise. That is, the terms or concepts used might be foreign to respondents, even though in their own language. They may not understand the questions and thus be unable to answer. Or they may answer without understanding, giving a useless response.

Quite apart from the terms used, respondents may be unable to cooperate effectively because they are asked to think in a way foreign to their normal thought patterns. They are being asked to react analytically rather than intuitively. Because they do not reason in the same way the research designer does, they may not be able to answer in a meaningful way. Even business respondents may have difficulty if they are asked in their own language about stock turnover or other business concepts which they have never used. Whatever the particular cause of the inability to respond, it is basically a translation problem. The research designer must be able to translate not only the words but also the *concepts*. The cultural gap must be bridged by the research designer.

**Infrastructure Constraints.**   In addition to the human and social difficulties just considered, the researcher in foreign marketing encounters technical problems that are not encountered at home. The problems here arise primarily in less developed countries. Good research is a function not only of proper design but also of implementation, which is often contingent upon factors the researcher cannot control. The researcher usually depends on some economic and commercial infrastructure in conducting research. This subject is touched on in Chapter 3.

Mail surveys, for example, require both literacy and a reliable postal service. Many less developed countries are largely rural, and postal service in these areas is not very dependable. Therefore, mail surveys may not be an available option. Data collection by telephone may not be, either. In the Philippines less than 10 percent of homes have a telephone.

If mail and telephone surveys are not practical, the researcher is left with personal interviewing as an alternative. With a largely rural population in the poorer countries, the problem then becomes physically reaching the people. Poor roads and lack of regular public transportation may make interviewing them economically unfeasible. In tropical areas many roads are impassible during the rainy season. Surveys may be limited primarily to urban areas.

Communications and transportation have been discussed, but there is an aspect of the commercial infrastructure that also bears on the conduct of marketing research. Especially in foreign markets, the firm is unlikely to be able to do 100 percent of the marketing research task. Because of its smaller market and staff there, it depends on supporting services available in the local economy. Such resources include personnel qualified to do research and firms that will handle all or part of the research. Because of the large U.S. market and the strong demand for marketing research, a great number of specialized supporting services are available in the United States.

Unfortunately, the smaller size of most foreign markets coupled with the lesser development of marketing there mean that research support services may not be available, especially where they are most needed. Organizations like A. C. Nielsen have moved into many industrialized countries but into few less-developed areas. Consumer panels and other techniques tend to be available in Western Europe and Japan, but absent from most other countries. Because such operations are too costly for any one firm to establish, these techniques and services are crossed off the list of available tools in many markets.

## Techniques for Dealing with International Marketing Research Problems

Defining a problem is the first step toward its solution. A preliminary identification of problem areas has been sketched above. The researcher in a company will need a more specific analysis of the problems peculiar to the firm's own situation. However, the problems would fall within the general outline given. Once the problems have been identified, what approaches are possible? A firm might, of course, forget about international marketing research since the problems are so great. However, the costs of missed opportunities or marketing mistakes must be compared to the costs of improved marketing intelligence.

An American tire producer built a plant in France without any special marketing research. The company felt it knew the market because of its experience in exporting there. However, driving habits were undergoing changes with resultant changes in the kind of tires wanted. Soon after the plant went on stream, costly production adjustments had to be made to match the new market demand. An initial result of this experience was the hiring of a skilled international marketing research executive. A few years later when another plant was to be built in Italy, the company conducted a detailed marketing analysis before giving the project a green light.

As another example, consider the case of Cluett Peabody, which closed down its Belgian factory after three years of operation. The plant was built as the keystone of Arrow's European distribution but it never really got off the ground. Cluett blamed high social-welfare costs, but Belgian retailers claim a complaisant Belgian management assented to American styling, pricing, and sizing out of keeping with European tastes and pocketbooks. Either cause of failure could have been avoided by appropriate preliminary research.

What the research activity requires is the enlistment of national participants, members of the cultures and markets being studied. There are various ways of getting this assistance. If the firm is new to a market, it can hire a national research agency to supply local knowledge (assuming such an agency is available). The national agency should help the firm avoid the cultural blunders and communication failures that result from an approach alien to the market.

If the firm already has some experience in a foreign market, it is in a much stronger position — first, because experience is the best teacher; and, second, because there are many more nationals it can call on. Its distributors and service agencies in the country can supply local understanding. Its own national employees can be even more useful in this regard. Again, Chapter 4 touches on this subject.

## Improvisation

Some improvisation is probably used in all marketing research, but a higher degree is needed in international markets, especially in communist and developing countries. *Improvisation* may be loosely defined as unconventional ways of getting the desired market information and/or finding proxy variables when data are not available on the primary variables. Some examples follow.

Hill studied the research methods of British firms selling capital goods to Eastern European countries. He found that very little useful published information was available, so the following approaches proved the most useful in studying the market:[4]

1. Discussions with Soviet importing organizations.
2. Participation in exhibitions in the U.S.S.R.
3. Contacts with the State Committee on Science and Technology.
4. Establishing an office in Moscow.
5. Participation in intergovernmental working parties.

Carr suggests borrowing a technique from anthropology to identify market areas in developing countries. The method uses the presence or absence of specialized institutions as an indicator of the size and development (and market potential) of communities. He cites an application from Thailand shown in Table 7–3. The value of this approach is that it gets around the lack of published data in developing countries. Data are gathered by observation as in an aerial survey or trip through the countryside. Furthermore, data do not need to be gathered on each item but only on the highest level

**Table 7–3**                            **Differentiation Scale of Rural Thailand and Associated Markets**

| Step | Content | Markets |
|------|---------|---------|
| 1. | Market square | Piece good cloth, light agricultural implements |
| 2. | Fair ground, food shops, farm support shops | Manufactured clothes, canned foods, radios, bikes, mopeds |
| 3. | Raimie fiber mill, Buddhist temple, elementary school, auto repair shop | Hardware, moped service, school supplies, light mechanical farm equipment |
| 4. | Government administration building, dispensary, secondary school, police | Doors and windows, social dresses, primitive plumbing supplies |
| 5. | Raimie sack mill, high school, sewer system | Light industrial machinery, cement, construction supplies, office supplies and equipment |

Source: Richard P. Carr. Jr., "Identifying Trade Areas for Consumer Goods in Foreign Markets," *Journal of Marketing* (October 1978): 76–80.

of differentiation, for example, a fairground, a temple, a government building, or a high school.[5]

A technique similar to Carr's use of the existence of certain kinds of marketplaces is the use of national consumption statistics for various items. Such statistics filter out exchange rate anomalies that arise in the use of currency-based economic indicators. Examples of such information are the following: the number of radios, televisions, and VCRs used; life expectancy at age one; the number of hospital beds available and doctors per 100,000 people; consumption of various food items on a per capita basis; the per capita availability of goods such as telephones, cars, motorcycles; the number of airline and train revenue passenger miles sold per year; consumption of electricity, steel; and the average number of years of schooling completed by the population.

All such indicators are generally available for a variety of countries and can be used to group countries and be correlated with market-size information.

**New Services to Aid the International Firm**

As international business continues to grow, more and more international marketing research services are appearing to aid firms. This includes the expansion of existing international marketing research organizations into more countries with more services, and the entry of new organizations into the field. It is not possible to catalog all of these but an example is International Information Services Ltd. (IIS), a global product pick-up service for consumer packaged goods manufacturers. It has 400 clients in over 30 countries, including Coca-Cola, General Foods, J. Walter Thompson, and Unilever. Each day supermarkets in 120 countries are "raided" by IIS shoppers buying products or searching for information needed by clients. They provide samples of competitive products, client products for monitoring of quality, and/or information on competing brands (ingredients, varieties, sizes, prices, etc.).[6]

| | |
|---|---|
| **Learn by Doing** | If the costs of primary marketing research would be too great, another way of learning about the market is to test it by exports. After a year or two of export experience, the firm will know more about actual market behavior than could be learned from a preliminary market study. If the market proves difficult or unprofitable, the firm can withdraw without major losses. If the market proves attractive, the firm might consider a heavier commitment in the country. |

## Other Techniques for Developing Countries

In the rich industrial countries, the marketing researcher can use all the analytical techniques that the firm uses in its domestic market. But many developing nations have small markets and inadequate data, making it impossible for the firm to conduct research in its regular fashion — or making the research prohibitively expensive in terms of the size of the market. In such cases, improvisation and special techniques may be useful. Reed Moyer has suggested several techniques that are relevant for researching the smaller, poorer markets.[7]

| | |
|---|---|
| **Analysis of Demand Patterns** | Countries at different levels of per capita income have diverse patterns of consumption and production. This commonplace observation is illustrated in Figure 7–2. Its importance lies in the fact that the researcher can usually get data at this macro level for most countries. This simple technique thus allows insights into the consumption-production profiles of many countries that cannot be studied using domestic techniques. Though relatively crude, it gives a clue both to a country's present position and the direction it is going. This in turn helps the firm identify possibilities for export or local production in that market. |
| **Multiple-Factor Indexes** | A multiple-factor index measures market potential indirectly, using as proxies variables that intuition or statistical analysis reveal to be closely correlated with the potential for the product in question. This technique is used in domestic marketing research, so we will not go into detail here but merely present an example.<br><br>Zoher Shipchandler was interested in forecasting the demand for television sets in international markets. His model said that sales of TV in a given country in a given year are a function of the market size for TV and consumers' capacity to buy TV. He operationalized this as follows: market size was indicated by the proxy variables number of households, percent of literacy, percent of urbanization, and percent in nonagricultural employment. Capacity to buy was indicated by per capita income, index of standard of living, price per unit, and price per unit per capita income.<br><br>Stepwise multiple regression was used in the study, which included 21 countries. The results conformed to expectations, and the model was considered useful for forecasting.[8] |

**Figure 7–2                                    Typical Patterns of Growth in Manufacturing Industries**

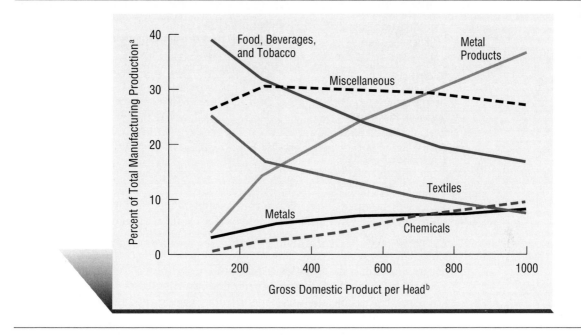

[a]Based on time-series analysis for selected years, 1899–1957, for seven to ten countries depending on commodity.
[b]Dollars at 1955 prices.

## Estimation by Analogy

For countries with limited data, estimating market potential can be a precarious exercise. Given the absence of hard data, there is one technique that can be helpful in getting a better feel for market potential in such countries: estimation by analogy. This can be done in two ways: (1) through cross-section comparisons and (2) through the displacement of a time series in time.

The *cross-section approach* involves taking the known market size of a product in one country and relating it to some gross economic indicator, such as disposable personal income, to derive a ratio. This ratio (of product consumption to disposable personal income in our illustration) is then applied to another country where disposable personal income is known in order to derive the market potential for the product in that country.

The *time-series approach* estimates the demand in the second country by assuming that it will have the same level of consumption that the first country had at the same level of development (or per capita income). This technique assumes that product usage moves through a cycle, the product being consumed in small quantities (or not at all) when countries are underdeveloped and in increasing amounts with economic growth.

Both approaches have limitations. The cross-section method assumes a linear consumption function. Both assume comparable consumption patterns among countries. When these assumptions are not true, the compar-

**Table 7–4**                          **Regression in Product in Use per 1,000 Population on per Capita GNP**

| Product | Number of Observations | Regression Equation | Unadjusted $R^2$ |
|---------|------------------------|---------------------|------------------|
| Autos | 37 | $-21.071 + 0.101x$ | 0.759 |
| Radio sets | 42 | $8.325 + 0.275x$ | 0.784 |
| TV sets | 31 | $-16.501 + 0.074x$ | 0.503 |
| Refrigerators | 24 | $-21.330 + 0.102x$ | 0.743 |
| Washing machines | 22 | $-15.623 + 0.094x$ | 0.736 |

Source: Reed Moyer, "International Market Analysis," *Journal of Marketing Research* (November 1968): 358.

isons will be misleading. When more sophisticated techniques are not feasible, however, estimation by analogy is a useful first step. Furthermore, it is an easy and inexpensive first step.

**Regression Analysis**

Regression analysis provides a quantitative technique to sharpen estimates derived by the deduction analogy method just discussed. Cross-section studies using regression analysis benefit from existing predictable demand patterns for many products in countries at different stages of growth. The researcher studies the relationship between gross economic indicators and demand for a specific product for countries with both kinds of data. The relationship derived can then be transferred to those countries that have only the gross economic data but not the product-consumption data. Moyer has illustrated this in Table 7–4. The equation used here was $y = a + bx$, where $y$ is the amount of product in use per thousand of population and $x$ is per capita GNP.

The regression results in Table 7–4 suggest that an increase of $100 in per capita GNP would result, on the average, in an increase of 10 automobiles, 10 refrigerators, 9 washing machines, 7 TV sets, and 27 radios per 1,000 population. Construction of such a table relevant to the products of a specific firm can be very useful.

We assume familiarity with regression analysis and will not discuss methodology here. There are limitations to its use, as well as benefits. For example, as a product approaches saturation levels, the rate of consumption would decline, requiring a different equation to explain the relationship. And some products do not lend themselves to a simple regression analysis. Moyer found a poor fit in trying to explain cement consumption per capita. Also, factors other than economic growth affect the patterns of consumption of different products. This technique assumes that relationships found in countries with data will hold for the countries lacking the data.

Nevertheless, even with these qualifications, regression analysis can provide useful insights. It is recommended as one way of beginning to understand markets for which good data are not available. Firms with operations in many countries have other resources to deal with data problems. As a company gathers information and experience in many foreign markets, it can use these to increase its understanding of all foreign markets through comparative analysis.

**Comparative Analysis**

Comparative analysis[9] is an attempt to organize information and experience to maximize their usefulness. In international marketing, this means that the company gathers and organizes its intelligence from all its global operations to see what new insights can be gained.

Grouping or classifying objects is an important step in understanding markets. Competing products can be grouped together to understand what are the different segments being targeted. Consumers can be grouped to assess customer segments. And countries can be grouped to determine which markets are similar to one another. This way, a generic strategy can be prepared for the countries belonging to a group, rather than approaching each country individually. Moreover, groups of countries can be compared in evaluating market performance. One of the difficulties of comparative market performance assessment is that markets are different, so the comparison may be unfair. Grouping similar countries mitigates this problem.

Parsimony is an important factor to keep in mind in conducting market research. Over 100 countries might be potential markets for a firm's products, and attempting to research every one of them would be foolhardy. What is needed is a way to identify the major markets for one's product, then examine this short list in greater detail.

**Cluster Analysis**

The approaches used to develop such a short list include comparative analysis of countries using macroeconomic and consumption data, with *cluster analysis* being a favored technique of identifying similar markets. The goal here is to ensure that the countries with the greatest potential make it to the short list for further investigation.

The mathematical techniques of cluster analysis were used by Sethi to develop seven distinct groups of countries. To develop these distinct groups, Sethi first used four sets of variables for each of the countries to be analyzed:[10]

1. *Production and transportation variables,* measured by items such as air passenger and cargo traffic, electricity usage, number of large cities, and population.
2. *Consumption variables,* based on income and GNP per capita, the number of cars, televisions, hospital beds, radios, and telephones per capita, and educational levels of the population.
3. *Trade data,* derived from import and export figures.
4. *Health and education variables,* using data such as life expectancy, school enrollment, and doctors per capita.

Once "scores" for these four variables were developed for each country, the countries themselves were grouped into seven distinct groups. The implication was that similarity of countries within the groups is sufficiently

**Figure 7–3**                          *BI* **Market Indexes: Size, Growth, and Intensity of 24 Largest Markets**

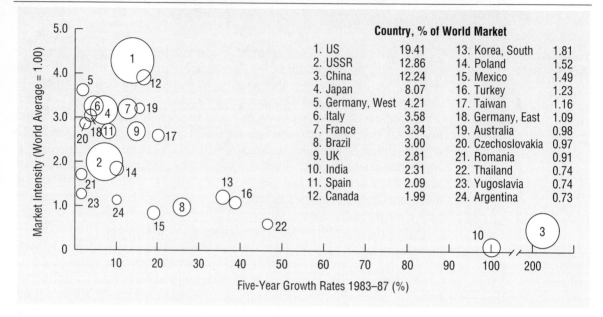

| Country, % of World Market | | | |
|---|---|---|---|
| 1. US | 19.41 | 13. Korea, South | 1.81 |
| 2. USSR | 12.86 | 14. Poland | 1.52 |
| 3. China | 12.24 | 15. Mexico | 1.49 |
| 4. Japan | 8.07 | 16. Turkey | 1.23 |
| 5. Germany, West | 4.21 | 17. Taiwan | 1.16 |
| 6. Italy | 3.58 | 18. Germany, East | 1.09 |
| 7. France | 3.34 | 19. Australia | 0.98 |
| 8. Brazil | 3.00 | 20. Czechoslovakia | 0.97 |
| 9. UK | 2.81 | 21. Romania | 0.91 |
| 10. India | 2.31 | 22. Thailand | 0.74 |
| 11. Spain | 2.09 | 23. Yugoslavia | 0.74 |
| 12. Canada | 1.99 | 24. Argentina | 0.73 |

Note: The position of the center of each circle shows the intensity of the market (when measured against the vertical axis) and its cumulative growth over the 1983–1987 period (when measured against the horizontal axis). The size of the circles indicates the relative size of the markets as a percentage of the total world market.

Source: "Indicators of Market Size for 117 Countries," *Business International,* July 3, 1989. Used with permission.

strong that similar marketing strategies can be used for all countries within a group.

Similar cluster analysis techniques are used by Business International (BI) to group markets based on the opportunities they offer (Figure 7–3). BI's indices cover market size, market growth rates, and market intensity (which measures the relative concentration of wealth and purchasing power in those countries). For example, the market-size index is derived from data on population, consumption statistics, steel consumption, cement and electricity production, and ownership of telephones, cars, and televisions. Note the similarity of the variables used at BI to those used by Sethi in his analysis.

**Screening Potential International Markets**

An example of using a screening process to derive a short list of key country markets is an application to the market for kidney dialysis equipment.[11] The first step is to determine which countries can afford such medical equipment. The high cost of kidney dialysis equipment and necessary supplies and personnel limit the market to wealthy countries. Hence, a *first screen* might be based on the wealth of a country, measured by

- A total GDP of over $15 billion.
- GDP per capita of at least $1,500.

## Global Marketing

### Pet-Food Market in Japan: An Opportunity?

The pet population in Japan was estimated at 10 million dogs and 5 million cats in 1988, indicating 18 percent of Japanese households having dogs and 7 percent having cats, compared with 38 percent U.S. dog ownership and 28 percent U.S. cat ownership. Pet-food sales aggregated 107 billion yen in 1986, a growth of 14.5 percent over the previous year. The entire pet market was estimated at about 500 billion yen in 1987. Thus, if the Japanese pet market were to approach U.S. levels, the total Japanese market could reach 80 trillion yen. Owning pets, pampering them, and spending money on their health, diet, and grooming, are all aspects common to advanced industrialized nations, which Japan is now a part of. The question is, having reached this economic milestone, will Japanese consumption habits also now approximate those of European advanced industrialized nations?

There are also demographic factors at work. Higher incomes, along with a crowded urban society, have led people to seek pets for company and solace. There are more people living by themselves in Japan than in the past: older people, unmarried single people, housewives whose children have left home: for them, the pet provides company, reduces stress, and enhances mental well-being. Even more important, the keeping of pets is seen as part of a new modern lifestyle, to which the young and newly wealthy middle class of Japan aspires.

Another facet of the pet-food market in Japan is the greater interest of Western pet-food companies such as General Foods, Heinz, and Purina. These companies have set up joint ventures with Japanese firms to introduce new pet foods, thus stimulating domestic competition. New kinds of firms revolving around the industry have sprung up, providing information on pet care and selling new species of dogs and cats and new species of animals, as well as pet accessories such as pet exercise aids, pet health products, and pet health care. An electrical appliance maker has introduced a kennel that retails for nearly $9,000, equipped with a floor-heating system, an air curtain to keep out mosquitoes, an insect-proof lamp, and ventilation and odor-killing devices. Furthermore, the kennel has a sun room and radio and television sets operated by remote control from the master's bedroom.

Another Japanese firm specializes in pet funerals, with a special hearse for pets, and a small smoke-free cremation furnace. On the market are pet showers and a home sanitation machine to catch fleas, kill odors, and clean pet stains from carpets. A variable peculiar to the Japanese market is the fact that living space is at a premium in Japan. A fundamental problem for apartment dwellers, which most Japanese are, is where to house the pet and how to keep the environment free of pet odor, hair, pet-food smells and pet wastes. This last is important, as Japanese neighbors are watchful and will exercise social pressure to prevent a pet owner from allowing his pet to soil the sidewalks, shrubs and telephone poles.

Source: Morio Murakami, "Profits in Pampered Pets," *Journal of Japanese Trade and Industry* (September–October 1988).

---

This screen alone reduces the number of potential markets to 28 countries outside North America.

Next, the markets must have specialized hospitals and doctors who can competently administer dialysis treatment. In addition, the treatment is expensive and requires a certain level of government support and subsidy, else the market for private patients alone would be too small to justify attempts at market penetration. Thus, a *second screen* would include

- No more than 200 people per hospital bed.
- No more than 1,000 people per doctor.

- Government health-care expenditures of at least $100 million.
- Government health-care expenditures of at least $20 per capita.

This results in a set of 19 countries as potential markets.

A *third screen* would analyze the markets in terms of the current market for dialysis equipment. Two factors are used:

- At least 1,000 deaths per year due to kidney-related causes. A lower number might indicate that the market for dialysis equipment is already being well served by competition.
- At least 40 percent growth in the number of patients being treated with dialysis equipment.

This results in just three markets being considered: Italy, Greece, and Spain.

A *fourth screen* consists of carefully evaluating the three countries in terms of existing competition, political risk, and other factors. Management subjectivity can enter here, since some managerial judgment is required in evaluating the strength of competition and political risk. Management may well decide to enter more than one of the three markets identified thus far. It may also go back to the third screening step and reduce the required rate of growth to, say, 30 percent, in order to gather some additional potential markets.

Once a short list of potential markets has been made up, individual markets must be studied more carefully. One approach is the Department of Commerce's Comparison Shopping Service (CSS). A CSS survey covers a product in a particular country market, answering questions about the product's overall marketability, chief competitors, comparative prices, customary entry, distribution and promotion practices, trade barriers, and how well the company's product competes. About 50 key countries are covered under this low-cost and timely service.

## Gap Analysis

The goal of gap analysis is to analyze the difference ("gap") between estimated total market potential and a company's sales.[12] The gap can be broken up into four categories:

1. *Usage gap.* This refers to total industry sales being less than the estimated total market potential. Such gaps may have their explanation either in estimation errors or in unpredictable changes in consumer tastes and behavior, such as, say, eggs being less in demand than expected. In the United States, such a usage gap would probably be traced to health-related concerns.

2. *Competitive gap.* This refers to existing market shares as against expected market share; analysis is needed to indicate why market share shifts have taken place, and what is needed to regain market share from competitors.

3. *Product-line gap.* This arises because a company does not have a full product line as compared to its competitors, thus losing sales. An example might be in the computer industry, where a part of the product line is small portable laptop computers. To the extent that IBM was late in marketing or did not have a laptop computer available, its market share was less than it would have been if it had fielded a full product line.

4. *Distribution gap.* Here the company is failing to target part of the market because of a lack of distribution facilities or agents. Closing such a gap would require that the firm extend distribution and product availability to cover all regions and segments of the market.

**Input-Output Analysis**

Input-output tables, discussed in Chapter 3, are an analytical tool of great value in studying demand in foreign markets. They are becoming increasingly available for many more countries, particularly for the advanced industrialized nations and the newly industrializing countries such as Brazil, Taiwan, and India. They are useful both for industrial product analysis and for the analysis of market demand for intermediate components and materials. Input-output tables give specific attention to how production functions vary among nations and thus allow the researcher to adjust market forecasts to take into account such country differences.

**Going Beyond Market Demand: Cost and Technology Trends**

Market research is focused mainly on market potential and consumer behavior. In international marketing, research into *cost and technology trends* is also essential. In addition, if the firm considers establishing a sales subsidiary, warehouses and service centers, and manufacturing operations, *political risk analysis* is necessary to assess whether it will be able to stay in the market for some length of time.

Cost trends shed light on relative cost competitiveness. For example, raw materials or components may be available from certain sources at lower cost than from others. Similarly, information about substituting newer low-cost materials — such as plastics for metal — and redesigning products to use fewer parts is relevant to a cost research study.

Technology trends reveal the future direction of new products and ultimately will affect sales and market share. Such research is generally focused on markets in which technological innovations are first presented. It aims to establish directions that the industry is likely to take and the relative position of key competitors in key technologies. For example, a major innovation in the computer industry is the growing use of specialized machines as file servers in a network. How soon such machines will become standard, how fast the current customer base will demand such file servers, and how quickly competition will introduce such machines are questions that research into technology trends attempts to solve.

## Evaluating Information

Because source materials are relatively abundant, the researcher's problem is often not how to find materials but how to select and evaluate them. Three criteria for evaluating international informational sources are: (1) the quality of the information, (2) its relevance to the decision maker's needs, and (3) its cost.

## Quality of Data

**Timeliness.** One quality of good data is *timeliness* — it should be up to date. All printed information is by nature historical, but some data are older than other data. The researcher needs especially the most recent material, but may also want that from earlier periods as a basis for determining trends. The number of years since data were published is usually, but not necessarily, an indicator of timeliness.

The researcher's objective is an accurate picture of the current situation. The timeliness of the data depends on what significant changes have occurred since their publication. For example, a public opinion poll in a political campaign may be out of date in a week. On the other hand, statistics on such items as per capita income, literacy rates, or the age distribution of a population might be reasonably valid five years or more after publication. Where the variables change rather slowly, the researcher can be less disturbed by having to work with "old" data, as is frequently necessary in international research.

**Accuracy.** Another aspect of the information's quality is its accuracy, which includes timeliness. However, statistics published at the same time may differ greatly in accuracy. If a demographic study were undertaken in a given year in both the United Kingdom and Zaire, it is highly probable that the latter study would be less accurate because of the research problems encountered.

*Definitions* are important to accuracy. In some instances, the statistical categories are too broad to be of value to the researcher. A category called "commercial vehicles" that includes taxis and all kinds of trucks is not very helpful to a firm supplying parts to a particular segment of that market.

*Objectivity* of the information supplier also affects the reliability of the information. If the supplier has an interest in encouraging a certain kind of behavior, the information may be inaccurate. Information provided for public relations purposes cannot be accepted on a par with more objective data. As a case in point, during a cholera epidemic in 1970 several countries did not report their cases because they feared such information would put a damper on their tourist trade as well as leave the rest of the world with an unflattering image of their country.

**Comparability.** Most international marketing research involves country comparisons. *Comparability,* discussed earlier in this chapter, is another important dimension of data quality. The company's information system can facilitate comparability by standardized reporting procedures for foreign subsidiaries. In any multi-nation study, however, the researcher will encounter several comparison problems mentioned earlier under "Problems in International Marketing Research." Skillful use of comparative analysis can help.

**Relevance of Data**

International market research is not the encyclopedia business; its only concern is with decision making in the firm. Therefore, the only relevant data are those that are useful for marketing decisions. Much information of good quality is not relevant. If the firm's information system is operating ideally, that information will not be sent to headquarters by the subsidiaries. This relevance criterion points again to the importance of a marketing information model to help set up an effective system. The model guides the establishment of the internal reporting system as well as the selection of outside information sources.

**Cost of Data**

Information is not free; its acquisition requires some outlay of funds. As with all outlays, the firm is concerned about the value received. Thus, in international marketing research, the firm should have some criteria to follow in deciding whether to hire another researcher, to buy an information service, or to hire an outside group to make a study. The benefits of improved decisions will be set against the costs incurred.

A food company executive wanted to change the reporting system for foreign subsidiaries in order to undertake some new comparative studies of foreign markets. A research assistant was hired, subsidiary reports were modified, and some new outside information sources were added. Traceable costs came to about $10,000 in the first year. The executive felt that this was modest in view of the better decisions he could make on marketing strategy and product policy in foreign markets. Once the adapted system was instituted, the extra costs went down greatly because the new approach was a modification of the old system rather than an addition to it.

Although some information comes to the company without a price tag or at a nominal cost, the firm still usually incurs expense in gathering, analyzing, storing, or discarding the data. Because these costs can be high, the researcher must be selective in choosing sources; in effect, one must look the gift horse in the mouth. *Redundancy* is a related issue. Some of the publications and information services cover the same ground. Of course, redundancy can be desirable if one source is a check on another, having used different inputs.

Cost must be related to the relevance of the information. Some information is low in cost but not very specific to the company's needs. A special market study by a consulting firm is apt to be quite expensive but also very specific to the company's needs. Part of the research task is to get the right mix of secondary sources along with more expensive primary sources. Before a market research group is hired or a researcher is sent on a trip overseas, less costly information inputs should be exhausted.

## Organizing for International Marketing Intelligence

How to find the best division of labor among the various parts of the international company — that is, between the international or regional headquarters and the national subsidiaries — is a major organizational problem. One aspect of the problem is the relation between domestic and international marketing research. Because the proper organizational arrangements will depend somewhat on the circumstances of each firm, we will discuss only general guidelines here. Some of the determinants are the level of decision making in the firm, its degree of foreign involvement, and its overall organization for international business.

**Level of Decision Making**

Marketing decisions can be made at several levels in the multinational company. Many are made at the national level, some at regional headquarters, others at the international division or corporate headquarters.

**Subsidiary.**   For decisions made within the foreign subsidiary, most information is gathered and stored locally. Such decentralization is probably most efficient. The market intelligence operation of a subsidiary, however, is not likely to be the same as that of a purely national company doing business in that country. The subsidiary should receive valuable inputs from its multinational affiliation, among them guidelines from the parent company and copies of studies from other operations of the parent firm.

**International Headquarters.**   At both regional and international headquarters the marketing information needed is broader and more general, corresponding to the types of decisions and studies made there. The basic sources of information at international headquarters are the country subsidiaries and the data gathering at headquarters itself. In order to coordinate multinational operations, headquarters needs to know conditions in all of its markets.

Data supplied by the subsidiaries serve two purposes. First, they provide a basis on which to make decisions for, or to give guidance to, the individual subsidiary. Second, they can be used for comparative studies of foreign markets. The marketing sophistication of the multinational company should be greater than that of a collection of national companies. Comparative studies are one means of achieving this increased sophistication.

International headquarters itself will do some marketing intelligence work. It will gather information that is not feasible to gather at the subsidiary level. Occasionally, even data on individual nations can be better obtained apart from the subsidiary. Whereas the subsidiary is concerned with daily operating problems, headquarters can take a broader view. Some international companies have regional or country desks where all kinds of information are gathered and analyzed. The political and economic pulse of the relevant nations is taken continually to keep the firm apprised of developments.

Data from international sources are probably best collected at international headquarters to avoid duplication of effort by the subsidiaries. Some examples are materials from the United Nations and its affiliated agencies, for example, the World Health Organization, the Food and Agricultural Organization, and the International Monetary Fund. Information on international economic and competitive conditions also would be gathered at headquarters. If a corporation has several subsidiaries in an area such as Latin America or Europe, the research on regional developments such as the Latin American Integration Association or the European Community should not be done at the subsidiary level where there would be great duplication. As can be seen, international marketing intelligence involves a division of labor among different levels of the organization.

Unilever has about 500 affiliated companies around the world. It has established an information system at headquarters to enable it to react quickly to events anywhere in the world. An extensive network of information units has a structure that ensures that information flows into corporate headquarters, where it is coordinated by a central information unit. These headquarters information services are "concern-oriented," meaning they focus on the total Unilever group on a worldwide basis. One key element in this scheme for handling external information is the Economics and Statistics Department. In London this group numbers about 70 people, half of whom are professional (college graduates). Some are data-processing specialists, some are country or industry specialists. A similar organization exists in Rotterdam for the Dutch side of Unilever, the binational multinational.

**Regional Headquarters.**   The simplest division of labor in information gathering is between the national subsidiary and international headquarters. Companies with regional headquarters may divide the labor further, that is, between the international and regional levels. Regional headquarters would do most of the intelligence work for its region, but international headquarters would still have to coordinate studies on a global scale.

Regional headquarters may have a large or a small role in marketing research, depending on the size of subsidiary operations. If individual subsidiary operations are large, the subsidiaries may have strong research activities of their own. These circumstances could lead to a small role for marketing research at regional headquarters, perhaps in coordination. By the same token, small subsidiary operations may not be able to support marketing research activity of their own. In the latter case, regional headquarters may play a big role because the necessary expertise and economies of scale are possible only on a regional basis.

One American consumer goods company has ten European subsidiaries. Whereas it once had a small marketing research activity in each country operation, it centralized all of these in London when it established a European regional headquarters there. The vice-president said: "We're centralizing our 'MR" to have one good department rather than ten half-baked operations. It operates on a service basis to all our European subs."

A contrary example is that of a much larger industrial-goods company with sales in Europe of several hundred million dollars. This firm had marketing research groups in each of eight major European countries, as well as at European headquarters in Paris (over 15 people), and at international headquarters in New York (over 40 people).

## Centralization or Decentralization?

Several factors contribute to a decentralization of marketing research activities. The larger a foreign subsidiary grows, the greater the possibility of national marketing research. If foreign subsidiaries are profit centers, they are more likely to carry on their own marketing research. As marketing research capability grows in different countries, more can be done in these markets. The more marketing decisions made locally, the greater the need is for local information. On the other side of the coin, the larger the firm's international business, the less able the firm is to centralize its marketing research activity effectively.

Decentralization does not eliminate the role of international headquarters. Each subsidiary receives guidance and expertise from the center, which coordinates activities among the subsidiaries and sees that duplication is avoided. Headquarters is the clearing house for all foreign operations, assuring the transmission of successful approaches and avoiding the repetition of ineffective methods. It serves as liaison with domestic marketing research, usually the source of the latest developments. Thus decentralization is a new division of labor. It does not eliminate the important role of international headquarters. If headquarters is not playing its coordinating role there will be suboptimization. The following quotation illustrates the problems:

> Often the only headquarters involvement in market research decisions is a review of the size of the market research budget. . . . The prevalence of this approach is surprising. It typically results in fragmentation of the company's total research effort, in duplication of research, and in incomparability of market data from country to country, because of the differing research methods chosen by various subsidiaries. Recognizing these problems, some companies have created at headquarters a position called "market research director to coordinate local efforts."[13]

Bayer, the German chemical giant, illustrates a compromise between centralization and decentralization, but with emphasis on centralization. It is organized into nine operating divisions with worldwide product responsibility. Each is a full manufacturing, marketing, and research and development operation. Bayer's system is decentralized as far as the gathering of information is concerned, with each division responsible for gathering what it needs. However, the processing of information (storage and retrieval) is managed centrally.

Bayer's guiding idea is to avoid divisionalization of information, and especially of information systems. The systems department works with experts from the operating divisions to develop a uniform information system applicable to all divisions so as to avoid costly duplication. The goal is to develop a means whereby information can be processed and retrieved in one centralized storage pool that every unit can tap, thus avoiding the installation of data processing units in every operating division. Extensive interaction is required between the systems people and the operating divisions.

# Information Sources for International Marketing

Because of the distance and cultural differences of foreign markets, the beginning international marketer knows little about them. Where and how can such knowledge be obtained? Fortunately, in spite of occasional data problems, there is a wealth of information on foreign markets. The discussions here will indicate the different kinds of information sources. Generally speaking, there are three basic sources of foreign market information: (1) secondary sources or published information, (2) knowledgeable individuals within the domestic market, and (3) travel to foreign markets for personal investigation. Most foreign market research should cover the first two sources before undertaking the third, relatively costly step. Our discussion will focus on the first two kinds of sources.

**United States Government**

**Department of Commerce.**   The Department of Commerce is the chief government source of foreign market information and it actively seeks to aid American firms in selling abroad. The umbrella organization for this purpose in the Department of Commerce is the International Trade Administration (ITA). It manages the U.S. Commercial Service, a network of 47 district offices in major cities around the country. These offices offer personal consultation to U.S. firms interested in doing business internationally.

Another service of ITA is the publication of information on many topics of interest to the international marketer. *Business America,* its biweekly magazine, is an excellent source of trade leads and information on developments in world trade. *Overseas Business Reports* is a regular series on most major markets of the world. Information covered in these reports includes economic and marketing data on the country, guidelines on how to do business there, copyright and trademark laws, and business and import regulations. In addition to international market information, the Department of Commerce offers specific guidance in locating customers, agents, or licensees in foreign markets (see Table 7–5).

Department of Commerce aids provide a good starting point for much foreign market research. First, they cover a wide range of subject matter as well as geography; and second, all this material and assistance is available at very modest cost.

**Other Government Departments.**   Other government departments also provide information on international trade matters. Among these are the Agency for International Development, the Federal Trade Commission, and the International Trade Commission. The Department of Agriculture publishes studies, for example, a 60-page analysis of *The Agricultural Economy of Tanzania,* and the Department of Labor publishes a periodical entitled *Labor Developments Abroad.* These examples are merely to indicate the extent of the United States government's interest in foreign countries and the way its information services can benefit the international marketer. In a sense, the government is a subsidized information service. The interna-

**Table 7–5**                                   **Department of Commerce Aid to Foreign Market Research**

A quick, easy to way to match your international business requirements to the programs, services, and publications described in this Guide.

| IF YOU ARE SEEKING INFORMATION OR ASSISTANCE REGARDING → <br><br> USE ↓ | Potential Markets | Market Research | Direct Sales Leads | Agents/ Distributors | Licenses |
|---|:---:|:---:|:---:|:---:|:---:|
| U.S. & Foreign Commercial Service | • | • | • |  | • |
| District Export Councils |  |  |  |  |  |
| Trade Opportunities Program |  |  | • | • | • |
| Agent/Distributor Service |  |  |  | • |  |
| Overseas Business Reports | • | • |  |  |  |
| Foreign Economic Trends | • | • |  |  |  |
| Small Business Administration |  | • |  |  |  |
| International Chambers of Commerce |  |  |  |  |  |
| Export Statistics Profiles | • | • |  |  |  |
| Export Information System Data Reports | • | • |  |  |  |
| Annual Worldwide Industry Reviews | • | • |  |  |  |
| International Market Research | • | • |  |  |  |
| Country Market Surveys | • | • |  |  |  |
| Custom Statistical Service | • | • |  |  |  |
| Product Market Profile | • | • |  |  |  |
| Market Share Reports | • | • |  |  |  |
| Country Market Profiles | • | • |  |  |  |
| Country Trade Statistics | • |  |  |  |  |
| Background Notes |  | • |  |  |  |
| International Economic Indicators | • | • |  |  |  |
| World Traders Data Reports |  |  |  |  |  |
| Commercial News USA | • |  | • | • |  |
| Export-Import Bank |  |  |  |  |  |
| Export Mailing List Service | • | • | • | • |  |
| Commerce Trade Shows | • | • | • | • | • |
| Commerce Trade Missions | • | • | • | • | • |
| Export Development Offices |  |  | • |  |  |
| Catalog Exhibitions |  |  | • |  |  |
| Major Projects Program |  |  |  |  |  |
| Overseas Private Investment Corporation |  |  |  |  |  |
| Private Export Funding Corporation |  |  |  |  |  |
| Foreign Sales Corporation |  |  |  |  |  |
| Commerce Business Daily | • |  | • |  |  |
| Free Ports & Free Trade Zones |  |  |  |  |  |

Source: A Basic Guide to Exporting (U.S. Department of Commerce, 1986).

| Credit Analysis | Financial Assistance | Risk Insurance | Tax Incentives | Export Counseling | Export Regulations | Overseas Contracts | Marketing Strategies | Trade Complaints |
|---|---|---|---|---|---|---|---|---|
|  |  |  |  | • | • |  | • | • |
|  |  |  |  | • |  |  |  |  |
|  |  |  |  |  |  | • |  |  |
|  | • |  |  | • |  |  |  |  |
|  |  |  |  |  | • |  |  |  |
| • |  |  |  |  |  |  |  |  |
|  | • |  |  |  |  |  |  |  |
| • |  |  |  |  |  |  |  |  |
| • |  |  |  |  |  |  | • |  |
|  |  |  |  |  |  |  | • |  |
|  |  |  |  |  |  | • |  |  |
| • |  | • |  |  |  |  |  |  |
|  | • |  |  |  |  |  |  |  |
|  | • |  | • |  |  |  |  |  |

tional marketing researcher should be aware of what is available and use whatever is relevant as a valuable and inexpensive input.

## Other Governments

No other government quite matches the American government in providing international trade information. Nonetheless, many have a large amount of data on their own economies, much of which is available through the country's embassy or consulate in America. In some cases, information can be obtained from a distributor or a subsidiary within the country. If the country is seeking to attract foreign investment, its information services are likely to be especially good. It will probably have a development office in the United States, like the Indian Investment Center in New York City. Foreign governments' information services tend to be inexpensive but valuable inputs to a foreign market study.

## International Organizations

Chief among international organizations, of course, is the United Nations and its affiliated organizations. There is no doubt about its major role in gathering and disseminating information about all aspects of the world economy. Its economic commissions conduct numerous studies and issue regular publications such as the *Economic Survey of Europe* and the *Economic Survey of Latin America*. The *United Nations Statistical Yearbook* is an invaluable source of data on over 200 countries. The International Monetary Fund issues the monthly *International Financial Statistics*. The General Agreement on Tariffs and Trade (GATT) publishes world trade data.

Many UN agencies are relatively unknown to the public, but they are doing work that is important to international corporations. For example, manufacturers of pharmaceuticals, foodstuffs, and hospital equipment must be up to date on the activities of the World Health Organization. Personnel managers in international companies need to be informed about the publications and services of ILO (International Labor Organization). Companies producing foodstuffs, fertilizers, or farm equipment are interested in the activities of the Food and Agriculture Organization (FAO). In fact, FAO has established the Industry Cooperation Program to promote closer relations with industry. Some of the international companies belonging to the program are General Foods, H. J. Heinz, Merck, Union Carbide, Nestlé, Massey-Ferguson, Unilever, and Shell. Other international organizations provide useful information. The Organization for Economic Cooperation and Development (OECD) is the most active. Its bimonthly *General Statistics* gives the major economic indicators for the member countries (the industrialized countries of the West). The OECD also publishes studies on many other topics of interest to the international marketer. The OECD now sells subscriptions to its valuable economic data on magnetic tape.

Other regional organizations supply information on their regions. The European Community (EC) is especially useful for information on developments affecting that area. A number of American companies located their European headquarters in Brussels partly to be near the power center of the EC. The EC also has an information center in Washington, D.C. and in New York City.

**Business and Trade Associations**

A number of business associations are concerned with international business. For industries that have international trade interests, the trade association will often provide information to its members. The chemical industry, for example, has such an association; and the office machine industry has the Business Equipment Manufacturer's Association (BEMA). These examples are American but there are counterparts in other industrialized countries.

One large producer of office machines was entering the Latin American market. In trying to evaluate the potential in the various countries, the firm found that the most useful and accurate guidelines were the export statistics and other information supplied by BEMA. At practically no cost to itself, the firm got a reading on all the Latin American markets, which helped it to establish appropriate quotas and marketing strategies.

Other business associations do not limit their interests to a particular industry or function. On a national level are the Chamber of Commerce of the United States and the National Foreign Trade Council. The former organization has a Foreign Commerce Department to serve its members. Most American Chambers of Commerce abroad are members of the Chamber of Commerce of the United States. These overseas members offer valuable services to both members and nonmembers. From their overseas position and experience, they can offer firsthand accounts of the situation in their national markets.

Within the United States, over 100 local Chambers of Commerce maintain foreign trade bureaus to serve members engaged in foreign commerce. One advantage of these local bureaus is the freedom members feel to ask questions when they know each other personally.

The *National Foreign Trade Council* is the principal association of American companies doing business abroad. Major banks, transportation companies, insurance companies, manufacturers, and others are members. It has area, country, and general committees made up of executives who have wide knowledge of international business. Consultative and informational services are available to members. The *American Management Association* has regular seminars on international business. *The Conference Board* publishes studies of interest to international management.

On a local level, there are over 50 foreign trade associations or *world trade clubs* in cities around the United States. These are especially strong in the port cities and in such large centers as Detroit and Chicago. However, they are also located in other inland points, such as Louisville, Memphis, Salt Lake City, and Denver. In membership and interests, these groups are small-scale versions of the National Foreign Trade Council. Small firms participate to a greater degree than in the National Foreign Trade Council.

The international trade clubs are extremely valuable for the personal exchange of information among members. As members get acquainted, they feel free to call on other members whose experience can help solve their problems. Those who have just returned from a tour of Latin America or who have been involved with trade problems in a given country, are generally willing to share their experiences. This is a valuable resource for firms in the area.

**Service Organizations**

Many companies are in the business of selling services to firms in international trade. To do their own job effectively, they must keep up with international developments. The information they gain is usually available free to their client companies. Some of the principal service organizations of interest here are banks, transportation companies, advertising agencies, and accounting firms.

The *major American banks* are doing increasing business with America's international companies. They have expanded overseas themselves and have developed a good intelligence system on the countries where they have interests. Both to encourage further client business and to keep the client from costly errors, the banks provide counsel and information on international business. In fact, this service is one of their major competitive tools vis-à-vis other banks. Trade leads, marketing reports, and country files are among the information the banks might supply. Bank information services may be available to clients in letters and in printed reports or through personal consultation with bank officers. Major banks in other leading industrial countries provide similar services.

Although the big New York banks are the American leaders in information services because of their size, location, and experience, large banks in many parts of the United States are getting more involved. For example, the National Bank of Detroit, an inland bank, makes available much of its international research material to customers. The officers of its international division frequently assist customers personally on international business questions.

By *transportation companies* we mean principally the international airlines and the steamship companies. Pan American Airlines (PAA) and Trans World Airlines (TWA) want to see U.S. companies expand their international business because then more business representatives and cargo will move by air. To promote this, they offer a variety of marketing and information services.

Other leading international airlines (British Airways, KLM, Air France, Japan Air Lines, for example) offer similar services. The Committee of American Steamship Lines offers international marketing help, as do individual shipping lines. Farrell Lines, for instance, ships primarily to Africa and can offer information and advice on problems and opportunities on that continent.

*Advertising agencies* with offices in foreign countries can provide marketing intelligence in their respective markets. Clients can draw on the agency's general knowledge of the market and also get specific guidance in marketing their own products. The *large accounting firms,* too, have expanded their international interests, becoming informed especially on financial, legal, and tax matters in international business. Besides offering client services in this area, some of the firms have extensive published material. Price Waterhouse has a series of *Information Guides* "for those doing business outside the United States." The *Guide to Argentina,* for example, is a 95-page booklet. *International Tax and Business Service* is the Haskins and Sells publication.

BBDO, the New York-based international advertising agency, has developed a satellite hookup to provide multinational marketers with early forecasts for international new product introductions. The mathematical model, stored in a central computer in New York, can be accessed by satellite in over a dozen countries in Asia, Latin America, and Europe. It helps clients evaluate new product introduction strategies without the time and expense of test markets, according to BBDO.

## Information for Sale

In all of the previous information sources, the provision of information was either free or at nominal cost. In the case of governments, the information service is subsidized. In the other cases, the supply of information is incidental to the main business of the supplier. Now we will discuss those organizations whose principal raison d'être is the provision of information for a price. Domestic examples of such organizations are A. C. Nielsen, Ward's (automotive reports), and Dodge (construction reports). Many of these information services have no counterpart in other countries because the market is too small. However, other organizations have extensive international coverage. (See Table 7–2.)

One important source on foreign business is found in the numerous *directories* of foreign firms in manufacturing, retailing, and other lines of business. Some cover just one country, but others are international in coverage. There are even guides to these directories so that it is possible to locate all those relevant to a particular need. An example is *Trade Directories of the World,* a loose-leaf volume by Croner Publications.

A number of companies publish information about international trade. Dun and Bradstreet is one of the companies actively providing international financial and marketing information to those who buy its services, both banks and manufacturers. Among the most important of its publications are *International Market Guide, Continental Europe* and *International Market Guide, Latin America.*

Two widely used services have an entirely international focus. The *Economist Intelligence Unit (EIU),* which is associated with the *Economist* magazine, is one. EIU services include quarterly reports on economic and political matters for most countries of the world, as well as regular reports on *Marketing in Europe* and other special topics. EIU also conducts specialized market studies for individual firms, but in this capacity it competes with other consulting firms.

The other widely used information service is *Business International (BI),* which has correspondents in all parts of the world. BI publishes weekly newsletters on developments affecting international business as well as on companies' international experiences and problems. The weekly letters specialize by area: Europe, Asia, China, Latin America, and Eastern Europe. Other BI services include *Investing, Licensing and Trading Conditions* (in over 50 countries) and *Financing Foreign Operations,* annual services with loose-leaf supplements.

Finally, major consulting and market research groups have overseas offices. As business has expanded abroad, these groups have followed their clients. Many can offer services abroad that are as good as those they offer at home. Not only American groups are available for foreign market intelligence; more and more, local organizations in the major industrial countries compete with the American consulting and research groups. Besides the general market research groups, such specialized market information services as A. C. Nielsen are operating in major world markets. As international business expands, the researcher can expect foreign market information services to grow along with it. There are already over 1,100 market research agencies in 60 different countries.[14]

## Company Experience

All the information sources considered until now have been outside the company. All are valuable either for the information or for the vicarious experience they provide. Nevertheless, the company's own experience is still its best resource. When a firm first considers some form of international business involvement, it must rely entirely on outside sources; but as the firm gains experience on its own, it will find this the most valuable resource of all. Although foreign operations provide the most comprehensive kind of familiarity with foreign markets, even operating through exports can be a very educational experience.

If the firm's only international involvement is in exporting, it is not physically present in foreign markets. Yet if the firm is aggressive in its export program, it can establish a good international intelligence system and gain valuable experience. Although the firm itself is not present in foreign markets, it has representation there, either through agents or distributors. Depending on the importance of its line to the foreign distributors, the exporting firm can make them a part of its international intelligence system. Even though the exporter cannot demand reports from distributors as a parent company can from its subsidiaries, some useful market feedback should be obtained from them in the normal course of business.

Good support by the exporter should increase the distributors' willingness to cooperate. Furthermore, travel to foreign markets by the export manager will give direct contact that will help management better interpret information from distributors as well as from other sources. If the firm later decides to establish foreign subsidiaries, it will have experience based on its export operations. Naturally, the firm that handles exports through outside firms or in a passive manner will not have this same experience. Thus the firm can gain intelligence on foreign markets through a limited form of involvement, and from this experience it can make better decisions about a heavier commitment to a market.

Multinational companies with many foreign subsidiaries are in the best position to benefit from local information sources and experience. They are not limited to requesting cooperation from independent distributors but can rely in large part on their own personnel. The firm will find the small size

**Figure 7–4**                          **GIMS Categories**

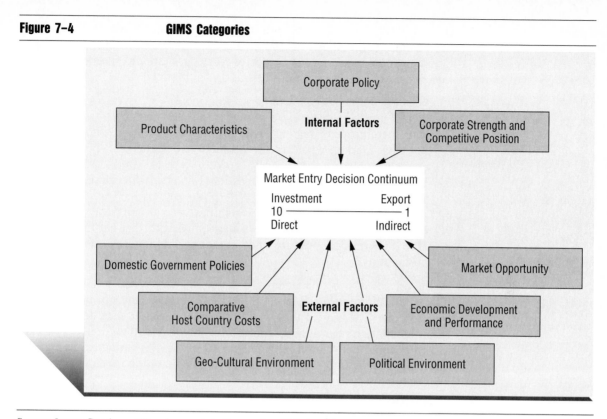

Source: James Goodnow, "Developments in International Mode of Entry Analysis," *International Marketing Review,* Autumn 1985.

of some of its foreign markets to be a disadvantage. Offsetting this, however, is the advantage of its experience in its domestic operations and in its foreign markets. By carefully analyzing its multinational experience and using some kind of comparative analysis, the multinational firm should be able to develop a market intelligence system which is more effective than that of its national competitors. The development of an effective market information system could be a competitive advantage of the international firm, as it is for the Japanese trading companies.

## Market Research Models: The Mode of Entry into Foreign Markets

The modeling of decisions that have to be taken in international markets is helpful in defining the nature of the marketing research task. We describe an application of market research that combines market data with a decision-support system to aid in deciding on the mode of entry into international markets. Goodnow notes that choosing the mode of entry is based on achieving a certain objective such as return-on-investment or market-share targets.[15] The constraints are relative costs, production efficiencies, product characteristics relative to competition, and environmental factors, all within the context of the strengths and weaknesses of the firm and its partners. Goodnow then breaks out the mode of entry decision into specific questions (see Figure 7–4 for a diagram illustrating his model):

1. Why does the firm want to go international?
2. Which products or services should it sell?
3. Which countries or regions should it market to, and in what sequence?
4. For each market, what are the resource and managerial-time commitments available?
5. For the commitment made (Question 4 above), what mode of entry is planned?
6. In the absence of direct sales, which partner will the firm select?
7. Has an acceptable contract been negotiated with this partner?
8. How will needed product and marketing adaptations affect ultimate profitability?

Based on the above questions, Goodnow has developed a GIMS model (Gauge for International Market Strategies), with nine sets of factors taken into account. There are a total of 140 separate variables used to arrive at a recommendation regarding the appropriate mode of entry. A task of market research would be to develop values for all of the 140 variables used in the model, thus providing data for the model to choose the mode of entry.

## Summary

International marketing research is complex primarily because of the difficulty of gathering information about multiple different foreign environments. The first step is to determine what information to gather. Other problem areas include the availability and quality of primary and secondary data, the comparability of data on different markets, and hindrances in gathering information about areas such as social organization and culture. While new services are springing up to help deal with these problems, improvisation and learning from experience are still important.

Techniques for market research in developing countries include analysis of demand patterns, the use of multiple-regression models, estimation by analogy, and cluster analysis. Gap analysis, input-output analysis, and estimation of cost and technology trends are other useful tools.

The information gathered through research must be evaluated for quality, timeliness, accuracy and comparability. Its cost must be balanced against its relevance. Data should be gathered at local, regional, and headquarters levels; a more difficult question is where such efforts should be supervised. Decentralization is helpful, and both in-house and outside expertise need to be tapped.

Information sources about foreign markets include the U.S. government, particularly the Department of Commerce, international organizations such as the OECD and the World Bank, industry and business associations, and consulting houses. A resource often ignored is information scattered within the company and derived from the company's own experience in various markets.

Models are an essential part of market research. The GIMS model by Goodnow is illustrative of such an approach.

## Questions

7.1  "International marketing intelligence is more comprehensive than domestic marketing research." Discuss.

7.2  Can domestic marketing research techniques be used in researching foreign markets? Explain.

7.3  Why is it often more difficult to get responses to marketing research in other countries than it is in the United States?

7.4  Explain how the economic and commercial infrastructure in a country can affect the marketing research task there.

7.5  Define the "data problems" in international marketing research.

7.6  How can international marketing researchers deal with the problems encountered in their task?

7.7  How can international marketers prepare a comparative analysis of their foreign markets?

7.8  How might comparative analysis and groupings of foreign markets aid in solving international marketing research problems?

7.9  Discuss the U.S. government as an information source for markets abroad.

7.10  Name some of the business and trade associations that provide assistance to the international marketing researcher.

7.11  Identify firms in your own community and determine what kinds of foreign market assistance are available to them locally or within the state.

7.12  Suggest criteria for evaluating information in international marketing research.

7.13  "Because marketing is done in the local market, marketing research needs to be decentralized." Discuss.

7.14  What kind of division of labor is feasible in the marketing research of the multinational company, that is, between subsidiary and international headquarters?

7.15  How should the firm decide whether to gather its own intelligence or to buy it outside?

7.16  Why is screening foreign markets important? Explain how screening was used in identifying key markets for kidney dialysis equipment (see discussion in Chapter 7).

## Endnotes

[1]Richard H. Holton, "Marketing Policies in Multinational Corporations," *Journal of International Business Studies* (Summer 1970): 1–20.

[2]*Marketing News,* September 18, 1981, 18.

[3]Charles S. Mayer, "Multinational Marketing Research," *European Research* 6 (March 1978): 77–83.

[4]M. R. Hill, "Desk Research Methods for the Soviet Capital Goods Market," *European Journal of Marketing,* 13, no. 5 (1979): 271–283.

[5]Richard P. Carr, Jr., "Identifying Trade Areas for Consumer Goods in Foreign Markets," *Journal of Marketing* (October 1978): 76–80.

[6]*Marketing News,* March 1, 1985, 19.

[7]Reed Moyer, "International Market Analysis," *Journal of Marketing Research* (November 1968): 353–360.

[8]Zoher E. Shipchandler, "Diffusion Patterns of Consumer Durables in International Markets" (PhD diss., Indiana University, 1973).

[9]The discussion here draws on research conducted by the author and M. Y. Yoshino of Harvard and reported in Bertil Liander, Vern Terpstra, M. Y. Yoshino, and Aziz A. Sherbini, *Comparative Analysis for International Marketing,* Marketing Science Institute (Boston: Allyn & Bacon, 1967).

[10]S. Prakash Sethi, "Comparative Cluster Analysis for World Markets," *Journal of Marketing Research* (August 1971).

[11]J. Jeannet and H. Hennessey, *International Marketing Management* (Boston: Houghton-Mifflin Co., 1988), 147–150.

[12]J. A. Weber, "Comparing Growth Opportunities in the International Marketplace," *Management International Review* 1 (1979).

[13]Ulrich E. Wiechmann, *Marketing Management in Multinational Firms* (New York: Praeger, 1976), 32.

[14]*The International Directory of Market Research Organizations* (London: Market Research Society, 1980).

[15]James D. Goodnow, "Developments in International Mode of Entry Analysis," *International Marketing Review* 2, no. 3 (Autumn 1985).

## Further Readings

Bergstrom, Gary L., and Mark England. "International Country Selection Strategies," *Columbia Journal of World Business* vol. 17, No. 1, (Summer 1982).

Carr, Richard P. Jr. "Identifying Trade Areas for Consumer Goods in Foreign Markets." *Journal of Marketing* (October 1978).

Cavusgil, S. Tamer. "Guidelines for Export Market Research." *Business Horizons* (November–December 1985).

Day, Ellen, R. J. Fox, and S. M. Huszagh. "Segmenting the Global Market for Industrial Goods: Issues and Implications." *International Marketing Review* 5, no. 3 (Autumn 1988).

Douglas, Susan P., and Samuel Craig. *International Marketing Research.* Englewood Cliffs, N. J.: Prentice-Hall, 1983.

Goodnow, James D. "Developments in International Mode of Entry Analysis." *International Marketing Review* 2, no. 3 (Autumn 1985).

Jeannet, Jean-Pierre, and H. Hennessey. *International Marketing Management.* New York: Houghton-Mifflin, 1988, 147–150.

Johansson, Johny K., and I. Nonaka. "Market Research the Japanese Way." *Harvard Business Review* vol. 65, no. 3, (May–June 1987).

Liander, Bertil, Vern Terpstra, M. Y. Yoshino, and A. Sherbini. *Comparative Analysis for International Marketing.* Boston: Allyn & Bacon, 1967.

Moyer, Reed. "International Market Analysis." *Journal of Marketing Research* (November 1968).

Parameswaran, Ravi, and Attila Yaprak. "A Cross-National Comparison of Consumer Research Measures." *Journal of International Business Studies* (Spring 1987).

Sekaran, Uma. "Methodological and Theoretical Issues and Advancements in Cross-Cultural Research." *Journal of International Business Studies* (Fall 1983).

Sethi, S. Prakash. "Comparative Cluster Analysis for World Markets." *Journal of Marketing Research* (August 1971).

Weber, J. A. "Comparing Growth Opportunities in the International Marketplace." *Management International Review* 1 (1979).

World Bank. *World Development Report.* (Published annually) New York: Oxford University Press.

# The Madrona Chemical Company Marketing Research for International Division

The Madrona Chemical Company manufactures a wide line of cosmetic, therapeutic, and household items, such as face creams, tonics, drugs, deodorizers, cleansers, and oils. Its sales have grown rapidly throughout the United States, but exports have not kept pace with overall growth.

Much of its success is attributed to dynamic marketing and aggressive promotion based on market research. According to William Tucker, the market research director of the company, all known methods of market study have to be utilized by the Madrona Company at different occasions to provide sound data for the marketing department. Some of the work is done by Madrona employees, but in most instances outside agencies are engaged to do the actual field work. Tucker and his research staff are primarily concerned with determining the types of projects to be undertaken at any time, negotiating with research agencies, and interpreting the findings to the company executives.

## International Division

The Madrona Company has been selling a modest volume of its output to foreign markets through a San Francisco export house which has branches in New York and a few foreign countries. These sales have been sporadic and have increased only modestly in the last 15 years. In the same period, domestic volume has nearly tripled. To stabilize its foreign sales and to get a larger share of the world market in its field, the company recently set up an international division with Craig Rivers as manager. Rivers has some 25 years of experience in selling Madrona products. He started as a junior sales representative and advanced rapidly to sales representative, field supervisor, district sales manager, and assistant sales manager in charge of promotion.

He had been in this latter capacity for nine years before becoming manager of the newly created International Division.

## Research Requirements

In his new capacity, Rivers sends an interoffice memo to Tucker requesting that a comprehensive market research program promptly be developed to provide data for the International Division. This program should consist of two major phases: (1) a worldwide market survey of a general nature to determine the overall sales potential in different countries for Madrona products and (2) a series of intensive studies in the most likely markets. These studies, Rivers suggests, should follow the same pattern as used in the domestic research.

A few days later Tucker informs Rivers that the project suggested by him is not feasible, for the cost of it would be prohibitive and the possibilities for utilizing findings relatively limited. In his opinion, no comprehensive study is economically justified, especially since his staff already has a backlog of research requests to be processed, and because new methods would have to be developed for foreign markets. This would be an extra burden on his professional personnel. He suggests that Rivers break the project down by individual countries and products or product groups and select the most pressing one for consideration by the research department. The individual problems should be evaluated and arranged into a sequence of priorities which can then be compared with research needs by the domestic sales department.

Rivers finds this answer entirely unsatisfactory. He insists it is only necessary to rerun domestic studies in the foreign countries and get the same data as the domestic sales people have.

Without such data he could not discharge the responsibilities the management has delegated to him. But Tucker does not agree. After several informal attempts, Rivers decides to study a number of domestic projects to gather ammunition with which to approach the executive committee of the company on a formal basis to have Tucker overruled and the research department compelled to undertake the foreign studies that he feels are essential.

The following briefly describes the studies that Rivers includes in his formal memorandum as indicative of the type of research that he wants to be carried out in overseas markets. He emphasizes that since these projects are or have recently been carried out in the United States, the cost of extending them to foreign areas should be modest at most. Very little if any will be added to the research overhead, which often accounts for a large share of the cost of market investigation.

**Project 020: Market Potential in the Far West.** The study consists of a compilation of official data on the 11 western states showing population figures, personal income, family units, retail sales of cosmetics and kindred products, and some geographical data. The study was prepared by Tucker's staff.

**Project 021: Brand Preferences for Face Creams and Hand Lotions.** A sample survey in 60 large cities recording what brand of these products is used in different households and the reasons therefore. The study was planned by Tucker's department, but the field work was farmed out to local research agencies in various cities, and the final tabulation and analysis were performed by a research consultant in San Francisco.

**Project 022: Consumer Shopping Habits.** Study made in ten test cities located in every major region of the United States. Study was planned by Tucker and executed as follows: In each city a local professor of marketing was retained as team coordinator. That individual, in turn, engaged the required number of field workers,

mostly seniors and graduate students in business, who were stationed at various stores to observe and record customer behavior. The coordinators made their own analysis of the results. Tucker summarized the findings and prepared the final report.

**Project 023: Effect of Package Change.** After a new type of container had been designed for one of the Madrona products, it was tested before converting production entirely to this new package. This was done by placing the new package for sale in some 15 different stores, 5 in New York, 5 in Los Angeles, and 5 in Chicago. Careful records were kept of daily sales in these stores, and a similar number of comparable test stores selling the product unchanged. Based on these findings, generalizations were drawn for the entire U.S. market.

**Project 024: Measuring Advertising Effectiveness.** Before embarking on a nationwide campaign of synchronized radio and TV commercials, the commercials were tested in two typical cities. This was done by having them run for a period of two weeks and collecting detailed sales data from all stores handling the product in these two cities. Similar data were collected from two other cities not having the commercials for the purpose of comparison. The findings were positive and the campaign was approved by the management.

**Project 025: Testing Advertising Appeal.** An ad was designed and shown to a random sample of people, whose responses were recorded by interviewers. On the basis of these findings the ad was improved before it was placed into a national magazine charging $55,000 for each issue of the ad.

**Project 026: Determining Distribution Costs as a Basis for Selling Prices in Different Sections of the U.S. Market.** An outside research agency was employed to conduct this study. It gathered data on freight rates, handling costs, delivery periods, insurance costs, state and local taxes, and warehouse rents in different states. While the cost of this study exceeded $200,000, it was considered well worth the expense, since it enabled the company to establish realistic prices that could be maintained and promoted over several years.

**Project 027: Current Market Conditions.**   This was a continuous project, or more correctly, series of different projects. Its purpose was to keep the management informed about local conditions important in planning company operations. The research department had developed a number of forms and questionnaires, which the field staff of Madrona regularly filled out and forwarded to Tucker for summarization and analysis. The people responsible for these data received detailed instructions from Tucker's staff as to how to maintain the data required. Among the data collected were: employment; payroll; strikes; "acts of God"; sales by brand; mileage traveled by sales representatives; number of sales interviews; number of orders; number of customers, old and new; and information regarding competing products and competitors' activities, official appointments and governmental changes, retailer markup practices, and the use of point-of-sale advertising and selling aids.

## Questions

1.  Evaluate the research projects with respect to their suitability and feasibility for foreign markets.

2.  What should Rivers do?

CASE

# 7.2   International Chemicals, Inc.

In the spring of 1986 International Chemicals, Inc. (ICI), a well-known American manufacturer of dry cell batteries, was exploring the possibility of establishing a dry battery manufacturing plant in Latinia. The company was one of the largest producers of dry cell batteries in the world; its "Thunder" trademark one of the best known brands. ICI had manufacturing plants throughout the United States and Europe, but no plant in Latin America. It once had a plant in Cuba but that was expropriated when Castro came into power there. Company headquarters were in New York.

For years, the sale of Thunder batteries in Latinia had been negligible, largely because the company's agent was very inactive in promoting and selling these products. The agent represented so many other product lines of heavy machinery and electrical equipment that batteries were of little importance to him. Because their sales in Latinia were so small, company officials in New York had little knowledge of the battery market in Latinia or of investment conditions in the country. They decided, therefore, that the first step they must take to consider a manufacturing plant in Latinia was to make a basic survey of the market for batteries there.

To do this job, they selected Mr. Robert Daane, a young man who had recently graduated from business college and joined the International Division of ICI, to travel to Latinia, study the market and prepare a report on his findings. Mr. Daane had two years of Spanish in high

Source: This case was prepared by E. J. Kolde, University of Washington. Used by permission.

school. Shortly thereafter, Mr. Daane arrived in Latinia and after contacting his embassy commercial office for basic orientation, began his market survey. He first contacted the ICI agent but found that the principal was on vacation having apparently not received his advance letter, and that the others in the office could give him very little help.

Much to Mr. Daane's surprise, there was little statistical information of any form available on battery consumption in Latinia. This disturbed him because his courses on market research at college had stressed the importance of a thorough statistical analysis in performing this type of study. After failing to find any battery statistics at the commercial library of his embassy, Mr. Daane went to Banco de Latinia, the Bureau of Statistics, the Ministry of Industry and Mines, and the Ministry of Customs.

At Banco de Latinia, where he had an introduction from the embassy, Mr. Daane was well received by the Chief of the Statistics Publications Department, but the only statistics available concerned basic national economic and monetary data or commodity prices. However, the department chief was very polite and discussed economic conditions in Latinia at some length.

Mr. Daane then visited the Bureau of Public Statistics, but was disappointed to learn that this agency was concerned only with population statistics. He obtained the latest such statistics since he thought they should be included in his report. But when he inquired about battery statistics, he was told that industrial statistics were gathered by the Ministry of Industry and Mines.

At the Ministry of Industry and Mines Mr. Daane found it difficult to locate the right people to talk with. No one seemed interested in his project, although everyone was polite to him. He finally located the Industrial Statistics Department where he had an opportunity to talk to several of the staff and was given a copy of the 1983 Statistical Yearbook, which was the most recent edition. This Yearbook gave some statistics on 12 basic industry groups, but, unfortunately, gave no information on dry batteries. The Chief of the Statistics Department explained that his responsibility was to collect statistics on established industries, and since dry batteries were not manufactured in Latinia, his department would not have information on them. He suggested that Mr. Daane visit the Ministry of Customs for import statistics.

At the Ministry of Customs, Mr. Daane spent several days searching and making inquiries until he found the section where import statistics were recorded. Unfortunately, however, customs duties on dry cell batteries were assessed on the basis of gross weight and there were no figures maintained on the actual number of batteries imported. The Assistant Chief of this section reminded Mr. Daane that the function of the Ministry of Customs was to collect customs duties and authorized commercial tax on imported goods—not to collect statistics. The figures that were available were simply a by-product of the Department's main job.

The statistics Mr. Daane obtained from customs are shown in Table 1. The figures show the peso value of shipments and the country from which imported. The gross weight included all packing materials, the wooden shipping crate and sometimes display cases. No breakdown as to the actual quantity or type of battery was available. The latest year for which figures were complete was 1983.

Since Mr. Daane was aware that the price of dry cell batteries varies widely depending on the country of origin, he knew that the peso value could not be used to determine the quantity of import and consumption. Therefore, after giving the problem some thought, he decided to approach the determination of actual quantity and breakdown by type of battery on the basis of weight and typical importers' order mix. Since the weight of a given type of battery was almost the same regardless of its quality, price, or country of origin, he reasoned that this was the best approach.

Following this decision, Mr. Daane spent the next three weeks interviewing various importers of batteries. From these interviews, he learned a good deal about the battery market and obtained

**Table 1  Dry Battery Imports Into Latinia**

| Country of Origin | Value in Pesos (000s) | | |
| --- | --- | --- | --- |
| | 1981 | 1982 | 1983 |
| Germany, FR | 15,358 | 6,320 | 5,521 |
| Great Britain | 46,704 | 38,627 | 50,334 |
| Japan | 18,251 | 14,319 | 39,485 |
| Hong Kong | 12,011 | 41,901 | 22,325 |
| United States | 4,631 | 1,668 | 2,319 |
| France | 1,584 | 1,602 | 2,828 |
| Denmark | 1,647 | 2,189 | 962 |
| Czechoslovakia | 102 | 474 | 690 |
| China | 55 | 2,805 | 2,262 |
| Singapore | — | 691 | 634 |
| Sweden | — | 1,083 | 519 |
| TOTAL | 100,343 | 111,679 | 127,879 |

numerous estimates on its size, growth prospects, price trends, and breakdown by type. Although some of these estimates were considerably divergent, he felt there was sufficient pattern to the response on which to base his report.

In the course of these interviews, he found two importers who were more cooperative than the rest and seemed interested in his study and more willing to help him. He persuaded both these importers, on the basis that he would share his market estimates with them, to permit him to unpack completely a number of recently imported battery shipments. Based on this process, Mr. Daane calculated that the average net weight of batteries was 82 percent of the gross weight of the shipment. This figure, together with the importers' estimates of consumption by type of battery based on their past ordering mix and opinions on current trends in the shift of consumer demands among battery types, gave him a basis for determining actual quantities consumed from the customs figures.

After completing his work with the importers, Mr. Daane spent another week analyzing the information and figures he had obtained and preparing his report. The report he submitted in New York after a total of two months in Latinia was as follows:

# Report:
# The Market for Dry Cell Batteries in Latinia

## Market Size and Growth

The market for dry cell batteries in Latinia for the year 1985 is estimated at 30 million units having a gross value of about 161 million pesos. My estimate is that this market will continue to expand, as it has in past years, at a rate of at least 10 to 12 percent per year.

An estimated breakdown of this market by product type is shown below:

## Breakdown of Product Type

| Battery Type | | Weight (Grams) | Units Consumed | Percent |
|---|---|---|---|---|
| Flat (Book) | 4.5v | 112.5 | 2,100,000 | 7% |
| Round (2LP) | 1.5v | 88.0 | 18,900,000 | 63 |
| Round (1LP) | 1.5v | 35.0 | 1,500,000 | 5 |
| Pen type | 1.5v | 9.5 | 5,100,000 | 17 |
| Long round | 3.0v | 40.0 | 2,400,000 | 8 |
| TOTAL | | | 30,000,000 | 100% |

My study indicates that there has been considerable shift in consumer demand for various battery types. Demand for the flat or book type and for the round (1 LP) has declined notably whereas demand for the large round (2 LP) and the pen type has increased substantially. The demand for the flat type has practically ceased in the large cities. I believe that eventually the same will happen in rural areas.

## Price Structure

The retail selling prices of dry cell batteries vary widely depending upon from which country they are imported. In general, batteries from Great Britain, the United States, and Sweden are highest priced whereas imports from Hong Kong and Japan are lowest priced. Typical prices encountered in the outdoor markets at the time of this study are shown below:

## Retail Battery Prices

| Type | | Retail Selling Price (Pesos) |
|---|---|---|
| Flat (Book) | 4.5v | 12 |
| Round (2 LP) | 1.5v | 5–12 |
| Round (1 LP) | 1.5v | 6–16 |
| Pen type | 1.5v | 3–6 |
| Long round | 3.0v | 8 |

A breakdown of battery imports in recent years by country is shown in Table 1, attached to this report. Peso figures in Table 1 are for landed value.

## Economic Factors

The following limited data on economic factors that have a bearing on future trends in dry battery consumption in Latinia are included in this report as background material.

**Population.** In 1984 the Bureau of Statistics published a population figure of 29,846,000. The last Latinian census was taken in 1970. Currently, the bureau is using a 2.4 percent per year increase to arrive at year-to-year figures. This places population for this year, 1986, at over 30 million.

The bureau does not maintain statistics which record population shifts from rural to urban areas. However, from this study, I estimate that at present about 20 percent of the population is urban, or 6 million out of 30 million. There is some migration movement from rural to urban which will increase this proportion somewhat in the years ahead. For example, in the next 15 to 20 years, the urban population will probably increase to 35 percent.

**Electrification.** Electrical power production has been on the increase. The past three years' figures based on available statistics are as follows:

| Year | KWH |
|------|-----|
| 1981 | 398,267,000 |
| 1982 | 519,786,000 |
| 1983 | 543,774,000 |

It should be noted that the bulk of this power consumption is in the large cities. Small towns, villages, and rural areas are still virtually unelectrified. The Third Development Plan of the Plan Organization programs an increase in demand and capacity at the rate of about 15 percent per year over the next five years. However, much of this increase will be required to support industrial expansion in the large cities.

**Radios.** The total number of radios imported in 1983 based on customs statistics was 422,027 with a value of 337,621,600 pesos. This figure included all types of radios, battery and electric. No separation is made by the Ministry of Customs of transistor radios from others. However,

based on the average import price of 800 pesos per radio, and with transistor radios retailing at from 600 to 2,400 pesos, it would appear that a large percentage of the radios are transistor type. No plant is in operation assembling transistor radios, although a license for an assembly plant has been issued by the Ministry of Industry and Mines.

**Flashlights.** Flashlights are available throughout Latinia. Many of the flat type batteries are used in old style flashlights. No flashlights are manufactured in Latinia and therefore all are imported. Following is a summary of importations for the past few years.

| Year | Kilos | Pesos |
|------|-------|-------|
| 1981 | 29,694 | 4,546,431 |
| 1982 | 50,108 | 6,517,613 |
| 1983 | 65,267 | 9,649,458 |

It is clear that the importation and use of flashlights increased tremendously from 1981 through 1983.

## Potential Competition

At present there are no factories manufacturing dry cell batteries in Latinia. At one time a small factory made flat batteries by hand, but this factory is no longer in operation. A license was issued in November 1985 to an Engineer Calderone for a factory to produce 2,600,000 single cell 1.5 volt batteries. I understand that he has gone to Japan either to gain experience in battery manufacture or to buy machinery.

An application was recently made to the Minister of Industry and Mines for a factory to produce 10,000,000 single cell 1.5 volt batteries. The application is now under study but no license has yet been issued.

## Protection

There is a law that provides protection from importations. In general, it states that if a company can manufacture all the needs of an item for Latinia, it may apply to the Ministry of Industry and Mines to stop importation. The word "all," in my interpretation, would cover the entire custom category of dry cell batteries, not just, for example, 1.5 volt cylindrical batteries.

License protection is vague and lies with the Ministry of Industry and Mines. Application for this license must be filed and approval obtained before machinery may be ordered or construction started for any factory. Generally speaking, any application is evaluated in light of existing factories already having a license and producing the items, their capacity to produce them, and any other license applications that may be in process. Once a license is granted, however, not much control is exercised as to quantity, quality, variety, or the actual range of products manufactured. Hence, it is possible for a factory with a license for one product gradually to enter into other related products using the same production facilities.

Latinia's laws and incentives pertaining to foreign investment are favorable. They include the Law on Attraction and Protection of Foreign Capital Investment of 1975 which provides for repatriation of capital and profits and guarantees equitable compensation in case of expropriation. This law also qualifies foreign-owned enterprises for the benefits of the Protection and Exports Encouragement Act of 1975 which provides for duty free importation of machinery and equipment and tax concessions for a five-year period for certain new industries established more than 60 kilometers from the capital. Finally, there is the United States Investment Guarantee Agreement with Latinia under which investments may be insured against currency inconvertibility and expropriation or confiscation.

My inquiries lead me to believe that the provisions of the Law on Attraction and Protection of Foreign Capital Investment can be relied upon.

There are no reports of a business that has lost its investment or has been unable to repatriate profits through government action in recent years. The president has repeatedly stated that foreign investment is essential for the success of industrial development and should be encouraged. This has been echoed by government officials, but foreign investors have apparently shown little response as there are still relatively few major foreign enterprises in Latinia.

It seems almost mandatory to enlist the aid of local investment to assure the success of a new business venture. Success does not always depend on a successful product but on contacts and goodwill, contacts in obtaining license in importation of raw materials, in banking circles, etc. Things appear to operate more smoothly when there is a capable Latinian partner. However, there is no legal requirement for Latinian control or majority ownership of foreign-owned enterprises.

I would recommend starting out with licensing rights, know-how, and management. Then advance to supplying specialized machinery, molds, and dies required for the manufacture of the items. Some companies have had success in sending their less automatic equipment as it is replaced. With the lower labor costs, its efficiency is not important. Latinian investment should be in land, buildings, and working capital.

Latinian capital is available, but it is costly. At present, the investment market is critical and there are no signs of its easing. As soon as the third five-year plan is approved and financing enlisted, this situation could change. Most important is to find the "right" investor-partner. This seems to be the most difficult part of investing in Latinia. I would suggest that this person or persons be found before any other step is taken.

Latinians do not seem to look at investments in the same way as we do. Their outlook will be on the short-term, quick-return basis. Five years is a long time and they seem to be skeptical of any investment that would not return in that time. They might not look kindly upon this return being reinvested or taken as a capital gain.

# Taxation

A new manufacturing industry approved by the Ministry of Finance that establishes itself 60 kilometers from the capital is exempt from income taxes for five years. If the business is established within the capital metropolitan area, an exemp-

tion of 50 percent may be granted. In any event, after five years, 50 percent is the maximum exemption allowed. In determining taxable income all joint stock companies are entitled to an exemption of 10 percent of income. A schedule of the present tax is shown below.

**Computation of Tax (in Pesos)**

| If the Net Taxable Income is not over 100,000 pesos | | No Tax | |
|---|---|---|---|
| **If the Net Taxable Income is:** | | **The Amount** | |
| **Over** | **But Not Over** | **of Tax is** | **of Income over** |
| 100,000 | 200,000 | 12,000 + 15% | 100,000 |
| 200,000 | 300,000 | 27,000 + 18% | 200,000 |
| 300,000 | 400,000 | 45,000 + 21% | 300,000 |
| 400,000 | 800,000 | 66,000 + 24% | 400,000 |
| 800,000 | 1,200,000 | 162,000 + 30% | 800,000 |
| 1,200,000 | 1,500,000 | 282,000 + 33% | 1,200,000 |
| 1,500,000 | 2,000,000 | 381,000 + 36% | 1,500,000 |
| 2,000,000 | 2,500,000 | 561,000 + 40% | 2,000,000 |
| 2,500,000 | 3,000,000 | 761,000 + 45% | 2,500,000 |
| 3,000,000 | 4,000,000 | 986,000 + 46% | 3,000,000 |
| 4,000,000 | 4,500,000 | 1,446,000 + 47% | 4,000,000 |
| 4,500,000 | 5,500,000 | 1,681,000 + 48% | 4,500,000 |
| 5,500,000 | 6,000,000 | 2,161,000 + 49% | 5,500,000 |
| 6,000,000 | — | 2,406,000 + 50% | 6,000,000 |

Note 1. Individuals are taxed at the same rates. They do not have the 10 percent exemption, but the first 48,000 pesos of income is not taxed, based on a 1980 revision of the tax law.

Note 2. One dollar equals approximately 30 pesos.

## Questions

1. Evaluate Mr. Daane's research into the dry cell battery market in Latinia. Identify strong and weak aspects of his research.
2. What would you have done if you were given Mr. Daane's assignment?
3. Evaluate Mr. Daane's report. What are the strengths and weaknesses of the report itself?
4. What should ICI do in Latinia?

CHAPTER 8

# International Product Policy
## The Basic Product and Its Attributes

International marketing is about satisfying consumer needs in foreign markets. The question often asked is, "Can I sell my product in overseas markets?" A better question would be, "What products should I be selling in foreign markets?" International product policy should be the cornerstone around which other aspects of the global marketing mix are designed and integrated.

The main goals of this chapter are to

1. Delineate the influences that lead a company to standardize or adapt its products.
2. Discuss the product attributes that are considered in addition to the basic product itself in formulating international product policy.
3. Examine approaches to market segmentation in foreign markets, and franchising as a mode of entry.

A central issue in approaching global markets is whether products sold in the domestic market should be *adapted* or *standardized*. A question of great practical interest is whether a company can successfully design and market a *global product.* Yet other questions have to do with the various product features, such as packaging and labeling, brands and trademarks, and warranty and service policies. How are these product features affected as the product moves internationally? Is international uniformity possible, or, if not, what modifications are necessary? In this chapter we consider the international parameters of these questions.

In Chapter 9 we will deal with two other aspects of international product policy: (1) the selection and management of the international product line and (2) product planning and development in international business.

## What to Sell Abroad: Product Policy for International Markets

Most international firms start off by selling domestic products in foreign markets. The central issue for them at that time is whether the product can be sold as is or needs adaptation to appeal to foreign customers. Most

251

companies choose between the two extremes of (1) adapting to the point of creating an entirely new product and (2) keeping the product exactly the same.

Standardization is more appropriate, of course, when customers are similar overseas, and such standardization can apply to services as well as to products. For example, Super Club, N.V., one of Belgium's largest video rental store chains, also has operations in other European countries, with a total of about 160 stores. The largest video chain in the highly fragmented European video market, its size and buying power allow it to achieve many cost economies. It also distributes video films through over 1,000 vending machines.

The United States is the biggest market for video rentals, with 1989 estimated revenues of $10 billion. Over 60 percent of U.S. homes have a VCR, and growth is projected to continue at 10 percent a year. The concept of renting videocassettes does not need to be changed significantly to cater to U.S. customers. Hence, Super Club established a U.S. headquarters office in Dallas at the beginning of 1989, and within six months had acquired 324 stores, including

- Record Bar, with 167 stores in the southeast and middle Atlantic United States.
- Turtle's, with 114 stores in Georgia, Alabama, Tennessee, and Florida.
- Movietime, with 21 stores in Louisiana, Mississippi, and Arkansas.
- Video Towne, with 22 stores in Ohio and Indiana.

Thus, the United States became its biggest single operation. In addition, it installed about thirty video vending machines on a trial basis. Super Club therefore became a credible competitor to established U.S. firms such as Blockbuster (with about 870 stores) and West Coast Video (with 700 stores). With U.S. market entry achieved, Super Club must next be concerned with issues such as economies of scale in inventory control, and costs of operation. It may also have to optimize the mix of videos available in each location, since customer tastes may differ by region within the United States.[1]

## The Product Itself

What is a product? Manufacturers may define it as the thing they sell: a tire, a deodorant, a cake mix, a computer. As such, it can be defined in terms of its physical or chemical characteristics. A more market-oriented definition might be based on the role it plays in the buyer's consumption system. The economist calls the product a bundle of *utilities,* which means everything the buyer receives, including psychological utility as well as physical and chemical dimensions. But when the adjective *foreign* or *international* is added to a product, any one of these definitions will change in some significant way.

The international products the firm sells are probably somewhat different, physically or chemically, from its domestic products. The foreign customer's definition of the firm's product is generally different from that of its domestic customers, either in terms of the role it performs or in terms of the utilities it offers. On a more prosaic level, the packaging, labeling, branding, and warranty aspects of the product are likely to be different. A rather close relation between the firm's foreign and domestic products is likely, however. The average firm's resources and competitive strengths will not allow it to attack both a new foreign market and a completely different product line at the same time. Therefore, although the soups, greeting cards, or automobiles sold abroad generally are not identical to their domestic counterparts, they are nevertheless in the same product category and require similar kinds of know-how, both in production and in marketing. There must be a core of expertise that the firm can carry abroad.

## Adaptation versus Standardization

In most cases, neither complete standardization nor total adaptation represent reasonable business responses. The goals of reducing costs and complexity lead companies to consider standardization, while a customer orientation sways them toward product adaptation.

**Factors Encouraging Standardization.**   The attractions of standardization are obvious. It can result in lowered costs and economies of scale in manufacturing, product development, and marketing. Managerial complexity is reduced, and export marketing is facilitated when the same product is exported to several countries.

*Economies of Scale in Production.*   If a product has only one production source, standardizing it will gain the economies of long production runs. As the company multiplies production facilities around the world, this advantage decreases. Similarly, as the optimum size of plant becomes a smaller proportion of world demand, pressure toward product uniformity will decrease.

*Economies in Research and Development.*   If the firm offers the identical product around the world, it gets more mileage out of its R&D efforts. Less research need be directed toward the peculiar desires of national markets, leaving more to be directed toward the search for new products. Uniformity yields a similar advantage in product-development expenses.

*Economies in Marketing.*   Even when marketing is done on a national basis, economies of scale are possible with uniform products. Although sales literature, salesforce training, and advertising may vary somewhat from country to country, they will be much more similar when the product is uniform than when it must be adapted for each national market. Service requirements and parts inventories are easier with a standardized product. When a promotional carry-over from one market to another occurs because of common language and media spillover, it is not a wasted carry-over but an extra return on the advertising.

*Consumer Mobility.*   If the product is one the consumer might purchase when traveling, product standardization is probably necessary to retain his loyalty. Examples of such products are Gillette razor blades, Kodak film, and Hilton Hotel services.

***The Home-Country Image.***   Products considered typically American might advantageously retain their American character in foreign markets. Wrigley's chewing gum, American cigarettes, and Levis are examples. French perfumes or fashion in women's clothing would be French examples. Electronic products, cameras, and small cars seem to benefit from a Japanese home-country image.

***Industrial Products.***   Products in which technical specifications are critical tend to be uniform internationally. Differences significant in international business are "people differences," that is, cultural differences; physical and chemical processes usually do not change when crossing boundaries. In general, then, industrial goods are more standardized than consumer goods. Even when industrial goods are modified, the changes are likely to be minor — an adaptation of the electric voltage or the use of metric measures.

***Operating via Exports.***   If a firm reaches foreign markets only through exports, very likely it is selling uniform products. Even if it is informed of foreign-market peculiarities, it may be deterred from undertaking product modification. Exporters from India chose among foreign markets primarily those in which little or no product adaptation was needed.[2]

**Factors Encouraging Adaptation.**   The greatest argument for adapting products is that by doing so the firm can realize greater profits. The economies referred to above represent cost minimization, not necessarily profit maximization. Modifying products for national or regional markets may raise revenues by more than the costs of adaptation. Apart from this general argument, there are several specific factors that encourage product adaptation.

***Differing Use Conditions.***   Although a given product fulfills a similar functional need in various countries, the conditions under which the product is used may vary greatly from country to country. Climate, for instance, has an effect on products sensitive to temperature or humidity, making it necessary to modify these products for tropical or arctic markets. Even within the United States, cars in northern markets tend to have heaters as standard equipment, whereas in southern markets they have air conditioners. Consider, too, the differences in oil drilling in the Sahara compared with offshore drilling in Alaska. Another factor is differences in the skill level of users, especially between consumers in industrialized nations and those in less developed countries. In regard to cars, trucks, and tires, differing road and traffic conditions may require product changes. Variations in national habits of wearing and washing clothes may necessitate different kinds of washing machines or soaps and detergents. In some countries, for example, clothes are worn a longer time between washings than they are in America. Thus a different washing process is needed. In some European countries, boiling water is used for washing, so the washing machine must have a special heater built in. In many countries, washing is done by a stream and not within some closed machine or container. Therefore, Procter & Gamble and Unilever sell soap or detergent *bars* in those markets.

***Other Market Factors.***   The income per capita of the world's nations ranges from over $18,000 to under $180. This affects not only the size and nature of consumer durables, but even the packaging of inexpensive consumer products. As recently as 1968, Italy passed a law forbidding the sale of cigarettes on a one-at-a-time basis. Also, consumer tastes are not identical around the world. Therefore, foods, fashions, and other items differ from market to market, even in neighboring countries. For example, in cars, the French show a strong preference for four-door models, whereas the Germans select two-door models.

***Influence of Government.***   Nations may forbid certain goods to be imported or manufactured in their country. Conversely, they may require that the product be manufactured locally and not imported. Demands for local production or a high degree of "local content" in the product often lead the international firm to modify it. Governments' taxation policies can affect the nature of the products offered in their markets, a notable example being the European tax on car and engine size that has been a predominant influence on car design there.

Government regulations on products, packaging, and labeling are an important cause of product variation among countries, especially in foods and drugs. For example, the required amount of sugar in a jar of jam or the number of units of penicillin in a bottle may be legally different from country to country. Government specifications affect some industrial goods, too: trucks, tractors, and tires often must meet different government specifications in different markets.

The rise of regional groupings provides a modifying influence, but the differences will not disappear rapidly as long as national producers find government regulations such an effective form of protection against foreign firms.

***Company History and Operations.***   Some firms have foreign operations that predate World War II. Because of the economic nationalism prevailing at that time, these subsidiaries were largely self-contained national operations. Many of them developed products for their markets without regard to international product uniformity within the company. Some carry-over of this practice still exists, even though markets are much more international today.

The firm that has production facilities in several countries will find product adaptation easier than will the firm that must rely on exports from domestic plants. The very fact that the firm has plants in various nations makes adaptation problems much less difficult than those facing the exporting firm. National subsidiaries also can exert pressure on the parent firm to localize products. Because they are interested in profits, they seek the product that will sell best in their market; and because they want to prevent having their functions taken over by a headquarters office they try to be as "national" as possible.

*Extent of Urbanization.*   An intriguing study by Hill and Still showed that products targeted to urban markets in developing countries required only minimal changes from those marketed in developed countries. Products targeted to semi-urban markets required more changes, while products targeted for national markets in developing countries needed even further adaptation to accommodate the requirements of the poorer, more culturally diverse population. These three levels of product adaptation were found through study of 61 subsidiaries operating in 22 less developed countries.[3]

**Convergence of Tastes.**   A major trend encouraging standardization is the convergence of tastes around the world. As the advanced nations grow more alike, with similar income levels, and global communications increase, differences in consumer tastes diminish. Standardized products can therefore appeal across national borders. To succeed, of course, the standardized product must offer value beyond that available from competition.

> Global competition spells the end of domestic territoriality . . . when a global producer offers his lower costs internationally, his patronage expands exponentially. He not only reaches into distant markets, but also attracts customers who previously held to local preferences and now capitulate to the attractions of lesser prices.[4]

Levitt thus sees globalization as succeeding because of the appeal of lower prices, coupled with world-standard technology, quality, and service, all of which persuade consumers to drop local preferences.

An example of such behavior comes from the washing machine industry in Europe. Market research conducted by Hoover, a major producer of washing machines, showed that consumers from the various European countries had distinct preferences. With regard to dimensions, Italians wanted a lower-height machine while most others wanted a 34-inch height; France, Italy, and Britain opted for a narrow machine, while West Germany and Sweden wanted a wide machine, as well as stainless steel drums, while the others were content with enamel drums. While Britain wanted a top-loading feature, the others preferred front-loading washing machines. With regard to washing machine capacity, Italians wanted 4 kilos, Britain and France 5 kilos, and West Germany and Sweden expressed a need for 6 kilos. Spin speed ranged from a preference for 60 rpm in France to medium speed (400 rpm) in Italy to high speed (700 to 850 rpm) in Britain, Sweden, and Germany. Britain and Sweden did not want a water-heating module in the washing machine (because homes in these countries have central hot water) while Italy, Germany and France did want such a feature. France and Britain preferred an agitator washing action, while the others wanted a tumble washing action. Each country also had a distinct preference with regard to external styling; British respondents wanted an inconspicuous appearance, Italy wanted brightly colored machines, the Germans an indestructible appearance, the French opted for elegance, and the Swedish respondents preferred a "strong" appearance.[5] But implementing changes to the machine produced in England to satisfy national preferences would have increased cost by about $18 per unit, as well as required additional capital investment.

Research also showed that the heavily promoted top-of-the-line German washing machine as well as the cheap Italian machine at half the price were both best sellers. In fact, the Italian machine was selling well even to the German market. Levitt inferred from this that an aggressively promoted low-priced washing machine with standard features would be the correct product choice. He notes, "Two things clearly influenced customers to buy: low price regardless of feature preferences, and heavy promotion regardless of price." That is, the low price is capable of convincing customers to accept the absence of certain features. But low price alone is not enough. Aggressive promotion, quality, and service are equally important ingredients of the marketing mix.

Hoover's experience with washing machines suggests that standardization can work as part of a well-thought-out marketing mix. It probably works better with products that do not directly influence a consumer's well-being. That is, products such as clothing, food items, cosmetics and footwear may be less amenable to standardization than industrial products and machines of various sorts. As the example in "Global Marketing" shows, food products are a class where standardization may be foolhardy.

**Adaptation in an Industrial Product Setting.**    Adaptation need not be restricted to consumer products. Lotus 1–2–3, the best-selling spreadsheet software package, underwent a major revision so as to serve the needs of the Japanese market. The adaptation took two years and involved a Japanese software developer as a partner. Major changes included

- Translation of all text (menus, help screens, documentation, etc. into Japanese).
- Incorporation of the latest techniques for entering the 7,000+ Japanese characters from a normal-size keyboard (kana-to-kanji conversion); this feature was licensed from the Japanese partner.
- Addition of a sort field to permit an ability to sort phonetically (based on the pronunciation of kanji).
- Addition of a Japanese data format, counting from the start of the Emperor's reign (Lotus was told politely to not even think of incorporating a provision for entering a new Emperor's name; culturally, one could not question the Emperor's immortality).
- New graph types commonly used by Japanese business, including "radar" charts and "high-low-open-close" charts; graphs could also be printed directly from within the program, unlike in the American version.
- New functions specifically used by Japanese business and analysts (in quality control, for instance).
- An option of disabling the beep that usually sounds when an inappropriate character is typed. Desks are close together in offices, and the Japanese might not want their mistakes to be broadcast within hearing range of their teammates.

# Global Marketing

## Food Products for the Japanese Market

BSN, the French food company, is famous for its Danone brand yogurt. Since yogurt consumption per person in Japan was only a tenth of French consumption, BSN viewed the Japanese market as having considerable untapped potential. Japan had many yogurt companies, but they made and sold yogurt drinks, with solid yogurt products only a quarter of the market. BSN conducted a six-month study with yogurt flown in from France. Then it introduced flavored yogurt to Japan, allying with Ajinomoto, a large food company, in a joint venture. But actual sales were only a fifth of forecasts, and after eight years BSN had not reached break-even.

One problem was that the Japanese did not have clear preferences for Western foods. Hence, they bought what was heavily promoted. When Danone was no longer heavily promoted, they moved to other products, or back to drinking Japanese yogurts. Thus, while BSN thought that it was introducing a healthy food, the Japanese consumers were using Danone products as a substitute for yogurt drinks. Understanding its competition better helped BSN compete slowly against the established Japanese yogurt manufacturers, Meiji Milk, Yakult, and Morinaga Milk. With a 10 percent market share it faces a long, slow haul to profits.

The breakfast-cereal market in Japan presents an interesting contrast. The Japanese consume an average of only half a box a year compared to the American average of 15 boxes a year. Until recently, breakfast cereals were considered a children's snack, and supermarkets stocked a few boxes next to the section with cookies and potato chips, to attract children. But sales have suddenly increased, up 60 percent in 1988 to $142 million (the U.S. market, in contrast, is about $5 billion). Kellogg has been in Japan for 27 years and has a 70 percent market share.

New competition has emerged, such as Nestlé, while the Japanese Cisco Co. now has 17 brands to Kellogg's 13. As the health-conscious Japanese are beginning to eat cereal for breakfast instead of rice and miso soup, new cereals are being introduced that contain bran, granola, whole rice, and even vegetables, sometimes in one-cup portions to allow customers to try new products. One such product, Kellogg's "Genmai Flakes" is made from ground whole rice (instead of corn) and is the second-best selling cereal after Corn Flakes. Nestlé's best-selling Vegetable Time is a salty corn-flakes cereal with vegetable powder, in three colors: green for spinach, orange for carrot and yellow for pumpkin.

As these two examples show, adaptation is more likely to lead to success when selling food products in Japan.

Sources: "A Hard Lesson to Swallow," *Financial Times,* July 14, 1988; and "Japanese are Snapping Up Cereals as Market Crackles with Entries," *The Wall Street Journal,* July 13, 1989.

---

- Capability of supporting several Japanese PC operating systems used on Japanese computers such as the NEC9800, the Toshiba J-3100, and the Fujitsu FM-R personal computer, in addition to the IBM 5500 family. (These are distinct from MS/DOS, which is customary on the IBM PC.)

Lotus indicated that it practically rebuilt the product from the ground up. The result was that the Japanese version was given a special Nikkei International award for Creative Excellence, Lotus being the only international company to receive such an award in 1986. More practically, the Japanese version of Lotus immediately became the best-selling business software product after its introduction in 1986.[6] It is clear that adaptation was crucial to Japanese success.

From the foregoing examples, variables that tend to foster product adaptation can be summarized as follows:

1.   Most important are variations in customer needs, conditions of use, and ability to buy; this can influence adaptation in the basic product, its attributes and features, as well as in ancillary areas such as packaging.
2.   Next in importance are market idiosyncrasies, such as different technical standards; a similar thrust toward adaptation is created by the existence of different languages, as illustrated in the Lotus software adaptation for the Japanese market.
3.   If competition has introduced adapted products that are well-received, a similar response might be tactically correct.
4.   If the costs of adaptation are not high, adaptation is more likely. Thus, a high-tech product will be adapted less than another type of product because of its high R&D costs.
5.   Local production parameters, such as available raw materials, skill level of labor force and nature of equipment might force adaptation.
6.   Government regulations leading to differences in standards might also force product adaptation: thus, cars imported into the United States must meet this country's emission controls. Some Volkswagen Beetles, manufactured in Mexico, cannot be imported for this reason.
7.   Cultural preferences are an important reason for adaptation, especially in personal-use products such as clothing or food and in products or services where design and taste are prominent.

## Product Attributes in International Markets

Product policy goes beyond the product itself — attributes such as brands and trademarks, country of origin, packaging and labeling, and warranty and service policies represent key decision areas.

**Brands and Trademarks**

One problem in international marketing is deciding how to protect the company's brands and trademarks. Another is deciding whether there should be one international brand or different national brands for a given product. A further question regards the role of private branding in international marketing (covered in a subsequent section). If the company uses its own brands, it may want to use multiple brands in the same market to target different customer segments (though this results in higher cost). The main question is whether to promote local country-specific brands, or to establish global and regional brands with appeal across countries.[7] Table 8–1 sets out the major branding choices in international marketing and summarizes their advantages and disadvantages.

**Global Brands.**   Building a global brand is inherent in using a standardized product. Its success depends on a growing convergence of consumer tastes and the coordination of global advertising and promotion. Also important is the development of communications media with multinational reach, such

**Table 8-1**                **A Perspective on Branding**

| Advantages | Disadvantages |
|---|---|
| **No Brand** | |
| Lower production cost | Severe price competition |
| Lower marketing cost | Lack of market identity |
| Lower legal cost | |
| Flexible quality and quantity control | |
| **Branding** | |
| Better identification and awareness | Higher production cost |
| Better chance for product | Higher marketing cost |
| differentiation | Higher legal cost |
| Possible brand loyalty | |
| Possible premium pricing | |
| **Private Brand** | |
| Better margins for dealers | Severe price competition |
| Possibility of larger market share | Lack of market identity |
| No promotional problems | |
| **Manufacturer's Brand** | |
| Better price due to more price | Difficult for small manufacturer with |
| inelasticity | unknown brand or identity |
| Retention of brand loyalty | Requiring brand promotion |
| Better bargaining power | |
| Better control of distribution | |
| **Multiple Brands (in One Market)** | |
| Market segmented for varying needs | Higher marketing cost |
| Creating competitive spirits | Higher inventory cost |
| Avoiding negative connotation of | Loss of economies of scale |
| existing brand | |
| Gaining more retail shelf space | |
| Not hurting existing brand's image | |

as the simultaneous transmission around the world of the Summer Olympics. In such cases, since the same transmission is received around the world, firms benefit if the brands featured in the transmission are familiar to the world audience.

The advantages of global branding include economies of scale in advertising. The uniform image can appeal to globe-trotting consumers. Global brands are also important in securing access to distribution channels. In cases where shelf space is at a premium, as with food products, a company has to convince retailers to carry its products rather than those of competitors. Having a global brand may help persuade them, since from the retailers' standpoint, a global brand is less likely to languish on the shelves.

The creation of a single European market provides additional impetus for creating global brands. A recent European survey[8] (see Table 8–2) quantifies the power of global brands, which is the resulting combination of "share of mind" (consumer awareness) and "esteem." However, "image-power"

| Advantages | Disadvantages |
|---|---|
| *Single Brand (in One Market)* | |
| Marketing efficiency | Assuming market homogeneity |
| Permitting more focused marketing | Existing brand's image hurt when |
| Elimination of brand confusion | trading up/down |
| Good for product with good reputation (halo effect) | Limited shelf space |
| *Local Brands* | |
| Meaningful names | Higher marketing cost |
| Local identification | Higher inventory cost |
| Avoidance of taxation on international brand | Loss of economies of scale |
| | Diffused image |
| Quick market penetration by acquiring local brand | |
| Allowing variations of quantity and quality across markets | |
| *Worldwide Brand* | |
| Maximum marketing efficiency | Assuming market homogeneity |
| Reduction of advertising costs | Problems with black and grey markets |
| Elimination of brand confusion | Possibility of negative connotation |
| Good for culture-free product | Requiring quality and quantity |
| Good for prestigious product | consistency |
| Easy identification/recognition for international travellers | LDCs' opposition and resentment |
| | Legal complications |
| Uniform worldwide image | |

Source: Sak Onkvisit and John J. Shaw, "The International Dimension of Branding," *International Marketing Review* 6, no. 3, Table I, p. 24.

does not translate into the highest market share. The top-ranking brand is Mercedes-Benz, but it has only 3.4 percent of the European car market. (Of course, one could argue that Benz does not compete in all segments of the car market, and that its brand-oriented advertising is aimed at dominating the luxury segment of the market.)

As this table shows, German companies have 11 of the top 50 brands (6 in the auto sector), while France has 10 (mainly high-fashion names), and U.S. and Japanese brands total 15. Global branding apparently appeals to a variety of multinationals from different countries and cuts across diverse industrial sectors.

**The Legal Dimension.**   There is a legal dimension that may limit the possibilities for a global brand. In the United States, brand ownership is established by priority in use. In markets that are under a code-law system, brand ownership is established by priority in registration. A firm that wishes

| Table 8-2 | Landor Associates First Annual Image Power Survey | | | |
| --- | --- | --- | --- | --- |
| | | Image-Power Rank | | Image-Power Rank |
| | Mercedes-Benz | 1 | Chanel | 26 |
| | Philips | 2 | Gillette | 27 |
| | Volkswagen | 3 | Lacoste | 28 |
| | Rolls-Royce | 4 | Honda | 29 |
| | Porsche | 5 | Fiat | 30 |
| | Coca-Cola | 6 | Schweppes | 31 |
| | Ferrari | 7 | Lego | 32 |
| | BMW | 8 | Renault | 33 |
| | Michelin | 9 | Audi | 34 |
| | Volvo | 10 | Grundig | 35 |
| | Adidas | 11 | Peugeot | 36 |
| | Jaguar | 12 | Rolex | 37 |
| | Ford | 13 | Canon | 38 |
| | Nivea | 14 | Cartier | 39 |
| | Esso | 15 | Palmolive | 40 |
| | Sony | 16 | Olivetti | 41 |
| | Nescafe | 17 | Yves St. Laurent | 42 |
| | Colgate | 18 | Citröen | 43 |
| | Christian Dior | 19 | Pierre Cardin | 44 |
| | Nestlé | 20 | Polaroid | 45 |
| | Alfa Romeo | 21 | Ajax | 46 |
| | Levi | 22 | Seiko | 47 |
| | Opel | 23 | Shell | 48 |
| | IBM | 24 | Telefunken | 49 |
| | Pepsi Cola | 25 | General Motors | 50 |

Source: "Building Brands for the New Europe," *Management Europe,* January 16, 1989.

to carry a brand name to foreign markets might find that in some of them, someone else has already registered that name. As an example, Ford Motor Company chose the name Mustang for one of its cars. Later on it found that it could not use this brand in Germany because an established firm was making bicycles under that name. However, Ford had successfully sold its cars in West Germany under the Taurus brand name enabling it to sell Mustangs in Germany using the Taurus name. In other situations, loss of rights to a brand name could be more serious.

*Brand piracy* is quite another matter. The "pirate" is someone who deliberately registers brand names to profit by selling them back to the firms that originated them. In markets where brand-name registration is easy and inexpensive, individuals can make a living by this practice. When a manufacturer wishes to enter a product in one of these markets under the regular brand name and finds that someone has already registered that name, the firm must negotiate with the legal owner. If they can agree on a price, the producer can obtain legal ownership of the brand. If they cannot reach an agreement, the producer must find another brand name — or keep the product off the market.

The most notorious example of brand and trademark piracy occurred in the mid-1960s. Robert Aries, a chemist, registered 330 trademarks in Monaco under a new international trademark convention. Some of the names registered were Bendix, Boeing, BBC, Du Pont, Chase, Morgan, Harpers, Mitsubishi, The New Yorker, Sears, and Texaco. Aries took advantage of loopholes in European laws and the fact that many companies missed filing deadlines.

Developing countries represent a special situation. Many governments in those countries resent the use of international brands, which they claim cause their people to pay higher prices. They also complain that the goodwill premium attached to these brands is created by massive advertising budgets, greater than those for R&D but without the benefits of R&D. They argue that their consumers pay for the advertising to build up the goodwill whose benefit rebounds to the multinational firm and thereby hinders the development of local competitive capacity. Because of these growing concerns, UNCTAD conducted a study on this issue.[9] Planning for international brand policy must take these concerns into consideration, as they may be translated into law.

**Protection: When and Where?**   How does a company protect its brands and trademarks, which are among its most valued possessions? The solution is primarily legal, and the first step is to have expert legal counsel. All we will do here is sketch some dimensions of the problem. The first decision is whether to seek protection for a brand or trademark and in what countries. Obviously, it is better to have registered a brand or mark in a country than to have to buy it back. This might suggest a policy of immediate registration of all of the firm's brands and trademarks in all countries, which would be a good solution if registration were free. Although actual registration fees are modest, the total expenses include legal fees that can raise the costs considerably higher.

Although protection may come through use in common-law countries or through registration in code-law countries, frequently registration must follow use in the one group, and use must follow registration in the other. This usually means two kinds of costs in protecting the mark — registration costs and use costs. Registration involves a fee; use is defined legally and varies from country to country. In order to meet the requirements of brand use, a product may have to be sold or even manufactured locally. But in some cases, the export sale of a few cases of a product has been sufficient to be defined as use of the brand for purposes of protection. In the latter situation, use costs are relatively modest.

Given the costs of protecting brands and trademarks, the firm must evaluate each market and each brand to determine whether to seek protection. Generally, the company name — Philips, IBM, Ford — and the major brands — Coca-Cola, Kodak, Gillette — would be protected in all markets. More selective coverage would be given to secondary brands. Some brands might have no foreign market protection at all if foreign sales of that brand were expected to be minimal. Blue Bell Inc., manufacturers of general apparel and blue jeans, have registered their major trademarks — Wrangler, Blue Bell, and the W switch design — in 135 countries, including the People's Republic of China.

A second decision on brand protection will be necessary in countries that require holders to renew their rights periodically and pay a renewal fee. As can be seen, international brand protection can be a complex task, involving both legal and marketing expertise.

Cost-benefit analysis would apply in deciding what price to pay in buying back rights from a brand pirate. The costs of purchasing the rights to the original brand and the sales with that brand would have to be compared with the costs of establishing a new brand name and the sales associated with it. A third alternative is to refrain from entering, which would mean no costs and no sales, but lost opportunities.

Sometimes brand piracy occurs in a different way. In some markets of the world, particularly Taiwan, Hong Kong, Singapore, South Korea and Mexico, international marketers find local imitations of their brands. In fact, the product, package, and brand are all designed to be as close as possible to the international product, so that customers will think they are getting the international product. Some examples are the following:

| Imitation | International Brand |
|---|---|
| Yalf locks | Yale |
| Coalgate, Goalgate, and so on | Colgate toothpaste |
| Del Mundo | Del Monte |
| Pang's Cold Cream | Pond's |
| Hotex, Potex, Katex, and so on | Kotex |

One Taiwanese drug maker confessed, "If our product doesn't look like the U.S. original, we can't sell it." Such imitation means lost sales to the multinational firm whose brand is being copied. The firm will have difficulty protecting itself against this form of brand piracy because legal action is of limited value in most of these countries. Consumer education through advertising is an expensive way to attack the problem — and probably an ineffective way in these low-literacy markets. For example, Colgate ran television advertising to protect its brand of toothbrushes in Thailand. In spite of this campaign, pirated "Colgate" brushes far outsold the authentic article. This burden is part of the cost of establishing a strong brand position in these markets. Trade in counterfeit goods amounts to $60 billion annually, according to the International Chamber of Commerce.

Levis and Chanel are two of the most pirated brands. Each company spends over $1 million yearly on security with only partial success. Chanel takes 40 to 60 cases to court each year. It feels this helps to deter some counterfeiters. Over 150 victimized firms have formed the International Anti-Counterfeiting Coalition (IACC). Among IACC members are Cartier, Coca-Cola, Playboy, Revlon, Ford, Jordache, Seiko, and Walt Disney.

**Cultural Aspects.**   Even if a firm has no legal problems in securing rights to its brand, it may encounter cultural barriers hindering its use. One problem may be that the name is just not pronounceable in the local language. Names developed for the U.S. market may not be able to travel to many countries. The longer the name and the more specifically American, the less likely it is to be suitable in other languages. Consider the contrary example of some names that have traveled well abroad: Ford, Kodak, Coca-Cola, Esso.

Choice of the name Esso was influenced by the fact that it can be identically pronounced in most of the world's languages. The shift from Esso to Exxon was governed by similar considerations. In its Spanish operation, Sears has not introduced its American brand names, such as Kenmore or Allstate, but simply labels most of the goods Sears. In Castillian Spanish, however, Sears sounds nearly the same as Seat, the name of Spain's automobile manufacturer. Because of the automobile producer's complaints, Sears agreed to add Roebuck to labels on goods having even a remote association with automobiles.

Another problem is that a brand name may have an undesirable connotation in the foreign language. A leather-care products manufacturer planned to market in the EC under the brand name Dreck. He chose the name because it "sounded virile" but changed his mind when he discovered that in German it means "dirt." For various reasons Maxwell House becomes Maxwell Kaffee in Germany, Legal in France, and Monky in Spain.

When faced with barriers to the use of one of its established brands, the firm must seek the best alternative. Occasionally, the firm is lucky and a small change in spelling is sufficient, as when Wrigley changed the spelling of Spearmint to Speermint in Germany to facilitate German pronunciation of the name. Exxon markets its Engro fertilizer around the world, but in French-speaking countries the name could be associated with the French expression *en gros,* which means "roughly, without taking consequences into account." This association was distracting rather than unpleasant, but to avoid it, Exxon added one letter to the name, making it Enagros for French-speaking countries. More frequently, however, the firm has to seek another brand name, as Pepsi did with Patio. Because Brazilians had difficulty pronouncing *Kentucky Fried Chicken,* the company changed to the name *Sanders* in Brazil.

When the Japanese electronics firm Matsushita came into the U.S. market, it found its name was awkward for Americans to pronounce. The brand name *National,* which it uses in many other countries, was being used by a U.S. firm. Therefore, the firm created a new brand name, *Panasonic,* for the U.S. and Canadian markets.

If a brand does have an undesirable connotation in a market, it is unlikely to carry over goodwill from its use elsewhere. The question then becomes whether to develop a new brand for just one market, for a number of foreign markets, or for all international marketing. There are advantages to minimizing the number of brand names on a given product. Wiechmann notes that "the establishment of an international brand name for a given product is generally regarded as an essential source of competitive strength by companies in the consumer goods field."[10] If barriers exist in several markets, the firm might decide to create a new brand for international markets but maintain the original brand name in the domestic market.

**Other Marketing Considerations.**   Several other influences bear on the number of international brands for the firm's products. First there is a difference between the firm's major brands and its secondary brands. On its leading products, the firm is likely to have the same brand all over the world; Coca-Cola and Pepsi Cola are global, for instance, even though these companies have multiple brands on secondary products. Firms maintain brands in part because international goodwill has been built up, and the costs of switching would be great. If the items are tourist goods or benefit from multinational advertising, the advantages of uniformity are so much the greater. Secondary brands may not be known in foreign markets, so choosing a new brand is more feasible.

Another factor is the importance of brand to the product sale. For many consumer products, the brand name is critical in the consumer's decision to purchase. Because of this, firms invest heavily to establish a strong brand image. For other products, factors such as price, services, product performance, or quality are more important. Where the brand is relatively unimportant, the firm does not spend heavily to promote it and does not mind using different brands in foreign markets. For example, when Goodrich's chemical operation in Mexico was forced by the government to link its brand with a new Mexican brand, the company merely dropped the Goodrich name and went with a single Spanish-language brand name. The costs of multiple brands are low in this case, because the firm is spending its marketing dollars in other areas.

Generally the brand of industrial goods is relatively unimportant, although the company name may be very important. The brand names on the individual products may be almost unknown, while the company name and/or trademark may tie diverse products together and play a significant role. The drug industry provides an example. Following is one pattern for a product of the Eli Lilly Company.

- Cordran-N (Flurandrenolone with Neomycin Sulfate, Lilly)
- Drenison with Neomycin     •   International English
- Drenison Avec Neomycine     •   French-speaking areas
- Sermaka-N     •   Germany
- Drenison Com Neomicina     •   Portuguese-speaking areas
- Drenison Con Neomicina     •   Spanish-speaking areas
- Alondra-F con Neomicina     •   Argentina
- Drenison-N     •   Venezuela
- Drocort Med Neomycin     •   Sweden

Often the company has too much investment in the brand on its established products to permit easy changing for foreign markets. If it has mostly new products, of course, it should choose brand names of international suitability.

*Dual brands* for similar products, arising from acquisition or joint venture, can pose a barrier to brand standardization. If the acquiring firm is operating in many markets of a region like Europe, there are probably promotional economies of scale in having just one brand on a product. But if the firm chooses its own brand, it will lose the goodwill attached to the existing national brand. As one food marketer noted: "Our name and symbol aren't important. What counts is getting in the market with a product. You keep the name you acquired, as that is part of what you paid for."

For example, Caterpillar acquired Towmotor, which was well established in the U.S. market. It retained the Towmotor brand for the U.S. market but used the Caterpillar brand overseas where Towmotor was not well known.

In some product areas, dual brands are a way of making a two-pronged attack on the market. We see that domestically, for example, when Procter & Gamble has multiple brands for similar kinds of detergents. Goodyear makes both Goodyear and Kelly tires in America and bought a German tire company called Fulda. In a new plant in Greece, Goodyear produces all three brands and probably gains much better distributor coverage thereby.

The firm's ability to use a multi-brand strategy on a line of products has been challenged by European consumer groups. The EC competition authorities studied Philips, AEG-Telefunken, Bosch-Siemens, Thompson-Brandt, Zanussi, Indesit, General Electric (U.K.), Hoover, and Electrolux, looking at "anomalies of competition." They concluded that there is much less variety available to the consumer than would appear from the number of brands on the market. Consumer groups claimed that multiple branding is "a devious way to double shelf space or create the illusion that the consumer has a wide selection." Product-testing organizations said multi-branding posed a problem in testing and reporting to consumers.

In Sweden, the ombudsman took Electrolux to court, charging that the firm misled consumers by offering virtually identical kitchen stoves under three different brand names. Earlier the ombudsman had taken a paint manufacturer to court on a similar complaint. In the paint case, the manufacturer was able to prove a substantive difference between the two brands. In the Electrolux case, the firm eliminated Swedish production of one of the three brands and agreed to provide "adequate information" to consumers about the other two brands.

**Product Piracy and Counterfeiting.**   As more trade becomes technology-intensive, intellectual property protection is essential to maintaining competitive advantage. Firms spend large amounts of money creating technology through R&D. It takes investment in people — programmers and musicians and directors and actors — to produce software, a best-selling record, or a successful film. Pharmaceutical companies can easily spend $100 million over ten years to develop a new pharmaceutical drug. Patent copyright law protects such investments.

Different nations have different regulations on what can be protected, the extent of protection, and period of protection. Developing nations need technology and are unwilling to pay large royalties to multinationals, while the triad economies increasingly depend on technology-based exports. Even within the developed nations, there are large differences in how technology is protected. A celebrated instance is the end of copyright protection in Japan for the Beatles' Sergeant Pepper's record. Japanese law limits copyright law for record companies to 20 years. Hence, in 1987, when the 20 years were up, a Japanese CD manufacturer introduced nine discount-priced collections of Beatles songs, while a branch of Marubeni Corp., a giant trading company, was able to buy master tapes and issue recordings of jazz classics by artists such as Miles Davis, John Coltrane, and Nat King Cole. In contrast, the U.S. copyright law provides 75 years of protection to producers, performers, and record companies.[11]

A similar problem arises in Thailand, whose copyright laws do not provide protection for software, allowing best-selling United States programs such as Lotus 1–2–3 to sell for about $15 as against an average price of $250 in the United States. Such piracy also hurts other industries where intellectual property is important such as pharmaceuticals and audio and video tapes.

**Protecting Brand Names.**   Protecting brands is as crucial as protecting technology in global marketing. Brands become increasingly important as consumers shop in impersonal environments such as mass-market outlets. The brand gives a product personality and reassures the customer of quality and service.

Marlboro is just such a global brand. The Marlboro man never speaks. The image, the American cowboy in a red flannel shirt, has universal appeal. Marlboro accounts for over one-quarter of Philip Morris's cigarette revenues, nearly 300 billion cigarettes a year. It is a quintessential American product, perhaps because of Hollywood's westerns seen the world over. The value of this brand alone to Philip Morris has been estimated at $10 billion.[12]

Undercutting such a brand presence could destroy Philip Morris's ability to maintain its competitive edge. Yet, recent EC legislation may have such a negative impact. In preparation for 1992, the EC has been harmonizing advertising. As part of such rules, it has proposed that cigarette print and poster ads (the only form of advertising open to cigarette manufacturers) be restricted to presentation of the cigarette packaging and information about tar and nicotine content, with health warnings to take up between 10 to 20 percent of the ad space. Such a restriction would prevent companies from using familiar images such as the Marlboro man and the Virginia Slims woman. Since prices are largely determined by excise taxes, creative advertising is the major approach to discriminating between brands. The legislation would take away any competitive edge enjoyed by Marlboro. Tobacco companies have few hopes of lobbying against such restrictions, as the EC bases its regulations on the fact that tobacco products kill 440,000 people every year in the EC.[13]

There may be a few benefits from a lack of brand and copyright protection. Consumers may pay less, though they may have to accept lower quality, which can be a health hazard, especially in an industry such as pharmaceuticals. Prestige brands may carry less status if they can be easily counterfeited, resulting in a reduction in purchase price. But manufacturers might attempt to raise prices to recover their R&D costs in a shorter time frame, and this would raise prices.

From the manufacturer's standpoint, the lack of protection can result in sales lost to the imitators, who are seen as competing unfairly. The reduced sales and cash flow in turn will reduce investment in innovation. Consumers may ultimately suffer from a lack of new high-technology and innovative products. Countries dependent on technology, such as the United States, will see their exports decrease, and job losses can result in the affected industries. Overseas, U.S. firms will lose sales to foreign companies that can copy technology or brand names or copyrighted material with impunity. In the short run, foreign industry and foreign consumers are the beneficiaries.[14] Overall, world welfare is likely to decline over time unless regulations allow a fair return to investments in technology and product differentiation.

**Private Branding.**  In private branding, which is common in consumer goods marketing, the manufacturer cedes control over marketing to the retailer or distributor. That is, the manufacturer supplies goods, but the retailer sells these goods under its own brand names. Thus, a marketer such as Spiegel might order quantities of dresses, linen, towels, lamps, and accessories, all to be sold through catalogs under the Spiegel brand name. Indeed, Spiegel has increased the proportion of private-label apparel that it sells to about 60 percent of total garment sales. Most of its purchases are from Far East clothing subcontractors. The original manufacturer's identity is lost, and its margins tend to be lower on private-brand sales.

Private branding provides a quick and relatively low-cost approach to penetrating foreign markets, though the seller fails to establish any relationship with the ultimate buyer and hence has little control over the marketing relationship. The manufacturer has no say in the prices charged and receives little direct feedback from the market. Nor can service and after-sales support be used as a means of forging long-term ties with the ultimate buyer. However, private branding is a useful means of test-marketing products in markets whose potential is likely to grow in the future. When product specifications are provided by a buyer such as Spiegel, which has a database of nearly 5 million active customers,[15] private-brand sales become a window on an emerging market and allow the manufacturer to better position itself for future direct entry. Spiegel benefits from its name becoming a well-known brand.

However, such private label experience may not easily transfer across national markets. For example, Sainsbury, Britain's largest supermarket operator, has been successful in the United Kingdom in selling private label products such as smoked salmon and its own brand of champagne. When it expanded into the United States it decided not to push its private label approach until it learnt how private label products in these product categories are evaluated by American consumers.

**Private Brands and Original Equipment Manufacturer (OEM) Sales.**   OEM contracts are related to brand strategies, especially in the marketing of components and sub-assemblies. For example, manufacturers of airbags, such as TRW or Morton International, would face the task of convincing automobile buyers to install their airbag as standard equipment on cars manufactured without an OEM contract. In the international arena, this would mean competing against other manufacturers of airbags. Since, instead, the sale is made to the auto manufacturer, the final consumer buys the airbags as part of the auto and does not specify the make of airbag he or she prefers.

OEM deals are an industrial marketing task, and the selling cycle may be long, entailing careful assessment by several executives and engineers. But when the sale is made, it is for large volumes, and repeat business is likely as long as price, delivery, and quality standards are satisfactory. OEM sales generally involve direct selling and close involvement with the buyers, often to the extent of redesigning products or adding features for large-volume customers. There is also a risk factor: if such a customer decides to switch suppliers, the loss of volume might result in unabsorbed overhead and excess capacity.

OEM sales are indirect means of penetrating different segments of a market, whether domestic or foreign. Tandy Corp., the operator of 4,800 Radio Shack computer stores in the United States, agreed to manufacture 16- and 32-bit portable computers for Matsushita, which would sell them in the United States under its Panasonic brand name. Matsushita's aim was to circumvent the 100 percent punitive tariffs imposed by the U.S. government on these imports. Tandy was happy to enhance its reputation for quality and low-cost manufacturing by being associated with the Panasonic label. At the same time, it obtains preferential access and low prices in buying Matsushita's memory chips — an item periodically in short supply. Furthermore, Matsushita will be selling the computers purchased from Tandy through office-products retailers; the segment of interest here are large corporations, a segment that Radio Shack has had difficulty in selling to.

Thus, the OEM sale to Matsushita allows Tandy to (indirectly) penetrate the Fortune 500 segment while selling to individuals and small businesses through the Radio Shack chain. Long term, the alliance will also help Tandy in developing products for the Japanese market.[16]

The Japanese have been very successful international marketers in recent years, and private branding has played a role in their success. Mitsubishi was an unknown factor in automobiles. By marketing initially under the Chrysler name (when Chrysler was strong), it was able to get quickly established in the U.S. market. Japanese producers led by Sony and Matsushita were marketing 80 percent of their video tape recorders under private brands, two of the leading ones being RCA and Zenith. Hitachi supplied large computers to Olivetti, BASF and National Advanced Systems for sale under their names. Fujitsu did the same with TRW, Amdahl, and Siemens. The president of Fujitsu said that lack of brand-name recognition was the major obstacle to foreign sales. The private-brand approach was the company's response. Similarly Toshiba markets consumer electronics items in Japan under its own name that are made by Tatung in Taiwan.

The newest firms using private branding to break into foreign markets are manufacturers from the "Four Tigers" — Hong Kong, Korea, Singapore, and Taiwan. They used the brands of their customers to make up for the lack of consumer recognition and acceptance of their own company names. Their customers included such established names as Mattel and IBM in addition to such prominent retailers as K Mart, Lord and Taylor, Nieman-Marcus, J. C. Penney, and Sears. But the owners of the brand may seek lower-cost suppliers, leaving the original producer without a market. Partly because of this fear, firms such as Tatung, Samsung, Lucky Goldstar, and Hyundai began promoting their own brand names.

Another situation may confront the smaller firm if it wishes to market abroad through an export management company (see Chapter 10) rather than through its own export department. The export management company may want its own brand on the goods to achieve greater control and protection in market development. If the manufacturer accedes, the producing firm is giving up developing a market for itself. This can hurt the firm later if it wants to go more directly into foreign markets.

**Private Brands as a Threat.**   We have looked at private branding as a way of breaking into a market. For firms already established in a market, private branding by retailers can be a threat to their survival. Large retailing groups in the major European countries are moving increasingly into their own brands. They like the greater control and higher margins this gives them. Because of the power of the retailing groups, they have been able to gain consumer acceptance and a reasonable reputation for quality, forcing producers' brands to fight very hard for space on the retailers' shelves. Producers will need to maintain a lead in product innovation and quality, conduct heavy advertising, and be very price-competitive at the same time — a difficult task.

In the United Kingdom, where private brands had achieved a 30 percent share of the packaged grocery market by 1985, Campbell's and the Nestlé affiliate there began supplying private branded products to retailers. Heinz, which had a strong number one position there, has instead fought back to maintain its retail distribution and the leading position of its own brands.

**Conclusions on International Brand Management**   One decision in international brand management is whether to register a brand and in which markets. The marketer and a lawyer should consult on this question. Another decision is whether to have uniform global brands or different national brands.

Reducing brand diversity involves phasing out one brand while minimizing the loss of goodwill associated with it. One way to do this is to emphasize the company name and trademark as a link between the old and new brand names. Even where a firm wants separate brands in different countries, it can use the company name, trademark, and package design for maximum visual similarity.

S. C. Johnson Company markets home-care products in many European countries and prefers nationalized brand names for greater local identification. However, to maximize visual similarity for promotion, the package shape, label design, and color are identical, including the company symbol. Thus, the products appear very much alike in different markets, even though the brand name and the copy on the label differ from country to country.

A *family brand approach* is another way a firm can reduce brand diversity. Sears simply uses the Sears label in Spain rather than all of its American brand names. Exxon uses the Atlas brand for its tire, battery, and accessory business in the United States but used the Esso brand exclusively when it introduced these items into Germany. Such an approach gave the promotional strength of the Esso name to all the products and economies of scale in promotion.

## Country-of-Origin Effect

Numerous studies have shown that consumers evaluate a product not only by its appearance and physical characteristics but also by the country in which it was produced. This is the country-of-origin effect. Certain countries have a good image for certain kinds of products — Germany for cars, France for women's fashion, Britain for men's fashion. If a firm is producing a product in a country that does not have a favorable image for that product, it will have a hard task marketing it.

Japan and Germany have replaced the United States as the favored source of cars. When Honda and Volkswagen began producing in America, customers wanted to buy the cars that came from Germany or Japan, rather than those produced or assembled in the United States. General Motors' joint venture with Toyota began producing the Nova, essentially a Toyota assembled in the United States. Part of the consumer reaction is indicated by the following quotation from one customer who replaced his Camaro with a Toyota Corolla after considering the Nova. "The Nova is new and partly made by Chevrolet. The Toyota is all Toyota."

Some products are *binational* in origin, such as the Honda Civic made in the United States. How would consumers rate such products? That is, which country of origin would they give more weight to? A study of color TVs and subcompact autos with binational origins found that both the source country and brand name affect perception of quality, although source country seems more important than the brand name. Further, the country of origin does not influence the consumer's perception of all attributes of the product in the same way. German products, for example, were rated high on quality but low on economy. The country effect may carry across product categories, so that a product from Germany may be regarded as being of high quality whether it is a car or a toaster.[17]

**Product
Standards**

Product standards in different markets determine whether a foreign product can be sold without adaptation. Standards can be divided into technical ones and government-mandated ones. An example of technical standards can be found in the personal computer industry, where IBM and its competitors all use Intel's 80286, 80386, or 80486 chips and Microsoft's MS/DOS or OS/2 operating systems. This means that foreign manufacturers who have not adopted the MS/DOS standard are at a disadvantage.

Currently, a struggle is taking place to establish a standard RISC (Reduced Instruction Set Computing) microprocessor around which a new class of 32-bit RISC engineering workstations will be built. Competing possibilities are the Sparc chip from Sun Microsystems, and chips from Motorola, Hewlett Packard, and MIPS Computer. Each of these firms is racing to get major manufacturers *around the world* to use its chip and thus make it the industry standard.[18] Given the expense of writing software, software developers will develop programs for the chip that has the highest installed base, further increasing demand and making the standard unassailable.

In an attempt to make the Sparc chip the global standard in workstations, Sun Microsystems has licensed its design to Philips in the Netherlands and Fujitsu in Japan. Similarly, Hewlett-Packard has formed an alliance with Japan's Hitachi and Samsung of Korea, letting Samsung manufacture both chips and workstations using HP technology. In response, MIPS Computer has licensed its chip to Japan's NEC, while Motorola has an agreement to let Thomson (of France) manufacture a version of its 32-bit RISC chip. Such agreements may seem a far cry from product-related marketing issues; but the market for RISC computers is expected to grow dramatically, and the firm whose chip becomes the industry standard will capture high market share in all major markets, not just in the United States. Thus, OEM agreements become important tools for establishing standards in high-technology products with short product life cycles.

Government legislation is another source of divergent product standards. As an example, the EC recently raised anti-pollution standards for small car engines, making such cars more expensive. The new standards impact heavily on manufacturers such as Peugeot and Renault, where small cars are about one-third of total output. The same standards benefit German car-makers, who already met stricter German anti-pollution standards. Hence, they gain a march on competition, as do the U.S. companies such as Ford and General Motors. The new standards will also increase demand for catalytic converters and fuel injection systems, as these are needed to control emissions to meet the new standards.

Often, government standards can become a means of keeping out foreign competition. Such standards may be considered as a non-tariff barrier. With new pharmaceuticals, Japan demands that tests be conducted in Japan before marketing approval is received. The fact that U.S. companies have already met rigorous U.S. FDA standards is not sufficient. One consequence is that U.S. pharmaceutical companies must spend additional time and money getting Japanese approvals, which acts as an impediment to entering the Japanese market. Such regulations also give the Japanese competitors additional time to study new products from overseas and develop a response.

In many Third World markets, the process of setting standards is just beginning. These countries often lack technical expertise and the financial resources to do an adequate job on their own. Therefore, they often turn to authorities from Europe, Japan, and the United States. Industries from the United States would certainly gain from helping in this process so that sales of U.S.-made products would be facilitated.

For example, the Saudi Arabian Standards Organization (SASO) has been receiving help from experts from Japan, the United Kingdom, France, and West Germany in updating product standards for over 42,000 products. And the standards being developed seem to favor manufacturers from those countries. Once Saudi Arabian standards are set, they are likely to be copied by smaller neighboring countries such as Bahrain, Kuwait, and the United Arab Emirates, all oil-producing countries with rising incomes.

The Saudi example is not unique. Brazil received a gift of several volumes of literature on German product standards in Portuguese, and European interests have helped India build a $16 million laboratory to certify that Indian electronic components meet European standards. The hope is that the labs will help India meet European standards and thus increase its exports to Europe; then it might use its hard currency earnings to import European telecommunication products. And Japan initiated a training program for standards personnel from 28 developing countries and sends out Japanese standards experts to provide training in developing countries.

While U.S. products may be safe and technically excellent, it is not enough that they meet Underwriters Laboratories (UL) standards alone. Unless U.S. firms as a group can influence other nations to accept UL standards as their own, they will probably lose some markets to foreign competitors that have become more adept at influencing and adhering to different national standards. Another way that standards can serve to exclude foreign products is the cumbersome certification requirements some countries enforce, raising costs to a prohibitive point.

## Packaging and Labeling

Many of the international considerations presented in the discussion of the basic product would apply with equal force to such auxiliary product features as the package, label, or warranty. Other special factors affect these product features, too, however, and we will discuss these separately. Note that much of Chapters 3 and 4 relate to this discussion.

**Packaging.** Many companies have spent great sums finding the best packaging. Whether this same packaging can be used in foreign markets depends on whether the conditions affecting package choice are similar. Packages need to be analyzed in both their protectional and their promotional aspects.

The kind of product protection needed in one market may differ from that needed elsewhere. A hot, humid climate probably requires a package different from that needed in a cooler, drier area. The kind of transportation and handling the product receives can also dictate packaging differences;

stronger protection must be built into the package if it will be subjected to bad roads, long distances, and frequent or rough handling.

Long, slow distribution channels also increase the demands on the package. If one market has a three-month cycle of production to final consumption and another market has a six-month cycle, the latter market probably will require a more durable and expensive package. This is especially true if the market with a slow distribution cycle also has bad transportation and other conditions punishing to packages, as is frequently the case. For this reason the poorer countries may require more expensive packaging in spite of their lower purchasing power. Furthermore, if the buyer has a slow usage rate and lacks appropriate storage facilities, the demands on the package are increased.

Promotional aspects of packaging, those attributes which help persuade channel members to handle the product and consumers to buy it, often vary among markets too. Channel members want minimum breakage and theft, plus ease of handling. The retailer is concerned about shelf storage and display. A country with a large number of very small retail outlets may want a different package than a country where self-service supermarkets are popular. Because of shopping habits and retail structure, detergent sold in France, Germany, and Spain is often packaged in 3½ kilogram round drums.

The kind of package that will help persuade the consumer to buy the product will depend on local cultural factors. What colors and shapes and materials do consumers prefer? Some products sold in aerosol or glass containers in America are sold in tubes in Europe. Countries exhibit differences in their preferences for metal over glass or plastic over paper, and so on. Gillette uses the cheaper squeeze bottle in poorer countries in contrast to the spray container used elsewhere. Procter & Gamble found that Mexicans prefer to buy their detergent in polyethylene bags rather than boxes or drums.

Package *size* is one of the most important packaging variables in international marketing. The major determinant of package size for consumer goods is the income level in the market. Low incomes usually mean low usage rates and small purchase amounts. For example, items such as razor blades are sold by the single unit rather than by the package. And, as mentioned earlier, single cigarettes were retailed until 1968 in Italy. In Latin America, Procter & Gamble sells one-use *Ace* detergent packages and one-use *Drene* shampoo packages. A drug company found four variables that affected its package size in various markets: (1) government reimbursement practices (with socialized medicine in most markets), (2) doctors' preferences, (3) patients' needs, (4) competitive practices.

Shopping habits often reinforce income constraints on package size. If daily rather than weekly shopping is the practice, the need for large packages is reduced. Furthermore, if the shopper has no car in which to carry the merchandise, the desirability of large packages diminishes. At the channel intermediaries, similar influences are at work. For example, one food processor that sells 48-can cases to the channel members in America sells only 12- or 24-can cases to different European markets.

*Packaging Decisions.* The first step in selecting a package for a market is to determine national preferences. Perhaps a package already in use in other markets will meet these preferences. If not, the firm must evaluate the costs of creating a new package, or of making changes in filling or packing machines. If a new plant is built for the new market, these problems recede. They become critical, however, when one production source serves several national markets.

If markets all require different packaging, the production and packaging operations will be less efficient. From the production point of view, standardization of shapes, sizes, and packaging materials is desirable, although differences in colors and aesthetics of the package can be introduced with relatively little expense. Even in aesthetics, however, standardization is desirable if the goods are promoted in international campaigns or are "tourist goods." For example, Kodak's yellow film packages are familiar to all international travelers. Also, 3M was fortunate enough to develop a global identity for its Scotch brand electronic recording products. After its research found global similarities in consumer demographics for the products, the company developed a uniform global packaging system that was tested in five countries. Favorable results led them to implement the new packaging in all their plants — in Brazil, Europe, Japan, and the United States.

The firm should be alert to the need for innovation in its packaging as consumer habits change, incomes rise, or retailing becomes more modern in a given market. And a new consideration in packaging has arisen in the European market — that of pollution caused by throwaway packages. Consumer groups and governments are pressing for action on this problem. The alert firm will take the lead in responding to these pressures. Firms that have already faced this problem in the United States should have an advantage in dealing with it as it arises in other countries.

**Labeling.** Labeling is related to packaging, but has its own particular parameters. The major elements are language and government regulations, with consumer information a continuous concern.

*Language.* Even if labels were standardized in content from country to country, the language would probably vary in each market. If the label contains important communication for consumers, usually it must be in their language, which means different language labels in most markets. The resulting economic loss is slight, since only printing diseconomies are involved. Occasionally, firms try to avoid even this cost. One way is through the use of multilingual labels; for example, one label might carry information in French, German, and Italian for a product serving all three markets. Some markets, such as Belgium, Canada, and Switzerland, are multilingual and thus require multilingual labels even within a single market. In Canada, bilingual French and English labeling is a requirement, and the government can confiscate goods that lack it.

Sometimes the nature of the product allows the use of the same language everywhere. For example, products such as perfumes or cosmetics might be labeled in French in non-French-speaking countries. For other products, an American or English image might be useful in all markets. A French producer of chewing gum, considered an American product, chose the brand name Hollywood and printed the label entirely in English, except for the word *Tirez* (pull) on the package opener. And an American bra manufacturer kept the American package and label intact all over the world.

Extensive information must be communicated to the customer about the use of some products. In this situation, the label may have brief, one-language copy but be supplemented by a detailed multilingual insert inside the package, as is done with photographic film and drugs.

**Government.**  Government requirements are of major importance in labeling, and labeling laws vary widely. Some aspects covered by government regulations are mark of origin, weight, description of contents and ingredients, name of producer, special information as to additives, and chemical or fat content. With all these variables, each country inevitably has somewhat different requirements. Equally inevitably, these requirements serve to give some protection to national producers.

In addition to meeting existing government requirements, the alert firm will be sensitive to new developments. For example, the common-market countries, Canada, Japan, and the United States, have all expressed interest in energy-use labeling for appliances. Even where this is not currently a government requirement, the firm should prepare for it, if it is in the consumer's interest.

Sometimes the firm may want to go beyond government requirements in developing countries. The poorer countries have the least consumer protection, yet need the most protection because of their consumers' lesser education and experience. Going beyond minimal legal requirements in its labeling to assure proper and safe usage of its products may not only increase consumer satisfaction with a company but also head off future conflicts. For example, the multinational drug companies have come under fierce attack for their alleged misleading promotion and labeling practices in developing countries, even though they claim to meet national requirements in those countries. And remember the famous case of Nestlé and the marketing of its infant formula in developing countries. Accused of using unsuitable — even dangerous — promotion and labeling practices for its baby formula, the company was boycotted by United States consumers.

A final aspect of labeling is the manufacturer's own interest in using the label to promote the product. Labeling is one avenue of communication with customers. The producer wants the label to encourage purchase and facilitate use of the product to assure consumer satisfaction and repeat purchase. The message that will accomplish these goals depends on the particular consumption system into which the product fits. These consumption systems are usually culturally determined and may vary from country to country. This may be a further source of lack of labeling standardization in international marketing.

Making decisions on labeling for foreign markets is easier than it is on other marketing questions for two reasons: (1) concerning government regulations, the firm has no choice — it must conform; (2) concerning costs, the firm can afford nonstandardized labeling because it is much less expensive than nonstandardized products or packages. Although this procedure could lead to different labels in each market, the firm's demands for international uniformity should be recognized where they are important. As some of the examples cited, international uniformity may be more important to the firm than national distinctiveness. Finally, the firm may work through industry associations in its various markets to try to attain greater uniformity in national regulations.

## Warranty and Service Policies

Consumers usually are buying performance, not the physical characteristics of a product. Thus the purchasing decision for certain products will be influenced by warranty and service policies offered. The manufacturer may consider warranty and service to be something apart from the product, but the firm is more attuned to its market if it sees them as integral parts thereof.

**Warranties.**   A *warranty* is a promise by the seller that the product will do what it is supposed to do. It can give buyers the reassurance they need in order to purchase. This reassurance can be especially important to companies selling in foreign markets. Uneasiness about purchasing from a foreign — that is, unreachable — company can be largely offset by strong warranty and service programs.

In international marketing the warranty questions are simple: (1) Should the firm have the same warranty internationally that it has domestically? (2) Should the firm keep the same warranty for all markets or adapt on a country-by-country basis? (3) Should the firm use the warranty as a competitive weapon?

From the manufacturer's point of view, warranties have both protective and promotional aspects. They help to protect the manufacturer against unreasonable claims by limiting the firm's liability. If the warranty also offers sufficient reassurance to buyers, it can be one of the factors persuading them to buy, especially if one producer's warranty promises more than another's. The promotional aspect of warranties is most likely to change in international marketing.

*Standardization?*   A number of parameters affect the decision to have a standardized international warranty policy. First, warranty standardization does not offer the economies of scale in production and promotion that standardization in product, packaging, or branding offers. Because the firm can expect little cost reduction from international warranty standardization, we might not expect to see serious efforts in this direction; however, some external pressures may encourage standardization:

1. If the market is truly international, having different warranties in different countries may be impossible. For example, the customers of the firm may themselves be international companies — in construction, mining, petroleum, or manufacturing. Such customers would probably be unwilling to accept a warranty on a product delivered to a Latin American operation if it were different from that on the same product delivered to a European operation.

2. If the product is purchased in one market but may need service in another market, it is desirable that the warranty be the same in both markets. This is why warranties are uniform throughout the U.S. market. On automobiles, for example, it will be necessary to have uniform warranties in a regional market like Western Europe. Indeed, the EC now requires community-wide warranties on automobiles. The growth of regional economic groupings around the world is further encouragement to standardized warranties.

3. On products where human life can be endangered, warranties are more likely to be uniform because the basic need of the user is the same all over the world. Products in this category include drugs, airplanes, and elevators.

4. If the company has just one production source for world markets, uniform warranties are more likely. But universal warranties can be offered only if the firm has the worldwide service programs to support them. This highlights the fact that a warranty is meaningful only to the extent that it has a service program backing it.

Although standardization in warranties is less rewarding to the firm than other kinds of standardization, we can see why some international firms — for example, Allis Chalmers, Bell & Howell, Brunswick (bowling equipment), Caterpillar, A. B. Dick, Parker Pen, and Sunbeam — are standardizing their warranties.

*Or Localization?*    Although a few strong pressures encourage uniform international warranties, several advantages influence the firm to tailor its warranties to the conditions of individual national markets.

1. Firms lack the incentive to standardize their warranties because they receive no significant economic gains by doing so.

2. Having many production sources, each with a different quality-control standard, can make it difficult for the firm to give a uniform guarantee to customers of the different plants.

3. Differing use conditions in various foreign markets can make a universal warranty too expensive. Operating equipment in extreme heat, cold, humidity, dust, or salty sea air can cause breakdowns that arise not from product defects but from adverse use conditions. Driving on primitive roads causes greater wear than driving the same mileage on an expressway.

4. Warranties can be useful as competitive promotional tools. Because the competitive situation of the firm varies from country to country, it often finds it desirable to vary its warranties to meet local conditions.

5.  If a firm does not have an international service network of fairly even quality, it will find it difficult to offer a uniform warranty. If the warranty is to be more than mere words, the firm must be capable of fulfilling its service requirements; that is, uniform warranty implies uniform service capability. This is difficult to achieve in global marketing.

General Motors provides a good illustration of how the various warranty constraints interact. Because of different government requirements and differing use conditions and competitive situations, General Motors' warranties range from three months or 4,000 miles up to 24 months and unlimited mileage. Furthermore, GM offers higher warranties on locally produced cars than on imports, because the local cars are designed for local conditions.

We have not provided a clear answer on warranty standardization. The situation of the firm and the industry needs to be examined before any decision can be made. Generally, however, warranty standardization is less critical in the firm's international operations than standardization of other product attributes.

***Warranties as a Competitive Tool.***   Given the promotional aspect of warranties, the possibility of using them as a means of competition arises. We see examples in the American market, ranging from the automobile industry to the blanket guarantee of satisfaction offered by Sears. Although this tool is also available in international marketing, whether it is used depends on the firm's circumstances in its various markets. First, the kind of competitive weapons a firm uses depends on its own strengths as well as on the strengths and practices of competitors. If rivals compete on warranty, the firm usually needs to be competitive. That is, the firm must offer a warranty as good as that offered by the others, unless it has offsetting advantages in other areas.

Second, the firm's position in the particular market can determine whether it competes on warranty. Someone has observed that it is the weakest firm that offers the most spectacular warranties. This may be because the warranty is a competitive weapon that can be quickly prepared.

The Simca Company was one of the smaller members of the French and European automobile industry. Not long after Chrysler became its majority stockholder, it became the first European manufacturer to guarantee certain essential parts of its new autos for two years or 60,000 kilometers. This significant expansion of warranty coverage in the European automobile industry was meant to give a boost to Simca's market penetration similar to the boost Chrysler had received earlier in the U.S. market when it introduced the five-year/50,000-mile warranty. Note also that Chrysler had warranties in Europe different from those in America. When it began selling Simcas in the United States, Chrysler did apply the five-year/50,000-mile warranty to the imported cars but maintained the two-year warranty in Europe.

Third, the firm's technological skill may determine how it uses the warranty. A warranty can be stronger if the product is more reliable than competitors' products. If increased quality and reliability are realized, the warranty can be increased without a corresponding increase in service costs.

Fourth, competitive use of warranty depends on the service facilities that support it. No lasting gain can be achieved by offering a warranty that cannot be fulfilled by product reliability and service support. Whether the firm uses the warranty competitively will depend further on the total competitive arsenal it has available. Although the warranty can be a useful tool, it is easily imitated. As one marketer noted, "If we can be first in warranty, we tell the story and get the benefit of leadership. Elsewhere we try not to disturb the market."

**Service.**   This section concerns postsale service. We consider presale service under "Personal Selling" in Chapter 13. Warranty and service policies are related in principle but differ in practice. Designing a warranty is largely a legal exercise, although with marketing implications. Creating an international service capability can involve investment in facilities, staffing, and training, and a distribution network. The question here is not one of standardization; it is rather how to offer the best service around the world. Because customers buying from a foreign firm tend to worry more about service than they do when buying from a national firm, the exporter or multinational company needs to be especially concerned about its service capability.

Product safety is related to the service problem. ITT has a common denominator of product safety policies applicable to all ITT products wherever made or sold. The company set up a Corporate Product Safety Committee to develop an overall product safety program. It has four area subcommittees, explicitly recognizing market differences.

The issue of standardization of service does not arise because it is impossible to fulfill. Even in the U.S. market where the automobile companies have uniform warranties, they do not offer uniform service. As any car owner knows, service varies from dealer to dealer even in the same city. Nevertheless, most companies try to offer the best service possible in all markets, because consumer satisfaction and repeat purchases will relate to the service received, especially as compared with the competition. Providing adequate service is a problem in international marketing. The customer's *need for service* is a function of his or her use and maintenance conditions, and these may vary from market to market.

For example, Japanese machine-tool producers found that their American customers used (punished) the machines more than their Japanese customers. Because of their higher labor costs, American firms used the machines more intensively and could not afford downtime for maintenance. The Japanese producers had to modify both their product and their service program in selling to the American market.

On the other hand, the manufacturer's *ability to supply service* is a function of the firm's international involvement. Most companies selling internationally do not have subsidiaries in all their foreign markets. They must rely on their distributors to provide service where they have no facilities of their own. Finding good distributors that can also service the product is critical. Often the distributors' service programs must be supplemented by the efforts of the producer.

***Handling Service Problems.***    International service problems can be attacked in several ways. One method is to establish a good distributor network with adequate service capabilities. Even before that, however, the product should be designed with both service and user in mind. If the product is designed with service in mind, repairs will be easier for the foreign distributor, whose capabilities may be less than those in the domestic market. If the product is designed with the user in mind, his or her use conditions and maintenance abilities (or lack of them) are accounted for. This suggests that a simple, sturdy, though primitive, product may be more suitable for some markets than the latest automatic device, which is more efficient but also in greater need of maintenance.

Because of the difficulties in finding international distributor networks with adequate service capability, many firms supplement their distributors' efforts by establishing service training programs. The three basic types of service training programs are illustrated below from the viewpoint of a U.S. firm.

1.    The firm invites distributor service personnel to the United States for training. The feasibility depends on the number of people involved and the complexity of the training program. Generally, the fewer the people and the more complex the training, the more desirable it is to bring them to the United States to get economies of scale. Overseas distributor personnel might participate in programs for American service trainees if the language problem can be overcome.

2.    When it is not economical to bring distributor personnel to the United States for training, the training must go to them. A traveling training program is one way to accomplish this. A team of trainers can be sent to cover the firm's distributor network, either on an individual-country or on a regional basis. The Armstrong Company, which sells flooring and ceiling materials, had a mobile training unit traveling around Europe in addition to fixed training centers in Germany and in Paris.

3.    As the Armstrong example shows, training of foreign distributor personnel can also be conducted by fixed-location training centers. Many multinational companies are setting up training centers around the world, usually on a regional basis. Caterpillar has established such training centers in São Paulo, Melbourne, Geneva, and at its home office in Peoria, Illinois.

One of the service difficulties in multinational marketing is the parts problem, which involves either expensive parts inventories in each market or shipping and importation delays in receiving the part from some central storage. No one has found an easy answer, but General Electric tried a novel approach. With each group of appliances sent to a distributor, GE sent along a spare parts kit, compiled on the basis of a statistical analysis of failure rates of various parts in various countries. It was expected to contain at least enough parts to cover the warranty period. This was sent out prepaid, supplanting the cumbersome system of giving distributors credit for each part replaced on the warranty. For GE the advantages were savings in freight and customs costs (because of bulk rates), elimination of wasteful accounting, and — most important — elimination of shipping delays.

Much of our discussion to this point applies to any product needing servicing. It is worthwhile to note the special factors bearing on the service of industrial products. The industrial customer requires uninterrupted production, therefore minimum downtime for repairs. One way to satisfy this requirement is through preventive maintenance, perhaps selling a service contract with the equipment. This is easier in concentrated markets than in markets where customers are spread out. For example, Otis Elevator visits its distant customers about every three months to check for signs of machine wear or stress. In concentrated markets where Otis has trained personnel, its visits are on a weekly basis.

Borg-Warner's Transmission Products Group established over 20 service centers around the world. These were in markets where Borg-Warner had important customers but no subsidiary. These allowed the company to guarantee quick service to customers who were not near a Borg-Warner plant. The Swedish robotics company, Asea, entered the Japanese and U.S. markets by initially setting up large service and support centers. A manager at Ford said, "We've been very pleased with their performance."

Another way to supply fast service is to send the part by air. In some instances, the part can be flown to a service center (or even to the United States), repaired, and flown back more quickly than it can be repaired under alternative service methods. General Electric, for example, requires that many mobile items be sent to the factory, but to make the process as rapid as possible, it has franchised independent service shops overseas to do repairs. By having these shops in enough markets, GE expects to accomplish reasonably prompt service. GE has 370 service centers around the world for industrial products — 156 for consumer goods, in 64 countries.

If the part or equipment cannot be flown, the individual who will repair it can fly to the customer, an approach unlikely except with very expensive, large products. For the manufacturer of such equipment, however, this centralized method offers some economies of scale in service operation. American Machine and Foundry (AMF) uses this approach, sending specialists from the United States or from overseas subsidiaries.

The nature of the firm's international involvement is another determinant of its service program. Firms operating exclusively via exporting must rely on the service capabilities of their *distributors.* As the firm establishes operations abroad, it gains a physical presence in foreign markets that adds greatly to its service capabilities. It is now dealing with its own employees rather than with outsiders. Operating through *licensees* has an advantage over exporting in that licensees should have greater expertise because they are manufacturing the product.

Administration of a multinational service program involves many dimensions. The goal is maximum consumer satisfaction at the lowest cost to the seller. Elements that contribute to this result include (1) product design, (2) service training programs, (3) parts inventories, (4) quality control, and (5) decisions as to kind of international involvement (that is, exports, licensing or foreign operations).

***Service as a Competitive Promotional Tool.***   The international marketer of technical products needs service capability to accredit the firm with foreign buyers. They will hesitate to purchase the product, however good, unless they are assured of service backup. The firm with a strong service program can gain a competitive edge. The multinational firm often has such an edge because of its size and experience.

The Japanese, being quick students of international marketing, have learned the importance of service. Seeing the potential of the Mideast market, Japanese auto manufacturers have begun training auto mechanics all over the region. In one venture, Toyota, Nissan, and Honda joined with Libya to set up service shops in 44 towns. They see two benefits. One is the income from the service business itself. Second is the boost to Japanese car sales. People in the market for a new car are likely to choose one that can be repaired locally.

Continuing on this theme, let us consider that when General Motors wanted to improve service to its 1,350 European dealers, it set up an automated communications network with a computer at each dealer. Once established, it provided numerous benefits to GM, the dealers, and their customers. Among other things, ordering errors were eliminated and processing time was cut. The improved service led to increased sales.[19]

Company-conducted service operations provide close, continuing contact with customers, which can yield insights into customer needs, ideas for new products, and opportunities for future sales. These advantages are realized most fully when a service contract is sold with the product. A U.S. chemical company, while servicing a major customer in Europe, found new uses and applications for some of its chemicals that it was able to market to its American customers. So important is this need for service that many companies set up service facilities for a market as soon as they begin selling there. In keeping with this practice, some companies will not accept an order from an area that they cannot service. When a program for international marketing is being prepared, service needs to receive attention equal to that given to such items as product development and promotion.

Service considerations may lead consumers to prefer domestic products on the premise that products of foreign origin may have less widely dispersed service networks. Providing global service capabilities may be critical then, in making sales worldwide, particularly to industrial clients with global operations. Johnson Mathey, a British multinational, recently chose to buy 24 IBM AS/400 minicomputers for installation at its offices around the world. The AS/400 was favored because it was available worldwide with a global support and maintenance network. Johnson Mathey wanted to standardize on one brand of computers so as to also standardize on software and facilitate worldwide data transfer and communication. Similar guarantees, such as service within 48 hours or free spare parts, have enabled Caterpillar to maintain a commanding share of global markets.

**Segmentation Across National Markets**

Marketing managers also decide, based on a product's attributes, which segments of the market they will target. Will segmentation decisions made for the domestic market be carried over to foreign markets? Also, the firm has to decide whether to standardize the positioning or image of a product across countries. Does it want to sell to the same customer segment across countries, or does it want to sell the same (standardized) product but to different segments in various countries (because a standardized product may appeal to different segments in different countries)?

Canon's positioning of the AE-1 camera (an affordable electronic auto exposure single-lens reflex camera) during its global introduction illustrates this concept. While the AE-1 was targeted to replacement buyers in Japan, it was intended for upscale first-time buyers in the United States and for an older, technologically knowledgeable buyer in West Germany. The differences in segments targeted dictated accompanying changes in other elements of the marketing mix. (See Table 8–3.)

**Alternatives to Direct Entry: Franchising Abroad**

Companies need not sell their product overseas in order to exploit market potential. Franchising, licensing and other indirect modes of entry are feasible approaches to obtaining profits and market share abroad.

United States franchising is becoming increasingly important to foreign companies. Franchising in the United States is, of course, regulated by law, and foreign firms must abide by these laws. Since United States laws require elaborate disclosure and registration, and make it difficult to take away a franchise once it is granted, foreign firms may prefer to test their concepts through company-owned stores. If it begins franchising, the firm's capital, commitment, and cultural knowledge must make its concepts work in the United States market.[20]

The fit between a franchise concept and a foreign market is not assured. The experience of United States franchisers in the United Kingdom is revealing. Computerland, a major computer distributor in the United States, found that the British were unwilling to buy high-priced personal computers from storefronts. Consumers wanted more hand-holding and a longer time to make a decision; as a result, Computerland had only franchised 20 stores in the United Kingdom by 1987, about a third of its goal.

The supervision of foreign franchisees is problematic, and requires a local management base that only becomes economical after a minimum number of outlets has been reached — about 50 in a market such as the United Kingdom. One solution is to use local partners in setting up a *master franchise* licensee and use this as a base to sub-license individual franchises. American International Group (AIG), a United States insurance company, has followed this approach by obtaining a master franchise for selected foreign markets and using its network of contacts in the East Asian markets to find local partners.[21] If necessary, it can also act like a venture capitalist, providing funding for interesting franchise concepts.

One danger in using master franchising agreements is that choosing the wrong company to receive the master franchise can destroy an entire market for the franchising company. Great care must be taken since the master

**Table 8–3**                     **Diverse Segment Positioning of Canon's AE-1 Camera**

| Marketing Activities | Japan | United States | Europe |
|---|---|---|---|
| Target audience | Replacement buyers among young people | First-time buyers of SLR cameras who can be converted from box cameras to SLR | Replacement buyers who can be converted from old-fashioned cameras to SLR |
| Advertising message | "Continuous-shooting SLR": single-lens reflex that allows sequences of two frames per second | "So advanced, it's simple": by using sports celebrities show the camera's ability to meet the challenge of fast-paced sport action and its suitability for nonprofessional photographers | No catch-phrase used in Europe: ads stress technological superiority resulting from use of microprocessor in the central processing unit or "brain" of the camera as well as speed and ease of use |
| Advertising media | Newspaper, television, magazine | Even split between television and newspaper/magazine: also official sponsor of Winter Olympics Games, Avon Tennis, Championship Professional Golfers Association, etc.: very substantial increase in promotional budget | Magazines, billboards, cinemas, bus/trains: substantial increase in promotional budget |
| Distribution | Speciality stores | Use AE-1 as means of shifting distribution from specialty stores to mass merchandisers: extensive dealer promotions and dealer training programs | Multi-unit specialty chains: some dealer promotions |
| Price | Retail list price of 85,000 yen (with 50 Fl.4 lens and case) or U.S. $290 at time of introduction | Determined locally; retail list price of $430 at time of introduction and actual selling price of below $300 | Differed from country to country |

Source: H. Takeuchi and M. Porter, "Three Roles of International Marketing in Global Strategy" in *Competition in Global Industries*, ed. M. Porter (Boston, HBS Press, 1986), 140.

franchisee will be a key partner in adapting the franchise product, obtaining government approvals, and negotiating with the informal network of suppliers and competitors. The importance of taking care in choosing the master franchisee can be seen in the contrasting results obtained by Kentucky Fried Chicken (KFC) and McDonald's in Hong Kong. KFC entered the Hong Kong market in 1973, opening eleven stores in the first year. Its local partner helped it secure chicken from China. But high prices, poor locations and quality problems (an unappealing taste) led to KFC closing its stores within two years (it subsequently reentered the market in 1985).

Meanwhile, McDonald's chose a master franchisee in 1973, opened one store in 1975, and added a second store a year later. By 1988, McDonald's had 30 stores in Hong Kong. Its success was due to an outstanding choice of partner, and its willingness to adapt the franchise concept. In Hong Kong, McDonald's changed its name to mean "at your service" in Chinese. While franchising is partly a service concept, many of the principles governing product and marketing mix adaptation apply equally as well.

## Summary

In deciding what products the company should sell overseas, the basic question is whether to standardize or adapt the product for foreign markets.

Factors encouraging standardization include economies of scale in manufacturing and marketing, preserving the country-of-origin image, and serving globe-trotting customers.

Factors encouraging adaptation include greater profit potential, differing use conditions, income levels and consumer tastes, local content laws, operating plants in many countries, consumer profiles, and competition. Adaptation is more likely if the costs are low and would not force the company to raise prices.

Consumer tastes are converging in the developed nations of the world, leading to greater acceptance of a standardized product in such countries. The washing machine industry example shows how careful standardization of product features and some elements of the marketing mix can be a successful strategy.

An important decision area in international markets is brand policy. The major choice is whether to opt for local brands or global brands. Global brands are consistent with a standardization approach to world markets.

Issues important to brand policy in international markets include protecting against brand piracy, paying attention to the cultural connotations of brand names, and dealing with government regulation in the area of brands and trademarks.

Another decision is whether to use private branding. While sales are made this way, the company has little contact with the ultimate consumer and learns little about changes at the consumer level. OEM sales are similar to private branding.

The country of origin of a product affects how it is perceived and accepted in foreign markets, and both technical and government-mandated standards affect a company's ability to market products in various foreign markets.

Packaging adaptation may be necessary to protect the product because of differences in climate or a longer than average time spent in the distribution channel. It may also be necessary to meet the package-size preference of local consumers, and cultural preferences regarding color, style, and materials.

Labeling may have to be adapted because of language differences, the need to inform consumers, and government requirements. Multilingual labels are one solution.

Warranties are standardized when possible. Multinational customers, "tourist" goods, competitive pressures, the nature of the product itself, and common sources of production are factors leading to standardization. However, cost savings, competitive actions, and the lack of even quality in the global service network may lead the firm to offer different warranties in different countries.

For certain products it is imperative that worldwide service be offered. Service training, the use of third parties such as distributors, and maintaining satisfied customers are some of the major factors to keep in mind.

Another interesting decision is whether to sell to the same segment in different foreign markets. This depends on product characteristics, and a standardized product may require that the company target different segments in different countries.

Franchising is a popular way to enter foreign markets. Cultural issues affect whether the franchise concept needs adaptation. The master franchise concept, which needs a strong local partner, is another useful approach to serving culturally distinct markets.

## Questions

8.1   What does selling a standardized product in global markets imply?

8.2   In what ways might a product be adapted for global markets?

8.3   What factors encourage global standardization of a product?

8.4   What factors encourage firms to adapt their product for foreign markets?

8.5   Are consumer tastes converging around the world? If so, what is the implication of this trend for international marketing?

8.6   Discuss the washing machine example cited in the text in terms of the standardization versus adaptation debate.

8.7   What are some approaches to brand policy in international markets?

8.8   Should a firm have one brand worldwide? Would your answer differ among products, for example, perfumes, photographic film, credit cards, and computers?

8.9   Why are trademark and brand piracy important? How can a firm protect itself against such actions?

8.10  What are the pros and cons of private branding in international markets?

8.11  What are OEM sales? How can they be used to increase foreign market penetration?

8.12  What is the importance of "country of origin" in international product marketing?

8.13  How do product standards affect international marketing? What can the firm do with respect to standards to bolster its foreign market position?

8.14  Discuss the promotional and protectionist aspects of packaging in international markets.

8.15  Evaluate the international labeling situation facing (1) a pharmaceutical firm and (2) a razor blade manufacturer.

8.16  What are the considerations involved in establishing a warranty policy for international markets?

8.17  Is offering worldwide service essential to international marketing?

8.18  Industrial Controls Corp. began exporting to Europe and Latin America two years ago. Now service problems are beginning to hurt its reputation and threaten future sales. What might the company do to improve its situation?

8.19   How does the existence of different customer segments overseas affect international marketing?

8.20   Discuss how Canon positioned its AE-1 camera worldwide in the face of divergent customer segments.

8.21   How is franchising relevant to international marketing? What are some issues in franchising abroad?

## Endnotes

[1]See "Video Firm Fast-Forwards into Ripening U.S. Market," *The Wall Street Journal,* September 25, 1989; and "Super Club Plans to Buy Georgia-Based Video Chain," *The Wall Street Journal,* October 9, 1989.

[2]Madhav P. Kacker, "Export Oriented Product Adaptation," *Management International Review* 6, no. 1 (1975):61.

[3]John S. Hill and Richard R. Still, "Effects of Urbanization of Multinational Product Planning," *Columbia Journal of World Business* (Summer 1984): 62–67.

[4]T. Levitt, "The Globalization of Markets," *Harvard Business Review* (May–June 1983).

[5]See Levitt, "Globalization of Markets," Exhibit 1.

[6]See "Lotus Announces #1 Ranking and Design Award for Its Japanese Version of 1–2–3," and, "Lotus Announces Shipment of Release 2J, A Japanese Version of 1–2–3," Lotus Development Corporation News Release, February 24, 1987, and September 10, 1986.

[7]For a detailed treatment, see Sak Onkvisit and John J. Shaw, "The International Dimensions of Branding: Strategic Considerations and Decisions," *International Marketing Review* 6, no. 3 (1989).

[8]"Building Brands for the New Europe," *Management Europe,* January 16, 1989.

[9]*The Role of Trademarks in Developing Countries* (Geneva: UNCTAD, 1979).

[10]Ulrich E. Wiechmann, *Marketing Management in Multinational Firms* (New York: Praeger, 1976), 23.

[11]"A Cruel Cut for Sergeant Pepper," *Business Week,* June 22, 1987.

[12]"Here's One Tough Cowboy," *Forbes,* February 9 1987.

[13]"EC May Chase Tobacco Symbols Like Marlboro Man Into Sunset," *The Wall Street Journal,* October 10, 1989.

[14]See Steven Globerman, "Addressing International Product Piracy," *Journal of International Business Studies* 19, no. 3 (Fall 1988); Richard S. Higgins and Paul Rubin, "Counterfeit Goods," *Journal of Law and Economics* (October 1986); and M. Harvey and I. Ronkainen, "International Counterfeiters: Marketing Success without Cost or Risk," *Columbia Journal of World Business* (Fall 1985).

[15]"Spiegel Resumes Strategy of Focusing on Goods Made Under Private Labels," *The Wall Street Journal,* July 13, 1988.

[16]"Tandy Corp. Fights Hard to Shake Radio Shack Image," *The Wall Street Journal,* December 8, 1988.

[17]Some interesting studies on the country-of-origin phenomenon include C. Min Han and Vern Terpstra, "Country of Origin Effects for Uni-National and Bi-national Products," *Journal of International Business Studies* Vol. 19, No. 2, (Summer 1988); Warren J. Bilkey and Erik Nes, "Country of Origin Effects on Product Evaluations," *Journal of International Business Studies* Vol. 13, No. 2 (Spring–Summer 1982); and Johny K. Johansson and Hans B. Thorelli, "International Product Positioning," *Journal of International Business Studies* 16, no. 3 (Fall 1985).

[18]See "HP Joins Forces with Samsung in Workstations," *The Wall Street Journal,* August 8, 1989; and "Sun Microsystems to License Division of N.V. Philips to Design, Sell its Chip," *The Wall Street Journal,* August 9, 1989.

[19]*Business International,* August 30, 1985, 274.

[20]"U.S. Franchising Grows Attractive to Foreign Firms," *The Wall Street Journal,* December 22, 1988.

[21]See "For U.S. Franchisers, a Common Tongue Isn't a Guarantee of Success in the U.K.," *The Wall Street Journal,* August 16, 1988; and, "U.S. Fast-Food Franchises Go East In American International Venture," November 15, 1988.

## Further Readings

Bilkey, Warren J., and Erik Nes. "Country of Origin Effects on Product Evaluations." *Journal of International Business Studies* Vol. 13, No. 2 (Spring–Summer 1982).

Christopher, R., R. Lancione, and J. Gattorna. "Managing International Customer Service." *International Marketing Review* (Spring 1985).

Globerman, Steven. "Addressing International Product Piracy." *Journal of International Business Studies* 19, no. 3 (Fall 1988).

Han, C. Min, and Vern Terpstra. "Country of Origin Effects for Uni-National and Bi-national Products." *Journal of International Business Studies,* Vol. 19, No. 2, (Summer 1988).

Hill, John S., and Richard R. Still. "Adapting Products to LDC Tastes." *Harvard Business Review,* (March–April 1984).

Johansson, Johny K., and Hans B. Thorelli. "International Product Positioning." *Journal of International Business Studies* 16, no. 3 (Fall 1985).

Levitt, T. "The Globalization of Markets." *Harvard Business Review,* (May–June 1983).

Onkvisit, Sak, and John J. Shaw. "The International Dimensions of Branding: Strategic Considerations and Decisions." *International Marketing Review* 6, no. 3 (1989).

Still, Richard R., and John S. Hill. "Multinational Product Planning: A Meta-Market Analysis." *International Marketing Review* (Spring 1985).

Walters, Peter G. P. "International Marketing Policy: A Discussion of the Standardization Construct and Its Relevance for Corporate Policy." *Journal of International Business Studies* Vol. 17, No. 2, (Summer 1986).

Wind, Yoram. "The Myth of Globalization." *Journal of Marketing* (Spring 1986).

Wind, Yoram, and Susan P. Douglas. "International Portfolio Analysis and Strategy: The Challenge of the 80s." *Journal of International Business Studies* Vol. 12, No. 3, (Fall 1981).

# CASE
# 8.1   **Ikea**

Ikea, founded in 1953, designs and sells inexpensive furniture and accessories from 77 stores in 18 countries, including Sweden, Norway, Denmark, the Netherlands, France, Belgium, W. Germany, Switzerland, Austria, Canada, United States, and Saudi Arabia, with smaller stores in Kuwait, Australia, Hong Kong, Singapore, Canary Islands, and Iceland. Ikea typically owns the larger stores while franchising the smaller stores. It distributes 45 million catalogs annually, and an equal number of customers visit it each year. Its 1986 sales were $1.7 billion, increasing to $2.1 billion for the fiscal year ended August 1987, with after-tax profits for that year of $155 million. Ikea's 7 percent after-tax margin is far above the 2.7 percent median for the U.S. retailing industry, and return on equity was 30 percent in 1987, despite little debt.

West Germany is the firm's largest market, at nearly one-third of turnover. Scandinavia (Sweden, Denmark, and Norway) accounts for another 30 percent, while 22 percent of Ikea's sales are in the rest of Europe and 14 percent in the rest of the world.

Its products are mainly manufactured in Scandinavia (50 percent), Western Europe (21 percent), and Eastern Europe (20 percent). In total, it has 1,500 suppliers manufacturing 12,000 items in 40 countries, such as standing lamps for $45, kitchen tables for $200, and tall wooden bookcases for $75. Even so, supply shortages cost the firm nearly $500 million in lost sales. As the furniture itself is sold in kit form, the pieces ac-

Case prepared by Associate Professor Ravi Sarathy for use in classroom discussion. All rights reserved. Source: Rita Martenson, "Is Standardization of Marketing feasible in Culture-Bound Industries? A European Case Study," *International Marketing Review* (Autumn 1987); "How a Major Swedish Retailer Chose a Beachhead in the U.S." *The Wall Street Journal,* April 7, 1987, Peter Fuhrman, "The Workers' Friend," *Forbes,* March 21, 1988; and James Cook, "A Better Mousetrap," *Forbes,* March 7, 1988.

tually are made in different locations, with Ikea purchasing from the manufacturers with the lowest prices.

Its furniture comes boxed and must be assembled at home. The boxed kits must be picked up by the customer after purchase from the adjacent self-service warehouse and lugged home. Since Ikea expects its customers to cart away their own purchases, it tends to locate near freeway exits and outside cities, where more space is available at lower rates. This allows the firm to provide ample parking space, and customers can easily get in and out of the store without facing discouraging traffic jams. Ikea also cooperates with local car-rental companies to facilitate the hiring of small trucks to transport a customers' orders.

The design is Scandinavian modern furniture built mainly of pine, with textiles in pastel colors. The international product line is less varied than that sold within the home markets of Scandinavia. Ikea's market is the "young of all ages." It has a flair for marketing to young couples with children: its warehouses are festively decorated, provide day care for children, and feature inexpensive restaurants specializing in Swedish meatballs. The focus on child care and the in-store restaurants aim to keep people in the stores till they buy something, preventing their exit due to bored and unmanageable children or the desire to get a meal.

The emphasis is on low-priced furniture, priced 30 to 50 percent below the fully assembled furniture of the competition. Prices vary for the same basic product from market to market, though not greatly.

Ikea's founder, Ingvar Kamprad, grew up on a farm in southern Sweden and began a business selling flower seeds and ballpoint pens through mail-order catalogs. He insists that employees be "cost-conscious to the point of stinginess." He has written: "Too many new and beautifully designed products can be afforded by only a small group of better-off people. We have decided to side with the many."

Ikea has always been innovative in selling furniture. When it entered Sweden in the early 1950s, furniture retailers were small firms, purchasing furniture to customer specifications and placing an order with the manufacturer only after receiving a commitment from the customer. Furniture was expensive and bought in sets, that is, a dining room suite for example, and credit was an important sales tool. Ikea entered into this market with large showrooms outside cities, the option to buy one piece of furniture at a time, self-service for cash, and low prices.

In 1973 Ikea entered Switzerland with its first store near Zurich. It had to decide whether to rely on the Ikea company name, to position Ikea as a Scandinavian furniture company (in which case, it might be confused with Danish furniture), or to identify Ikea as a distinctive Swedish company. Ikea knew that it would have to address Swiss concerns (for they were perceived to be a conservative group) about a Swedish company and its way of selling furniture.

Ikea prepared a set of ads that deliberately brought up typical conservative Swiss opinions of and reactions to Ikea (see Table 1). These ads consisted of letters sent by a conservative Herrn Bunzli to Ikea saying what he thinks of the company's ideas and way of selling furniture in Switz-

erland. The aim of the campaign was to joke about the old-fashioned values of the Swiss and appeal to those who would like to change. The ads exemplify Ikea's philosophy, which is to take advantage of being an unknown foreigner and use advertising that is attention-getting and provocative. Managers in all countries are required to follow this advertising strategy, though they can use local agencies, following guidelines from headquarters.

The first year Ikea was in Switzerland, 650,000 people visited its stores. The next year, Ikea entered the huge West German market, and subsequently, France, drawing on its experiences with the German and French-speaking parts of Switzerland.

Ikea has a special organization structure dedicated to smooth and speedy entry into foreign markets. This foreign-expansion group has several key subunits: a European deco-manager, a manager of construction, and a first-year group whose responsibility is to create and manage new overseas outlets during its first year. The construction manager selects a site and supervises the creation of the new store, overseeing inventories, installation of fixtures, communications networks, etc., while the first-year manager oversees hiring, the borrowing of experienced employees from other Ikea locations, training, advertising campaigns, and deciding on the "assortment" of product line to be carried. Fur-

**Table 1    Themes in Ikea's Swiss Advertising Campaign**

| Theme of Ikea's Sales Approach | Message: Joke about Swiss Conservatism |
| --- | --- |
| *No delivery* by Ikea | The Swiss will not transport and assemble furniture themselves even if the price is low. |
| You have to *assemble your own furniture* | What a stupid idea. You can't make us Swiss do that. |
| Ikea makes *pine furniture* | We don't use pine: we aren't Swedish. |
| The Swiss's need for *status furniture* | Swedes, go home. |
| Ikea does make *quality furniture* | Only Swiss-made goods can be high quality. |

Source: Adapted from "Cross-cultural Similarities and Differences in Multinational Retailing."

niture is typically ordered from a central warehouse in Sweden and starts arriving three months before opening day.

Planning of a new outlet begins about ten months before opening day. Since Ikea has expanded rapidly, the first-year group cannot spend a whole year nurturing new outlets as originally envisaged. Training has to be speeded up to allow local management to take over earlier. Staff begin working about two months before opening day to familiarize themselves completely with Ikea's mode of operations and product line, so as to ensure a smooth opening. Advertising begins at about the same time. The staff generally takes a trip to Ikea's outlets in Scandinavia, culminating in a press conference the day before store inauguration.

## Ikea Enters the United States

Already established, with nine stores in Canada, Ikea prompts the question, "Why aren't you in California?" California was its first pick, with Boston the second choice. But executives who set out to study the California market encountered some obstacles. California has unique standards for upholstered furniture that would have raised costs by 15 percent. Its system of unitary taxation by which it taxed California's "share" of Ikea's worldwide income was unpalatable to that private company.

Boston was attractive because of its huge itinerant student and yuppie population. But government regulations and lack of responsiveness on the part of state officials led the company to establish its first warehouse and retail operation in suburban Philadelphia instead.

Philadelphia made special efforts to help Ikea. Why? Jobs, and tax revenues. Through the Greater Philadelphia International Network, a small-business backed office that tries to attract foreign investment, Ikea officials were introduced to bankers and real estate brokers, given a helicopter tour of the city, and invited to cocktail parties every evening of their three-day stay.

The Philadelphia market area, which includes Delaware and southern New Jersey, had large numbers of young middle-income families and cheap commercial real estate. The Network helped Ikea find space in a mall next to a turnpike exit in the suburb of Plymouth Meeting. Location, of course, is critical to this kind of company. "Pennsylvania Turnpike, Exit 25" is the sort of address it seeks. (Forty percent of its customers were likely to be from out of state.)

The store attracted 130,000 customers during its inauguration in June 1985 and averages 30,000 a week. Ikea has shifted its North American headquarters from Vancouver to Philadelphia. It opened a second store in the Virginia suburb of Dale City, near Washington, D.C., in the spring of 1986, where weekend crowds are averaging 15,000. Together, the two stores had total sales of $77 million in 1987, and Ikea admits that it underestimated the market by 50 percent. Severe inventory shortages have consequently developed. Future expansion sites include Baltimore, Pittsburgh, and suburban New York. The plan is to have several stores served by a major central warehouse. By 1992 Ikea plans to have ten stores operating in the United States.

Success breeds imitation. A California company, Stor, plans to open 30 stores similar to Ikea on the West Coast, carbon copies, including toy-filled day-care rooms. Ikea is five times as large as Habitat, the British multinational furniture retailer. And the knock-down kit idea has spread to other market niches. Bush Industries, another furniture company, has grown from $14 million sales in 1982 to $93 million in 1987 by manufacturing and selling kit furniture for electronic products: furniture to house and display audio and video products, VCRs and personal computers and printers. By 1987 Bush was selling 115 different furniture models ranging in price from $20 to $500, in 6,000 stores such as Sears and Best Products. Other U.S. manufacturers competing with Bush include Tandy Corp.'s O'Sullivan Industries and Sauder Woodworking.

Paul Bush, president, notes that ready-to-assemble (RTA) furniture is perhaps 40 percent of the furniture market in Europe, but only about $2 billion in sales in the United States; dealers dislike it. Bush was able to sell its furniture by going through new channels such as electronic retailers, mail-order office supply houses, catalog stores, and the audio, video and microwave departments of big stores such as Sears and J. C. Penney.

Bush has adapted the ideas of RTA furniture to U.S. needs. It must be easy to assemble. And precision fit is important, since the user will assemble it and will not be satisfied with less than

perfect fit. Bush pioneered soft forms, with smooth curved edges. Oak furniture is traditional in the United States, conveying a solid heavy feel, darker in tone than pine, which is light and feels insubstantial. Hence, Bush introduced oak RTA by combining oak solids with oak veneers. The lower price and immediate delivery have gradually increased the share of RTA in the U.S. market; in fall of 1987 Bush introduced RTA bedroom furniture in oak.

## Questions

1. Analyze Ikea's international expansion. Why was it successful?
2. To what extent does its product line need to be adapted to foreign markets?
3. Did Ikea have to adapt other aspects of the marketing mix when entering foreign markets?
4. Prepare a time chart showing how Ikea proceeds in opening a new international store.

5. How did Ikea enter the United States? Why did it choose Pennsylvania?
6. How might have Ikea's success stimulated the ready-to-assemble (RTA) market in the United States?
7. How did Bush adapt RTA furniture to fit U.S. market needs? Does the success of Bush Industries represent a niche that Ikea should consider expanding into?

CASE

# 8.2  Domino's Pizza in Japan

When Michael Jackson was in Tokyo and wanted a snack between concerts, he called on Domino's Pizza, for a vegetable special, with no cheese — and within 30 minutes it was ready, served piping hot in his dressing room. All Tokyo seems to like Domino's pizza: the busy housewife faced with hungry kids and no time to make dinner, the officeworker with her friends over for an evening of chatter and music — it goes better with pizza. As always, the Japanese love the service: one phone call, and 30 minutes later, pizza delivered to the home.

## Domino's Pizza International (DPI)

Domino's first foreign venture was in Canada. Company officials viewed this as the logical first step toward globalization because of Canada's proximity to the United States, both geographically and culturally. In Canada the corporate-owned and the franchised stores were both moderately successful. Again following the logic of cultural and language similarity, Domino's entered the Australian market. Rather rapidly during the middle and late 1980s, Domino's entered a total of 16 foreign markets from China to Hong Kong to Honduras to Western Europe.

## Domino's to Japan

When Domino's was considering entry into the Japanese market, it could count on no cultural or linguistic similarity to help its analysis. Therefore, it hired a consultant, who expressed the following concerns: the Japanese do not eat much cheese; fast-food restaurants are not considered desirable employers; the Japanese are not entrepreneurial; real estate is very expensive; and banks do not like to lend to small businesses. On the other hand, Japan does have a high population density, high per capita income, substantial westernization, and wide acceptance of the delivery concept. The consultant concluded that Japan was not ready for a pizza delivery service.

## Higa-San Meets Tom Monaghan

Y. Higa, a Japanese businessman, and Tom Monaghan, did not accept the consultant's recommendation. At first Higa was uncertain about the wisdom of a tie-up between the food business and Higa Corp., originally a Japanese trading company dealing in lumber and medical equipment. However, when he visited Monaghan in 1984 at Domino's Ann Arbor headquarters, he was impressed by several things: the rapid growth of Domino's in the United States and abroad; the fact that this growth allowed Monaghan to buy the Detroit Tiger baseball team for $53 million; and Monaghan's enthusiastic description of Domino's operating methods.

Higa decided he wanted to bring the Domino's concept and operating method to Japan. Higa felt that the "secret ingredient" he could bring to the deal was his knowledge and feel for the marketplace, the culture, and the people. He thought that with more Japanese women working and coming home tired, home delivery of food would work. Also, more Japanese were traveling abroad and developing a taste for new foods. The previous success of McDonald's and Kentucky Fried Chicken was a good omen, too.

Higa's undergraduate degree from Wharton and his M.B.A. from Columbia helped him to also have a good feel for Domino's U.S. operations. Furthermore, there was some relevant experience in the Higa family. His father, Yetsuo Higa, helped bring Pepsi Cola to Japan in the 1950s, and his brother-in-law, Shin Ohkawara, is president of Kentucky Fried Chicken Japan Ltd. Higa made an agreement with Domino's giving him the exclusive right to develop and franchise stores in Japan.

## Domino's in Japan

The first Domino's opened in Tokyo's Azabu district in 1985. Azabu is a trendy, westernized district. From that start, Domino's Pizza of Japan became the company's most successful foreign operation. Royalty income per store was almost twice as high as in Britain, the second-best foreign market in terms of royalty income. By 1989 there were 54 Domino's Pizza outlets in Japan, and sales in 1988 reached $43 million. By starting with the innovators and westernized Japanese in the Azabu district, Domino's found a group ready to consume home-delivered pizza. These consumption leaders also influenced other segments of the population, increasing Domino's popularity in Tokyo.

The pizza is sold by Y. Higa Corporation, Domino's licensee for Japan. Home delivery itself is familiar to the Japanese, accounting for a large share of the estimated 12 trillion yen in annual restaurant sales. The problem in a city as crowded as Tokyo, is how to get the pizza to the house fast, and still hot.

Higa wanted to copy Domino's U.S. promise of a guaranteed delivery by car in 30 minutes or your money back. But not only are Japanese cities crowded, finding an address in Japan is quite difficult. Streets are not straight, are not named, and houses are numbered according to when they were built; it is possible for two houses built at about the same time to have the same number. Population density is also much greater in Japanese cities as compared to the United States; a Japanese store might have 14 times as many people in its territory in Tokyo, when compared to the number of people in an average territory that a U.S. pizza store might serve. On top of these differences, the horrendous traffic in Tokyo almost guaranteed that the 30-minute delivery promise would be impossible to meet, especially since each order is made up fresh after the phone call.

The solution was to design special three-wheeled Honda scooters that could maneuver easily in Tokyo's traffic. Painted with Domino's red, white, and blue logo (a moving Domino billboard), the scooters have sloping windscreens and protective roofs. The pizzas cost from $7 to $23, and a refund of about $5 is given if the delivery does not arrive in the trademark 30 minutes — Domino's version of just-in-time logistics. (These figures are at average 1989 exchange rates.)

The original fleet of five scooters was inadequate to meet the demand, so five more were added the second week of operation, five more the third week, until the original store had twenty-five three-wheelers. Each store now may have up to twenty three-wheelers.

The scooter driver is the delivery person, often a part-timer and a college student earning extra money. The driver wears a distinctive uniform, different from other Japanese delivery people, who usually come in a white smock.

The full-color menu is on expensive laminated paper, unlike the usual paper flyers. Customers are impressed, and hold on to their menus, which are left in their mailboxes by part-time workers.

Domino's Japanese locations do not provide on-premises restaurant service. If you want pizza, you have to order it and wait to eat it at home. Real estate is expensive in Tokyo and hard to find, and such a policy allows Domino's outlets to be located in small spaces.

There are no franchisees. Higa owns and operates all the shops itself and buys fresh ingredients from a sister company (owned by another member of the Higa family), which are then cooked into pizzas immediately from scratch, beginning with tossing of the dough. As one might expect, extensive training in the art of pizza-making is provided by a Domino's University.

Domino's strives for international uniformity of both product and operating methods. The pizza dough, cheese, and sauce are as uniform as possible internationally. Toppings, however, may vary. In Japan, pepperoni is the most popular, but tuna and corn are offered, too. Each store is limited to a total of 12 varieties.

Each store pays 3 percent of sales into a promotional fund. Door hangings and direct mail, including the fancy menu, are used for advertising rather than TV or radio.

## A Success Story?

Domino's Pizza International (DPI) is pleased with its decision to enter the Japanese market and with its Japanese employees. "They do exactly what you tell them." Diligent, hard-working, and team-oriented, they follow the rules to the letter, allowing Domino's system to operate at its most efficient.

Higa gives some of the credit to DPI for sending one of its most experienced veterans for an extended time in Japan to help establish the operation. And, of course, the company set up a "Domino's University" for local training.

## Questions

1. In Japan, Domino's is marketing both a product and a service. Review Domino's Japanese marketing program in detail. For each item in the program, identify how it was standardized internationally or adapted to the Japanese market.

2. Explain why this standardization or adaptation was used.

3. Identify and explain all the factors that appear to have contributed to Domino's success in Japan, in spite of the consultant's recommendation against the operation.

# CASE

# 8.3    Kellogg's Corn Flakes

Kellogg Company is a leading food products manufacturing company based in Battle Creek, Michigan (1989 sales were over $4.5 billion). The company produces a wide variety of ready-to-eat cereals and other food products including toaster pastries, frozen waffles, soups, dessert mixes, Salada tea, snack items, and other convenience foods. The company also engages in supporting

## Figure 1    What's on the Nutrition Label?

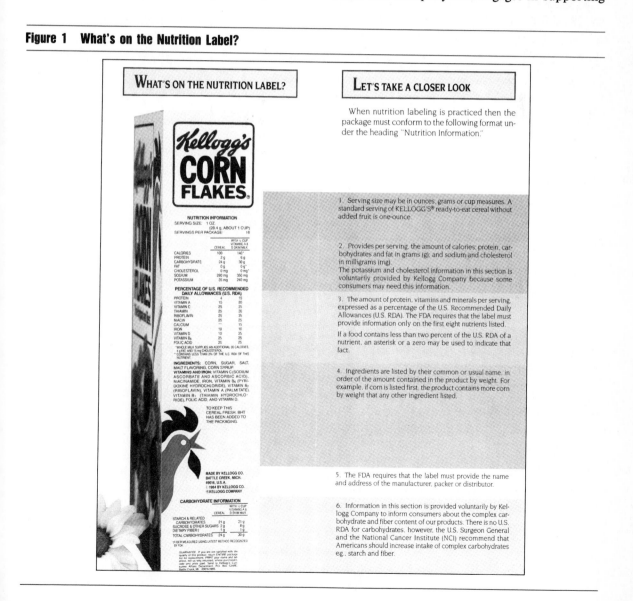

activities such as grain milling and carton print-ing in a number of countries where principal manufacturing operations exist.

Kellogg International handles the company business outside the United States and Canada. Sales outside the United States account for one-third of the total. Kellogg has 22 manufacturing locations on six continents with Europe and Latin America accounting for most of them. Japan and Australia are also good markets.

Kellogg Company markets through its own salesforce in major world markets and through broker and distributor arrangements in less de-veloped market areas.

A basic thrust of the company's advertising and promotion is designed to further consumer knowledge regarding the nutritional worth of Kellogg's products. Both advertising and pack-aging are oriented to the theme of health and nutrition information (see Figure 1).

Kellogg's Corn Flakes is the company's most famous product. It is sold in many world mar-kets.

## Questions

Putting yourself in the position of international brand manager for Kellogg's Corn Flakes, make brief recommendations on the following:

1.  Should the product itself (cornflakes) be stan-dardized or adapted for world markets?

2.  Should the brand and trademark Kellogg's Corn Flakes and the familiar red script be uni-form in all markets?

3.  What is the appropriate packaging for foreign markets?

4.  What is an appropriate labeling strategy for world markets?

C A S E

# 8.4 Chrysler–Jeep: International Product Policy

In August 1987 Chrysler bought American Mo-tors–Jeep from Renault for about $750 million dollars. The major assets acquired by Chrysler were the Jeep brand, the Jeep production facili-ties in Toledo, Ohio and the new plant in Bra-malea, Ontario, and Jeep's overseas distribution facilities, especially in Europe. Chrysler had withdrawn from international markets in the late 1970s and was reentering them in the late 1980s. Jeep's established presence abroad could be a big help in that reentry. Jeep also gave Chrysler a new kind of vehicle to add to its automotive product line — four-wheel-drive/sport-utility ve-hicles.

Worldwide Jeep sales reached 320,000 vehicles by 1989, with about 275,000 of that in the North American market, primarily the United States and Canada, but also including sales in Mexico. The total world market for four-wheel-drive/ sport-utility vehicles was about 1,000,000 units. The Japanese were the major competitors to Jeep, but Land Rover of Britain was also a factor. Jeeps were sold in most world markets apart from the Communist countries and the United Kingdom — in the latter case because of the cost of adaptation to right-hand drive.

Most of the Jeeps were manufactured in one plant, located in Toledo, Ohio. The majority of Jeep sales abroad were of built-up units shipped from the United States, but about one-fourth were shipped CKD (completely knocked down) to assembly plants abroad. There were joint-venture assembly plants in China, Egypt, and Venezuela and independent assembly operations in Australia and Turkey. The plant in Australia made adaptations for right-hand drive. The joint venture Beijing-Jeep in China was aiming for 50 percent local content but had achieved only about 20 percent by 1989.

Chrysler International handles Jeep sales abroad. The International group has about 200 people covering all of Chrysler's sales outside of North America. It includes an engineering function called Vehicle Homologation, which is charged with verifying compliance with foreign market specifications. Sales abroad are through independent distributors in most markets. In Europe, however, which accounts for about 60 percent of international sales, Chrysler has some different distribution arrangements. Renault has the distributorship for France, Italy, Spain, and Portugal and accounted for over one-half of European sales in 1989. Chrysler has its own marketing subsidiaries in Belgium, Germany, the Netherlands, and Switzerland.

The four-door Jeep Cherokee is the largest seller abroad, followed by the Wrangler — the army-style jeep. Jeep also sells over 1,000 vehicles annually to foreign countries for army or military use. In developed countries, Jeeps are used mostly as recreational vehicles. In developing countries, they are seen as multipurpose vehicles for transporting people or cargo, for tactical uses and emergency vehicles. In some countries they serve as taxis or minibuses (the famous Jeepney in the Philippines). Cargo transport is important in rural areas — for example, coffee in Colombia, oil drums or cattle in Venezuela. In Egypt, the army uses Jeeps for tactical maneuvers. In Mexico, they are used as tow-trucks and as ambulances in Norway. Obviously, Jeeps are used in countries with very different economic, environmental, and use conditions.

## Questions

Putting yourself in the position of international marketing manager for Jeep vehicles, suggest and defend appropriate policies on the following:

1. To what degree should Jeep vehicles be adapted for foreign markets?

2. Should Jeep have a uniform brand for world markets?
3. Should the Jeep warranty be the same in every market?
4. What should be the service policy for world markets?

CHAPTER 9

# International Product Policy
## New-Product Development and Product-Line Policies

*Learning Objectives*

In Chapter 8, we discussed how a firm's basic product fits into global markets. We considered product features such as packaging, labeling, brand name, and warranties, and how these may change as they encounter global markets. This chapter considers additional aspects of product policy concerning new-product development and product-line policies.

The main goals of this chapter are to

1. Discuss the challenge of developing new products for foreign markets.
2. Discuss the selection and management of the international product line.
3. Explain how the decision is made about which foreign markets to enter with which products. This decision is about matching products and markets. In Chapter 7, we studied market research in an international context; here we look at which foreign markets to enter from a product-line perspective.

## New-Product Development

New-product development consists of three primary activities:

1. Searching for new product ideas.
2. Evaluating these ideas and selecting some of them for development.
3. Developing the selected ideas as new products.

In all three phases, the goal of selling into global markets will affect the firm's ideas and behavior in various ways that we will explore in this chapter.

**Table 9–1**                                            **Market Characteristics and Product-Line Strategies**

|            | **If:** |          | **Then:** |
|------------|---------|----------|-----------|
| **Customer Need** | **Conditions of Use** | **Ability to Buy** | **Product-Line Strategy** |
| Same | Same | Exists | Product and Communications Extension |
| Different | Same | Exists | Product Extension and Communications Adaptation |
| Same | Different | Exists | Product Adaptation and Communications Extension |
| Different | Different | Exists | Product and Communications Adaptation (with new products in the future) |
| Same | Not Applicable | Low to None | *New* Product and Communications |

Source: Warren J. Keegan, "Multinational Product Planning: Strategic Alternatives," *Journal of Marketing* (January 1969).

**Importance of Consumer Needs**

Consumer needs are the starting point for product development, whether for domestic or global markets. Take pianos, for instance. It takes time and effort to play a piano well, so there are a great many pianos gathering dust in living rooms around the world — 40 million of them by one estimate. Yamaha, with 40 percent of the global market, and facing declining demand, had to rethink customer needs. It chose to retrofit pianos (for about $2,500) with a computer board that could capture music from the piano as it was played; the piano can then be used as a playback instrument. It can even play back performances by great piano artists. The piano is linked to a computer that "reads" disks of piano music, then causes the piano to play the music back. This is the player piano concept all over again, with disks substituting for paper rolls.[1] What was a dead business is being revived by creating a value-added product in response to consumer needs.

**Products for Foreign Markets: A Conceptual Framework**

In addition to consumer needs, conditions of use and ability to buy the product form a framework for decisions on new-product development for foreign markets. The strategy may be product extension, with or without significant product adaptation, or new products for specific foreign markets, or design of a global product for all markets. In using this framework, the development process encompasses the product itself as well as the communication about the product, that is, advertising, etc. Table 9–1 summarizes the implications of this concept.

When consumer needs and conditions of use are not taken into account, failure is the result. Heinz Co., attracted by the size of the Brazilian market, set up a joint venture with Citrosuco, an orange-juice exporter, to launch its first product, Frutsi, a fruit drink that had been successful in Venezuela and Mexico. But every street corner in Brazil has a little store selling freshly squeezed orange juice at low prices. And while Heinz could keep pure fruit-juice content at 10 percent in most countries, Brazilian regulations set a minimum of 30 percent. This raised prices and made Frutsi uncompetitive with the fresh-squeezed variety. To complicate matters, the additional fruit juice shortened shelf life, necessitating new packaging.

To penetrate the market, Heinz gave cases of Frutsi to retailers on consignment, to be paid for after the product was sold. This led to overstocking and many cases of spoiled product had to be returned (brownouts and electric supply interruptions are common in Brazil, and the hot climate hastened product deterioration when refrigeration failed). Then Heinz spent $200,000 on TV advertising featuring a robot character that wasn't considered friendly enough. Although a name change to "Suco da Monica," based on a popular Brazilian cartoon character, helped sales, Heinz decided to pull out. All three of the factors in Table 9–1 — customer need, ability to buy, and conditions of use — were unfavorable to Heinz in Brazil.[2]

**Adoption and Diffusion of New Products**

New-product introduction entails adoption and diffusion (use). There are five stages: awareness, interest (knowledge), evaluation (of information, to decide whether to try or not try), trial, and finally adoption (continuing use).[3] *Awareness* is the stage of communicating the existence of the new product or innovation to potential adopters/consumers. The second stage of deepening *interest* is related to obtaining detailed knowledge about the new product or innovation. Next, consumers must *evaluate* the knowledge gathered to decide whether to break old habits and take the risk of trying the new product. The *trial* phase is when the new product is actually being used for the first time. Lastly, consumers assess their experience from first use and decide whether to continue using the product — *adoption*.

Mirroring the stages by which consumers decide to adopt new products are the stages of decision making that firms go through in introducing the products. First there is idea or concept generation, then screening of (several) competing new product ideas, then evaluation of a short list of such ideas in view of consumer needs, costs of production, current revenues, and competitive actions. Next, the firm enters the prototype stage, where trial runs of the new product are made. After ascertaining product viability and quality from an engineering and production standpoint, the firm then moves to product testing in the marketplace. If testing is successful, the product is launched into the wider market, perhaps with additional modifications based on results from the testing phase. Results from the product launch are then evaluated, and the product is kept on the market, completing market entry. Competition is a complicating factor, since retaliatory moves by competitors may hinder an accurate assessment of market acceptance. Success breeds imitation, so rarely will a new product have the market to itself unless protected by strong patents and copyrights (as in the case of the Apple Macintosh computer).

## Generation of Product Ideas

The first step in product planning is to generate a list of new product ideas. Some of the many sources of new product ideas are (1) company employees, (2) company research and development activity, (3) customers, (4) distributors, (5) sales representatives, (6) inventors, and (7) competitors. All of these are available to the international company as well as to the domestic firm. An added dimension to the international firm's situation, however, is the use it makes of these idea sources in all its foreign markets. In other words, is the firm an international marketer with a purely domestic product-planning activity?

Organizations and publications that report internationally on new inventions — including new patents — represent a source of product ideas especially interesting to the international firm. For example, a major American chemical company maintains an office in its Swiss headquarters that notes new product ideas in European trade, company, government, and patent office publications. Visits to international trade fairs, especially in Europe, are important even for domestic companies. Some of the fairs are general industrial expositions, but others are formed around a specific industry, for example, photo, automotive, or aircraft and space equipment, as is the Paris Air Show.

The planning programs of governments and international agencies are another source of ideas. These planning reports yield sales leads, so they are publicized by the U.S. Commerce Department and other organizations. In addition to sales leads, companies can get new product ideas from studying the plans of nations. Projects in agriculture, infrastructure development, health, education, housing, and so on, can mean new product opportunities to equipment and chemical manufacturers, food and pharmaceutical firms, publishing houses, and school supply companies.

As an example, Sweden's Tetra Pak has been one of Europe's leading manufacturers of packaging machinery. For over a decade it has had a close association with two United Nations agencies — the Food and Agriculture Organization (FAO) and the United Nations Children's Fund (UNICEF). As a result, Tetra Pak has supplied machinery for over 100 projects throughout the developing countries and is usually in on the planning stage. This kind of new product idea source has several advantages. First, because the idea is generated by a market need, it is less speculative than an idea based only on technological possibilities. Second, these market needs are high-priority items, thus quite assured of financing. Third, responding to market needs represents a healthy market-oriented way to get new product ideas. Besides the possible market payoffs, the firm can acquire a more favorable company image by identifying itself with the problems of its market in this way. For example when Coca-Cola developed "Samson" — a high-protein beverage — in Mexico, the Mexican government felt this was a very useful product and helped Coca-Cola introduce it to the market. Fourth, the firm may reap rewards in other markets by selling there the product originally developed for one particular country.

Goodyear experienced this good fortune when it developed a tire for tough driving conditions on Peru's roads. These tires contained a higher percentage of natural rubber than those manufactured elsewhere, and they had better tread. As a result, Peruvians preferred them to imported tires. The performance reputation spread to other countries with similar problems. And Procter & Gamble first developed enzyme detergents to meet special conditions in the Spanish market. Later enzyme detergents found a market in the United States. A related source of new product ideas is to be found in the visualization of products in terms of the foreign buyer's consumption system. This concept is not new, but it needs more extensive application in international marketing.

The marketer must first visualize the firm's product as part of the foreign user's overall consumption system. Then cultural bias in interpreting that consumption system must be eliminated. Many products have status as well as functional aspects, and these will often vary from market to market. Cultural bias can easily cause the marketer to misinterpret the relative role of function and status and make errors in product design and promotion. The same holds true in analyzing the way a product is used. All over the world people engage in the same activities: eating, sleeping, playing, working in agriculture or other kinds of production. Although the activities are the same, the way they are carried out can vary, and the differences are important for product development.

Colgate Palmolive Company, for example, sells soaps and detergents all over the world. Detergent sales are very low in many less developed countries, although clothes are washed in those countries with reasonable frequency. A major deterrent to detergent sales is the fact that women wash their clothes by streams where detergents would be wasted. Colgate asked an inventor to develop a simple manually operated washer. The device resembles an old-fashioned butter churn and is operated by a pumping action. It gets clothes clean and eliminates some of the drudgery of the earlier method — and detergents work well in it. Although this device was not ultimately successful, it illustrates a creative way to address the foreign user's consumption system.

The value of international idea sources for international marketing needs to be stressed. Consider these examples of American firms who found profitable product ideas abroad.

- 3M bought the Italian firm Ferrania to improve its own film products. The first result was a new medical X-ray film that did not need to be developed in a darkroom.
- TRW acquired Pleuger of Germany which had superior pump technology. This helped TRW to develop a line of submersible pumps that it markets around the world.
- The director of Gillette's British laboratories did a microphotographic study of shaving. This led to the double bladed Trac II, one of Gillette's most successful razors ever.
- NCR sells its 230 electronic cash register around the world. It was developed by its Japanese subsidiary.
- Citibank and Morgan Guaranty are learning new banking services from the Swiss and German "universal bank" model. They want to offer these in a deregulated U.S. market.

Much is made today of the economies of scale in large centers. But although their output has indeed been respectable, the engineers, scientists, and thinkers working in these centers are all subject to the same environmental conditions and influences; their newspapers, recreation and social concerns are similar. Such a homogenous situation can lead to a certain conformity in thinking, or a form of "tunnel vision." More idea centers spread out among different countries are likely to provide a more complete range of new-product ideas.

A study by the National Science Foundation (NSF) is related to the idea of scale economies in R&D. NSF found that small businesses (fewer than 1,000 employees) came up with 24 times as many research innovations per dollar as the largest companies. One-half of all major inventions came from such companies. Furthermore, independent inventors register one-fourth of all patents in the United States.[4]

In regard to the products where market conditions are more important than technological conditions, the argument for international inputs on new product ideas is much stronger. Even for IBM, a company strong in technology, product specifications include inputs from at least 20 countries around the world.

If international input is desired for new product planning, how can it be achieved? Much depends on the volume of the firm's international business and the nature of its involvement in foreign markets. The firm with small foreign sales has fewer resources for getting new product ideas from abroad. As foreign sales grow, the options available to the firm increase.

**Exporter.**  The firm involved only via exporting is concerned about ideas from its foreign markets, but it is not physically present there. Distributors can be counted as part of the company's intelligence network. As their salesforce contacts the market, the insights they gain relative to the firm's product line should be available to the firm.

The exporting firm may also receive some feedback from customers. More importantly, the export manager and perhaps marketing or technical specialists from the firm can visit foreign markets personally. This specialized observation of differing competitive environments and use conditions can be highly rewarding in ideas for new products or applications.

**Licensor.**  Licensees are independent parties bound to pay royalties on what they produce and sell but usually not bound to cooperate in other ways. However, licensees have technical expertise relating to the licensor's product that helps them come up with new applications or product ideas. This happens often enough that many licensors make provision to benefit from it. Contracts can include cross-licensing clauses whereby new-product developments connected with the licensed product are made available to the other party, whether developed by the licensee or the licensor.

**Joint Venture.**  The joint-venture approach to foreign markets gives the international firm a management voice in the local company. If the national partner has significant equity in the venture, it will have interest in claiming, or at least sharing, new product ideas and development. It will have less interest in product ideas for other markets, however, and may resist joint-venture participation in such projects.

**Wholly Owned Subsidiaries.**   The only limitations to using foreign subsidiaries as part of product planning lie in the size of the foreign subsidiaries and in the company's international organization. Where the subsidiary is small, it is able to do less product planning.

The minimum role for the subsidiary is the assignment of responsibility to one person for new product ideas. The other extreme is for the subsidiary to duplicate the product-planning organization of the domestic operation. The synergism of multinational operations comes from elimination of duplication and the appropriate international division of labor. Thus, although all subsidiaries are represented, not all have to have a complete activity, as would purely national concerns in these markets.

Until now we have mentioned only the international side of the company's operations. For many multinational companies, domestic operations are the principal source of new product ideas. The international activity should be part of the total corporate program. It bears repeating that there must be appropriate integration of the domestic and international sides of such activity. Otherwise, the firm will have duplication of effort in its operations. Concerning Eaton's foreign affiliates, Chairman E. M. de Windt noted:

> They're no longer the ugly in-laws which used to irritate the domestic plants with their requests for drawings and technical assistance. Now there is a constant interchange between domestic and international operations and many new ideas are finding their way back into the United States.

**Location of Product Development for Global Markets**

Where a global product is developed and who participates in developing it are both important. Product development may be centered in one country, perhaps at headquarters. But because the product is to be a global product, it is important to receive information from key markets around the world. Hence, involving foreign subsidiaries at the early stage of product-concept development is crucial to success. This way, features of importance to a variety of consumers in different markets can be considered.[5] Firms must recognize, however, that development teams tend to "own" products, and are reluctant to accept designs from other teams even when these designs originate within the company. In theory it appears sound to assign central responsibility for designing a particular product to a particular team in a particular country, the assumption being that this team's design will then be adopted globally. But organizational conflicts can undermine this sort of plan, and a company may be forced to compromise and accept two versions of what was meant to be a global product.

**Pressures from within Organization.**   Companies with well-established foreign subsidiaries usually encounter demands for more local autonomy. This may be reinforced by the nationalistic feelings of subsidiary personnel, most of whom are probably citizens of the local country. Participation in such a fundamental corporate activity as development of new products is one of the most forceful ways of showing that one has "a piece of the action." In this situation, the firm must weigh the payoff in improved morale against any loss of efficiency in product development. For example, Sperry Vickers began product development in Europe because its affiliates there demanded a "fair share" of this activity.

Multinational companies may have inherited foreign operations with existing product-development activities. Subsidiaries may have been operating mostly on a national market basis. Because high tariffs and economic nationalism prevented them from exporting or importing, it was natural for each subsidiary to be rather self-contained, even engaging in local product development. With the liberalizing of trade in recent decades, these subsidiaries have been integrated into a regional or international operation. Nevertheless, for the parent company to eliminate their product development activity is not easy. Perhaps the best alternative in these cases is to assure that product development is coordinated internationally.

Many companies that began their foreign operations recently, have expanded internationally partly through acquisition of existing foreign businesses. Acquisition has proved the quickest way to get in on expanding markets such as the EC. But an acquired firm usually comes with its own product-development activity, which may be difficult to eliminate. The acquiring firm may seek instead to integrate it with the rest of its operation. There may be strong local pressures in this regard, especially from the government.

In industries where product development is very slow and costly, companies may be forced to go outside for new products. The pharmaceutical industry provides a good illustration. Though most firms in the industry are research-intensive, none can have a very complete product line from internal research only. It takes too many years and too much money to bring a new drug to market. In this industry therefore, we see a fourfold approach to product development.

1. Internal R&D.
2. Acquisition of firms with new products.
3. Licensing a new product from the firm that developed it for markets where that firm is not represented.
4. Joint venturing with a firm that has complementary products.

Firms in industries with slow, high-cost product development are able to have a satisfactory international product line with an appropriate blend of the four strategies. Getting the appropriate blend is the challenge for management as over-reliance on any single approach can leave the firm vulnerable. For example, American Home Products (AHP) spent less on R&D than other major drug firms and relied heavily on licensing drugs from foreign firms. In the 1980s the French firm Rhone Poulenc and the British giant ICI, which had licensed several major drugs to AHP, decided to enter the U.S. market themselves. That meant that AHP lost a significant part of its product line, including its best-selling product.

Occasionally company policy leads to decentralized product development. Hewlett-Packard (H-P) has set up European operations that were encouraged to tap local expertise to develop products for global markets. Partly as a result of this, foreign sales topped domestic sales for the first time in 1980. From its German operations, where this policy has been particularly successful, H-P has developed a leading position in such products as a fetal heart-monitoring system and a liquid chromatograph instrument. Furthermore, more than half of the German subsidiary's sales of $500 million derive from German-developed products.

The increasing importance and complexity of product development in the firm may lead to a need for expansion, with foreign operations being involved. Merck, for example, found its primary R&D facilities in the United States had reached a saturation point and that a new center was needed. In line with its growing overseas business, Merck decided to put the new center in France. In the mid-1980s, Merck added 14 laboratories in four different countries.

The work on very large-scale projects may be too much for any group to handle, and decentralization may be a better approach. Similar pressures would be present if the company were working under a time constraint. These and other factors can be illustrated by the following examples.

In 1985 Procter & Gamble successfully introduced liquid TIDE in the U.S. market. It was the result of collaboration in product development among its Cincinnati, Brussels, and Tokyo labs. The water-softening ingredients were developed in Brussels because water there averages twice the mineral content of U.S. wash water. The surfactants were developed in Japan because the Japanese wash their clothes in colder water than do consumers in the United States or Europe.

As another example, when Kodak was developing its instant camera, it became necessary to come up with a fast film using a high-speed emulsion four times as responsive to light as any then known. A team began working on this. It involved 1,000 employees in Europe and the United States for an entire year. The final product used an emulsion developed in England, refined in Rochester, and made commercial with the help of French expertise in emulsion control.

Another reason for foreign R&D may be the need to monitor developments in countries of leading technological activity. In many industries, Europe and Japan are on a technological par with the United States. Firms from any one of these three areas cannot afford to ignore new developments in the other two. A development lab is the best way to monitor competitive activity because it is an ongoing operation staffed with qualified specialists.

Although a major argument for centralized product development involves efficiency and economies of scale, sometimes efficiency may be greater with an international division of labor. In production the largest plant is not always the optimum size, and the same is probably true of development activities. After a certain point, economies of scale may turn into diseconomies. The fact that engineering and scientific personnel are less expensive abroad can mean more development for the dollar internationally. While this is no longer true in Europe, it is true in Israel, Taiwan, and India. Control Data, Motorola, Intel, and National Semiconductor have all set up R&D centers in Israel because of the availability and low cost of scientific and technical personnel. If additional payoffs can be gained in training and morale in the subsidiaries as well as in local public relations, the arguments grow in favor of some foreign product development.

Unilever is one international company that deliberately seeks the advantages of *international* research development. The company has development activities in four European countries as well as close liaison with its associated companies in the United States and India. As one vice-chairman put it, "By locating research and development activities in a number of countries, an international company can take advantage of its unique ability to do research in a variety of national environments. . . . The probability of success is increased if there is good liaison between the laboratories. . . . There is a greater chance of sparking off new ideas."

**Pressures from Environment.**   The governments of countries where subsidiaries are operating often exert strong pressure for local R&D activity. The government wants the international company to operate locally as it does in its home country. In other words, the government does not want its country to be a disfavored member of the international company.

If the firm exports to the country, the government would prefer local production. If it gets local production, it then wants local product development. Because the firm must depend on a government's favor, it does well to consider these wishes even if it does not always yield to them. Furthermore, sometimes the firm can gain advertising benefits if it can say that certain products were developed nationally for national tastes.

India, for example, wants multinationals to establish local R&D. Sperry Vickers responded to the government's request because the Indian market was sufficiently important to the firm. Hoechst, the German multinational, also has R&D in India. Because it has one of the larger such operations there, Hoechst has received very favorable press coverage.

**Local Market Needs.**   Another encouragement to decentralized product development are local market needs. Some products require continuous local testing during the development process if they are being designed primarily to meet market specifications (tastes, use conditions, and so on) rather than technological standards. Development close to the market is practical because these use conditions usually cannot be simulated in the firm's domestic laboratories. According to this reasoning, one would expect to find consumer goods developed locally more often than industrial goods. Furthermore, when demand for a product is limited to one market, it is usually developed in that market. The game *Trivial Pursuit* is sold in over 25 countries. The questions for each country had to be developed locally.

American tire technology, also, cannot be adapted easily to European roads and weather, so Goodyear and Goodrich had European R&D facilities. Firestone was behind on this score but began a $7-million facility near Rome. While awaiting completion, the company worked jointly with Ferrari to design and produce a new racing tire. A by-product of this effort was a new passenger-car tire designed especially for Europe.

Beacham's Brazilian subsidiary felt there was a local demand for a deodorant with a strictly feminine image. The Brazilian staff developed the product and made extensive local tests of the deodorant and perfume element. From these tests, it developed and introduced the product. Within one year it was already vying for number one position in the market.

**Research versus Development.**   Until now, we have made no distinction between research and development in our discussion. Actually, the process loosely called R&D has several different stages. Distinguishing among them is important in making decisions about internationalizing them. Basic research is, almost by definition, something in which purely technical considerations of physics or chemistry predominate. As the process moves through applied research, development of products, and adaptation of products, the need for decentralizing the activity increases. Thus many foreign subsidiaries will have facilities for making product adaptations for local markets, far fewer will have a real product-development activity, and fewer still will be doing basic research.

**Some Generalizations.**[6]

1.   Multinationals conduct most of their R&D in their home country. The exception may be Canadian firms, which have transferred large segments of their R&D to the United States.
2.   Multinationals are increasingly conducting R&D on a decentralized basis in foreign markets. The drug industry illustrates both generalizations: most R&D is done at home, while a growing percentage is done abroad. Some of the reasons explaining multinationals' R&D logistics will be given later, with examples.
3.   The larger markets of the multinational firm will have the earliest and largest of its foreign R&D activity. This is evidenced by the location of U.S. multinationals' foreign R&D in the major European countries, Canada, and Japan. Dow Chemical put its Latin American R&D center in Brazil. European multinationals conduct above-average amounts of R&D in the large U.S. market. Canada-based multinationals have even transferred significant segments of R&D to the United States from Canada.
4.   For a country to be chosen as an R&D location, it must possess sufficient technical and scientific personnel. With this kind of personnel, even a smaller or less developed country can attract R&D. For example, the Swedish multinational SKF chose Holland as the location for a major R&D center. Cyanamid chose the Philippines for a regional R and D center. In both cases personnel considerations were critical. On the other hand, General Motors developed its Basic Transportation Vehicle in the United States because of a lack of qualified personnel in the target markets.

5.   Entering foreign markets by acquisition is a major way multinationals expand their foreign R&D. This is true even though the major reason for the acquisition usually has nothing to do with R&D but is primarily a means of market entry. Firms tend to keep the acquired R&D activity. Gillette acquired Braun (small appliances) in Germany and Du Pont (Cricket lighter) in France. R&D for these new lines is done in the acquired company. ICI acquired Atlas Chemical in the United States and not only continued local R&D but switched over to the United States some products that were being developed in Britain.

6.   Industry and product lines are variables. There is more decentralized R&D in consumer goods than in industrial goods. Whenever local market characteristics, adaptation, and testing become important, there is more local R&D than when technical considerations predominate. For example, there is more decentralized R&D in food than in nonfood consumer goods, more decentralization with automobiles than with tractors or diesel engines, and more with pharmaceuticals than with chemicals.

7.   Host government pressures and incentives do influence location of R&D. Britain required Chrysler to maintain the existing R&D in Britain when Rootes was acquired. NCR began a new research program in Canada for which half of the funds were supplied by the Canadian government. IBM and Control Data also received help in expanding their Canadian R&D. France, Spain, Brazil, and India have had some success in inducing local R&D by multinationals.

8.   An important variable in the decentralization of R&D is the *divisibility* of it as a corporate activity. It is divisible on at least two bases: (1) product line and (2) the nature or level of the R&D. For example, Dow acquired Le Petit, an Italian drug firm. This was Dow's first pharmaceutical venture, and the company continued its drug R&D in Italy. Gillette does its R&D on small appliances and lighters in Germany and France, where it got these product lines by acquisition.

R&D decentralization by product line is especially common when a multinational enters a new product area by acquisition. It also happens, however, independently of the acquisition approach. The computer industry provides several good examples. Burroughs, Honeywell, and IBM all do significant R&D outside the United States for varied parts of their product line.

9.   Two final company variables will be noted. The longer the firm has been engaged in international business and the larger this business is relative to the total, the more decentralized is the firm's R&D. This has been shown for the U.S. pharmaceutical industry and can be illustrated in the case histories of most multinationals.

**Screening Product Ideas**

An effective search for new product ideas will turn up candidates from all the firm's markets. The next step is to evaluate these and select the ones most promising for further research and development. The relevant questions are where the screening is done and how it is done.

**Where?**   An initial screening of a product idea should be conducted in the market where the idea originates. There are two advantages to doing the initial screening at the national level: (1) It helps to assure that the ideas have met at least a preliminary feasibility test. (2) It educates subsidiary management in product-market analysis. The initial national screening should not be too rigorous. Subsidiary personnel lack inputs from the rest of the international operation, and several subsidiaries might come up with similar product ideas. For all to do comprehensive screening on the same idea would be wasteful. Furthermore, each subsidiary might reject an idea on the basis of its own market, whereas in a multinational context the idea might be viable. A modest market in many countries could add up to a profitable volume internationally.

After evaluation at the national level, a more comprehensive review can be conducted at either the regional or the international level. Although the regional organization can play a useful role in coordinating new product activity in the region, its review is no substitute for the global view of international headquarters. Although the regional organization might conduct the intermediate screening, it should not be responsible for the final evaluation of new product ideas.

General Foods Europe, for example, has a Product Development Committee composed of the product-development managers from each European subsidiary. They meet twice a year to evaluate new product ideas from the subsidiaries. This allows early region-wide screening in General Foods' major foreign markets.

Not only in the initial screening can national organizations participate. The national companies must market new products, if adopted, and their knowledge of their own markets can add useful second-level evaluations to ideas originating in other countries. In this way, each new product idea gets a comprehensive global evaluation.

The top management of the Singer Company made a decision to market white goods (appliances) in Europe. When the idea was presented in Europe, the German subsidiary disagreed and suggested they market TV sets instead of white goods. The subsidiary's position was supported by market research and local experience. Shortly after, the white-goods cartel in Germany collapsed and prices declined severely. TV prices, however, remained stable. In short, the subsidiary's viewpoint saved management from a serious error.

When an IBM World Trade company has an idea for a new product, it draws up a documented study known as a market requirement procedure that goes to IBM World Trade headquarters for review. The case study includes factual and intuitive data and covers such items as specifications for the machine, functions of the machine, and sales estimates. The details are then disseminated to all local and foreign offices, which in turn document their need for such a machine. If enough demand for the product is assured, the original request is sent to IBM's systems development division for a feasibility study, a look at the proposed equipment from the point of view of development and production costs and other factors.

**The Screening Process.**   The purpose of generating new product ideas is to have a list of alternatives from which to choose. The goal of the screening process is to assure that the best products are chosen from this list. As usual, we define the best products as those with the greatest probability of increasing long-run company growth and profits.

*Organizational Implications.*   An effective new-product activity must have continuing support. Funds must be allocated to it and personnel made responsible for it. One method used by some companies is to establish a corporate "new product" or "product planning" committee, perhaps headed by a high-level executive as a vice-president for research and development. This corporate group can either have total international responsibility or else coordinate subgroups in the international and domestic divisions.

At the regional or national level is a product-planning person or group that reports to the corporate group. As noted earlier, each national organization in the company should devote some effort to product planning, even though the amount will vary according to the size of the firm's operations in the country. We gave some indication of an appropriate division of labor in the preceding section: (1) initial screening of an idea in the national organization where it originates, (2) total international screening by a corporate group; and (3) the major ideas circulated to all national organizations so that all ideas receive a screening in terms of national market suitability.

*Screening Criteria.*   Because of the many ramifications in developing a new product, product ideas are best screened on the basis of several criteria rather than only one. Expected profit might be one suitable criterion, but it is itself a function of many other variables. In the screening process, these variables should be specifically identified to show how the expected-profit figure is derived. When a number of criteria are used for screening, generally the product ideas scoring highest on the greatest number of criteria are those selected for development. We will use a twofold classification of criteria to simplify discussion: (1) production factors and (2) marketing factors.

*Production Criteria.*   A product is more likely to be profitable if it relates favorably to the existing production capabilities of the firm. The more the new product utilizes existing plant, technical know-how, and labor skills, the less the product will cost in money and learning time. If the product uses raw materials already used by the firm, so much the better. The diversified company has a wider range of product choices because of its diversified production skills and facilities.

As regards product choice, these international differences in production skills mean that the product not suited to an American plant might nevertheless fit in well at the company's French or Brazilian plant. Conversely, although a product idea from a foreign subsidiary might not match local production capability, it may be well suited to the production facilities in another country or in the firm's domestic facilities. Thus, the internationalization of production facilities in the multinational company gives it a wider range of alternatives when evaluating new product ideas.

*Marketing Criteria.* The checklist of production variables helps the evaluator to envision the supply side of the new product picture. For the demand side, marketing criteria are needed. Again the firm would benefit if the new product fit in with the marketing skills and facilities it is currently using. Some of the marketing criteria considered by the firm are its marketing skills, distribution channels, goodwill attached to the company name or brands, life cycles of existing products, and the relation of new product sales to existing product sales: Does the new product enhance or replace the old? Also affecting the marketing evaluation are the competitive situation and the potential demand for the new product.

Marketing considerations for new product evaluation can vary considerably in the firm's foreign markets. The firm's *marketing know-how* should be a common denominator running through its international operations, but such uniformity is usually more a goal than an accomplished fact. The *distribution channels* used by the firm are seldom identical in all markets. Except for a few names such as IBM, Coca-Cola, and Singer, the *goodwill* attached to the company name and brands will probably vary widely from market to market.

The *life cycles* of products, too, will tend to vary in different markets. This can be an advantage for the firm in that it can count on a longer overall product life in its international operations than in any of its national operations. The competitive opportunities for new products will vary from country to country. Market *demand* for the new product will be a function of factors peculiar to each country, such as tastes, habits, and income levels.

In an evaluation of product ideas according to these marketing variables, each potential new product will probably have a different score in each country. Those products with the highest total scores on an international basis would be the best candidates for development. For a meaningful international score, of course, the individual country scores would have to be weighted by their market size.

If the most desirable market, a global market, is not feasible for the product, groups of countries may constitute an interesting market. These groups can be regions, such as Latin America or Europe, or groups of industrialized or less-developed countries. Finally, the firm can occasionally find single national markets that are large enough to warrant a new product development. More frequently, though, carrying a product to international markets is the best course. This is especially true for products with heavy research and/or development costs, such as automobiles and pharmaceuticals. Food products can be more economically developed or adapted for a single-country market.

**Legal and Other Influences.** The legal part of the new product screening is very technical and must be done by corporate legal staff or outside experts. Some of the questions they must answer are listed below:

1. Does the product fall within the legal scope of the company's charter? Is the idea already patented?

2. Can we patent it in the relevant markets? What conflicts are possible on the product claim? (The same questions apply to brand and trademark protection.)
3. What import or export regulations might apply to this product?
4. What packaging, labeling, or other product requirements affect this product in our foreign markets?

Two other factors may be important in the new product evaluation process: (1) the existence of company goals in addition to profits and growth and (2) the global logistics situation of the firm. In the former case, the product-selection process may lead to different results; that is, some products may be accepted even if they do not score highest on the profit and growth indicators. For example, a firm might make such a decision on the basis of certain problems in its markets or because it wishes to create a particular image for itself — say, good citizen, progressive, concerned.

Products selected to meet these goals might not be immediately related to profit maximization. Yet, long-run profit and growth are increasingly related to overall corporate behavior and image. Food companies asked to develop high-protein low-cost foods in less-developed countries where they are operating might find it difficult to refuse. Although they will try to seek the most profitable solution to the problem, they will also be concerned about government relations, company image and the international repercussions of any decision.

The logistics situation of the firm can be another constraint on product selection. We have been considering the advantages of multinational markets for new products, but the availability of these markets cannot be automatically assumed. The costs of international distribution can restrict market accessibility.

Perishable products or those with high transport costs may be limited to serving national or regional markets from a given production source. However, transportation barriers tend to diminish with technical progress. Developments in transportation such as pipelines, containerization, and giant jets, and in processing such as freezing, dehydrating, and liquefying mean that yesterday's domestic product becomes tomorrow's international product. Tariff barriers were also greatly reduced in the years following World War II.

Finally, we should note an important development affecting product selection. That is the growth of *consumerism* and increasing product liability imposed on the manufacturer. Firms that have encountered this in the U.S. market should be prepared for it as the trend continues around the world. European requirements may be more stringent than American. Firms marketing internationally must choose products which maximize safety and performance, both for consumer satisfaction and to minimize their own liability. As these requirements spread, firms will not be able to have different standards and practices in different countries. International coordination will be necessary.

**Market Testing**

In a sense, a product is tested in a market whenever it is introduced there; but our concern here is market testing before full-scale introduction of the product. How extensive must preliminary market testing be? Does domestic experience suffice, or must testing be done in every market? Even for technical products, a domestic market test is unlikely to be sufficient. Because of differing use conditions, some foreign market testing is necessary. Fortunately for the international firm, although no one country is exactly like any other, there are enough similarities that full-scale market testing is probably not necessary in every country.

If the firm conducts a comparative analysis of its foreign markets (see Chapter 7), it should be able to form country groupings based on criteria relevant to the product at hand. From these groupings, then, the firm can select certain countries as test-markets for their groups. Just as American firms use test-market cities that acceptably represent the United States market for them, so the international firm can choose test-market countries.

Unilever wanted to introduce a new deodorant in nine European countries. However, it did not wish to have to conduct nine individual market tests. After a discussion among several company delegates, a region in France was selected as representative of the average overall development of the deodorant market in Europe, halfway between the more developed northern countries and the less developed southern countries. This region was to be the test-market for all nine countries.

After a market test in France showed strong sales performance, the product, Rexona deodorant, was launched successfully in the eight remaining subsidiary countries. To get this success required cooperation among the nine subsidiaries, as well as overall coordination from headquarters.

**Example of Product Development: Nestlé**

In discussing international product development, we have cited many company examples. These examples were very brief and were meant to illustrate some part of the development process. It is helpful to give a more extended example to show how the various aspects of international product development relate to each other in a one-company situation. In Nestlé, new-product development may originate either at the subsidiary level or at the headquarters level (in Vevey, Switzerland); i.e., a *bottom-up* or *top-down* process.

**Bottom-Up Process**

1. A product manager or marketer in a subsidiary believes there is a market in that country for a new or modified product.
2. The initiator contacts the production manager of the subsidiary about the proposed product, with a rough estimate of demand.
3. The production manager writes Vevey asking for a formula and information about the proposed product.
4. Vevey develops and sends the requested information.
5. The local production manager and initiator develop a version of the product.

6.  A sample is sent to Vevey with a request for a number of units, say 5,000 jars, for market testing.
7.  The market test is conducted. The subsidiary management will make a decision based on the results. Their decision must be approved by Vevey.
8.  Vevey assures maintenance of standards for quality, branding, and packaging.

**Top-Down Process**

1.  From subsidiary reports, a Vevey marketing manager recognizes a latent demand for a new or modified product.
2.  He contacts the Vevey production chief, who experiments with versions of the new product (say, a new kind of instant coffee).
3.  Once an acceptable product is found, taste tests are conducted in the laboratory.
4.  A preliminary cost and business analysis is conducted for the product.
5.  The marketing manager discusses a market test with Nestlé management in the region where the product is best suited.
6.  If the regional manager agrees, subsidiary management in the target country is asked to conduct the test.
7.  If the subsidiary agrees, the market test is conducted. If it is successful, the product will be introduced.

It is apparent that Nestlé is very centralized both in research and in development. Nevertheless, the company manages to get foreign markets involved in the important stages of product development. The role of Vevey is central, but it does not neglect the contribution of local markets.

## Cooperation in Developing Products

As the costs of developing new products rise, and diverse technologies are needed, consortium approaches have greater appeal. The consortium partners typically have complementary assets in design or technology, and the alliance is initiated to develop new products more speedily. IBM and Toshiba began collaborating in the design of lightweight computer screen displays used in laptop computers, because they had complementary technologies. Small color screens that use low energy are essential for the next generation of laptops. IBM joined Toshiba in order to learn from Toshiba's expertise in manufacturing. Product development is expected to take two years.[7]

**Creating a Common Standard.**    Such collaboration can also result in a common standard being adopted. A new data-storage device called CD-I, compact disc interactive, can combine text, sound, and video pictures. Such disks can be used by computers for complex simulation and interactive training programs. When RCA announced its own, different, system named Digital Video Interactive, which uses compression techniques to record more video images, Philips and Sony decided to forge a common standard for CD-I technology in an effort to reduce risk and stimulate demand.[8]

**Strategic Fit.**    Recently, a joint venture between Merck and Johnson & Johnson acquired the over-the-counter drug business of ICI, the British multinational.[9] ICI's total U.S. sales were about $125 million annually, of which $90 million was from Mylanta antacid, one of the top 25 U.S. over-the-counter drugs. The joint venture between J&J and Merck had been set up to develop and market over-the-counter versions of prescription drugs. They were developing a compound called Pepcid based on an anti-ulcer drug, and it would be three to four years before Pepcid would be approved for non-prescription sale. The agreement with ICI gives the joint venture a product to sell in the meantime.

**National Consortia.**   Governments have formed national consortia to develop new products in the face of global competition. Examples of this are the organizations Sematech and Microelectronics and Computer Consortium (MCC), created as consortia of U.S. companies in the semiconductor and semiconductor production equipment fields, to pool knowledge, share financial risk, and create common standards on which to base product development. These initiatives were taken in response to the growing Japanese domination of these product areas.

# Incremental Innovation

Much of new-product development consists of small but steady improvements to existing products. This is especially true of industrial products. As product use increases, customer feedback provides suggestions for additional features that should be incorporated. Matching competitive products provide another source of ideas. Periodic evaluation of one's product in relation to those of the competition will enable a checklist of areas where competitors' products have an advantage. This activity is essential to keeping and gaining market share. By the same token, incremental innovations based on information from existing customers and focus groups allow a company to keep one step ahead of competition, continually providing differentiated products for a higher price rather than being forced to compete on a lowest-cost basis.

An example of such an approach is Mitsubishi Electric's changes to its line of residential air conditioners.[10] Between 1979 and 1985, Mitsubishi first introduced integrated circuits to control the air conditioning cycle. Then, the next year, it replaced the integrated circuits with microprocessors. Moreover, it made the product easier to install and more reliable. Specifically:

1.  It used quick-connect precharged freon lines that clicked together to replace the older version of freon lines which had to be cut to length from copper tubing, then bent, soldered together, purged and then filled with freon. This older process was costly, requiring skilled labor, and the fabrication process inherently created the possibility of a higher defect rate.
2.  It used simpler wiring, a two-wire connection with neutral polarity replacing the older model, which used six color-coded wires. Because the product was easier to install, the new air conditioner could be sold through mass-market outlets, and local contractors could install it more easily.

Next, in 1982 Mitsubishi introduced a high-efficiency rotary compressor to replace the obsolete reciprocating compressor. The condensing unit was designed with louvered and inner fin tubes for better heat transfer, all of which made the air conditioner more energy-efficient. In 1983 it added sensors and more computing power, resulting in further energy-efficiency gains. In 1984 it added an inverter, with additional electronic controls, which afforded greater control over the speed of the electric motor, again increasing the unit's efficiency. Thus, through a series of small steps, Mitsubishi was able to offer customers a technologically advanced product that also saved energy.

While research and development is necessary to creating new products, converting research into commercially viable products is not a trivial task. This is why product testing is crucial to the product-development process.

**Product Testing**

As part of the development process, the product must be tested under realistic use conditions. A further reason for testing in a number of markets is to meet national requirements as to product specifications and performance. For example, in the case of food products, drugs, and electrical or transportation equipment, some local testing may be necessary for government authorization to sell. In the case of pharmaceuticals, there is often a special factor. The U.S. Food and Drug Administration (FDA) approval of new drugs is a very time-consuming process. Drug manufacturers often test and certify their drugs in other markets and begin marketing there before getting final approval in the United States, thus expediting international introduction of the product. The firm should be virtually certain of FDA approval, however, or it will be in an awkward position abroad if its product is deemed unfit for users in the United States.

Finally, local product testing may be advisable for promotional reasons. Although the firm must test its own products vigorously, there may be advantages in having local testing done outside the firm. The firm may improve its local public relations by using national testing organizations. In Europe, which has many testing organizations, the firm may use one for the promotional value gained from its certification. Such certification may be valuable to an international firm if it is advantageous for the international firm to appear more native.

Although Abbott Laboratories develops its new drug products in the United States, it then sends them to universities and hospitals around the world for testing. Findings are reported in various national medical journals. This has the dual advantages of extensive international testing under different conditions plus the publicity value when findings are reported.

## Product-Line Management

Beyond deciding which products will be sold in which countries, firms must also decide on the product line that will be sold in each overseas market. They must decide whether to replicate the product line from the domestic market or develop some subset of the full line, with additional new products that are not sold in the domestic market for individual country markets.

**Domestic versus International Product Line**

If a firm has a diversified product line, its international product line is quite unlikely to be identical to its domestic line. The history and rationale for each are different. The domestic line of a firm is a function of many different influences.

Since the domestic product mix is less than ideal in many companies, the firm has a good opportunity to start with a clean slate internationally. As the vice-president of a pharmaceutical company noted: "We were fortunate in our international product line in being able to start from scratch. We didn't have to carry anybody's favorites or any weak products." In international markets the firm may be able to field an "all-star team" with no weak players on it. The strongest products can be selected, making use of the firm's greatest competitive advantage.

The foreign product line frequently is shorter than the domestic for several reasons. Because of financial or market limitations, the firm usually is not able to carry its full domestic line when it first moves abroad. By entering a limited product line into foreign markets, the firm can test the market before taking a bigger plunge. As a few strong products prove themselves, they pave the way for other products. The initial foreign line cannot be too narrow, however, because it would spread the entry cost over too few products. Marketing and administrative costs of foreign sales bear less heavily as they are spread over a wider line.

**Extending the Domestic Product Line**

One possible product-line strategy is to extend the domestic product line to foreign markets. *Nintendo* provides an example. Nintendo broke into the U.S. market with a family entertainment computer that was already a best-seller in Japan and is following a similar strategy in marketing its portable "Game-Boy" — a small hand-held version of the Nintendo computer. When the Game-Boy was introduced in Japan, it sold 200,000 units in the first two weeks.[11] The company hopes to achieve a similar success in the United States.

Nintendo is also expanding its U.S. product line to take advantage of its installed base of over 20 million Nintendo machines. It formed a joint venture with Fidelity Investments, the mutual funds group, to develop and sell a home-trading system for financial services. This would allow Nintendo owners to use their machines to trade stocks and check on the latest market information. The company already operates a communications network in Japan with Nomura Securities offering financial information and a trading service. To develop the national network, it is attempting to set up a venture with AT&T and other telecommunications companies.[12] Thus, Nintendo's U.S. product strategy is a copy of its product policies in Japan. Just as it worked with Nomura in Japan, it intends to cooperate with AT&T as the key to obtaining a U.S.–wide communications capability.

A strong factor in product extension to foreign markets is *client needs* — that is, the needs of the company's home customers as those customers travel abroad. As Japan becomes prosperous, the number of Japanese tourists going overseas is increasing. Several Japanese companies have responded by diversifying in order to gather additional revenues from their client base. For example, Japan Air Lines manages 23 Nikko International Hotels and its Seibu/Saison Group purchased 100 Intercontinental hotels. Seibu's travel agents in Japan can thus bring their clients to Intercontinental hotels worldwide, and let them charge purchases with Seibu credit cards.[13]

Credit cards are a business dominated by American firms. Visa had issued about 187 million cards by the end of 1988, and American Express nearly 31 million. (There are about 220 million credit cards in circulation in the United States.) In comparison, JCB Co., Japan's largest credit card company, with 39 percent of the Japanese market, had issued 16 million cards. Only 30,000 of these cardholders are outside Japan. JCB wants foreign cardholders to account for at least 10 percent of its total, while also increasing the number of Japanese cardholders. As the Japanese travel overseas, JCB has to convince shops around the world to accept the JCB card. Holiday Inn has agreed to do so at its 1,500 hotels in 52 countries, and JCB has signed agreements with two U.S. ATM networks to allow JCB cardholders to use their cards at over 27,000 automatic teller machines in the United States.

JCB has also been attempting to differentiate itself from its global competitors by certain innovations. It allows cardholders to buy gift certificates that are accepted by all merchants who accept the JCB credit card. JCB gets a commission when the certificates are exchanged for goods, and it also earns interest on the "float," the funds it receives for the gift certificates but that do not have to be paid out till the certificates are actually used.

JCB also offers a monthly catalog of goods that cardholders can purchase, and it provides a service wherein it will handle customer complaints with merchants from whom purchases were bought with JCB cards.

But JCB has little doubt that real growth can come only by expanding overseas.[14] And expanding overseas is not easy, even for the dominant American firms. Italy, for example, has only 3 million cards in use, and credit card transactions account for about 1 percent of all transactions. Part of the reason for the limited diffusion of credit cards in Italy is the profusion of small family-owned retailers who prefer to bargain with individual clients for cash. Italian merchants, for example, would prefer that their clients not use the American Express card, since a higher commission is charged by American Express (about 6 percent, with discounts for large-volume merchants, as against 2 to 4 percent charged by firms such as Visa), and there are greater delays in receiving payment. The Visa franchise for Italy is owned by a local bank, and merchants can cash their credit card receipts at any one of over 100 branches of the Banca d'America & d'Italia (BAI), and have their funds transferred to their accounts immediately. American Express at one time required that merchants mail their receipts to Rome, which delayed payment by about 15 business days (although it now also uses BAI branches to speed payment). Local competition is increasing as Italian banks realize the profit potential from consumer credit. For example, a consortium of Italian banks launched the Carta Si card in 1986, which soon captured about 32 percent of the market to Visa's 27 percent and American Express's 18 percent.[15]

**Table 9–2**                              **Luxury-Car Segment in United States, 1988**

| Make | Market Share | Model | Price |
|------|------|------|------|
| Cadillac | 26.9% | Fleetwood 60 | $34,325 |
| Lincoln | 19.5 | Continental | 29,910 |
| Buick/Oldsmobile | 18.8 | | |
| Mercedes-Benz | 7.3 | 420 SEL | 61,210 |
| Acura | 7.2 | Legend | 29,960 |
| Volvo | 5.9 | | |
| Chrysler | 5.2 | | |
| Audi | 3.1 | Quattro V-8 | |
| Jaguar | 1.6 | XJ6 | 43,500 |
| BMW | 1.4 | 735i | 54,000 |
| Other | 3.2 | | |
| | | | |
| New Entrants: | | | |
| Toyota | — | Lexus LS 400 | 35,000 |
| Nissan | — | Infiniti Q45 | 38,000 |

Source: *The Wall Street Journal,* August 7, 1989.

**Competitive Influences on the Product Line**

Competition serves as a benchmark in assessing how to satisfy customer needs worldwide. The competition's product line is particularly relevant. If a firm wants to be one of the top three or four players in an industry, it must match competitors' product lines. The powerful competitive impetus to match product lines can best be appreciated in the auto industry in the United States.

The luxury-car segment can be divided into two sub-segments, with GM/Cadillac and Ford/Lincoln appealing to older buyers, and the prestigious, highly engineered super-expensive European cars such as BMW and Mercedes catering to the young rich. As shown in Table 9–2, Cadillac, Lincoln, and Buick/Oldsmobile dominate this segment in number of units sold. On a price basis, the American luxury cars are attractively priced. It is this market that the Japanese have targeted. Their theory is that as their consumers, the owners of Sentras and Maximas and Camrys, get older, they may trade up, and the Japanese want to have cars that they can trade up to. Profit margins are higher on these cars, which is important as the yen gets stronger and the Japanese lose their competitive advantage in the economy-car segment. The Japanese product-development goal is simple: to match the German cars in engineering and styling and compete on price. As shown in Table 9–2, the price differential may be sufficiently large to overcome the prestige factor.

The first Japanese company to follow this upscale-segment entry strategy was Honda when it insisted that a separate Acura brand identity be established, with physically separate dealers and distinctive buildings. The Lexus and Infiniti follow the same approach, choosing from the best dealers and then requiring them to build new facilities to sell only Lexus or Infiniti. The entire luxury segment was only about half a million cars in 1988, and the new Japanese entries, if successful, will mean trouble for the bread-and-butter lines of the Big Three American auto makers.[16]

## Other Influences on the Product Line

Product-line choices for individual markets are affected by additional factors, such as government regulations, the level of economic development of the market, the company's growth patterns, and the length of time the firm has been in a particular foreign market. The mode of entry into a foreign market, whether through exports or licensing or joint ventures, also plays a role.

*Government regulation,* domestic and foreign, often affects product lines. Some governments prohibit export of certain products for national security reasons. This keeps some domestic products from foreign product lines. The Export Control Act gives the U.S. president power to restrict exports to Communist countries. Such controls are being relaxed with better East–West relations.

Host-country governments have shown increasing interest in local product lines of multinationals. They may bar certain products from their markets, such as liquor in some Islamic countries. Because of this, Anheuser-Busch is working on a nonalcoholic beer for Islamic markets. Host-country pressures can also encourage firms to enter completely new product areas to please the local government. International Protein Corporation for example began a boat-building operation in Panama as a condition for participating in fishmeal and shrimp operations. And because of the Indian government's restrictions on foreign involvement in low-technology industries, Hindustan Lever (Unilever's Indian subsidiary) switched its emphasis from toilet articles to animal feeds and chemicals.

The *level of economic development* in a country will affect the choice of products to be sold there. Established firms usually have a domestic product line that ranges from mature products to advanced, higher-technology products. Firms from industrialized countries will find that the choice of products from this line for foreign markets will depend on the level of development of those markets. This is as true in consumer goods, such as for CPC International or General Foods, as for industrial marketers, such as Dow Chemical or General Electric. A GE executive remarked:

> We've placed to track right up the development curve with countries growing economically. Our first businesses in a country are those necessary for infrastructure building such as power generation and transmission and locomotives. As light industry starts we can take in our small motors and other low-technology industrial products. As electrification spreads, our consumer housewares find a market. Finally, when advanced manufacturing begins, we can take in our engineering plastics and other high-technology products.

A company's *method of growth* will also affect its product lines in foreign markets. Firms that stress internal growth will generally have narrower and more homogeneous product lines internationally than those who stress growth by acquisition. The firm that expands abroad by acquisition has both its own and the acquired line from which to draw. The acquiring firm may sell off or drop some of the acquired products but it may also carry some of them to other markets.

Finally, *length of time in a market* will affect the firm's product line there. Firms generally enter a market with a narrow line of "all-star" products. As the firm gains experience, it finds opportunities and the skills to expand its offerings. The experience of almost every firm is a growing product line over time in foreign markets. Silentnight, a British bedding firm, is an example. It established a mattress manufacturing operation in Kenya. Over time, the firm branched out into the production of bedframes, upholstered furniture, contract furniture for hotels, and then into office furniture.

**Impact of Method of Entry.**   The nature of the firm's involvement in foreign markets is another product-line determinant. If the firm enters a market through *exports* only, it theoretically has freedom to choose as many or as few products as it wants in each market. Once it establishes an export operation, however, it will feel some pressure to expand the product line to gain economies of scale; if it uses an export middleman, this pressure becomes less because the intermediary can spread the cost over other products carried. "Buy national" policies, tariffs, and transport costs are other restraints on the export line.

*Licensing* offers less freedom in product selection. Appropriate licensees may not be available for all the products a firm wants to enter in a market; licensees may not have satisfactory technology, or the best candidates may be licensed to competitors. Even if the firm finds suitable licensees, possibly they are producing products that compete with those of the licensor. The product line of the licensee can limit the product line of the licensor in that market.

For example, Pepsi Cola pulled a coup on entering the French market when it obtained Perrier as licensee. Perrier gave Pepsi instant widespread distribution in France. However, Perrier also had a line of soft drinks in the non-cola areas, which restricted Pepsi's ability to sell its own non-cola line in France.

Occasionally the firm can overcome such limitations by using different licensees in a country. The feasibility depends on the availability of licensees and the divisibility of the licensor's product line. If the licensor's products are competitive, the licensee would not want another firm in the country to be involved.

The positive licensing impact on the national product line is that it can avoid tariff and transport cost restrictions that can eliminate items from the export line. Also, preference for national suppliers favors licensing over exporting.

The *joint-venture* approach can restrict the firm's foreign-product line, too. Most joint ventures of international firms bring together two companies, each with a particular product line, just as does licensing. If the national partner has complementary products, this will confine the product line possibilities of the international partner.

*Wholly owned foreign operations* appear to offer the greatest product line flexibility. The firm can produce any or all of its products in its own plants abroad. Eaton's experience with national product lines was described by its chairman, E. M. deWindt:

> Originally, our automotive customers suggested we establish manufacturing abroad where they were building cars. Soon, however, these plants acquired a life of their own. They had to develop new engineering, manufacturing, and marketing capabilities for the local market. Today our overseas operations are no longer carbon copies of what we do in Cleveland and Detroit. We make components that differ substantially from our U.S. products for local customers in these markets.

We discussed the impact of foreign involvement on product line as if the firm were entering a market by one method exclusively. Actually, many firms enter some markets using two or more approaches in combination. The limitations inherent in any one approach no longer apply when different approaches are combined.

The Westinghouse Company chose the licensing approach for several of its products in the European market. It overcame, at least partially, the product-line limitations in licensing by two methods. First, it expanded its European line with a wide range of complementary licensees in different countries of the Common Market. Its EC product line could thus be rather broad even though limited in any one country.

Second, by integrating its licensee suppliers with components from the United States, Westinghouse landed some large equipment orders that would normally be impossible to obtain by a licensing approach, or even by export, because of national preferences. As this example indicates, product-line strategies abroad cannot be determined merely by considering the advantages and disadvantages of different approaches. It is rather a question of overall strategy in foreign markets.

**Adding Products.**   As new products come from product development, mergers and acquisitions, and so on, decisions must be made as to their addition to the existing line. The standard decision rule is simple to state: Add the product if this course of action represents the most profitable use of company resources.

In the international company, cost-benefit analysis would need to be done on either a national-market or a regional-grouping basis. Not only does the number of markets make the problem complex; the variations in both company situation and external environment among markets make evaluating cost-benefit factors uncertain.

Procter & Gamble (P&G) has added many products to its original soaps and detergents line in the United States. In Europe, the company initially stayed with soaps and detergents. However, Mr. Morgens, the president, said, "We want to build an organization and business in Europe as strong as we have in the U.S. When we decide the organization in Europe is ready, we will add other products just as we have here."

On the *cost* side, the company may have several possible production sources for the new product. Production costs will vary from nation to nation, as will other cost factors such as tariffs, taxes, and regulations. Marketing costs also differ for the firm in its different markets. The firm's own marketing mix might not be the same in neighboring countries.

On the *benefit* side, the benefits to the firm of adding the new product are dissimilar in its various markets. In each country, sales of the product will depend on local tastes, income levels, and the nature of competitive offerings. Because of imperfect information, it is not easy for the firm to evaluate the benefits of adding a product in foreign markets.

Drop/add practices involve a number of national decisions. These decisions are different from those facing national firms in the same markets for two reasons: (1) the multinational firm wants to optimize its global profits, not just those in certain national markets; (2) an international decision must take into account more variables both on the supply and demand side and on the cost and benefit side. As a result, the international firm may not add a product even though it would be profitable to do so in a particular country, or, on the other hand, it may add a product that is not profitable in a particular country.

**Dropping Products.**   In theory, a product should be dropped when it is unprofitable — or even when it is profitable, if the resources allocated to it could earn a higher return elsewhere. Some of the parameters involved are the costs of maintaining the product; its importance to consumers and retailers; costs and rewards of product rejuvenation; and costs and returns of other alternatives.

Although the product may not be profitable in the domestic market, it could be in the growth phase of its life cycle in foreign markets. The firm might drop the product domestically but accelerate marketing in the product's growth markets abroad. At first, the situation could involve domestic production but exclusively foreign marketing of the product, but eventually foreign production, too, would be likely.

**Divestment within a Product Line.**   Divestment of specific products from the product line is another option. As the following example of Zenith's laptop-computer division shows, divestment may have less to do with a product's intrinsic attractiveness than with resources and a firm's strategies.

Zenith's sale of its PC division to Bull (the French state-owned computer company) to concentrate on consumer electronics presents an interesting example of how companies can have opposite views on product diversification and divestment in international markets. Zenith Data Systems held a 28 percent, or number one, market share worldwide in the portable or laptop-computer segment. The parent Zenith Corp. also owns the Zenith consumer electronics division. Zenith decided to sell off the portable-computer segment to Bull for over $600 million, using the proceeds to reposition itself in the worldwide color-television market, which faces stiff competition from low-cost Far Eastern producers that has prompted major U.S. producers such as GTE (Sylvania), Motorola and GE/RCA to sell off their TV lines. Zenith could not afford to be in both the PC market and the television market; it opted for the TV market.

The industry is now dominated by Japanese companies, European companies such as Thomson and Philips, and South Korean companies such as Samsung and Goldstar. A major future opportunity lies in high-definition TV (HDTV), which will incorporate wide, sharp, cinema-like pictures and compact-disk quality sound. The American Electronics Association forecasts HDTV sales of $11 billion in the year 2010, and worldwide sales of $40 billion.[17] Zenith has decided to concentrate its resources on developing HDTV products for this future global market. It is one of the few American companies doing so.

At the same time, even as Zenith is abandoning the laptop market where it has the lead, Bull is seeking to enter it. Bull's market presence is mainly in the mainframe and minicomputer markets, so why did it want the Zenith PC line?

1.   It immediately gained a commanding market share in the PC segment by taking over the Zenith computer line.
2.   Zenith is strong in the United States, and the acquisition doubled Bull's U.S. revenues.
3.   Zenith also had significant U.S. government orders ($560 million in 1988), including an Air Force computer order, and was a bidder in the $1 billion federal Desktop III contract. Thus, the Zenith acquisition gave Bull a strong presence in selling to the U.S. government.
4.   In addition, Zenith has been developing an advanced PC as part of a consortium, using an EISA (Extended Industry Standard Architecture) bus as an alternative to IBM's Micro Channel based PS/2 computers.[18] Since Bull had already backed the IBM standard, the Zenith acquisition also gives it a stake in the alternative standard being developed by IBM's competitors. In effect, the Zenith acquisition allows Bull to hedge its bets with regard to technical standards for advanced PCs.

Both Zenith's reason for divestment and Bull's reasons for the acquisition make sense when viewed in light of each firm's global product policies.

Firms within the same industry can thus arrive at different decisions about product diversification. As shown in Table 9–3 , multinational pharmaceutical companies selling prescription drugs have made divergent decisions about complementary lines of business. Given the divergences, competitive behavior may lie in entering product lines in which competition is entrenched. For example, the table shows Glaxo as unrepresented in the over-the-counter (OTC) sector. When SmithKline merged with Beecham, thus giving SmithKline an OTC capability for its Tagamet anti-ulcer prescription drug, Glaxo then had to match this by finding a similar OTC channel for a version of its anti-ulcer drug Zantac. Glaxo's defensive move was an alliance with the Swiss firm Sandoz, giving it U.S. marketing rights for a nonprescription version of Zantac.[19]

**Table 9-3**                    **Product Lines of Major Multinational Pharmaceutical Companies**

| Areas | Companies | | | | | | | |
|---|---|---|---|---|---|---|---|---|
| | Eli Lilly | Merck | Ciba Geigy | Sandoz | Bayer | UpJohn | Beecham | Glaxo |
| Ethical Drugs | X | X | X | X | X | X | X | X |
| Over-the-Counter Drugs | | | | X | X | X | X | |
| Biotechnology | X | | | | X | | | |
| Diagnostics | X | | | | X | | | |
| Medical Instruments | X | | | | X | | | |
| Agriculture | X | X | X | X | X | X | | |
| Animal Health | X | X | X | | X | X | | |
| Consumer Products | | | | | | | X | |
| Chemicals | | X | X | X | X | X | | |
| Contact Lenses | | | X | | | | | |
| Photography | | | | | X | | | |
| Nutrition | | | | X | | | | |

Source: Annual Reports.

## Banned at Home, Sold Abroad

Ethical considerations sometimes also affect the nature of the product line sold overseas. Cigarettes present an instance. U.S. public sentiment opposed to the spread of cigarette smoking has steadily increased to the point that smoking is banned in most public places, and growth prospects for cigarette usage in the United States are negative. At the same time, there is a huge potential for increasing the sale of tobacco products in developing countries such as China or Thailand. The U.S. government opposes discriminatory measures taken by the Thai government that restrict the sale of tobacco products from U.S. multinationals at the same time that it is opposed to the spread of cigarette smoking in the United States. The question is, is it correct for governments and companies to promote the sale of products such as cigarettes in overseas markets while restricting their consumption at home?

A similar controversy surrounds the sale of a drug that induces abortions early in pregnancy. The pill, RU486, is marketed by a French company, Roussel-Uclaf S.A. It is considered an inexpensive, safe, and less traumatic way to end pregnancies as opposed to surgical abortions (it is sometimes referred to as the "morning-after pill"). While the drug has been legally approved for sale in France and China and has undergone extensive testing, the company had decided against marketing the drug because of fear of protests from anti-abortion forces. It was then ordered by the French government to reinstate marketing of the pill. But the company does not plan to export the drug to the United States, and it will therefore be available only on the black market in the United States (the FDA permits citizens to bring into the U.S. unapproved drugs for personal use).[20]

The issues here are complex and controversial and they are increasingly important for international marketers, especially after the Bhopal disaster.

Governments have different product and safety standards. To what extent can firms take advantage of these differences? Their resolution will depend on the informed judgment and the conscience of the decision maker.

Consumer groups, such as the International Organization of Consumers' Unions, accuse multinationals of taking advantage of developing countries' low levels of literacy, vaguely drafted and unenforced consumer-protection laws, and desire for foreign investment at almost any price. A spokesman for the National Association of Manufacturers said, "The standards are cultural issues. U.S. exports should not be hampered in foreign markets because of standards designed for the U.S. The foreign country has the opportunity to refuse the product. The firm's responsibility is met by notification."[21] The firm must make its own decision in this sensitive area. After Bhopal, however, on products where there is a serious question of product safety, it would seem that the ethical and economic decisions would concur — don't have a dual standard.

In closing our discussion of product line, it is useful to look at the actual international product line of a multinational company. Table 9–4 shows the collection of national product lines of an American consumer goods firm. It illustrates many of the points made earlier in this chapter. The reader can compare the U.S. product line with that in other countries. It is hard to find two countries with identical lines. Some products sold abroad aren't sold in the United States and vice versa. Only one product is found in all markets. Such a matrix is a valuable way to analyze a firm's international marketing.

## Foreign-Market Choice: Matching Products to Markets

Each international marketer has to decide which products to sell to which countries. Several steps make up this decision:

1. Using the international product life cycle (IPLC) to identify potential markets.
2. Screening markets to extract a short list of those with highest potential.
3. Assessing individual markets in terms of how well they meet the firm's objectives (market share, or return on investment, or matching competition).
4. Conducting a competitive audit to isolate markets where risk-return trade-offs are most attractive.
5. Finally, for the markets chosen, deciding on realistic market-share objectives.

**Table 9–4**                     **National Product Lines of an American Consumer Goods Firm**

COUNTRIES

| Product Category | United States | Belgium | Britain | Canada | France | Germany | Holland | Italy | Japan | Libya | Mexico | Morocco | Peru | Philippines | Saudi Arabia | Spain | Sweden | Venezuela |
|---|---|---|---|---|---|---|---|---|---|---|---|---|---|---|---|---|---|---|
| **Detergents** | | | | | | | | | | | | | | | | | | |
| heavy duty synthetic granules | X | X | X | X | X | X | X | X | X | X | X | X | X | X | X | X | X | X |
| light duty synthetic granules | X | X | X | X |  | X | X |  | X |  |  |  |  |  |  | X | X |  |
| paste in tube |  |  |  |  | X |  |  |  |  |  |  |  |  |  |  |  |  |  |
| **Other Household Products** | | | | | | | | | | | | | | | | | | |
| abrasive cleanser | X |  |  | X |  |  |  |  |  |  |  |  | X |  |  |  |  |  |
| auto. dishwashing gran. | X |  |  | X |  |  |  |  |  |  |  |  | X |  |  |  |  |  |
| liquid bleach |  |  |  |  |  |  |  | X |  |  |  |  |  |  |  |  |  |  |
| pre-soak | X |  |  |  |  |  |  |  |  |  |  |  |  |  |  |  |  |  |
| **Bar Soaps** | | | | | | | | | | | | | | | | | | |
| toilet | X | X | X | X | X | X |  | X | X |  | X | X | X | X | X | X | X | X |
| laundry |  |  | X |  |  |  |  |  | X |  | X |  |  |  | X |  |  |  |
| **Food Products** | | | | | | | | | | | | | | | | | | |
| shortening | X |  |  | X |  |  |  |  |  |  |  |  |  | X | X |  |  |  |
| salad cooking oil | X |  |  | X |  |  |  |  |  |  |  |  |  |  | X |  |  |  |
| margarine |  |  |  |  |  |  |  |  |  |  |  |  |  | X |  |  |  |  |
| cake mix | X |  |  | X |  |  |  |  |  |  |  |  |  |  |  |  |  |  |
| potato chips | X |  |  | X |  |  |  |  |  |  |  |  |  |  |  | X |  |  |
| cookie mix | X |  |  | X |  |  |  |  |  |  |  |  |  |  |  |  |  |  |
| peanut butter | X |  |  |  |  |  |  |  |  |  |  |  |  |  |  |  |  |  |
| roast coffee — packaged, ground | X |  |  |  |  |  |  |  | X |  |  |  |  |  |  |  |  |  |
| roast coffee — packaged, bean |  |  |  |  |  |  |  |  | X |  |  |  |  |  |  |  |  |  |
| instant coffee — regular | X |  |  |  |  |  |  |  |  |  |  |  |  |  |  |  |  |  |
| **Toiletries** | | | | | | | | | | | | | | | | | | |
| dentifrice | X |  | X | X |  |  |  |  |  |  | X |  |  |  |  | X |  | X |
| shampoo | X |  | X | X |  |  |  |  |  |  |  |  |  | X | X |  |  | X |
| deodorant | X |  |  | X |  |  |  |  |  |  |  |  |  |  |  |  |  |  |
| mouthwash | X |  |  | X |  |  |  |  |  |  |  |  |  |  |  |  |  |  |
| shaving soap |  |  |  |  | X |  |  |  |  |  |  |  |  |  |  |  |  |  |
| home permanent | X |  |  |  |  |  |  |  |  |  |  |  |  |  |  |  |  |  |
| **Paper and Related Products** | | | | | | | | | | | | | | | | | | |
| disposable diapers | X | X |  | X | X | X | X | X | X |  | X |  | X |  |  | X | X | X |
| toilet tissue | X |  |  |  |  |  |  |  |  |  |  |  |  |  |  |  |  |  |
| paper towels | X |  |  |  |  |  |  |  |  |  |  |  |  |  |  |  |  |  |
| facial tissue | X |  |  |  |  |  |  |  |  |  |  |  |  |  |  |  |  |  |

**International
Product Life
Cycle (IPLC)**

The international product life cycle (referred to here as the IPLC) was described in Chapter 2. It comprises stages of demand growth, staggered in time across countries, representing lags in income and development of consumer demand in the various countries. Typically, demand first grows in the innovating country and in other advanced industrial nations similar to the innovating country. Only later does demand begin in the less-developed countries. Production, consequently, first takes place in the innovating country, with excess production (greater than domestic demand) being exported to satisfy demand elsewhere. As the product matures and technology is diffused, production occurs in other advanced industrialized countries and then in less-developed countries (see Figure 9–1).

This sequential introduction of new products means that the firm will have different product lines in different markets. As noted by a Gillette executive, "Yesterday's product in the U.S. is today's product in Latin America and tomorrow's in Africa. The razor blade we launch in 1985 in the U.S. will be a brand new product in New Guinea in 1998. We can write the marketing plan for New Guinea in 1998 right now."[22]

A further implication of this life cycle is that as products become mature in the firm's home market, they may be dropped there while continuing to be sold in other markets. In other words, the sequence for dropping products generally follows the same order as for adding products. This again leads to different product lines in different countries. This is a strength of the international marketing firm. It can continue to exploit its mature products, even when they are no longer sold in its home country or the other industrialized nations.

A concrete example of product life cycles is seen in Figure 9–2, which illustrates the demand curve for fuel-injection systems and anti-skid braking systems, both products from the innovative German company, Robert Bosch. Fuel-injection systems were a luxury found initially only on expensive cars, but with stricter emission controls, auto manufacturers began using them on all cars to precisely regulate the amount of gasoline delivered to the engine, leading to a cleaner burn and cutting pollution. Gas-conservation measures also stimulated demand for fuel-injection systems. Thus, while demand grew hardly at all between 1952 and 1965, it jumped from 1965 to 1980, then further accelerated from 1985 onward. The market seems to have reached the mature stage in the United States, with 90 percent of all cars expected to have fuel-injection systems by 1990. In Japan, about 60 percent of cars will have them. The comparable figure for Europe is 47 percent.

Anti-skid braking systems (ABS) display much the same profile. First installed on Mercedes-Benz and BMW cars, early ABS systems contained as many as 1,000 components and were somewhat unreliable. Innovation reduced the number of parts to 140, then 80, then 40. Weight also has dropped, to only one-sixth of the original weight. These innovations in turn cut production costs, and volume production has led to further economies, making ABS systems more affordable, and speeding their acceptance as standard equipment. As Figure 9–2 shows, sales were slow from 1978 to

**Figure 9-1**                               **International Trade and Production in the Product Cycle**

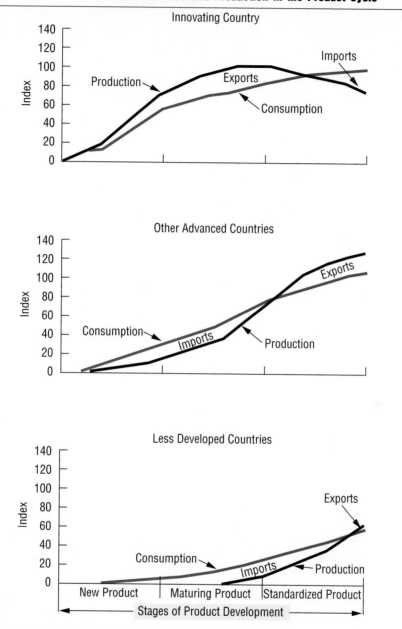

Source: Raymond Vernon and Louis T. Wells, Jr., *Manager in the International Economy,* 5/e, © 1986, p. 83. Reprinted by permission of Prentice Hall, Inc., Englewood Cliffs, New Jersey.

1982, with moderate acceptance, then accelerated after 1984, with sales almost doubling between 1986 and 1987. Bosch has an 80 percent share of an expanding world market and will open a U.S. production site for ABS

**Figure 9–2**                **Product Life Cycles in Action: Fuel-injection and Anti-skid Braking Systems**

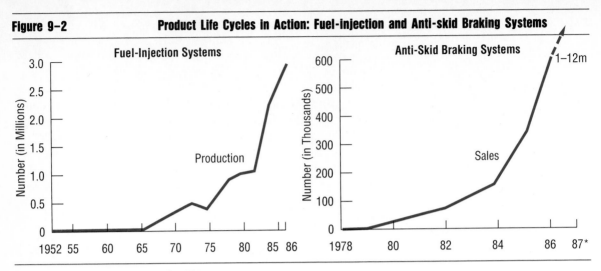

Source: *The Economist,* January 3, 1987.

as soon as sales reach the 100,000 unit mark.[23] Such a shift is in line with IPLC theory.

**Technology and the IPLC.**   Technology can compress product cycles, increasing risk and underlining the importance of maintaining product leadership through technological innovation. Ford had designed a new 2 liter engine with two valves per cylinder to be used as the base engine for a variety of cars built in factories around the world. But the Japanese moved quickly to develop and introduce a 16-valve high-performance engine, which shortened the life of Ford's new engine to only four years, too short to satisfactorily recover product-development costs and earn a return on investment. Yet, Ford had to match its competition by introducing a 16-valve engine of its own.

Alternative technologies can also present an interesting conundrum for the IPLC. If recognized as superior in the marketplace, they can suddenly make an existing product obsolete before its life cycle has had a chance to play itself out. Consider the way the Beta-format VCR introduced by Sony lost ground, when the VHS standard was adopted in the less-developed countries as the VCR diffused into these markets.

Cellular car telephones, a rapidly growing industry, present another example. Cellular phones rely on powerful base stations that relay call signals to the next station or cell as the driver moves out of range of a station. A new mobile phone service based on cordless phones has been developed in the United Kingdom whereby customers can place calls anywhere in the world by punching in a special code and then the number when they are within range (100 to 200 yards) of a local transceiver. It is cheaper than cellular phones, though the customer cannot receive calls. This service, known as CT2 or Telepoint, is being tested in France as well as England. It will require an investment of about $70 million to build a U.K.–wide network of 20,000 base stations, roughly a fifth of the cost of Britain's cellular phone network. Costs to the individual user will be about one-third to one-half lower. CT2 can also be used in the home as a multi-extension cordless system, costing about $200 to replace up to eight hard-wired extensions.

The question is whether there will be much demand for a phone system that cannot receive calls. Ericsson of Sweden is working on a two-way system, but CT2 backers expect that they have about 10 years before such a two-way system would be available at commercially competitive prices. IPLC theory then dictates that they introduce the CT2 approach immediately to as many countries as possible so as to reap maximum revenues from their R&D investment thus far.[24]

Even low-technology products such as toys have an IPLC. Tonka had enormous success in the United States with its Mask line of toys, which were subsequently introduced to Europe, where sales increased just at the time they began petering out in the United States. Lagged marketing and advertising caused a lag in the stimulation of demand for Mask toys in Europe. The important point is that Tonka was able to generate additional sales and profits from a toy line whose product-development costs had already been amortized.

The Tonka example also suggests that if there is no lag in marketing a product in the triad economies, demand is likely to grow simultaneously in them. As multinationals move to global marketing and develop global brands, and as communications media instantaneously bring news of market developments to all of the advanced nations, corporations may not be able to delay a product introduction into some advanced countries. If they do, their competitors might steal the market. And as the example of Ford's engine obsoleted within four years shows, a phased introduction of a new product into advanced nations may be a luxury companies can ill afford. Short IPLCs dictate that a firm move expeditiously to stimulate and take advantage of demand in all of the key markets of the world. And if the firm lacks the cash or other resources necessary for such simultaneous market penetration, the logical step is for it to develop strategic alliances.

## Market Potential and Market-Entry Decisions

In considering which markets to enter, a key issue is unrealized market potential. Consider the market in Europe for carbonated drinks.[25] While the average American drinks 170 liters a year of carbonated drinks, the European average is only 48 liters. But it is not that Europeans drink significantly less. Average total beverage consumption is 542 liters per year in America compared to 472 liters in Europe. The difference is that Europeans prefer drinks other than carbonated soft drinks: the French like to mix juice concentrate (squash) with water, and they also drink more wine. As Figure 9–3 shows, carbonated soft drink consumption is highest in West Germany, and yet even there it is only 43 percent of the American average. French consumption is the lowest while consumption in Britain and Italy is rapidly growing. Soft drink firms seeking greater European sales, then, have to decide whether to focus on France which has the greatest unrealized potential, or the faster-growing markets in Italy and England — or whether to attempt to increase

**Figure 9–3**                                **European Carbonated Soft Drink Consumption**

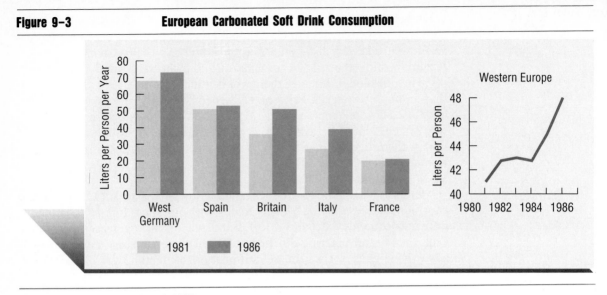

Source: *The Economist,* May 16, 1987.

consumption in the West German market, which has already shown the greatest inclination to drink carbonated beverages. But without data of the sort embodied in Figure 9–3, companies have no way to effectively screen and rank market attractiveness.

Companies might be better off targeting markets where significant market shares are likely to be achieved. In such fast-growing markets, new customers are emerging who do not have preestablished links with suppliers; growth makes the established competitors slack and inattentive to new entrants; and demand may exceed supply from established suppliers, leading to openings for other firms seeking entry. Ryans[26] found that firms adapting the product achieve highest market share in the introductory and growth phases of the market and less during maturity and decline phases.

The market-entry decision must weigh unrealized market potential against the strength of competition. Multinationals within an industry are all likely to have similar data, leading them to similar rankings of individual country market attractiveness. Hence, the strength of competition likely to be encountered is important. *Competitive audits* are a formal way of judging the strength of competition in markets of interest. Table 9–5 sets out the basic questions that form part of a competitive audit.

Results from the competitive audit can be combined with assessment of market potential to begin estimating market share likely to be achieved by the company. Then, depending on objectives, the company will assess whether a specific market represents an attractive opportunity for entry.

Government regulations and attitudes may also be factors in market attractiveness. Import-substituting governments often use tariffs and regulations to keep out foreign multinationals and foster the growth of domestic companies. In such instances, foreign firms have to decide whether they

# Global Marketing

## Will Chilled Food Charm U.S. Shoppers?

Marks & Spencers, the British retailing giant, has pioneered the selling of fresh refrigerated foods in England.[27] Under its St. Michael brand, it offers dishes such as Salmon en Croute with cream sauce, Spaghetti Carbonara, and Crepes Suzettes, priced at about $2.12 for the spaghetti to $5.34 for the salmon (two servings). Chilled food is not frozen food; rather, it is freshly prepared and needs to be heated or lightly cooked before serving.

Marks & Spencers plans to sell similar fresh refrigerated foods in the United States through its upscale chain of New Jersey stores, Kings Supermarkets Inc., which it had just acquired. But bringing this concept over to the United States is not simple. Consider the following aspects:

1. *Logistics.* Chilled foods spoil easily unless a constant temperature is maintained. Consequently, Marks & Spencers has developed close ties to farms and factories in the United Kingdom, using its own fleet of trucks, called the Cold Chain, to deliver these foods across Britain to 264 stores daily.

The United States is much bigger, and maintaining a complex distribution system would be more difficult and costly here. Truckers would have to be aware of the nature of the foods they are delivering, and supermarkets would need to pay attention to shelf life, rotating stock more often. Moreover, the United States does not have much experience operating a smoothly functioning refrigerated trucking and warehouse system.

2. *Substitutes.* U.S. supermarkets stock other varieties of take-home and premium easy-to-prepare foods in delis, salad bars, and in-store bakeries. Wide choice in deli sections and in precooked carry-out meals make chilled foods less appealing.

3. *U.S. tastes.* American food tastes may be more faddish, changing often compared with European tastes. And nutritional issues are more important here, too. Safeway, for example, is offering take-out Chinese food in some stores. American shoppers may be concerned with whether the chilled foods are low-fat, or high in fiber, something that Marks & Spencers has not had to worry about with British customers.

4. *Price.* Chilled food is marketed as gourmet food and is accordingly high-priced, sold to the young and affluent. This may limit its U.S. market to certain regions, such as downtown Manhattan in the state of New York.

5. *Suppliers.* In moving to the United States, Marks & Spencers will need to develop closer U.S.–based suppliers in a new food category. Will it be able to find quality suppliers as needed?

6. *Shopping habits.* The British shop every day in stores with perishables replenished every day. Refrigerated food may be less appealing to customers who prefer to shop once a week; frozen microwaveable food is much easier to store for a few days.

7. *Competition.* Other large U.S. food companies are also interested in the fresh refrigerated food concept and are working with their own recipes. Campbell is test-marketing the "Fresh Kitchen" line of refrigerated sauces, entrees, and desserts; Campbell uses a temperature-sensitive patch that turns blue if the food has not been refrigerated properly. General Foods abandoned its Cullinova line of fresh refrigerated foods because of distribution problems. Kraft has been test-marketing its Chillery line, featuring beef teriyaki at $3.49, seafood salad at $2.89, and cheesecake for $1.39. Mary Kay Haben, a Kraft General Foods vice-president, has said, "It's an energizer to see how the chilled foods category has developed in the United Kingdom and to think about what it could be here (in the United States)"[28]. Nestlé has also entered this area, with its Carnation division selling refrigerated pastas and sauces, and the Nestlé Enterprises subsidiary test-marketing upscale entrees and salads under the "FreshNes" brand.

**Table 9–5**                                              **Competitive Audit of a Foreign Market**

*Basic Information*

1. Which competitive products are sold in country X?
2. What are the market shares of competitive products?
3. How do competitive products compare with our own in reputation, features, and other attributes?
4. Which support facilities (production, warehousing, sales branches, and so on) do competitors have in country X?
5. Which problems do competitors face?
6. Which relationships do competitors have with the local government? Do they enjoy special preferences?

*Marketing Information*

1. Which distribution channels are used by competitors?
2. How do competitors' prices compare with our own?
3. What credit terms, commissions, and other compensation are extended by competitors to their channel members?
4. What promotion programs are used by competitors? How successful are they?
5. How good are competitors' post-sales services?

*Market Supply Information*

1. How do competitive products get into the market?

If they are imported:

2. Who are the importers?
3. How do importers operate?
4. What credit, pricing, and other terms are extended to importers by foreign suppliers?
5. How long has each importer worked with a foreign supplier? Is he/she satisfied with the supplier?

If they are produced locally:

6. Who are the producers?
7. Are the producers entirely locally owned, or is there foreign participation?
8. What advantages do local manufacturers have over importing competitors?

Source: Franklin R. Root, *Entry Strategies for International Markets* (Lexington, MA: Lexington Books, 1987), 42–44.

want to participate in local markets by licensing technology to the local firm in the hope of eventually securing entry once the government liberalizes its economic policies regarding foreign multinational participation in the domestic economy. Table 9–6 sets out a framework for analyzing government's role in influencing market attractiveness. While the analysis was designed to assess attractiveness for export opportunities, it can also be used in judging market attractiveness for other modes of entry.

In sum, a firm will evaluate risk, competition, likely returns, and resource commitments needed before judging whether it should enter a particular market. A checklist for screening foreign market entry might include

1. The product's competitive position at home (what is transferable to overseas markets). Is the product new?

**Table 9–6**                     **Consumer Product Export Opportunities to Liberalizing LDCs: A Life-Cycle Approach**

| Stage | Policies | Market Characteristics | Foreign Exporter Opportunities |
|---|---|---|---|
| Pre-Liberalization | • Encouragement of import substitution<br>• Severe restrictions on consumer imports<br>• Possible production limitations on consumer products<br>• Heavy taxation on consumption and/or higher incomes, discouragement of conspicuous consumption | • Sellers' market<br>• Restricted competition<br>• Pent-up consumer demand | • Very restricted |
| Liberalization | • Greater encouragement of free enterprise and competition<br>• Encouragement of export orientation<br>• Allowance of wider income disparities | • Greater availability of consumer products<br>• Wider choice of products<br>• Increased consumption of consumer products | • Substantially increased |
| Partial Retraction | • Reenactment of higher tariffs, quotas and/or decreased importer access to foreign exchange<br>• Reenactment of import substitution | • Slower consumption growth likely<br>• Competition from local production | • Curtailed or threatened<br>• Continued access via foreign investment may be possible |

Source: Kate Gillespie and D. Alden, "Consumer Product Export Opportunities to Liberalizing LDC's," *Journal of International Business Studies* (Spring 1989).

2. Is there a market? What is its size? How does the product relate to consumers' needs, ability to buy, and conditions of use in that market? Is adaptation necessary in product attributes, the physical product and its packaging?

3. Is the market growing? How attractive is the market? What is the level of product saturation (as exemplified by the soft drink example in Figure 9–3)?

4. Is there much competition? What does the competitive audit show?

5. Will government regulations diminish chances of success?

6. Will the product require much training, after-sales service, and complementary products?

7. Is the product likely to be obsolete soon? (That is, is this type of product undergoing rapid technological change?)

8. What resources (management time, financial resources) will have to be committed to this market?

9. What are the potential returns from the market, and what is its level of risk? Where does it rank when compared with alternatives?

10. What are the objectives for this market? (Possible objectives include market share, profits, defending against a competitor, responding to local government, and maintaining a presence in lead markets.) The firm must also distinguish between strategic and short-term objectives for the market.

11. If entry into the market is through a partnership, such as a joint venture or strategic alliance, is there agreement on objectives? Is there likely to be conflict over goals?

12. How patient is the company? How long will top management be prepared to wait until success is achieved? For example, if a firm has few managers that speak Japanese, and if it has little knowledge of day-to-day management problems of doing business in Japan and few personal business contacts there, then it cannot expect early success from Japanese market entry.[27]

Based on the foregoing, companies will generally be selective in their foreign-market expansion. The steps outlined above should lead to a short list of potentially attractive markets, from which one or two are chosen for entry after exhaustive investigation. The process is, of course, not static. Markets discarded as being unattractive can be assessed more favorably with the passage of time and changing economic conditions. This constant revaluation of markets is seen in Coca-Cola's approach to certain foreign markets.

**Coca-Cola: Rethinking Foreign-Market Entry.**    Coca-Cola has traditionally been content with supplying the syrup to prepare the soft drink, while letting the local bottlers market the drink. But as Coca-Cola grows more dependent on foreign earnings (about 80 percent of total earnings), and as the U.S. market becomes saturated (5 percent growth a year, whereas foreign growth is about 16 percent), managing growth in foreign markets becomes more important. It has tailored its strategy to match product penetration and future potential of each market thusly:

1.  *Japan.* It continues to rely on a dozen bottlers who are Japan's largest food and trading companies, such as Kirin, Mitsubishi, Mitsui, and Kikkoman.

2.  *United Kingdom.* It formed a 49 percent owned joint venture with Cadbury and took over bottling from franchises held by Grand Met and Beecham. It has been able to double U.K. sales between the mid 1980s and 1989.

3.  *France.* It bought back bottling rights from Pernod-Ricard, which had sold Coke in France for 40 years. Consumption in France is only 13 percent of the American average of 46 gallons per person. Coca-Cola paid 2 billion francs for an operation earning a pretax profit of 150 million francs. It hopes to raise consumption by controlling the marketing directly. Paris may also have an important role as the center from which to ship concentrate and cans to other parts of Europe, an important capability with a single European market on the horizon.

4. *Brazil.* In the world's third largest market for soft drinks, with a hot climate and 140 million thirsty people, Coke is being challenged by Pepsi; Pepsi had formed an alliance with Brahma, Brazil's biggest beer company, and had been able to capture 25 percent of the cola market in Sao Paulo within a year. As Brazil's per capita consumption is only about a quarter of U.S. consumption, there is much future potential. Coca-Cola began introducing large plastic bottle containers of Coke (2 liter bottles to Pepsi's 1.5 liters), and diet versions of Coke, which did not receive government approval until 1988. Heavy investment and advertising are seen as the key to maintaining a 50 percent market share in this fast-growing market.

5. *Australia.* Coca-Cola purchased a 41 percent interest in Amatil, the largest local Coke bottler. Australia has the third largest per capita consumption of Coke after the United States and Mexico, and Coca-Cola has a 53 percent market share there. It also formed a joint venture to buy out its bottler in New Zealand, a small market.

Coca-Cola is also focusing on *developing countries.* It is attempting to return to India, where soft drink consumption is growing at 20 percent a year, partly in response to Pepsi-Cola's 39.9 percent share in a joint-venture local bottling operation. It awarded the Coke bottling franchise in China to the government in order to win market share. Clearly, Coca-Cola will do what it takes in each market to be successful. While Coke is a global brand, this does not imply standardization of the entire marketing mix.[28]

## Summary

Three major issues for an international company are (1) deciding which new products to develop for global markets, (2) selecting the product line for individual foreign markets, and (3) deciding which foreign market to enter.

New-product development has three stages: (1) searching for new product ideas, (2) screening these to select some for development, and (3) carrying out development to the point of commercial launch.

As always, the starting point is consumer needs. Together with conditions of use and ability to buy, consumer needs indicate whether extension, adaptation, or completely new development of products and marketing mix is the appropriate strategy.

Ideas for new products should be sought in all major markets, both domestic and foreign. Distributors, licensees, joint-venture partners, and overseas subsidiary personnel are all potential sources. So are the competition, new patent filings, the plans of governments and international agencies, and the foreign buyer's consumption system.

Where the new-product development activity is located is important. Multiple sites may prevent the "not-invented-here" syndrome, in which all "foreign" ideas are rejected on the basis of not having been invented at home, from taking hold.

R&D is typically carried out in a firm's largest markets, provided that the necessary scientific and technical personnel are available. It can be decentralized within the product line or across the product line. Sometimes basic R&D work is carried out in one or two central locations and applications of lesser import at more distant locations.

R&D may be decentralized because of demands for local autonomy or in order to monitor technological developments in key lead markets. Government pressures and adaptation to the local market also influence the diffusion of R&D activity. Budgets and communication networks are tools helpful in coordinating geographically dispersed R&D labs.

New product ideas must be screened to select the more promising ones for further development. Screening may be done successively at the national, regional, and headquarters levels. Screening criteria should include production and marketing considerations, as well as legal factors, financial returns, logistics constraints, and government views.

Foreign market testing is another essential step. Representative markets may be used as a surrogate for testing in every potential foreign market.

Product development through consortia and strategic alliances is becoming more common. Cooperation may lead to agreement on common standards, and may arise because of a strategic fit among complementary skills.

Incremental innovation — keeping ahead of competition through continuous improvements — is as important as radical changes and major new product introductions.

Product testing in foreign markets may be necessary because of different use conditions and government regulations. There are also promotional benefits from testing specifically for foreign markets.

A general question in product-line management is whether to replicate the domestic product line in foreign markets. Market similarity and similar client needs would predispose toward such product-line extension. Other determinants of the product line for overseas markets include competitive response, government regulation, level of economic development of the market, the firm's growth targets, and the length of time it has been in a market.

The mode of market entry also affects product line. And a joint-venture agreement may prohibit certain domestic products in a line from being introduced.

Adding and divesting products from the product line are equally important decisions. Legal considerations are involved, as well as cost, competition, market, and financial considerations.

The international product life cycle (IPLC) helps identify promising foreign markets. Technology diffusion and the presence of competing technologies are important elements in assessing foreign-market potential according to the product life cycle.

Market potential must be balanced with market-saturation assessment. Markets should be chosen such that significant market share gains can be achieved.

Competitive audits are important in arriving at realistic market share targets. Government policies also delineate the extent to which foreign firm participation is encouraged.

Risk, competition, likely returns and resource commitments together suggest which foreign markets the firm should enter. These factors form the basis of a suggested checklist.

## Questions

9.1   Explain how consumer needs, conditions of use, and ability to buy affect new-product development.

9.2   Explain how Yamaha's attention to consumer needs enabled it to revitalize the worldwide piano market.

9.3   How are ideas diffused and new products adopted? How are these concepts relevant to new-product development in international markets?

9.4   What are some potential sources of ideas for new-product development? How can a firm obtain international inputs? Contrast the new product possibilities at American Remedies, which only exports, with those at Pharmaceuticals International, which has several wholly owned foreign plants.

9.5   Where should new-product development activity be located? What are the advantages and disadvantages of decentralization?

9.6   What are some common patterns in global R&D? What pressures lead management to decentralize global R&D? How can such decentralized new-product development be coordinated and controlled?

9.7   How and where should new-product screening be done? What should be the role of the foreign subsidiary in this process?

9.8   How are marketing and production considerations used in screening new products for international markets?

9.9   Why are strategic alliances used in new-product development?

9.10  Analyze the Mitsubishi air conditioner example cited in the text as an example of incremental innovation. What are the benefits of using an incremental innovation approach?

9.11  Product testing must be done locally even if product development is centralized. Discuss.

9.12  Is market testing necessary before a firm introduces new products into foreign markets?

9.13  What are the determinants of a firm's product line in foreign markets?

9.14  How does the nature of a firm's involvement in foreign markets affect the composition of its product line? Contrast the product-line alternatives open to an exporter with those available to a licensor.

9.15  Discuss the decision to add or drop products to or from the product line in international markets. Explain how these considerations affected the divestment of the personal computer line by Zenith and its sale to Bull.

9.16  How does competition affect product-line composition? Illustrate your answer with reference to the luxury-car segment in the United States.

9.17  What factors are relevant to the choice of foreign markets?

9.18  How does the international product life cycle (IPLC) help screen foreign markets for possible entry?

9.19  What is a competitive audit? How can it help in choosing foreign markets for possible entry?

9.20  Analyze how and why Coca-Cola has been rethinking its foreign market entry choices.

## Endnotes

[1] See Kenichi Ohmae, "Getting Back to Strategy," *Harvard Business Review* (November–December 1988).

[2] "Why Heinz Went Sour in Brazil," *Advertising Age*, December 5, 1988.

[3] E. M. Rogers, *Diffusion of Innovation* (New York: Free Press, 1983).

[4] *Business Week*, March 10, 1980, 83.

[5] See H. Takeuchi & I. Nonaka, "The New-New Product Development Game," *Harvard Business Review* (January–February 1986).

[6] Vern Terpstra, "International Product Policy: The Role of Foreign R and D," *Columbia Journal of World Business* (Winter 1977): 24–32.

[7]"IBM, Toshiba to Produce Screens Jointly," *The Wall Street Journal,* August 31, 1989.

[8]"The Multi-media Encyclopedia," *The Economist,* May 2, 1987.

[9]"Drug Firms Set Plan to Acquire Some ICI Assets," *The Wall Street Journal,* October 10, 1989.

[10]See George Stalk Jr., "Time-The Next Source of Competitive Advantage," *Harvard Business Review,* July-August 1988, 49–50.

[11]"Nintendo Goes Portable, Stores Go Gaga," *The Wall Street Journal,* October 4, 1989.

[12]"Nintendo, Fidelity to Develop Jointly Financial Software," *The Wall Street Journal,* October 3, 1989.

[13]"The Japanese Go Globe-trotting, but the Yen Stays Home," *Business Week,* October 17, 1988.

[14]"Credit Card Firm a Success in Japan, Looks Overseas," *The Wall Street Journal,* July 26, 1989.

[15]"American Express Card Users in Italy Meet Some Resistance from Merchants," *The Wall Street Journal,* August 10, 1989.

[16]See "The Coming Traffic Jam in the Luxury Lane," *Business Week,* January 30, 1989, and "Trying to Crack the Luxury Car Market," *The Wall Street Journal,* August 7, 1989.

[17]See "Zenith's Return to Roots is Risky Plunge," *The Wall Street Journal,* October 5, 1989, and "Super Television," *Business Week,* January 30, 1989.

[18]"Bull to Acquire Zenith Data," *Electronic News,* October 9, 1989.

[19]"Glaxo Plans Non-prescription Ulcer Drug for U.S., Intensifying Industry Battle," *The Wall Street Journal,* December 23, 1987.

[20]"Abortion Pill Is Expected to Generate U.S. Black Market, More Controversy," *The Wall Street Journal,* October 31, 1988.

[21]*New York Times,* April 2, 1984, 13.

[22]*Business Week,* August 31, 1984, 131.

[23]See "Bosch: A Very Private Enterprise," *The Economist,* January 3, 1987; and Andrew Fisher, "West German Electronics Switch into Overdrive," *Financial Times,* July 1988.

[24]"A Phone Booth You Can Put in Your Pocket," *Business Week,* January 30, 1989.

[25]"Bubbles in Europe's Bellies," *The Economist,* May 16, 1987.

[26]Adrian B. Ryans, "Strategic Market Entry Factors and Market Share Achievement in Japan," *Journal of International Business Studies* (Fall 1988).

[27]Will U.S. Warm to Refrigerated Dishes?" *The Wall Street Journal,* June 18, 1989.

[28]Ibid.

[29]Kenichi Ohmae, "Planting for a Global Harvest," *Harvard Business Review* (July–August 1989). See also Hermann Simon, "Market Entry in Japan: Barriers, Problems and Strategies," *International Journal of Research in Marketing* 3, no. 2 (1986).

[30]See "Soft Drinks get the Hard Sell in Europe," *The Wall Street Journal,* November 21, 1988; "Foreign Fizz," *The Economist,* July 15, 1989; "Pepsi Aims to Liberate Big Market in Brazil from Coke's Domination," *The Wall Street Journal,* November 30, 1988; "France's Pernod-Ricard to Sell to Coke," *The Wall Street Journal,* May 26, 1989; and "Coca Cola Continuing Overseas Push Plans to Acquire New Zealand Bottler," *The Wall Street Journal,* August 10, 1989.

## Further Readings

Ayal, Igal. "International Product Life Cycle: A Reassessment and Product Policy Implications." *Journal of Marketing* (Fall 1981).

Bilkey, Warren J. and Erik Nes. "Country of Origin Effects on Product Evaluations." *Journal of International Business Studies* (Spring–Summer 1982).

Giddy, Ian H. "The Demise of the Product Life Cycle in International Business Theory." *Columbia Journal of World Business* (Spring 1978).

Johansson, Johny K. and Hans B. Thorelli. "International Product Positioning." *Journal of International Business Studies* 16, no. 3 (Fall 1985).

Johansson, Johny K., S. P. Douglas and I. Nonaka. "Assessing the Impact of Country-of-Origin on Product Evaluation: A New Methodological Perspective." *Journal of Marketing Research* 22 (November 1985).

Keegan, Warren. "Multi-National Product Planning: Strategic Alternatives." *Journal of Marketing* (January 1969).

Keshani, Kamran. "Beware the Pitfalls of Global Marketing." *Harvard Business Review* (September–October 1989).

Ohmae, Kenichi. "Getting Back to Strategy." *Harvard Business Review* (November–December 1988).

Ohmae, Kenichi. "Planting for a Global Harvest." *Harvard Business Review* (July–August 1989).

Onkvisit, Sak and John J. Shaw. "An Examination of the International Product Life Cycle and Its Application within Marketing." *Columbia Journal of World Business* (Fall 1983).

Root, Franklin. *Entry Strategies for International Markets.* Lexington Books, 1987.

Terpstra, Vern. "International Product Policy: The Role of Foreign R&D." *Columbia Journal of World Business* (Winter 1977).

Wind, Yoram. "The Myth of Globalization." *Journal of Marketing* (Spring 1986).

# Grand Met: The Development of World Brands

Grand Met (GM) is a British conglomerate whose lines of business include wines and spirits, beer, dog food, a chain of stores selling contact lenses and glasses, and over 1,700 retail betting shops in the United Kingdom and Ireland. GM once owned the Intercontinental chain of hotels. In 1987 its revenue totaled nearly $10 billion, divided as follows:

|  | Percent of Sales |
| --- | --- |
| Wines and Spirits | 39 |
| Brewing and Retailing | 20 |
| Foods | 16 |
| Consumer Products | 19 |
| Hotels | 6 |

In October 1988 the company launched a take-over bid for Pillsbury, the U.S. food products conglomerate based in Minneapolis, for $5.2 billion. The successful acquisition transformed GM into one of the world's largest food companies, ranking with Nestlé and Philip Morris. Earlier, it had announced the sale of its Intercontinental hotel subsidiary to a Japanese group, Seibu/Saison, for $2.3 billion, thus refocusing its business and gathering resources for the Pillsbury bid.

## The Pillsbury Acquisition

What does GM get by buying Pillsbury? Pillsbury is a $10 billion company, deriving 35 percent of its sales from foods. Its leading brands are Green Giant, Pillsbury, Le Sueur, Jeno's, Bumble Bee Seafood, and Haagen-Daz. The remaining 65 percent of its sales come from its restaurants, which are Burger King, Bennigan's and Steak & Ale. About 86 percent of Pillsbury's sales, by volume, come from products with a number one or number two market share.

GM hopes to use its retailing skills to increase Pillsbury food sales overseas, especially in Europe, where Green Giant and Haagen-Daz are already well-known. It feels that what it learned in selling liquor — about appealing to the psyche of the buyers — applies equally to selling food. In marketing liquor, image matters at least as much as price.

"Do you promote microwave pizza like you do Absolut vodka? Yes. A lot of the basics are the same," claims one GM executive. Pillsbury pioneered microwave foods, and GM plans to capitalize on these items, since they are just beginning to catch on in Europe. Its strength is its ability to add value to brands by pushing them through its strong distribution networks and throwing the weight of increased advertising behind them, thus creating the required image that is viewed as so important to gaining market share. Lower costs are also achievable, as the acquisition makes GM the eighth largest international food processor. The company has always been run with few staff personnel: Ian Martin, who became Pillsbury's chairman, says, "The primacy of the line manager is one of our most fundamental beliefs." And, "The three basics are

Case prepared by Associate Professor Ravi Sarathy for use in classroom discussion. All rights reserved. Source: "With Bid for Pillsbury, Grand Met Tries to Join Top Consumer Firms," *The Wall Street Journal,* October 5, 1988; "Pillsbury Could Be a Grand Coup for Grand Met," *Business Week,* October 17, 1988; "Pillsbury's Burger King Could Be Hard to Digest," *The Wall Street Journal,* October 6, 1988; "Brothers Who Run Japan's Seibu Empire Step Up Their Rivalry," *The Wall Street Journal,* December 21, 1988; "European Liquor Giants Pursue a Jackpot" *The Wall Street Journal,* October 4, 1988; "Now Alpo Wants to Dish It Out to Kitty," *Business Week,* September 19, 1988; "U.K.'s Grand Met Says It Will Sell Alpo Subsidiary," *Business Week,* February 9, 1990; "Can a New CEO Pull Burger King Out of the Fire?" *Business Week,* May 22, 1989; "Grand Met Unit to Acquire Christian Brothers," *The Wall Street Journal,* May 17, 1989; "Pillsbury Puts 2 Seafood Lines on the Block," *The Wall Street Journal,* May 23, 1989; "Going Soft," *The Economist,* May 16, 1987; and Pillsbury Co. 1988 Annual Report and Grand Metropolitan Annual Report 1988.

to cut costs, build brands, and develop new products — in that order." GM has a central staff in London and at U.S. headquarters in New Jersey of just 160, while Pillsbury, with half GM's revenues, had a staff of 350.

GM is also ready to drop the weak brands. After acquiring Pillsbury, it decided to sell off Bumble Bee — which falls behind Starkist (Heinz Co.) and Chicken of the Sea — and Van de Kamp — which falls behind Gorton's (General Mills) and Mrs. Paul (Campbell Soup). These product lines might appeal to other foreign companies wanting an immediate entry into the U.S. market, as well as to U.S. competitors such as Campbell's Soup and ConAgra.

## The Burger King Challenge

But Burger King represents the biggest challenge and gamble. GM is a restauranteur, owning 2,000 pubs and franchising 4,500 more pubs in the United Kingdom; it had also revived the failing chain of Berni's Steak houses, in many cases converting them to the "Pastificio" Italian-style restaurant chains. It expanded into Germany by buying Wienerwald, a 231-store spit-roasted chicken chain. But selling "bangers and mash" in the United Kingdom is a far cry from competing with McDonald's worldwide. There are about 240 units in the Berni chain of restaurants compared to about 5,600 Burger Kings.

Of the 5,600 Burger King stores, only about 600 are overseas; McDonald's overseas stores constitute about 25 percent of its total. The Burger King stores were unevenly managed, considered by observers to be scruffy-looking at times. In fast foods, it is important to provide an identical experience from store to store, hence the need for carbon-copy consistency. Burger King franchise owners have complained of shoddy service and high prices on food supplies provided by the Pillsbury-owned subsidiary Distron. Pillsbury has had four separate advertising campaigns in four years for Burger King and spent $164 million on advertising for it, compared to $650 million spent at McDonald's. But per-store sales have actually fallen:

**Burger King Store Statistics**

|                           | 1988          | 1987          |
| ------------------------- | ------------- | ------------- |
| Worldwide Sales           | $5.4 billion  | $5.05 billion |
| Number of Stores          | 5,687         | 5,179         |
| Average Store Sales, U.S. | $996,000      | $1,020,000    |

Barry Gibbons, the GM executive put in charge of turning around Burger King, plans to focus on cleanliness and good service. He notes, "A bad cup of coffee at the end of a meal is just as damaging as a bad advertising campaign." He laid off about 550 management personnel, consolidating field-office marketing, financial and personnel functions at headquarters and doing away with a couple of layers of staff functions. He also began searching for a new ad agency for the $150 million plus account. Gibbons wants to attract the "snack and grazing" set, which means diversifying the menu.

He also wants routine problems handled at regional offices: "My philosophy is that if a snake walks in through the door, kill it, don't call McKinsey & Co." He split up the food service subsidiary, Distron, into separate procurement and distribution operations, allowing franchisees to choose services that they needed; some 40 percent of the franchisees were already buying their supplies elsewhere. Since GM owns only 15 percent of the Burger King franchises, maintaining conformity is difficult. Communication and morale building are necessary. Accordingly, Gibbons has videotaped talks and delivered some in person.

GM does have some experience with franchising: its pubs in the United Kingdom, and the 1,300 Pearle Vision outlets that it operates in the United States. Sales increases could come from overseas expansion, and from menu changes, such as providing breakfasts at Burger King.

## The Alcohol Business: A Mature Product Line?

GM's acquisition of Pillsbury may have been a case of swallowing or being swallowed. GM's liquor business is a mature business with low growth prospects. GM is the world's largest liquor-marketing concern, selling 34.8 million cases in 1987.

**World's Leading Liquor Concerns**
**Based on 100 Top-Selling Brands**
**(Millions of Cases)**

| | |
|---|---|
| Grand Metropolitan | 34.8 |
| Guinness | 30.9 |
| Seagram | 22.8 |
| Bacardi | 21.8 |
| Suntory | 17.9 |
| Allied-Lyons | 17.3 |
| Pernod-Ricard | 12.5 |
| Brown-Forman | 11.3 |
| American Brands | |
|   (Jim Beam) | 9.2 |
| Pedro Domecq | 7.7 |

Liquor consumption is declining at about 2 percent annually in the developed countries. As a result, Seagram, for example, is deemphasizing liquor and moving into other product lines such as orange juice, acquiring Tropicana Products for $1.2 billion. Seagram also moved to dominate the wine cooler business, where it has a 36 percent market share. It is refocusing its portfolio of brands, dropping poor-selling brands, such as Calvert whiskey and gin, and Wolfschmidt and Crown Russe vodkas, and aiming for a higher-priced, loftier image by concentrating on high-margin brands such as Chivas Regal. As part of this strategy, Seagram purchased Martell and Cie., the prestigious French cognac maker, by beating out GM in a bidding contest. GM ended up with a profit on its 20 percent stake in Martell and retained rights to distribute Martell in East Asia.

## Acquisitions in Wines and Spirits

GM, on the other hand, increased its market share in the liquor business by acquiring Heublein for $1.2 billion in 1987 so as to gain control of Smirnoff vodka. The purchase was negotiated in four days, at about 11 times earnings. (Recently, Seagram paid 38 times earnings for the French cognac company Martell.) GM acts speedily when necessary; it is a strategically opportunistic company. It has been successful in marketing original creations such as Bailey's, a milky-sweet concoction of cream and Irish whiskey that is now the world's best-selling liqueur.

It also expanded into the U.S. wine business by purchasing Almaden vineyards for $128 million. In 1989 it followed up by acquiring Christian Brothers for over $100 million. Christian Brothers controls 1,200 acres in the Napa valley, about 3 percent of the wine-growing area. Its Greystone cellars in St. Helena draw 400,000 visitors a year, making it California's second-largest tourist destination after Disneyland. This purchase allowed GM to become the largest owner of vineyards in the Napa valley. Christian Brothers had not been faring well, with its wine shipments declining 14 percent in 1988 and brandy shipments down 21 percent. Christian Brothers' brandy is number two in the United States; Gallo Winery is number one.

GM clearly expects to do a better job of marketing than Christian Brothers did. Prior to the Christian Brothers acquisition, GM had 13 percent of the U.S. table wine market, and 12 percent of the spirits market. An insurance policy comes in the form of the 1,200 acres of Napa valley, a real estate position that is unique.

GM's major liquor brands include Smirnoff and Popov Vodka, J&B, Bailey's Irish Cream, Gilbey's gin and vodka, Croft sherry and port, Almaden, Inglenook and Lancers wine, Le Piat d'Or, a table wine exported from France, Black Velvet Canadian whiskey, Dreher Brandy (Brazil), Malibu, a coconut rum, and Heublein cocktails. In addition, it is the importer of Cinzano, Absolut vodka, and Cuervo tequila.

## Global Competition in Liquor:
## Pernod of France

As part of this acquisition strategy, GM also tried to gain control of Irish Distillers PLC, the sole maker of Irish whiskey. Its opponent was Pernod-Ricard S.A., of France. Both Pernod and GM were trying to gain control of the Irish whiskey market segment, including two of the best known independent brands, Jameson and Bushmills. As Pernod's president, Thierry Jacquillat, has noted, "You can buy any of several bourbon whiskey companies, but there's just one Irish whiskey company."

Pernod-Ricard was formed when France's two leading makers of pastis (a strong anise-flavored aperitif) merged in 1975. Pernod is now the biggest seller of alcoholic drinks in Europe, and third largest in the world, after GM and Seagram. It bought out 18 competitors in France and abroad in recent years. Equally significantly, it has focused on soft drinks. In 1975, 75 percent of its revenues came from alcoholic drinks; by 1987, 64 percent did, and the goal is to reduce that to 50 percent. Its big seller is Orangina, a fizzy orange-juice drink. Pernod also marketed Coca-Cola in France before recently selling the franchise back to Coca-Cola Co.

Pernod's need for Irish Distillers was perhaps greater than GM's. Pernod is not a global player and lacks international brands. Its Ricard anisette is the world's third-largest selling brand but almost unknown outside of France. "As consumers switch to international brands, domestic products such as aniseed spirits in France are in decline," notes Michelle Proud, a stock analyst at NatWest. Pernod did acquire Austin Nichols Co., the maker of Wild Turkey bourbon, in 1980. Its other well-known brands are Dubonnet aperitif and Biscuit cognac. If Pernod had failed in its acquisition bid for Irish Distillers, it could well have been bought out, as it becomes harder for an independent firm with a few brands to succeed in a global marketplace dominated by global brands.

GM's reasons for wanting to buy Irish Distillers were similar to its motives in its other acquisitions: Irish Distillers had no international distribution network, and GM hoped to increase profits by marketing whiskies such as Jameson through its worldwide distribution network. "Putting another brand through its existing distribution network would cost next to nothing," is Mary Hall's opinion, the editor of *International Drinks Bulletin* of London. GM's global presence can also filter back to the United States. For example, it test-marketed a juice drink, Aqua Libra, which is a mixture of sparkling water, passion-fruit juice and apple juice, in England. After a successful national introduction there, it began selling the drink on the U.S. East Coast.

Building a brand name from scratch is expensive, time-consuming, and risky. And well-known U.S. brands have potential to be "exported" to markets around the world. After the Pillsbury acquisition, GM would have roughly equal contributions from foods, liquor, and retailing and property. Interestingly, GM currently values its existing brands on its balance sheet at 588 million pounds, while the Pillsbury acquisition would add to its books about $2 billion of intangible assets from Pillsbury. Thus, the acquisition cost of the Pillsbury family of brands would be about twice the value of GM's existing brands. Further, GM's brands are weak in the United States, except for Alpo, and sales of GM brands might be strengthened through the use of Pillsbury channels and with access to Pillsbury customers.

## Alpo: The Pet-Food Business

There is always a danger that acquisitions might draw attention away from existing lines of business, leading to their neglect. For example, GM's Alpo line of pet food is marketed as a dog food. But in the United States, pet cats outnumber dogs by 58 million to 49 million, according to the Pet Food Institute. The trend is away from dogs, who need more attention, to the self-reliant cat. Hence, Alpo wanted to build cat food into about 40 percent of its business, developing a feline image without losing its "meaty, masculine" dog-food image. The question was, should it launch a national line of Alpo cat food, or experiment regionally with its small Tabby line of cat food? Furthermore, Alpo is strong mainly in canned dog food, with a 24 percent market share, and sales of $439 million. Overall, though, its share is less than 8 percent. It has performed less well in new products such as dog treats and diet dog food. It spends $35 million a year in advertising, and a push into cat food would bring it into competition with Ralston-Purina, Heinz, and Carnation.

### Pet-Food Market-Share Leaders, 1988

|                | Market Share Percent |
| -------------- | -------------------- |
| Ralston-Purina | 28.8                 |
| Carnation      | 11.8                 |
| Quaker Oats    | 11.6                 |
| Heinz          | 10.2                 |
| Kal Kan        | 9.4                  |
| Alpo           | 7.7                  |

Alpo launched a $70 million promotion to sell a new line of canned and dry cat food featuring cartoon character Garfield on the package. By the end of 1989, through aggressive price-cutting, it was able to get a 5 percent share of the canned cat-food market and about 3 percent of the dry cat-food market. Then, in February 1990, GM announced that it wanted to sell off the Alpo line, which earned about $45 million on sales of about $400 million in 1989.

An essential part of GM's product-line reshuffling was the sale of its hotel business; it used the proceeds to help pay for a portion of Pillsbury's purchase price. The question arises, why did Seibu/Saison want to buy the Intercontinental Hotels that GM wanted to get rid of? Seibu Department stores are stylish, with high prices. Seiji Tsutsumi, the owner of the Seibu chain, expanded by guessing that the Japanese would become bigger spenders, and that a segment of this market would prefer to buy one stylish but expensive suit to two lower-quality ones; and that the future of retailing in Japan would lie in selling style, not brands. Seibu/Saison became Japan's biggest retail group, with annual sales (1987) of about 3.5 trillion yen.

He further decided that department stores could sell one-stop consumerism. It was a short step, then, to provide travel and tourism services as part of the Seibu/Saison chain. Thus, Seibu's strategy of catering to the globe-trotting Japanese customer required that it buy into an existing hotel chain, while GM perhaps saw its small stake in the hotel business as peripheral to its goal of concentrating on global brands and global marketing of these brands.

## Questions

1. Outline the international marketing strategy of Grand Met (GM), as made apparent through its acquisition and divestment moves internationally.
2. How have GM's moves led to a refocusing of its product lines into three main areas: food, alcoholic beverages, and restaurants? What are the keys to success in these three product lines?
3. What strengths/weaknesses does GM have that might help and/or hinder its achievement of its international strategy?
4. What should GM do with Burger King, in the United States and internationally?
5. What synergies, if any, exist between GM's liquor lines and the Pillsbury acquisition?
6. Do you agree with the decision to sell the Intercontinental hotel chain? In what ways does this help fulfill GM's overall international strategy?
7. Is GM too thinly spread? That is, is it in too many product lines? For example, should it be getting rid of its Alpo pet-food line?

CASE

# 9.2 Boeing and Airbus: Competing Product Lines

The aerospace industry is important to the U.S. economy. In 1985 the U.S. aerospace industry accounted for about 9 percent of U.S. exports and had a favorable balance of trade of $12.5 billion, as compared to an overall merchandise trade deficit of $136.6 billion. Boeing is the world industry leader, accounting for $6.5 billion of exports. It had $15.8 billion in international orders and is among the largest U.S. exporters. It sold 738 aircraft in 1987, valued at $39 billion. Its only competitors are Airbus and McDonnell Douglas (MD).

Airbus Industries is a multinational consortium consisting of two state-owned enterprises — France's Aerospatiale (with 37.9 percent of Airbus) and Spain's CASA (4.2 percent) — the semi-private Deutsche Airbus from West Germany (37.9 percent), and the wholly private British Aerospace (20 percent), all of whom receive subsidies for aircraft development and customer financing of aircraft sales.

Airbus has estimated world market demand to total 7,275 aircraft, valued at $403 billion, through the year 2005, of which 3,298 will be narrowbodied, 2,005 widebody twins, and 1,972 three- to four-engine widebodies.

## Commercial Jet Transport Industry

The commercial jet transport industry has been characterized as a "sporty game,"[1] where introducing each new aircraft involves betting the continued survival of the company. When the 747 was being developed, Boeing almost went bankrupt in 1969–1971; aircraft development expenditures resulted in negative cash flow, and employment declined from a peak of 101,000 in 1968 to about 37,000 in 1971. Now, 16 years later, Boeing is on its fourth version of the 747, which, priced at over $110 million per plane, is a major source of earnings, while employment is over 125,000 (at the end of 1986). The industry is an oligopoly, with Boeing, Airbus, and McDonnell Douglas being the only three remaining manufacturers of large civilian jets. They work hand-in-glove with three aircraft engine manufacturers, GE (and its French joint venture, GE-Snecma), Pratt and Whitney (a subsidiary of United Technologies), and Rolls Royce, a British state-owned company recently "privatized." New airframe models typically require new engines, and development of new airframes and engines is estimated to cost about $1.5 to $2 billion apiece, with total investment in the aircraft reaching $3 to $4 billion five to six years after the launch of a model.[2]

New aircraft development faces long lead times and low unit volumes; planning the introduction of a new aircraft involves looking ahead about 20 years: 5 years for the planning, and a product life of 15 years or more. Hence, considerable market-forecasting abilities are required, particularly since airline demand is highly cyclical. For example, Boeing delivered 376 aircraft in 1968, 97 units in 1972, then reached a peak of 299 units in 1980, before declining to 146 in 1984. In dollars, Boeing's revenues from commercial jets declined from $7.7 billion in 1980 to $5.4 billion in 1984. Despite these fluctuations, Boeing has consistently maintained a dominant market share, as shown in Figure 1. However, Boeing's market share has been dropping since 1980, particularly in segments where competition from Airbus and McDonnell Douglas (MD)

Source: Case prepared by Associate Professor Ravi Sarathy for use in classroom discussion. All rights reserved.
[1]John Newhouse, *The Sporty Game* (New York: Knopf, 1985).

[2]"Eternal Triangles: Aircraft Industry Survey," *The Economist,* June 1, 1985.

**Figure 1  Orders Received, Number of Aircraft, All Models**

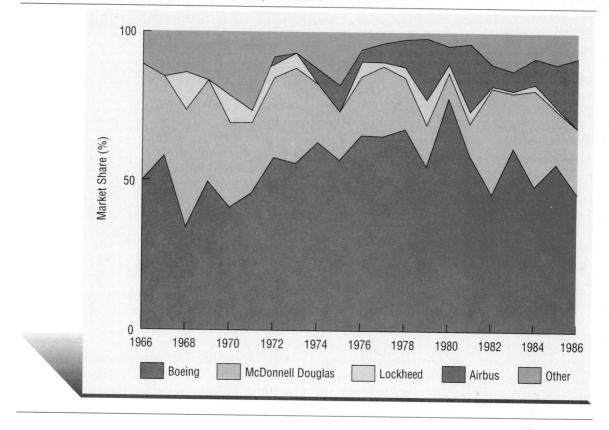

has intensified. Table 1 breaks out orders by segments for each of the three manufacturers and further tracks orders over three distinct time frames.

Once an aircraft model moves beyond development into production, the cost of production of initial batches of aircraft will be far higher than, say, the 300th unit manufactured, owing to learning-curve-driven cost reduction; hence, it is vital that the gamble represented by development of a new aircraft model be transformed into continuing sales. Yet, few aircraft have yielded volume sales sufficient to generate profits to their manufacturers. The De Havilland Comet, the pioneer jet introduced in 1952, sold only 112 units, while the Boeing 707, introduced in 1958, sold nearly 1,000 units. Given a breakeven volume of

about 600 units for the smaller jets,[3] Boeing has achieved profitability with its 707 (980 sold), 727 (about 1,900 sold) and 737 (over 2,000 sold), while the 747 (with about 700 units sold) is also a profit contributor, given its far higher unit price of about $100 million, and higher margins due to its monopoly position. (As a consequence, breakeven volume is lower, at about 300 units.) MD may have reached breakeven with its DC-9/MD-80 family, as also Airbus with its A300/310, though development costs of extending the product family at both MD and Airbus may have raised the breakeven volume significantly.

[3]Assuming aircraft development costs of $3.5 billion, a sales price of $30 million and margins of about 20 percent, breakeven volume is 584 units; these assumptions are for a current generation small jet such as the A320.

**Table 1   Aircraft Orders in Units, by Segments**

| Aircraft Segment | 1970–1980 | 1981–1985 | 1986–1987 |
|---|---|---|---|
| **Short-Range, Small Capacity** | | | |
| Boeing 727 | 960 | 50 | 0 |
| Boeing 737 | 600 | 681 | 399 |
| Boeing Total | 1,560 | 731 | 399 |
| MD: DC-9, MD-80 | 442 | 369 | 219 |
| Airbus A320 | 0 | 90 | 219 |
| **Long-Range, Large Capacity** | | | |
| Boeing 747 | 378 | 124 | 150 |
| MD-11 | 0 | 0 | 87 |
| Airbus A330/340 | 0 | 0 | 80 |
| **Medium-Range, Medium Capacity** | | | |
| Boeing 757/767   (Available 1978) | 264 | 117 | 136 |
| Lockheed L-1011 | 166 | 10 | 0 |
| Airbus A300/310 | 268 | 159 | 80 |
| MD: DC-10 | 278 | 19 | 0 |

Moreover, introducing derivatives further pushes back the payback period, as additional development costs are incurred, though it also extends product life. Thus, a company seeking to make commercial jets must be prepared to wait ten years or more to recover its investments, with profits being even further away. Price-cutting by a less profit-oriented competitor will reduce margins and contribution and so push back the breakeven point further, and will decrease the willingness of top management to approve funding for new-generation aircraft development projects. At the same time, lower prices and margins reduce cash flows and prejudice the ability of a firm to fund new aircraft development from internal sources.

Future growth and the bulk of the market for aircraft would appear to lie overseas. U.S. traffic is expected to represent only about one-third of world traffic, with Europe and Canada, and the rest of the world representing another third each.[4] Foreign airlines will thus be the major customers for aircraft manufacturers, with government-owned airlines representing a significant share of the customer group. Political pressures can in this

way hinder a private company that cannot obtain government help.

Yet, aircraft manufacturing can be highly profitable. Operating leverage beyond breakeven is high: with over 2,000 737 aircraft sold, total contribution is about $7 billion.[5] It is the possibility of demand growth fueled by rising world incomes, trade, and airline traffic, that attracts firms to this industry. If an aircraft model is successful, as in the case of the 747 where Boeing had no competition, profits can be enormous.

## Airbus, McDonnell Douglas and Boeing: Their Competing Product Portfolios

**How Do Airlines Buy Planes?**   Airlines sell perishable commodities: an empty seat is revenue that is lost forever. They would like to fly their planes with every seat sold, which means that they would like aircraft with *different passenger capacities for different routes,* based on traffic de-

[4]Ibid, p. 56.

[5]Adding incremental development costs of $1.5 billion to initial development costs of $3.5 billion, against contribution per 737 aircraft of $6 million, or $12 billion for 2,000 aircraft sold, yielding a net contribution of $7 billion.

mand patterns. Routes can also vary in distance, with major transcontinental routes such as New York–Tokyo or London-Sydney requiring long-range aircraft. In addition, the gradual development of international hub-and-spoke systems means that different-sized but short-range aircraft may be needed, depending on passenger density within each hub-and-spoke system.

Further, the larger the plane, the heavier the engine needs to be, and matching engine thrust to aircraft size determines fuel economy and speed, which become important as more and more airlines seek nonstop flight schedules. Aging aircraft fleets are another factor. The costs of replacing fully depreciated aircraft must be balanced against fuel and maintenance costs, which are comparatively higher with the older aircraft. Environmental controls and noise-abatement provisions complicate this trade-off as airline freedom to operate older noisy aircraft over crowded cities is gradually circumscribed. Technical obsolescence of the existing fleet, with improved safety arising from advanced avionics also color demand for new jet aircraft.

If existing model planes are sufficiently discounted in price and cheap fuel reduces the economic gains to be had from the more expensive new generation aircraft, airlines might prefer to buy the (cheaper) older models and hope to squeeze the manufacturers into financing the aircraft at low risk to the consumers (the airlines).

Airlines buying jet aircraft are hence guided by their route structure, the balancing of fuel versus labor versus capital costs, and would probably prefer a family of aircraft (of differing ranges and passenger capacity) from one manufacturer in order to economize on flight crew training, inventory of spare parts, spare engines, maintenance and related expenses. But the business cycle and outlook for traffic growth influence the willingness of airlines to buy expensive new aircraft and add on large amounts of long-term debt. Therefore, offering attractive aircraft financing and flexible delivery of aircraft become important. As in any new product launch, firms gamble that the product will appeal to the market. The risks of being wrong are magnified in the com-

mercial jet market because the costs of development are so high.

In sum, aircraft product offerings from the manufacturers must meet niches set by the confluence of range, passenger capacity, and engine choices desired, and with the requisite speed, fuel economy, and personnel savings — all this at a reasonable and competitive price, while also matching financing terms offered by competitors. (An example is Boeing's sale of fifteen 767–300 aircraft to All Nippon Airways, with EximBank having to guarantee $300 million of the $857 million purchase, against strong financing support from the export credit agencies of the United Kingdom, France and West Germany as part of the terms of sale offered for the competing Airbus A300-600 aircraft.)

**Profile of Competing Product Lines.** Airframe manufacturers work within their customers' decision calculus to design and manufacture aircraft, relying on forecasts of expected modal route ranges and passenger densities. Figure 2 sets out the current product portfolios of the three competing manufacturers. The launch of the newest commercial jet aircraft models, namely the A320, the A330 and A340, all from Airbus, the MD-11 from McDonnell Douglas, and the 7J7 and the 737–500 from Boeing, can best be understood in light of the product map represented in the figure.

Figure 2 concentrates on two dimensions: range and passenger capacity. Other factors, such as speed, fuel economy, number and type of engines, number of required flight crew, aircraft-reliability experience, and financing terms, also influence the choice between competing aircraft. However, range and capacity are helpful in demarcating broad product segments within which the factors mentioned above can play a further role. Figure 2 includes

- Aircraft that have been recently discontinued (the DC-9, L-1011, DC-10, B727).
- Aircraft currently in service.
- Aircraft that have been launched and have received orders, with delivery set over the next

**Figure 2**          **Boeing, Airbus, McDonnell Douglas, and Lockheed Jet Aircraft:**
                      **Number of Seats and Mileage Range**

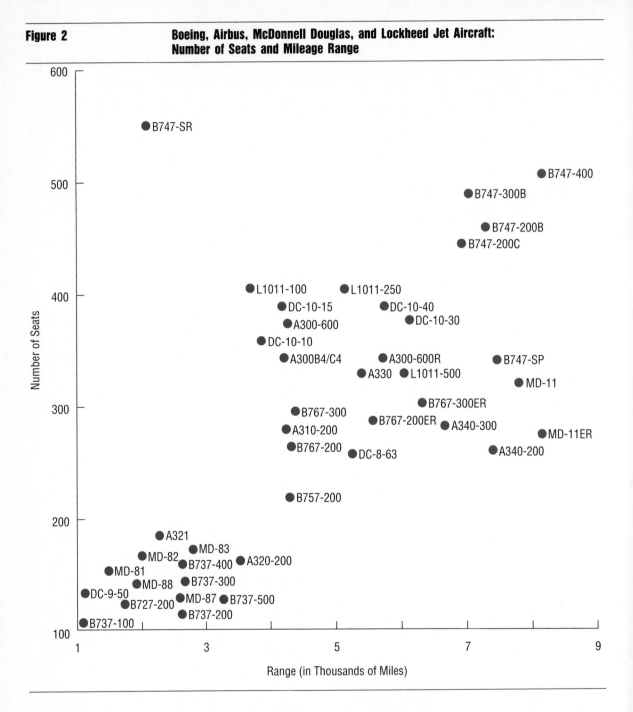

few years (the A320, A330 and A340, the MD-11, the 737–400 and 737–500, and the 747–400).

Three distinct groups emerge: a crowded, short-haul, short-capacity segment; a competitive, medium-haul, medium-sized segment;

and a long-range segment that is the object of new product launches.

**Boeing.** Boeing has long been successful because of its canny product-forecasting abilities. Its first product, the 707, was successful despite being several years behind the British Comet. Since then, the company has offered jets to meet demand in a variety of segments:

1. *The 727 and 737 for short-range, small-capacity routes.* These compete against new aircraft launched by competitors, the MD-80 series, and the A320 from Airbus; the 727 and 737 are the two most successful aircraft ever introduced, with respective sales of about 1,900 and 2,000 units. While the 727 has been withdrawn from production because it is an outdated design, inefficient in fuel consumption and noisy, the 737 is still in production. Two derivative model aircraft, the 737–400 and the 737–500, were recently introduced, both in response to competition from Mc-Donnell Douglas and Airbus.

2. *The 747 for large-capacity, long-range routes.* Boeing pioneered this segment at the insistence of Pan Am and nearly bankrupted itself in the process; but the aircraft is high-priced, at about $100 million each, and provides profit margins of 25 percent or more, principally because Boeing has had a monopoly in this segment. The recent emergence of new offerings such as the MD-11 and the A330/340 will begin to provide competition, mainly at the lower-capacity levels in this segment.

3. *The 757 and 767 for medium-range, medium-capacity and small-capacity, long-range routes.* These are new offerings from Boeing, a response to the Airbus A300/310 aircraft. They are smaller in capacity than the Airbus aircraft but are two-engine, fuel-efficient aircraft. The 767 is gradually carving out a role in long-distance over-water trans-Atlantic and trans-Pacific flights. Sales of these two models have not matched the success of their predecessors, and it is still unclear whether they will be profitable models.

The market segments identified are not rigid, chiefly due to the ability to vary seating capacity on a particular model of aircraft. Airlines have some flexibility to adapt capacity by offering one or multiple classes of seating, and by putting seats closer together; and aircraft manufacturers can adapt airframes by stretching them, literally extending the fuselage to hold more passengers while upgrading the engines to provide more thrust for the now-heavier aircraft, and perhaps redesigning the wings, using winglets and so forth to increase aerodynamic efficiency and fuel burn.

Developing such so-called *derivative* aircraft is less costly and therefore less risky than developing completely new ideas. This approach enabled MD to launch its MD-11, a derivative of the DC-10, at a cost of about $500 million versus more than $2.5 billion at Airbus for its competing A330/340 aircraft. Boeing has used this approach in offering the 747–400, thus protecting its monopoly position in the 747 segment and extending the product family while conserving cash and reducing risk associated with developing a completely new plane.

But sticking to derivative aircraft, while safe, may invite a bolder competitor to pioneer a new aircraft model in a new segment of the market and develop a monopoly position, much as Boeing did with the 747. Such an opportunity may be presenting itself now with the likelihood of a successful Ultra-High Bypass (UHB) engine being available for use on the next generation of jet aircraft. A UHB engine would result in considerable fuel economies and render the previous generation of models obsolete.[6]

**Airbus.** Airbus's product strategy has been one of catching up to Boeing, with two central goals:

1. Matching Boeing's broad product range by providing an Airbus *family* of aircraft to meet a variety of range and passenger capacity needs:

[6]AWST, "Airframe Manufacturers near Landmark UHB Decisions," April 13, 1987, 52–55.

single and twin-aisle aircraft for short, medium, and long-range flights; that is, Airbus had to grow beyond its two available models (the A300 & A310), and develop aircraft that could match Boeing offerings across the entire product line.

2. At the same time, utilizing advanced technology, including the so-called "fly-by-wire" avionics and more fuel-efficient engines and airframe design, thus making the Airbus offerings efficient and attractive, and capable of being flown by two-pilot crews. (The use of advanced cockpit instrumentation in the A300 and the follow-on A310 allowed them to be certified with a minimum crew of two pilots, eliminating the need for a flight engineer and resulting in considerable personnel cost reductions.)

Airbus's initial product offerings were the A300 and the A310. The A300 was designed to meet a gap in the market for twin-engine medium-size aircraft, and designed with the route needs of the major European airlines in mind. The 310 was a longer-range derivative, introduced in 1978. Both aircraft were expected to suit the needs of European airliners, whose routes did not cover long distances but needed passenger capacities of around 250 seats, hence the term "airbus." Cost reduction was achieved by using the same jigs and tooling and a shared assembly line for the 300/310 program, though they did not share the wing, which is one of the most expensive components of an aircraft. However, this initial narrow-market focus also reduced the appeal of the Airbus aircraft to U.S. airlines as they generally fly longer routes.

Airbus therefore launched two derivatives: the long-range 310–300, with a fuel tank in the horizontal stabilizer, and a stretched A300-600. Over 300 A300s have been ordered, with about 275 delivered, while about 150 A310s have been ordered with 95 delivered (as of June 1987). With only 450 aircraft sold, it is unlikely that payback has been achieved on these programs, and a private enterprise firm would have lacked the cash flow with which to embark on further new aircraft product development.

Yet, despite the disappointing A300/310 sales, Airbus moved on to the 150-seat market, with the A320 undergoing certification with fly-by-wire controls. This refers to the use of computer-based controls of the aileron, rudder, and other aircraft responses, replacing the more traditional mechanical controls. The A320 is a short-haul twin-engined aircraft seating between 150 and 180 passengers in a single-aisle configuration, with 150 being a popular size. It is conventionally powered in that it uses tried and tested GE turbofan engines and achieves fuel economies with design innovations.

Given the lack of cash flow and profits from the A300/310 program, the A320 program was entirely dependent on government funding for its development costs. But market prospects looked attractive, as airlines would be considering replacement of the aging DC-9s and 727s. As Boeing was deep in the launch of the 757/767 model family, it would be less able to launch yet another program for a new-model 150-seat aircraft.

Airbus has been successful with the A320. It had received 439 orders for the A-320 by its maiden flight on February 22, 1987, including 262 firm orders, 157 options, and 20 commitments. It is likely to obtain over 600 orders and thus become the first aircraft in the Airbus family to break even (though actual payback will not occur till deliveries reach about 600 units, which might not be till 1996–1997). Even more important, there seems to be no directly competitive product offering that can match the Airbus in passenger capacity and fuel economy and in its use of advanced technology. Boeing's derivative 737–400 is the closest competitive offering, and it is of an older design.

And with the 150-seat and mid-size (200 to 250 seats) segments covered, Airbus has just launched the long-range high-capacity A330/340 series, again with shared design, such as the twin-aisle cross section of the 300/310, and a variable-camber high-efficiency wing, and a shared new final assembly line. Its existing A300/A310 models need new wings to improve range and efficiency (wings are the single most critical and expensive element of the airframe, costing perhaps one-third of the total plane cost), and adapting the same wing to the A330 and A340 could further reduce the joint aircraft-development costs.

The A330, a high-capacity medium-range jet, is to carry 330 passengers within a range of about 5,500 miles; it is intended as a twin-engine replacement for widebody trijets such as the DC-10 and the L-1011, with sufficient range to operate on transatlantic routes. The A340 is designed as a four-engine long-range aircraft with 260 to 290 passengers, and will be offered in two versions: the A340–200, seating 262, and capable of flying 7,650 nautical miles, or, nonstop from New York to Hong Kong; while the A340–300 is to carry 295 passengers over a distance of 6,850 nautical miles. The A340–300 will sell for $84 to $86 million (in 1987 dollars), while the A340–200 should sell for $80 to $82 million.

The A330/340 program is, of course, subsidized, and represents the latest provision of subsidies that have benefited the Airbus consortium. Since Airbus does not publish its accounts, it is difficult to estimate the extent of subsidies made available to it. But Airbus began taking orders in 1972, with first deliveries in 1974, and by the end of 1986 had sold a total of 271 planes, or a little over 20 aircraft per year. Since the breakeven volume for a single model has been estimated at around 600 units, it is a certainty that Airbus has recorded continual losses: Demisch[7] has estimated total subsidies to Airbus over the years of its existence at between $12 to 15 billion, including launch aid for its new models, the A320 and the A330/340 series. U.S. Treasury estimates are similar, with $10 billion having been spent by the consortium, and an additional $3.2 billion earmarked for the A330/340 programs.[8]

The surety of government subsidies and the early commitment from the French government may have emboldened Airbus to gamble on obtaining enough unit volume to derive profits from new aircraft product launches despite the presence of Boeing and MD. Or perhaps Airbus had reasoned that its government backing could enable it to sustain losses while sapping MD's will to remain in the commercial aircraft market.

Airbus's success with aircraft sales, particularly the A320, will have a direct effect on its costs, and thus its competitive position, as it expects to produce four times more aircraft per month in 1990 than it did in June 1987. Orders for the A310/300 transports totaled 450 units (June 1987), and production was therefore to be increased to four per month from three currently; A320 success (with orders and options totaling 439) has Airbus planning production of between 11 and 14 aircraft per month, plus 4 to 5 of the A330/340s as that program takes off. From Boeing's viewpoint, Airbus will be less inefficient than it used to be, as considerable scale economies and cost reductions are expected. Investment needs will, of course, be high, while risks will also increase due to a higher fixed-cost base.[9]

**McDonnell Douglas.** McDonnell Douglas (MD) also chose to attack Boeing's monopoly position in the long-range widebody jet market, its 747 market, with the launch of the MD-11, a 330-seat, very long-range plane, and a replacement for the L-1011–500s, the DC-10–30s and the 747-SPs. The driving argument for a derivative stretched version seems to be the airport gate shortages and airspace congestion faced by U.S. airlines. In an effort to optimize revenues in a capacity-constrained environment (airlines cannot fly as many flights as they would like), they are trading fuel economy and range for more seats, meaning more short-range high-volume aircraft; and the stretched MD-11 version is aimed at this need, seating up to 500 passengers on shorter-range routes.

The MD-11, a trijet requiring a two-pilot crew, is supposed to fill a void between the 747 and 767. MD plans to invest $500 million in non-recurring costs in addition to funds from risk-

[7]Wolfgang Demisch and Christopher Demisch, *"Boeing Company Report"* (New York: First Boston Co., January 27, 1987), p. 3.

[8]"U.S. Says Talks with Common Market over Airbus Subsidies Are Deadlocked," *The Wall Street Journal,* December 18, 1987.

[9]AWST, "Airbus Charts Long-Term Plan for Civil Aircraft Product Line," June 1, 1987, 40.

sharing partners, who include GE, P&W, Sperry, Rohr, Aeritalia, and CASA.

Plans are to deliver the first MD-11 in April 1990 and reach a production rate of one aircraft per week by 1991. Existing DC-10 manufacturing facilities will be refurbished and used, thus further reducing costs. Four versions are to be offered, the standard MD-11, the longer range MD-11ER, the MD-11 Combi, and the MD-11F cargo aircraft. McDonnell Douglas is planning a stretched shorter-range version of the MD-11 to compete directly with the A330. Such an aircraft would be 35 to 40 feet longer and would carry 425 passengers in a two-class configuration over routes as long as Chicago to Honolulu.

In the face of competition from Airbus, Boeing has sought U.S. government help in attempting to limit the product development and export financing subsidies given Airbus by the consortium-member governments. It has attempted to prevent Airbus gains in market share, particularly with long-established Boeing customers. And it has launched new aircraft models to compete directly against the new Airbus aircraft.

However, Boeing has had little success in countering Airbus in the 150-seat segment of the market. Airbus's A-320's launch success may in part be traced to Boeing's product strategy of delaying the launch of a competing similar-sized, new-technology aircraft, the 7J7, and ultimately canceling this project.

The 7J7 represents an interesting case of product development. Boeing decided to cancel its launch[10] for several reasons:

1. Low fuel prices reduced the incentive to buy an expensive new-technology aircraft such as the 7J7, as its promised fuel economy was less attractive economically.

2. Price was a factor, as the 7J7 would compete with Boeing's own 737-400 and the A320; Boeing estimated that the 7J7 should be priced at about $27 million (1987 U.S. dollars), about the price at which the 737 was on offer. Airlines

seemed unwilling to pay more for the new technology under existing economic conditions and did not want to commit the traditional one-third advance payment over the four-year development period.

3. Airlines disagreed on the desired passenger capacity for a new aircraft (somewhere between 150 and 170 seats).

4. The version of the unducted-fan UHB engine that GE was to provide could not accommodate a stretched version of a 170-seat jet, which would have been a likely product development move at Boeing in the future; therefore, waiting till the UHB engine was better defined seemed prudent both to Boeing and to its customers.

5. Further, as Boeing's backlog was high and employment at almost 140,000 people, scarcity of human resources that could be committed to the 7J7 program became a constraining factor.

Instead, Boeing launched a derivative version of the 737, the 737-500, seating between 100 and 125 passengers, and with a range of between 1,700 and 2,800 nautical miles. Boeing's launch of the 737-500 put it in a crowded small-jet segment with competition from small manufacturers such as British Aerospace, with its BAe146 four-engine short-haul transport. A competing aircraft for this market segment is from Fokker of Netherlands — the Fokker 50 (with 39 firm orders and 12 options) and the Fokker 100 (with 87 firm orders and 91 options).

As commuter airlines become affiliates and subsidiaries of the major carriers, with their principal role being that of providing feeder traffic for longer routes, their purchases of these smaller jets become subject to their major airlines partner's approval. This may be another reason for Boeing's decision to launch the 737-500, and it could also explain Boeing's recent acquisition of De Havilland from the Canadian government, as De Havilland is one of the major suppliers of turboprop-powered aircraft seating around 40 to 60 passengers, representing the segment just below the small-jet market.

Boeing must make decisions soon concerning the launch of a new-model aircraft, for delivery

[10]AWST, "Boeing Delays 7J7 Program; Mid-1993 Certification Expected," August 31, 1987, 28–31.

around 1995. Should Boeing bet the company again? Should it continue to press ahead with the 737–500, hoping airlines do not want to pay the additional price of the new-generation A320? Or should it be targeting a totally new segment of the market, avoiding competing with the Airbus A320 altogether?

## Questions

1. What are the market segments within the commercial aircraft industry? How have the three major competitors approached these segments?
2. Is Boeing the strongest company in the industry in terms of product line?
3. Compare Boeing's and Airbus's competing products.
4. Trace how Airbus has filled out its product line. Can its product introductions be seen as competitive responses to Boeing?
5. How do customers influence the aircraft product line?
6. What factors influence an airline in buying jet aircraft?
7. What should Boeing do?
8. How relevant are subsidies in this industry? How should Boeing react to Airbus subsidies in developing a new aircraft?

# CHAPTER 10

# Distribution
## Entering Foreign Markets

*Learning Objectives*

Once the firm has chosen target markets abroad, the question arises as to the best way to enter those markets. We consider the major entry methods and criteria for selecting them here.

The main goals of this chapter are to

1. Explore the many types of indirect exporting possible, including export management companies, which provide a firm with instant experience and contacts in markets abroad.
2. Explain how cooperation among companies wishing to export can increase effectiveness and offer cost economies.
3. Discuss the challenges, problems, and rewards of do-it-yourself, direct exporting.
4. Give the reasons for assembling products abroad as a way to enter the market.
5. Discuss the advantages and disadvantages of contract manufacturing, licensing, joint ventures, and wholly owned operations as ways of entering foreign markets.

The distribution question facing the international marketer is very simple to state: How can I most profitably get my products to foreign customers? The marketer must deal with this question in two stages: (1) the firm's method of *entry* into foreign markets and (2) the selection of distribution channels *within* each of the firm's foreign markets. A subsequent management task is the coordination of global logistics. This chapter will deal with the first of these stages.

## How to Enter Foreign Markets

We cannot overemphasize the importance of the choice of method of entry into foreign markets. It is one of the most critical decisions in international marketing. This is because the entry decision is a macrodecision. That is, when the firm chooses a level of involvement in foreign markets, it is also

**Figure 10–1**                                    **Alternative Methods of Foreign Market Entry**

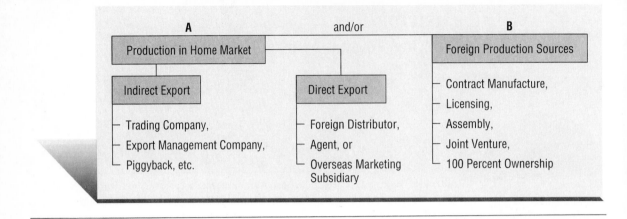

making choices about its marketing program there. For example, if the firm enters a market through a distributor or licensee, it is limiting its marketing freedom in such areas as marketing research, product policy, pricing, and promotion. The constraining influence of the level of involvement will be a recurring theme as we discuss the firm's international marketing program.

We will assume that the firm has made a decision to sell internationally and that it has selected its markets. The firm then faces the question of how to reach these markets. The range of alternatives is wide enough that almost any company in any product area can find some appropriate way to reach foreign markets. The nature of entry ranges from indirect exporting to wholly owned production in foreign markets (see Figure 10–1).

Before exploring these alternatives, the firm should decide what it wants from its channel to foreign markets, since this will help it choose the one that best meets the needs of the firm.

**Decision Criteria for Entry Method**

The selection of the method of entry to foreign markets depends on some factors peculiar to the firm and its industry — for example: (1) *company goals* regarding the volume of international business desired, geographic coverage, and the time span of foreign involvement; (2) the *size* of the company in sales and assets; (3) the company's *product line* and the nature of its products (industrial or consumer, high or low price, technological content); and (4) *competition* abroad. The firm must evaluate these factors for itself; we merely note them here because our decision model will not help in evaluating them — that is, a case-by-case approach is necessary.

Beyond the factors peculiar to the firm and its industry are other criteria that relate more generally to the method of entry to foreign markets and are relatively independent of the firm and its industry.

**Number of Markets.**   Companies have different ambitions in international marketing, including the number of countries they want to enter. Different entry methods offer different coverage of international markets. For example, wholly owned foreign operations are not permitted in some countries; the licensing approach may be impossible in other markets because the firm cannot find qualified licensees; or a trading company might cover certain markets very well but have no representation in other markets. To get the kind of international market coverage it wants, the firm will probably have to combine different entry methods. In some markets, it may have wholly owned operations; in others, marketing subsidiaries; in yet others, local distributors. For example, DuPont has 40 countries with manufacturing operations, wholly owned or joint venture, 20 countries with marketing subsidiaries, and over 60 countries with distributors.

**Penetration within Markets.**    Related to the number of markets covered is the quality of that coverage. An export management company, for example, might claim to give the producer access to 60 countries. The producer must probe further to find out if this "access" is to the whole national market or if it is limited to the capital or a few large cities.

**Market Feedback.**    If it is important that the firm know what is going on in its foreign markets, it must choose an entry method that will provide this feedback. Although in general the more direct methods of entry offer better possibilities of market information, feedback opportunities will depend in part on how the firm manages a particular form of market entry.

**Learning by Experience.**    Experience is the best teacher, and the firm will get more international marketing experience the more directly it is involved in foreign markets. The firm with international marketing ambitions should choose an entry method to help it gain some experience and realize these ambitions. The firm cannot "learn by doing" if others are doing the international marketing.

**Control.**    Management control over foreign marketing ranges from none at all — for example, selling through a trading company — to complete control, as in a wholly owned subsidiary. The firm may want a voice in several aspects of its foreign marketing, for instance, pricing and credit terms, promotion, and servicing of its products. The extent to which such control is critical to the firm will bear heavily on its choice of entry method.

**Incremental Marketing Costs.**    There are costs associated with international marketing, no matter who does it. However, the *producer's* incremental marketing outlays and working capital requirements will vary with the directness of the international marketing channel. For example, with indirect exporting there would be practically no additional outlays by the producer.

**Profit Possibilities.**    In evaluating the profit potential of different entry methods, the long-run sales and costs associated with each entry method must be estimated. Costs and profit margins are less important than total

# Global Marketing
## Japanese Entry and Expansion Strategies

| | | | |
|---|---|---|---|
| TOYOTA | Build new factories around the world. Diversify through acquisitions in electronics, telecommunications, factory automation, and possibly aerospace. Buy into or create joint ventures with other automakers, most likely in Europe. | TOSHIBA | Buy foreign companies that have strong positions in computers, integrated circuits, medical equipment, telecommunications, ceramics, and superconductivity. Build more plants throughout the world. |
| MATSUSHITA | Buy foreign software companies, particularly those involved in office automation, factory automation, and computer networks. Build more overseas plants. | NIPPON OIL | Become a major global oil producer by buying proven oil reserves anywhere in the world, or foreign oil companies that have big reserves. |
| HITACHI | Expand production around the world. Buy foreign computer and telecommunications companies that have global sales and distribution networks. | | |

Source: *Fortune,* November 21, 1988, 198.

---

profit possibilities. For example, one entry method may offer a 25 percent profit margin on a sales volume of $2 million, but another may offer a 17 percent profit margin on a sales volume of $10 million. The latter entry method probably would be more attractive, even though it has lower profit margins.

**Investment Requirements.**   Investment requirements are obviously highest in wholly owned foreign operations. Plant investment, however, is not the only consideration; capital also may be required to finance inventories and to extend credit. Since the amount of capital required varies greatly by method of entry, this financial need will be an important determinant for most firms.

**Administrative Requirements.**   The administrative burdens and costs of international marketing vary by entry method. These include documentation and red tape, as well as the management time required. For example, indirect exporting or licensing may involve very little additional burden on management.

**Personnel Requirements.**    Not only capital requirements vary by method of entry; so do personnel needs. Generally, the more direct kinds of involvement require a large number of skilled international personnel. If the firm is short of "internationalists," it will be constrained in its alternatives.

**Exposure to Foreign Problems.**    The more directly the firm is involved in foreign markets, the more management will have to deal directly with new kinds of legislation, regulation, taxes, labor problems, and other foreign market peculiarities. If the firm is unable or unwilling to deal with those problems, it must choose an entry method that lets someone else handle them.

**Flexibility.**    If the firm expects to be in foreign markets for the long run, some flexibility in its method of entry is important. Any entry method optimal at one point in time may be less than optimal five years later. Not only do the environment and the market change, so, too, do the company situation and goals. The firm therefore wants *flexibility* — the ability to change to meet new conditions. It may wish either to expand its involvement to take advantage of rapidly growing markets, or to contract its operations because of adverse developments.

Although not easy to achieve, this flexibility will be greater where the firm has planned for it in choosing its method of entry. For this reason, firms sometimes gain experience with limited forms of involvement before committing themselves heavily to a market.

**Risk.**    Foreign markets are usually perceived as riskier than the domestic market. The amount of risk the firm faces is not only a function of the market itself but also of its method of involvement there. In addition to its investment, the firm risks inventories, receivables and — perhaps — even the market itself. When planning its method of entry, the firm must do a risk analysis both of the market and of its method of entry. Exchange rate risk is another variable.

Risks are not only commercial; in foreign markets the firm is also faced with political risks. The firm's political vulnerability may differ from market to market as we saw in Chapter 5. The level of involvement will be one factor in that variability. Generally, the more direct and the more visible the entry of the international firm in the foreign market, the more vulnerable it is politically.

**A Simple Decision Model**

The criteria for evaluating foreign market entry methods can be combined in a matrix, as is done in Table 10–1. The firm will find that each of the entry methods will have a different score on the different dimensions. By relating these scores to the firm's own situation and needs, management can choose the most appropriate entry strategy.

The approach illustrated by Table 10–1 seeks to answer two questions: (1) How well can the firm market through any particular entry strategy?

**Table 10–1**                                 **Matrix for Comparing Alternative Methods of Market Entry**

| Evaluation Criteria | Entry Methods | | | | | | |
|---|---|---|---|---|---|---|---|
| | Indirect Export | Direct Export | Marketing Subsidiary | Marketing Subsidiary — Local Assembly | Licensing | Joint Venture | Wholly Owned Operation |
| 1. Number of Markets | | | | | | | |
| 2. Market Penetration | | | | | | | |
| 3. Market Feedback | | | | | | | |
| 4. International Marketing Learning | | | | | | | |
| 5. Control | | | | | | | |
| 6. Marketing Costs | | | | | | | |
| 7. Profits | | | | | | | |
| 8. Investment | | | | | | | |
| 9. Administration | | | | | | | |
| 10. Foreign Problems | | | | | | | |
| 11. Flexibility | | | | | | | |
| 12. Risk | | | | | | | |

(2) What are the costs and benefits of different entry strategies? Depending on its needs, the firm can use the matrix to select entry strategy for individual markets, for regions, or for the whole international market. The large firm could apply this approach by product line or division. The matrix is also useful for evaluating specific channel candidates in a given country. For example, a firm could modify it and use it to help evaluate three distributor candidates in the German market. Or to decide between a distributor, licensee, and joint venture partner in Brazil. We now turn to a consideration of the entry methods themselves.

Usually the decision facing a manager is to choose one entry method from among several alternatives. However, many times a firm will use a number of entry methods in combination — different entry methods for different countries or different product divisions, for example. Two company illustrations will show some of the real-world complexity that we simplify in our discussion. The first involves a Honeywell division using five entry methods for world markets; the second, General Electric using four different entry methods in one market, for different divisions.

The Aerospace and Defense Group (ADG) is a major division of Honeywell. It has five different ways of interacting with foreign markets. In order of priority, they are

1.  Honeywell Control Systems' foreign subsidiaries.
2.  The ADG international salesforce.
3.  Manufacturer's representatives abroad.

4.   Licensees abroad.
5.   Control Systems' foreign distributors.

In Mexico, General Electric (GE) has four different kinds of involvement for different parts of the company. GE has wholly owned factories for several of its industrial electrical products. It has a joint venture for major appliances. There is a marketing sub for distributing imports from the United States. Finally, there are licensees for locomotives and lighting systems.

## Indirect Exporting

The firm is an *indirect exporter* when its products are sold in foreign markets, but no special activity for this purpose is carried on within the firm. In indirect exporting, the sale is handled like a domestic sale. In fact, the firm is not engaging in international marketing, in any real sense, with indirect exporting. Its products are carried abroad by others, and its distribution problems are similar to those in domestic sales. Although exporting in this indirect way can open up new markets without special expertise or investment, the firm's control over market selection and marketing strategy is very limited. There are several different methods of indirect exporting.

**Foreign Sales through Domestic Sales Organization**

A firm likes to have a buyer come to it. Occasionally even a foreign buyer will do this. Products are sold in the domestic market but used or resold abroad in several ways:

1.   Foreign department stores or wholesale or retail organizations that have buying offices in the firm's home country may find the firm's product desirable for their market. For example, Macy's has buying offices in 30 countries. If the potential volume is adequate, the producer may even modify the product to assure that it meets the foreign buyer's desires.

2.   Manufacturers and firms in extractive industries often have U.S. offices to procure equipment and supplies for their foreign operations. In selling to the U.S. firms in this category, a company would have the advantage if it is already supplying their domestic operations. Reaching the foreign firms in this group would require special marketing. A similar example would be selling to the United States for post exchanges or embassies abroad.

3.   A slightly different situation arises when companies with multinational operations buy certain equipment and supplies for them through their regular domestic purchasing. In this case, a domestic supplier of the multinational company would have an advantage. Many smaller industrial marketers can trace their international involvement to such a beginning. Indeed, many exporters receive their initial export orders unsolicited.

Suppose a national company builds a plant in a foreign market. It buys a machine from its domestic supplier through the normal domestic procedure. The machine is shipped and installed in the new foreign plant. A foreign producer visits the plant and takes note of the machine. Sometime later the supplying firm receives its first foreign order. Such a sequence of events has often led to an active export involvement by the supplying firm.

It has benefited from the demonstration effect and received a free introduction to the foreign market. Although such experiences can lead to profitable exporting, they are too random to be part of a firm's strategy.
4.   International trading companies with local offices are very important
for some markets of the world. If these markets are on the firm's select list,
it should consider using one of these companies. Most large trading companies are of European or Japanese origin. In Japan, for example, some of
the largest enterprises are trading companies, such as Mitsui and Mitsubishi.
They handle the majority of all Japanese imports. The trading companies
of European origin are important primarily in trade with former European
colonies, particularly Africa and Southeast Asia. The United Africa Company, which is part of Unilever, is the largest trader in Africa and would
give the best market coverage, especially in West Africa.

The size and market coverage of these trading companies make them
attractive distributors, especially with their credit reliability. They cover
their markets well, and can also service the products they sell. For example,
Unisys uses United Africa Company for selling computers, a very technical
product.

There are some potential drawbacks to the use of trading companies,
however. They are likely to carry competing lines, and the latest product
added might not receive the attention its producer desires. In addition, some
of the developing countries resent trading companies associated with the
former colonial master. A few countries have even nationalized their foreign
trade (for example, Burma and Egypt) in part to get rid of foreign influence.

The sales from these kinds of indirect exporting are as good as domestic
sales, but they may be less stable. Because it is so far removed from the
ultimate market, the firm has very little control. Although the firm welcomes
any new sales, those arising from the sources mentioned here may prove too
uncertain to be included in long-run planning. This might move the firm
in the direction of more control over its foreign sales.

## Export Management Companies (EMCs)

Another form of indirect exporting is the export management company
(EMC), often considered as constituting the export department of the producer. That is, the producer gets the performance of an export department
without establishing one in the firm. The economic advantage arises because
the EMC performs this export function for several firms at the same time.

Compared with other indirect approaches, working with an EMC generally means the firm has closer cooperation and more control. The EMC
often uses the letterhead of the manufacturer, negotiates on the firm's behalf,
and gets its approval on orders and quotations. Theoretically at least, the
EMC approach to indirect exporting seems ideal for the medium-sized or
smaller firm contemplating exports, because the firm can overcome its limitations in size and foreign market knowledge while retaining some control.

The following list enumerates the potential advantages of using an EMC.

1.   The producer gains instant foreign market knowledge and contacts
     through the operations and experience of the EMC.

2. The commission method of payment means that costs are variable and the EMC is motivated to expand sales.
3. The manufacturer is spared the burden of developing in-house expertise in exporting, a significant cost saving, because the EMC's costs are spread over the sales of several manufacturers.
4. Consolidated shipments offer freight savings to the EMC's client.
5. A line of complementary products can get better foreign representation than the products of just one manufacturer, and perhaps better foreign market feedback also.
6. Most EMCs accept foreign credit responsibility, taking this burden away from the manufacturer.

***Evaluating the EMC.***  Because of their potential advantages, EMCs can be very attractive for a new exporter. Over 10,000 American manufacturers have used the EMC for exporting to all or some of their foreign markets. In evaluating this alternative, the exporter should determine to what degree all the potential advantages apply in its particular case. Some EMCs may be too new or too small to have adequate foreign market knowledge and contacts. Some may handle too many lines to give proper attention to a new exporter. EMCs may represent as few as 3 or 4 clients or as many as 50 or more. Many tend to be market specialists rather than product specialists, so product expertise may be weak, especially if they handle many lines. Their market coverage is often regional rather than global, in contrast to, say a Japanese trading company. That means the exporter may need more than one EMC or more than one entry method to cover all its potential markets.

One advantage cited for the EMC is that it gives the manufacturer access to instant foreign market knowledge and exporting know-how. But this can be a potential disadvantage if the producer never develops such capabilities because of continual reliance on the EMC. As foreign sales grow, it may become important for the firm to do its own exporting. Although initially the EMC may offer great economies, at some volume of sales it is more profitable for the manufacturing firm to set up its own export department. When the firm reaches this point, it will want its own foreign market knowledge and exporting know-how.

Looking at the relationship from the EMC's viewpoint is revealing. It is often vulnerable to the extent that it does a good job. It builds up foreign markets in the manufacturer's name and with the manufacturer's brands. When the market is well secured, the manufacturer may decide to take over the exporting to this now large foreign market. The EMC, of course, then loses a major source of revenue.

To protect themselves, many EMCs have changed the nature of their operations, using their *own letterhead* to establish their own identification. Instead of selling on commission, they *buy for resale* to control prices and terms and they use their own brand on some products. Brasch found that about half of all EMCs always buy the products they handle and over 90 percent take title at least some of the time.[1] Also, they try for a *larger list of clients* so that the loss of one or two is not so damaging. Brasch found that three out of four EMCs were actively seeking new clients, and most of the rest were willing to consider new lines to handle. The manufacturer doesn't have as close relations or as much control over the new type of EMC, but that doesn't mean that it is less effective than the more traditional type.

We have noted many potential advantages and limitations to using an EMC. In conclusion, we suggest that most smaller firms should consider the EMC alternative when evaluating export possibilities. The exporter-to-be needs to develop a list of export requirements and targets and then match these against the capabilities and market coverage of various EMC candidates. The potential exporter might find the EMC better than the alternatives.

The United States has over 1,000 export management companies. Because they provide necessary economies of scale and other advantages in international marketing, they are a continuing factor in U.S. international trade. They are a far cry from the Japanese trading companies, but the same economic logic underlies their operations. They are not just for small companies either. Over one-third of their clients have sales over $50 million and more than one in eight has over $500 million in sales. Even General Electric used an EMC for its airport-lighting division.

## Cooperation in Exporting

Cooperation in exporting is another way to enter foreign markets without bearing the costs and burdens of an in-house export department. Among the forms of cooperation in exporting are Webb-Pomerene associations, export trading companies (ETCs) and piggybacking.

**Webb-Pomerene Associations.**   Notable in that it permits competing firms to cooperate for export marketing, a Webb-Pomerene association can act as the single exporting arm of all the member companies, presenting a united front to world markets and gaining significant economies of scale. Its major functions are

1. Exporting in the name of the association.
2. Freight consolidation, rate negotiation, and ship chartering.
3. Market research.
4. Appointing selling agents in the United States or abroad.
5. Obtaining credit information and collecting debts.
6. Setting prices for export.
7. Allowing uniform contracts and terms of sale.
8. Allowing cooperative bids and sales negotiation.

Firms joining in a Webb-Pomerene association can research foreign markets more effectively together and obtain better representation in them. They may find that by establishing one organization to replace several sellers, they can realize more stable prices. Selling costs can be reduced just as in the EMC approach. Through consolidating shipments and avoiding duplicated effort, firms can realize transportation savings. And a group can achieve standardization of product grading and create a stronger brand name, just

**Table 10-2**   **Webb-Pomerene Associations**

| Association | Number of Members |
|---|---|
| Afram Films, Inc. | 6 |
| Alimenta Peanut Co. | 3 |
| American Cotton Exporters Association | 60 |
| American Motion Picture Export Co. Inc. | 7 |
| American Natural Soda Ash Corp. | 6 |
| American Phosphate Export Association | 8 |
| American Poultry, U.S.A., Inc. | 12 |
| American Sulphur Export Corp. | 2 |
| American Wood Chip Export Association | 5 |
| California Dried Fruit Export Association | 37 |
| Motion Picture Export Association of America, Inc. | 8 |
| North Coast Export Company | 2 |
| Northwest Fruit Exporters | 18 |
| Pacific Agricultural Cooperative for Export, Inc. | 11 |
| Phosphate Chemicals Export Association | 5 |
| Phosphate Rock Export Association | 5 |
| Pulp Paper and Paperboard Export Association | 9 |
| Sodium Bicarbonate Export Corporation | 3 |
| Sulfate of Potash Magnesia Export Association | 2 |
| Talmex Export Corporation | 6 |
| Texas Produce Export Association | 14 |
| Tri-State Export Corporation | 7 |
| UAN Solutions Export Association | 3 |
| United States Cigarette Export Association | 3 |

Source: Federal Trade Commission, May, 1989.

as the California fruit growers did with Sunkist products. Most of the benefits derive from economies of scale and the countervailing power made available through joint efforts. Flexibility is a final advantage. Many degrees of cooperation and product and market coverage are possible, so joining a Webb-Pomerene association is not an all-or-nothing affair.

With the many attractions of Webb-Pomerene associations, it is surprising that not more of them are operating. As shown in Table 10–2, there were only 24 registered as of 1989, down from 36 associations in 1981. Over 200 associations were formed under the Webb-Pomerene Act of 1918, but many were organized optimistically soon after the act was passed and never actually operated.

The great majority of associations are in some kind of commodity business, often with a large number of members as with the cotton exporters. On the other hand, other commodity groups include some of America's largest companies, such as the soda ash group that includes FMC, Kerr-McGee, Stauffer Chemical, and Tenneco. Some of the other groups deal in manufactured goods or services and also include some of America's larger companies. The cigarette exporters include the leading American cigarette makers, and the film-exporting groups have all the major U.S. movie producers, such as Columbia, MGM-UA, Paramount, and Warner Bros. It is interesting that there are three Webb-Pomerene associations of film producers, with generally the same membership. The three associations cover different parts of the world.

**Export Trading Companies.**   Export trading companies (ETCs), permitted in the United States since 1982, are an American attempt to emulate the Japanese trading companies. An ETC acts as the export arm of a number of manufacturers. Because EMCs and Webb-Pomerene associations play a small role in exports from the United States, the government wanted a more powerful mechanism to assist U.S. exporters. ETCs allow giant American corporations or banks to form a trading company with the size, resources, sophistication, and international network more comparable to that of the Japanese trading companies. The advantages to an exporter using an ETC would be much like those offered by EMCs and Webb-Pomerene associations (foreign market knowledge, economies of scale, etc.) but to a greater degree because of the greater resources and coverage of the ETC.

Some major U.S. banks, such as Bank of America, First National of Boston, Citicorp, and First National of Chicago, and major corporations, such as Borg-Warner, Control Data, GE, GM, and Sears, have formed ETCs so the groundwork has been prepared. GE has formed the largest ETC. It has 60 bilingual engineers with MBAs in its countertrade department alone. GE's ETC does about 90 percent of its business in GE products, however. GE has had limited success in getting exports from other U.S. firms. That illustrates the problem of American ETCs. They are slow in getting off the ground. Indeed, the Sears ETC folded completely after less than five years of operation. This is not surprising. A major international trading company does not reach maturity overnight. The Japanese have been at it a long time, and there may be successful American ETCs as time goes by. The exporter should consider the ETC alternative. Information can be obtained from the local Department of Commerce Field Office.

**Piggyback Exporting.**   In *piggyback exporting,* one manufacturer uses its overseas distribution facilities to sell another company's product along with its own. Although not new — General Electric was doing it some 50 years ago — this method is becoming more important today. Two parties with somewhat different interests make up the piggyback operation — the carrier and the rider.

The *carrier,* the firm actually doing the exporting, is usually the larger firm with established export facilities and foreign distribution. It may have several reasons for adding the product of another manufacturer. The new noncompetitive product may round out a gap in its product line, or it may mean greater economies of scale and profits in exporting. Borg-Warner had as much as one-sixth of its export sales and profits from piggybacking.

By piggybacking, companies can please foreign distributors by giving them a more complete line of complementary products. Also, it can mean extra customer convenience by offering related products. For example, Singer sells fabrics, patterns, and sewing accessories in addition to sewing machines. Finally, firms with seasonal sales may piggyback to keep their export operation working at full capacity throughout the year. It might be noted that for the carrier firm, piggybacking is a sale of know-how and services rather than a sale of products.

Schick Safety Razor tried piggybacking after encountering difficulty in entering the German market. After dissatisfaction with a German distributor and a temporary alliance with another consumer goods company, Schick set up its own sales subsidiary in Germany, hiring an executive from Gillette. A large salesforce was hired to give the necessary retail coverage. The costs of this approach would have been very high if only Schick products were sold. Fortunately, American Cyanamid wanted a distributor for its Breck hair products. Cyanamid had its own salesforce in Germany, but it was selling industrial products to markets that didn't overlap with Breck's. Schick became Breck distributor for Germany. This worked so well that Schick later agreed to distribute the cosmetic products of another American firm. Perhaps most important, Schick's own market share in Germany rose from 3 to 7 percent in one year. The large salesforce made possible by piggybacking was a major factor in this outcome.

***Piggyback Decisions: The Carrier.*** A firm that has a gap in its product line, or excess capacity in its export operation has two options. One is to develop internally the products necessary to round out its line and fill up its exporting capacity. The other option is to acquire the necessary products outside by piggybacking (or acquisition). Piggybacking may be attractive because the firm can get the product quickly (someone already has it). It is also a low-cost way to get the product in that the carrier firm does not have to invest in R&D, production facilities, or market testing for the new product. It can just pick up the product from another firm.

While piggybacking can be extremely attractive for the carrier, some concerns exist about quality control and warranty. Will the rider maintain the quality of the products sold by another firm? It will depend in part on whose brand name is on the product. If the rider's name is on the product, the quality incentive might be stronger. A second concern is continuity of supply. If the carrier develops a substantial market abroad, will the rider firm favor its own marketing needs in tight demand conditions? Each of these items should be a subject in the agreement between the two parties. If the piggybacking arrangement works out well, there is another potential advantage for the carrier. It might find the rider is a good acquisition candidate or joint-venture partner for a stronger relationship.

***The Rider.*** For the rider, piggybacking is one alternative route to foreign markets. It offers established export and distribution facilities and shared expenses, benefits similar to those offered by the EMC, the ETC, or a Webb-Pomerene association. The rider must compare a piggybacking opportunity to these other alternatives as to how well each meets the needs of geographic diversification and market coverage, economies of scale in exporting, entry into markets with high entry barriers, testing foreign markets, and learning international marketing. Given the growth of piggybacking in recent years, it appears that it is frequently a satisfactory answer to these needs.

***Method of Operation.***    Although piggyback agreements may be more flexible than agreements with export management companies or Webb-Pomerene associations, the same points must be considered for the protection of carrier and rider. Among these are terms of sale, promotional arrangements, market coverage, and provisions for termination of the agreement. The Schick-Cyanamid agreement again serves as an example. The contract provided that Schick sell Breck cosmetics in its own name, but for the account of Cyanamid; that is, the products remained Cyanamid property until sold. Schick agreed not to sell its own similar products or similar products of a third company. Should any questions arise concerning "similarity" of a new product, Cyanamid had to be consulted before a marketing decision was made.

The contract stipulated that Schick was to receive a higher commission during the launching period. Cyanamid was authorized to check Schick's accounts with an independent auditor and to withdraw Breck cosmetics from the market if sales were disappointing. Should Schick be taken over by a third company, Cyanamid had the right to cancel the contract.

In selling, piggybacking offers two types of arrangements: (1) the carrier sells the rider's product on a commission basis, as an agent or EMC might do; (2) the carrier buys the products outright from the manufacturing company, acting more like an independent distributor. The latter alternative is more common, but the appropriate choice depends on the situation of the two firms.

Branding and promotional policy is variable in piggybacking. In some instances, the carrier may buy the products, put its own brand on them, and market them as its own products. In this case, the company does the total marketing job, as Borg-Warner does with auto replacement parts it buys from other manufacturers. More commonly, the carrier retains the brand name of the producer and the two work out promotional arrangements between them. The choice of branding and promotional strategy is a function of the importance of brand to the product and of the degree to which the brand is well established. Borg-Warner kept the producer's name on the small appliances it bought from Hamilton Beach. It had similar agreements for the Toastmaster products of McGraw-Edison and the garbage disposers of In-Sink-Erator Company.

The piggyback approach can be flexible also as to product and market coverage. The carrier may handle just one or all of the rider's products. For example, in Thailand DuPont markets its own industrial chemicals but piggybacks its agrochemicals with Shell. WYKO, a smaller firm, sells its full line of optical-testing equipment through Matsushita in Japan.

In terms of country coverage, piggybacking may offer just one market — or the whole world. For example, AT&T used Toshiba just for the Japanese market whereas Hitachi used NAS only for the U.S. market. Uniflow, a producer of ice-making and beverage-cooling equipment, had successfully exported to Europe, Africa, and Latin America but was unable to enter Japan till it piggybacked with Matsushita, who it used just for the Japanese market. By contrast, Champion Spark Plug offered markets throughout Southeast Asia for several Australian and European auto parts makers. Sankyo Seiki, a robotics firm, used the global coverage of IBM, as did Stratus minicomputers.

Other advantages of piggyback to the carrier and the rider can be seen in the following examples of Whirlpool and Sony and IBM and Minolta: Whirlpool had been exporting appliances to a Japanese distributor for 12 years. In the late 1970s it switched to piggybacking with Sony in Japan and found its sales increasing. Sony not only had good distribution and service capabilities, it gave more sophisticated promotion, and association with the Sony reputation. For Sony, the gains came from a wider complementary product line to distribute.

Minolta began selling small copiers in the United States through IBM with the IBM brand. Although Minolta had its own American distribution under its own name, IBM gave it much greater coverage of the U.S. market. The advantage to IBM was in gaining a low-priced copier without all the time and expense of developing one itself.

## Direct Exporting

In our discussion of indirect exporting we examined ways of reaching foreign markets without working very hard. Indeed, in the indirect approaches, foreign sales are handled the same way as domestic sales; the manufacturing firm engages in international marketing only by proxy, that is, through the firm that carries its products overseas. Both the international marketing know-how and the sales achieved by these indirect approaches, however, are probably limited. The firm can commit itself further by going to direct exporting.

The difference between indirect and direct exporting is that in the latter, the manufacturer performs the export task rather than delegating it to others. In *direct exporting,* the tasks of market contact, market research, physical distribution, export documentation, pricing, and so on, all fall on the export department of the firm. Direct exporting usually results in greater sales than does indirect exporting. Whether it also yields greater profits will depend on whether the sales increase is greater than the increase in costs from an in-house export operation. Table 10–3 gives an overview of the export marketing task.

The choice between indirect exporting and direct exporting is analogous to the choice between selling through a manufacturer's representative and the firm's own salesforce in domestic marketing. The advantages of directness are not only greater sales, but also greater control, better market information and development of expertise in international marketing. The costs of going direct are high because the direct exporter bears them alone, whereas they are shared in the indirect or cooperative approaches. Although we are contrasting direct and indirect exporting, they are not mutually ex-

| **Table 10-3** | **Outline for an Export Plan** |
| --- | --- |

**Table of Contents**

*Part I — An export policy commitment statement*

*Part II — The situation/background analysis*
- Product
- Operations
- Personnel and export organization
- Resources of the firm
- Industry structure, competition and demand

*Part III — The marketing component*
- Identification, evaluation and selection of target markets
- Product selection & pricing
- Distribution method
- Terms and conditions
- Internal organization & procedures
- Sales goals: Profit (loss) forecasts

*Part IV — Tactics: Action steps*
- Countries where firm has special advantages (e.g. family ties)
- Primary target countries
- Secondary target countries
- Indirect marketing efforts

*Part V — An export budget*
- Pro forma financial statements

*Part VI — An implementation schedule*
- Followup
- Periodic operational/management review (measuring results against Plan)

*Addenda — Background data on target countries & market*
- Basic market statistics: Historical & projected
- Background facts
- Competitive environment

Source: *Basic Guide to Exporting,* U.S. Department of Commerce (Washington, D.C., 1987), p 4.

clusive. A firm might export directly to large markets but export indirectly to smaller markets.

## The Task of Export Management

To gain the benefits of direct exporting, the firm must pay the costs of performing the export management task. Depending on the size of foreign sales, export management may range from a part-time activity for one person to a large export department with a specialized staff and a full-time export manager. As a further variation, the export department could be a part of the international division, or there could be separate export departments in the product divisions. Regardless of the volume of export sales or the organizational structure, however, export management has certain tasks. The first is choosing export markets.

**Choosing Foreign Markets.** In indirect exporting, foreign-market coverage is usually dictated by the company that takes the product abroad; that is, it is already selling in certain markets, and these are the ones it can offer the manufacturer. Of course, the manufacturer can add other markets by using other intermediaries that cover the additional markets wanted. By direct exporting, management can make its own selection of markets.

In theory, the firm could have the whole world as its market. In practice, it is usually limited to a part of the world's markets. For an American company, U.S. restrictions on trading with Communist countries might eliminate those countries from consideration. However, East-West trade is expanding and opportunities will be found there, all in accord with government policy. The firm may eliminate other markets in order to concentrate on those offering the greatest potential. Some markets may be too small; others may have too much competition; yet others may have tariff barriers or trade restrictions on the firm's products.

To choose the best export markets, the firm needs some analytical approach to help it evaluate and rank markets according to potential. Among the variables are demand factors, competition, and government. The kinds of approaches and information sources needed for such an analysis were discussed in Chapter 7.

**Choosing Representatives in the Target Markets.** Once the firm has selected its markets, it must have representation there. If both the markets and the firm are large enough, the firm can establish its own sales subsidiary, exporting to itself in the foreign market and controlling its marketing program there. The more frequent approach, especially in smaller markets, is to select local representatives to distribute the firm's products.

The firm would do well to have several distributor candidates in each target market, the names of which can be obtained from many different sources: Department of Commerce, foreign business directories, commercial banks, steamship companies, airlines, and so on. After the firm obtains a list of candidates, it must secure information about each one in order to select the best. The firm will want to know their method of operation — whether they buy for their own account, whether they carry inventory, how many on their sales staff, what product lines they carry — and their effectiveness and reliability in marketing and in paying their bills.

A Dun and Bradstreet report or a Department of Commerce *World Traders Data Report* (WTDR) can give information on several of these questions. For example, a WTDR gives background information on the company, number of employees, sales area, products handled, general reputation of company, names of foreign companies represented, and so on. (See the example in Figure 10–2.) These sources can be followed up with inquiries through banks, other American clients of the candidate, and their other references to get a fuller picture. All this can be done in the home country of the exporter.

After all this information has been gathered, however, the exporter should visit the market before making the final choice of a distributor. Such

**Figure 10–2**          **World Traders Data Report**

U.S. DEPARTMENT OF COMMERCE
International Trade Administration
1140 McNamara Building
477 Michigan Avenue
Detroit, Michigan 48226

This report, submitted to the U.S.
Department of Commerce by the U.S.
Foreign Service—Department of State, is
transmitted in confidence. No
responsibility can be assumed by the
Government or its officers for any
transactions had with any persons or
firms herein mentioned. The report is not
for publication.

SECONDARY DISTRIBUTION PROHIBITED.

```
R 1008202 APR 77
FR AMEMBASSY LONDON
TO USDOC WASHDC
BT
UNCLAS LONDON 0128
EO  11652: N/A
TAGS:  BBSR, UK
SUBJ:  WTDR/FTI: FRANKLIN, CLAYTON-WRIGHT LTD.
       (REQUESTED AS: F.C. WRIGHT)

REF: USDOC 18269

1. UNITED KINGDOM
OFFICE USE:  2. 412   3. 0705400   4. 01

5. FRANKLIN, CLAYTON-WRIGHT LTD.
6. P.O.BOX 189; 56 OXFORD ST.
7. LONDON WC2H 8BA

8. CONTACT: ROBERT PETERSON
9. TITLE: MANAGING DIRECTOR
   OTHER OFFICIALS ARE: ARTHUR SMYTHE, PRESIDENT AND
   JOHN S. CARLYLE, FOREIGN SALES MANAGER.
10. PHONE: 01/9924321  11. TELEX: 889352
12. CABLE: CLAYTONITE LONDON
13. ESTABL: 1952  14. EMPL: 1300  15. SIZE: VERY LARGE
16. REPUTATION: Y-SATISFACTORY  17. RPT DATE: 04/77
OFFICE USE:  18. K  19. X  20. X  21. N/A  22. A3582

23A. 20650/M04    MFR, DIST, EXP, OF CONFECTIONERY
                  PRODUCTS AND
23B. 20665/OM4    CHOCOLATE AND COCOA PRODUCTS
23C. 20231/SG     IMP. OF DRY MILK PRODUCTS; INTERESTED IN
                  LICENSE TO PRODUCE
23D. 35514/F      INTERESTED IN PURCHASING CONFECTIONERY
                  PACKAGING EQUIP

24. FOREIGN SALES: FRANCE 35%, SPAIN 28%, GERMANY
AND USA (BY VALUE).

25. FINANCIAL REFS: INTERNATIONAL BANK, 739 PARK
AVE., NEW YORK, MORRISON BANK LTD., 17 NORTHURP CT.,
LONDON W1VOE, ENGLAND.

26. TRADE REFS:  JOHNSON MACHINERY, INC. 862 S. LOS
ANGELES ST., LOS ANGELES, CA 96102; TEDENSON CO., INC.
125 SOUTH STREET, BOSTON, MA 02111.

27. FOREIGN FIRMS REPRESENTED: AGENCY REP. OF NORTH-AM CHICLE
CO., INC., P.O.BOX 245, WASHINGTON DC 20001 FOR CHEWING GUM,
ACQUIRED 1954; LICENSEE OF HOBART CANDY CO., 1215 N EADS ST.,
ATLANTA, GA 37259 FOR PEANUT BRITTLE & CHOC. COVERED PEANUT
BUTTER.

28. POST EVALUATION:  THIS FIRM IS ONE OF THE LEADING MANUFACTURERS
OF ALL TYPES OF CONFECTIONERY IN THE UNITED KINGDOM.  THE FIRM
HAS A BASIC CAPITAL OF 3 MILLION POUNDS AND FIXED ASSETS VALUED
AT 1.5 MILLION POUNDS.  ITS CENTER OF OPERATIONS, INCLUDING
MANUFACTURING FACILITY, IS IN LONDON.  IT HAS DISTRIBUTION
FACILITIES IN GLASGOW, LIVERPOOL AND LONDON.  THE FIRM'S MAJOR
STOCKHOLDER IS BURTON'S LTD., A HOLDING COMPANY.  LOCAL CREDIT
SOURCES REPORT SATISFACTORY EXPERIENCE ON LOANS IN THE LOW FIVE
FIGURES; THE FIRM'S FINANCES APPEAR SOUND AND OBLIGATIONS ARE
PROMPTLY MET; IT HAS, HOWEVER, RECENTLY ENCOUNTERED CASH FLOW
PROBLEMS.  THE EMBASSY CONSIDERS COMPANY A SATISFACTORY TRADE
CONTACT FOR U.S. FIRMS.
```

Source: U.S. Department of Commerce, International Trade Administration, 1140
McNamara Building, 477 Michigan Ave, Detroit, MI 48226.

a visit provides a feeling for the market that written reports can't convey, but more important, it gives further insights on the distributor — probably the most important single factor in export performance. As noted by an international marketer at Corning Glass, "The key to export success is a strong presence in the market." Furthermore, once the contract has been signed, the laws of the country may make it very difficult to break the contract and get another distributor. Finally, the choice of a distributor is important because it may play a role in the future as joint-venture partner or acquisition candidate. For example, when 3M established a marketing subsidiary in the Netherlands, it did so by acquiring its distributor there. For these reasons, the initial selection must be made very carefully.

Paying a visit to the better candidates and viewing their operations will help the export manager make the best choice. Establishing personal familiarity will make future written communication more meaningful. In some markets, the firm will not be able to develop a list of acceptable distributor candidates, in which case it might be happy to find even one that is being used by a competitor.

**Physical Distribution and Export Documentation.**   Once the firm has made agreements with foreign distributors, it must get the product to them. This task of physical distribution differs from the same task in the domestic market. Different shipping companies and modes of transportation are necessary; for example, the use of ships and airplanes is more common in exporting. Packaging for export is usually more costly because the greater distances and numerous changes in modes of transportation require that the product be handled more frequently. Of course, air shipments can avoid some of these problems.

A further complication of shipping to foreign markets is export documentation. The paperwork required for exports is greater than for domestic shipping, and the importing nation requires documents of its own. An average shipment requires over 40 documents and several hundred copies. This is not unmanageable, however, as over 80,000 American firms are exporting. Finally, insuring shipments to foreign markets is more complicated than insuring domestic shipments.

The complications noted here, combined with firms' lack of familiarity with foreign markets, have deterred many managers from giving adequate consideration to foreign opportunities. Although paperwork and other complications involve extra work and cost, many sources of expertise are ready to help the exporter. Overseas freight forwarders are skilled in handling physical distribution and documentation; banks take care of the international financial aspects; insurance companies handle foreign shipments and can even insure credit to foreign customers. There are also companies that do export packaging.

Most exporters use some outside expertise, the amount often depending on the volume of export sales. The exporter has, in effect, a make-or-buy decision. Can we do these tasks more efficiently in-house, or should we

## Global Marketing

### The Most Common Mistakes of New Exporters

1. Failure to get export counseling and to develop an international marketing plan before starting exports.
2. Insufficient commitment by top management.
3. Insufficient care in selecting overseas agents or distributors.
4. Chasing orders from around the world instead of establishing a basis for profitable and orderly growth.
5. Neglecting export business when the U.S. market booms.
6. Failure to treat international distributors on an equal basis with domestic counterparts.
7. Assuming that a given product and marketing technique will succeed everywhere.
8. Unwillingness to modify products to meet preferences or regulations of other countries.
9. Failure to print sales, service, and warranty messages in local languages.
10. Failure to consider use of an export management company.
11. Failure to consider licensing or joint-venture agreements.
12. Failure to provide readily available servicing for the product.

Source: *Basic Guide to Exporting,* U.S. Department of Commerce (Washington, D.C., 1987), 85, 86.

---

purchase them outside? As export volume increases, the exporter will tend to do more and more in-house.

**Other Marketing Tasks.**   Additional responsibilities of export management include market intelligence, pricing, and promotion. In indirect exporting, marketing information is gathered by the firm selling abroad, if it is gathered at all. The firm supplying the goods may receive little market feedback. To perform effectively, the export manager must have continuing market information. Some market information is available from domestic sources. Foreign distributors are another important source. When export volume is large enough, the export manager should visit foreign markets to keep informed. We have described the market-intelligence function more fully in Chapter 7.

Pricing for foreign markets involves several new dimensions. First the manager must decide whether to quote in U.S. dollars or other currencies. Then it is necessary to determine whether the quote should be *f.o.b.* (free on board — plant or port of exit), *c.i.f.* (cost, insurance, freight) to foreign port, or one of several other possible quotes. Should exports be at full cost or marginal cost pricing? How should the firm handle tariffs and the other add-ons to the plant price? If promotion is needed for exported products, the export manager must take the responsibility for it. One may work with an export advertising agency and/or with national distributors in cooperative advertising programs. The questions of export pricing and promotion are discussed in detail in Chapters 12, 13, and 14.

**Marketing through Foreign Distributors.**   We have noted some of the major marketing tasks the exporter must perform from its home-country base. The actual marketing to final customers abroad must be done by the firm's distributor in that market. One of the most challenging jobs for export managers is to obtain the cooperation of the independent distributor in the foreign market in the marketing effort. Various strategies and tactics for doing so are discussed in Chapter 11 under the heading of "Marketing through Foreign Distributors."

**Conclusions on Direct Exporting.**    Our discussion here has been primarily from the viewpoint of the firm whose only involvement is by exporting. Of course, exporting is a continuing part of a firm's international business and will be done by those who also engage in licensing, joint ventures, and other kinds of involvement. We gave quite a bit of space to direct exporting because it is the most common form of international marketing. We will not try to summarize that discussion. Rather, we conclude with a list in "Global Marketing" that highlights many of the important issues for the direct exporter. The list was prepared by those with long experience with many American exporters.

# Foreign Manufacturing as Foreign-Market Entry

So far we have assumed that the firm entering foreign markets was supplying them from domestic plants. This is implicit in any form of exporting. However, under certain conditions the firm may find it either impossible or undesirable to supply all foreign markets from domestic production sources.

Several factors may encourage, or indeed force, the firm to produce in foreign markets if it wishes to sell in them. For example, transportation costs may render heavy or bulky products noncompetitive. Tariffs or quotas can prevent entry of an exporter's products. In many countries, the government's preference for national suppliers can also shut the door to goods produced outside the country. Where governments practice such preferences, a firm that sells to governments must produce locally. Any of these conditions could force the firm to manufacture in foreign markets in order to sell there.

More positive factors also encourage a firm to produce abroad. Some markets are large enough to warrant an efficient plant size, especially regional groupings such as the European Common Market. In addition, local production allows better interaction with local market needs concerning product design, delivery, and service. Sometimes foreign production costs are lower, especially when transportation and tariff savings are added in. The firm might undertake foreign production to gain any of these advantages even though it has the option of serving the market, at least partly, by exports. Britain's chemical firm, ICI, gave these reasons for beginning production on the European continent:

1.  You are more credible to your customers if they know your plant is close.
2.  You are more acceptable to local authorities and have more influence on them.

3. Britain is an island and is especially vulnerable to interruption of supplies.
4. Perhaps most important, with a local plant you force your own company to commit itself to the market.

**Approaches to Foreign Manufacture: Assembly**

Once the firm has decided to enter certain markets by manufacturing in them, it has several alternatives. Foreign production may range from assembly plants, contract manufacturing, licensing, or joint ventures to wholly owned plants. In each approach, foreign manufacturing is the source of the firm's product in the market, but the extent of its involvement in production and marketing varies with the approach it chooses.

In *foreign assembly,* the firm produces domestically all or most of the components or ingredients of its product and ships them to foreign markets to be put together as a finished product. Assembly operations abroad involve less than full-scale manufacturing but still require that significant value be added in the local market. Notable examples of foreign assembly are the automobile and farm equipment industries. Where transportation costs on a fully assembled vehicle or piece of equipment are very high, the firm might be more competitive by shipping CKD (completely knocked down) and putting the product together within the market. Another reason for local assembly is the tariff barrier; many countries have much lower tariffs on unassembled equipment than on assembled. By forcing local assembly, governments increase local employment.

The pharmaceutical industry is another example of extensive assembly operations, although in this case they should be called *compounding* or *mixing operations.* Again because of transportation or tariff barriers, a firm will ship key ingredients to foreign markets and add bulky liquids or other ingredients locally, plus the capsule and packaging. In similar fashion, Coca-Cola ships its syrup to foreign markets, where local bottlers add the water and the container. These assembly or mixing plants abroad represent partial local manufacturing by the firm; they are a compromise between exports and local production.

If an assembly plant involves foreign investment by the firm, the firm must make an investment decision as well as a decision on how to enter the market. However, the investment commitment is not necessarily included in a decision to assemble abroad. The firm can assemble its products in foreign markets through licensing arrangements without making a capital outlay. For example, Jeep licensed Renault to assemble its cars in Belgium.

Company-owned assembly operations usually are combined with a company marketing subsidiary in the same market. A licensee who runs assembling or mixing operations may handle local distribution as well. For example, Renault distributed Jeep vehicles in some parts of Europe, whereas Jeep handled the distribution in other European countries through its Swiss sales subsidiary.

Coca-Cola is usually distributed by national organizations licensed by the company. This allows the company to earn over half of its revenue abroad with a very small amount of investment outside of its home market. Coca-

Cola has the following division of labor with its foreign franchised bottlers. Coca-Cola supplies:

1. The syrup
2. Engineering services
3. Quality control
4. Marketing advice

The bottlers do everything else, including the local marketing.

## Contract Manufacturing

*Contract manufacturing* abroad is foreign manufacturing by proxy. That is, the firm's product is produced in the foreign market by another producer under contract with the firm. Because the contract covers only manufacturing, marketing is handled by the firm. Contract manufacturing is feasible when the firm can locate foreign producers with the capability of manufacturing the product in satisfactory quantity and quality. In some markets such capability cannot be found, so contract manufacturing is not an alternative. One enterprising manufacturer in Honduras was producing under contract for three American firms: American Home Products, Colgate, and Procter & Gamble (P&G).

Contract manufacturing may be an attractive alternative if the firm's competitive advantage lies in marketing and service rather than in production. For example, P&G in Italy had several products manufactured under contract. It concentrated its own efforts on marketing the products. Contract manufacturing obviates the need for plant investment, something the firm may wish to avoid if the market is politically uncertain or if the firm is short of capital.

Contract manufacturing enables the firm to avoid labor and other problems that may arise from its lack of familiarity with the country. At the same time the firm gets the advantage of advertising its product as locally made. This may be useful in public relations or for government procurement purposes. If a market proves too small or risky, it is easier and less costly to terminate a manufacturing contract than to shut down the firm's own plant. Other advantages include transportation savings (compared to exports), occasionally lower production costs abroad, and possible exports of components or supplies to the contract manufacturer.

Drawbacks to the contract-manufacturing approach may limit its application. For one, the manufacturing profit goes to the local firm rather than to the international firm. This is not serious if sufficient profit remains in marketing activities. For another, finding a satisfactory manufacturer in the foreign market may be difficult. Quality control, too, is usually a greater problem when production is done by another firm.

From our discussion, the advantages of contract manufacturing appear to outweigh the drawbacks. One should not, however, underestimate the problems of locating and working with a contract manufacturer. Nevertheless, this avenue should be given serious attention in markets where foreign investment is not feasible or desirable for the firm.

Del Monte chose contract manufacturing as a low-cost way of producing in Central America. It had been exporting there for many years and felt the time had come for local production. Del Monte began by signing a contract with Del Campo, a Costa Rican producer of canned foods. Del Campo put out 20 different Del Monte products, using Del Monte recipes. The agreement was a straight price per item with Del Monte handling the distribution.

After a couple of years, Del Monte decided it had a good local partner, so a closer relation was worked out. Del Monte began to assist Del Campo with production and marketing, and Del Campo began to produce Del Monte products for other Central American countries. Del Monte negotiated an option to buy up to 67 percent of Del Campo's equity.

## Licensing

Licensing is another way the firm can establish local production in foreign markets without capital investment. It differs from contract manufacturing in that it is usually for a longer term and involves much greater responsibilities for the national party. A *licensing* agreement is an arrangement wherein the licensor gives something of value to the licensee in exchange for certain performance and payments from the licensee. The licensor (the international company) may give the licensee (the national firm) one or more of the following things: (1) patent rights, (2) trademark rights, (3) copyrights, (4) know-how on products or processes. Any of these may be given for use in a particular foreign market, or the licensee may have rights in several countries or on a whole continent.

In return for the use of the know-how or rights received, the licensee usually promises (1) to produce the licensor's products covered by the rights, (2) to market these products in an assigned territory, and (3) to pay the licensor some amount related to the sales volume of such products. The licensee takes on a much greater role than the foreign manufacturer who produces under contract. The licensee takes over the marketing task in addition to production and is thus the complete foreign-market presence of the international firm for the products covered.

**Evaluating Licensing.**   Several features of licensing are attractive. First, it requires no capital outlay and thus need not deter even small companies. Second, it is often the quickest and easiest way to enter a foreign market. Even the firm that has capital may otherwise face a slow process to establish local production and get distribution. Third, the firm immediately gains local knowledge.

A fourth advantage is that many governments favor licensing over direct investment because licensing brings technology into the country with fewer strings and costs attached. Thus licensing may gain government approval more quickly than direct investment. And from the licensor's viewpoint, there is no investment to be expropriated. Finally, the general advantages of foreign production also apply to licensing — savings in tariff and transport costs, local production where national suppliers are favored, and so on.

Philip Morris has a special reason for licensing. Because many governments have tobacco monopolies, the only way Philip Morris can get into their markets is to license a government to produce and sell its brands. Philip Morris does this in six Western European and four Eastern European countries.

The disadvantages of licensing are less numerous, but they may carry greater weight. The chief fear about licensing is that the licensor may establish its own competitor. During the five or ten years of the licensing agreement, the licensor may transfer enough expertise that the licensee can get along alone, and thus the licensor may lose that market, and perhaps neighboring markets, to the former licensee. This is less likely where strong brands or trademarks are involved.

Westinghouse encountered this problem. In 1972 when the French company Framatome signed a licensing agreement with Westinghouse, Framatome was an insignificant factor in the market for atomic power. By 1980, Framatome was second only to Westinghouse, and the two parted company. An executive at Westinghouse acknowledged that Framatome had developed the capability to design around its patents, "but we'll attempt to stay six months to a year ahead of them."

Another reason for hesitancy about licensing is the limited returns it provides. Although no capital outlay is necessary, the royalties and fees from licensing are not "gravy" to the licensor, who must invest management and engineering time. A direct investment approach to the foreign market requires greater effort and resources from the firm, but it may yield much greater profits. Licensing returns are limited primarily to a percentage of the licensee's sales, commonly 3 to 5 percent. Indeed, less developed countries are trying to reduce even further the royalties and fees paid to licensors.

Yet another possible drawback is the problem of controlling the licensee. Although the contract should spell out the responsibilities of each party, misunderstandings and conflicts can arise in its implementation. Frequent areas of conflict are quality control, the marketing effort of the licensee, and interpretation of the exclusiveness and extent of the territorial coverage. These problems arise partly because an agreement that met both parties' interests at the time of signing can become unsuitable to one or both as years go by and conditions change. And again, host countries are trying to reduce the licensor's control over the licensee.

One U.S. equipment producer had a French licensee for over 30 years. The licensee was capable and aggressive in developing the French market, and the licensor was very satisfied. However, when the European Common Market eliminated territorial restrictions between member nations, the licensor found the French licensee competing with its own subsidiaries in other member countries. The U.S. firm was unhappy but was afraid to terminate the agreement for fear the licensee would go off on his own and be an even more dangerous competitor, taking the French market with him.

**Managing Licensing.**   Firms that are successful in licensing have developed certain approaches and techniques for minimizing the pitfalls of licensing and accentuating its potential benefits. We note some of them here:

1. Have a deliberate policy and plan for licensing; that is, give it proper attention.
2. Fix licensing responsibility in the firm by means of a licensing manager or department. Pfizer has nine licensing directors, one for each major business unit.
3. Select licensees carefully.
4. Draft careful agreement and review with licensee. Some items to include are territorial coverage, duration, royalties, trade secrets, quality control, and minimum-performance clause.
5. Supply licensee with critical ingredients.
6. Obtain equity in licensee.
7. Limit product and territorial coverage.
8. Keep patent and trademark registration in licensor's name.
9. Be a reasonably important part of licensee's business. Canon deliberately chose a smaller firm for its copier licensee in India to get better performance.

International licensing can be an important part of company strategy. American firms receive over $10 billion a year from licensing agreements. It should be noted that licensing income is not limited to royalties but includes such items as (1) technical assistance fees, (2) sale of materials or components to licensee (3) lump-sum payments for transfer of rights or technology, (4) technology feedback, (5) reciprocal license rights, (6) fees for engineering services, (7) sales of machinery or equipment and (8) management fees. The typical company receives five different types of return on its licensing agreements, but a study by Contractor showed that over 80 percent of the income tends to be from royalties.[2]

Juste Quimico Pharmaceutica, a Spanish pharmaceutical company, signed a contract with an Indian licensee. Juste will receive no know-how, royalty, or trademark fees. Because of this, government approvals were not required. Juste is seeking its return by selling critical ingredients to the licensee and by getting better market access rather than depending on the limited royalties and technical fees allowed by the Indian government. Juste hopes for a good foothold in the large Indian health-care market, plus exports to several countries in Asia and Africa, including the U.S.S.R.[3]

**Licensing as a Fallback Strategy.**   Another way licensing can be attractive is as a fallback position when other approaches run into trouble. An exporter may find that tariffs or other trade restrictions have taken away one of its export markets. If it is not feasible or desirable for the firm to set up local production in that market, the firm could maintain a position there by licensing. In a similar vein, a firm producing in a country may find political or economic problems have made its operation untenable. If it is unable to export to that market from another plant, it could find licensing an attractive way to maintain some position in that market. In both cases, licensing could prove effective, not as a primary strategy, but as a fallback position to hold onto some share in the otherwise lost market.

**A Final Example.**  A brief case study of an American company's licensing experience will conclude our discussion of licensing: The Manhattan Shirt Company had licensees in over 30 countries, many of them in the developing nation category. These were administered by the company's International Licensing Division, whose manager spent 40 percent of his time traveling abroad. Though Manhattan shirts are a nonpatentable product, the company felt that its brand name and know-how were very licensable.

The company's method of operation is instructive. Manhattan began with a market survey. This was followed up by a search for licensee candidates in the more attractive markets. The licensing manager visited all the prospective licensees on their home grounds before making a selection. One criterion was that Manhattan shirts be an important part of the licensee's business, so that they could be given proper attention. The licensee's production people were required to come to the United States for training. Sales training was given in the licensee's country.

The licensee was required to advertise. Whereas sales and production training were included in the royalty fee, advertising had to be at the expense of the licensee, although the size of the commitment varied by country. Often the company took a part of the first year's royalties and rebated a portion to be used by the licensee for advertising, above his or her regular commitment.

Manhattan set up an exchange of information between members of its licensing "family." This was good for morale and also for the exchange of experiences. Most of the important technical information came from Manhattan's domestic operations. The data were supplied to licensees at the same time they became available in the United States. The manager felt that periodic visits to licensees not only helped their performance, but helped Manhattan control the agreement.

For quality control, the company required random samples of every licensee's production. Revenue control was maintained by traveling auditors who checked licensees' production and sales reports. The company preferred to limit the territory of a licensee. If a licensee was given more than one country, Manhattan liked separate performance clauses for each market.

# Joint Ventures in Foreign Markets

Foreign joint ventures in manufacturing have something in common with foreign licensing. Both usually involve foreign manufacturing and distribution by a foreign firm. The major difference is that in the joint venture, the international firm has equity and a management voice in the foreign firm. The equity share of the international company can range between 10 and 90 percent, but generally it is between 25 and 75 percent. Instead of seeking a technical or legal definition of a joint venture, however, we will use the following practical one: A joint venture is a foreign operation in which the international company has enough equity to have a voice in management but not enough to completely dominate the venture. Note also that we consider only joint ventures between an international firm and a firm that is native to the country where the venture is located.

Contract manufacturing and licensing are joint ventures of a sort, and so is the exporter working with the foreign distributor, but in none of these relationships are the ties so strong as in the joint venture. As in the progression from going steady to being engaged to being married, each step represents a stronger tie. With the expansion of international operations, joint ventures have become increasingly important. Whereas three-quarters of all foreign manufacturing subsidiaries established before 1946 were wholly owned, the percentage had dropped to half by 1970.

**To Join or Not to Join.**   In evaluating the joint-venture approach, its advantages and disadvantages must be compared with both the lesser commitment of contract manufacturing and licensing and the greater commitment of wholly owned foreign production. Whatever benefits derive from foreign manufacture will, of course, be obtained in the joint-venture approach as well as in any other. As compared with a lesser commitment, joint ventures have the following advantages: (1) potentially greater returns from equity participation as opposed to royalties, (2) greater control over production and marketing, (3) better market feedback, and (4) more experience in international marketing. Disadvantages include a need for greater investment of capital and management resources and a potentially greater risk than with a nonequity approach.

When the partial ownership in joint ventures is compared with wholly owned foreign production, a different picture emerges: (1) A joint venture requires fewer capital and management resources and thus is more open to smaller companies. (2) A given amount of capital can be spread out among more countries. (3) The danger of expropriation is less when a firm has a national partner than when the international firm is sole owner. Because of this last point, Club Méditerranée has a policy of minority ownership in its foreign operations, or "villages." An analyst noted, "They always make sure that local interests are big enough that if Club Med is thrown out, those interests will suffer first."

Many foreign governments prefer or even demand joint ventures because they feel that their nations get more of the profits and technological benefit if nationals have a share. India and Mexico have been especially restrictive about foreigners owning over 50 percent of any venture in their countries. Also, finding a national partner may be the only way to invest in some markets that are too competitive or crowded to admit a completely new operation. This latter point is important for many Japanese firms in the U.S. market. Fujitsu, Japan's largest computer manufacturer, found it almost impossible to break into the competitive U.S. market by itself. Therefore, it formed a marketing joint venture with TRW, to get the marketing know-how and distribution it couldn't get alone.

Joint ventures compare unfavorably with wholly owned operations on only a few, but critical, points. The interests of one partner may conflict with those of the other. The interests of the national partner relate primarily to the operation in the local market. The international firm's interests, on the other hand, relate to the totality of its international operations; actions it takes to further global operations may not appear beneficial from the viewpoint of the national partner. Some points over which conflict arises are (1) transfer pricing, (2) earnings — pay out or plow back, and (3) product-line and market coverage of the joint venture.

Shared equity may also involve an unequal sharing of the burden. Occasionally, international companies with 50-50 joint ventures feel that they are giving more than 50 percent of the technology, management skill, and other factors that contribute to the success of the operation, but receiving only half the profits. Of course, the national partner contributes local knowledge and other intangibles that may be underestimated. Nevertheless, some international companies feel that the local partner gets too much of a "free ride."

The major complaint about joint ventures compared with 100-percent ownership is that it is difficult to integrate them into a synergistic international operation. When the international firm wishes to standardize product design, quality standards or other activities, it may encounter disagreement from its national partners. Thus, where standardization, international exchange, and integration are important to the company, the joint-venture approach can be a hindrance. The U.S. automobile companies and IBM prefer 100-percent ownership for this reason. Conversely, where the national operations have differing product lines and localized marketing — as in packaged foods — joint ventures pose less of a problem.

**Strategic Considerations.**   It is worthwhile noting that marketing considerations play a primary role when international firms evaluate the joint-venture approach. Local market knowledge is usually the foreign firm's major lack when entering a host country. Joining with a national firm may be the best way to obtain the critical local marketing skills and contacts. The national partner can provide quick access through its existing market position. The foreign firm can effectively piggyback with its national partner.

One place where many firms feel the need for such local marketing help is in the difficult Japanese market. A few examples will illustrate this. Morton Thiokol joined with a Japanese firm to be able to sell its air bags to Japanese auto producers. Kodak formed a marketing venture with a Japanese distributor to strengthen its local marketing. Allied Lyons, the British distiller, and Anheuser-Busch each formed a joint venture with Suntory in Japan to sell their liquor and beer there. In each case, the firm made an evaluation that its marketing in Japan wouldn't be effective without a local partner.

Firms coming into the U.S. market also frequently feel the need for an American marketing partner. For example, Volvo, which does its own car marketing in the United States, joined with General Motors for the U.S. truck market. After a lack of success in the U.S. market, Nikko Securities joined with Wells Fargo to build its American business. The benefit for Wells Fargo is a better entry into Japan.

A second major consideration favoring joint-venture entry is oligopolistic competition. In industries characterized by a small number of competitors, the foreign firm may find entry barriers too high for solo entry into

a competitive foreign market. It may need to join with a competing firm —
or a firm in a complementary line — to have a viable presence in the market.
For example, Bols and Heineken formed a joint venture to survive the
European market of 1992. Molson and Elders joined together to maintain
a share of the U.S. beer market. When Coca-Cola joined with Cadbury-
Schweppes in the United Kingdom, Pepsi responded by joining with three
British brewers. In Brazil, Pepsi joined with Brahma, Brazil's largest brewer,
to gain market share against leader Coke.

Two case histories will illustrate contrasting aspects of company philosophy and practice in joint ventures. First consider this statement of the
Scott Paper Company, a firm believer in joint ventures.

> Our foreign policy: Get there early and get married. Scott was an early
> arrival in 15 countries. And our growth overseas is as spectacular as the
> opportunities there. We are across the world from Europe to Latin America
> to Japan. Our markets there are growing faster than at home.
>
> All in all, there are some 500 million people in Scott's markets outside
> the United States. Which means our manufacturing and marketing facil-
> ities now can serve at least 80 percent of the Free World purchasing power.
> The potential is there. And so is Scott.
>
> We're there in an unusual relationship, too, as the 50-50 partner in
> most of our overseas affiliates. Not 51-49. 50-50. That 1 percent we don't
> have has yielded substantial dividends. In mutual trust. In the higher
> caliber of the corporate partners it has brought us in each country. In the
> knowledgeable people *they* bring us. It's a successful marriage if ever we
> heard of one. And the honeymoon has only just begun.

The sad and costly experience of Xerox provides a second example. In
its early years, Xerox Corp. experienced tremendous growth in the United
States market. Faced with difficulty in meeting rapidly growing American
demand, the company felt it could not begin to tackle the rest of the world.
Xerox therefore joined with the Rank Organization in the United Kingdom
to form a 50-50 joint venture, Rank-Xerox (RX). Xerox gave the venture
an exclusive license *in perpetuity* to manufacture and sell all xerographic
machines outside North America.

This was a rather generous gift to the Rank Organization. Most of the
world was its to sell Xerox machines in. As time went by, Xerox realized
that it had been too generous. It had begun to expand capacity and to meet
the demands of the North American market. Now it wanted the ability to
sell its machines in other countries without having to share the profits with
its partner. Since the markets outside North America legally belonged to
the joint venture, Rank-Xerox, Xerox had to buy back the right to market
its own products abroad.

A series of agreements over the years sought to rectify the initial error
made by Xerox in giving away its world markets. In one agreement, RX
*sold* marketing rights for Latin America in return for a 5 percent royalty on
all Xerox sales and rentals there — plus several million dollars of Xerox
stock. Later Xerox paid Rank $12.5 million for the right to name 13 RX
directors to Rank's 12. There were several other adjustments over the years

as Xerox tried to extricate itself from its "original sin." Analysts estimate that the careless entry by Xerox into the RX joint venture would cost Xerox stockholders almost $300 million in its first 20 years.

## Strategic Alliances

Almost every entry method involves an alliance with a partner. It may be an export management company, a distributor, a licensee, or a joint-venture partner. In the 1980s, however, a new term arose to describe a different kind of international cooperative venture. *Strategic alliance* has no precise definition but covers a variety of contractual relationships, frequently between competitors, and frequently between competitors in different countries. For example, Philips links with Siemens, Texas Instruments links with Hitachi, and General Motors links with Toyota. In these and hundreds of other examples, competitors from different countries decide to contract together in some venture that meets a strategic need of each party. Because the relationship does not fit the definition of a licensing arrangement or joint venture, the looser term, "strategic alliance," is used. Some other terms have also been used: international coalitions, competitive alliances, and strategic partnerships.

Strategic alliances have a variety of objectives but a frequent objective is market entry, which is why they are discussed here. Many firms find that a contractual arrangement with a foreign competitor is a better way to enter a market than the traditional distributor, licensee, or joint-venture approach. For example, Harris Corp. allied with Matsushita in Japan and Philips in Europe to distribute PACnet, a data communications product. Unisys and Hewlett-Packard both allied with Canon to distribute microcomputers in Japan. Glaxo contracted with E. Merck to market Zantac in the large German drug market.

Why would a firm help a competitor enter its home market? The answer is that the local firm is getting a new product for its line, one that is complementary rather than directly competitive. Thus, E. Merck has many drugs in its line but no ulcer remedy like Zantac. In effect, market-entry strategic alliances are a form of piggybacking. Stated differently, piggybacking is an early form of strategic alliance. Finally, we should note that though these alliances are called "strategic," every entry method the firm uses should be equally strategic.

## Wholly Owned Foreign Production

Wholly owned foreign production represents the greatest commitment to foreign markets. In principle, "wholly owned" means 100 percent ownership by the international firm. In practice, the firm usually achieves the same results by owning 95 percent or even less. The chief practical criterion for wholly owned ventures is not the completeness of ownership but the completeness of control by the international company. Complete management control is often achieved with something less than 100 percent ownership.

**Make or Buy?**   The international firm can obtain wholly owned foreign production facilities in two ways: (1) it can buy out an existing foreign producer — the acquisition route, or (2) it can develop its own facilities from the ground up. As a variation on the acquisition route, the firm can buy out the equity of a joint venture partner. The acquisition route is especially popular, and it offers certain advantages.

*Acquisition* is a quicker way for a firm to get into a market than building its own facilities. Acquiring a going concern usually means acquiring a qualified labor force along with it. By acquiring an existing concern, a firm also gains national management, local knowledge, and contacts with local markets and government. And in some markets, acquisition may be the only way to enter if the industry has no room for a completely new competitor. The example of a Swedish firm coming into the U.S. market illustrates some of the rationale of the acquisition approach.

[AB] Electrolux is a billion-dollar firm selling consumer and industrial goods. It reentered the U.S. market by acquiring National Union Electric (NUE), a maker of vacuum cleaners and room air conditioners. Electrolux's rationale was as follows:

1. Complementarity of product lines and distribution channels made synergy possible.
2. Immediate access to the U.S. market for many Electrolux products through NUE's network of 37,000 independent dealers.
3. NUE's product line could be carried throughout the world via Electrolux's worldwide marketing organization.

The alternative to acquisition is the *establishment of a new facility,* a method that may be desirable or necessary in certain circumstances. For example, in some markets, the international firm will not be able to find a national producer willing to sell, or else the local government will not allow the firm to sell to the international company. In other markets, producers may be willing to sell but lack the caliber of facilities needed by the technology of the international firm.

For its part, the international firm may prefer a new facility to an acquisition. If the target market has no personnel or management shortages, the firm feels less pressure toward the acquisition route. Furthermore, if the firm builds a new plant, it can not only incorporate the latest technology and equipment, it can also avoid the problems of trying to change the traditional practices of an established concern. A new facility means a fresh start and an opportunity for the international company to shape the local firm into its own image and requirements.

Xomox, for example, a small American-based multinational, believes in starting foreign manufacturing entirely on its own in preference to acquiring an established facility. It believes acquisitions can lead to resentment on the part of local management and workers. Also, through going it alone, the firm can show its contributions to the local economy — jobs, exports, investments — that were not there before it came.

**Deciding on Solo Operations.**    Evaluation of the sole-ownership approach to foreign markets is easier now that we have considered the other alternatives. The advantages of wholly owned ventures are few but powerful.

Ownership of 100 percent means 100 percent of the profits go to the international firm, eliminating the possibility of a national partner's getting a "free ride." Complete ownership also permits the international firm to acquire greater experience in international operations and better market contact.

With no national partner, no inefficiencies arise from conflicts of interest. Perhaps the overriding argument for complete control, however, is the possibility of integrating various national operations into a synergistic international system. Lesser degrees of involvement are likely to lead to suboptimization, as national partners have goals that conflict with those of the international firm.

The limitations to the 100 percent ownership approach are several. For one thing, it is costly in terms of capital and management resources. The capital requirements prevent many firms from practicing a complete ownership strategy. Although very large firms do not often find capital availability a constraint, they may face a shortage of management personnel.

One of America's largest companies (in Fortune's top 20) conducted all of its international business via exports and licensing for many years. Management decided that an equity approach would mean greater long-run profits. The company began to implement this decision, but progress was very slow. The impediment was not a lack of capital but a shortage of company managers with the necessary international experience. The company also had problems locating desirable firms to acquire. It had begun the equity approach a bit late in the game.

Another drawback to 100 percent ownership is the probable negative host-government and public-relations effect. Most nations feel their participation in the venture should not be limited to supplying just labor or raw materials. Some governments go so far as to prohibit 100 percent ownership by the international firm and demand licensing or joint ventures instead. A further risk deriving from these national feelings is expropriation, which is much more likely and more costly with wholly owned operations. The firm has more to lose because it has more eggs in one basket.

Finally, 100 percent ownership may deprive the firm of the local knowledge and contacts of a national partner. The local collaborator often would serve as a buffer between the international firm and its various national audiences. This role of the national partner as a cultural bridge can be its major contribution, helping the firm to avoid mistakes in its encounters with nationals in business or government. By taking the acquisition route, the firm has more chance of retaining such nationals than it does in setting up a new operation. The same applies to a wholly owned operation developed from a joint venture. With a new establishment the firm can develop nationals who can be a culture bridge, but the process is slow compared with other kinds of involvement.

## Conclusions on Foreign-Market Entry Methods

In this chapter, we discussed many methods of foreign market entry, noting the advantages and disadvantages of each. We cannot say that there is one best way to enter a foreign market. The way best for the firm depends not

**Table 10–4**  **International Flows by Level of Involvement**

| Type of Foreign Operation | Flow of Goods and Materials | | | | | | Flow of Financial Capital | | | | | | | Flow of Physical Capital | | | Flow of Human Capital | |
|---|---|---|---|---|---|---|---|---|---|---|---|---|---|---|---|---|---|---|
| Indirect export | X[a] | | | | X[a] | | X[a] | | | | | | | | | | | |
| Direct export | X | | | | X | | X | | | | | | | | | X | | |
| Own export (Marketing subsidiary) | X | | | X[c] | X | | X | | | X | X | X | X | | X | X | | X |
| Licensing | | | | | | | | X | X | | | | | X[d] | X[d] | X | X | X |
| Contract manufacturing | | | | | | | X | | | | | | | X[d] | X[d] | X[d] | | |
| Co-production | | | | | | | | | X | | | | | X | X | X | | X |
| Own assembling | X[b] | X | X | | | | X | X | | X | X | X | X | X | X | X | | X |
| Own manufacturing | X[b] | X | X | | | X | X | X | X[b] | X | X | X | X | X | X | X | X[b] | X |

[a] If the middleman in the home country is a buying middleman, the different flows in the first stage of operation take place in the home country.

[b] May be included as a suboperation or as a supplementary operation.

[c] Easily assembled parts may be assembled in a sales outlet.

[d] May be included in the contract.

Source: Reijo Luostarinen, *Foreign Operations of the Firm* (Helsinki, Finland: Helsinki School of Economics, 1975), 10.

only on its own size, capabilities, and needs, but also on the opportunities and conditions in the target markets. The firm must analyze its own situation, considering how the variables discussed here apply. A careful analysis of alternatives should lead to more optimal results than merely responding to initiatives coming from outside the firm, which is the way many firms have carried on their international business.

Earlier in this chapter, we presented a matrix relating the various entry methods to some of the principal decision variables (see Table 10–1). Now that we have discussed the nature of the different approaches, another matrix may be helpful. Table 10–4 distinguishes among the entry methods according to the various flows involved (goods, money, equipment, and so on). This matrix, developed by Reijo Luostarinen, is a useful way of summarizing many of the operational differences among the levels of involvement.

Flexibility is an important aspect of the firm's choice of entry strategy. Rather than rigidly following a single approach, the firm may want variation, depending on conditions within its different markets. Larger markets may permit more direct approaches, whereas smaller markets may be better served by less direct entry. In some firms, it may be appropriate to use different entry strategies for different product lines or divisions. Flexibility over time is also a major consideration. As conditions change, the optimum strategy may change. The firm can gain only by anticipating developments and adapting to them, rather than fighting against them. One such development is the desire of most nations for licensing or joint ventures rather than 100 percent ownership by the international firm. Finding creative answers to such developments is the key to the viability of the international corporation. The following two examples show how strategies change over time.

Weyerhaeuser set up its own sales offices in Europe, South America, Australia, and the Far East. This was a departure from the traditional policy of U.S. forest products companies to sell overseas only in conditions of excess supply or when overseas prices were higher than domestic. Weyerhaeuser committed to foreign markets permanently when exports topped 8 percent of company sales. By 1989, exports reached $1.5 billion and the company was among America's top 20 exporters, the only firm in its industry in the top 50.

A large European chemical company had a five-stage strategy in its approach to foreign markets:

- *Stage 1.* Limited sales, a form of market testing, through trading companies or independent distributors who bought for their own account.
- *Stage 2.* Where markets looked promising, the company sent field representatives to aid the distributor. This was done in Nigeria and East Africa, for example.
- *Stage 3.* Where the field representatives reported strong sales possibilities in a sizeable market, the company moved to establish its own sales organization.
- *Stage 4.* If the company sales subsidiary developed the market to a highly profitable degree, the company considered plant investment. The first step was a compounding or assembly plant to mix and package ingredients imported from Europe. Two examples of this are Brazil and Mexico.
- *Stage 5.* The final step is a complete manufacturing plant. Such a plant might produce only a few of the many products of the firm depending on local raw material supply and markets. The company has such a plant in India.

## Level of Involvement — A Two-Way Street

The normal progression of the firm in world markets is from exporting to heavier kinds of involvement, usually ending up with wholly owned manufacturing operations abroad, as with the European chemical company just cited. Indeed, that is the history of most multinationals — a life cycle pattern of international involvement. However, just as life cycles have a decline phase, so the firm's involvement in a market may undergo retrenchment and a regression to lesser kinds of involvement. The extreme case would be where expropriation or other political action forces the firm to leave wholly owned operations and have nothing left in the country, such as in Cuba or Iran. More common is the situation where changes in a market or in the firm's position there cause a strategic reassessment. The factors that made the firm seek a certain level of involvement may have changed or the firm may not have been successful in maintaining that involvement, so the appropriate strategy is to accept a lesser involvement in the market.

It should be noted that such strategic withdrawals or retreats are not necessarily defeats. They are often merely the more sensible business response to a new situation. Just as discretion may be the better part of valor in some military situations, so may strategic changes of involvement be the most profitable response of the firm to certain problems in foreign markets. A few examples will illustrate some of these situations:

1.   Bulova, a strong international marketer of traditional watches, was being buffeted by the new electronic and quartz watches. Losses overseas caused Bulova to change from its own marketing subsidiaries to less expensive independent agents.
2.   Unilever is one of the most powerful multinationals. In Mexico, Unilever had wholly owned production facilities for soaps and detergents. Severe competition from Colgate, Procter & Gamble, and La Corona (a Mexican firm) prevented satisfactory profits for Unilever. The company decided to sell its factory, maintain a marketing subsidiary, and contract manufacture its product with La Corona.
3.   Several American firms had wholly owned operations in the Japanese market. After several years of unsatisfactory performance, they changed to joint ventures with Japanese partners. They needed the cultural bridge to help them in the misunderstood Japanese market.

## Summary

Firms with limited resources can find quick and easy entry to foreign markets through indirect exporting. They can make a domestic sale to companies with buying offices in the United States. These buyers may be foreign retail groups, foreign trade organizations, or corporations supplying foreign subsidiaries from the United States.

Export management companies (EMCs) are another form of indirect exporting, but they are specialized intermediaries who sell their export marketing services. This is a low-cost way to obtain the use of an export department without setting one up in the firm. They offer instant market access as well as economies of scale by serving several producers. These miniversions of a foreign trading company are used by thousands of American firms.

Another way to get economies of scale in exporting is by joining with other producers. One form of such legal cooperation is the Webb-Pomerene association, which act as the exporting arm of their members and are used primarily by agriculture and commodity groups. The new American export trading companies (ETCs) offer another form of cooperation. They are meant to be more powerful than the EMCs and emulate the Japanese trading companies, but they have had very limited success thus far. Piggybacking is a form of cooperation between two producers wherein one carries the other's product(s) to export markets. This is a popular form of exporting because the rider gets instant, inexpensive export marketing while the carrier gets a complementary product to round out its line.

Direct exporting, where the firm does the whole exporting job in-house, is much more demanding than indirect exporting. There are greater personnel, administrative, and financial requirements. The firm itself must choose its foreign markets, find representatives in those markets, arrange the logistics, and then try to manage its foreign marketing, working through independent distributors.

When foreign production is desired, assembly in foreign markets is a compromise approach. It is a blend of exporting and local production as the firm ships parts or ingredients from home which are then processed locally. It reduces transport and tariff costs and helps the firm respond better to local needs.

Contract manufacturing allows the firm to produce abroad without plant investment by contracting to use a local firm's production facilities. It saves on transport and tariff costs and avoids local investment and labor problems. It is useful when governments/customers favor local supply.

Working with a licensee avoids any major commitment to a foreign market. The local licensee produces *and* markets the firm's product. It gives the advantages of local supply at low cost, but a disadvantage is that it limits the control and returns of the firm. What's more, it may mean training a competitor.

Joint ventures — producing and marketing abroad with a local partner — can be an effective market entry. In addition to the advantages of local production, the firm may gain local market knowledge and contacts as well as potential conflicts. Joint venturing is more costly than other forms of entry except for wholly owned operations. Today, looser forms of partnering, called *strategic alliances,* are popular. These contractual, nonequity links may offer some of the advantages of joint venturing but with a lesser commitment.

Wholly owned operations involve the greatest commitment to a foreign market. In return for this commitment the firm receives complete control, greater international integration, and usually greater profits, but also greater exposure to foreign problems. Wholly owned operations can start with a new establishment or by acquiring a local firm. Acquisitions are currently very popular as they allow quicker entry and an established market position. They may also be necessary in markets that have no room for completely new entrants.

## Questions

10.1   Explain market feedback, investment requirements, and exposure to foreign problems as variables in choosing an entry method to foreign markets.

10.2   Identify the ways to reach foreign markets by making a domestic sale.

10.3   Why do international trading companies offer the best entry to some markets?

10.4   Why might a small new-to-export company be interested in using an export management company?

10.5   How can the carrier and the rider both benefit from a piggyback arrangement?

10.6   When a firm begins direct exporting, what tasks must it perform?

10.7   "When exporting to a market, you're only as good as your distributor there." Discuss.

10.8   What procedures should a firm follow in se-
       lecting a distributor?

10.9   What are the benefits to local manufacture
       as a form of market entry? What are the
       costs?

10.10  "Foreign assembly represents a compromise
       between exporting and local production."
       Discuss.

10.11  When is contract manufacturing desirable?

10.12  What are the pros and cons of licensing as
       a form of market entry?

10.13  How do successful licensors manage their li-
       censing program?

10.14  Why is acquisition often the preferred way
       to establish wholly owned operations
       abroad?

## Endnotes

[1]John J. Brasch, "Export Management Companies," *Journal of International Business Studies* (Spring–Summer 1978): 59–72.

[2]Farok J. Contractor, "The Profitability of Technology Licensing by U.S. Multinationals," *Journal of International Business Studies* (Fall 1980): 40.

[3]*Business Asia,* July 18, 1988, 231.

## Further Readings

Bello, Daniel C., and Nicholas Williamson. "Contractual Arrangements and Marketing Practices in the Indirect Export Channel." *Journal of International Business Studies* (Summer, 1985): 65–82.

Bilkey, Warren J. "Development of Export Marketing Guidelines." *International Marketing Review* (Spring 1985): 31–40.

Contractor, Farok J. *Licensing in International Strategy.* Westport, Conn.: Quorum Books, 1985.

Goodnow, James D. "Developments in International Mode of Entry Analysis." *International Marketing Review* (Autumn 1985): 17–30.

Hall, R. Duane, and Ralph Gilbert. *Multinational Distribution: Channel, Tax, and Legal Strategies.* New York: Praeger, 1985.

Howard, Donald G., and James M. Maskulka. "Will American Export Trading Companies Replace Export Management Companies?" *International Marketing Review* (Winter 1988): 41–50.

Rosson, Philip J. and Stanley D. Reid. *Managing Export Entry and Expansion.* New York: Praeger, 1987.

Sarathy, Ravi. "Japanese Trading Companies: Can They Be Copied?" *Journal of International Business Studies* (Summer 1985): 101–120.

Shipley, David, David Cook, and Eileen Barnett. "Recruitment, Motivation, Training and Evaluation of Overseas Distributors." *European Journal of Marketing* 23, no. 2 (1989), 79–93.

# 10.1 BMW: Marketing Subsidiaries in Foreign Markets

BMW is a German manufacturer of quality motor cars. About half of its sales are in the German market, with the other half from exports outside Germany. In reappraising its marketing and distribution strategy both in Germany and abroad, the company felt that its multiple layers of distribution were causing inefficiencies in its marketing efforts.

## BMW Germany

Originally, BMW had a dual distribution system in Germany. It employed a strong wholesaler system along with direct distribution by BMW to large dealers. This system seemed to work effectively, because BMW's market share in Germany doubled in ten years. However, the company found severe competitive distortions with this dual approach. For example, the wholesalers who received the same commission for wholesale transactions as for retail sales had gone into direct competition with retailers. The larger direct dealers sometimes sold more than the wholesalers but received the smaller dealer discount. The problems arising from BMW's distribution strategy caused the company to abolish its German wholesaler network. BMW expanded its direct dealer system to replace the business formerly handled by the wholesalers.

## BMW Abroad

The company was planning to initiate a more direct selling method in its foreign markets as well as at home. It realized the need for care in order not to disturb existing import channels. However, the company felt that it was desirable to replace the present independent importers in foreign markets with company-owned marketing subsidiaries. The independent importers buy the cars from Germany and then resell to accredited dealers — who sell them to the public. In moving to company-owned marketing subsidiaries, BMW was following the international marketing approach of Volkswagen and Daimler-Benz (with Mercedes). One of the major arguments presented for going direct was that BMW could save the 15 percent commission the company paid to its importer distributors in foreign markets.

## France

In line with its new policy of more direct distribution in foreign markets, BMW formed its first marketing subsidiary in France. BMW Import SA replaced the former independent French importer (which had been called BMW France but now was renamed SFAM France). SFAM France continued to sell BMW cars to *consumers* through its retail outlets in Paris and in the provinces. Sales to *dealers* henceforth were made only by BMW Import SA, the company's wholly owned marketing subsidiary. It is too early to evaluate the results of this changeover in France.

## United States

In implementing its new direct marketing approach in the U.S. market, BMW faced two alternatives. It could either take over its present American importer-distributor or establish a new and separate BMW marketing subsidiary as was done in France. The company wondered which of these alternatives would be best for the important U.S. market. BMW had about 250 dealers in the United States.

## Questions

1. Do you see any potential problems or disadvantages for BMW in going to direct distribution in foreign markets?
2. What advantages might the company realize by operating through its own marketing subsidiaries?

3. In making the decision for the U.S. market, what questions would you ask? What variables would you consider?

CASE

# 10.2 Metro Corporation: Technology Licensing Negotiation

Negotiations between Metro Corporation and Impecina Construcciones S.A. of Peru, for the licensing of Petroleum Tank Technology:

## 1. The Licensor Firm

Metro Corporation is a diversified steel rolling, fabricating and construction company based in the midwest and considers itself to be in a mature industry. Innovations are few and far between. With transport and tariff barriers, and the support given by many governments to their own companies, exporting as a means of doing foreign business is rather limited. Similarly, given the large investment, modest return and political sensitivity of the industry, direct foreign investment is all but a closed option. In a global strategic sense then, Metro Corporation has far more frequently focused on licensing as a market entry method, with technologies confined to a) processes and engineering peripheral to the basic steel making process, e.g., mining methods, coke oven door designs, galvanizing, etc., and b) applications of steel in construction and other industries, e.g., petroleum tank design, welding methods, thermo-adhesion, etc.

All Metro's licensing is handled by its international division, International Construction

and Engineering (ICE) which is beginning to develop a reputation in Western Europe and South America as a good source for specialized construction technology.

## 2. The Proposed Licensee

Impecina, a private firm, is the largest construction company in Peru and operates throughout Latin America. Impecina has a broad range of interests including residential and commercial buildings, hydraulic works, transportation, and maritime works. Employing several thousand personnel, engineers and technicians, its sales had doubled in the last five years. It was still primarily a Peruvian business with most turnover in Peru, but was in the process of expanding into Colombia, the North African Mediterranean countries, and Argentina, Brazil and Venezuela. Impecina has advanced computer capacity with a large IBM and other computers at their branches. In oil-storage tanks, Impecina experience was limited to the smaller fixed-cone roof designs under 150 feet diameter.

## 3. The Technology

National Tank Inc., a fabrication division of Metro, had designed a computerized design procedure for floating-roof oil storage tanks, which minimized the use of steel within American Petroleum Institute or any other oil industry standards. Particularly for the larger tanks, for in-

Source: This case was prepared by Professor Farok Contractor, Rutgers University, as a basis for class discussion rather than to illustrate either effective or ineffective handling of an administrative situation. Copyright © by Farok J. Contractor. Used with permission.

stance 150 feet diameter and above, this would confer upon the bidding contractor a significant cost advantage. National Tank had spent one man-year, at a direct cost of $225,000, to write the computer program alone. Patents were involved in an incidental manner, only for the seals on the floating roof. Metro had not bothered to file for this patent except in the U.S.

## 4. The Market

Peru's indigenous oil output is very low, but it imports and refines annually 50 million tons mostly for domestic demand. Following the escalation of oil prices and tightening of supplies in 1973, the Peruvian government determinedly set about to formulate a program to augment Peru's oil-storage capacity. Impecina's representatives, at a preliminary meeting with ICE in U.S. headquarters, said their government planned $200 million expenditures on oil storage facilities, over the next three years (mostly in large sized tanks). Of this, Impecina's "ambition" was to capture a one-third market share. That this appeared to be a credible target was illustrated by their existing 30% share of the "fixed-cone type under 150 feet diameter". Additionally, they estimated private sector construction value over the next three years to total $40 million.

Approximately half of a storage systems construction cost goes for the tank alone, the remainder being excavation, foundation, piping, instrumentation and other ancillary equipment, all of which Impecina's engineers were very familiar with.

Neighboring Colombia was building a twelve million ton refinery, but the tank installation plans of other South American nations were not known according to the Impecina representative.

Each of Impecina's competitors in Peru, for this business, was affiliated with a prominent company; Umbertomas with Jefferson Inc. in the United States, Zapa with Philadelphia Iron & Steel, Cosmas with Peoria-Duluth Construction Inc., and so on. Thus association with Metro would help Impecina in bidding.

## 5. The First Meeting

National Tank Division had in the past year bid jointly with Impecina on a project in southern Peru. Though that bid was unsuccessful, Impecina had learned about Metro's computerized design capabilities and initiated a formal first round of negotiations which were to lead to a licensing agreement. The meeting took place in the United States. Two Impecina executives of Sub-Director rank were accompanied by an American consultant. Metro was represented by the Vice-President of ICE, the ICE attorney and an executive from National Tank Division.

Minutes of this meeting show it was exploratory. Both genuine and rhetorical questions were asked. Important information and perceptions were exchanged and the groundwork laid for concluding negotiations. Following is a bare summary of important issues gleaned from the somewhat circular discussion:

a) *Licensee Market Coverage:* Impecina tried to represent itself as essentially a Peruvian firm. They reviewed their governments expenditure plans and their hoped-for market share. Yet through the meeting, there kept cropping up the issue of the license also covering Libya, Algeria, Morocco, Colombia, Argentina, Brazil and Venezuela.

b) *Exclusivity:* For Peru, Metro negotiators had no difficulty conceding exclusivity. They mentioned that granting exclusivity to a licensee for any territory was agreeable in principle, provided a minimum performance guarantee was given. At this, the question was deferred for future discussion. At one point a Metro executive remarked, "We could give Impecina a non-exclusive — and say for example, we wouldn't give another (licensee) a license for one year (in those nations)", proposing the idea of a trial period for Impecina to generate business in a territory.

c) *Agreement Life:* Impecina very quickly agreed to a ten year term, payment in U.S. dollars, and other minor issues.

d) *Trade Name:* The Impecina negotiators placed great emphasis on their ability to use the

Metro name in bidding, explaining how their competition in Peru had technical collaboration with three U.S. companies (see above).

"Did that mean Metro's National Tank Division could compete with Impecina in Peru?" they were asked rhetorically. (Actually both sides seem to have tacitly agreed that it was not possible for Metro to do business directly in Peru.)

e) *Licensee Market Size:* Attention turned to the dollar value of the future large (floating-roof) tank market in Peru. Impecina threw out an estimate of $200 million government expenditures and $40 million private-sector spending, over the coming three years, of which they targeted a one-third share. Later, a lower market size estimate of $150 million (government *and* private) with a share of $50 million received by Impecina over three years, was arrived at (memories are not clear on how the estimates were revised). "Will Impecina guarantee us they will obtain one-third of the market?" brought the response "That's an optimistic figure but we hope we can realize." Impecina offered as evidence their existing one-third share of the "fixed roof under 150 feet" market, an impressive achievement.

f) *Product-Mix Covered By License:* It became clear that Impecina wanted floating-roof technology for *all* sizes, *and* fixed-roof over 100 feet diameter. They suggested the agreement cover tanks over 100 feet in size. "Would Impecina pay on all tanks (of any size)" to simplify royalty calculation and monitoring? After considerable discussion, Metro seems to have acceded to Impecina's proposal (to cover both types, only over 100 feet) based on consensus over three points.

1. The competition probably does not pay (their licensors) on small tanks and therefore Impecina would be at a disadvantage if they had to pay on small tanks also.

2. The market in floating-roof tanks was over 100 feet anyway, usually.

3. Impecina claimed that customers normally dictate the dimensions of the tanks, so Impecina cannot vary them in order to avoid paying a royalty to Metro.

g) *Compensation Formula:* Metro proposed an initial lump-sum payment (in two installments, one when the agreement is signed, the second on delivery of the computer program and designs), *plus* engineers and executives for bid assistance on a per diem rate, *plus* a royalty on successful bids based on the barrel capacity installed by Impecina. Impecina's American consultant countered with the idea of royalties on a sliding scale, lower with larger capacity tanks, indicating talk about "one million barrel capacity tanks." The (rhetorical?) question, "What is Peru's oil capacity?" seems to have brought the discussion down to earth and veered it off on a tangent, while both sides mentally regrouped.

On returning to this topic, Impecina executives on being asked, ventured that as a rule of thumb, their profit markup on a turn-key job was 6%. (However on excluding the more price-sensitive portions such as excavation, piping and ancillary equipment, which typically constitute half the value, Impecina conceded that on the tank alone they might markup as much as 12%, although they kept insisting 5–6% was enough.)

Impecina executives later offered only royalties (preferably sliding) *and* per-diem fees for bid assistance from Metro executives and engineers.

Metro countered by pointing out that per-diem fees of say $225 plus travel costs, amounted at best to recovering costs, not profit.

The compensation design question was left at this stage, deferred for later negotiation, the broad outlines having been laid. Metro's starting formal offer, which would mention specific numbers, was to be telexed to Lima in a week.

h) The *Royalty Basis:* Metro entertained the idea that Impecina engineers were very familiar with excavation, piping wiring, and other ancillary equipment. Metro was transferring technology *for the tank alone,* which typically comprised half of overall installed value.

i) *Government Intervention:* Toward the end of the discussions, Impecina brought up the question of the Peruvian government having to approve of the agreement. This led to their retreat from the idea of a ten year term, agreed to earlier, and Impecina then mentioned five years. No agreement was reached. (Incidentally, Peru had in the last two years passed legislation indicating a "guideline" of five years for foreign licenses.)

# 6. Internal Discussion in Metro Leading to the Formal Offer

The advantages derived by the licensee would be acquisition of floating-roof technology, time and money saved in attempting to generate the computerized design procedure in-house, somewhat of a cost and efficiency advantage in bidding on larger tanks, and finally the use of Metro's name.

a) It was estimated that National Tank division had spent $225,000 (one man-year = two executives for six months, plus other costs) in developing the computer program. Additionally, it may cost $ 40,000 (three-quarters of a man-year) to convert the program into Spanish, the metric system, and adapt it to the material availability and labor cost factors peculiar to Peru. Simultaneously, there would be semi-formal instruction of Impecina engineers in the use of the program, petroleum industry codes and Metro fabrication methods. All this had to be done before the licensee would be ready for a single bid.

b) It was visualized that Metro would then assist Impecina for two man-weeks for each bid preparation, and four man-weeks on successful receipt of a contract award. Additionally, if Metro's specialized construction equipment were used, three man-months of on-site training would be needed.

As the licensee's personnel moved along their learning curve, assistance of the type described in paragraph (b) would diminish until it was no longer needed after a few successful bids.

Additional considerations that went into a determination of the initial offer:

i) Metro obligations (and sunk costs) under paragraph (a) above were fairly determinate, whereas its obligations under (b) depended on the technical sophistication and absorbtive capacity of the licensee's engineers, their success rate in bidding and so on.

ii) If Impecina's market estimates were used, over the next three years, they would generate large tank orders worth $50 million, on which they would make a profit of $3 million (at 6% on $50 million or 12% on half the amount.)

iii) The market beyond three years was an unknown.

iv) Exclusive rights might be given to Impecina in Peru and Colombia, with perhaps ICE reserving the right of conversion to non-exclusive if minimum market share was not captured.

v) While Impecina's multinational expansion plans were unknown, their business in the other nations was too small to justify granting them exclusivity. They may be satisfied with a vague promise of future consideration as exclusive licensees in those territories.

vi) Metro would try for an agreement term of ten years. It was felt that Impecina computer and engineering capability was strong enough so they would not need Metro assistance after a few bids.

Surprisingly, the discussions reveal no explicit consideration given to the idea that Impecina may emerge some day as a multinational competitor.

In view of the uncertainty about how successful the licensee would actually be in securing orders, the uncertainty surrounding the Peruvian government's attitude, a safe strategy seemed to be to try and get as large a front-end fee as possible. Almost arbitrarily, a figure of $400,000 was thrown up. (This was roughly 150% the development costs plus the initial costs of transferring the technology to the licensee). There would be sufficient margin for negotiations and to cover uncertainties. In order that the licensee's competitiveness not be diminished by the large lump-sum fee, a formula may be devised whereby the first five years' royalties could be reduced. (See below.)

# 7. The Formal Offer

The formal offer communicated in a telex a week later called for the following payment terms:

• $400,000 lump-sum fee payable in two installments,

• A 2% royalty on any tanks constructed of a size over 100 feet diameter, with up to one half of royalties owed in each of the first five years reduced by an amount up to $40,000 each year, without carryovers from year to year. The royalty % would apply to the total contract value less excavation, foundation, dikes, piping, instrumentation, and pumps.

• Agreement life of ten years.

• Metro to provide services to Impecina described in paragraph 6(a) above, in consideration of the lump-sum and royalty fees.

• For additional services, described in 6(b) above, Metro would provide on request, personnel at up to $225 per day, plus travel and living costs while away from their place of business. The per diem rates would be subject to escalation based on a representative cost index. There would be a ceiling placed on the number of mandays Impecina could request in any year.

• All payments to be made in U.S. dollars, net after all local witholding, and other taxes.

• Impecina would receive exclusive rights for Peru and Colombia only, and non-exclusive rights for Morocco, Libya, Algeria, Argentina, Venezuela, Brazil and Colombia. These could be converted to an exclusive basis on demonstration of sufficient business in the future. For Peru and Colombia, Metro reserves the right to treat the agreement as non-exclusive if Impecina fails to get at least 30% of installed capacity of a type covered by the agreement.

• Impecina would have the right to sub-license only to any of its controlled subsidiaries.

• Impecina would supply free of charge to ICE all improvements made by it on the technology, during the term of the agreement.

• Impecina wold be entitled to advertise its association with Metro in assigned territories, on prior approval of ICE as to wording, form, and content.

## 8. The Final Agreement

ICE executives report that the Peruvians "did not bat an eyelid" at their demands, and that an agreement was soon reached in a matter of weeks. The only significant change was Metro agreeing to take a lump sum of $300,000 (still a large margin over costs). In return, the provision for reducing one half of the royalties up to $40,000 per year was *dropped*. The final arrangement called for a straight 2% royalty payment (on tank valve alone, as before). Other changes were minor: Impecina to continue to receive benefit of further R & D; ICE to provide, at cost, a construction engineer if specialized welding equipment was used; the per-diem fee fixed at $200 per day (indexed by an average hourly wage escalation factor used by the U.S. Department of Labor); and the $300,000 lump-sum fee to be paid in installments over the first year.

In other respects such as territory, royalty rate, exclusivity, travel allowances, etc., the agreement conformed with Metro's initial offer.

## 9. An Upset

The Peruvian government disallowed a ten year agreement life. By then, both parties had gone too far to want to reopen the entire negotiations and Metro appears to have resigned itself to an agreement life of five years, with a further extension of another five years subject to mutual consent. Given Impecina's in-house engineering and computer capability, extension of the agreement life was a very open question.

## Questions

Analyze the negotiations from each party's perspective:

1. List what each party is offering and what it hopes to receive.

2. Identify the elements in each list that are "musts" and those on which flexibility may be shown, and state why.

3. Compute net cash flows for each party under several scenarios. For example:

Licensee fails to get a single order; licensee gets one-third market share in Peru for three years, no orders thereafter, and no orders in any other nation; licensee gets one-third share in Peru for ten years and half again as much in business in other nations; and so forth.

In computing the licensor's cash flows, remember that, in addition to the direct costs of implementing an agreement, there are sometimes substantial indirect costs. What are they? How would you apply the licensor's development costs to this exercise?

What do you think of the rule-of-thumb, encountered in licensing literature, that licensors should settle for roughly one-quarter to one-half of the licensee's incremental profit? Describe negotiating tactics or ploys each party did or could have used. Discuss the role of government intervention in licensing negotiations in general.

# CHAPTER 11

# Distribution
## Foreign Market Channels and Global Logistics

Once a firm has arranged for its products to be available in a foreign market, it must discover and manage the distribution channels to the final customers there. In this chapter we consider the major elements in managing foreign channels.

The main goals of this chapter are to

1. Discuss how exporters, who market through foreign distributors, can influence distributors to be effective marketing partners.
2. Discuss the ways in which wholesalers and retailers can differ internationally, requiring adjustment by the international marketer.
3. Note some major distribution trends that should be monitored by the international marketer.
4. Explore some of the questions a firm must answer in regard to marketing through foreign channels: Should the firm duplicate its domestic approach? Should it use direct or indirect channels, selective or intensive distribution? How should it work with the channel? How can it keep distribution up-to-date?
5. Explain how a firm can discover appropriate logistics patterns within a given foreign market and between multiple markets and determine its use of facilities and technology in those markets.

The preceding chapter considered one question facing the international marketer: How do I get my products into foreign markets? We saw that there are many alternative answers — and combinations of answers — to that question. Once the firm has chosen a strategy to get its products *into* foreign markets, its next challenge is distribution of the product *within* foreign markets. Our first topic in this chapter, therefore, will be the management of foreign distribution; our second topic will be the management of international logistics.

# Managing Foreign Distribution

Some firms who sell in foreign markets do not have the task of managing distribution within those markets. For them, this question was resolved, for better or for worse, when they decided on their method of entry. Firms that sell through trading companies, export management companies, or other indirect methods must accept the foreign distribution offered by these intermediaries. The same is true for those that sell through licensing, and generally, for those engaged in direct exporting. The firms having direct responsibility for their foreign-market distribution are those having marketing subsidiaries or complete manufacturing and marketing operations there. Having responsibility is different, of course, from having complete control. For example, the manager in a joint venture is constrained by the desires of the national partner. The wholly owned venture that resulted from an acquisition will also find its distribution options affected by the practices inherited from the acquired firm.

The first step in managing foreign distribution is to identify the firm's *goals* in the foreign market. The marketing program, including distribution, is a means toward achieving those goals. Then the international marketer must identify the specific *tasks* to be performed by the channel in that market. What role is the channel expected to play — inventory, promotion, credit extension, physical distribution, service? Finally, the marketer must try to match this job description with the channel possibilities available in the market. There will seldom be a perfect match between the firm's specifications and what is available in the market. Many factors will be beyond the control of the marketer, so compromise will often be necessary.

We begin by considering how exporters can manage foreign distribution. Although they work through independent distributors abroad, export managers can have an impact on the foreign marketing of their products.

# Marketing through Distributors in Foreign Markets

Direct exporting through distributors abroad is the major form of international marketing. It is the best method of reaching foreign markets for the thousands of smaller firms in every exporting country who lack the resources for a greater commitment. It is also an important form of international marketing for large multinationals who do not have their own production and/or marketing presence in all of their global markets — and most do not.

The international marketer's success in export markets will depend largely on the performance of the independent distributors it uses there. The challenge, then, is, "How can we get the distributor to do a good job for us?" The key is to make the relationship continually rewarding to the distributor as well as to the international marketer. In addition, distributors should be carefully selected, the distributing agreement carefully drawn up, and various types of marketing support offered.

**Initial
Distributor
Selection**

In distributor selection, as in marriage, choosing the right partner is the major factor in the success of the relationship. We discussed distributor selection earlier under market entry, but we shall note a few other items here. First, careful specification of what is wanted from the distributor will help a firm choose the most suitable candidate. Not all distributor candidates in a country will match a firm's specifications equally well.

Second, the firm should evaluate the distributor's track record. Past performance is the best predictor of future behavior and this can be determined in part by talking with other clients who have worked with this distributor over the years.

Third, the firm should try to ascertain whether its product line will be a reasonably important share of the distributor's business. The more important it is to the distributor, the better treatment its products will receive. Avery International tries to account for at least 10 percent of its distributors' business.

**Distributor
Agreement**

The distributor agreement is a legal document that should spell out the responsibilities and interests of each party, protecting both. Careful preparation of such an agreement and reviewing it with the distributor should help to minimize later misunderstandings. Though it is a legal document, the agreement is too important to be left to the lawyers. Managers from both sides should review it and agree on its provisions. Finally, the contract should be a "living" document that can adjust to new circumstances so that the relationship can grow beyond the original agreement.

**Financial
and Pricing
Considerations**

The distributor wants to make as much money as possible and work as conveniently as possible. The firm's use of financial and pricing variables will affect the distributor's ability to reach those goals. For example, the international marketer must determine what *margins or commissions* are needed to motivate the distributor. Should the firm just match the competition, or are higher margins needed to break into the market or to overcome competitive disadvantages? Conversely, the firm may offer lower margins because of competitive strengths in its total offering — a form of nonprice competition. The same questions apply to *credit terms*. Does the firm need to be generous on credit to break into the market or merely competitive?

The firm's use of *price quotations* will also have an effect. For example, the distributor would generally prefer a *c.i.f. quote* (cost, insurance, and freight) to an *f.o.b. plant quote* (free-on-board plant). The c.i.f. quote gives a clearer picture of landed cost and also means less work and responsibility for the distributor. (See our later discussion on pricing for more details on price quotes.)

A second aspect of export pricing is *choice of currency* for the quotation. The distributor generally prefers a quote in the currency of its country rather than a quote in U.S. dollars. This facilitates the accounting and eliminates foreign exchange exposure for the distributor.

# Global Marketing
## Globalizing Retailers

Though distribution problems and local cultures stand in the way, some retailers flourish in foreign markets. Take Ikea, a privately owned Swedish furniture retailer, which has 83 stores in 20 countries. The company's next target market is Eastern Europe.

Delhaize, a Belgian food retailer, is another successful internationalist. It has been opening 100 supermarkets a year for the past couple of years in America — it now has close to 600 stores. Thanks to this expansion it has increased earnings by 30 percent a year. Around 80 percent of Delhaize's annual profits now come from America.

Ahold, a Dutch food retailer, has a better balance. It has broken into the ranks of the top ten American food retailers and earns 40 percent of its 190 million guilder ($85 million) post-tax profits there. Ahold has also taken tentative steps to link up with two other European food retailers, Argyll, a British supermarket chain, and Casino, a French chain. Such an alliance could produce savings from pooling purchasing power and even the possibility of joint brands and joint takeovers.

Some of the biggest West German retailers, such as Tengelmann, Europe's largest supermarket chain, have also expanded internationally. Tengelmann, which is privately owned, controls the American supermarket chain, A&P.

Such European successes pale beside Japanese achievements in other parts of Asia. In Hong Kong, Singapore, and Bangkok, Japanese retailers, led by companies such as Yaohan, Daimaru, and Isetan, have used their "scientific retailing techniques" (i.e., being well-organized and efficient) to elbow the locals aside and grab between 40 percent and 50 percent of department store sales.

The Japanese stores might have to rely more on international expansion because of shifts in the domestic economy. True, consumer sales in Japan are booming; but the Japanese are spending more of their cash on holidays — good for companies such as Seibu Saison, which own in-store travel agents and hotels, but not so good for other, purer stores.

Source: "Bad Bargains on the High Street," *The Economist,* December 16, 1989, 77.

---

One other financial consideration important to the distributor is the *payment terms* used. For example, the use of open-account terms by the international marketer shows trust in the distributor — and saves him or her the several hundred dollars required to open a letter of credit at the bank. The exporting firm must balance its need for financial security with its need to satisfy and motivate the distributor.

## Marketing Support Considerations

There are a number of other marketing considerations that will encourage distributor performance. A well-established brand name and customer franchise will make the distributor's marketing task much easier. Names such as Coca-Cola, IBM, Philips, and Sony mean that the product is partially presold. Heavy advertising and promotional support by the producer also make the distributor's job easier. In addition to the producer's promotional efforts, there may be a program of cooperative advertising with the distributor. Another kind of marketing support is producer participation in national or regional trade fairs, preferably in cooperation with the distributors in the region.

Exporters usually will train the distributor's salesforce as a necessary aid to marketing. This would be done at the beginning of the relationship and as new products are added to the line. Distributors should be supplied on a timely basis with product and promotional materials from the home office. Establishing a regional warehouse (e.g. for Europe or Asia) can assure better product supply and service to the distributor.

## Communications

If the distributor is to be an effective member of the firm's international marketing network, regular and easy communications are important. Telephone contact, preferably with an international 800 number, can assure timely response to problems and opportunities. Periodic visits from the home office allow the face-to-face contact that humanizes the long-distance relationship. Corporate travelers could include the export manager, product engineer, and occasionally the CEO.

Establishing a regional headquarters allows closer contact and support of all the distributors in a region. A company newsletter can help create a corporate spirit among the "family" of distributors. Such a newsletter or magazine would include news and pictures about the distributors as well as the company.

Regional meetings of distributors, as in the Toro example which follows, can further encourage the family spirit and also provide for economies of scale for training or motivation sessions. A computer link with distributors means on-line communication that can provide instant information, reduced transaction time, and fewer errors. General Motors realized these benefits when it established such a system with its European dealers. The dealers benefited from a quicker, more accurate service and better availability of product and supplies. Levi Strauss has implemented a similar system with major department store accounts in Europe.

Toro Manufacturing Company held its first international sales conference in Switzerland. The three-day conference was attended by Toro distributors from 13 Western European countries. These distributors had previously attended the firm's annual meetings in the United States but felt these meetings were not oriented to their particular marketing needs. The face-to-face contact between Toro personnel and the European agents helped Toro gain better insights into the marketing problems of each of the countries represented. The language problem was solved by the use of simultaneous translations by personnel borrowed from United Nations operations.

## Other Considerations

Some firms use contests to provide some excitement and motivation for distributors. In any case, rewards for superior performance give recognition and encouragement to distant distributors. One popular reward is a visit to the home country of the supplier. This usually includes a home office and plant visit plus other points of tourist interest. For American firms, it often means a trip to Disneyworld. Indeed, some American firms hold distributor meetings in Orlando, Florida, to take advantage of that area's popularity with foreign distributors.

Giving the distributor an exclusive territory means that the marketing efforts put forth in that market will rebound to the distributor's benefit. One further way to have leverage over the distributor is to take an equity position in the distributor. This gives the firm a different but useful kind of influence.

In a study by Rosson and Ford,[1] distributor performance was highest when the manufacturer-distributor relationship exhibited the following characteristics:

1. The roles and routines were not rigidly fixed but were adapted over time to changing circumstances.
2. Marketing decisions were made jointly by the manufacturer and distributor, rather than being imposed on the distributor.
3. There was a high degree of contact between distributor and manufacturer (letters, visits, phone calls).

## Marketing through the Firm's Own Presence

When the firm has its own staff in a foreign market, it will generally have responsibility for its own local distribution, but it will still have to deal with the existing distribution infrastructure (i.e., the wholesale, retail, and transport system), which will certainly differ in some ways from that of the firm's home market. The marketer must become familiar with the distribution environment in a given market to be able to fashion an appropriate distribution strategy there.

**Wholesaling in Foreign Markets**

The wholesaling functions (gathering assortments, breaking bulk, distribution to retailers) are performed in all countries but with varying degrees of efficiency. Differences in the economy, its level of development, and its infrastructure all cause variation in the wholesaling function.

**Size.** One of the notable international differences in wholesaling is the relative size and number of wholesalers from country to country. Generally, the industrialized countries have large-scale wholesaling organizations serving a large number of retailers, while the developing countries are more likely to have fragmented wholesaling — firms with a small number of employees serving a limited number of retailers. Finland and India illustrate this generalization. Finland has one of the most concentrated wholesaling operations in the world. Four groups account for most of the wholesale trade. Kesko (the Wholesale Company of Finnish Retailers) is the largest, with a market share over 20 percent, and it services over 11,000 retailers. India, on the other hand, has thousands of stockists (like wholesalers) serving hundreds of thousands of small retailers. Because of the large number of small stockists, manufacturers frequently use agents to sell to the stockists, adding an extra step in the channel.

Unfortunately, there are many exceptions to the generalization. In other words, there are industrialized countries that have small-scale wholesaling much like some developing countries. Italy and Japan are examples. Because of Italy's fragmented distribution system, Procter & Gamble had to use an intermediary to reach the wholesale level, much as firms in India have to

**Table 11-1**                                **Average Wholesaler Size in Selected Countries**

| Country | Number of Employees per Wholesaler |
|---|---|
| Turkey | 3.5 |
| Greece | 3.7 |
| South Korea | 3.8 |
| Singapore | 5.7 |
| Argentina | 6.0 |
| Sweden | 6.9 |
| Malaysia | 7.3 |
| Philippines | 7.4 |
| United Kingdom | 8.3 |
| Peru | 9.0 |
| Australia | 9.2 |
| Japan | 9.5 |
| New Zealand | 9.5 |
| Brazil | 9.6 |
| France | 10.4 |
| Finland | 10.4 |
| Austria | 11.5 |
| Kenya | 13.0 |

Source: Derived from *United Nations Statistical Yearbook,* (New York, 1986), 866–889.

do. Japan is notorious for its fragmented distribution system, with wholesalers selling to other wholesalers. Half of Japan's wholesalers have fewer than four employees. Japan has almost as many wholesalers as the United States, with only half the population. Wholesaler sales are five times retailer sales in Japan, four times the U.S. ratio. Table 11–1 gives average wholesaler size for selected countries.

As the table shows, there is no easily determined pattern in the size of wholesaling operations around the world. A rough correlation exists with the level of economic development, but one finds European countries on the list next to countries in Asia and Latin America. An African country, Kenya, has the largest wholesalers. Many former colonies have large trading houses started during the colonial period. In many African nations, for example, a Unilever subsidiary — the United Africa Company — has large-scale operations. Given this unpredictable pattern, the marketer must evaluate each country individually. (Data for the United States were not included in the *United Nations Statistical Yearbook.*)

The varied wholesaling picture in world markets presents a challenge for the international marketer. For efficient wholesalers it presents an opportunity to internationalize. For example, Makro, a Dutch wholesaler, set up an operation in Argentina. It hoped to gain business because of its large facilities and economies of scale compared to existing wholesalers in Argentina. Makro was encouraged to take this step because of its experience in Brazil, where it was already doing business of $500 million a year.

**Service.** The most important difference in wholesaling abroad is in the services offered to the manufacturer. The quality of service usually relates to the size of operations. Smaller operators generally have limited capital and less know-how, as well as small staffs, and are thus unable to give the same service as large wholesalers. Wholesaling service also relates to the level of economic development.

In some markets, the manufacturer is tempted to bypass the wholesaler because of its costs or inefficiencies. Although this might lead to more efficient distribution, its feasibility needs to be carefully evaluated. Various factors, such as the power of wholesalers or the critical functions they perform, may preclude the manufacturer's bypassing them. In Germany, for example, Kraft Foods found it would be more efficient to ship directly to the retailer. However, the wholesaler's control over the channel was strong enough to force Kraft to give it a payment, even though its services were not being used.

Colgate has a manufacturing and marketing subsidiary in Thailand. Nevertheless, Colgate finds it desirable to use a Thai distributor for the actual selling and physical distribution to retailers. To make this agreement most effective, the company recruits and trains the distributor's salesforce and pays operating and depreciation costs on the distributor's trucks.

In Japan, international firms have encountered problems that led some of them to ship directly to larger retailers. This did not work, however, because then the wholesalers would not cover the other outlets. Thus the firm usually has but two alternatives: 100 percent direct sales or no direct sales. Some firms, such as Coca-Cola or Nestlé, have gone completely to direct sales, but the cost is high. Because many small dealers are financially weak, Japanese wholesalers extend them liberal credit, sometimes as long as ten months. The manufacturer who wishes to go direct may have the financial burden instead of the wholesaler.

Levi Strauss worked with wholesalers in Japan for ten years. Capitalizing on the craze for jeans, it decided to set up its own direct salesforce. Levi Strauss normally demanded monthly payment, but Japanese department stores pay vendors on a six-month basis. Reconciling these differences was critical to the success of the company's new distribution system.

Our major observation about wholesaling is that in a majority of world markets it is small scale and fragmented compared with the United States and some other industrialized countries. Where that is true, there will be less service by the wholesaler and greater responsibility for the producer. The following problems can arise when the marketer faces a fragmented wholesaling structure.

1. Where the number of wholesalers is large relative to the size of the market, the contact and *transaction costs* of the manufacturer may be high. This raises the consumer price, too, further limiting market penetration.
2. Instead of providing *credit* to the channel, the wholesaler may be a demander of credit, placing a financial burden on the manufacturer.

3. Small wholesalers carry a narrow *assortment* of goods. This may force the manufacturer to omit some products from the line or seek out other wholesalers to carry them.
4. Small wholesalers give limited geographic *coverage.* The marketer can either forget about covering the whole national market or try to find other wholesalers for the neglected regions.
5. Small wholesalers give limited *service* in other ways, too. They carry less inventory. They give less effective selling and promotional efforts. They provide less market feedback to the producer.

In markets with fragmented wholesaling, the firm must resign itself to incomplete market coverage or try to overcome the weakness by a pull strategy, company distribution, or other means. (A *pull strategy* involves heavy consumer advertising to "pull" products through the channel.) When facing fragmented wholesaling in Italy, Procter & Gamble took a twofold approach. It emphasized its traditional pull strategy *and* inserted an extra level in the channel, using a master wholesaler who reached smaller wholesalers who contacted the retailers. U.S. firms usually find Japanese channels of distribution the most complex. For many, the best answer is to use a Japanese partner as a guide.

Many of the considerations discussed here apply as well to the distribution of industrial goods, but the producer's needs for know-how and service are greater than with consumer goods. This might keep industrial marketers out of certain countries or force them to seek other solutions. For example, Unisys is able to use United Africa Company in several African nations and piggybacks with Plessey, a British electronics firm, in Southeast Asia.

The following example illustrates how some very large American electronics companies have adapted their distribution by going indirect in one of their largest markets: Semiconductor Specialists, Inc., Chicago, formed a sales and stocking facility in London, then distributed the products of several U.S. manufacturers in the solid-state circuit and integrated circuit fields to buyers in the British market. Among U.S. firms represented in England by Semiconductor Specialists were Fairchild, Motorola, RCA, Westinghouse, Signetics, ITT, Siliconix, General Electric, Clevite, and Augat.

## Retailing in Foreign Markets

International differences in retailing are as extensive and unpredictable as we saw in the case of wholesaling. The marketer must study retail patterns in each market to see how they constrain the firm's marketing there. We shall note some of the major differences.

**Greater Numbers, Smaller Size.**   The major variable in retailing in world markets is the great difference in numbers and size of retail businesses. The United States and the advanced industrial countries tend to have larger retail outlets and a smaller number per capita than the developing countries. That means they enjoy greater economies of scale and efficiency. Some industrialized countries do not have an extensive modern retail sector, however.

Among them are Japan, Italy, Belgium, and France. Japan has about as many retailers as the United States with only half the population. The United States and Germany have 6 shops per 1,000 people; Japan has 13 and France 11. In Germany, 75 percent of retailing is done by large units, whereas in Italy over 75 percent is done by small independents.

A major reason for the lack of growth in efficient large-scale retailing in Belgium, Japan, France, and Italy is the legislation in these countries. Though France was one of the creators of the hypermarket (a giant supermarket), in 1973 France passed the *Loi Royer* regulating the establishment or expansion of retail stores. The effect of this law, and of similar laws in Belgium and Italy, is to give existing retailers a veto over the establishment of any new large-scale retailers. Naturally, these retailers don't want to see a big new competitor come in, so they don't give out any licenses. Japan has a similar law, *Daiten Ho.*

Japan's law states that no one can open a store larger than 5,382 square feet without permission from the community's store owners. The government administers the law such that it takes eight to ten years for a store to get approval. Even then there are problems. The Lawson chain opened a store in Shizuoka, and shopkeepers beat up a construction worker. Later, they stormed the store at night, screaming at employees and intimidating customers. Late night calls harassed the owners' families. Finally, someone dumped excrement outside the store.[2]

In France and Japan, powerful retail groups are fighting the restrictive laws. Daiei, Seiyu, and Jusco are leading the fight in Japan. Edouard Leclerc is leading the fight in France, with some success. He has 500 supermarkets with over $5 billion in business and is very popular with French consumers. If these groups win, retailing in those two countries will more closely resemble that in the United States.

Table 11–2 shows some of the international differences in retailer size. Generally, average retailer size increases with economic development, but there are a number of exceptions. For example, a rich country, Belgium, is similar to Iraq and Turkey on this dimension. Also, Japan is not much different from Brazil. Caution is necessary with United Nations data, however, since they are not always directly comparable and have many gaps. Even the United States' figures are missing from the *United Nations Statistical Yearbook!*

Anyone who visits only the capitals or largest cities of developing nations will not get a true picture of the retailing structure of the country. The capital cities may have a few department stores and supermarkets like those the tourist sees at home. Such evidences in the small, modernized sector of the economy, however, are not typical of the nation as a whole. Rather, they reflect the "dual economy" phenomenon; that is, the same country has two different economies, one of which includes the majority of the population in the villages and rural areas, and the other, the few large cities where some industrialization and commercial development have taken place.

**Retailing Services.**   Another variable in world markets is the services provided by the retailer to the manufacturer. Services a producer might desire from retailers include the following: stocking the product; displaying the

**Table 11-2**                    **Retailer Size in Selected Countries**

| Country | Employees per Retail Establishment |
|---|---|
| Iraq | 1.4 |
| Belgium | 1.5 |
| South Korea | 1.7 |
| Greece | 1.8 |
| Turkey | 1.8 |
| Peru | 1.9 |
| Ecuador | 1.9 |
| Ethiopia | 2.2 |
| Malaysia | 2.5 |
| Philippines | 2.5 |
| Cuba | 2.6 |
| Ghana | 2.8 |
| Brazil | 3.0 |
| Japan | 3.7 |
| France | 3.7 |
| Sweden | 4.2 |
| Netherlands | 5.0 |
| New Zealand | 5.0 |
| Australia | 6.6 |
| United Kingdom | 7.8 |

Source: Derived from *United Nations Statistical Yearbook* (New York, 1986), 866–889.

product; selling the product; promoting the product (orally, by display or by advertising); extending credit to customers; servicing the product; and gathering market information.

***Carrying Inventory.***   Stocking products is a basic function of retailers in every country. The services offered, however, are not identical. Small retailers carry very limited inventories and may be frequently out of stock in certain items. This is lost business for the manufacturer. Limited inventory means a limited line of products. New entrants to the market can have difficulty getting their products accepted by retailers.

Because they are financially weak, small retailers may be able to carry certain products only if they do not have to invest in them; that is, the retailer carries the inventory physically, but the wholesaler or manufacturer carries it financially. This is a problem even in Japan, where small dealers may get credit up to ten months from their suppliers. Consignment sales are another possible answer to the retailers' inventory problem. A U.S. firm selling prepared foods partially dealt with the problem by changing its case size from 48-can cases in the United States to 24-can and 12-can cases in other markets.

***Product Display.***   Where the package plays a role in persuading the consumer to purchase, display is important. The kind of display a product gets in a retail outlet depends on the physical facilities (space, shelves, lighting).

The producer will find great international variations in these. At one extreme, an African *duka* may have less than 200 square feet of store space, no electric lighting, one door and one window, a few shelves running around two or three walls, and one or two tables. The seller in the open market or bazaar would have equally limited facilities. Retail facilities range from these examples all the way up to the 250,000 square foot hypermarket or large department store found in the United States or Europe.

General Foods in Brazil had to deal with "Mom and Pop" stores, usually with less than 200 square feet of space and almost no room for display. The customer would ask for the item and the retailer would get it from under the counter. Local GF managers hoped to develop a display counter that could be suspended from the ceiling by wires. They also investigated self-dispensing units that could be nailed to the wall of the store. The customer would take a piece of candy or gum, and gravity would replace it with another piece.

Merchandising skills correlate somewhat with the level of economic development, although many retailers in poorer countries have a flair for product display. Many firms in the United States do not rely on the retailers for display of their product, except for shelf space. Representatives of the manufacturer will arrange the display themselves, with the concurrence of the retailer. This will not be possible in many markets because of the small size and dispersion of retail businesses and because the firm may have a narrower line there, offering too small a base over which to spread these promotional costs.

Cooperation will also be affected by the retailer's overall relations with the producer, as in the case of Kimberly-Clark, when it was distributing Kotex in France through the *pharmacie,* which differs from an American drug store in that it is limited to dispensing medicines and selling related items. The company wanted to add supermarket-type outlets for Kotex, as in the United States. The supermarkets were willing to handle the product, but the *pharmaciens* were angry about the competition. As a result, they put all Kimberly-Clark products under the counter and refused to display them.

***Promotion of the Product.***   Product display is frequently all that a manufacturer can expect. Occasionally, however, retailers might do some personal selling or advertising. This is more likely if the retailers have a favorable attitude toward the product and it is an important part of their sales. Use of point-of-purchase materials is another form of retailer promotion, but the small size of retail outlets makes most such displays impractical. Retailer product advertising is a form of promotion that also tends to be limited in most markets because of the small resources of retailers. These limitations force the manufacturer to rely on its own advertising in many markets.

***Other Retailing Services.***   Credit extension, product service, and market information are other services a manufacturer might desire from retailers. After our repeated mention of the limited resources available to retailers in most countries, it is obvious that the manufacturer is more likely to be involved in extending credit than in finding retailers who can ease the financial flow. Where product service is necessary, the retailers' ability to perform it will depend on their resources and technical skills. Usually, the smaller the retailers, the less able they are to give service. The burden of assuring product service thus falls on the producer. Where the manufacturer is unable to assure adequate service, it may have to forgo entering some markets.

In Turkey at one time about 60 percent of all farm tractors were estimated to be incapacitated. International Harvester could find only about 50 qualified repairmen in its own Turkish organization and in the government equipment centers. To maintain its franchise with the consumers and the government, International Harvester undertook an extensive training program.

Market feedback for the manufacturer is not something retailers consider their job. Only to the extent that the manufacturer has contacts with retailers can it get market information from them. In large markets the producer often has contact with retailers or retail organizations. Furthermore, retail audit services are available in some large markets. In small markets and in rural areas, very little retailer contact is practical.

Another problem may arise when the producer wants retailer cooperation for marketing or advertising testing. Retailers may be reluctant to cooperate, either because they do not understand how it can benefit them, or because they are suspicious of any outsiders looking at their business. Retailers in many countries are secretive about their operations and afraid of tax investigators. This secretiveness affects their relations with the producer. For example, one large cosmetics firm wanted to do "before and after" retail product audits to test an advertising campaign in a Latin American country. Only after great difficulty did it finally secure the participation of enough retailers to conduct the test.

## Distribution Trends in World Markets

Because most countries are experiencing economic and social change, to observe the wholesale or retail structure at just one point in time is not sufficient. Channel decisions must be based on what the structures will be like tomorrow, as well as what they are today. Statistics on distribution are limited for most less-developed nations. Fortunately, the marketing manager can still get an idea of distribution trends there. Since the nature of wholesaling and retailing is related to economic development, the marketer can follow economic growth as a rough guide to predict distribution changes.

For the international marketer, a review of the development of wholesaling and retailing in the United States is instructive. Developments elsewhere often parallel those in the United States in earlier periods. This is because those nations are experiencing economic and social changes similar to those that occurred in the United States. Another reason is that U.S. retailers have carried their techniques abroad. For example, Jewel Companies, the Chicago-based retailer, entered a joint venture with Aurrera, a Mexican retailer. At that time, Aurrera was tenth in Mexican retailing. By adopting many of Jewel's techniques, Aurrera rose to the number one position in Mexico. Another aid to the marketer is the comparative-study approach. Studies of markets where the firm is already selling should give insights into markets with similar characteristics.

Kacker notes four major ways in which retailing technology is transferred internationally:[3]

1. *Seminars and training programs.* Programs of the American Supermarket Institute and National Cash Register Co. (NCR) played a major role in the spread of the supermarket concept in the 1950s.
2. *Foreign direct investment.* By establishing or acquiring stores abroad, retailers transfer know-how within their international family. Safeway, Sears, and Woolworth are American examples. Ikea and Mothercare are European examples.
3. *Management contracts and joint ventures.* Sears has a contract with Seibu for the transfer of a total package of retail technology, including systems manuals. Printemps has a joint venture with Daiei for trademarks, merchandising, and training know-how.
4. *Franchising.* The most visible contemporary symbol of the international transfer of retailing know-how is the franchise. McDonald's and Kentucky Fried Chicken are notable American examples. Benetton is a famous European example.

We note four major distribution trends in world markets. One is the growth of large-scale retailing. A second is the continuing internationalization of retailing. Another is the growth of direct marketing. The fourth is the spread of discounting.

**Larger Scale, Greater Retailer Power.**   In the affluent nations, distribution developments are similar to the United States' pattern of recent decades. Of course, not all retail developments originate in America. The hypermarket, for example, was a French invention. The trend in the industrialized countries is toward larger units and more self-service. Almost everywhere, the number of retail outlets is dwindling, and the average size is increasing. Sweden, for example, had 30,000 food stores in 1955 but only 5,000 in 1988. Inexorably, though at differing rates in different countries, the trend is the same. Everywhere, the forces are the same also: (1) rising affluence, (2) greater car ownership, (3) more households with refrigerators, and (4) more wives working outside the home.

Even Japan and Italy are joining the bandwagon, though at the end of it. Italy, which still had 850,000 retailers in 1987, was seeing a yearly 5 percent drop in the numbers. And Japan saw a drop in the number of Mom-and-Pop stores of 8 percent over a three-year period in the late 1980s. Furthermore, many Seven-Eleven franchises in Japan were former mom-and-pop store owners.

Even some developing nations, especially the newly industrializing countries, are seeing a growth in large-scale retailing. In Korea, the first supermarket appeared in 1971. With tax incentives and consumer support, the number grew to over 1,500 in one decade. In Hong Kong, the number of supermarkets increased six-fold from 1975 to 1983, while the number of traditional grocery stores declined 30 percent. Many of the forces behind these developments are the same as those that led to modern retailing in the United States and Europe: rising incomes, more automobiles, more working wives. Thus, the life cycle of retailing works its way around the world.

These trends mean stronger retailing and greater countervailing power vis-à-vis the manufacturer. The power of channel members is further reinforced by the growth of large-scale cooperative wholesaling, often on an international basis. For example, Spar International is a voluntary chain of several hundred wholesalers and about 40,000 retailers in 12 Western European countries. As a result of larger operations and greater power, European retailers are demanding more private (distributor) brands. These groups also bargain strongly on prices. Private brands already have a greater share in Europe than in the United States, and 1992 will strengthen distributors in Europe.

**Internationalization of Retailing.**   The continuing integration of the world economy is internationalizing not only the advertising, banking, and manufacturing industries; it is also reaching retailing. The life cycle of today's large retailers began with a store in one city. This slowly grew into a national operation and today it is going international. Retailers in the United States, Europe, and Japan are expanding their international ties, both with respect to procurement and to marketing. Macy's of New York, for example, has buying offices in over 30 countries. Leading examples in marketing would be the U.S. franchisors who have over 25,000 outlets outside the United States. Southland Corp. ranks first with over 4,000 Seven-Eleven stores abroad. McDonald's and H&R Block have 2,000 each. Avon and Tupperware, specializing in direct sales, are a different kind of American retailer abroad. Goodyear, IBM, Tandy-Radio Shack, and Singer are U.S. manufacturers who are also retailers abroad. K Mart, Safeway, and Sears are examples of more traditional retailers with sales abroad.

U.S. retailers are not the only internationalists. Europeans own over 10 percent of the American grocery business and have very important department and specialty store holdings. Ikea, the Swedish furniture retailer, and boutique retailers like Benetton and Laura Ashley are increasingly visible in the United States. Carrefour has stores in Argentina, Brazil and the United States, as well as Europe. Printemps, the famous French department store, is in Japan, Singapore, Saudi Arabia, the United States, Korea, and Turkey.

### Some American Stores Owned by Foreigners

| | |
|---|---|
| A & P | Gimbels |
| Bloomingdale's | Grand Union |
| Bonwit Teller | Lazarus |
| Brooks Brothers | Rich's |
| Burdines | Saks Fifth Avenue |
| Eddie Bauer | Spiegel |

The Japanese are relative newcomers to this internationalization of retailing, but they are getting deeply involved. Jusco has supermarkets in Hong Kong, Thailand, and Malaysia. Southeast Asia seems to be the natural zone of influence for Japanese retailers, and they have spread throughout the region. However, they have not limited themselves to that area. Wacoal, the lingerie firm, has boutiques in the United States. Major Japanese retailing groups like Daiei, Seiyu, and Jusco have ties with such American retailers as K Mart, Kroger, Safeway, and Sears.

**Direct Marketing.**   Another distribution trend is the growth in direct marketing, especially mail order. In 1973 European mail-order business surpassed the volume of U.S. mail-order sales for the first time. Mail order is expanding in most major Western European countries, including Italy, but it is also growing in Japan and Mexico. One attraction of mail order for the consumer is that in inflationary periods the catalog prices stay the same for six months at a time.

Using a salesforce to go direct to the consumer is not a new way of direct marketing, but it continues to be important. Avon and Tupperware are the most famous American examples abroad, but Sara Lee is also doing it overseas, though not domestically. In Indonesia, Sara Lee is selling cosmetics direct to consumers with a salesforce of 400 women. Electrolux, the Swedish appliance producer, has direct salesforces in ten Asian countries from Japan to India. Electrolux could not compete successfully against the Japanese through its network of agents, so it switched to the more powerful direct sales channel.

Telephone marketing, sometimes combined with direct mail, has been the rapid growth area in direct marketing, both in the United States and in Europe. For example, Harrod's of London has an international 800 number for American customers. Even IBM uses telemarketing in Europe. Specialized organizations have arisen to handle direct marketing for firms. Ogilvy and Mather Direct is Europe's largest such firm and includes as clients American Express, Royal Viking Line, and Trans World Airways. This type of marketing has been very effective for many firms. It is being attacked however, by several groups, including a consumer group in the Netherlands and the Office of Fair Trading in the United Kingdom, who complain of high-pressure techniques and the invasion of privacy.

**Discounting.**   Among other distribution trends is the increasing popularity of discount merchandising. Several factors have contributed to discounting's popularity, including the demise of resale price maintenance, consumerism, and inflation. In Japan, discount chain stores have replaced department stores as the country's largest retailers. A Parker pen is 25 percent less in a supermarket than in a department store there. In France, Leclerc has become the darling of the consumer, with his 500-unit chain of discount stores.

As more and larger discount stores, mail-order operations, and retailer or wholesaler organizations are formed, there will be pressure on manufacturers' pricing and distribution practices. Firms that have become acquainted with these organizations in the United States should have an advantage as the same developments occur in other countries.

## Marketing through Foreign Distribution Channels

Having considered some of the principal constraints on distribution in foreign markets, we will now look at the strategic decisions facing the international marketer:

1. Should the firm extend its domestic distribution approach uniformly to foreign markets or adapt its distribution strategy to each national market?
2. Should the firm use direct or indirect channels in foreign markets?
3. Should the firm use selective or widespread distribution?
4. How can the firm manage the channel?
5. How can the firm keep its distribution strategy up to date?

**International or National Patterns**

The important question is not whether the firm should have uniform distribution patterns in foreign markets; it is the question of which channels in each market are most profitable. A few factors may favor a standardized approach, particularly the possibility of economies of scale. Although these are not as easily attainable in distribution as in production, there may be some. For example, the international marketing manager may work more efficiently the more similar the task in different markets. Also as with the integration of Europe in 1992, the more similar the conditions, the more easily experience in one country can be transferred to another.

Occasionally executive desire for uniformity is also a factor, but not one that should weigh heavily on the channel decision. It can be argued that channels used in one market should be tried in another because they have been tested. Although success in one market does give a presumption in favor of trying the same thing elsewhere, it is not a sufficient reason. Market analysis should be done before deciding on local channels.

Numerous pressures deter the firm from standardized distribution. One consideration is the existing distribution structure in a country, that is, the number, size, and nature of wholesale and retail operations. Because the distribution structure varies from country to country, the firm's alternatives also vary. Storage and transportation possibilities, plus the dispersion of the market, also help to determine channel alternatives. For example, Pepsi Cola uses similar channels all over the world — that is, local bottler to truck driver/sales representative to retailer. However, in sparse market areas, the truck driver/sales representative is too expensive and the company must find another method.

Another channel determinant is the market. Consumer income and buying habits are important considerations in deciding on distribution. Still another variable is the strength and behavior of competitors. On the one hand, competitors may force a firm to use the same channel they are using because they have educated the market to that channel; on the other, competitors' strength may effectively preempt that channel and force the new-comer to find some other way to the market.

The initial application of Allstate Insurance for Japan was rejected by Japanese protectionism. Its entry "would disrupt existing firms." In a different approach, Allstate joined with Seibu, the Japanese retailer. This gave Allstate a powerful sales channel. It also fulfilled an entry requirement that it "provide something new to customers" — the opportunity to buy insurance over the counter.

Finally, differences in the manufacturer's own situation might suggest channel differences from market to market. An important determinant is the firm's level of involvement in a market. Where the firm supplies a market through an importer-distributor, it has less freedom than where it supplies through a local plant. Similarly, working through a licensee or joint venture is more restrictive of channel selection than is working through a wholly owned operation. Even where the level of involvement is the same in two markets, the firm's product line and sales volume may differ. The smaller the line and the volume of sales, the less direct the channels that the firm can afford to use.

The international firm generally tries to use the same distribution channels from market to market. Although adaptations are frequently necessary, a firm's channels will be similar around the world, especially in industrial goods. Even in consumer goods, there can be a carry-over from country to country.

When Tupperware entered Japan, the only channel it was familiar with was selling by parties in the home with a housewife as hostess. It used the same direct channel in Japan and found it successful. Avon is another direct seller at home and abroad. In Taiwan, for example, there are 11,000 Avon ladies selling to customers at home. And Amway has a force of 500,000 direct sellers in Japan.[4]

As another example, consider the situation of Shaklee Pharmaceuticals. Because vitamin pills are not "drugs" in Japan, they can be sold door-to-door. Shaklee Pharmaceuticals uses that channel in the United States and entered Japan the same way. It was the only firm in that channel and became number one in vitamins. Japanese firms hesitated to follow suit for fear of offending their traditional channels on which they depended for sales of prescription drugs.

**Direct versus Indirect Channels**

Because direct channels are almost always more effective than indirect channels, firms like to go as direct as they can. The major determinant is the volume of sales attainable. Where volume is large, the firm can afford to go directly to the market. When a U.S. firm considers foreign markets, it usually finds less possibility of going direct than in the United States. Many elements combine to make most other markets smaller, for example, lower incomes, narrower product line of the firm, fewer large-scale buying organizations, and so on.

Where foreign markets are small, many firms accept indirect distribution as the only feasible alternative. In India, for example, Unilever and other consumer goods companies sell through agents, who reach the stockists, who reach the retailers. Procter & Gamble in Italy used a similar three-stage channel. Channels in Japan may be even more indirect than those in India and Italy. In these cases, the fragmented nature of wholesaling and retailing forces the firm to go less direct than it would like. These conditions characterize most world markets, especially for consumer goods.

Some firms, however, insist on trying for more direct distribution as the best way to get a strong market position. This is especially true of consumer durables or industrial goods producers. Goodyear was establishing its own franchised dealers in Europe, just like those it has in the United States. The vice-president of Massey-Ferguson said, "The first to have a controlled system of outlets in Europe will be the winner. You have to have your own outlets with people you can control. That is the reason for Singer's success."

IBM has always gone direct to its customers with its large equipment. When the company began selling smaller equipment (copiers and computers) to smaller customers, it found its direct salesforce too expensive. IBM experimented with its own retail outlets, first in Europe and Argentina. When these proved successful, IBM began opening its own retail outlets in the United States.

In Japan, the Erina Company defied the conventional wisdom by going direct to consumers with its pantyhose. It developed a salesforce of about 200,000 agents (99 percent are housewives). Because this was more efficient than traditional methods in Japan, its price was about half that of pantyhose sold in other channels and Erina quickly got one-sixth of the market. The company then began looking for other products to add to its distribution system.

## Selective versus Intensive Distribution

*Intensive distribution* refers to the policy of selling through any retailer that wishes to handle the product. *Selective distribution* means choosing a limited number of resellers in a market area. Although a firm usually wants to make its product as widely available as possible, it may be necessary to select a limited number of distributors to make it worth their while to carry inventory and to provide service and promotion. For shopping or specialty goods, retailers may demand selective distribution, which protects their market by limiting competition. For industrial goods or consumer durables, selective distribution may be the only way to induce intermediaries to cooperate in providing service.

In foreign markets, the decision factors are the same but the environment is different. Marketing abroad, manufacturers usually give exclusive franchises to importers or wholesalers at the *national* level. However, selectivity at the retail level depends on local market conditions. With a multiplicity of small retailers, the firm might have difficulty locating those that can handle its product effectively. Low consumer mobility also limits the value of selective distribution.

General Motors in Belgium tried to hinder the import of GM cars by others than the company-owned distributor in Belgium. However, the European Community Commission said the GM distributor charged excessive prices for inspections and conformity certificates for cars bought outside the GM channel. The commission levied a fine on GM of $120,000 for "abuse of a dominant position." Thus GM was effectively prevented from having an exclusive distributorship in Belgium.

As the General Motors example suggests, governments are beginning to have a greater influence on a firm's distribution decisions. Outboard Marine in Norway tried to implement a selective distribution system but the Norwegian courts ruled against the company, saying that this practice would reduce competition in outboard engines. On a broader level, the European Bureau of Consumer Unions asked the EC Commission to investigate the selective distribution practices of Grundig, Telefunken, and Saba, saying, "Such distribution seriously harms the interests of consumers." The commission is investigating these practices to find the extent to which they raise price "artificially."

Firms must be alert for such government actions affecting their distribution policy. In countries with very uneven income distribution, the firm might well use selective distribution, if it sells only to a group above a certain income level. For consumer durables or industrial products, the distribution in smaller markets might be more selective than in larger markets because of the thinness of the market and its relative concentration. The channel follows the market.

## Working with the Channel

Managing the channel is easiest when the firm sells directly to the retailer or to the consumer. The costs of direct distribution bring the benefits of control as well as the flexibility to respond to market conditions and better market feedback. When the firm cannot afford to go direct, it must deal with independent intermediaries. The problem then becomes one of getting cooperation rather than one of maintaining control. Although this problem is not peculiar to foreign markets, the firm's own situation and market conditions will vary from country to country, making channel management a somewhat different task in each market.

Effective channel management is critical because the firm's success in a market often depends on how well independent intermediaries do their job. Thus, helping them to do their job becomes a major responsibility of the marketer. Coca-Cola ran into trouble in Japan, a market accounting for 10 percent of company sales. Its response was to put in a new manager whose forte was dealing with franchised bottlers. He practiced this in Japan by visiting, listening to their problems, improving inventory service, and introducing better training programs.

Manufacturers have developed many different techniques for encouraging cooperation from members of the channel, including margins, exclusive territories, a valuable franchise, advertising support and cooperative advertising, financing, salesforce or service training, business advisory service, market research assistance, and missionary selling. All of these are known to students of marketing. We will discuss just their international application. Levi provides a European example. In the early 1980s, it found a weakness in the retail link of its channel in Europe. In response, it decided to use more selective distribution and give more support to those retailers who were willing to emphasize Levi products. This extra support included special discounts, local advertising help, merchandising assistance, and training of retailer sales staff. Also, it began computer links with retailers.

A firm needs to be competitive on margins in each of its markets. Sometimes to break into a market, the firm is tempted to beat competitors' margins, a form of price cutting and the easiest form of competition to imitate. Usually the weak firm that has no other advantages will try this approach, but once the firm has made its entry, it may have difficulty adjusting its margins.

The international firm may or may not have a valuable franchise to offer its channel members. When the firm enters a new market, its brand is usually unknown. Middlemen may be reluctant to carry the product unless the firm gives strong advertising support. Some larger international companies, such as Philips, Unilever, IBM, or Sony, are in a different position. Because of their size and reputation, they are usually considered as desirable suppliers in any market they enter.

Indonesia poses a special problem for international firms, because all local marketing activities must be handled by Indonesian nationals, and marketing skills are not well developed there. To get effective marketing, foreign firms must lend considerable assistance to their Indonesian distributor. Some firms have taken the quasi-legal approach of setting up a sales company and getting an Indonesian with a distributor's license to serve as front man. Another way to influence local marketing is through a management contract with the Indonesian distributor. This approach appears to be legally acceptable.

Strong advertising support of a product makes the intermediaries more cooperative. International firms have an advantage over national firms in this respect. First, they have the financial resources to advertise extensively; second, they have more expertise in advertising than most of their national competitors. A German competitor of Procter & Gamble noted that the company was able to enter any Western European country and "buy" a 15 percent market share just on the strength of its advertising. The resources and experience of the international company also help in developing cooperative advertising with channel members. The same financial resources make the international company more than competitive in extending credit for financing the channel.

Rosenthal, the German porcelain maker, created a subsidiary called Table Top Retail with an annual budget of $3 million. Its purpose is to support Rosenthal dealers to prevent erosion of the firm's market coverage. The company was losing some of its best dealers from a variety of forces, including retirement. The fund will keep these valuable specialty stores in operation till strong new management can be found. Faced with similar problems, Grunding, the German electronics firm, formed its own franchising system to maintain and support its dealer network. Both of these moves are especially important in view of the increased competition expected in 1992.

The size and experience of multinational companies give them an advantage in other avenues of obtaining cooperation, such as training of sales or service personnel, business advisory service, and market research assistance. A firm with operations in several countries can draw on its experience in helping any one market. It can gain economies of scale in developing training personnel, or in operating a centralized training center for several countries. Most national firms cannot match these advantages. Furthermore, the international firm can give additional prestige by holding regional meetings with representatives from several countries.

Ford Motor Company (Overseas Tractor Operations) conducts training programs in Latin America for its own and dealers' employees. The training is in repair, maintenance, and utilization of tractors and equipment. The program has paid good returns in dealer relations. Prestige has been associated with training at a large Ford facility as well as with the foreign travel often required to attend training programs. The instructors are drawn from the United Kingdom, where one of Ford's three major tractor plants is located.

As another example, an auto firm found a new way to train its far-flung network of dealers by leasing a plane and outfitting it as a classroom with cutaway training units of rear axles, engines, transmissions, and so on, plus movies, slides, and other visual aids. The first trip was an 18-stop swing through Central and Latin America, with four days at each stop. The six-man training team gave sessions (in Spanish) on technical and product training, as well as sales and management methods. The dealers plus their sales and service personnel were included.

A unique way the international firm can increase intermediaries' cooperation is by increasing its commitment to the local market. When the firm changes from imports to local production, it increases its involvement in the market and reassures local dealers. Its reliability and image are enhanced in the dealers' eyes, and it can give better delivery and service. Transportation, customs, inventory, and communications problems are all lessened once the international firm establishes local production.

*Missionary selling* is a way to maintain contact with channel members and to help them sell the product. In markets with many small retailers, it is more difficult, but where the market is not too thin, missionary selling can play the same role it does in the United States. The Wrigley Company provides an illustration. As chewing gum caught on in Europe, European competitors arose and used a low-price strategy to attack Wrigley's position. Rather than responding with price cuts, Wrigley used missionary selling to convince retailers of the greater profits they could obtain with Wrigley's well-established, strongly advertised brand. The strategy was successful in maintaining the company's position.

**Keeping Channels Up to Date**

The challenge of management is to keep on top of change. In international marketing the problem is compounded because the changes in the environment and in the firm are occurring at different rates in different markets. Even if we assume that the firm had an appropriate distribution strategy when it entered each market, this strategy is unlikely to remain the most desirable over time.

The variables affecting channels are numerous. In any market, the situation of the firm evolves. Generally, the volume of sales increases, the product line expands, and the level of involvement undergoes a change, that is, from importer-distributor to marketing subsidiary, or from licensee to joint venture, and so on. Environmental changes occur. Developments in wholesaling and retailing are taking place in all markets. Technological change in distribution as well as evolution in the purchasing behavior of buyers exert pressure on the firm's channels. Laws affecting distribution are being changed. Finally, political developments such as regional groupings are changing the horizons of the firm.

**Growth of Firm in a Market.**   The international firm in most of its markets is expanding. As it gets established in a market, its sales volume should increase, and this will lead to expansion of the product line. At some level of sales, the firm will find it profitable to increase its involvement in that market. Where this growth occurs, the firm is able to take stronger control of its distribution, that is, to go more direct. In fact, this is the strategy of many international companies.

Union Carbide had been selling its consumer products in the fragmented Philippine market through one national distributor, an indirect channel. When the company expanded its involvement by building a dry cell battery plant in the Philippines, it wanted a more vigorous sales effort. To get this, Union Carbide established 4,000 Class A dealers who, while functioning as retailers, served primarily as wholesalers to Class B and C dealers. Then UC appointed 100 of its own salespeople to work with the Class A dealers. This system resulted in more aggressive marketing with more control.

**Environmental Change: Large-Scale Retailing.**   Changes in the environment have a complex impact on the firm's marketing. The trends toward retail concentration and buying co-ops in Europe, for example, have twofold impact. The concentration of the market in larger units means not only a greater possibility of direct distribution but also increased demand for private brands. The growth of large mail-order operations has the same result. The bargaining power of these large groups affects the pricing policy of the manufacturer. Even large Japanese retailers, such as Daiei and Takashimaya, are buying direct from foreign producers.

The strategic response of the firm to large-scale retailing may be either direct channels or dual channels, that is, selling directly to large retail groups and indirectly to small retailers. The private-brand approach might become necessary. In other cases, private branding may be the way to open up new markets. For example, some American firms had been unable to enter the German market because German wholesalers were unwilling to carry their products. The wholesalers' associations in Germany often have been strong enough to prevent the manufacturer from bypassing them. German manufacturers have agreed to this restriction on the condition that the wholesalers in turn act as a sort of buffer against foreign firms' coming in. The rise of large retail groups buying directly opens the way for non-German firms to break into the market, although perhaps with private branding.

Large-scale retailing organizations have caused manufacturers to make still other adaptations. The situation in the United Kingdom, which is a leader in European distribution trends, can be taken as an example. Manufacturers have increased their promotional activities to the large retailers, using missionary selling with them, but at the same time they have reduced their efforts with smaller retailers. Even as they sell more directly to large retailers, they leave small independent retailers to be serviced by wholesalers; in effect, they adopt a dual-channel strategy. This strategy is used not only by a food company like Heinz, but also by a consumer durables firm like Philips. For example, when Heinz found that fewer than 300 buying points controlled over 80 percent of the market for its products, it stopped deliveries to the small independent retailers, leaving them to wholesalers.

**Other Changes.**    The firm must monitor other developments affecting distribution. In some markets, rising wages are drawing people out of low-wage retailing. More self-service retailing is one result. Such a situation caused the Nissan Motor Company in Japan to change its distribution channel. The company was sending sales representatives door to door, but the diminishing availability of labor for this kind of retailing caused the company to consider switching to American-style automobile showrooms.

Technological developments, such as the *cold chain* — meaning the availability of refrigeration in warehouses, trucks, and retail outlets — emerging in Europe and Japan, will enlarge product-line possibilities. Unilever found the major deterrent to growth to be the retail link of the cold chain. Many retailers could not afford the freezer unit. Unilever helped retailers finance a frozen-food unit in the expectation that the growth in the company's frozen-food sales would be enough to cover financing costs.

Managing distribution often requires changing the channel when conditions change; for example, the firm may add a new channel or type of outlet. After World War II, the leading U.S. producer of ice cream faced a dilemma. Its traditional outlets were drug stores, but the new supermarkets were beginning to sell ice cream. Because adding supermarket outlets would irritate the members of the existing channel, the company decided to stay with its traditional channel. Eventually, of course, supermarkets became the overwhelming favorite outlet for ice cream. This is the kind of challenge facing firms in many markets. Multinational operating experience helps answer such questions in individual markets. Although the firm may reap ill will from existing channels, it also may gain goodwill and a strong place in the new outlet by being the first to change.

Hans Guldenberg, A. C. Nielsen director for Germany, has analyzed the impact of 1992 on retailing and distribution in Europe as follows:[5]

1.  Retailers will become even larger and more powerful with continuing concentration and integration.
2.  Private brands will increase further and there will be retailer Eurobrands.
3.  Retailer power will mean lower supplier (manufacturer) margins.
4.  Logistics, including warehouse and production locations, must adjust for the integrated market and retailer concentration.

5. Mail order will continue to grow and become international. Already Le Redoute in France and Quelle and Otto in Germany plan to go European with their mail-order operation.
6. There will be greater price uniformity in Europe with a more open market. This means less pricing freedom for manufacturers.

## Logistics for International Marketing

Up to this point, we have been discussing distribution from the viewpoint of the financial and ownership flows of goods in international marketing, touching only incidentally on the physical movement of goods, what is usually called *physical distribution.* A somewhat broader term — *logistics* — has become popular in business usage and can be defined as including those activities involved with the choice of the number and location of facilities to be used and the materials or product to be stored or transported from suppliers to customers in all the firm's markets.

The important point about logistics is that it is much more than transportation or the mere physical movement of goods. And international logistics decisions affect the number and location of production and storage facilities, production schedules, inventory management, and even the firm's level of involvement in foreign markets. According to Davies, international logistics differs from domestic in several ways:

1. Documentation for an international sale (a) costs more, (b) involves more parties, (c) has a higher penalty for error and (d) requires more data.
2. The average export order is much larger than a domestic sale, requiring more rigorous credit checks of foreign buyers.
3. There is a new intermediary in export sales — the international freight forwarder.[6]

Physical distribution problems can limit market opportunities on the supply side as severely as low incomes can do so on the demand side. By the same token, however, improvements in logistics can open up new markets. Logistics management can offer the international marketer two ways for increasing profits: cost reduction and market expansion.

**Logistics within the Foreign Market**

In each market where the firm has a subsidiary, it must seek to optimize its physical distribution system. In countries where it is represented by distributors or licensees, it will have only a limited role in local logistics. Its approach abroad will be similar to the one it uses at home, but there will be variations resulting from differences in the size of the market, the way the market is supplied, the degree of urbanization, the topography, and the transportation and storage facilities.

Zaire provides an illustration of physical distribution problems within a national market. Imported goods destined for the eastern part of Zaire take the following path: (1) Ocean shipping arrives inland on the Zaire River at Matadi, where it is unloaded and put on a train. (2) The train goes to

Kinshasa, the capital, bypassing the falls and rapids between Matadi and the capital. (3) At Kinshasa, the goods are put on a boat for a 1,000-mile river trip to Kisangani, where the river again is unnavigable. (4) There, the goods are put on a train for Kindu. (5) At Kindu, goods are trans-shipped by truck. It is not hard to imagine, therefore, that for many goods, physical distribution costs constitute the biggest element in the price. This is reinforced by inadequate storage facilities and adverse climatic conditions causing damage and loss en route.

We discussed in Chapter 3 how nations differ in their transportation and communications infrastructure. Developing nations generally have a weak infrastructure and this, combined with poorer markets, forces logistic adjustments by the firm from an affluent, industrialized home market. At one time Pepsico acquired a Mexican company whose "fleet" was 37 bicycles. Over the years, Pepsico expanded the operation and now covers Mexico with over 1,000 trucks. Even in industrialized countries, a fragmented wholesale-retail structure can lead to distribution inefficiencies as we have seen. Because of the difficulty of covering the whole Japanese market, for example, many firms limit their initial marketing efforts to just the Tokyo and Osaka metropolitan areas. On the other hand, Coca-Cola felt it was necessary to cover the whole Japanese market so the company circumvented the existing multitiered wholesale system by franchising 54 bottlers who distribute from 500 warehouses on 8,500 trucks.

We also saw in Chapter 3 that topography is one aspect of a nation's physical endowment. The existence of rivers, deserts, mountains, or tropical forests can pose opportunities or challenges to physical distribution. Some Latin American countries, for example, are divided into almost inaccessible regions by the Andes Mountains. Because these are not affluent markets, some firms do not even try to cover the whole country but content themselves with reaching major urban areas. Bata Shoe Company in Peru is one of the rare firms that does more business in the rural areas than in the major cities. To cover these areas, Bata uses air, truck, rail, plus occasionally mule or launch to reach distant outlets. In Europe, inland waterways can have the opposite effect, tying several nations together for the physical movement of goods.

**Multimarket Logistics**

If there were one world market, the logistics problems of international marketing would be basically the same as those in the domestic market. The world, however, is not one market but a collection of individual national markets, each under the control of a sovereign government. Governments have various methods of separating their markets from others, for example:

1. Tariff barriers.
2. Import quotas and licenses.
3. Local content laws.
4. National currencies and monetary systems, exchange control.
5. Differing tax systems and rates.
6. Differing transportation policies.
7. Differing laws on products (food, drug, labeling, safety).

# Global Marketing
## India's Urban Sector — Where the Money Is

For firms marketing in India, city dwellers are the name of the game. Although over three-fourths of India's population lives in the countryside, the city dwellers have over one-half of the total purchasing power and buy over two-thirds of most packaged consumer goods.

|  | Urban India Percent | Rural India Percent |
|---|---|---|
| Population | 23 | 77 |
| National Income | 53 | 47 |
| 1987 Sales |  |  |
|   Batteries | 59 | 41 |
|   Soap | 62 | 38 |
|   Toothpaste | 83 | 17 |
|   Shampoo | 96 | 4 |
|   Packaged Consumer Products (44 Items) | 71 | 29 |

Source: Indian Market Research Bureau; and *Business Asia,* May 1, 1989, 141.

Because the world is made up of national markets, logistics management must adapt to, or overcome, the barriers in order to achieve, as nearly as possible, an integrated world market in its own physical distribution. The goal is not merely reduction of costs but greater sales. Sales will increase if logistics improvements lead to improvements in the customer service level. The appropriate customer service level varies among countries because of competition and customer expectations. (*Customer service level* refers to delivery times, availability of parts and service, and other elements required to meet customer needs and desires.)

The firm's ability to develop an integrated logistics system is affected by its level of involvement. Where the firm has wholly owned subsidiaries, it has the most potential for controlling the customer service level; joint ventures offer less control, and licensee and distributor markets offer the least control. This is one reason many firms prefer wholly owned ventures.

If the firm had a choice, the favored logistics arrangement would be to concentrate production at home and export to world markets. This allows economies of scale in production and eliminates many international business problems, such as dealing with foreign labor or governments or operating in an unknown environment. The Japanese have had success with this approach. There are several factors working against it, however: (1) transportation costs, (2) trade barriers, (3) foreign exchange risk, (4) customer service needs, and (5) political resistance. These factors often force a firm to choose a deeper commitment to the foreign market.

For example, Volkswagen bought a factory in the United States because of exchange rate problems. The Japanese built auto plants in the United States and Europe because of protectionist pressures. American firms expanded production in Europe also because of protectionist fears. Coca-Cola built a concentrate plant in India because of trade restrictions; and Wacoal, a Japanese lingerie firm, built a factory in Puerto Rico to avoid U.S. tariffs. In each case, it was an involuntary change from exporting from home.

## The Dynamic Environment

Designing an optimal logistics system for international markets is a continuing task. Almost every parameter of the system is subject to change. Not only are markets and competition dynamic, but transportation possibilities also undergo a continuous revolution. We cannot assume that our current transportation achievements represent the end of technological change. Rather, continuing improvements are probable, opening new logistics possibilities.

Government barriers also change, not always for the worse. Tariff barriers have been reduced in recent decades through GATT negotiations. Other trade restrictions have been lessened because of GATT, IMF and similar activities. The formation of regional groupings has had a favorable effect, allowing greater rationalization of the firm's logistics, at least on a regional basis. The U.S.–Canada free-trade agreements and projections for 1992 in Europe are noteworthy here. Negative governmental changes have included decreasing import allowances and demands for greater local content. Furthermore, many nations demand exports from the international firms in their country. Changing international relations — for example, East-West or Arab-Israeli — also influence physical distribution patterns.

## The Flexible Response

Considering the dynamic nature of the international logistics environment, the marketer might reach one major conclusion: There is no definitive solution. This is a useful guideline if it helps the firm avoid large investments aimed at a definitive answer. The firm might better seek ad hoc, temporizing solutions that meet present constraints. These can then be changed as the situation changes, without major new investment. Although perhaps representing second-best answers at any given time, in the long run they may add up to the best feasible solution.

Although a firm can make major investments in facilities on the basis of a currently ideal international logistics system, as changes occur in technology, the political situation, or its own goals, the firm may find it necessary to make costly adjustments. Ideally, the firm should make investments in such a way that they can be adjusted to a variety of possible future environments — technological, political, and strategic. The manager must keep all options open insofar as possible. Contingency planning is an inherent part of the *modus operandi.*

## Management of International Logistics

Physical distribution is a major cost in international marketing, and profits often can be increased through cost reductions in the movement of goods. Profits can be increased further if sales rise because logistics changes lead to an improvement in customer service. For these reasons, logistics deserves attention in the international company. We consider the principal elements in the management of international logistics, including the facilities and technology as well as the need for international coordination.

**Facilities and Technology**

The facilities available to the manager of international logistics include (1) service organizations such as transportation companies and freight forwarders, (2) institutions such as free-trade zones and public warehouses, and (3) modern hardware such as computers, the telex, containerization, and jumbo jet planes.

**Freight Forwarder.**   Foreign freight forwarders are specialists in both transportation and documentation for international shipments. The full-service foreign freight forwarder can relieve the producer of most of the burdens of distribution across national borders. They not only handle all the documentation but also provide information on shipping and foreign import regulations. They arrange both for shipment and insurance. They may consolidate shipments for lower costs. Because of their expertise in this technically detailed area, they are used by a majority of companies to take care of overseas shipment. Their efficiency makes them valuable to both large and small companies.

**Free-Trade Zones.**   Aware of the problems posed by their barriers to trade, some 50 nations have established over 300 free-trade zones, free ports, bonded warehouses and similar devices to overcome some of the self-created problems. There are over 100 foreign-trade zones in the United States. These facilities are usually government-owned, supervised by customs officials. They permit the firm to bring merchandise into the country without paying duties as long as it remains in the free-trade zone or bonded warehouse. Many allow processing, assembly, sorting, repacking, and the like within the zone. Countries provide these zones because they gain employment that would normally be driven away by their trade barriers.

*Potential Advantages.*   Among the potential advantages offered by free-trade zones are the following:

1.   They permit the firm to realize the economies of *bulk shipping* to a country without the burden of custom duties. Duties need to be paid only when the goods are released on a *small-lot* basis from the zone.
2.   They permit manufacturers to carry a local inventory at less cost than in facilities they own, because in their own facilities they must pay the duty as soon as the goods enter the country. If duties are high, the financial burden of covering the duty on goods in inventory is significant.

Bausch & Lomb, Inc., for example, leased 500 square meters in the public bonded warehouses at the Netherland's Schipol Airport and shipped merchandise there at bulk rates from the United States. The company used Schipol as its European distribution center. It realized big savings by concentrating European inventories at one spot, yet it provided two-day delivery in Europe. This system also permitted its distributors and agents to reduce their own inventories, which improved distributor relations.

3.  U.S. foreign trade zones offer the same advantages as others and are used by U.S. and foreign firms, though more by the latter. Among the major American users are General Motors and Ford with 13 and 12 free zones, respectively.

One advantage for firms is that they can ship ingredients or components into the zone without paying the U.S. duty on them. After assembly, the complete product can be shipped into the U.S. market at the lower rate applying to the finished good. Thus, AOC, a Taiwanese TV producer, ships tubes and components into a U.S. zone without paying the 22 percent U.S. duty on them. After assembly it ships them out at the lower 11 percent duty that applies to complete sets.

4.  The ability to engage in local processing, assembly, repacking, and similar operations can mean savings to the firm. It can ship to the market in bulk or CKD for advantageous freight rates. Then it can process, assemble, or repack for local distribution. For U.S., European, or Japanese firms, the local labor costs may be less than at home. The free zones in Panama and Colombia have been popular with European and U.S. firms such as, for example, Ronson, Goodyear, Kodak, Ericsson, and Celanese.

A variation on free-trade zones allows a company to have all or part of its own plant declared a free-trade zone or bonded warehouse. The advantages are the same but it is even more convenient for the firm. Honda's motorcycle plant in Ohio and Olivetti's Pennsylvania typewriter plant are located in free-trade zones. Ford has one for its tractor plant in Romeo, Michigan. In a similar manner, Brazil permitted Caterpillar to have an on-site free zone. The savings are significant for Caterpillar because duties on its imports average 50 percent and goods have to be financed for about one year. Because such zones attract or keep companies in a country, they are a growing development. Olivetti was threatening to leave the U.S. market until it received a free-trade zone.

***Evaluation of Free Zones.***   The firm should consider foreign-trade zones to see if their potential advantages apply to its own situation. Their usefulness depends on duty rates. Since free zones are primarily aimed at overcoming the inconvenience of tariff barriers, they are less important for products with low duties. Furthermore, the economies of bulk shipments and the use of low-cost local labor are benefits that can be obtained *apart* from the use of free zones.

The logistics planner must decide in which markets free zones can play a useful role and in which markets the firm is better off with its own or distributor facilities. The free zone must be considered as just one part of the overall system. Each zone must be individually evaluated, because not all deliver the promised advantages. A review of Latin American free zones found some that were excellent and some that were unsatisfactory. Other benefits of free zones are that they minimize the investment needs of the firm and have built-in flexibility. If they do not work out well, other alternatives can be tried and the firm has lost little.

**Modern Technology.**   Supertankers, containerization, jumbo jets and computers all are the result of modern technology, and they all affect the costs of moving goods in international marketing. Physical distribution is dependent on the state of the art in transportation and storage. Therefore, the logistics planner must make sure that the distribution system reflects the economies possible with modern technology but at the same time is flexible enough to adapt to new developments without major investments having to be written off.

In view of the increased European integration expected in 1992, Philips has spent heavily on superautomated Eurodistribution centers for each product division. Comprehensive computer systems run the entire operation on an ordering-to-forwarding basis.

Computers and communications are other aspects of modern technology that aid international logistics. They permit the speedy information flow necessary for prompt response. With almost instant communication, the firm's markets and supply sources around the world can effectively be made part of the same physical distribution network. Communications is as much a part of logistics as the movement of goods. They are interdependent, of course. The varied roles of modern technology can be illustrated best by an actual example.

The Limited is a very successful American retail chain with 3,200 outlets and three different kinds of stores: The Limited, Express, and Victoria's Secret. Part of its success may result from its mastery of modern technology in its international logistics. As the following steps indicate, The Limited has been able to raise its customer service level and gain significant competitive advantage by aggressive logistics management.

1. From point-of-sale computers in all its stores, daily sales reports flow back to company headquarters in Columbus, Ohio.
2. To restock its best sellers, The Limited sends production orders by satellite to plants in the United States, Hong Kong, South Korea, Singapore, and Sri Lanka.
3. When the goods are finished, they are flown back to Columbus on a chartered 747 that makes four flights weekly.
4. At its automated distribution center in Columbus, apparel is sorted, priced, and shipped within 48 hours.
5. Trucks and planes carry the goods from Columbus to the 3,200 stores.
6. Within 60 days of the order, the apparel is on sale. Most competitors order six months or more in advance.

This example demonstrates not only the role of modern technology, but also how logistics is a total system, integrating production, distribution, and communications as complementary parts of international marketing.

## Coordination of International Logistics

Physical distribution can be a major cost element affecting competitiveness. In international marketing, logistics almost inevitably involves more than one country. This means that some corporate coordination is necessary. Some ITT Europe companies lost major orders because their distribution costs were too high. The company studied the problem and made some interesting findings. Managers perceived their distribution costs to be about 1 to 1.5 percent. In reality, they were at least 6 percent, or over $700 million for ITT Europe. A reporting and cost control system was installed, leading to significant savings in all aspects of physical distribution, from deliveries by suppliers, warehousing, and transportation, to designing a new cardboard box for shipping. We discuss some aspects of the coordination of international logistics.

**For One Market.**   Within each of the firm's markets, physical distribution will be handled primarily by the subsidiary or distributor there. However, corporate headquarters should provide assistance in the planning of local physical distribution. It can contribute ideas and analytical techniques, such as distribution cost analysis, so that the best technology is available in each market. Furthermore, some governments, for example, Mexico, may require that the firm balance each dollar of imported components with a dollar of export. Obviously, the local subsidiary cannot solve this problem on its own.

To improve its customer service level in North America, BMW established three parts distribution centers for its 420 auto dealers and 290 motorcycle dealers. By calling the nearest center they can hook into BMW's inventory network.

**For Regional Markets.**   Operations within regional groupings will also need coordination. As these groups achieve economic integration, a subsidiary or distributor in one member country cannot be considered merely a national operation. It becomes part of the larger regional market. For example, as the EC reaches a common transport policy, physical distribution will have to be organized on an EC-wide basis. Even in LAIA, which has not achieved much integration overall, individual firms and industries are obtaining integration on a multinational basis through complementation agreements. We examined these in Chapter 5.

SKF, the Swedish firm, is the world's largest producer of ball bearings. SKF chose Singapore as its sales, service, and distribution center for Southeast Asia. Singapore was chosen because it has excellent shipping and airfreight services, and it offered a free port, enabling the company to avoid tariffs and sales taxes on trans-shipments. In addition to its marketing and logistics activities in Singapore, SKF added a bearing factory. The output of this plant that is not used in the region will be sold elsewhere, using the central marketing coordination of SKF's German subsidiary.

**Internationally.**   Firms that have many markets and supply sources need overall coordination for optimum integration of supply and demand. Coordination is necessary to achieve synergism. The firm will want each plant operating at an efficient level as well as adequate inventories and customer service in each market. Such coordination is possible only on a centralized basis.

Centralized control of exports is one way to achieve international logistics coordination. One office, not necessarily at company headquarters, coordinates all export orders and assigns production sources for the order. Eaton, for example, produces in 43 countries in addition to the United States. All products are exported to more than 100 countries through a worldwide marketing organization based in Switzerland.

Centralized control of exports is often tied in with regional distribution centers where inventories are held for faster local delivery. For example, Caterpillar has a parts depot in the Far East from which it ships inventory and provides services to dealers and customers in 19 Asian countries. Texas Instruments (TI) stocks materials in 16 major market areas. TI uses a computer-teletype-telephone hookup with this global system. With appropriate planning, distributors and licensees can be included in the integrated logistics program. Automatic Radio International has accomplished this successfully with 160 distributors and licensees in 80 countries.

The firm can assure integrated international logistics under various arrangements. The particular setup must fit the situation of the firm, but, some centralized control will be necessary if the *overall* corporate interests are to be satisfied. In review, the benefit of efficient international logistics planning should be increased profits produced by (1) more efficient and stable production levels at plants in different countries, (2) lower-cost distribution, resulting in part from the possibility of combining small orders into carload or planeload lots (for example, Squibb does this by using five major exporting points with intermediate break-bulk points around the globe), and (3) better customer service levels in international markets.

In one year, Dow Chemical Company processed 25,000 foreign orders and made 12,000 export shipments. Ocean freight costs came to $12 million. Dow handled these shipments from its Midland, Michigan, headquarters through its International Distribution and Traffic Department, which had 55 employees. Dow had overseas manufacturing in 20 locations and bulk terminals or package storage facilities in more than 35 locations.

One of the projects of the department was the preparation of price lists enabling sales representatives to quote a price on any chemical in more than 100 markets. Information necessary for these lists included insurance and freight costs, consular fees, and duties. Since some of these are constantly changing, maintaining a currently valid list was difficult. Computerizing helped here, and updated computer printouts were sent to sales representatives in each country as changes occurred.

One reason freight rates were changing was that the department was bargaining with over 30 steamship conferences on rates and classifications on its chemicals. By getting one chemical, *Dowpon,* reclassified, Dow cut its freight rate from $64 to $42 per long ton. This opened new markets by making it competitive with a similar German product.

Because of the importance of volume shipping of bulky chemicals, the firm operated three vessels under long-term contract for bulk shipments. This was in addition to its regular-spot and medium-term charter arrangements. Dow's engineers also collaborated with marine engineers on the design of specialized vessels. The great majority of company shipments were made in bulk to overseas bulk terminals.

Although Dow did all of its own logistics planning, it did use the service of freight forwarders — two on the Gulf Coast, one each on the East Coast, West Coast, and Great Lakes. One exception to the centralized physical distribution management at Dow was the European market. As its manufacturing and marketing operations grew in Europe, Dow found that decentralization was appropriate for control of shipments *within* Europe.

## Summary

There are several ways exporters can influence foreign distributors' marketing. The first step is careful distributor selection. This requires a job specification and evaluation of the distributor's track record according to the exporter's criteria. A second step is writing the distributor agreement to recognize the interests of both parties. A third step is in making suitable financial arrangements. The exporter must choose margins, price quotes, the currency, and payment terms to satisfy both parties. A fourth ingredient is marketing support, which may include a strong brand, advertising support, training distributor's salesforce, supplying promotional materials, and establishing a regional warehouse. A fifth dimension is communication, which may include an 800 telephone number, visits, a regional headquarters, and a company newsletter. Some other potential motivators include contests, rewards for good performance, an exclusive territory, and taking equity in the distributor.

Wholesalers around the world differ greatly in size and capability. Wholesaling efficiency generally rises with the level of economic development, but there are many exceptions to that trend. Where wholesaling is fragmented and small-scale, it constrains the local marketing of the firm by increasing transaction costs and credit requirements and limiting the product line and geographic coverage and services offered.

Retailing shows great international variation with a majority of countries having large numbers of small retailers. In such markets, the firm may find it difficult to secure retailer cooperation in carrying inventory, displaying the product, promoting the product, and giving market feedback.

The international marketer must monitor distribution trends. As economies develop, their distribution structures change as wholesaling and retailing become modernized and the channel members become more powerful. The internationalization of retailing is predicted to continue, with American, European, and Japanese retailers spreading their wings abroad. Direct marketing remains important and mail-order and telephone marketing are growing. Discounting and retail price competition are spreading to more countries.

A firm would like to use the same channels in every market, but exact duplication is never possible. Differing wholesale and retail structures and consumer income and buying behavior force adjustments. Also the manufacturer's own situation varies from market to market.

Also, the firm would like to go as direct as possible to its customers, however, in foreign markets that is usually less feasible than at home because of smaller markets and fragmented channels.

In deciding on selective or intensive distribution coverage, the firm may find that its wishes are overruled by political or economic conditions.

In working with the channel abroad, the firm may be able to employ the techniques learned at home (e.g., margins, advertising, financing, training, advisory services, market research assistance and missionary selling).

The firm must keep its channels up to date as its sales and product line grow. It must learn to respond to powerful retailers who demand private brands and price cuts.

In each foreign market, the firm must analyze the logistics environment and infrastructure and design an appropriate physical distribution system for it. In addition, the firm must try to link its many foreign markets into an effective global network. This network should be flexible enough to adapt to its dynamic environment where government, competitive, and technological parameters are changing.

In managing its international logistics, the firm will use such facilities as the foreign freight forwarder and free-trade zones where they can increase efficiency. Modern technology can be a big help in managing international logistics. The firm will need to coordinate its international physical distribution to gain the necessary efficiencies to be competitive.

## Questions

11.1   Discuss the financial and pricing techniques for motivating foreign distributors.

11.2   Discuss the various ways of communicating with foreign distributors.

11.3   What are some of the international differences in wholesaling?

11.4   What problems arise when the firm faces fragmented wholesaling in a country?

11.5   Many markets have relatively large numbers of small retailers. How does this constrain the local marketing of the international firm?

11.6   What services would the manufacturer like to receive from the retailer?

11.7   What are the ways in which retailing know-how is transferred internationally?

11.8   Discuss the implications for the international marketer of the trend toward larger-scale retailing.

11.9   Discuss current distribution trends in world markets.

11.10   Why do American firms tend to have somewhat different distribution channels abroad?

11.11   Identify some of the ways a manufacturer can work with the distribution channel abroad.

11.12   What will be the impact of 1992 on retailing in the European Community?

11.13   How do export logistics differ from logistics in domestic marketing?

11.14   What are the advantages offered by using the foreign freight forwarder?

11.15   Discuss the potential benefits of using foreign-trade zones.

## Endnotes

[1]Philip J. Rosson and I. David Ford, "Manufacturer-Distributor Relations and Export Performance," *Journal of International Business Studies* (Fall 1982): 52–72.

[2]*The Wall Street Journal* November 14, 1988, p 1.

[3]Madhav Kacker, "International Flow of Retailing Know-how," *Journal of Retailing* (Spring 1988): 41–67.

[4]*Business Week,* September 4, 1989, 47.

[5]*Management Europe,* February 13, 1989, 13–16.

[6]G. J. Davies, "The International Logistics Concept," *The International Journal of Physical Distribution* 17, no 2 (1987): 20–27.

## Further Readings

Bello, Daniel C, and Lee D. Dahringer. "The Influence of Country and Product on Retailer Practices." *International Marketing Review* (Summer 1985): 45–52.

Czinkota, Michael R. "Distribution of Consumer Products in Japan." *International Marketing Review* (Autumn 1985): 39–51.

Ho, Suk-Ching, and Ho-Fuk Lau. "Development of Supermarket Technology. The Incomplete Transfer Phenomenon." *International Marketing Review* (Spring 1988): 20–30.

Kacker, Madhav P. *Transatlantic Trends in Retailing.* Westport, Conn.: Quorum Books, 1985.

Robles, Ferdinand, and George C. Hozier, Jr. "Understanding Free Trade Zones." *International Marketing Review* (Summer 1986): 44–54.

Stock, James R., and Douglas M. Lambert. "Physical Distribution Management in International Marketing." *International Marketing Review* (Autumn 1983): 28–41.

In early April 1973, the vice-president of Latin America/Pacific Division of General Foods Corporation was preparing a final report to the executive committee on whether its manufacturing and sales subsidiary in Japan should continue to operate alone or enter a joint venture with Ajinomoto, Japan's largest food company. Ajinomoto recently expressed interest in acquiring for cash half the stock of GF's wholly owned subsidiary. Ajinomoto had annual sales of more than $500 million and sold a broad line of products, including seasonings, salad oils, soups, frozen food, and amino acids. Established in 1909, the company has well-established distribution channels and marketing contacts. Ajinomoto, the company name, is also the Japanese word for monosodium glutamate, one of the company's major products.

## The Company

General Foods Corporation is a major New York–based food company with 15 subsidiaries in Canada, Europe, Latin America, and Japan. Its sales in fiscal 1973 reached $2.6 billion. The company was divided into three business groups: domestic grocery operations, U.S. non-grocery units, and operations outside the United States. Overseas operations were under two vice-presidents, in charge of Latin America/Pacific and Europe, respectively. Overseas sales were increasing more rapidly than domestic and accounted for 17 percent of total sales in fiscal 1973. Coffee was a major item in more than half of the countries in which General Foods had operations. However, General Food's product line abroad included a number of items not sold in North America — for example, ice cream, spices, soup, and bottled soft drinks.

General Foods had entered the Japanese market in 1954 by acquiring 100 percent of an orange juice concentrate manufacturer. This operation, which sold exclusively to a bottler who marketed the finished product, was still going strong. In 1960, General Foods opened its first coffee plant in Japan and focused on expanding sales of coffee, under the name of Maxwell. Though well established as a brand name by U.S. occupation forces, *Maxwell House* is not easy for Japanese to say, so it was shortened to Maxwell, as in France and Germany. By 1973 General Foods managed to share, with Nestlé, about 90 percent of the Japanese packaged coffee market, although Nestlé's share was much larger.

Coffee represented by far the largest sales item of its $25 million annual turnover in Japan. General Foods had a sales staff of about 200 at over 30 sales offices in all major Japanese cities, including Tokyo, Osaka, Sapporo, and Nagoya.

General Food's operations in Japan had been growing at a moderate pace. However, in recent years, the company faced increasing competitive pressures there. Its earnings in fiscal 1973 were also adversely affected by the heavy investment in trying to establish a dog-food business in Japan where dog-feeding habits were quite different from those in the U.S. market. General Foods Japan was a wholly owned venture, but almost all the staff were Japanese. Nevertheless, the company had only partially adopted Japanese management and business practices.

## Marketing Strategy

During the early 1960s, General Foods' marketing strategy focused on wholesalers. Through these wholesalers, General Foods progressively extended its retail network to include, besides general grocery stores, confectionery, fruit, bread, and tea shops. With the rising popularity of the supermarket in Japan (since the mid-sixties),

443

General Foods intensified its marketing efforts and extended its promotion all the way down the distribution channel to the retail level. More than 60 percent of General Foods products were sold through supermarkets in 1973, although these stores accounted for less than one-sixth of all food sales in Japan.

The company also expanded its selling directly to small retail stores along with supermarkets, because its experience in Japan revealed that Japanese demand was drawn down through the distribution system from the consumer/retailer end, rather than being pushed down from wholesaler levels. Once a retail store felt that it must carry an item because of customer demand, it would reorder. However, the wholesaler could not be relied upon to push products to the retailer. General Foods sold directly to store owners from trucks manned by company personnel, almost in the same manner as bread or milk is sold.

This strategy of intensive distribution was working well enough that General Foods had access to stores selling 70 percent of the soluble coffee market. Yet the company could not continue its efforts in selling to small stores, because volume did not justify the cost. To make competition tougher, Nestlé, its main competitor, which had a much broader range of products and a larger sales staff, could approach the smallest stores with a wide range of goods without depending on sales of any particular line.

General Foods' product lines in Japan were soluble coffees, sauce mixes, nondairy creamers, and dog foods. The recent dog-food introduction had proved a difficult and expensive undertaking. The company did not have at present any intention of introducing in Japan other product lines carried by the U.S. or other overseas operations.

The vice-president of General Foods Latin America/Pacific thought that the joint venture with Ajinomoto would be desirable if the new alliance added another ten percentage points to General Foods' market penetration. On the other hand, he was concerned that the joint venture could have some adverse effects, including some loss of control and conflicts on transfer pricing and product line.

## Questions

1. Should General Foods — Japan enter a joint venture with Ajinomoto? Give the arguments and considerations for and against such a joint venture.

2. Identify and evaluate any alternative courses of action to the joint venture.

CASE

# 11.2 Protective Devices Division Case

My name is Steve Ball. This story is true but all the names in it have been changed. My job was assistant marketing manager of the Protective Devices Division of Electronic Systems, Inc. (ESI), an electronics manufacturer whose major

Source: This case was prepared by Robert M. Ballinger of Siena College, based on a personal experience. Used by permission.

markets were in the aerospace industry. Protective Devices Division (PDD) was an acquisition in a fairly unrelated business, the intrusion-alarm industry.

ESI's products were custom-engineered and required an electronics engineer to sell them. In contrast, PDD's products were sold in a commercial market. Although PDD's products were electronic, PDD's customers were fairly unsophisticated in electronics. Thus, PDD's markets were quite unlike any with which its parent corporation, ESI, had any experience.

ESI's sales were in the $80 million range and PDD's were in the $4 million range. PDD had about 75 employees.

My story begins one sunny, hot day in August when I was on vacation. The phone rang. My general manager, Andy Smith (see Figure 1), was on the phone.

"Steve, this is Andy. Is your passport up-to-date?"

"Yes it is, Andy."

"Good, something has come up here. I won't be able to take that European trip I had planned, so I want you to go in my place. Is that okay with you?"

"Oh sure, Andy, I'll start planning for it right away."

When I hung up, I really had mixed feelings. It would be fun to go to Europe again. The itinerary included Germany, France, Sweden, and England. It would be in September, so the weather should be pleasant. But, I also knew that now I would have to negotiate with our French distributor's manager, who was really upset with us. I'd hoped that since Andy got us in this mess he would have the "pleasure" of dealing with Monsieur Dupuis. Also, I wondered why Andy skipped my immediate boss, Tom Daniels.

## Background

Two years before I had convinced Andy that we should exhibit at the Security Equipment Trade Show sponsored by the U.S. Department of Commerce at the U.S. Trade Center in Milan, Italy. At that time, we had not exported any products. I had recently joined PDD after having been employed by a competitor in the alarm-manufacturing business in international marketing.

Although we did not find a distributor in Italy, we did obtain a good lead in France. I visited our prospective distributor, Systemes de Securite

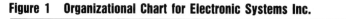

**Figure 1    Organizational Chart for Electronic Systems Inc.**

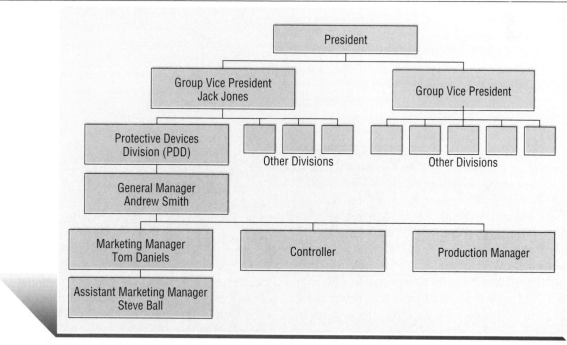

(SDS), which placed a substantial trial order for ultrasonic intrusion detection systems. SDS asked for the usual exclusive agreement to market our products in France. Because ESI's corporate policy did not permit exclusive distributorships, I was not able to accede to its request. However, I tried to resolve this difficulty by promising to refer any inquiries to SDS that we received from France. This I did on a number of occasions. SDS was pleased with our equipment and reordered several times.

Eventually we became so comfortable with SDS that we no longer required our sight drafts to be secured by SDS's letters of credit. By the next year, SDS was our third largest customer, following two of the largest intrusion-alarm installation companies in the United States.

About a year and a half after appointing SDS, the Telex rattled with a message from Paris. It was from another potential distributor that wished to import our products into France. In fact, it was sending a Bob Peters over to visit us in a week. I wanted to refer Peters to SDS but was overruled by Andy Smith.

"Remember, Steve, ESI's Group Vice President, Jack Jones, was really adamant. He said there would be no exclusive distributorships and that means we have to talk to Bob Peters."

"Well, Andy, I can tell you right now. The SDS people are going to be very upset if they see us 'going behind their back.' "

"Oh heck, Steve, if they like our products, they'll continue to buy. Don't worry about it. We'll work something out."

Bob Peters visited the next week. He was an expatriate American who had lived in Paris for a number of years. He represented some wealthy businessmen who wanted to enter the alarm business. He claimed that the French market "had not yet been scratched." Bob made a good impression on everyone at PDD, even me. He placed a fairly significant initial order for some $8,000. At this time, SDS was purchasing about $100,000 of our products annually. Peters placed a couple of follow-up orders over the next several months.

Although I later tried to get SDS to serve Peters' company, I could reach no satisfactory conclusion with SDS, and Peters continued to order directly from PDD. Meanwhile, our relations with SDS deteriorated.

First, SDS fell behind in paying its sight drafts. Second, it complained that some new PDD microwave intrusion-detection systems it had ordered did not work properly. In fact, the new system did "false-alarm." (It signaled the police that a protected building was being burglarized, but when the police responded, no evidence was found to indicate that a burglary had taken place. A few such occurrences are acceptable, but our new system was doing this much too often.)

At this time, we were no longer sure that SDS would continue to be a good distributor. Maybe Peters' group would be better, we thought. At least, it was easier to communicate with Peters than it was to communicate with SDS.

We then learned that another Security Equipment Show was to be held at the U.S. Trade Center in Paris. It seemed like a good idea to exhibit at this show to attract sales leads for our French distributor. Also, we could resolve the French distributor problem and perhaps find distributors for the other European countries.

Andy Smith decided to represent us in Paris, to visit ESI's subsidiary in England, and to visit a German and a Swedish prospect. Although disappointed that I was not to make this trip, I also was gleeful that Andy would "have to work something out" with SDS.

## The European Trip

This brings my story up to the point where the phone rang during my vacation. I went to Europe as requested. First, I visited a German prospect near Frankfurt. Then, I took the Trans-European Express to Paris. Upon arrival, I attempted to contact Monsieur Dupuis. He was "not available." Bob Peters, however, welcomed me, and I was taken around to see the sights of Paris by Peters and his French associates.

I then made sure that the exhibit was correctly installed at the U.S. Trade Center. After I had repeatedly phoned Dupuis' office, he showed up at the exhibition without notice. He was furious.

"Ball, you assured me that I would be your French distributor. But you have been dealing with this upstart Peters behind my back."

"Now wait a minute, Monsieur Dupuis," I responded, "We did refer Peters to you, but you chose not to deal with him. Furthermore, SDS has been delinquent in paying for about $50,000 on orders we shipped. What are you going to do about that?"

## Questions

1. Detail the origin and nature of the problems PDD is having with its French distributor.

2. From the exporter's viewpoint, what are the arguments for and against exclusive distributorships in foreign markets?

3. What can Ball and PDD do now?

CHAPTER 12

# International Promotion
## Advertising

*Learning Objectives*

Advertising is a major form of promotion in international as well as in domestic marketing. In this chapter we examine the parameters of an effective international advertising program, including the subjects of international constraints, agency selection, the message and the media, the budget, and ways of evaluating, organizing for, and sharing the advertising effort.

The main goals of this chapter are to

1. Discuss how languages, controls, and infrastructure modify the advertising task.
2. Identify the criteria used for agency selection, and explain the growing role for international agencies.
3. Discuss the role of language, media, market segments, and new-product introductions in the international advertising message.
4. Show how media diversity and media developments affect the options available in a market.
5. Describe the techniques available and appropriate for setting the ad budget in foreign markets.
6. Discuss the difficulties in evaluating advertising in foreign markets.
7. Describe the different ways of organizing for international advertising — that is, the degree of centralization, decentralization, or compromise that is most effective.
8. Identify the advantages and problems of cooperative advertising.

*Marketing* includes the whole collection of activities the firm performs in relating to its market. Promotion is the most visible as well as the most culture-bound of the firm's marketing functions. In the other functions the firm relates to the market in a quieter, more passive way. With the promotional function, the firm is standing up and speaking out, wanting to be seen and heard. We will define *promotion* as the communication by the firm with its various audiences, with a view to informing and influencing them.

The subject matter of Chapters 12 and 13 is not really international promotion, but rather promotion in international marketing. Since relatively little promotion is truly international, we concerned primarily with the management of promotion in a number of separate nations. The international aspect is the coordination of the various national activities to make up the firm's integrated international program. Promotion in international marketing plays the same role it does in domestic operations, that is, communication with the firm's audiences to achieve certain goals. Variations from country to country will occur, however, in all three dimensions: means of communication, audience, and even company goals.

Promotion is aimed at selling products and enhancing the image of the company. We have seen, however, that the situation of the company and its product line often are not the same from one country to another. Therefore, the promotional task will not be exactly the same in every market either. Another dimension is nationality; that is, the firm must decide whether to present itself as a local, foreign, or multinational company.

Our approach will be to examine the various elements of promotion in international marketing. We will discuss the following major topics: advertising, personal selling, sales promotion, the marketing mix, special forms of promotion, and public relations. We will give a picture of the state of the art in these areas and highlight problems and decisions facing the international marketing manager. Our examination begins in Chapter 12 with advertising; in Chapter 13 we will discuss the other elements of international promotion.

*Advertising* is the paid communication of company messages through impersonal media. The messages may be audio, as in radio; visual, as in billboards or magazines; or audiovisual, as in television or cinema advertising. Advertising everywhere is used to achieve various marketing goals. These goals include paving the way for the salesforce, gaining distribution, product sales, improving brand image, and so on. In every country, advertising is just one element of the marketing mix. Its role will depend on the other elements of the mix in that country.

Because the principles of advertising do not vary internationally, but only the practice, we will not discuss principles. We begin our discussion of advertising in the international company with a review of the environmental constraints, after which we consider the advertising decisions facing the international marketing manager.

## Constraints on International Advertising

The international advertising program of a company is determined by two sets of constraints, one posed by the internal situation of the company, and the other by the international environment of advertising. We look first at the important elements of the international environment. Figure 12–1 illustrates some of the constraints on international marketing communication.

**Figure 12-1**                              **Constraints on International Marketing Communication**

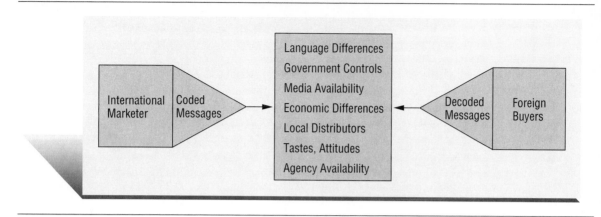

| | Languages: The Tower of Babel | |
| --- | --- | --- |

## Languages: The Tower of Babel

We discussed language in Chapter 4; here we examine its significance for international advertising. Construction of the biblical tower of Babel stopped when the workers could no longer communicate with each other. The manager of international advertising may feel a similar constraint when facing the diversity of languages in world markets. Although some languages are used in more than one country, there are many more languages than countries. The international advertiser does not have to know all the languages of all markets, but the firm's advertising must communicate in these languages. Even in the few cases where the product and its advertising appeals are universal, the language will not be.

Technical accuracy or perfect translations are not sufficient, either; persuasive messages must speak the "language of the heart," and for this, intimate local knowledge is required. The local help available is of two kinds: national personnel in countries where the firm has subsidiaries, and the advertising agency located in the market. In either case, the company gets the benefit of employees in whose native language the company wants to advertise. In other markets, the firm may rely on its distributor for the advertising.

## Role of Advertising in Society

Another constraint on the international advertiser is the different role of advertising in each country. About half of the world's advertising expenditures are in the United States. In 1988 and 1989 ad outlays abroad surpassed those in the United States after trailing them during most of the 1980s. As Table 12-1 shows, the United States still leads all other countries in relative expenditures on advertising, spending, for example, ten times as much as Indonesia and over six times as much as India. Given the great differences in size of GNP, the absolute differences in ad outlays are much greater still. However, ad outlays in many overseas markets are growing much faster than in the United States. For example, in the late 1980s, countries such as Spain, Korea, Taiwan, and Thailand had advertising growth rates of 15 percent or more per annum.

**Table 12-1**                          **Role of Advertising in the Economy: Selected Countries**

| Country | Advertising as Percent of GNP |
|---|---|
| *United States* | 1.50% |
| *Latin America* | |
| Argentina | 1.03 |
| Brazil | 1.00 |
| Mexico | 0.22 |
| *Asia* | |
| Australia | 1.42 |
| India | 0.23 |
| Indonesia | 0.16 |
| Japan | 1.15 |
| Malaysia | 0.56 |
| South Korea | 0.86 |
| *Europe* | |
| Belgium | 0.56 |
| France | 0.63 |
| Germany | 0.89 |
| Norway | 1.25 |
| Sweden | 1.12 |
| United Kingdom | 1.34 |

Source: Calculated from *International Marketing Data and Statistics, 1988–89*; and *World Bank Atlas 1988*.

The level of economic development is only one factor in advertising spending. Regulations on advertising and media and other cultural factors are also important. Mexico spends only one-fourth as much as its Latin neighbors at a similar level of development. Britain and Norway spend twice as much as their equally wealthy neighbors, Belgium and France.

**Media Availability**

Some of the media used by advertisers in the United States may not be available abroad. Two factors are at work here. One is government regulation, such as Indonesia and Norway not allowing commercials on TV. Another variable is the communications infrastructure. For example, newspaper availability ranges from 1 daily paper per 2 persons in Japan and 1 per 4 persons in the United States to a range of 1 to 10–20 in Latin America, and in extreme cases, 1 to 200 persons in such countries as Bangladesh, Nigeria, and Sudan.

As another example of variation in communications infrastructure, TV set ownership ranges from 1 set per 2 persons in countries like the United States and Japan to 1 to 25 in Indonesia, 1 to 200 in India, 1 to 330 in Bangladesh, and 1 to 4,000 in Burma.

## Government Controls

A problem for marketers in both industrialized and developing countries is government regulation of advertising. American marketers will often find foreign countries more restrictive of advertising than their home market. Government regulations can affect the product, the media, the message, the budget, and agency ownership.

1.   Tobacco, alcohol, and drugs are special targets. For example, cigarette advertising is partially or totally banned in most Western European countries, but also in several communist countries, and even in India and Argentina.
2.   Some media are not available or are very limited for commercial use. In addition to communist countries, five Western European countries had no commercials on TV and/or radio as of 1988. Indonesia cancelled advertising on TV after earlier restricting advertising pages in newspapers.
3.   Advertising messages have a variety of restrictions. Some countries regulate the languages that can be used. Many countries have rather strong limits on comparative advertising. About 25 countries require preclearance of certain commercials.
4.   The ad budget can draw government attention. India attacked the ad budgets of foreign tire companies there. Britain made a similar attack on the ad budgets of Unilever and Procter & Gamble, which were considered too large. Developing countries are concerned about the ad budgets of drug firms.
5.   Some countries restrict ownership of ad agencies. Boddewyn found 21 percent of his sample allowed only minority foreign ownership, and Indonesia, Nigeria, and Pakistan allow none at all.[1]

## Competition

The competitive situation is another variable. In some markets, an international company will compete against other international companies. In others, the competition will be purely national. Sound advertising strategy in one market will not necessarily be sound in another market with a different competitive situation. Furthermore, the approach of the international company will provoke different kinds of reactions. In some countries, the international company causes national competitors to follow its course of action. For example, Procter & Gamble's entry into Western European countries caused national competitors to increase their advertising. In another case, British American Tobacco's (BAT) entry into the Dutch market led to a strong defensive advertising attack by a local Dutch firm. The battle finally ended up in the Dutch courts.

## Agency Availability

Another constraint on the international advertiser is the availability of ad agencies in different world markets. This runs a very broad range. For example, the 1989 *Advertising Age* survey showed 9 countries (mostly in Africa) with just one agency, and many, such as China, Panama, Paraguay, and Saudi Arabia, with just two.[2] At the other extreme are the United States and the United Kingdom, with over 500 agencies each. The quality of agency service in a country corresponds roughly to its economic development *and*

## Global Marketing

### Japanese Ads Take Earthiness to Levels Out of This World

TOKYO—If television advertising is a window on a society's culture, the Japanese aren't as uptight as Westerners think. Picture this: A small pile of gray clay, coiled like the top of a Dairy Queen cone, waddles up to the front of the television screen and stares out with puppy-dog eyes. It looks suspiciously like something unmentionable on American TV. But it isn't unmentionable in Japan.

"Sorry for being stinky all the time," the little clay coil says in a squeaky voice after identifying itself. "But humans who do nothing about my stinkiness are bad, too." Whereupon a strong shot of a toilet-bowl deodorizer called "Shut" swiftly dissolves the problem.

Japanese use earthy humor to advertise products that Americans sell ever so delicately. One hemorrhoid-preparation commercial features a man in an outlandish costume, his trousers around his ankles, sitting on a toilet and whining about pain. Another ad for a toilet-bowl cleaner is shot from inside the toilet so you can watch a wife urge her husband to stick his head inside the bowl to see how clean she got it. A tampon is advertised by a famous Japanese actress dressed up as a tampon.

"People think it is fun," says Yuya Furukawa, who created both the "Shut" and hemorrhoid ads for Dentsu Inc., the giant Japanese ad agency. If all this frankness seems un-Japanese it isn't. Casualness about bodily functions has always come naturally in Japanese culture.

Source: Quoted from Damon Darlin, "Japanese Ads Take Earthiness to Levels Out of this World," *The Wall Street Journal,* August 30, 1988, 1. Reprinted by permission of *The Wall Street Journal,* © 1988 Dow Jones & Company, Inc. All rights reserved Worldwide.

---

the size of its economy. Thus, India, a poor nation in per capita income, has several good agencies because its total market is large. J. Walter Thompson has over 500 employees in its several offices there. Though Nigeria has just one agency, it is a rather well-staffed affiliate of the Saatchi and Saatchi group.

## Advertising Decisions Facing the International Marketer

The international advertiser must assure the development of appropriate campaigns for each market and also try to get the right degree of coordination among the various national programs. We will examine seven decision areas in international advertising: (1) selecting the agency (or agencies), (2) choosing the message, (3) selecting the media, (4) determining the budget, (5) evaluating advertising effectiveness, (6) organizing for advertising, and (7) deciding whether to engage in cooperative advertising abroad.

**Selecting the Agency**

Many marketing functions are performed within the company. With advertising, the firm almost always relies on outside expertise from the advertising agency. Agency selection will usually be the first advertising decision the marketer has to make. Two major alternatives are open: (1) an international agency with domestic and overseas offices or (2) local agencies in each national market. Various modifications of these alternatives are often available.

**Selection Criteria.**   Naturally, the firm should choose the agency or agencies that will best help it achieve its goals. Because this selection criterion is not easy to determine directly, it is helpful to identify subsidiary criteria that can aid in the choice. First, the specific agency alternatives that are available should be identified. For example: What agencies are located in each market? Which are preempted by competitors? Second, each agency should be evaluated using the following criteria.

*Market Coverage.*   Does the particular agency or package of agencies cover all the relevant markets?

*Quality of Coverage.*   How good a job does this package of agencies do in each market?

*Market Research, Public Relations, and Other Marketing Services.*   If the firm needs these services in world markets, in addition to advertising, how do the different agencies compare on their offerings?

*Relative Roles of Company Advertising Department and Agency.*   Some firms have a large staff that does much of the work of preparing advertising campaigns. These firms require less of an agency than do companies that rely on the agency for almost everything relating to advertising. Thus a weak company advertising department needs a strong agency.

*Communication and Control.*   If the firm wants frequent communication with agencies in foreign markets and wishes to oversee their efforts, it will be inclined to tie up with the domestic agency that has overseas offices. The internal communications system of this agency network would facilitate communication for the international marketer.

*International Coordination.*   Does the firm wish to have advertising tailor-made to each national market? Or does it desire coordination of national advertising with that done in other markets? One of the major differences among agency groups will be their ability to aid in attaining international coordination.

*Size of Company's International Business.*   The smaller the firm's international advertising expenditures, the less there is to be divided among many different agencies. The firm's advertising volume may determine agency choice to assure some minimum level of service. A small volume multiplied by a number of markets could be of interest to an international agency even if it is of no interest to an agency in any one market.

*Image.*   Does the firm want a national or international image? If it wants good local identification, it should probably choose national agencies rather than an international one. This is the practice of IBM.

*Company Organization.*   Companies that are very decentralized, with national profit centers, might wish to leave agency selection to the local subsidiary. S. C. Johnson does this.

*Level of Involvement.*   In joint-venture arrangements, the international firm shares decision making. The national partner may have experience with a national agency, which could be the decisive factor. In licensing agreements, advertising is largely in the hands of the licensee. Selling through distributors also reduces the control of the international company. Generally, international marketers can choose only the agencies for the advertising paid for by their firms. Where the firm has a cooperative program with its distributors, it may have some voice in agency selection.

**Trend to International Agencies.**   Increasingly choices are being made in favor of the agencies with offices abroad, especially among U.S. companies. Many U.S. firms feel that choosing an American international agency yields cost savings because it avoids duplication of the creative activity involved in preparing advertising campaigns and facilitates communication with the agency's foreign branches. Where centralized control is desired, it is facilitated by dealing with one agency with a similar international organization.

When companies want to present a united front to the world, the task is easier if the firm uses the same agency everywhere. For example, when the Kodak Instamatic was introduced globally at the same time it was introduced in the United States, some of Eastman Kodak's foreign subsidiaries switched to the local office of J. Walter Thompson. Thompson's American account executive for Kodak was coordinating global advertising for the introduction. The choice of an international agency is especially common in industrial marketing, where the appeals are more common from country to country and the advertising budgets are generally smaller. Consider these examples:

- American Express uses Ogilvie & Mather to coordinate its domestic and international advertising in all its markets.
- AMF was dealing with 18 different agencies internationally. When it switched to one international agency, it found its corporate awareness improved considerably.
- Texas Instruments (TI) had 26 different agencies at home and abroad. Then it switched to one agency, McCann-Erickson. "We were looking for an international approach and McCann has more experience than any other agency," said TI.
- Xerox uses Young & Rubicam almost everywhere that agency has an office or affiliate, even though Xerox uses also local advertising in some of its markets.

Some consumer goods marketers, too, find that the same basic appeals can be used everywhere and therefore an international agency can be chosen. Several examples follow:

- Levi Strauss tries for similarity of appeals abroad and uses McCann-Erickson in the majority of its foreign markets.
- For Philip Morris, Leo Burnett Co. developed the famous Marlboro theme for the U.S. market. As Marlboro went international, Leo Burnett was given the foreign markets as well.
- Pepsi Cola believes in global appeals and relies on BBDO as its international agency to achieve the coordinating in world markets.

**Table 12-2**                    **World Top 20 Advertising Agencies, 1984 and 1988**

| 1984 Rank | Agency | 1988 Rank | Agency |
|---|---|---|---|
| 1 | Young & Rubicam | 1 | Dentsu |
| 2 | Dentsu | 2 | Young & Rubicam |
| 3 | Ted Bates | 3 | Saatchi & Saatchi |
| 4 | Ogilvy & Mather | 4 | Backer Spielvogel Bates |
| 5 | J. Walter Thompson | 5 | McCann-Erickson |
| 6 | BBDO | 6 | FCB-Publicis |
| 7 | Saatchi & Saatchi Compton (SSC) | 7 | Ogilvy & Mather |
| 8 | McCann-Erickson | 8 | BBDO |
| 9 | Foote, Cone & Belding (FCB) | 9 | J. Walter Thompson |
| 10 | Leo Burnett | 10 | Lintas |
| 11 | Grey Advertising | 11 | Hakuhodo |
| 12 | Doyle Dane Bernbach (DDB) | 12 | Grey Advertising |
| 13 | D'Arcy MacManus Masius | 13 | D'Arcy Masius Benton & Bowles |
| 14 | Hakuhodo | 14 | Leo Burnett |
| 15 | SSC & B: Lintas | 15 | DDB-Needham |
| 16 | Benton & Bowles | 16 | WCRS |
| 17 | Marschalk Campbell Ewall | 17 | HDM |
| 18 | Needham Harper | 18 | Roux, Seguela, Cayzac & Goudard |
| 19 | Dancer Fitzgerald Sample | 19 | Lowe, Howard-Spink & Bell |
| 20 | N. W. Ayer | 20 | N. W. Ayer |

Source: *Advertising Age,* April 22, 1985, and March 29, 1989.

• Coca-Cola is a pioneer in internationally similar advertising. It found it desirable to use McCann-Erickson to coordinate on a global basis.

Table 12–2 shows the dominance of the international agencies. Except for the Japanese firms, all of the top 20 are internationalists, and the Japanese are moving in that direction. The membership of the group has remained steady, with 16 of 20 repeating, and two others surviving in mergers, (DDB-Needham and D'Arcy–Benton & Bowles). The table shows the continuing consolidation in the industry, with newcomers joining the list by mergers and acquisitions, and the pecking order changing because of the same activity. The internationals' share of world advertising is growing and will continue to do so as the industry consolidates further. For example, in 1989 three of the top Canadian agencies were acquired by U.S. firms. While the pecking order changes, the internationals continue to lead the industry.

A majority of the top 20 are U.S.–based. This isn't surprising, as the Americans were the first internationalists. They went abroad to follow their clients who were going international. Their great expansion came in the last three decades. In 1927 there were only four U.S. agencies abroad, with a total of 21 offices. By 1990 there were about 100, with over 1,700 offices. Table 12–3 shows that the top U.S. agencies are all internationals, and for

**Table 12-3**                **Top Ten U.S. Agencies, 1988**

| Rank | Agency | Total Billings (Billions of Dollars) | Foreign Billings (Billions of Dollars) |
|------|--------|--------------------------------------|-----------------------------------------|
| 1 | Young & Rubicam | $5.4 | $2.6 |
| 2 | Saatchi & Saatchi | 5.1 | 2.9 |
| 3 | Backer Spielvogel Bates | 4.7 | 2.7 |
| 4 | McCann-Erickson | 4.4 | 3.1 |
| 5 | FCB-Publicis | 4.4 | 2.6 |
| 6 | Ogilvy & Mather | 4.1 | 2.2 |
| 7 | BBDO | 4.1 | 1.7 |
| 8 | J. Walter Thompson | 3.9 | 2.1 |
| 9 | Lintas | 3.6 | 2.2 |
| 10 | D'Arcy Masius Benton & Bowles | 3.4 | 1.6 |

Source: *Advertising Age,* March 29, 1989, 2.

most of them, foreign billings are well over half their total business. McCann-Erickson is the leader here with over 70 percent of billings abroad.

The American leadership has not gone unchallenged. Agencies abroad have gone international also to serve the international interests of their clients. Indeed, two British firms, through acquisitions, have joined the list of the top agencies (Saatchi and Saatchi and WPP). In Japan, Dentsu dominated the market and did almost all of its business there. Realizing the need to go international in the 1980s, it began ties with China and entered a joint venture with Young & Rubicam. This was to help Dentsu enter foreign markets (which also helped Young & Rubicam in Japan).

The relentless growth of the multinational agencies puts pressure on those agencies that serve only one market. For example, in looking toward 1992, mid-size British agencies faced tough choices. They either had to forge a European network or sell out to one, if they wanted to keep their clients who would be operating in the larger integrated European market. It was the same integration pressures of the U.S.–Canada Free Trade Agreement that led to U.S. agencies acquiring a number of Canadian agencies. Many misfortunes have befallen single country agencies that have multinational clients. The Volkswagen advertising in America, for example, was handled very successfully by Doyle Dane Bernbach. When this American agency opened an office in Germany, the Volkswagen company dropped its national agency there and gave the account in Germany to the German office of Doyle Dane Bernbach (now DDB-Needham).

A case well remembered on Madison Avenue is that of the giant Coca-Cola account. Once held by the D'Arcy agency, the account was lost to McCann-Erickson in the United States after McCann got its foot in the door abroad. Thereafter D'Arcy, too, moved into foreign markets. Also, Leo Burnett won the international account for Seven-Up in 1980 and in 1985 was awarded the U.S. account also.

In many instances an international agency covering foreign markets for a firm has obtained its domestic advertising as well. This reflects the firm's desire for coordination and convenience in its advertising program.

The dominance of the international agencies is shown again in Table 12–4. Some indication of their global spread is given by their positions in the 30 markets in the table. They cover many markets and tend to have strong positions in them. The pioneering agency, J. Walter Thompson, is first, second, or third in 12 of the 30 markets. We must add a word of caution here lest we paint a one-sided picture. As recently as 1988 one study showed that of U.S. brands sold abroad, only one-third were handled by the same agency both at home and abroad.[3] The internationals have not yet conquered the world.

**The Local Agency Survives.**    National agencies are a continuing alternative for the international marketer for several reasons. Although international agencies offer multimarket coverage, their networks are not always of even quality. Their offices in some markets might be very strong, whereas in others they might be only average. If the firm needs high-quality advertising in all of its markets, it might decide to use the best local agency in each market even if it does not belong to an international family.

Also, if a firm does not require coordination of its advertising in different markets, it has less need to employ an international agency. The coordination provided by international agencies is not always effective, either.

Other reasons for choosing local agencies include the desire for local image and the desire to give national subsidiaries responsibility for their own promotion. As one vice-president for European operations told the author: "Our gains from improved morale and performance from giving them this responsibility far outweigh any loss of efficiency from not requiring international coordination." For a variety of reasons, Ford Motor Company chose to work with 30 different agencies in world markets.

Of the several reasons for choosing national agencies, most of those we have discussed have been negative, in the sense that they are based on weaknesses in, or a lack of need for, the international agency approach. A more positive reason is the special quality a national agency has to offer. Although it is not uncommon for some of the best agencies in a market to be offices of an international group, in some cases the best agency for a firm will be an independent national agency — just as some relatively small but very creative shops in the United States can exist and compete with the giants of the industry. Sometimes their very independence and lack of size give them a flair and flexibility that may be just what the firm needs in that market. Some of the most successful campaigns are carried out by such agencies, and that is a major reason for the firm to consider them. For example, when looking for a new creative approach to the United States, Perrier chose the small Hal Riney agency rather than one of the internationals. GM also chose Hal Riney for its new Saturn car.

Having made an appropriate bow to the independent national agencies, we again note the persistent trend toward the selection of international agen-

**Table 12–4**

**Global Networks of 12 International Advertising Agencies: Rankings in Individual Markets**

| Country | Young & Rubicam | J. Walter Thompson | McCann-Erickson | Ogilvy & Mather | Leo Burnett | Ted Bates | BBDO | SSC & B:Lintas | Foote, Cone & Belding | D'Arcy MacManus Masius | Grey Advertising | Saatchi & Saatchi |
|---|---|---|---|---|---|---|---|---|---|---|---|---|
| Argentina | 13 | 1 | 7 | 8 | 12 | 14 | 5 | 11 | 9 | | 3 | |
| Australia | 6 | | 5 | 4 | 7 | 1 | 2 | | | 11 | | 8 |
| Austria | 11 | 9 | 3 | 10 | | | | 2 | | 17 | 18 | 7 |
| Brazil | 12 | 5 | 8 | 7 | 17 | 9 | 15 | 16 | 20 | | | 14 |
| Britain | 6 | 2 | 10 | 5 | 19 | 4 | 29 | 24 | 12 | 3 | 23 | 1 |
| Canada | 5 | 1 | 7 | 4 | 13 | 14 | 17 | 28 | 16 | 29 | 15 | |
| Chile | 9 | 1 | 3 | 11 | 14 | 10 | 2 | 4 | | | 7 | 13 |
| Colombia | | 2 | 5 | 1 | | | 4 | | 9 | | | 3 |
| Dom. Republic | 1 | | 2 | | 3 | | | | 4 | | | |
| Ecuador | | | 2 | 3 | | | | | 4 | | | |
| Finland | | 1 | | 19 | | 7 | | 10 | | 25 | | |
| France | 5 | 20 | 18 | 13 | 30 | 16 | 26 | 5 | 22 | 27 | 24 | 10 |
| Germany | 7 | 3 | 4 | 6 | 14 | 16 | 1 | 2 | 19 | 9 | 5 | 13 |
| Greece | | 1 | 9 | | 15 | 3 | 4 | 10 | 11 | 17 | | 5 |
| Hong Kong | 3 | 7 | 5 | 2 | 1 | 4 | 21 | 18 | 16 | 14 | 10 | 12 |
| India | | 1 | | 3 | | | | 2 | | | | 9 |
| Italy | 5 | 2 | 1 | 10 | 20 | 18 | 6 | 9 | 3 | 24 | 12 | 14 |
| Japan | 20 | 17 | 7 | | 29 | | 8 | | 34 | 11 | 25 | |
| Malaysia | 7 | 2 | 8 | 6 | 4 | 1 | 9 | 3 | | | | 10 |
| Mexico | 7 | 3 | 2 | 6 | 8 | | 9 | 21 | 17 | 12 | 18 | 19 |
| Netherlands | 4 | 7 | 6 | 2 | 8 | 27 | 1 | 3 | 19 | 14 | 24 | 11 |
| New Zealand | | 8 | | 5 | 7 | | 1 | 10 | 12 | 4 | 11 | |
| Norway | 4 | | 6 | 3 | | 1 | | 8 | 10 | 11 | 12 | 7 |
| Singapore | 4 | 14 | 5 | 2 | 6 | 11 | 1 | 10 | 12 | 18 | 13 | 16 |
| South Africa | 4 | 7 | 12 | 6 | | 3 | 1 | 8 | 5 | 10 | 2 | 9 |
| Spain | 13 | 1 | 5 | 11 | 19 | 2 | 4 | 3 | 29 | 18 | 28 | 23 |
| Sweden | 6 | 19 | 14 | 9 | | 1 | 7 | 12 | 15 | 18 | 3 | |
| Switzerland | 7 | 16 | 4 | 12 | 27 | | 6 | 10 | | 23 | 24 | 14 |
| Thailand | | 14 | 5 | 2 | 4 | 3 | | 1 | | 13 | 9 | 15 |
| Venezuela | 8 | 1 | | 2 | 3 | | | | 9 | | 7 | 6 |

Source: Reprinted with permission from the April 22, 1985, issue of *Advertising Age.* Copyright 1985 by Crain Communications, Inc.

cies by international companies. Although there will always be room for a certain number of quality independent agencies in each market, their relative importance is likely to decline.

Pepsico is an example of a company that uses American international agencies in many markets. When it moved into Japan, however, Pepsico chose a Japanese agency rather than an American office or affiliate. The executive explained, "We were moving into a very complex market. We wanted a large Japanese agency that knew its way around the key media. The American affiliates just weren't big enough, *at that time,* to do the job."

We should note one more reason local agencies may survive in some countries—nationalism. Many countries resent the role played by foreign firms in their economy and restrict them in various ways. These restrictions often apply to ad agencies too. In the Philippines, for example, national agencies pressured the government to ban foreign ad agencies. They said that the industry would become dominated by the multinationals. They claimed that although they were able to handle local campaigns, the internationals' affiliates would win the major accounts because of their global ties with multinational clients. Along with a dozen other countries, the Philippines now allows only minority foreign ownership of agencies (a maximum of 30 percent). Indonesia, Nigeria, and Pakistan allow no foreign ownership at all. Such protectionism is one barrier to the growth of the multinational agencies.

**Future Developments.**    As the advertising industry evolves in the 1990s, certain trends should continue:

1.   Further industry consolidation through mergers and acquisitions.
2.   Even greater internationalization, including more ties between U.S. and Canadian agencies under the Free Trade Agreement, more European networks by agencies there, and more foreign involvement in U.S. agencies.
3.   A continuing shift by advertisers to international agencies who will increase market share.
4.   Expanded geographic coverage by the internationals. The communist countries are now opening up. Saatchi and Saatchi and Grey are in Moscow; Young & Rubicam is in Budapest; others are in China and Yugoslavia. The *Global Village* in advertising is coming.
5.   Even fuller service from full-service internationals. In addition to advertising, they are acquiring capabilities in public relations, sales promotion, direct marketing, and other marketing services.
6.   An erosion of the 15 percent commission payment system, with more fees and other payment schemes arising.[4]

**Choosing the Advertising Message**

A major decision for the international marketer is whether the firm should use national or international advertising appeals, a localized or standardized approach. The goal in either case is to fit the market. The principles of effective advertising are the same the world over, and can be found in any advertising textbook, so we concern ourselves here with the international aspects of advertising.

# Global Marketing

## Young & Rubicam's Moscow Men

New York—For Young & Rubicam's ambassadors of marketing to Moscow, it's not just a job, it's an adventure.

"To be a part of the first U.S. communications team in Moscow is somewhat historic," said Gary Burandt, who last week was named CEO of Young & Rubicam Sovero, the agency's joint venture with V/O Vneshtorgreklama, the leading Soviet communications company. *Sovero* is short for Soviet Export Organization.

"I'm not sure what we're going to find," Mr. Burandt said. "It's not going to be an ad agency as you and I know it for the first couple of years. But I think the opportunity to be there and watch *perestroika* unfold and watch the opening of that economy, the development of a marketing orientation, I think is very significant. I'm looking forward to that.

"There will be a lot of personal hardships, but I think the experience will be worth it."

Mr. Burandt said E. I. du Pont de Nemours & Co., which already does business in the Soviet Union, will be a Y&R Sovero client. He added that the members of a consortium recently formed to do business in the Soviet Union — Eastman Kodak Co., Ford Motor Co., RJR Nabisco, Johnson & Johnson and Chevron Corp. — are all Y&R clients. "We anticipate doing business with them," he said.

Mr. Burandt also said the Soviets are bringing their own client list to the joint venture, for doing business both in the Soviet Union and in Soviet export markets. Most exports handled by the venture are likely to be business-to-business products, possibly including selling space on the Soviet space shuttle.

Source: Reprinted with permission from *Advertising Age*, December 5, 1988, 67, ©Crain Communications Inc.

---

Although people's basic needs and desires are the same around the world, the way these desires are satisfied may vary from country to country. Because it is impossible to know each national market intimately, help must be obtained from the local subsidiary or distributor and the local advertising agency. The firm may, in fact, completely decentralize responsibility so that each national operation prepares its own advertising.

**Localized or Standardized?**   In the preparation of advertising campaigns in the international company, there are usually arguments for both an individualized national approach and a standardized international approach. The arguments reflect the self-interested evaluations of the parties involved as well as the objective factors in the situation. In general, two groups tend to be biased in favor of a separate national approach: the management of the local subsidiary and the independent local agency. In each case, the argument depends in large part on the special local knowledge they contribute. The more practical it is for the international firm to treat their market as it does its other markets, the less necessary they are. Because of this vulnerability, both tend to be defensive about the uniqueness of their market and the need for special approaches there. They will argue in terms of objective factors, but their position is influenced by their perceived vulnerability.

Subjective factors influence the other side of the argument also. The international agency and the international advertising manager naturally tend to favor an international approach. For example, assume the international agency makes its bid for the company's business in competition with an independent national agency. The international agency's competitive advantage may well lie in its internationalism and its ability to coordinate advertising. Therefore, it will argue on the basis of its strong points and their appropriateness to the company's need, suggesting the international approach as the best solution as well as the one it is best equipped to provide. Saatchi and Saatchi is a leading proponent of the global approach.

The international manager also would have some bias toward an international approach. If each of the firm's markets is indeed unique, thus requiring a national approach by those located there, the need for an international manager is diminished. Another element that sometimes enters in here is the desire of top management to have "one name, one image, worldwide." When executives travel abroad, many of them like to see the same company advertising as they go from market to market. This desire may not be a decisive element, but it does play some role.

The decision on international uniformity in advertising appeals will be affected by the human and organizational elements discussed above. However, it should also rest on objective data. Ultimately, the needs of the market should determine the approach used. The international marketer should choose the approach that is the most profitable in terms of sales and costs. Because measuring the sales results of advertising is difficult, however, other variables must be considered.

By way of clarification, we use the words *localized* and *standardized* to refer to the two extremes of the international advertising spectrum. Completely localized advertising would have only accidental similarity with that done in other countries. Completely standardized advertising would be identical in all markets. Neither extreme is usually practiced. The issue for the firm is the degree to which it should move toward one or the other end of the spectrum. Thus from country to country standardized advertising has a high degree of similarity, but it is not identical.

**Market Considerations.**    Several factors influence the ability of the firm to use similar appeals from market to market. One is the role the firm's product plays in the *buyers' consumption system*. If the product is used in the same way and meets the same needs from country to country, similar appeals are more feasible. The international success of Coca-Cola, which takes a standardized approach in its advertising appeals, suggests that the product meets similar consumer needs or desires everywhere. This is probably true for some other low-priced consumer goods, a famous example of which is Esso gasoline as promoted by Esso's "tiger" campaign.[5] With small modifications and language changes, this campaign traveled all around the world. Some examples of the slogan in different languages:

- Put a tiger in your tank.
- Putt en tiger pa tanken.
- Ponga un tigre en su tanque.

- Kom en tiger i tanken.
- Metti um tigre nel motore.
- Tu den tiger in den tank.
- Pankaa tiikeri tankum.
- Mettez un tigre dans votre moteur.

Another market consideration is the similarity of buying motives from country to country. The same product may be purchased for a mixture of functional, convenience, and status reasons, but with a different combination of motivations in each country. The more alike buying motives are, the more desirable the use of common appeals. This is often the case with industrial goods but is less common with consumer durables. Procter & Gamble, for example, found with its fluoride toothpaste that decay prevention was an important motive in Denmark, Germany, and the Netherlands. In England, France, and Italy, however, cosmetic considerations were more important.

General Electric used an international approach with its industrial goods but took a national approach with its consumer durables. The automobile market offers conflicting examples. Volvo emphasized economy, durability, and safety in both Sweden and the United States, whereas its advertisements stressed status and leisure in France, performance in Germany, and safety in Switzerland (scene of many fatal accidents). On the other hand, BMW, selling in 30 countries, tried to maintain a uniform international image.

***Language.***   Another market factor is language overlap from market to market. One world language would obviously facilitate uniform international advertising. Fortunately for those who use the English language, English is gradually coming to fill that role. Of course, the present role of English in the world does not yet permit international campaigns in English, except in the case of some industrial goods or goods that appeal to some international jet set.

Although language overlap among countries is not sufficient to permit global advertising campaigns, a few multi-language areas do facilitate multinational advertising on a less-than-global basis. Minor examples are found in Europe, where the German language covers Austria and most of Switzerland in addition to Germany, and the French language covers parts of Belgium, Switzerland, Luxembourg, and Monaco, as well as France. More important examples are the following: (1) the English-speaking world, covering up to 600 million people in dozens of nations; (2) the French-speaking world, including the former French colonies in addition to the European countries mentioned above; and (3) the Spanish-speaking world, including most of the Americas south of the United States. Even though not all residents of these areas are fluent in the dominant language, its role is large enough to facilitate the internationalization of advertising campaigns there.

Two examples illustrate the practical importance of language overlap to international marketing: Unilever introduced its Radion detergent into Germany with a heavy ad campaign. Because several of the German media overlap into Austria, many Austrian consumers sought to find Radion in

Austrian stores. Unfortunately for Unilever, Radion had not yet been introduced into Austria so Unilever lost the benefit of the free advertising carry-over.

As another example, Anheuser-Busch, a heavy advertiser of Budweiser beer in the United States, began marketing "Bud" in Canada hoping for a 1 to 2 percent market share. It was pleasantly surprised to gain almost 8 percent of the market in a few months. One reason was the big carry-over of U.S. TV commercials for "Bud" into the Canadian market.

***A Note on Translations.***   Language diversity in the world does not, by itself, prevent the use of international appeals. If a translation is the only adaptation needed in an advertising message, it does not modify the similarity of the appeal. The many humorous examples of advertising translation errors — for example, *corpse* for *body* — are recounted frequently because they make interesting copy, but statistically they are not significant.

David Kerr, vice-president of Kenyon & Eckhardt, gives some guidelines for translation. He suggests that English-language advertising to be used in international campaigns should be of the 5th- or 6th-grade vocabulary level and contain no slang or idioms. Furthermore, copy should be relatively short because other languages invariably take more space to say the same thing the English copy says. The growing use of visual presentation — pictures and illustrations — minimizes the need for translation. Thus, more and more European and Japanese advertisements are purely visual, showing something, evoking a mood, and citing the company name. Emphasis on such simple illustrations also avoids part of the problem of illiteracy in poorer nations.

Libby made a commercial to be used by its subsidiaries around the world showing a clown pantomiming enjoyment of Libby products. And in Saatchi and Saatchi's famous "Manhattan Landing" commercial for British Airways, a representation of the island of Manhattan is "flying" across the Atlantic. It had such recognition that it ran unchanged, except for voice-overs, in 45 countries.

***International Market Segments.***   Another factor is the existence of international market segments; that is, certain markets within a nation often have counterparts in a number of other nations. In many ways, these markets resemble their counterparts in other countries more than they do other markets in their own country. The international jet set is one example. The youth market is another, and probably includes two segments: the adolescent group and the college-age group. The concerns of college students on all continents seem remarkably similar. Such similarities among age groups can provide a truly international market. There are numerous examples of successful appeals to these national market segments which together constitute an international market for a product. American Express used Ogilvy & Mather to carry its "Membership has its privileges" campaign to its international market segment in over 30 countries.

Levi Strauss & Company has found an international market segment for its Levis. The company prepares its international advertising by beginning with its United States ads. One purpose of the advertising campaigns abroad is to achieve a similarity of appearance and image from country to country. Company sales seem to attest to the correctness of this approach. Overseas sales rose 500 percent in five years. As someone has said, the groups who buy Levis do speak a common language — the language of youth.

Similarly, Young & Rubicam was able to develop an international campaign for Oil of Olay. The commercials featured women from various countries, all of whom "share the secret of Olay." Though ages, incomes, and languages varied, they found groups of women everywhere concerned about wrinkles.

A final market consideration is the gradual development of the world or regional consumer. What we already see in certain market segments will gradually expand to broader segments of the world's population. Advances in communications, transportation, and production lead to an international democratizing of consumption. People will not be alike, but market segments will become more international in scope, making possible greater use of similar appeals in advertising. The European Common Market is accelerating the emergence of the European consumer. In the United States, marketers speak of market segments on a national basis. They usually do not separate Michigan consumers from Maine or Missouri consumers. The United States, in a sense, is merely the first and most successful of the regional groupings. We already see advertising campaigns coordinated for groupings of countries. Such industrial marketers as Bayer, IBM, and Sulzer organize one campaign for a group of industrialized country markets and another for a group of developing country markets.

The impact of forecasted events of 1992 in Europe is dramatic. Beginning already in 1988, dozens of major advertisers from Japan, the United States, and Europe switched one or more of their products to pan-European campaigns and switched to a single agency for Europe. The following list indicates some of the scope and variety of firms going pan-European:

> Alfa Romeo, Canon, Continental Tire, Federal Express, Fruit of the Loom, Gillette, Helena Rubenstein, Henkel, Hewlett-Packard, International Wool Secretariat, Johnson Wax, Johnson and Johnson, Kimberly-Clark, 3M, Northern Telecom, Olivetti, Philips, Quaker, SEAT, Sara Lee, Seagrams, Texaco, and Trans World Airlines.[6]

**Other Considerations.**   If market considerations permit similarity in international advertising, the marketer must then evaluate the other factors affecting its feasibility. One of these factors is economics. Are there any gains in efficiency in taking an international approach to advertising?

*Economics.*   As long as agencies are paid on the commission basis, there would seem to be no savings with a uniform international message, because the payment would be the same whether an international agency or separate national agencies were used. Although this is true for commission payments, gains could still come in other areas. If the company uses a national approach to advertising, the creative work will probably vary greatly in quality from country to country. Small markets have small agencies and small budgets for doing creative work, not to mention a shortage of skilled personnel.

An international approach would permit more to be spent on developing a quality campaign with the best personnel. The best agencies in the larger markets could create the campaign and that expenditure could then be "amortized" over many countries. The better campaign that results should more than pay for itself in increased revenues. Grey Advertising produced an ad for 12 countries for a new Playtex bra. It cost $250,000 to develop. However, the average cost to develop a single U.S. ad was $100,000.

***Agency Relations.***   A uniform approach is also facilitated by the use of the same agency in all or most of the company's markets. By using an international agency the company gains efficiencies in communication and coordination. Additionally, the preparation of the international campaign, including inputs and testing in various markets, is much easier if the same agency is working in all the markets. The use of closed-circuit TV aids in the preparation and coordination of international campaigns, eliminating time and travel costs involved in consultations among representatives of agencies in various nations. When Playtex wanted to create a global campaign for its new Wow bra, it switched from using 30 different agencies around the world to a single international agency — Grey Advertising.

Because Goodyear and Coca-Cola use McCann-Erickson as their major international agency, they can benefit from McCann's "International Team," which has a staff of 25 "creatives" from Japan, Africa, Brazil, China, Britain and the United States. It creates advertising for 43 clients in three or more countries.[7]

Another factor affecting the feasibility of similar campaigns is the internal organization of the company. If the firm's international operations are very decentralized, international campaigns will be more difficult. Conversely, if the firm is centralized and has a marketing or advertising manager with global responsibility, international campaigns are easier.

***Media Developments.***   The availability of media also affects the development of an international campaign. If the same media were available everywhere, international campaigns would benefit greatly. The fact that this situation does not exist hampers an internationally similar approach. The media do "massage the message" to some degree, and a campaign prepared for TV probably would not be identical to one prepared for radio or print media. This lack of media uniformity does not, in itself, prevent international campaigns, however, as is evidenced by domestic campaigns that use the same appeals in several different kinds of media simultaneously.

Similarity in international media conditions is increasing steadily. Commercial TV and radio are coming to more and more countries. Satellite TV is becoming a truly international medium, bringing to the whole world such events as the Olympic Games, a royal wedding, or a space spectacular. Satellite TV is gradually coming to Europe and will have a Europeanizing effect on campaigns there. Gillette, for example, signed with Sky Channel for advertising to 17 European countries. A study of European advertising and agency executives produced the following predictions about the effects of the coming of satellite/cable TV in Europe:[8]

1.  Brand awareness of non-European products will increase. It will be easier for non-European firms to break into Europe.
2.  It will lead to the use of Europe-wide promotional campaigns and themes.
3.  Local ad agencies will lose out to those that operate across national boundaries. (This is already happening, as we noted above.)
4.  Surprisingly, it was predicted that global brands will *not* dominate European markets in the next decade.

Print media are going aggressively international also. *Reader's Digest* already reaches 40 countries in their own languages, and other American magazines and newspapers also have extensive international coverage. The European print media are going more Europe-wide and also beyond Europe. The internationalization of media ownership will reinforce this trend. Already European groups are among the largest owners of American magazines. Media internationalization will contribute to the internationalization of advertising messages.

**Regional or Global Product Introductions.**   Companies are going to more uniform campaigns as they develop products for a regional or global market, and introducing them simultaneously (or sequentially) in the region or the world. An early example of this was the around-the-world send-off given the Instamatic camera by Kodak. Another one was by NCR in introducing its Century computer on all five continents, with simultaneous showings in 120 cities around the world. As product development becomes more international, and as firms prepare for the Europeanization of campaigns in 1992, there is more motivation to create advertising that is as international as the rest of the marketing program.

When Johnson & Johnson chose its Silhouettes sanitary napkin for its first Europe-wide product roll-out, it selected Saatchi & Saatchi to manage the campaign, in part because of that agency's good European coverage. When Philip Morris took Marlboro cigarettes into world markets, it successfully carried much of the "Marlboro Man" ad campaign along with them.

*Government Regulations.*   Government restrictions are a fact of life for advertisers as countries regulate the content of advertisements. The maze of government regulations makes it difficult to create a universal advertising campaign. There has been a push in particular to restrict advertisements for cigarettes, children's products, liquor, and pharmaceuticals. Events in 1992 should help the regulatory environment for European advertisers, as more uniform regulations are promised as part of the open market.

The Marlboro cowboy has been sidelined altogether by stiff regulations in Britain. The reasoning: Heroic figures in cigarette advertisements might have special appeal and encourage people to start smoking.

Kellogg has found how European regulations would undermine a 30-second commercial produced for British TV. References to iron and vitamins would have to be deleted in the Netherlands; a child wearing a Kellogg T-shirt would be edited out in France where children are forbidden from endorsing products on TV. And in Germany, the line, "Kellogg makes their cornflakes the best they have ever been," would be dropped because of rules against making competitive claims. An executive of the Kellogg account at J. Walter Thompson remarked, "After the required changes, the 30-second commercial would be about five seconds long."

Nationalistic policies also restrict advertisers' freedom. More countries now are requiring local production of at least a portion of TV commercials to build their film industries and create more jobs. When Playtex created the international ad for its new bra, it was filmed in Australia because Australian TV will run only those commercials produced there. The other markets for the bra did not have such a restriction.

***Industrial Products.***   The industrial market is more homogeneous internationally than the consumer market. Therefore, industrial marketers are generally more able to implement international campaigns than their consumer counterparts. For example, Siemens of Germany has been working on internationally coordinated advertising in 52 foreign markets ever since 1955.

**Making a Choice.**   All the variables discussed above must be weighed in deciding what kinds of advertising appeals to use. Although agencies and subsidiaries in each country must help to determine the appeals for their market, it is unlikely that a purely national approach will be taken in many markets. There will probably be some internationalizing of the advertising. For Europe, it has been suggested that a multinational campaign with a distinctive national touch in each country flatters national sensitivities.

The task is not to find global uniformity but to determine what will make the firm's advertising most effective. Multimarket advertising on a regional basis may be desirable because of regional groupings, regional tourism, and media overlap. Or it may be possible to use common appeals in common-language areas. In any case, by seeking common denominators and by playing down national differences, a firm can probably be effective with similar appeals in many countries. We have mentioned a few firms that use basically the same appeals all over the world. Some others are Maidenform, Revlon, and Helena Rubenstein. Although the products associated with these names are of a personal nature, they succeed internationally with universal appeals.

**Multinational Coordination in Practice: The Pattern, or Prototype, Approach.**   Because of client demands for more uniform — though not standardized — international advertising, McCann-Erickson created a division called the International Team. Its membership with nationals from more than six countries was noted earlier. Since the "Coke Is It" ads of 1981, no Coca-Cola campaign has been created without using McCann's International Team. For each new campaign, McCann variations on the standard theme are based on research on the customs of target markets. This allows much uniformity along with the necessary localization.

Goodyear International provides a more detailed example through its *prototype* approach, in which international advertising is guided from Akron using prototype campaigns based on common denominators drawn from consumer research in representative markets around the world. The finished ads are prepared nationally for a more effective result.

This prototype, "pattern standardization" approach has been used in the firm's 11 major markets. Other developed markets, such as Brazil, Mexico, South Africa, and Japan, received copies of pattern campaigns and could adopt all or part of them. However, these markets had more discretion about adopting them than the 11 major markets. It should be recognized, however, that for lesser-developed markets, the pattern itself became the best source of high-quality advertising material and strategy.

Several characteristics of Goodyear International favor the use of the pattern approach. First, Goodyear operates through wholly owned subsidiaries, giving it a strong basis for control. Second, Goodyear's consumer products have a standardized use and potentially common appeals. Third, the firm's ad budget is large enough to make it attractive to an agency. This assures high-level agency support in developing the pattern campaign and following it through in local markets.

Although Akron headquarters could have commanded subsidiaries to adopt the pattern campaign, the firm preferred to enlist cooperation. Goodyear International and its network agency (McCann) worked directly with both the agency's and the firm's subsidiary representatives throughout the development of the campaign.

Union Carbide provides another example. Wanting to move its Prestone brand of car care products into Europe, it called on its ad agency, Young & Rubicam (Y&R) to survey dealers and consumers in 11 European countries. Research showed that the ideas and approaches that had been used in the United States would also be suitable for the European market. The basic American advertising campaign was therefore used in Europe. It proved to be a successful illustration of the pattern approach.

**Selecting the Media**

A third decision in international advertising is the selection of media for each national market. The desirable media in every country are those that reach the target markets efficiently. The target markets — the purchase decision influencers — will not always be the same individuals or groups as in the domestic market. The relative roles of different family members in consumer buying, or of the purchasing agent, engineer, or president in industrial procurement, will vary from country to country.

Those most familiar with the local scene — the advertising agency and the company representative within the country — will do much of the local media selection. Studies have found the greatest role of subsidiaries in advertising was in media selection. To the extent that subsidiaries do the job, international managers need not get involved. However, international managers might wish to have some voice in local media selection. Through their experience in many countries, they may have insights to contribute.

Or managers may wish to use international media alongside of, or in place of, strictly national media. Since international media cover a number of markets, this would require some centralization. For example, Continental Bank, Deltona, and Monsanto handle their international media planning through Tatham-Laird & Kudner, a Chicago agency. Then, too, international managers may be able to contribute sophisticated techniques of media selection. Because more money is spent on advertising in the United States than elsewhere the technology is generally more advanced here. International managers can assure that these techniques are made available to company operations everywhere.

**Media Diversity.**   International media selection is complicated by the international differences in media availability. One cannot take a successful media configuration from domestic operations and apply it abroad, because the same facilities will often not be available. We saw earlier how nations differ in their communications infrastructure, that is, the availability of TV, radio, and newspapers. In addition to that disparity, there is a great difference in how these media are used for advertising. Table 12–5 illustrates these differences. For example, TV's share of the ad dollar ranges from zero in Indonesia and Sweden to as high as 64 percent in Venezuela. (Sweden has since permitted commercial TV.) Radio's share ranges from zero to 20 percent; the print media from 15 to 96 percent; and outdoor advertising from less than 1 percent up to 22 percent. These are the international extremes; the table shows, however, that even within regions like Europe or Asia, there are great differences in media usage.

*Diversity Means Adaptation.*   When media availability differs from market to market, international marketers have to decentralize media selection and adapt to local possibilities. Since local managers cannot follow the media patterns used elsewhere, they must find the local media that reach their markets effectively. They will therefore experiment with different media and promotional mixes.

In Peru, Orange Crush used a wide variety of media ranging from newspapers, TV and radio, to cinema and point-of-purchase materials. Outside the capital, Lima, the company used billboards more heavily because taxes were lower in the provinces. On the other hand, the use of cinema slides was reduced in the provinces because it was not found very effective.

**Whom Does the Medium Massage?**   Another factor hampering media decisions in many countries is the lack of reliable information on circulation and audience characteristics. Advertisers in the United States are accustomed to audited data on the size of audience reached by the various media. In addition, they often have a breakdown on audience characteristics, such as occupation, education, and income level. No other country has the same amount of information available, and the supply decreases rapidly with the

**Table 12-5**                 **Advertising Expenditure by Media—Selected Countries**

| Countries | Media Percentage | | | |
|---|---|---|---|---|
| | TV | Radio | Print | Outdoor |
| United States | 22% | 6% | 32% | 1% |
| Canada | 17 | 9 | 36 | 7 |
| Asia | | | | |
| India | 13 | 3 | 58 | 4 |
| Indonesia | 0 | 18 | 72 | 4 |
| Japan | 35 | 5 | 36 | 22 |
| South Korea | 37 | 5 | 41 | 4 |
| Thailand | 49 | 20 | 32 | 0 |
| Europe | | | | |
| France | 19 | 9 | 59 | 13 |
| Italy | 49 | 4 | 42 | 5 |
| Sweden | 0 | 0 | 96 | 3 |
| United Kingdom | 33 | 2 | 61 | 4 |
| West Germany | 10 | 4 | 81 | 4 |
| Latin America | | | | |
| Argentina | 31 | 10 | 32 | 8 |
| Brazil | 56 | 8 | 33 | 2 |
| Mexico | 45 | 18 | 15 | 8 |
| Venezuela | 64 | 5 | 27 | 3 |

Source: Drawn from *International Marketing Data and Statistics 1988–81* (London: Euromonitor, 1988), 401; and "Advertising Statistics," *International Journal of Advertising* 7 (1988): 17–93.

level of economic development. In many countries, the only figures are those supplied by the media themselves. Such unaudited figures are somewhat suspect.

Another consideration complicating media evaluation is that whatever figures can be obtained for the circulation of a medium do not necessarily indicate its true coverage. In countries where data can be obtained as to the number of TV or radio sets, the true audience may be much larger than the figures suggest. For example, in countries with low literacy rates, the average number of viewers per TV set is apt to be at least twice as large as in the United States. This principle also applies to the number of radio listeners, especially in less developed countries where a few receivers may reach a whole village.

Even with print media, the average readership varies from country to country. In less developed countries, one literate villager will read a newspaper or magazine for his illiterate neighbors. Even in more developed countries, one issue may pass from the initial purchaser through several other readers. A French magazine with a circulation of 1.5 million estimated its total readership at 8.3 million.

This lack of accurate media information makes media selection difficult. The answer in the long run is to expand media auditing services. In the short run, advertisers must depend on their own ingenuity. As firms gain experience in a market, they learn about the relative effectiveness of different media there. Comparative analysis of similar markets can again be useful.

**International or Local Media?**   The manager will sometimes have the alternative of using either national media or media that cover several markets; both print and broadcast media, for example, have multimarket coverage. The print media with international market coverage include such U.S. general-interest magazines as the *Reader's Digest* and *Time,* which reach most of the world's major markets, and *Paris Match* or *Vision,* which reach several European and Latin American markets, respectively. *Elle,* the French fashion magazine, has 13 editions outside France. Numerous technical and trade publications (usually American) in the engineering, chemistry, electronics, and automotive industry, and so on, also have an extensive and influential circulation around the world.

The scope of international media and the expenditures are rising steadily. Magazines, newspapers, and TV are all expanding in the global village, as we shall see. In each medium the geographic coverage is expanding. For example, *Business Week* has gone to China, and *Fortune* has French and Japanese editions and is considering one in Spanish. Satellite TV will blanket Europe.

*Magazines, the First Internationalists.*   International magazines can offer advantages to the marketer where they correspond to target markets. Among these advantages are audited circulation and audience data, good-quality reproduction of advertisements, an influential audience, regional market coverage for marketing to specific areas, and the lending of the magazines' prestige to products advertised. An additional boon is that advertisements can be placed and paid for at one source, rather than through many separate national organizations.

The internationalization of magazines, and thus the convenience of advertising in them, is increasing with the international consolidation of the industry. Through purchases of American magazine publishers, Bertelsmann of Germany and Hachette of France have become the world's largest media companies after Capital Cities–ABC and TIME Inc. Hachette is now the publisher of *Woman's Day* and *Car and Driver,* for example.

The drawbacks of international magazines are that they usually have only English, French, or Spanish editions (except for the *Reader's Digest*) and give only partial coverage of any national market. These advantages and limitations have to be evaluated in terms of the markets of the firm. International magazines are less likely to be used for mass-consumption items because of their limited coverage. However, for certain industrial goods, and for consumer goods and services that appeal to an affluent or sophisticated market, the international magazines may give just the coverage the advertiser wants.

Surveys of European executives continually show their cosmopolitan reading habits. Publications like the *Financial Times* and *The Economist* (London), *Fortune* and *Business Week,* and leading European business publications are read in a number of countries besides their country of origin.

***The Internationalizing Newspapers.***  Whereas the *International Herald Tribune* used to be the only international paper, it now has lots of company. The *Financial Times* covers Europe and is trying to enter the United States. *The Wall Street Journal* has European and Asian editions. Even the *China Daily,* the official English-language publication of China, is published simultaneously (by satellite) in China, the United States, and Europe. European integration is forcing major national papers to try to regionalize their coverage. We'll note some of the efforts briefly, because only time will tell which shall survive as European newspapers.

- *Die Welt, Le Monde, La Stampa,* and *The Times* launched *Europa,* a business paper with common editorial content but in the local language for the German, French, Italian, and British markets.
- *USA Today* is expanding in Europe.
- Robert Maxwell launched *The European* as the European counterpart of *USA Today.*
- Eight major European papers are discussing joint publication of a weekly paper.

***Radio.***  Although broadcast media traditionally have played a smaller international role than print media, their growing commercialization is increasing their importance. International commercial radio is most important in Western Europe, where at least four stations reach several nations. Because they have transmitting power up to 275,000 watts (United States limit is 50,000 watts), these stations truly can cover most of Western Europe. The leading station is Radio Luxembourg, which works three frequencies — longwave, medium, and short-wave — and broadcasts in five languages. It counts over 40 million listeners from the British Isles to southern France and eastward into both Germanies, Austria, and Switzerland. Many of the advertisers on this station are U.S. firms: Procter & Gamble, Colgate-Palmolive, Gillette, Nabisco, John Deere, 3M, and Coca-Cola. Radio Luxembourg's coverage corresponds to their markets.

If the national radio networks in the major European nations ever go commercial, it would threaten these "international" stations, all of which are located in tiny principalities. Until that time, however, they are the major commercial radio available in Europe; Latin America, by contrast, has many commercial radio stations *within* the various nations. Clearly, commercial radio is especially useful for reaching nonliterate populations.

A good example of radio as an international medium is the case of Saudi Arabia. Because of restrictions on broadcast advertising, the best buy for spot radio advertising in Saudi Arabia is Radio Monte Carlo, one of the European international stations. It is a favorite of Saudis who have lived abroad.

*Television.*   Commercial TV for international advertising is an area of great potential growth. Some such advertising occurs almost accidentally now as U.S. broadcasts reach into Canada (and vice versa) or German television commercials spill over into Austria and Switzerland. However, there has been no internationally organized approach to commercial TV. That is changing now with Sky Channel and several other proposed satellite channels in Europe. UNIVISION operates in several Spanish-speaking countries, and there is the Worldvision organization of ABC International.

ABC, the American company, has pioneered a network of TV stations in Canada, Latin America, the Caribbean, Spain, Africa, the Middle East, the Far East, and Australia, an area of 25 nations with over 25 million television homes. An advertiser can buy various packages of nations in this network for an international campaign. For example, Pan American Life Insurance sponsored the Academy Awards program, on a delayed basis, in 14 Latin American countries. Other firms that use parts of this international network include Ford, Sterling Drug, Nestlé, Goodyear, Kellogg, Quaker Oats, and Pepsi Cola.

Advancing technology, increasing set ownership, and the needs of international business all suggest an expansion of international commercial television. About 140 nations have TV service, and the majority have some commercial TV. The number increases each year. Also, a potentially large number of hours can be devoted to the same broadcasting material all over the world; for example, programs on the Olympic Games, space shots, royal or presidential accessions (or funerals), important political events or acts of God. The international popularity of some of America's television series is an indicator of the potential.

*Other International Media.*   Magazines, radio, and TV are the major international media. Yet there can be other kinds. John Deere found no suitable medium in which to advertise to farmers, so it started a magazine called *Furrow* back in 1895. As Deere went international, so did the magazine, which now has 22 different editions in ten languages and a circulation of about 2,500,000. It is easily the world's most widely read farm magazine and the most effective medium John Deere could use. An equivalent campaign in other farm periodicals would be at least twice as expensive. In a similar way Abbott Labs reaches 300,000 doctors around the world with its quarterly magazine *Abottempo,* printed in nine languages. Ronald McDonald, the clown, also represents another kind of media. Used first in Washington, D.C., in 1963, he went national in 1967 and made his first international TV appearance in 1969. Today Ronald speaks a dozen languages, including Chinese, Dutch, French, German, Gaelic, Japanese, Papiemento, Portuguese, and Swedish. A clown seems to be popular everywhere, and Ronald may be the best-known character since Santa Claus. Ronald not only opens stores but is a goodwill ambassador who visits hospitals and raises funds for children. There are 90 Ronald McDonald Houses in countries abroad, although, in Japan, he is known as "Donald McDonald" to avoid the difficult *R* sound, and in Hong Kong, he is known as McDonlo-Suk Suk or "Uncle McDonald."

*Local Media.*   We have discussed international media at some length because they are an option peculiar to international marketing and because they will be a more significant alternative tomorrow than they are today. Nevertheless, the amount of advertising in national media is vastly greater than that done in international media. National media predominate, even for the international advertiser, because they offer certain advantages. They offer more possibilities, ranging from newspapers, magazines, direct mail, cinema, and billboards to the broadcast media (where available commercially). They permit the use of the local languages and provide greater flexibility in market segmentation and test marketing. In general, local media do a better job of reaching and adapting to the local market, especially for consumer goods.

Disadvantages, however, occasionally arise in using local media. Although the industrialized countries frequently offer the same media quality as the United States, in many other countries print reproduction may be poor, rates may not be fixed, and audited circulation data may not be available. The need to place the advertising as well as pay for it locally can be a drawback if the firm has centralized control. Nevertheless, these disadvantages are not sufficient to seriously limit the use of local media by advertisers who need to reach a wide local market.

Most companies do most of their advertising in the local media of the foreign market. Generally, the more decentralized the firm, the more it uses local campaigns, and the more it relies on local ad agencies, the more it will use local media rather than international media.

Colgate knows well how to use the local media in its foreign markets. As an example, Colgate is credited with creating the Mexican soap opera and one of the more popular programs broadcast in Mexico. Thus, the company successfully carried to Mexico a form more commonly associated with its competitor, Procter & Gamble, in the United States.

## International Advertising Budget

Among the controversial aspects of advertising is determining the proper method for setting the advertising budget. This is a problem domestically as it is internationally. Yet because the international advertiser must try to find an optimum outlay for a number of markets, the problem is more complex on the international level. In theory, it is not difficult to state the amount of money the firm should put into advertising abroad. In each of its markets, the firm should continue to put more money into advertising as long as an advertising dollar returns more than a dollar spent on anything else. In practice, this equimarginal principle is difficult to apply because of the impossibility of measuring accurately the returns, not only from advertising but also from other company outlays.

Because of the difficulty in determining the theoretically optimum advertising budget, companies have developed more practical guidelines. We will examine the relevance of these guidelines for the international advertiser. Although the equimarginal principle noted above is difficult to apply, it must nevertheless serve as an initial rough guide. In other words, the manager must remember that the advertising budget is not set in a vacuum, but that it is just one element of the overall marketing mix. Therefore, it is necessary to have some idea as to whether a sum of money should go into advertising or personal selling or price reductions or product or package improvements or something else.

Coca-Cola may be the world's most advertised product. The company spends yearly over $700 million, about half of it outside the United States. And the bottlers approximately match the corporate outlay.

**Percentage-of-Sales Approach.**   An easy method for setting the advertising appropriation in a country is based on percentage of sales. Besides its convenience, this method has the advantage of relating advertising to the volume of sales in a country and thus keeping advertising from "getting out of hand." This approach, perhaps the easiest to justify in the budget meeting, appeals to financially oriented managers who like to think in terms of ratios and costs per unit. And when the firm is selling in many markets, it has the further advantage of appearing to guarantee equality among them. Each market seems to get the advertising it deserves.

For the firm that centralizes control over international advertising, the percentage-of-sales approach is very attractive. A manager at headquarters would have difficulty using any other budgeting approach for 50 or 100 markets. Rabino studied 80 of the *Fortune* 1,000 companies and found this to be the most popular method.[9] The Europeans favor this approach as much as the Americans.

Despite its attractions, the percentage-of-sales approach has limitations. The purpose of advertising is to cause sales, but this method perversely makes the volume of sales determine the amount of advertising. When sales are declining, advertising will decline, although long-range considerations might suggest that advertising should be stepped up. When a firm is entering a foreign market, it may need a disproportionate amount of advertising to break in. Limiting the advertising to the same percentage-of-sales figure used elsewhere would be undesirable during the firm's first years in the market. Even Hershey, the famous nonadvertiser in the U.S. market, began advertising when it entered Canada.

The same is true in the introduction of new products into a market. As firms expand international marketing, they introduce more products into their markets. The advertising budget for these introductions should relate to the introductory needs rather than to some percentage of sales applied to existing products — or to the same products being sold in other countries. Significant advertising outlays are usually required of firms that want to expand their presence in world markets.

When Panasonic tried to launch its batteries into the whole U.S. market in 1989, it set an ad budget that was a small fraction of those of its competitors. An analyst commented "Unless they inundate the airways, people won't even notice Panasonic batteries."[10]

The major weakness in applying a standard percentage-of-sales figure for advertising in foreign markets is that this method does not relate to the firm's situation in each market. The examples given — entering a market and introducing new products — are just two illustrations of the need for special treatment for special situations. In some countries the firm may be well-established with no strong competitors, whereas in others it may have difficulty getting a consumer franchise. Advertising needs are different in these two instances. The second group might need twice the percentage of sales in advertising as the first. For example, European firms are raising their ad budgets now in anticipation of the larger market of 1992.

Other factors differentiating the firm's situation from country to country are variations in media availability and the firm's level of involvement. Differences in media possibilities might mean that the firm will spend more on personal selling or other promotional tools in certain markets and less on advertising. In countries where the firm has its own subsidiaries, the advertising appropriation usually will be determined differently from the way it is in countries where the firm is represented by a licensee or distributor.

Until more sophisticated techniques are made operational, many companies will continue to use some percentage-of-sales method despite its limitations. This is not necessarily bad if the percentage is shown from company experience to be reasonably successful and if the method is somewhat flexible, allowing different percentages to be applied in different markets according to need.

**Competitive-Parity Approach.**   Matching competitors' advertising outlays — the *competitive-parity* approach — is used by some companies. Although it may offer the firm some benefit of collective wisdom and a feeling that it is not losing ground to its competitors, the merit of this approach is dubious in domestic operations, and it is especially to be challenged in international marketing. As a practical matter, in most markets the firm is not able to determine advertising figures of national competitors.

Another danger in following the practice of competitors is that they are not necessarily right. In fact, the international firm is almost always a heavier advertiser than national firms in the same industry, probably because of its more aggressive marketing posture. If anything, the international firm sets the standard for national competitors to follow rather than the reverse. This was evident in Procter & Gamble's experience in Europe, for example. The fact that different competitors may employ different promotional mixes also hampers the use of this approach. In the United States, for instance, Revlon is a heavy advertiser, whereas Avon relies almost entirely on personal selling. Who should follow whom?

A final limitation to the competitive-parity approach in foreign markets is the difference in the situation of the international firm. Since it is a foreigner in the market, it may have a relationship with consumers different from that of national companies. This would be reflected in its promotion. Its product line and marketing program are also likely to differ from those of national competitors. For all these reasons, it is improbable that matching competitors' advertising outlays would prove to be a sound strategy in foreign markets.

**Objective-and-Task Approach.**   The recognized weaknesses of the above approaches have led some advertisers to the *objective-and-task* method, which begins by determining the advertising objectives, expressed in terms of sales, brand awareness, or something else; then ascertaining the tasks needed to attain these objectives; and finally estimating the costs of performing these tasks. If this approach includes a cost-benefit analysis, relating the objectives to the cost of reaching them, it is a desirable way to approach the problem.

The objective-and-task method is as relevant for markets abroad as it is at home. It logically seeks to relate the advertising budget in a country to the firm's situation and goals there. To use it satisfactorily, however, the firm must have good knowledge of the local market situation so that it is able to set appropriate objectives. Unfortunately, except where it has strong local subsidiaries, the international firm will not have intimate knowledge of the market, so setting specific objectives may be difficult.

Lack of familiarity with foreign markets will also make the marketer less able to define the task of advertising there. In such cases, a percentage-of-sales method may be more feasible. This is one instance where it is more important to be operational than to be "scientifically correct." The Europeans have equally low usage of the objective-and-task method as the Americans.

**Comparative-Analysis Approach.**   Between applying a uniform percentage to all markets and letting each market go its own way lies a middle ground — *comparative analysis,* in which markets are grouped into two or more categories according to characteristics relevant to advertising. This method yields more flexibility than the uniform approach and more control than the laissez-faire approach. Categories might be based on size (markets with over $1 million sales and those with under $1 million), media situation (markets with commercial TV and those with no commercial TV), or other pertinent characteristics. Different budgeting methods or percentages could be tried for each group. One country could serve as a test-market for the other countries of that group. This technique can be useful for the international advertiser who has a large number of markets.

**Some Special Considerations.**   Several special factors affect the amount of advertising the firm will do in foreign markets.

*Media Restrictions.*   In markets where certain media do not exist or cannot be used commercially, the firm's advertising budget is apt to be relatively low. For example, many firms that advertise heavily on TV in the United States have smaller relative outlays in markets where that medium is not available. Conversely, many firms greatly increase their budgets when commercial TV becomes available. When media regulations are very restrictive, the firm may place greater reliance on other promotional tools.

*Low-Income Markets.*   Two-thirds of the world's countries are less developed. Generally a limited amount of advertising is done in these economies and consumers have limited discretionary income. Although these factors usually combine to lower the level of advertising, there can be exceptions. Some firms selling low-priced consumer goods have successfully used rather heavy advertising outlays in low-income countries, for example, Colgate-Palmolive and Unilever. One study found that both TV and print media were rather heavily used in developing countries.[11]

***Company Organization.***   The degree to which the firm centralizes its international operations will affect advertising budgeting. The more centralized the advertising control, the more uniform the budget process is likely to be from country to country. The percentage-of-sales approach is probable in this case. If the firm has highly autonomous subsidiaries, however, each one is likely to determine its own advertising appropriation, resulting in greater variability.

***Level of Involvement.***   A firm's involvement in foreign markets often ranges from a distributor in some markets to ownership of subsidiaries in others. As the firm's position and control vary greatly from one situation to another, so will its approach to budgeting advertising. Subsidiaries were discussed in the preceding paragraph. Advertising budgeting of *joint ventures* will be constrained by the other partner. *Licensees* may be entirely on their own or the agreement may require them to do some advertising. *Distributors* also may be on their own or have a cooperative advertising program with the international firm.

The Culligan Company provides a fairly typical example. Culligan adds 2 percent to the basic purchase price paid by the distributor and matches this with an additional 2 percent from the corporation. This is a percentage-of-sales method of administering local advertising on a cooperative basis. In this case 4 percent of local sales is applied to local advertising.

**Evaluating International Advertising Effectiveness**

Testing advertising effectiveness is even more difficult in international markets than in the United States. One reason is that the markets are smaller and therefore budgets are smaller. A more important reason is that few markets have experience in this work. Consequently, in most markets international marketers have to rely primarily on their own capabilities. Because they have less contact with foreign markets, their ability to investigate advertising effectiveness is limited. Thus three factors restrict the measurement of advertising's effectiveness in world markets: (1) smallness of the market, (2) lack of facilities, and (3) the distance and communications gap between the market and international marketers. As a result, many firms try to use sales results as the measure of advertising effectiveness.

In this area, international marketers must again exercise ingenuity. Some evidence of effectiveness is needed to develop sound advertising budgets. Once more, comparative analysis may be useful. If the firm's markets can be grouped according to similar characteristics, experiments with advertising programs can be conducted using one or two countries in a group as test markets. Variables to be tested might include the amount of advertising, the media mix, the appeals, frequency of placement, and so on. Experience needs to be built up on a cross-sectional basis — that is, between countries — as well as on a historical basis. Such experience, developed on a comparative basis, can help to overcome some of the handicaps in measuring advertising effectiveness in foreign markets. The continuing internationalization of marketing research and ad agencies will eventually help with this problem.

## Organizing for International Advertising

The firm has basically three organizational alternatives: (1) it can centralize all decision making for international advertising at headquarters; (2) it can decentralize the decision making to foreign markets; (3) it can use some blend of these two alternatives. Of course, the question of organizing for international advertising cannot be separated from the company's overall organization for international business. The firm is unlikely to be highly centralized for one function and decentralized for another. We discuss overall organization in Chapter 16. Here we consider the special factors affecting organization for international advertising.

**Centralization.** Complete centralization of international advertising implies that campaign preparation, media and agency selection, and budgeting are all done in the headquarters country. This might be necessary if the firm's international business is small or if it is confined to dealing with distributors or licensees. Complete centralization is less likely where the firm operates through foreign subsidiaries. In reality, control at headquarters of international advertising is seldom complete. We use the term *centralized* to refer to the situation where headquarters plays a major coordinating role, as in the Goodyear example cited earlier, or the ITT example that will be presented soon.

Centralized control of advertising is more feasible when the firm works with one international agency that has branches covering all of its markets, when the firm can have standardized international advertising, and when the market and media conditions are similar from market to market. As we saw, these conditions were met by American Express when it used Ogilvy & Mather to carry its message around the world.

On the personnel side, centralized control implies that staff at headquarters know the foreign markets and media well enough to make the appropriate decisions. Communications must be adequate for controlling the actual placement of the advertising in each market. It might be possible to rely on an international agency for help. Industrial marketers, such as Timken, Rockwell, and DuPont rely on the U.S. office of their international agency. Where subsidiaries are involved, there must be some line authority over the subsidiary personnel in advertising, just as the agency works with its own people in the same market.

The centralized approach creates demands for advertising personnel at headquarters but minimal demands for them at the subsidiary level. Economies of scale in staffing and in administration are arguments for centralization. The potential dangers are rigidity, failure to adapt to local needs, and stifling of local initiative, which can lead to morale problems in the subsidiary.

ITT provides an example of strong headquarters coordination of international advertising. ITT headquarters is in New York and so is its global advertising department. Under this office are advertising staff in the area organizations: Europe, Latin America, the Far East, and the Pacific. The department also monitors the efforts of 80 advertising agencies for ITT worldwide. The global budget is over $300 million. The department's responsibilities include selection of ad agencies around the world and hiring and indoctrination of ad managers for ITT divisions.

The coordination process starts with an annual subsidiary advertising plan, which is explained in a *Standard Planning Guide*. The guide also spells out standard practices and procedures. Another control device is the monthly progress report from each unit's ad manager. A final important form of communication is the annual face-to-face group meetings. It is a two-day session where staff from New York meet with ad managers from the four regions.

There is an increasing trend for centralizing international advertising as more companies push for regional or global marketing. Plans for 1992 have increased centralized control for European firms, as we have seen. Continuing integration of world markets is leading American and Japanese multinationals in the same direction. For American firms with well-established foreign subsidiaries, the main resistance comes from subsidiary managers who view global advertising as a threat to their autonomy.

**Decentralization.**   With complete decentralization of international advertising, each market would make all its own advertising decisions. Where this laissez-faire method is company policy, it may result from several different considerations: (1) The volume of international business and advertising is too small to warrant attention at headquarters. (2) The communications problems between home and field render a centralized approach impossible. (3) The firm feels it can allow local decision making to gain a more national image. (4) The firm feels that nationals know the local scene best and will be more highly motivated if given this responsibility.

Decentralized control is likely to be associated with national rather than international advertising campaigns and with the employment of independent local agencies in each market. It requires more expertise and personnel at the subsidiary level. In markets where the firm does not have subsidiaries, performance would depend on the advertising skills and interest of the firm's licensee or distributor. The advantages of decentralization are the motivation given to the national operation and the possibility of getting more effective tailor-made advertising programs. The dangers are duplication of effort and ineffective advertising, especially in smaller markets. Honeywell is a practitioner of the decentralized, or "hands off" approach, allowing its major operating units to create their own advertising. This is quite a contrast to the coordination practiced by IBM.

**A Compromise Approach.**   Between the extremes of complete centralization and complete decentralization are programs that use elements of both approaches. A compromise approach should entail finding the appropriate division of labor between headquarters and country operations, with each making its contribution according to its comparative advantage. One expert has called this *coordinated decentralization.* However, this same expert emphasizes the coordination more than decentralization. IBM, Matsushita, and N. V. Philips follow this approach, for example.

In a compromise approach, headquarters usually will play the more important role, being "more equal" than the national operations. The central advertising manager will be responsible for international advertising policy and guidelines. The basic creative work and selection of overall themes and appeals will generally be centralized. Headquarters will also work with the coordinator from the international agency, if such an agency is used.

When the Kodak Instamatic was introduced around the world, the Kodak vice-president for marketing and the Instamatic account executive of J. Walter Thompson not only planned strategy together, they also traveled around the world together, visiting local subsidiaries and agencies. Rank-Xerox had a similar collaboration with Young & Rubicam in its European operations.

The advertising manager at headquarters will establish standard operating procedures and prepare a manual for subsidiary advertising management, including budget and reporting forms, as in ITT. Common formats make budgets comparable from country to country so that they can be better evaluated. The manager will also act as a clearinghouse for international advertising, transferring relevant experience between countries and from domestic operations, and organizing meetings of advertising personnel to improve communications.

CPC International has held annual worldwide marketing conferences to help advertising coordination. These meetings took place sometimes in the United States, sometimes abroad. In addition, meetings were held on a regional basis where marketing personnel discussed advertising programs and agency operations. The company used more than one agency in many markets because of the number of different brands it sold. In Europe, the company's largest region, the firm had a consumer goods policy council, whose duties included selection of agencies and coordination of advertising programs.

In this compromise approach, the role of subsidiary personnel will be strongest in media selection and in the adaptation of advertising appeals to local market needs, while the role of headquarters will be greatest in setting objectives and establishing the budget. Subsidiaries will not have major creative and administrative responsibilities, but they will have a voice in the decisions related to their own market. As compared with a decentralized approach, this compromise requires a smaller staff and less expertise within the subsidiary.

The three American auto companies practice central coordination, but in differing degrees and with different approaches. For example, General Motors markets in 176 countries and uses McCann-Erickson as the main agent of coordination. GM coordinates on a regional basis, that is, for Latin America, Europe, and Asia. McCann is GM's agency in 35 countries. Other agencies are used elsewhere, but they are in consultation with McCann and regional and corporate marketing staff in GM. Though control is regional, Detroit has final approval on campaign budgets. In Europe, McCann's office in Zurich coordinates European advertising in conjunction with GM's European headquarters there.

Ford, on the other hand, markets in 185 countries and uses more agencies, though J. Walter Thompson, Ogilvy & Mather, and Young & Rubicam have 25 major country accounts between them. Rather than using a single agency for coordination as GM does, Ford has its own international coordinating group in Detroit that "coordinates, counsels, advises and assists." It does this through regular advertising exchange, including videos, advertising cost reviews, and annual agency reviews.

As still a different example, Chrysler is basically only an export marketer abroad. Thus, it uses an American international agency, Bozell, Jacobs, Kenyon & Eckhardt, to handle its international promotion. BJKE has an office in Detroit to work with Chrysler's international arm there.

## Cooperative Advertising

A firm that sells through licensees or distributors can choose one of three ways to advertise in its foreign markets: (1) it can handle such advertising itself; (2) it can cooperate with the local distributor; or (3) it can try to encourage the distributor or licensee to do such advertising by itself. The last alternative is not really feasible, so the choice is primarily between going it alone or cooperating.

**Advertising Made in U.S.A.**   When the firm chooses to handle its own advertising for distributor markets, it must arrange for the complete advertising program at home with few inputs from the markets concerned. Going it alone poses some difficulty because the international firm is not very familiar with those markets where its only contact is an independent distributor. This problem is alleviated somewhat when the firm's agency has offices in those markets. However, the agency's network is unlikely to mesh very closely with the company's foreign markets. The agency tends to have offices in the larger markets, whereas many of the firm's distributors are likely to be in smaller markets. The company may have its own subsidiaries in the larger markets.

In spite of the problems involved in centralized management of advertising for distributor markets, some firms choose this approach, implementing it through an international advertising agency. Their feeling is that even with its limitations, this way offers more control and greater effectiveness than the alternatives. Working on a centralized basis with its agency gives the firm a voice in the management of the advertising and general control over its quality and placement even in markets far from company headquarters.

**Cooperative Local Advertising.**   Many other firms choose the alternative of developing their foreign market advertising programs in cooperation with their local distributors. They do so in an attempt to obtain the advantages claimed for coordinated decentralization — the appropriate division of labor and a contribution from each party according to its comparative advantage.

Several advantages are claimed for the cooperative approach. For one, the exporter hopes to get more advertising for the money, either through a greater amount of advertising or through the same amount done on a shared basis rather than solely by the exporter. Furthermore, the cooperative program itself may motivate the distributor to do more promotion. In markets where the distributor is well known, the exporter can trade on the distributor's reputation. The distributor, through knowledge of the local market and media, can help choose the advertising that best fits the local situation. The distributor may also get better media rates as a national.

One problem with cooperative advertising is that advertising quality will be uneven from country to country. If the advertising is poor, it could be a waste. A related difficulty is that distributors sometimes emphasize their own business rather than the exporter's. Also, it is difficult to ascertain whether distributors actually spend their advertising allowance on advertising. Occasionally the money is taken but no advertising placed. Bogus invoices might be sent.

The problems of cooperative advertising need not prevent its being used. The manager can minimize the problems. Working with an agency with good foreign-market coverage can help to control distributor placement of ads. Development of prototype advertising will help standardize the quality of work. The exporter's partial payment of the cost provides for some control. Still another way to combat the problem of uncooperative distributors is to establish agreed upon guidelines. If the firm can implement these steps, it has a good chance of success with a cooperative program.

The Culligan Company prepared three different advertising approaches with its domestic agency. Then it met jointly with its European licensees to review them. A majority vote by the licensees decided which approach should be used. The licensee's agency placed the ads.

Another success story involved the MEM Company (maker of "English Leather" products), which distributed United States ad copy to licensees and allowed them discretion as to its use. Many did use these advertisements, finding them well done and convenient. If the licensee used its own ad material, it had to have it approved by MEM. Of course, to have this kind of control, the firm must pay for at least part of the local advertising. For example, Culligan and MEM paid one-half of the expense, sharing equally with the licensee.

## Summary

Several factors affect the job of the international advertiser. *Languages* vary by market, and the advertising must be in the local language. This requires local help, from the local ad agency or subsidiary of the firm. *Media availability* (TV, radio, newspaper) varies between countries requiring adjustment by the advertiser. *Governments* restrict advertisers' freedom by limits on products advertised, appeals used, media use, and agency ownership. *Com-*

*petition* in the local market will influence the firm's advertising there. *Agency availability* differs between markets for political and economic reasons. That can hinder the firm's ability to find a good agency or get international coordination.

Major *advertising decisions* involve selecting the agency, the message, and the media; determining the budget, evaluating the effectiveness of the advertising, and determining the degree of centralization or decentralization appropriate.

Using its own international marketing criteria, the firm must choose an agency for each foreign market. The trend is to multi-country agencies who are gaining market share. However, some good local agencies will survive in most markets.

In choosing the message, the issue is whether the firm should use local or international campaigns. The use of internationalized campaigns will be affected by language requirements, the existence of international market segments, the use of local versus international agencies, and the degree of decentralization in the firm. To maximize similarities, many firms use a pattern, or prototype, approach.

The firm's media configuration will often vary from country to country because of government restrictions or media infrastructure in the country. Some firms will be able to use international media for multicountry coverage, but local media predominate for most international marketers.

It is difficult to apply the various formulas for determining the ad budget in the firm's foreign markets. Because of this, the percentage-of-sales approach is the most common. The ad budget in a country will be a function of its overall promotional mix there, local media availability, and the firm's own level of involvement in that country.

Evaluating advertising is more difficult in foreign markets than at home. For this reason, firms frequently use sales as the measure of effectiveness. The internationalization of research and advertising agencies is helping on this score.

A major question is, how centralized should the firm be for international advertising? Favoring centralization are potential economies, international coordination, and higher quality. Favoring decentralization are local adaptation and encouraging autonomy in the local subsidiary. Most firms compromise between the two extremes, making coordination more common.

The firm must also decide how to advertise in markets where it is represented by independent licensees or distributors. Should it rely on them, go it alone, or cooperate? Cooperative programs with the local licensee or distributor appear to be the most common and effective approach.

## Questions

12.1   Discuss government controls and agency and media availability as constraints on the international advertising manager.

12.2   Identify the seven advertising decisions facing the international marketer.

12.3   Home Care Products Co. just opened a marketing subsidiary in Spain. The company has been selling in 12 other European countries since 1950. The advertising manager at European headquarters must choose between the Madrid office of a large American agency and a leading Spanish agency. What questions would you ask in advising her?

12.4   Why have the international agencies been growing so strong?

12.5   Why do local agencies survive in view of the internationals' growth?

12.6   What are the factors encouraging standardized international advertising?

12.7   What are the factors encouraging localized advertising in a firm's foreign markets?

12.8   Explain "pattern" or "prototype" advertising.

12.9   Why is it difficult for the international advertising manager to use the same media configuration in all markets?

12.10  Discuss the growth of the international media.

12.11  Why do local media predominate, even for international marketers?

12.12  Evaluate the percentage-of-sales approach to setting advertising budgets in foreign markets.

12.13  What are the arguments for and against centralization of advertising decision making in the international firm?

12.14  Discuss the benefits and problems in a program of cooperative advertising with local distributors in export markets.

# Endnotes

[1] J. J. Boddewyn, "Barriers to Advertising," *International Advertiser* (May–June 1989):21,22.

[2] *Advertising Age,* March 29, 1989, 72–77.

[3] Barry Rosen, J. J. Boddewyn, and Ernst Louis, "Participation by U.S. Agencies in International Brand Advertising," *Journal of Advertising* 17, no. 4 (1988), 14–22.

[4] "The Ad Agency of the Future," *International Advertiser,* May–June, 1989, 18–20.

[5] John Ryans, "A Tiger in Every Tank?" *Columbia Journal of World Business* (March–April 1969):71.

[6] *Advertising Age,* June 5, 1989, 42.

[7] *New York Times,* February 27, 1989, Y37.

[8] Donald G. Howard and John K. Ryans, Jr. "The Probable Effect of Satellite TV," *Journal of Advertising Research,* January, 1989, 41–46.

[9] Samuel Rabino, "Is Advertising Budgeting Changing?" *International Journal of Advertising* 3, no. 2 (1984).

[10] *The Wall Street Journal*, February 3, 1989, B1.

[11] John Hill and Unal Boya, "Consumer Goods Promotion in Developing Countries," *International Journal of Advertising* 6, no. 3 (1987):246–264.

# Further Readings

Aydin, Nizam, Vern Terpstra, and Attila Yaprak. "The American Challenge in International Advertising." *Journal of Advertising* 13, no. 4 (1984):49–57.

Boddewyn, J. J. *Barriers to Trade and Investment in Advertising,* New York: International Advertising Association, 1989.

Callahan, Francis X. "Advertising and Economic Development." *International Journal of Advertising* 5 no. 3 (1986):215–224.

Peebles, Dean M., and John K. Ryans, Jr. *Management of International Advertising,* Boston: Allyn & Bacon, 1984.

Rau, Pradeep A. "Awareness Advertising and International Market Segmentation." *International Journal of Advertising* 6 (1987):313–321.

Rijkens, Rein, and Gordon Miracle. *European Regulation of Advertising,* Amsterdam: North Holland, 1986.

Rosen, Barry N., J. J. Boddewyn, and Ernst A. Louis. "Participation by US Agencies in International Brand Advertising." *Journal of Advertising* 17, no. 4 (1988):14–22.

Ryans, John K., Jr., and David G. Ratz. "Advertising Standardization: A Reexamination." *International Journal of Advertising* 6 no. 2 (1987):145–158.

Synodinos, Nicholas E., Charles Keown, and Laurence Jacobs. "Transnational Advertising Practice." *Journal of Advertising Research* (April–May 1989):43–49.

# 12.1 Nestlé (A): The Case of the Dying Babies

In June 1976 Nestlé Alimentana S.A. (Nestlé) was told by a Swiss court to "carry out a fundamental reconsideration" of the methods it uses in Third World nations to sell milk powder for babies. The Nestlé managing director wondered what actions should be taken on the court judgment.

## The Company

Nestlé is one of the world's largest food companies, with 110 years of history. It is based in Vevey, Switzerland. In 1975 its group sales with 300 factories in 49 countries totalled 18.3 billion Swiss francs, and the number of employees reached more than 140,000, of which only some 7,000 actually worked in Switzerland. Nestlé's most important products are instant drinks and other beverages, which yield nearly one-third of sales, and dairy products, which account for one-fourth. Infant foods and dietetic products account for 7.5 percent of sales. Nestlé has many marketing and manufacturing facilities in the Third World, including 19 factories in 10 African countries.

Like other multinational giants, Nestlé is increasingly exposed to criticism from activists in the home country as well as nationalists in the foreign countries in which it operates. Nestlé has more reason for trepidation than most: Only 3 percent of its business is in its home market.

## The Libel Suit

In early 1974 the British aid-for-development organization War on Want published a report entitled "The Baby Killer." As the picture on the first page showed, the killer was the baby's nursing bottle. The author, Mike Muller, said that powdered-formula manufacturers contributed to the death of Third World infants by hard-selling

their products to people incapable of using them properly. Too often the powdered milk was mixed with impure water, or excessively diluted in order to economize. In the 28-page pamphlet, he accused the industry of encouraging mothers to give up breast feeding, but added the qualification that other factors, such as working at a job, also influence women to switch to bottle feeding.

In 1974 the World Health Organization had also called for a code of good practice in advertising of baby foods. And in May 1974 the Bern-based Third World Working Group (which lobbies in Switzerland for support of less developed countries) published the Muller pamphlet with a few changes. Muller had criticized the industry as a whole, but the Bern activists titled their pamphlet "Nestlé Kills Babies," making the company the killer rather than the bottle-feeding process. They also omitted some of Muller's qualifying remarks and included a preface that singled out Nestlé for an accusation of using dishonest sales techniques in the developing world. Nestlé sued for libel, and the trial took place in Bern.

One of the activists said that the powdered formulas should be provided in pharmacies or through doctors. They should not be advertised on the radio in native languages such as Swahili, which are understood by illiterates. Nestlé's managing director countered, "No one has yet hit on the idea of demanding that wine be sold through doctors or pharmacies because hundreds of thousands of people get drunk on it and sometimes cause fatal accidents." Nestlé officials insisted that their advertising has always stressed, as one billboard in Nigeria put it, that "Breast Milk Is Best."

When the final hearing began, Nestlé withdrew three of the four libel counts it had made against the group. These charges had concerned the allegations that Nestlé dresses sales representatives as nurses to increase sales of its Lactogen milk powder and asserts in advertisements that Lactogen makes children healthier and more intelligent. The only charge retained by Nestlé involved the title on the pamphlet, "Nestlé Kills Babies."

In what *The Economist* (December 6, 1975, 92) called a "happy coincidence," a new ethical code drawn up by an international baby food makers' council appeared in November 1975. The code governs advertising and promotional materials for Third World consumers. It was adopted by nine infant-food processors, including Nestlé. The code had been under discussion for five years.

## The Decision

In June 1976 the court ruled that the pamphlet's title was indeed defamatory. In his decision, the judge stated that the cause behind the injuries and deaths was not Nestlé's products; rather it was the unhygienic way they were prepared by end users. However, the judge ordered the 13 members of the group found guilty to pay only token fines; $120 each plus an additional $160 toward Nestlé's legal expenses. Furthermore, the judgment then stated, "Nestlé has to carry out a fundamental reconsideration of its promotion methods if in the future it wants to avoid charges of immoral and unethical behavior."

The defendants indicated they would appeal the verdict.

## Questions

1. What problem is Nestlé facing here?
2. In view of the judge's order to Nestlé, review its promotional program in detail (see the Appendix to Chapter 11). Evaluate this promotional program and suggest potential changes in Nestlé's marketing program for the Third World.
3. What responsibilities do manufacturers have to assure the safe usage of their products? Would your answer differ for developed and Third World markets? Why?

On November 28, 1975, Dr. Arthur Furer, Managing Director of Nestlé Alimentana S.A., held a press conference in Bern to defend the company against its attackers. Following are extracts from that press conference (from 1975 Annual Report supplement 1–4):

*We have been making and selling baby foods in the world for over 100 years. We have been doing the same in the developing countries for over 50 years. During this period, infant mortality has considerably declined in these countries. Our products have greatly contributed to this. So much so that the more zealous members blame us for the population explosion in the developing countries.*

*In 1974, the British aid-for-development organization War on Want published a report entitled "The Baby Killer." As the title on the first page shows, the target is the feeding bottle. The author, Mike Muller, refers in his report to mothers wrongly using baby milk in the developing countries; he blames the manufacturers who advertise these products.*

*Professor Mauron and Dr. Muller have reminded you of the situation of babies in the developing countries. We have been concerned with this matter for several decades, not merely since the existence of "War on Want" and a group called "Arbeitsgruppe Dritte Welt." The two speakers who have just addressed you have clearly explained that these countries need milk formula foods if many infants are to survive. The problem is not solved by ordering mothers to breast-feed their infants until they are four years old. Nor is*

*the problem solved by having baby foods sold exclusively by doctors, pharmacies and dispensaries. There are far too few of them. Nor would a ban on advertising help solve the problem, since there is an urgent need for these foods. Mothers must be made aware of these products and the manufacturer has the right to draw their attention to them. The governments of the countries concerned have always understood this.*

*However, this right also creates obligations. The first obligation is self-evident. It is the obligation on the manufacturer's part to make good products.*

*The manufacturer's second obligation relates to the advertising he does. In my opinion, it is obvious that the advertising must not contain any false indications leading to possible error. In the developing countries there is the added fact that a fair percentage of mothers are illiterate, disregard the fundamental rules of hygiene and do not have the means to buy our products. To begin with — let's be quite open about it — we are not responsible for this state of affairs. We can help to keep children alive with our products, but we can't teach large sections of the population to read and write any more than we can radically change the living conditions of millions of people. The only thing the producer can do is to instruct and advise the mothers. We have been doing this for decades, and we shall improve our efforts in the light of experience as time goes on. The methods employed by our allied companies to sell milk foods for infants can be summarized as follows:*

• Our subsidiaries take the greatest trouble to instruct expectant mothers by means of specialized brochures, tables, leaflets and films on the care to be given to nursing infants. We have also consulted old brochures and found that for very many years we have drawn attention to the fact that breast feeding is best. We have always stressed the fact that infant milk formulas are primarily intended to supplement mother's milk which, if the mother is feeding the baby herself, is not always sufficient to meet the infant's growing needs.

• These brochures have been so clearly illustrated for many years that even the illiterate can understand them.

• The packages contain all the relevant instructions, set out in a simple manner, for preparing the food hygienically.

• Mothers and expectant mothers receive advice mainly through the clinics, doctors and consultations.

• To advise young mothers, we also engage the services of qualified midwives or nurses in various countries who work closely together with those responsible for consultation.

• Newspaper advertising seldom occurs.

• Slogans relating to our milk formula foods have been broadcast on the radio in various countries.

• The TV medium has been used only in a few countries.

*In spite of everything, I am willing to admit that the War on Want report has made public opinion aware of a real problem. However, one fails to understand why the matter is blown up like this in a country such as ours where hygienic conditions are satisfactory.*

*There are plenty of other problems of hygiene and common sense that deserve attention in the developed countries.*

*But no one has yet hit on the idea of demanding that wine be sold through doctors and dispensing chemists because hundreds and thousands of people get drunk on it, cause fatal accidents or take the risk of a cirrhosis which may endanger their lives.*

*No one has called for a ban on automobile advertising, despite the fact that many drivers are really incapable of driving properly, with the result that hundreds of thousands of people are killed on the road every year.*

*No one has thought of banning television just because some program or other brings cruelty, violence, shooting and murder to the remotest homes day after day. Such programs are jointly responsible for the increase in brutality and for corrupting the minds of viewers; thus the program sponsors bear their share of responsibility for the frequent crimes that are being committed in Switzerland.*

*These problems are serious — one man's meat is another man's poison — and no one can be prevented from drawing public attention to them.*

*But it is reasonable to expect that those who are criticized should deal with the matter and closely examine all possible ways and means of improving the situation.*

*This is what we ourselves did once again after the publication of the War on Want report, if only for the simple reason that even in a large organization there are matters that have not been given sufficient thought.*

*We are surprised at the extent to which some radio and television stations have been carried away by this flood of propaganda. It's no excuse to say that we were also invited to put forth our views. Firstly because this wasn't always the case, and secondly because when we were invited, the public could at least have been told of the reason for our absence, namely that we did not wish to make a public pronouncement before the initial hearings of the case.*

*The first act in the libel suit took place before the Court yesterday and the day before. At a public hearing the judge has listened to the plaintiff and the defendants. Thus we now think it appropriate to take a public stand.*

*Finally, I should like to give those who claim they have interests of the Third World at heart, a little further food for thought:*

*The women of the Third World, they too have a right to avail themselves of modern feeding methods if they are unable to breast-feed their babies because of physical incapacity, because of the work they do, or for any other reason. Before insisting that they nurse their children for three or four years, one would do well to ask Swiss*

*mothers what they think about it. White women are not the only ones entitled to some relief in feeding their babies or to keeping their figures attractive.*

CASE

# 12.2 Saatchi & Saatchi: Becoming Number One in Global Advertising

Saatchi & Saatchi was started 15 years ago as a small London-based ad agency owned by the two Saatchi brothers. It became famous for the pregnant-man ad, prepared on behalf of Britain's Health Education Council: the ad encouraged men to think responsibly about pregnancy by showing a pregnant man and the caption: *"Would you be more careful if it was you that got pregnant?"* Later, in another famous ad, it showed unemployed people in a line waiting for benefits, with the caption: "Labour isn't working." This was an ad seeking votes for the Conservative Party during British elections in 1979.

Saatchi now consists of two major agencies: Saatchi & Saatchi Advertising Worldwide, and, Backer Spielvogel Bates, along with a public relations arm, Rowland Worldwide, and a newly established management consulting division, on which much management attention has been lavished; Saatchi is one of the world's largest advertising agencies, and aims to become world leader in consulting too. It has about 5 percent of the world advertising market and 1 percent of the consultancy market. It has achieved its po-

Case prepared by Associate Professor Ravi Sarathy for use in classroom discussion. All rights reserved.
Sources: "Is the New, Improved, Giant Economy-Size Saatchi Really Better?" *Business Week*, December 21, 1987; "Berkeley Square Takes on Madison Avenue." *The Economist*, September 17, 1988; "Avenue Madison." *The Economist*, July 23, 1988; "Saatchi & Saatchi: Back to Basics." *The Economist*, June 17, 1989; Thomas Doorley. "Saatchi & Saatchi Is Down, but Is It Out?" *The Wall Street Journal*, April 24, 1989; Saatchi & Saatchi Company. PLC *Annual Report* 1988.

sition by acquisitions, issuing its own high-priced stock to buy lower price/earnings companies, thus patching together a giant company.

The attraction of advertising as a global business is its rapid rate of growth worldwide, as shown in Table 1. Advertising spending is growing faster than inflation; and growth is now faster in overseas markets, catching up with the U.S. advertising spending.

Roughly 60 to 65 percent of advertising spending within the United States is spent on promotion (coupons, price cuts, etc.). There is some indication that this may be peaking, with more money moving back from promotion dollars into traditional advertising.

Advertising expenditures grew in every European market from 1980 to 1989, particularly where commercial TV has emerged and in economies that have been freed from government regulation. Such liberalization has encouraged the formation of large retail groups that have focused on selling branded merchandise backed by considerable market research and heightened advertising. By 1990 the world advertising market could total $275 billion, with more growth overseas than in the United States.

It is in this context that Saatchi launched its goal of being the world's largest advertising agency. Figuring that the advertising industry would grow mainly in response to client demand in the various national markets, and perceiving that it was a fragmented industry, Saatchi be-

**Table 1    Spending on Advertising, U.S. and Overseas**

| | U.S. (Billions of Dollars) | Overseas (Billions of Dollars) |
|---|---|---|
| 1982 | $ 66.6 | $ 58.3 |
| 1983 | 75.8 | 58.2 |
| 1984 | 87.8 | 58.6 |
| 1985 | 94.8 | 63.3 |
| 1986 | 102.1 | 79.8 |
| 1987 | 109.7 | 102.9 |
| 1988 | 118.1 | 121.4 |
| 1989 (est.) | 126.2 | 133.5 |

Source: Robert Coen, McCann-Erickson, as quoted in *The Wall Street Journal,* June 15, 1989.

lieved that an opportunity existed to create an integrated global advertising multinational.

Its growth strategy is based on the fact that advertising is a stable business, with fewer than 5 percent of clients switching their ad agencies in a given year; thus, cash flow is predictable and stable. Saatchi also tied the total purchase price of agencies that it acquired to their performance after acquisition in this manner: Saatchi generally made a down payment to the principals of the agency, then offered a contingency payout based on subsequent profit performance, thus buying agencies with their own future cash flow.

Table 2 summarizes Saatchi's meteoric rise to the top of the global advertising industry. Some key assumptions of the company's strategy follow:

• Multinationals will increasingly use sophisticated marketing, advertising, and promotion techniques.
• Such demand for marketing services will require worldwide support.
• There will be a proliferation of advertising media.
• Clients will move to a global advertising strategy, with similar advertising used to sell homogeneous products in various national markets (such as using the Marlboro cowboy in advertising around the world, or Coke, which is advertised in the same way in 50 countries).

Saatchi's goal is to offer one-stop shopping for multinationals, coordinating global or at least

**Table 2    Saatchi: An Acquisitions Chronology**

| | |
|---|---|
| 1974 | Garland Compton, a British ad firm, much larger than Saatchi |
| 1982 | Compton of New York |
| 1985 | Hay Group (human resources consulting) |
| 1986 | U.S.–based Dancer, Fitzgerald & Sample |
| 1986 | U.S.–based Backer, Spielvogel |
| 1986 | U.S.–based Ted Bates |
| 1987 | U.S.–based Peterson Co. and Litigation Sciences (both litigation consulting firms) |
| 1988 | U.S.: Gartner Group (information systems consulting) |
| 1988 | Formation of Zenith, Saatchi's centralized buying company |
| 1988 | Option to acquire control of Information Consulting Group, a spinoff from Arthur Andersen and Co. |

## Table 3   Saatchi's Lines of Business

| Communications | Consulting |
|---|---|
| Advertising | Strategic Analysis |
| Sales Promotion | Market Research |
| Public Relations | External Information |
| Design: Corporate Identity, product | Information Systems Services |
| and packaging design | Human Resources |
| Direct Marketing | Technology Development |
| Marketing and Sales Analysis | Logistics and Operations |
| | Management Development |
| | Litigation Services |
| | Transition Management |

pan-European advertising campaigns, and providing services ranging from advertising to management and human resources consulting, public relations, and even financial advice. The company recently launched an advertising program across Europe for Natrel, Gillette's new deodorant, as well as for Silhouette tampons manufactured by Johnson & Johnson. In both cases, Saatchi was responding to its clients' desires to create a pan-European brand.

Such pan-European campaigns are likely to be in increasing demand as the pace of acquisition in Europe quickens. As companies such as Nestlé buy up British chocolate-manufacturer Rowntrees, or BSN (France) buys HP sauce (an all-purpose brown sauce quite popular in Britain), they will want to advertise these products in other European countries so as to increase sales and recover their investment. The promise of a single Europe after 1992 also makes marketing across Europe more attractive and necessitates more careful consideration of pan-European advertising. In many countries advertising plays a smaller role than in the United States or England, and there is much potential for growth. Saatchi has begun to dominate pan-European advertising, winning seven $10 million–plus accounts, totaling $200 million, out of more than $1 billion in pan-European advertising business put up for bids in 1988.

Saatchi's divisions and business lines can be divided into two major categories: communica-

tions and consulting, each further subdivided into a range of activities as shown in Table 3. Saatchi has derived about half of its sales and profits from the United States, 18 percent from the United Kingdom, and 30 percent from the rest of the world. Communications represent about 80 percent of revenues, with the rest coming from consulting. The company's long-term goal is to obtain about half of its revenues from consulting.

Advertising may elicit smiles and win awards, but the client who pays for it is interested only in whether it enhances sales. If it does, then ad budgets will grow, and the agency will get more business, which implies that it can hire better personnel, do more research, reap economies of scale and do even better advertising. In turn, this should help clients' sales, which will further increase the ad agency billings and help attract new clients, and so on.

The main issue is, are clients benefiting from the growing size and number one position of Saatchi? The client will not reward size, only performance. The client's only question is, will your growing size help you make better ads for me, so that I can sell more?

Acquiring ad agencies also expands the number of clients doing business with a Saatchi agency. But as distinct ad agencies become part of the Saatchi conglomerate, clients may begin to worry about conflict of interest, and loss of confidentiality. That is, a different agency within

**Table 4   Saatchi & Saatchi Financial Performance**

| | Millions of Pounds | | | | |
|---|---|---|---|---|---|
| | **1984** | **1985** | **1986** | **1987** | **1988** |
| Total Billings: | 855 | 1,307 | 2,088 | 3,954 | 3,796 |
| Cost of Sales | 708 | 1,006 | 1,644 | 3,180 | 2,934 |
| Revenues (Margin) | 147 | 302 | 444 | 774 | 862 |
| U.K. | — | — | 98 | 124 | 157 |
| U.S. | — | — | 253 | 430 | 448 |
| Rest of World | — | — | 93 | 221 | 257 |
| Expenses: | | | | | |
| Salaries | 63 | 141 | 208 | 347 | 372 |
| Social Security Taxes | 5 | 12 | 19 | 33 | 37 |
| Pension Expenses | 4 | 6 | 10 | 15 | 16 |
| Total Labor | 71 | 159 | 238 | 395 | 425 |
| Sales, General, and Administrative | 55 | 100 | 116 | 213 | 251 |
| Operating Profit | 20 | 43 | 90 | 165 | 186 |
| Profit after other expenses, pretax | — | — | 70 | 124 | 138 |
| Profit after Taxes | 12 | 25 | 44 | 79 | 88 |

Saatchi could be handling advertising for a client's competitor, and sensitive information that the company provides to its agency could thus leak to the Saatchi division handling that competitor's account. For example, at one time, Saatchi handled five different automobile accounts within various divisions. When Saatchi acquired Ted Bates, it lost clients worth $300 million in billings, some of whom probably left because of fears of loss of confidentiality.

The managerial problem becomes one of maintaining a high quality of offerings in services as disparate as advertising, promotion, and other marketing services, executive search, and consulting. At a minimum, cooperation will be essential. Will formerly independent units with strong cultures be willing to merge? Just as important, these advertising conglomerates need to keep turnover low and ensure that the creative staff of the acquired agencies do not leave, taking ideas and future business with them.

Saatchi also expects to gain additional work through cross-division referrals of existing clients; for example, an ad client may use Saatchi's Hay unit to evaluate personnel positions and salaries, and later use the Rowland public rela-

tions unit. Since Saatchi buys about 20 percent of all network ad time, it hopes to negotiate discounts that can lower the cost of advertising to the client. It combined its 1986 acquisitions, Backer & Spielvogel and Ted Bates, into Backer Spielvogel Bates Worldwide (BSBW), thus merging a creative hot agency (Backer) with Bates, a profitable agency with a well-developed overseas network. Similarly, Compton and Dancer have been merged into Saatchi & Saatchi Worldwide. The two Saatchi divisions were competitors in the runoff for Electrolux's $10 million U.S. advertising account.

Saatchi's approach to forming an advertising conglomerate through acquisition has imitators: Martin Sorrell, formerly with Saatchi, started the WPP group, and has become the largest agency in the world by acquiring J. Walter Thompson (1987) in a hostile takeover, then Hill & Knowlton, the largest U.S. public relations firm, and most recently, Ogilvy Group (1989), also initially as an unfriendly takeover bid. As a result, five of the ten largest U.S. ad agencies in 1980 are no longer independent. WPP's focus is somewhat different, aiming to be the world's foremost marketing services company, while Saatchi has publicly proclaimed its desire to become the world's premier global know-how company. Further, Saatchi's goal is to be the number one advertising agency in the world as well as number one in each major national market. Table 4 summarizes Saatchi's recent financial performance.

## Questions

1. Explain how advertising has become a global business.
2. Discuss the actions Saatchi has taken to develop a global strategy in the advertising industry.
3. Why did Saatchi decide to launch a complementary product line, management consulting, in addition to its basic business of communications/advertising?
4. Will Saatchi succeed with its strategy of becoming the key global company in both advertising and consulting? What are the dangers facing Saatchi?
5. From a client perspective, why might Saatchi be a better choice than a purely local agency?

# CHAPTER 13

# International Promotion
## Other Factors

Advertising is a major but not the only form of promotion in world markets. In this chapter we consider a number of other ingredients in the promotional mix: personal selling, sales promotion, marketing mix, and public relations.

The main goals of this chapter are to

1. Explore the ways in which personal selling varies in world markets, requiring different methods of recruitment and management of the salesforce.
2. Describe how differing national cultures and requirements affect the possibilities for sales promotion in foreign markets.
3. Explain how the firm can use the total marketing mix as a form of promotion in foreign markets.
4. Detail special forms of promotion, such as government assistance, trade fairs, traveling exhibits, seminars, countertrade, and bribery.
5. Answer the question of whether an effective public relations program in foreign markets can make the firm a better marketer there.

Although advertising is often the most prominent element in the promotional mix of the international marketer, for some firms, especially those in industrial marketing, it is a minor form of promotion. Certainly, in every case, a sound promotional program involves more than advertising. In this chapter we will examine some of the other considerations, namely, (1) personal selling, (2) sales promotion, (3) the marketing mix as promotion, (4) special forms of promotion, and (5) public relations.

## Personal Selling

After advertising, personal selling is the major promotional tool. Often it is more important in international marketing than domestically. That is, it commonly takes a greater percentage of the promotional budget, for two reasons: (1) restrictions on advertising and media availability may limit the amount of advertising the firm can do, and (2) low wages in many countries allow the company to hire a larger salesforce. This second reason is especially applicable in less developed nations. Working in the opposite direction is the low status associated with sales work in most countries of the world.

The experience of Philip Morris in Venezuela illustrates the role personal selling can have in a market. Low wages in Venezuela permitted the company's sales department to employ 300 men. However, only one-third of these were salesmen. The rest were assistants who helped them with deliveries, distribution of sales materials, and so on. The younger sales assistants were provided with bikes (a prized possession), which were cheaper than four-wheeled transportation. The missionary-selling activities of these younger sales assistants provided a very effective complement to the regular salesforce.

Sunbeam also had success with its appliances in Peru with a heavy emphasis on personal selling. Sunbeam had a dual-brand policy. The distributor's salesforce and the Sunbeam subsidiary's salesforce overlapped in their market coverage — with the two different brands. This double coverage meant increased sales and market penetration.

## National, Not International

The subject we are considering is essentially personal selling in the firm's foreign markets; it cannot really be called *international* personal selling. In discussing advertising, we could speak of international campaigns and international media, but personal selling involves personal contact and is more culture-bound than impersonal advertising. As a result, even though international business has expanded tremendously in recent decades, personal selling activities are still conducted primarily on a national basis. In fact, many national markets are divided into sales territories served by salespeople recruited *only* from their respective territories. They do not even cover a national market.

A limited amount of personal selling does cross national boundaries, most commonly that of industrial goods, and especially big-ticket items. However, as international as IBM is, it still uses national sales representatives in each of its markets. Although the growth of regionalism should encourage more international personal selling, economic integration is not the same as cultural integration. Experience in the EC shows that personal-selling activities are very slow to cross cultural-political boundaries.

A study of international selling by the Fortune 100 made this observation: "Foreign competition, expanding global markets, and 1992 in Europe will cause U.S. companies to place significantly higher priority on salesforce management in the 1990s."[1] Observations about other countries were as follows:

1. *Japan.* Individual recognition of sales reps is still at odds with the nation's team approach to business.
2. *Saudi Arabia.* Finding qualified sales reps is difficult because of a labor shortage and the low prestige of selling.
3. *India.* Salesforce management is difficult in a market fragmented by language divisions and the caste system.

4. *Brazil.* Salesforce compensation is complicated by rampant inflation.
5. *Hong Kong.* Many qualified natives are leaving in fear of the China takeover in 1997.

One task of the international marketer is to determine the role personal selling should play in each market. Comparative analysis of markets will be helpful. Once the role of personal selling has been decided, the actual administration of the salesforce in a market will be similar to that in the home market. That is, the same general functions must be performed: recruitment, selection, training, motivation, supervision, and compensation. We will touch on them here only as they take on special international dimensions.

Since the sales task varies by country and personal selling takes place on a national basis, sales management must be decentralized to the national market. International marketers will not have a salesforce to manage but will generally serve as advisors to national operations. For example, Manufacturing Data Systems, Inc. (MDSI), a producer of computer software, finds that a sale in the United States requires an average of two calls per firm. In Europe, there are frequent callbacks, each with a higher level of management. This means more time and higher cost. In Japan, MDSI's selling is different in terms of contact and negotiation, requiring even more time than in Europe.

Also in Japan, another company, Wella, finds its salesforce productivity far below that in its Western markets because of differences in sales management there. In other Asian markets, Electrolux finds its direct salesforce requires an average of only five demonstrations to make a sale in Malaysia but twenty demonstrations in the Philippines.

## Recruitment and Selection of the Salesforce

Recruiting and selecting sales representatives will be done in the local market by those who know the situation best. Two problems may arise in trying to find salespeople in certain markets: (1) selling is a low-status occupation in many countries, which causes the most attractive candidates to seek other employment; and (2) finding people with the desired characteristics, educational and otherwise, is often difficult. Shortcomings encountered in the recruitment and selection process may have to be compensated for in training and managing the salesforce.

NCR has been in Japan for over 70 years but only in the past 20 years has it been able to recruit college graduates for its salesforce, since selling used to be considered a low-prestige job. And recruitment is a major part of Electrolux's sales management task in Hong Kong, where it must interview 400 applicants to find 10 it accepts for sales training.

As an aid in recruitment and selection of salespeople, many companies develop job descriptions and specification lists. Both may vary internationally. In a foreign market, the sales job will be a function of the firm's product line, its distribution channels, and its marketing mix. Thus the job will not be exactly the same in all markets, but the greater the carry-over from country to country, the more international direction is possible. The international marketer will search for similarities and common denominators to aid supervision.

A question also arises as to whether there is a universal "sales type," even for one industry. As job descriptions and market situations vary from country to country, so do other cultural influences. In many markets, a variety of religious, educational, and racial or tribal characteristics must be considered. Where markets are segmented in these dimensions, the salesforce may have to be segmented also. Just as German sales representatives generally are not used in France, so salespeople from one tribal or religious group often cannot sell to another group in their own country. The world is full of examples of group conflicts that can be reflected in salesforce requirements: English versus Irish, black versus white, French-speaking versus English-speaking Canadians, Hindu versus Muslim, Sinhalese versus Tamil, Ibo versus Hausa, and so on.

In some parts of the world, a particular group will be the major source of businesspeople, as were the Jews throughout Europe prior to World War II. The Chinese are prominent merchants in many Asian nations today. Within the nation itself, a particular group or tribe may play this role. For example, the Parsees are a chief supplier of business enterprise in India; in Nigeria, the Ibos occupied a majority of positions in government and business until the Biafran War. In many countries the important commercial role played by a minority group, such as the Chinese, is resented by the majority. Laws may be passed forcing greater hiring of the major national group. In Malaysia the group favored by legislation is called "Bumiputra" — sons of the soil. Similar laws exist in the Philippines and Indonesia.

Although recruitment and selection are done in the country, international marketers can make contributions. For example, they may introduce tests or techniques that have proved successful in domestic operations or in other subsidiaries. Each country is not completely different from all others, and some carry-over of these techniques will be possible. By comparative analysis of company experience and by collaborating with subsidiary personnel, international marketers should optimize the use of these experiences in local operations.

When industrial marketers enter a foreign market, they often find their lack of a local salesforce to be an important barrier. To accelerate and ease their entry, they may find it desirable to join with — or acquire — a local firm for its salesforce capability. When Merck wanted to expand in the salesforce-intensive Japanese pharmaceutical industry, it acquired Banyu Pharmaceutical, which enabled it to field a salesforce of more than 1,000. In Japan, where relationships are so important, personal selling is especially critical.

IBM, long number one in Japan, dropped down to number three, partly because it had only about 10,000 sales-engineer hand-holders, whereas Hitachi had 17,000 and Fujitsu, 23,000. Nomura Securities, the largest in its field in the world, is famous for its 3,000-man salesforce that meets demanding quotas. This is supplemented by a part-time force of 2,500 women who sell to the home.

**Training the
Salesforce**

Training of salespeople is done primarily in the national market. The nature of the training program will be determined by the demands of the job and the previous preparation of the salesforce. These vary from country to country. Nevertheless, the international marketer will have a voice in the local training program. Because of the similarity in company products from market to market, national training programs will have common denominators.

Drawing on the firm's multinational experience, the international marketer will seek to improve each training program. This can be accomplished in part by supplying training materials, program formats, and ideas to each country. International meetings of subsidiary personnel responsible for sales training can also promote the exchange of experiences.

Squibb, the pharmaceutical firm, gives special attention to sales training in developing countries. Training programs are developed by the corporate medical affairs division and product planning division. Squibb has medical directors in its Latin American, Pacific, Indian, and Middle East regions who help in subsidiary training programs. All national salespeople receive basic training in anatomy, pharmacology, and diseases, as well as in salesmanship. Then they receive detailed information on Squibb products, including contraindications and possible complications in their use.

For some high-priced or high-technology products, sales training may be at the international or regional level. Because the industrial market has more similarities internationally, and because selling is more complicated, centralizing training for several countries is more feasible. For example, a company's European or Latin American headquarters could conduct training. This would allow better facilities, highly skilled trainers, and economies of scale. IBM has a European training center with average attendance of 5,000 people a day. Bank of America managed its training from its Tokyo, Caracas, and London offices. Upjohn has one in Kalamazoo, Michigan.

Another training technique is the traveling team of experts from regional or international headquarters. As the company finds new product applications, adds new products, or enters new market segments, the sales task might be changed. The new selling task usually requires additional training, which can be accomplished either at a regional center or by a traveling team of experts. As we have seen, Kodak and NCR used such extra training in introducing new products into several countries simultaneously.

Where the firm sells through independent distributors or licensees, it has little control over the salesforce, except to some extent in the initial selection of the distributor. Nevertheless, it is not unusual for firms selling industrial goods to give specialized training to the sales staff of their distributors or licensees. This is generally done at no charge and turns out to be a profitable expenditure because of its contribution to sales as well as to relations with the licensee or distributor.

A particular problem faces international companies in many markets. Because they are usually better marketers and have a better trained sales staff, they tend to be "raided" by national companies. This means that they must either train more salespeople than they need or find some way of keeping their salesforce with them, usually higher compensation.

## Motivating and Compensating the Salesforce

Motivation and compensation of the sales force are closely related. Indeed, attractive compensation is often the chief motivator. Motivation can be more of a challenge abroad than at home, for two reasons: (1) the low esteem in which selling is held, and (2) the cultural reluctance of prospective sales representatives to talk to strangers, especially to try to persuade them — two essential elements of selling.

Although compensation is a prime motivator, there are other ways to motivate. Since much will depend on cultural factors, motivation must be designed to meet local needs. In countries where selling has especially low status, the firm must try to overcome this handicap. Training, titles, and perquisites are all helpful, as well as financial rewards. In addition, special recognition can help the salesperson's self-image. For example, Philip Morris in Venezuela publicizes the achievements of its best salespeople and also gives them financial and other awards; periodically it gives a special party and banquet for the top four. Electrolux in Asia also finds such "hoopla" to be a major motivation for its salesforce (see "Global Marketing" feature).

Foreign travel is another kind of reward employed by international companies. Few members of the salesforce in foreign markets would be able to afford a trip to the United States or Europe. Their ability to earn such a trip through good performance is a very strong incentive. In addition to providing access to tourist attractions, the company will usually entertain the visitors at headquarters. International companies are better able to do this than national companies, both because of their size and because their internal logistics facilitate such efforts. They also gain economies of scale by entertaining sales representatives from a number of countries at the same time. Electrolux rewards winning sales teams in Asia with international trips. Incentive travel is growing in the United States also.[2]

A British engineering firm was having trouble motivating its East European sales representatives. Direct cash bonuses were illegal, so it had to find something else. It came up with a program of periodic one-week training visits to the plant in England. Maximum benefit resulted when the company invited sales reps from Western countries at the same time. While much of the week is devoted to actual training on new products and applications, ample time remains for shopping and tourism. The firm has found these visits an effective motivator.

Chesterton Packing & Seal Company working through its Japanese distributor, Nitta, offered one-week vacation trips to those sales representatives who topped their quotas. The trips were to such Far East holiday spots as Hong Kong, Taiwan, and Manila. The first year of the program, sales of Chesterton products jumped 212 percent. The distributor, Nitta, was so impressed that it adopted an incentive program for its other products.

In motivating and compensating the salesforce, one challenge is to find the mix of monetary and nonmonetary rewards appropriate for each market. Some nonmonetary factors are training, counseling, supervision, and the

# Global Marketing
## Selling Asian Consumers with Hoopla

Sweden-based Electrolux has taken advantage of the Asian consumer's rising affluence by reapplying a concept it developed for Europe of the 1920s — direct sales on the installment plan — to Asia of the 1980s.

"Direct selling is very efficient in a virgin market," says Gunnar Bruberg, who started Electrolux operations in Singapore, Malaysia, Thailand, Indonesia, India, the Philippines, and Taiwan. "The active selling of this method enables the individual sales rep to build need and product awareness among consumers who are completely unfamiliar with the product."

The sales pitch has been tailored to mesh with the cultural characteristics of individual customers. Muslims and Indians tend to own fine carpets that last longer with proper care; the Chinese preference for stone floors creates an opportunity to sell a floor polisher. On average, Electrolux sales reps close one in three demonstrations.

Since direct-selling is labor-intensive, the key ingredient in achieving high sales volume is attracting and motivating a quality salesforce. High commissions and special incentives form the backbone of the salesforce's commitment. The primary motivator of the Electrolux salesforce, though, is a management style best characterized as *hoopla* — celebrating sales victories in a way that makes everyone feel like a winner.

Electrolux has found that its hoopla style is more effective in Asia than in its home base in Europe. The twice-daily rowdy sales meetings include committing to targets, handing out awards, and singing the company song. "Europeans won't sing the company song," laughs one Electrolux manager. The same techniques easily transfer across Asian borders, with few modifications necessary for the different cultures. The company sports club is another rallying point, with tournaments held against neighboring countries.

Headquarters in Sweden sponsors the biggest opportunity for hoopla: the world championship. Every two years, all countries in Electrolux's world compete for the world championship of direct selling. The contest, set in terms of percentage of target to even out differences in size and market conditions, lasts six months and includes a large cash purse. When Malaysia won in 1982, the prize was used to sponsor incentive trips to Sweden, Taiwan, and Thailand. The Philippines took the title in 1984.

Source: *Business International,* June 28, 1985, 204.

---

use of quotas and contests. In monetary compensation, the question usually arises as to whether payment should be a salary or a commission.

In many countries, salespeople are reluctant to accept an incentive form of payment such as a commission. They feel that this reinforces the cultural conflict and the negative image of personal selling. In such markets the firm will tend to rely on a salary payment rather than a commission. Some U.S. companies, however, have been able to introduce incentive elements into their sales representatives' remuneration even in these markets.

NCR for example, pioneered, the use of commission selling in Japan, a country where incentive payments were felt to be against the cultural pattern. However, a decade of experience in which NCR sales quadrupled and sales representatives were increasingly satisfied seemed to argue to the contrary. In fact, the evidence convinced others to follow. Not only foreign firms, such as IBM, but even a number of Japanese firms began to model commission systems on the NCR example. Commission systems are still the exception in Japan, though.

## Controlling the Salesforce

With a commission form of remuneration, close control over the sales staff is less necessary than with a straight salary. Regardless of the mode of payment, however, some control is necessary. Some of the control techinques are establishment of sale territories, setting of itineraries and call frequencies, use of quotas, and reporting arrangements. Because all these must reflect local conditions, they must be determined in part at the local level. For example, when some territories are less attractive than others, the firm may offer extra reward in those areas to assure equal coverage of the market. Philip Morris did this in Venezuela, offering higher commissions in the rural provinces.

Even though this activity is decentralized, international managers should participate in establishing control techinques for the national salesforce. They have contact with domestic operations, which are probably the most sophisticated in these techniques, and their experience can be a source of know-how for foreign markets. They can advise on establishing sales territories, norms for sales calls, reporting arrangements, and so on.

The local knowledge of national management is complemented by the international knowledge of international marketers. A comparative analysis of similar markets provides a better idea of what range of performance is possible. Thus international managers can aid local managers in setting appropriate norms. Especially when introducing a new product, local management can learn from experience in the firm's other markets. In the United States, firms make comparisons among sales territories. With appropriate modifications, the same kind of comparative analysis should be conducted for foreign markets. The comparisons should be among groups of similar countries. This is one way managers can realize the benefits of multinational experience in salesforce management.

## Evaluating Salesforce Performance

Although far removed from day-to-day selling activities in foreign markets, international marketers have a twofold interest in evaluating them. First, the performance of the salesforce helps determine the firm's success in a market. International marketers will want to be sure that local management is getting good performance. To this purpose they will help them in applying the best techniques of evaluation. They can assist with ideas, reporting forms, ratios, and other criteria used elsewhere in the company.

The second interest in evaluating performance is in making international comparisons. It is important to know not only how each country is performing in its local context — that is, relative to last year or to quota — but also how it compares with other markets. Such comparisons identify the countries needing help. They can be used to motivate below-average markets to improve their performance. Some criteria for comparing countries can be personal selling cost as a percentage of sales, number of salespeople per $1 million sales (to eliminate differences in wage costs), or units sold per sales representative.

There are obviously many differences that hinder such comparisons. In fact, the differences are so evident that some firms try to avoid comparing countries. We say "try to" because every international executive inevitably makes such comparisons subjectively. It is better that they be made explicitly, on the basis of criteria which take account of relevant differences. For example, the European division of Singer developed such a comparative framework for its 16 European subsidiaries, including such diverse countries as Sweden and Spain. This framework became operational in the sense that it was understood and accepted by management in the 16 subsidiaries.

## Level of Involvement and Personal Selling

Our discussion until now has been concerned with markets where the firm has subsidiaries and, therefore, company salesforces. Where the firm sells through independent distributors or licensees, the international marketer has no line authority. Because of this, it is all the more important to exercise great care in the initial selection of a representative. One of the main things a distributor has to offer the international firm is a salesforce, which makes quality of salesforce a major criterion in choosing a distributor. The international firm usually can aid the licensee's or distributor's salesforce by providing sales aids and even special training. This is useful, but provides only a limited form of control.

The licensee's or distributor's salesforce is important for another reason. When an international firm wishes to expand its involvement in a market, a common method is to take over the licensee or distributor. In such a case, the salesforce becomes the company's own. Although it is theoretically possible to dismiss the acquired salesforce, there are many political and marketing (and often legal) arguments against this.

In joint ventures the international marketer may have a small or a big voice in selling, depending on the capabilities of both partners. The greater the control given to the international firm in the marketing of the joint venture, the more the situation resembles that of a wholly owned subsidiary. The less the control, the more the situation resembles that in a licensing or distributor agreement.

## Sales Promotion

*Sales promotion* is defined as those selling activities that do not fall directly into the advertising or personal-selling category, such as the use of contests, coupons, sampling, premiums, cents-off deals, point-of-purchase materials, and the like. In the United States, sales promotion budgets have been larger than advertising budgets since before 1980, with a 60/40 ratio by the end of the 1980s. The factors that created that situation are coming to other world markets too.

The firm is interested in any approach that will persuade customers to buy. Firms that use sales promotion devices in the U.S. market generally find them as effective in other markets, if not more effective. Where incomes are lower, people are usually even more interested in "something for nothing," such as free samples, premiums, or contests.

Apart from economics, other constraints affect the international use of sales promotion, one of which is legal. Laws in foreign markets may restrict

| Table 13-1 | **Regulation of Premiums, Gifts, Competitions: Selected Countries** |
| --- | --- |

*Liberal Countries (minor restrictions)*

| | |
| --- | --- |
| Australia | Philippines |
| Canada | Singapore |
| France | Spain |
| Hong Kong | Sweden |
| Ireland | United Kingdom |
| Malaysia | United States |
| New Zealand | |

*Restrictive Countries*

| | |
| --- | --- |
| Austria | Korea |
| Belgium | Mexico |
| Denmark | Netherlands |
| Germany | Switzerland |
| Italy | Venezuela |
| Japan | |

Source: J. J. Boddewyn, *Premiums, Gifts and Competitions,* New York: International Advertising Association, 1988.

both the size and the nature of the sample, premium, or prize. The value of the item received free must often be limited to a percent (say, 5 percent, as in France) of the value of the product purchased. In other cases, the nature of the item received free must be related to the nature of the product purchased, such as cups with coffee — but not steak knives with laundry detergent.

Table 13–1 shows some of these variations. There are industrialized and developing countries on each list, so generalization is difficult. Each country must be studied separately. The restrictions are limiting but not crippling. For example, *Reader's Digest* successfully used contests in Italy even though they are taxed there, giving away such prizes as automobiles. Vicks was able to distribute over 30 million samples of Oil of Olay in many different countries.

Another constraint is cultural. The premiums or other devices used must be attractive to the local consumer. For example, Procter & Gamble successfully used nativity scene characters in packages of detergent in the Spanish market for many years. Premiums require greater adaptation than products. Meeting local consumer desires is one cultural problem. Another is the capabilities of retailers and other intermediaries.

Many sales promotion activities require some retail involvement, that is, processing coupons, handling odd-shaped combination or premium packages, posting display materials, and so on. Getting retailers to cooperate may be difficult where they lack the appropriate facilities. Among the problems that arise with small retailers are that they are difficult to contact, they have limited space, and they will often handle the materials in a way that the producer did not intend.

A further challenge is to be found in the local competitive situation. On the one hand, a firm can feel itself "forced" to use a particular sales promotion because competitors are using it. It may see no advantage to the particular gimmick but nevertheless feel that it will lose sales without it. A different situation can occur when an aggressive international company makes significant gains in a market with a strong sales promotion. National competitors may react to restrain such methods, either through trade-association action or political-legal channels.

A General Electric joint venture in Japan had noticeable success in breaking into the air conditioning market there. Two factors behind the successful entry were (1) offering overseas trips as prizes to outstanding dealers and (2) offering a free color TV set to purchasers of high-priced models.

The result was that the trade association drew up rules banning overseas trips as prizes *for sales of air conditioners* and setting a limit on the size of premium that could be offered. These rules were approved by the Japanese Fair Trade Commission. Company complaints led to a modification of the rules — no overseas trips as prizes for *any* home electric appliance dealers.

Sales promotion is becoming more important in foreign markets just as in the United States. It is also becoming more international to meet the needs of multinational marketers. This internationalization is taking place within marketing firms and in service organizations. Consider the joint venture of Stratmar Systems, Inc., a U.S. firm, with TMG Participations S.A., a Swiss firm. Both specialize in marketing services, particularly couponing, sampling, and point-of-purchase efforts. Together they offer clients service in the United States, 16 European countries plus Nigeria and South Africa.

By 1985 a much broader international sales promotion group was formed. KLP International of London brought together sales promotion specialist groups from the United States and six European countries. Looking to 1992, the Point of Purchase Advertising Institute (POPAI) formed POPAI Europe with 200 point-of-purchase firms in Europe.

The international firm should have some advantages over its national competitors in sales promotion. For example, there may be economies of scale in generating ideas and in buying materials. Ideas and materials may be suitable for several markets. One country can be used as a test-market for others that are similar. Analysis of company experience in different markets will help in evaluating sales promotion and setting budgets.

## Marketing Mix as Promotion

We have discussed the principal elements of promotion: advertising, personal selling, and sales promotion. The purpose of these activities is to induce purchase of the company's products. As marketers well know, however, other factors also help persuade customers to buy — or not to buy — the firm's products. All elements of the marketing mix influence the sale of goods and services. Because the elements of the mix have a different influence from country to country, the appropriate mix for a given market will have some degree of individuality.

The idea of the complementarity and substitutability of the various elements of the mix is familiar to students of marketing. What we note here are some of the international applications of the mix concept as related to promotion. Since we have already examined product policy and distribution, as well as the other elements of promotion, our treatment will be brief.

## Product

Although the quality of the product is presumably the major reason a consumer buys it, consumer desires for a given product often differ from country to country. By modifying products for national markets, the firm can persuade more customers to buy. Affluent markets may demand more style and power, or larger size. Poorer markets may require smaller sizes, durability, and simplicity. Food products will vary in the degree of sweetness or spiciness desired. Further differences will be found in the form, color, and texture of products.

**Package.**   For many goods, the package is an important element of the product. Adapting packaging to the individual market may be effective promotion. In Latin America, Gillette sells Silkience shampoo in one-half ounce plastic bubbles. It sells Right Guard deodorant in plastic squeeze bottles, "the poor man's aerosol." In some markets, dual-use packages attract the consumer because they can be retained for some other use. Plastic squeeze containers are popular in some markets, whereas traditional metal or glass are preferred elsewhere. Form and color are important, too. The label on the package should also serve a promotional role in its design and color, in the language used, and in the text printed on it.

**Brand.**   Brand policy can affect the attractiveness of the product. For some goods, an international brand name will be more prestigious and trusted than a national brand. On the other hand, for many products, such as food and household items, individualized national brands are favored by international companies. Johnson's Wax and CPC International are examples of firms that pursue a national brand policy.

**Warranty and Service.**   Many companies use warranties defensively; that is, they meet competitors' warranties. Warranties, however, can also be used aggressively to promote sales. If the international company has a stronger quality control program and a more reliable product than national competitors, it may gain a promotional edge through using a more liberal warranty. Many producers of electrical and mechanical products have used a strong warranty as part of their foreign-market entry strategy. When Chrysler reentered Europe, it offered a generous three-year, 100,000-kilometer warranty.

Consumers everywhere are concerned about product service, which includes delivery, installation, repair and maintenance facilities, and spare parts inventories. International firms are handicapped in some markets because they are not represented well enough to offer service as good as that of national firms. A weakness in this area can offset strengths in other areas, and by the same token, a strong service capability can be effective promotion. It has been a strength of Singer and IBM in many markets and of the German and Japanese auto producers in the U.S. market.

**Distribution or Level of Involvement**

Domestic marketers are aware of the promotional implications of different distribution strategies. Where convenience is important to the buyer, the firm must have widespread distribution. Where dealer "push" is important, more selective distribution is necessary. The same considerations apply in foreign markets. Where the international firm sells through distributors, it invariably gives them an exclusive franchise to encourage support of the product. This exclusive franchise is almost always necessary to get effective dealer support.

When a firm goes from an indirect to a direct channel, it means that the distribution system is bearing a greater part of the promotion. The more direct the channel, the greater push it gives the product. Going direct can have a special significance for the international firm in reference to its level of involvement in a market. An indirect channel means many intermediaries between producer and consumer. In international marketing, an indirect channel would be exporting.

The way the firm can develop a more direct channel in export markets is to establish its own presence there with a marketing subsidiary. As with any more direct method, the firm's cost will increase. Many marketing benefits are associated with such a move, however, one of which is a favorable promotional effect. One way of illustrating the benefits is to note the disadvantages of exporting which are usually overcome by establishing a local subsidiary.

Studies have shown the following complaints expressed by foreign buyers in dealing with American exporters.

1. American exporters do not familiarize themselves with the market.
2. Management gives less attention to foreign business. Foreign inquiries are sometimes ignored.
3. There is a lack of reliability in delivery dates.
4. Price quotations are f.o.b. — United States plant.
5. Little or no local language material is available describing the firm's products. Some of what is available is poor.
6. Domestic customers get open account terms. Foreign buyers receive harsher terms, such as a letter of credit.

The establishment of a foreign subsidiary is almost certain to eliminate all these problems. It can be one of the most powerful promotional tools the firm can use. Of course, the potential market must warrant the costs involved.

**Price and Terms**

The idea behind the demand curve and the elasticity concept is that buyers are sensitive to price. By changing the price, the marketer affects the attractiveness of the product. In other words, pricing has promotional aspects. If consumers in different countries have differing degrees of price sensitivity, the marketer should try to adjust prices accordingly, if costs permit.

Price may be able to be used promotionally in other ways. On products where there is a price-quality association, the firm might wish to price above competitors to gain the quality image. Of course, this is most meaningful if the product in fact has a quality advantage. In countries where purchasing power is low, prices might be reduced by modifying the product, for example, giving it fewer features and greater simplicity, or using smaller sizes.

**Export Pricing.**   Export prices and terms can be used to promotional advantage in several ways. One is in choosing the currency for the price quotation. Although exporters usually prefer to quote in their own currency, importers like price quotations in *their* currency because it protects them against variations in the exchange rate.

Another promotional aspect of export pricing is the specific quotation used. As noted in our chapter on pricing, f.o.b. plant prices are favored by exporters. However, there is a promotional advantage in using a c.i.f. quotation, which is preferred by importers.

A third promotional aspect of export pricing is in the terms extended to the buyer. Exporters often discriminate against foreign buyers. For example, domestic buyers may be given open account terms, whereas foreign importers have to pay by letter of credit. Foreign buyers would generally like to have the same terms as domestic buyers. Although this may not always be feasible, exporters who want to use pricing as a promotional tool will respond insofar as possible. They would move toward local currency price quotations, c.i.f. pricing, and more liberal payment terms.

**Credit.**   A final promotional aspect of payment terms is the use of credit. The credit needs of buyers vary from country to country. Sellers of industrial equipment abroad often find that the factor determining the choice of supplier is the credit terms. For some countries, it has meant greater working capital to cover more liberal credit. Cincinnati Milacron lost a contract to supply capital equipment for a new canning factory in Georgia even though it had the low bid. The factory chose a Japanese supplier because it offered a complete credit package.

For consumer goods marketers, credit extension can be a promotional weapon directed at both channel members and consumers. In many countries, wholesalers and retailers are financially weak. The seller has to cover their credit needs in what seems to be extremely liberal fashion compared with domestic practices. Very liberal credit may be needed to sell durable goods. For example, credit extension is one reason Singer has been able to maintain a market position in sewing machines in spite of lower-priced competition.

Automobile dealers in Brazil have found an ingenious way to sell cars in a money-tight economy without credit, through a *consorcio,* or lottery. Every member of the *consorcio* is guaranteed a new car in 60 months. Each group includes 120 people. The monthly payment is pegged to the price of the car and divided by the number of members. At each month's drawing there are two winners. Each member pays for the whole 60 months, of course.

Members avoid Brazil's high interest charges and the large down payments normally required. They pay a 10 percent administrative fee, however. Ford's Brazilian subsidiary has parlayed these clubs into a major marketing tool. Ford runs 2,300 such *consorcios* and sells one-fifth of its total Brazilian output this way. Ford do Brazil has aroused the interest of Ford subsidiaries elsewhere in this promotional technique.

## The Total Mix at Work

We discussed the promotional aspects of the various elements of the marketing mix taken in isolation. In reality, of course, these elements interact synergistically. Two examples will illustrate the mix elements as part of an overall marketing strategy. First, consider how the Japanese auto firms successfully entered the German market, gaining a 10 percent share. They took the following steps:

1. *Product.* Improved suspension and steering for autobahn driving, and sold multivalve engines as standard equipment, an option on German cars. Introduced cars with catalytic converters to capitalize on German environmental concerns.
2. *Product line.* Introduced minivans and four-wheel drive, which were not available from German producers.
3. *Distribution.* Expanded and strengthened dealer networks.
4. *Warranty.* Nissan and Mitsubishi gave three-year warranties, greater than they gave elsewhere in Europe and greater than German producers offered.
5. *Price.* Entered the market in the lower and mid-price range.
6. *Promotion.* Established a new ad agency for Toyota in Germany. Honda introduced its four-wheel drive at the Frankfurt Auto Show rather than the Tokyo Auto Show and emphasized its Formula 1 racing activities.

Now consider how Kodak strengthened its position in the Japanese film market:

1. *Product.* Conducted an early rollout of its new Ektar 25 film.
2. *Packaging.* Added Japanese-language labels to packaging. Only English was used before.
3. *Service.* Established a Kodak photofinishing operation to give one-day turnaround versus three days when competitor facilities were used.
4. *Level of involvement.* Greatly expanded commitment to the Japanese market: workforce was more than doubled, photofinishing operation was opened, and a $74 million R&D operation was established.
5. *Distribution.* Moved to direct distribution to retailers versus previous distributor. Marketed Kodak's increased commitment in Japan to encourage retailer support. Gave free trips to Olympics as dealer incentives for good performance.
6. *Promotion.* Expanded promotion along with increased market commitment: expanded advertising, used yellow Kodak blimp, set up Kodak neon signs on major streets, and offered free Kodak film with Kodak photofinishing.

## Special Forms of International Promotion

Certain forms of promotion have special international dimensions. Because they are not usually considered in the promotional mix, we discuss them separately here. They include the activities of governments, international trade fairs, and the Washington representative. Barter and bribery, along with other miscellaneous efforts, will also be discussed.

**Government Assistance in Promotion.** Many governments assist their industry in export marketing. This assistance usually takes three forms: information, financing, and promotion. It is only the latter form that will concern us here. The other forms of governmental assistance are discussed in Chapters 7 and 14. Since most of the readers of this book will be in the United States, we take that country as our example. Most developed and some developing nations have programs similar to those described here. In addition, the joint GATT-UNCTAD International Trade Centre in Geneva serves less-developed countries for export promotion.

## The National Level

In looking at the United States, it is necessary to distinguish between the national government and the state governments. Promotional assistance for international selling is often available at each level, especially for firms located in the industrial states. We will first look at the efforts of the federal government. The Department of State and the Department of Commerce are the principal sources of help.

**Department of State.** U.S. international trade promotion activities were affected by the presidential reorganization in 1980. The commercial activities previously administered by the Department of State in the leading 65 country markets were transferred to the Foreign Commercial Service under the Department of Commerce. The Department of State remains active in secondary markets and through projects administered by the Agency for International Development.

Though the U.S. program is large in absolute terms, it ranks near the bottom in relative terms. Only 29 cents of each $1,000 of federal spending in the United States is spent on export promotion. Germany, which is also low, spends 68 cents, and Canada is way ahead at $6.02, or over 20 times the U.S. figure.[3]

**Department of Commerce.** The most active department in promoting the international business of U.S. firms is the Department of Commerce. We saw in Chapter 7 how it supplies information on world markets. It is equally active in promotion. Its major promotional efforts are as follows:

1. *Commercial News USA.* This monthly magazine promotes the products or services of U.S. firms to more than 85,000 overseas agents, distributors, government officials, and end-users. Exporters may submit a black-and-white photo and a brief description of their product or service for inclusion in the magazine.

2. *Foreign buyer program.* Exporters can meet qualified foreign purchasers for their product or service at trade shows here in the United States. The department promotes the shows worldwide to attract foreign buyer delegations, manages an international business center, counsels participating firms, and brings together buyer and seller.

3. *Overseas catalog and video-catalog shows.* Companies can gain market exposure for their product or service without the cost of traveling overseas by participating in a catalog or video-catalog show sponsored by the department. Provided with the firm's product literature or promotional video, the department will send an industry expert to display the material to select foreign audiences in several countries.

4. *Overseas trade missions.* Officials of U.S. firms can participate in a trade mission that will give them an opportunity to confer with influential foreign business and government representatives. Department staff will identify and arrange a full schedule of appointments in each country to be visited.

5. *Overseas trade fairs.* U.S. exporters may participate in overseas trade fairs that will enable them to meet customers face to face and also to assess the competition. The department creates a U.S. presence at international trade fairs, making it easier for U.S. firms to exhibit and gain international recognition. The department also selects international trade fairs for special endorsement, called *certification.* This cooperation with the private show organizers enables U.S. exhibitors to receive special services designed to enhance their market promotion efforts.

There is a service charge to the exporter for these special Department of Commerce services.

**States' Role in Promoting International Business.**    All 50 states have export development programs, and the budgets allocated to them doubled between 1984 and 1989. Over half of the states run a total of 108 offices in over 15 countries. Tokyo is the most popular location, with 32 states represented. California is represented in Tokyo, London, and Mexico City; Michigan and Ohio each have offices in Tokyo, Brussels, and Lagos; Montana has an office in Taipei. Minnesota has eight offices abroad, four in Asia and four in Europe. And the activities of state export agencies are expanding. Twenty-seven states have set up export financing programs, and several have set up Export Trading Companies and/or shared Foreign Sales Corporations (see Chapter 5). The range of their activities is shown in Table 13–2. As can be seen, state activities sometimes complement and sometimes overlap those of the federal government.

**Relevance of Federal and State Programs for International Marketing.**    As a citizen and taxpayer, the firm is entitled to both federal and state assistance. Because both are subsidized efforts, the cost to the firm is usually low. Therefore, if there are benefits to be derived, the firm should make federal and state support a part of its own promotional mix for international marketing. It should be aware of those programs and evaluate their potential contribution.

**Table 13–2**   **State Foreign-Trade Development Programs**

| | Seminars/conferences | One-on-one counseling | Market studies prepared | Language bank | Referrals to local export services | Newsletters | How-to handbook | Sales leads disseminated | Trade shows | Trade missions | Foreign office reps | Operational financing program |
|---|---|---|---|---|---|---|---|---|---|---|---|---|
| Alabama | • | • | | | • | | • | • | • | • | • | |
| Alaska | | | | | | | | | • | • | • | |
| Arizona | • | • | • | | | • | | • | • | • | | |
| Arkansas | • | • | • | • | • | • | | • | • | • | | • |
| California | • | • | • | • | | • | | • | • | • | | • |
| Colorado | • | • | • | | | | | • | • | • | | |
| Connecticut | • | • | • | | • | • | | • | • | • | • | |
| Delaware | • | | | | | | | • | • | • | | |
| Florida | • | • | • | | | | | • | • | • | • | |
| Georgia | • | • | • | | • | | | • | • | • | • | |
| Hawaii | • | • | | | | | | • | • | • | | |
| Idaho | • | | | | | | | • | • | • | | |
| Illinois | • | • | • | | • | | | • | • | • | • | • |
| Indiana | • | • | | • | | | | • | • | • | • | • |
| Iowa | • | • | • | • | | | • | • | • | • | • | |
| Kansas | • | • | | • | • | | • | • | • | • | • | |
| Kentucky | • | • | | | • | | • | • | | • | • | |
| Louisiana | | | | | | | | | | | | |
| Maine | • | | | | | | | • | | • | | |
| Maryland | • | • | | | | • | | • | | • | • | |
| Massachusetts | • | • | • | | • | | | | • | | | |
| Michigan | • | • | | | | | | • | • | • | • | |
| Minnesota | • | • | | | • | | | • | • | • | • | • |
| Mississippi | • | • | | | • | | | • | • | • | | • |
| Missouri | • | • | • | | • | • | • | • | • | | • | |

**International Trade Fairs.**   Over 1,800 international trade fairs take place in over 70 nations. Although trade fairs are not uncommon in the United States, they play a greater role in other countries. In the United Kingdom, for example, manufacturing firms spend almost one-fourth of their promotion budget on trade fairs. In the United States they tend to be exhibitions, whereas abroad the emphasis is on "show and sell." American fairs often draw many visitors from the general public. Abroad, most fairgoers are businesspeople — managers, purchasing agents, sales representatives, and engineers.

International trade fairs are either general, covering many product categories, or specialized, displaying the products of a single industry. The

**Table 13-2**                    **(continued)**

| | Seminars/conferences | One-on-one counseling | Market studies prepared | Language bank | Referrals to local export services | Newsletters | How-to handbook | Sales leads disseminated | Trade shows | Trade missions | Foreign office reps | Operational financing program |
|---|---|---|---|---|---|---|---|---|---|---|---|---|
| Montana | • | • | • | | • | | • | • | • | • | | |
| Nebraska | • | • | | • | • | | • | • | • | • | | |
| Nevada | • | | | • | | • | | | | • | | |
| New Hampshire | • | • | | | • | | • | • | | | | |
| New Jersey | • | • | | | • | • | | • | • | • | | |
| New Mexico | • | • | | | • | | • | • | | | • | |
| New York | • | • | | | • | • | • | • | • | • | • | |
| North Carolina | • | • | • | • | • | | | • | • | • | • | |
| North Dakota | • | • | | | | | | • | • | | | |
| Ohio | • | • | • | • | • | • | | • | • | • | • | • |
| Oklahoma | • | • | • | • | • | • | • | • | • | • | | |
| Oregon | • | | | | | • | • | • | • | | | |
| Pennsylvania | • | • | • | | • | • | | • | | | • | |
| Rhode Island | • | • | • | | • | • | | • | • | | • | |
| South Carolina | • | • | • | | • | | | • | • | | • | |
| South Dakota | • | • | • | • | | | | • | | | | |
| Tennessee | • | • | • | | • | | • | • | • | | | |
| Texas | • | • | | | | | • | • | • | | • | |
| Utah | • | • | | | | | • | • | • | • | • | |
| Vermont | • | | | | | | | | | | • | |
| Virginia | • | • | • | | | | | • | | | | |
| Washington | • | • | • | • | • | | | • | • | • | • | |
| West Virginia | • | | | | | | | | | | • | |
| Wisconsin | • | • | | | • | • | • | • | • | | • | |
| Wyoming | | | | | | | | | | | • | |

Source: National Association of State Development Agencies.

annual Hanover Fair in Germany is the largest of the general fairs, with over 5,000 exhibitors in 20 major categories, and 500,000 visitors. Because so many buyers and sellers from different nations gather at a big general fair, contacts can often be made that might take years otherwise. Said one international marketer: "We had been trying to crack the European market for three years. After we came to the Hanover Fair last year, we soon had a complete network of European distributors lined up." Potential licensees or joint-venture partners might also be found at a fair.

Fair time can also be test-market time. A firm can test sales and potential distributor reactions in a market before committing itself there. If sales potential is proved, the fair will help the firm contact candidates for distributorships or licensing agreements. Potential distributors or licensees favor the fair for the same reasons. They can see the firm's products and observe the market reaction to them. The fair provides a test-market situation for both parties.

A further value of trade fairs is the opportunity they offer to do some research on the competition. Because of the strategic audience and the publicity given to the major fairs, firms use them to show their latest products and services. Therefore, a firm can note initial market reaction to competitive developments and get a comparative evaluation of its own offerings.

The specialized, or vertical, fair fulfills basically the same role but for a single product category. Two of the more famous specialized fairs are the Paris Air Show and the *Fotokina*, or photo products fair, in Cologne. The *Fotokina* is the major international showplace and battleground of German, Japanese, U.S., and other producers of photo products.

At the 1989 Paris Air Show, a biennial event, the Department of Commerce coordinated the American presence, which included 305 U.S. firms. There were obviously many small U.S. firms there as well as the aerospace giants. Altogether there were 1,600 exhibitors from 34 countries. The Americans had their best results in 22 years at the show. Not only did they register more than 15,000 industry visitors from over 25 countries, they also had the best preliminary sales.

***East European Fairs.***   For firms wishing to trade with East European countries, both general and one-industry fairs are available. In principle, these fairs are the same as those described above. A major advantage for Western firms is the opportunity to meet the end users of their products and other contacts whom they do not meet when negotiating with the foreign trade organizations of these countries. Drawbacks of these fairs are that they are relatively expensive and include many nonbusiness visitors. Selling displayed products for hard currency is also more difficult than in the trade fairs of Western countries. Nevertheless, because of the difficulty of conducting regular marketing in Eastern Europe, trade fairs can be even more important there than in the West. A firm wishing to participate should work through its home government, industry group, or specialized agency.

***The Use of Trade Fairs.***   International trade fairs can offer many advantages. International marketers must consider them when planning promotional programs. If the decision is made to use fairs, the first step is to identify those relevant to their products and markets. The publication of the Department of Commerce, *Business America,* has a periodic listing of international trade fairs. Next, the firm's participation in the selected fairs must be incorporated into the planning of the annual promotional mix. Merely adding it on will result in wasted effort.

In the planning stage, the firm should include its subsidiaries, distributors, and licensees to assure their participation so that maximum value can be obtained by all of the firm's operations. An annual review of inter-

## Global Marketing

### Marylanders Report Abundant Trade Leads at Medica '88

"Medica '88 — The results were phenomenal," reports John Powers, president of BioClinical Systems of Columbia.

"Within a week of the show, I had an order on my desk for monthly shipments. I've had serious inquiries from 32 qualified distributors representing every West European country."

Held in Dusseldorf, West Germany, on November 16–19, Medica is Europe's largest medical trade show. The six Maryland companies that participated in the show through the Maryland Office of International Trade reported more than 300 serious trade leads and opportunities. By the end of the show, more than six new distributors had been signed up, while negotiations were in progress for others. The companies project $2.25 million worth

of sales over the next 18 months as a result of attending Medica with the Office of International Trade.

**A Turning Point.** Powers went to Medica to test the European market for a new 30-second diagnostic test for urinary tract infections. "They were very receptive," he said. The positive response marks a turning point for Powers, who has found the European market tough to penetrate. "Medica provided exactly the market exposure we were looking for to test-market receptivity to our new product."

An added bonus: A distributor in Spain is also interested in marketing BioClinical's current product list. "We're looking at sales of $6,000 to $10,000 a month," says Powers.

Source: *Maryland Trader,* March, 1989, 3.

---

national fairs will indicate some that might be added and others that might be dropped.

**The Washington Representative.** Over 700 American firms maintain Washington offices, and more than 15,000 lobbyists work the halls of Congress and the regulatory agencies. Over 100 Japanese firms also have representatives in Washington. When the office has several people, one will usually be responsible for looking at the firm's international interests from a marketing and intelligence viewpoint. Washington, D.C., is one of the largest markets in the world. The international side of that includes the foreign embassies, the World Bank, the Inter-American Development Bank, and the continuing flow of high-level visitors. Together, these banks (with the Export-Import Bank) add up to many billions of dollars per year in sales opportunities. The Washington rep is a high-level salesperson in a very strategic market.

The task involves marketing to purchase influencers. This is the international part of the Washington representative's job: to cultivate the market among international agencies, embassies, and important foreign visitors. After a sale, the representative may even help customers arrange financing with the Export-Import Bank. Some of the work is long-range market development and may not result in immediate sales. The goal is the same, however: to increase the company's international business.

A firm with significant international business should consider a Washington rep for both the intelligence and promotional contributions he or she can make. It is hard to include this position as a part of the international promotional mix, but it can often be a valuable addition to the firm's overall effectiveness.

**Miscellaneous Efforts.**   Because each market is to some degree unique, the varieties of promotional efforts possible are limited only by the ingenuity of the marketer. Special programs can be designed to meet particular situations. The international marketer is interested in these particular promotions not only for their success in one country but also in terms of their potential application in other markets. One country or region may serve as a test-market for such promotions. Here we note briefly a few of the diverse efforts used in international promotion.

*The Traveling Exhibit.*   Whereas trade fairs are at specific locations, some firms or industries have organized a traveling exhibit that can be a one-company or industry trade fair covering countries or products not normally covered by trade fairs. This can best be illustrated by examples.

1.   Automatic Radio International (ARI) organized a ten-week flying-show-case promotion for 22 Western Hemisphere nations from Canada through Latin America. The purpose was to expand ARI's involvement and business in this area, which was lagging behind the rest of ARI's international sales. The 37,000-mile trip stopped in 27 cities and received more than 6,000 visitors, including presidents and prime ministers as well as business prospects. All of these visitors saw and heard demonstrations of ARI's full line of radio, stereo, air conditioning, and refrigeration equipment — 32 different products in operation.

The results were in line with ARI's goals. Eleven new distributors and licensees were acquired, dealers were added in existing markets and several agreements were expanded. The firm considered the publicity received a valuable extra benefit for its continuing operations there.

2.   Westinghouse chartered a cargo jet and sent 25 tons of equipment to stage what it called the largest private exhibit ever presented in Saudi Arabia. Displays featured virtually all the company's products and services applicable to current or anticipated projects in the development of Saudi Arabia's infrastructure. Many Westinghouse divisions had products in the exhibit.

3.   Rank-Xerox used an exhibition train for the Communist countries of Eastern Europe. This was rather expensive so it later replaced the train with mobile display vans that ran twice a year.

Traveling exhibits share features of international trade fairs. For a single company, they are more costly than participation in trade fairs. However, they can cover market opportunities not available and give one company a monopoly of the exhibit. The Westinghouse exhibit in Saudi Arabia illustrates these advantages.

*International 800.*   Telemarketing is now international. Service 800 S.A. is a firm offering toll-free dialing in more than 40 countries on five continents, much as firms use 800 numbers for telemarketing in the United States. The firm has over 600 clients and service is available in over 110 cities around the world. Financial services account for 40 percent of clients and many others are in the travel industry. However, firms such as DuPont, Digital Equipment, and Lee's Jeans are among the 60 American clients. Many firms use this service as an intermediate step before establishing a sales office in a country. If the volume of business reaches a certain level in one location, a sales office can be justified there. Harrod's of London has an 800 number for customers in America.

Another modern technology marketing device is the videodisc. IBM Europe is using videodiscs linked to touch screen TV to market its personal computer through its European dealers. The sales/training message is interactive, allowing the viewer to call up various programs. This means that the PC can be demonstrated at a uniformly high level in all European countries. IBM has supplied videodiscs in Danish, Dutch, English, French, German, Italian, and Spanish.

**Reducing Level of Involvement or Sharing Production.**   A firm's level of involvement in foreign markets is a critical determinant of its marketing program there. Here we consider its use as a special form of promotion. We've noted how an exporting firm can increase its attractiveness and credibility in a country by establishing a subsidiary there. Interestingly, a firm can also promote its business by *reducing* its level of involvement in a market.

Many countries want to reduce the power of multinational firms in their countries. Foreign firms with wholly owned operations in such countries may find that their business opportunities increase as their equity percentage decreases. This can be true for markets as diverse as Canada, Europe, India, and Latin America.

Hindustan Ciba-Geigy reduced its equity from 65 percent to 40 percent. This allowed it to be classified as an Indian company. It was also free to produce drug formulations valued at 10 times the sale of its bulk drugs. Effectively, its equity dilution strategy allowed Ciba-Geigy to double its pharmaceutical sales.

ITT was induced by the French government to sell out completely to a French firm one of its two French subsidiaries. One return to ITT was $160 million for its two-thirds interest in the subsidiary. The primary gain by ITT, however, was the right of its other French subsidiary to share in $10 billion worth of telecommunications business budgeted by the government.

The aerospace industry illustrates another kind of "sharing as promotion." Such firms as Boeing, General Electric, and McDonnell Douglas have formed joint ventures in Europe and Japan to land business there. By joint-venturing and guaranteeing employment, research, and value added in the host country, the aerospace firms can be assured of continuing business in these markets. In getting this business, the major promotional tool is the agreement to joint venture and subcontract rather than exporting finished products from the United States. Host government pressures play an important role here, of course.

McDonnell Douglas won a $1 billion military airplane contract in Britain over a British competitor. Critical to the success of its bid was its promise to build the 60 planes in the United Kingdom and to use Rolls Royce engines in the planes sold to the U.S. Marine Corps. Several British government committees and eventually Prime Minister Thatcher got involved.

As another example, to clinch an Awacs sale to Britain and France, Boeing agreed to offsets of $1.85 billion on a contract valued at $1.5 billion.

**Seminars and Symposia.** Industrial marketers find that company-sponsored seminars or symposia can be effective marketing tools in markets from developing countries to Eastern Europe. A company *seminar* usually includes lectures as well as demonstrations and/or films of new products, applications, or developments in the industry. The firm invites customers and potential customers, and perhaps purchase influencers. At one seminar, for example, Caterpillar had 425 users in attendance, plus 59 bankers. Also included are the company's own distributors and personnel, both for updating and for marketing contact at the seminars. Alcan found its seminar in Indonesia to be the most important factor in its sales one year. Seminars may cover just one country or a whole region. Alcan has them in Indonesia every couple of years. 3M uses them in Hong Kong, but includes some participants from the Peoples Republic of China. Caterpillar has had seminars in Singapore for all ten Asian countries in its Far East division.

More and more Western companies are finding *symposia* a cost-effective way to reach customers in Eastern Europe. Rising costs at trade fairs in Eastern Europe are causing firms to look at a single-company symposium as a better alternative. A symposium is something like the seminars described above, though more restricted. The firm must get permission from and work with the appropriate ministries in the country so it has less freedom in what it can do. There is a smaller audience. However, the symposium offers the benefit of a critical audience of appropriate government and industry personnel, which can make it more efficient than the trade-fair approach in Eastern Europe.

**Bribery?** There is no question that bribery has been an effective and extensive form of promotion in international marketing. The SEC estimated that U.S. corporations alone made over $400 million in questionable payments in the years 1970 to 1976. The questions concerning bribery are not about its effectiveness, but about its legality and morality. For U.S. firms, bribery of foreign government officials or political parties has been illegal since the passage of the 1977 Foreign Corrupt Practices Act. The law makes it a crime to make payments to anyone if the firm has reason to believe that some of the money will go to a government official. Excluded from the act are payments made to lower-level government officials for the purpose of obtaining permits or expediting goods through customs, so-called "grease" payments.

The fact that bribery is now illegal for U.S. firms' international marketing should simplify the decision making. Do not act illegally. The situation is not clear-cut, however. One problem for the U.S. firm is that its competitors from other countries are not forbidden to bribe in their foreign business. They thus enjoy a competitive advantage over U.S. firms in the use of this promotional technique. In some countries and some industries, U.S. firms may feel they are fighting with one hand tied behind their back.

Western European countries are generally permissive of payoffs abroad. Italy passed a law in 1980 saying that they are a legal way of doing business abroad. They are even tax-deductible in many countries. A confidential West German government memo suggested that firms be prepared to pay up to 20 percent of the contract price.[4]

A second problem is that bribery is not illegal in some countries where the firm conducts business. The firm may feel uncomfortable imperially imposing U.S. laws and values on the host society. While the U.S. law may be essentially noble, host-country officials may resent its extraterritorial application and its holier-than-thou implications. As Aburish puts it, "The idea of giving and receiving is part and parcel of Arab history."[5]

The third problem for U.S. firms is the ambiguity in the law itself. Bribery can take an endless variety of forms, so the firm will often be uncertain whether or not a particular payment will be illegal. Clearer guidelines would help American business to comply. What U.S. firms would really like, of course, is a uniform international code applying to all firms and all countries. In spite of work on codes of behavior by OECD and UNCTAD, however, there is little immediate prospect of this.

Because no international anti-bribery law is in sight, American firms, to compete, will need even greater marketing skills and will need to be extra-competitive on things like product, service, price, and financing. One advantage of the law is that it is easier for American firms to refuse requests for bribes, because foreign customers generally know about the U.S. law and its penalties. For executives, the penalty is up to five years in prison — plus the shame of public exposure and publicity that usually accompanies these cases. In an extreme case, the president of United Brands committed suicide by leaping from his office atop the Pan Am building. Perhaps the most encouraging note is the growing international disapproval of bribery whenever cases are reported. Companies in Sweden and Germany have been embarrassed by publicity about bribery in recent years, and the Recruit scandal in Japan even removed the Prime Minister, as did the earlier Lockheed scandal.

American firms have learned to live with the law. One of the first reactions of many major firms was to write company codes of conduct. Some enforce them severely. Rand Araskog at ITT did not hesitate to fire high-level executives who did not comply with company policy. In closing our discussion, we will quote from the bribery section of one of these codes. This code had to be signed by managers with Eaton Corp.:

> Bribes and illegal payments subvert the very essence of competition and erode the moral fiber of those involved. Such activities are not condoned and will not be tolerated.

**Barter and Countertrade.** One of the biggest markets in the world is the nonmonetary world of barter and countertrade. Modern countertrade is much more complex than the barter trade of ancient times. It includes barter, compensation deals, counterpurchase, and product buy-back. Whatever form it takes, the basic principle is the same — the exporter agrees to take products from the importer in full or partial payment for its exports. Instead of the convenience of money, the exporter accepts, at least partially, the awkward form of payment in goods.

Countertrade is truly a giant market. Estimates of its size range up to 10 percent of world trade, or over $250 billion. Over 100 countries practice countertrade, and over 90 have government-mandated countertrade. There are many participants on the export side also. In the United States about one-half of the Fortune 500 companies are involved in countertrade. Of GE's exports one year, over 40 percent depended on countertrade. Not only large firms are involved, however. Bates found that half of the countertrading firms in Florida had fewer than 100 employees.[6]

Why is such an awkward form of commerce the growth market in world trade? The primary reason is that many would-be importing countries lack the international money (foreign exchange) to buy the foreign goods they want. Therefore, they seek to use their goods as a means of payment. Countertrade is most prominent in the communist countries and the developing countries, because these are the countries with chronic balance-of-payments deficits and consequent shortage of foreign exchange. It is not limited to these countries, however. Even Switzerland used countertrade when it bought Northrop fighter planes with GE engines. It required the two firms to find markets for Swiss products equal to 50 percent of the value of the planes. They had to be products the Swiss could not sell themselves.

Why are firms willing to supply their goods for such an inconvenient form of payment? The major reason is that they would miss out on many sales and many markets if they insisted on monetary payments. Obviously, any firm that can make all the sales it wants for hard cash should do so. In today's competitive world, with a majority of countries short of foreign exchange, few firms are in that ideal situation. The alternative then is some form of countertrade or nothing.

For the exporting firm, the use of countertrade becomes a major form of promotion. In trying to sell to the many countries with chronic foreign exchange shortages, the most persuasive argument to induce the country to choose the firm's products will be its degree of acceptance of a nonmonetary form of payment. A buying country faced with two suppliers offering equivalent goods and prices will invariably choose the supplier who will countertrade over the one demanding money payment. In other words, a firm's willingness to countertrade will often be its major form of persuasion, and may even offset competitive handicaps in price and quality.

Because of the great variety and complexity of countertrade transactions, we have gathered a series of examples to convey some of the flavor of this important kind of international marketing.

1.   NEC, which assembles TVs in Egypt, has half the market there. To keep the business, NEC agreed to export Japanese tourists to Egypt on Egypt Air (3,000 yearly). Half of the airfare and all local spending by the tourists is used to buy parts from NEC.

2.   Coca-Cola operated a tomato paste factory in Turkey, sold Polish beer in the United States, and marketed Yugoslavian wine in Japan — all to sell Coke in Eastern and Southern Europe.

3.   Wilkinson Sword built a razor-blade plant in Russia for sales in that country. As one form of payment, Wilkinson will be taking back a proportion of the blades produced.

4.   Singer supplied its name and technical expertise for a sewing-machine plant in Poland. As payment for its name and services, Singer receives part of the plant's output for sale in Singer's other markets.

5.   Gillette's British subsidiary was selling 20 percent of its exports to Eastern Europe. Barter deals were an important factor in its success there. The company has taken "anything from rabbit skins to butter, from carpets to pajamas" in exchange for razor blades. However, it relied on a specialized London barter house to handle the mechanics of the trade.

If the firm decides to enter the difficult but potentially profitable world of countertrade, it must make special provisions. This kind of international marketing requires special skills. The firm may decide to rely on outside expertise, as in the Gillette example above. If countertrade will be an important part of the firm's business, however, it may wish to develop the skills in-house. Ford of Britain appointed one executive as Special Transactions Manager. General Motors formed a separate Motors Trading Corporation for such trade. In 1979 GE set up a one-man department to handle countertrading. By 1985, the department had 200 people and expected to have $4 billion of countertrade deals a year.

## Public Relations — Corporate Communications

Public relations is concerned with images. The firm is trying to present itself in a favorable light with one or more of its constituencies. Too often it has been associated with telling the world how good the company is, or explaining away the company's mistakes. In an ideal sense, good public relations is corporate diplomacy — the firm seeking to relate constructively to its various stakeholders to the benefit of both parties. Thus it involves more than corporate *communications*. It requires appropriate corporate *behavior*. Public relations is often more important to the firm in a foreign market than it is domestically. A Conference Board survey that identified the major problems facing international executives found that number one was relations with governments and number two was marketing. The two are often related.

Public relations is not marketing, but good relations with the public are essential to marketing success. A firm that is seen as a bad citizen may also find itself *persona non grata* in the marketplace. One reaction could be a boycott of the firm's products. In another sense, public relations can be considered as the marketing of a product, the product being the firm itself. The firm's products can enjoy continued success in the market only because of their performance. The image of the product cannot be maintained if product performance is not consistent with it. The same reasoning applies to the image and behavior of the firm. The experience of ITT provides a good example.

ITT has one of the most extensive and effective public relations programs anywhere. All its sophisticated programs, however, did not prevent one of the costliest public relations failures ever — the punishing publicity ITT got from its attempted intervention in Chilean politics to prevent Allende from becoming president. Although ITT is generally a good citizen in all its markets, this one blunder offset much of its investment in public relations. Public relations cannot be more effective than the corporate behavior behind it.

The publics of the firm are broader than its market. They include all those who are affected by the firm's operations — and all those who can have an effect on the firm's success. These publics, stakeholders, or constituencies include:

1. Customers
2. General public
3. Stockholders
4. Government
5. Media

6. Suppliers
7. Employees
8. Activist groups
9. Financial community
10. Distributors

The importance of any particular group will vary from country to country. The firm's level of involvement in a market will also affect the publics it must deal with.

## The Public Relations Task Today

**Research.**   Just as the first job in marketing is to become familiar with the market, so the first task of international public relations is to become familiar with the various publics of the firm in each of its markets. This involves two processes: (1) seeing others as they see themselves, rather than using a foreign viewpoint or stereotype, and (2) seeing the company as others see it. Thus public relations should begin with market intelligence. By being informed, the firm can practice preventive medicine rather than finding itself forced into drastic surgery after serious trouble has developed. Too often, public relations is used to fight fires rather than to prevent them. Inadequate intelligence can lead to many problems.

**Response to the Public.**   The purpose of intelligence gathering is to serve as a basis for action. The appropriate action depends on the nature of the intelligence. Occasionally the appropriate action will involve a statement or press release by the firm, as for instance, when false statements are circulating. In other instances, it may be a change in the behavior of the firm. Where change is inevitable, it is preferable to initiate the change voluntarily rather than to be forced into it. For example, Nestlé was reluctant to change its baby-food marketing in developing countries. This led to a boycott of

**Table 13-3**                                        **Ten Commandments for the Foreign Firm**

1. Maintain a high degree of local autonomy in decision making.
2. Retain some earnings within the country.
3. Allow and encourage exports.
4. Process locally our natural resources.
5. Conduct local R&D.
6. Search out and develop local sources of supply (local content).
7. Offer equity to national investors.
8. Provide employment and career opportunities at all levels.
9. Maintain fair prices locally and in transfer pricing.
10. Provide information and maintain transparency in your operations.

its products in the United States. On the other hand, Procter & Gamble immediately withdrew its Rely tampons from the market when unwanted side effects were discovered. This quick action minimized the problem and maintained customer goodwill. In yet other circumstances, the correct response may be to do nothing and maintain a low profile. This would be true if the firm were unable or unwilling to change its behavior in a given situation and if a public response would exacerbate the problem.

Avon Products took a constructive response to the rise of consumerism: (1) It created Avon Cares Network to respond to inquiries and complaints, (2) it published consumer information pamphlets, (3) it sought out consumer leaders and groups, (4) it held conferences on consumer issues, (5) it invited consumer leaders to meet Avon managers, and (6) it sought guidance from experts.

Noting host-country complaints about the "foreign" company is a helpful way to see problems the firm must deal with. In addition to problems peculiar to individual countries, certain complaints tend to appear in most of the foreign markets of a firm. They arise primarily because the international firm is a foreigner in the market. The common thread among them is that the foreign firm takes unfair advantage of the host country and otherwise abuses its position as a guest. These complaints are often expressed in emotional language, such as "imperialistic exploitation." A reasonable statement of the kinds of things a host country wants from a foreign firm is given in Table 13–3. It is based on an advisory of the Canadian government. The efforts of the United Nations and the OECD to develop codes of conduct for multinationals are another useful intelligence input.

The best defense probably is a good offense. An imaginative public relations program is the best way to reduce the probability of extreme reaction against the company. Many companies have won praise and awards from host governments for their behavior and beneficial programs. Thomas Watson, former chairman of IBM, was decorated by no fewer than nine governments. Although expropriated in Peru, Esso has a better image in Colombia since it organized a collection of Colombian art and sponsored its presentation in the United States. The acclaim this exhibit received in the United States led to the Colombian government's highest decoration for

Esso. Obviously, the foreign marketing task is easier for a company that enjoys an attractive image.

**Organizational Aspects.**   Because of its need to be sensitive to local publics, the firm must rely heavily on local staff. BASF and ITT are firms with highly centralized control of public relations, while Citibank and John Deere exemplify the decentralized approach. The firm can centralize policymaking, but day-to-day operations will be up to people within the market. The firm will have nationals on its staff in each country and may use a local public relations agency. The international corporate communications manager will assure consistency from country to country and also act as a clearinghouse of ideas and experience. Aiding in this task is the increasing availability of international public relations firms, even in China. Such groups can aid coordination much as the multinational agency does in advertising.

A promising development for improved external affairs is the European Advisory Committee. Many large firms, such as Exxon, General Motors, IBM, ITT, and Thyssen, have formed such committees. The groups are composed of prominent European leaders from various fields and countries. They meet regularly and advise the company on economic, social, and political trends. The group also acts as a sounding board, interprets events, and contributes to strategies. A major value of such committees is the members' independence from company management. They are not "yes men" but give the outsider's objective and critical view.

Public relations is important to effective marketing, but the two functions should be organizationally separate. Although public relations is a profitable activity, its purpose is not immediate sales. By lumping the public relations and marketing functions together, the firm runs the risk that public relations might take a short-run view, focusing on the annual profit-and-loss statement. Public relations should be sufficiently independent of functional management to be able to consider the interest of the public as well as the long-run interest of the firm.

**Megamarketing.**   Public relations *(external relations* or *corporate communications)* has evolved into a new role called *megamarketing,* or the "fifth P" of marketing. The idea is that marketing today must do more than manage the four Ps of the marketing mix; it must also try to manage the environment — the fifth P of political power and public opinion — a much broader role than traditional public relations. In megamarketing, in other words, the firm attempts to make changes in the external environment so that the marketplace will be more receptive to the firm, its products, and marketing program. This new function is implemented in a variety of ways:

1. *Making the chairman or chief executive officer the principal communicator for the company.* Akio Morita fulfilled that role for Sony, John Sculley for Apple, and Lee Iacocca for Chrysler.

2.   *Investing in corporate advertising.* Some American and Japanese firms are advertising in China even though their products are not available there. They are trying to create familiarity and an image that will facilitate their eventual entry into that market. Hitachi had image problems in the United States, so it took out a number of full-page ads in major American papers, like *The Wall Street Journal.* They showed a picture of Tsuneo Tanaka, president of Hitachi America. The heading read, "Toward a Truly American Corporation," and Tanaka discussed Hitachi's "commitment to becoming an active member of America's corporate community."

3.   *Using the home government to support the firm's sales abroad.* AT&T entered the lucrative Italian (and European) telephone market as the government-appointed partner to government-owned Italtel. It was helped by President Reagan. A Ford vice-president returned from the Mideast complaining about the competition. Margaret Thatcher had been there supporting a British system. The Queen of England entertained Saudi Crown Prince Abdullah in her box at the Ascot races. The Saudis are buying $25 billion worth of weapons from Britain over the next 10 years.

4.   *Developing government negotiation and lobbying skills.* In Japan, Motorola retained as advisers former officials of MITI and the Ministry of Post and Telecommunications. In Korea, Goodyear received permission for a wholly owned plant rather than the suggested joint venture. It was the result of a careful and extensive negotiation with different parts of the Korean government.

The Japanese have become adept at megamarketing. An examination of their budget for the United States in 1988 reveals some of their approaches.[7]

**Japanese Megamarketing**

|                                      | Millions of Dollars, 1988 |
| ------------------------------------ | ------------------------- |
| Corporate Philanthropy               | $140                      |
| Washington Lobbying                  | 50                        |
| Public Relations                     | 45                        |
| Research Contracts to Universities   | 30                        |
| Foreign Affairs Ministry             | 17                        |
| JETRO                                | 15                        |
| Japan Foundation                     | 5                         |
| Public Television                    | 5                         |
| U.S.—Japan Foundation                | 3                         |
| Total                                | $310                      |

## Summary

Personal selling is often more important in the promotional mix abroad than in the domestic market. Although it is done almost entirely on a national basis, headquarters management can contribute something to almost all the tasks of salesforce management in the firm's foreign markets: recruitment and selection, training, motivation, compensation, control and evaluation. Successful techniques can be transferred from the home market to similar foreign markets. Economies of scale can be employed for some tasks. The firm will also frequently train or assist distributors' or licensees' salesforces. And international comparisons help in evaluating and thus improving international performance.

Sales promotion is usually effective in most foreign markets in spite of national restrictions. It often must be adapted to meet local legal and cultural differences, but it will play the same role in the marketing mix abroad as at home.

Each of the four Ps of the marketing mix can attract the customer and therefore serve as promotion. *Product* modifications abroad (including package, brand, warranty, and service) can persuade customers to buy the firm's products. By going to more direct *distribution* abroad, the firm can usually increase sales and respond better to the local market. Various *pricing* and credit terms can make the firm's marketing more productive, such as c.i.f. quotes and open account terms.

Government assistance is a special form of promotion in international marketing. Many governments support the export sales of their companies. In the United States, the Department of Commerce is the main supporter and has several programs — publications, shows, and missions. All 50 state governments also have support programs, sometimes overlapping and sometimes complementing those of the federal government.

International trade fairs are very valuable marketing tools, not only for market entry but for keeping up in markets abroad. They can also be used in communist countries.

The Washington representative can market to a critical clientele in Washington, D.C.

Other special forms of promotion include (1) traveling exhibits that involve extra costs but special advantages; (2) international 800 numbers for distributors or customers (these should become more popular); (3) reducing its level of involvement in a market to give a firm a bigger market share because of favorable government treatment; (4) seminars and symposia, offering a special entry to some countries and some industry sectors; (5) bribery which, though illegal for American firms, is used by competitors; and (6) barter and countertrade, which are very big markets today; the firm will often find its willingness to countertrade is its most persuasive marketing tool.

Public relations is a very important and sensitive task for international marketing. The first step in successful public relations is reseach to familiarize the firm with all the constituencies that can affect its success in the market. The second is designing a company program and behavior appropriate to the market. The new megamarketing concept suggests that firms should not only respond to the environment but should try to manage it, thus achieving more favorable outcomes in the marketplace through political power and public opinion — the "fifth P" of marketing.

# Questions

13.1   Why does personal selling often play a proportionately larger promotional role in foreign markets than in the domestic market?

13.2   Why is personal selling done largely within national boundaries rather than internationally?

13.3   Since most of the task of salesforce management must be done within the national market, what contributions can the international marketing manager make?

13.4   How can comparative analysis of the firm's foreign markets help the international marketer with local salesforce management?

13.5   Explain how the multinational firm may have an advantage over local firms in training the salesforce and evaluating its performance.

13.6   Discuss the influence of the firm's level of involvement on the personal-selling function in foreign markets.

13.7   Discuss the potential competitive advantages of the multinational firm in sales promotion activities in foreign markets.

13.8   How does the establishment of local operations aid the firm's promotion in foreign markets?

13.9   Review the promotional services of the U.S. Department of Commerce. Who might use these, and how?

13.10  How might the firm use international trade fairs?

13.11  Discuss the role of the Washington representative in international marketing.

13.12  Identify the various publics of the firm in foreign markets.

13.13  What are the elements of a sound public relations program?

13.14  What is the relationship of public relations to marketing?

13.15  Federated Motors, a large U.S. manufacturer of automobiles, has plants in several Latin American countries. Recently, the firm (along with several others) has been attacked in the newspapers of some of these countries. The general tenor of the attacks is anti-capitalist, anti-Yankee, and anti-imperialist, although some more specific charges are listed also. Advise the firm on its public relations program.

13.16  What constitutes megamarketing for the international marketer?

# Endnotes

[1]*Marketing News,* May 8, 1989, 7.
[2]Ibid., March 13, 1989, 1.
[3]*The Economist,* January 21, 1989, 68.
[4]*Time,* March 16, 1981, 67.
[5]*The Economist,* February 8, 1986, 86.

[6]Constance Bates, "A Study of Countertrading Firms in Florida," paper presented at the Academy of International Business, New York, October 1985.
[7]*Business Week,* July 11, 1989, 64.

# Further Readings

Bates, Constance. "Are Companies Ready for Countertrade?" *International Marketing Review* (Summer 1986): 28–36.

Crespy, Charles T. "Global Marketing is the New Public Relations Challenge." *Public Relations Quarterly* (Summer 1986): 5–8.

Flynn, Brian H. "The Challenge of Multinational Sales Training." *Training and Development Journal* (Winter 1987): 54–55.

Foxman, Ellen R., Patriya S. Tansuhaj, and John Wong. "Evaluating Cross-National Sales Promotion Strategy." *International Marketing Review* (Winter 1988): 7–15.

Graham, John L. "The Foreign Corrupt Practices Act." *Journal of International Business Studies* (Winter 1984): 107–121.

Hill, John S., and Unal O. Boya. "Consumer Goods Promotions in Developing Countries." *International Journal of Advertising* 6, no 3 (1987): 249–264.

Huszagh, Sandra M., and Frederick Huszagh. "International Barter and Countertrade." *International Marketing Review* (Summer 1986): 7–19.

Kaikati, Jack G., and Wayne Label. American Bribery Legislation: An Obstacle to International Marketing." *Journal of Marketing* (Fall 1980): 38–43.

Yoffie, David B. "How an Industry Builds Political Advantage." *Harvard Business Review* (May–June 1988): 82–89.

# 13.1 Nestlé(B): More Trouble in the Baby Market

On October 12, 1988, the International Organization of Consumers Unions (IOCU) called for a renewal of the boycott against Nestlé. Because of the deaths of babies in developing countries that were alleged to be related to the use of infant formula (see Case 12.1), IOCU encouraged an international boycott of Nestlé products from 1977 to 1984. During that time, Nestlé responded by changing its marketing practices for infant formula, working with the industry and the World Health Organization (WHO) on a code for marketing infant formula, and forming a prestigious committee (headed by Senator Muskie) to investigate the claims and advise Nestlé. By 1984 the company was perceived as a leading firm in support of the WHO code, and the boycott was dropped.

Calls for a renewed boycott arose because some observers claimed that Nestlé and some other firms were breaking the spirit of the code by supplying large amounts of free formula to hospitals in developing countries with the result that too many mothers became dependent on formula and lost the ability to nurse their babies. Nestlé's response was that the WHO code allows the free distribution of supplies to hospitals who request it, and that the amounts supplied were not excessive.

## Nestlé in the United States' Baby Market

The American market for infant formula amounts to over $1.6 billion, and until 1988 none of it belonged to Nestlé. (Abbott and Bristol Myers had 90 percent of the market between them.) In June 1988 Nestlé introduced Good Start H.A., which it said was able to prevent or reduce fussiness, sleeplessness, colic, rash, and other worrisome ailments because it is hypoallergenic — which the labels indicated in bold type. Carnation, Nestlé's American subsidiary, introduced the product and called it "a medical breakthrough."

The market-entry strategy for Good Start H.A. included the product-differentiation feature of being hypoallergenic while having a taste similar to other infant formula products. By contrast, Nutramigen, another hypoallergenic product, had a distinctive, less pleasant taste. Good Start H.A. was priced competitively with the leading infant formula brands, although Bristol Myers' hypoallergenic Nutramigen, a niche product, cost twice as much as Good Start H.A. To further speed market entry, Carnation broke with industry practice and publicized the hypoallergenic feature directly to parents without waiting for pediatricians to recommend it.

About three months after the introduction of Good Start H.A., there were scattered reports of severe reactions. Some mothers of severely milk-allergic babies tried the formula and reported that their babies vomited violently and went limp. Nestlé's competitors helped to publicize these incidents. Some leading pediatricians criticized Nestlé's marketing as misleading, and the American Academy of Pediatrics strongly protested against advertising directly to mothers and bypassing the physician. James Strain, director of the academy said, "These ailments (fussiness, colic, etc.) happen to 90 percent of all babies and aren't really symptoms of anything. The advertising just raises the level of anxiety in mothers about something being wrong with their babies."

One mother, Mrs. Elizabeth Strickler, was interviewed by *The Wall Street Journal*.[1] Her son, Zachary, hadn't tolerated other formulas well, so she was eager to try Good Start H.A. After two weeks of use, Zachary had severe vomiting. She discontinued usage, but for two months she had to feed him Maalox to soothe his gastrointestinal tract. "If you call something hypoallergenic, that means a lot to me," she said. "I thought it was the best thing and that's why I bought it."

William Spivak, pediatrician and Mrs. Strickler's doctor, said, "My concern is that long after physicians realize that this formula isn't as hypoallergenic as claimed, parents with milk-allergic babies will be grabbing it off the shelf because of its attractive hypoallergenic labeling, and thereby exposing their babies to a potentially dangerous formula without physician supervision." Other pediatricians pointed out that while Good Start is easier to digest than ordinary milk-based formulas, it isn't mild enough for the approximately 2 percent of babies who, like Zachary, are severely allergic to cows' milk. The mothers of these babies were most likely to be attracted by the hypoallergenic claim.

Good Start had received preliminary approval of the Food and Drug Administration (FDA) before introductory marketing, but the FDA had asked for more data backing up the formula's extra claims that it could reduce allergies. After the severe reactions were reported, the FDA began a new investigation of the company's claims as well as the six reports of severe reaction.

Following the widespread publicity given to the cases of severe reaction to the Good Start formula, several state attorneys general also began an investigation of Nestlé's Head Start marketing. The company had to submit copies of Good Start's print, radio, and TV advertising that had appeared in California, New York, and Texas. It also had to provide scientific studies supporting the formula's health and nutrition claims as well as studies showing consumer perception of the term "hypoallergenic."

Robert Roth, an assistant attorney general in New York, said "This case is a little unusual in that it involves the health of infants. We are pursuing it more urgently than we would a matter which is purely economic."[2]

In responding to the publicity and the criticisms, Nestlé and Carnation pointed out that all formulas have isolated cases of bad reactions. They argued that the severe reactions to Good Start resulted from its misuse with highly milk-allergic babies. Pierre Guesry, a Nestlé vice-president in Switzerland, said, "I don't understand why our product should work in 100 percent of cases. If we wanted to say it was foolproof, we would have called it allergy-free. We call it hypo- or less-allergenic."

## A Product from Europe

Nestlé, which has the largest share of the infant formula market outside of the United States, had introduced Beba H.A., a version of Good Start H.A., in Germany two years before bringing it into the U.S. market. While mothers are in the hospital after giving birth, Nestlé supplies them information about hypoallergenic formulas and infant allergies. It doesn't name the company or the product, but Beba H.A. is the only major hypoallergenic brand available. Other formula makers also distribute information to mothers, but some critics say Nestlé goes too far. Judith Phillipoa of the Geneva Infant Feeding Association, an anti-Nestlé activist group, said, "In Europe, Nestlé is blowing up the allergy problem as a way of creating demand for their product. Now they're exporting this system to the United States."

Pierre Guesry said that Good Start was introduced in the United States because "we felt American babies should have the same rights to a good formula as German, Belgian, or French babies." He pointed out that no problems were reported in Europe as have occurred in the United States and that most of the 40,000 American babies who had tried Good Start had no problems with it.

## Nestlé Responds

Nestlé's first response to the publicity and criticism was to remove the term "hypoallergenic" from the front of the can where it had been displayed in large type. Some critics were not satisfied, because H.A. was still in the product name — Good Start H.A. — and "hypoallergenic" was in the fine print on the back of the can. Also, Good Start was still advertised in medical journals as a "breakthrough hypoallergenic infant formula."[3]

In July 1989 Nestlé reached a settlement with nine states' attorneys general about its Good Start marketing. The agreement specified (1) Carnation could not use the word hypoallergenic in advertising Good Start; (2) it could not use expert endorsers that had been paid by the company; and (3) it could not make claims that were not scientifically supported. Carnation also agreed to pay $90,000 to cover the costs of the investigation.[4]

Nestlé also hired Olgilvy & Mather's public relations unit to help its relations with the FDA and the other publics involved. Among Ogilvy's proposals were

1. Get people into the groups organizing and supporting the boycott. This was meant to be an early warning system for Nestlé.

2. Create a Nestlé positive-image campaign — a daily 12-minute news program to reach 8,000 high schools. This was not to advertise but to buy public service time such as a "Nestlé News Network."

3. Create a Carnation image campaign to inoculate the Nestlé subsidiary from any negative effects of the boycott.

The game plan included a Carnation National Homework Help Line and a foster care fund for children with AIDS.

## Questions

1. Identify in some detail and evaluate Nestlé's marketing strategy (the four Ps) for entering the U.S. infant formula market.

2. Suggest a program for Nestlé to deal with its public relations problems, for example, the renewed boycott and the negative publicity about Good Start. Would you use the Ogilvy & Mather recommendations?

## Endnotes

[1]*The Wall Street Journal,* February 16, 1989, 1.
[2]Ibid., February 24, 1989, B6.

[3]Ibid., March 13, 1989, B6.
[4]Ibid., July 7, 1989, B4.

CASE
# 13.2 Eberhard Faber's Special Forms of Promotion

The board of directors of Eberhard Faber, Inc., was discussing the matter of establishing a joint venture in a Third World country. The joint venture was to supply the know-how to enable a local pencil company there to expand and improve its operations and to use Eberhard Faber's name. In return, Eberhard Faber would receive 35 percent equity of the local company, which could be expected to provide dividend income in the years ahead. However, no cash was required of Eberhard Faber for the equity position. The deal also envisaged that Eberhard Faber would supply equipment for the expected venture over a five-year period at a pretty good profit. After two years' effort, the deal was consummated in principle. Only the approval of the board was lacking.

## The Company

Eberhard Faber, Inc., was founded in 1849 by the original Eberhard Faber. It is known for quality pencils and other stationery supplies including the well-known brands, Mongol and Colorbrite pencils, Dart pens, Pink Pearl erasers, and Star rubber bands. It is owned by the Faber family, and the present chairman is the fourth Eberhard Faber. It has no immediate plans to go public.

Although sales were only $30 million, the company did business in many countries. In addition to the U.S. operation based in Wilkes-Barre, Pennsylvania, it had wholly owned subsidiaries in Canada and Germany and joint ventures in Venezuela and Colombia. There were also licensees using its name and know-how in Argentina, Brazil, Central America, Peru, Syria, and the Philippines. Eberhard Faber's board of directors has been on record for several years in favor of further expansion into foreign markets.

Following the board's policy of international growth, a substantial contract that included know-how for a factory to make Eberhard Faber products was signed with the Syrian government. Soon after, there was an expansion of the licensing agreement in Brazil. The proposed joint venture was the next step in this program of international development.

The company had a good reputation, both for product quality and business dealings. Recently, for example, it refused to ship large quantities of its newest Dart pen because the quality didn't meet its standards — even though the company knew that its customers would accept the merchandise. The board of directors was always very concerned for the company's reputation.

## Board Meeting

After discussing the other major agenda items, Eberhard Faber, chairman and chief executive officer, introduced the proposal for the joint venture with a ten-minute summary of the conditions of the deal. He explained that it would increase this year's budgeted profit by more than one-quarter. In addition, he mentioned that the local pencil company under consideration was paying off the government of its country in order to do business. Although the laws of the country prohibited bribery, it was a common and accepted practice there. Eberhard Faber, Inc., however, would be a minority shareholder in the venture, so there seemed to be no legal exposure. (Later it was confirmed by legal counsel that there was no legal exposure, and the company had informal advice from the IRS that its concern was primarily with U.S.–controlled companies that made illegal payoffs and deductions.)

A number of board members insisted that the problem was not the legal exposure but the ethics of taking an equity position in a company that was paying off its country's government. Faber argued, however, that aside from the rights and wrongs of payoffs in a country where they were common practice, the board's own company would be doing no paying off. Furthermore, it could not hope to change the practices of another company in which it held only a minority stock interest. He also said, "Don't you realize that if we adopt this type of policy, we'll be shut out of half the world? Don't you realize that our competition in Europe, if not the United States, won't have any such ethical qualms and will take over this opportunity in a flash, shutting us out of this market permanently? Whatever happened to our policy of international expansion?"

## Questions

1.  If you were a board member, what would be your decision? Why?

2.  What guidelines for international business expansion would you suggest for Eberhard Faber, Inc.?

CASE
# 13.3  Raytheon's Offset Adventure

As Bill Stevenson, contracts administrator for Raytheon Company Limited, waited for clearance from Korea on his proposal to use Lucky-Goldstar as a supplier for advanced electronic components, he worried about the offset requirements. Raytheon had to "offset" its sale of a radar system to Korea by purchases in Korea for export. Even if Lucky-Goldstar were selected to fulfill the offset agreement, it was an unknown company in the United States. He had limited information on whether its components would sell or whether they could be used internally by Raytheon. Stevenson had no doubt about the desirability of making the sale to Korea, but he wondered if the offset demands were becoming too stringent.

Only two months earlier, Stevenson had been encouraged when he made contact with Lucky-Goldstar in Seoul, Korea, to supply quality electronic components to Raytheon in order to satisfy the "like product" percentage of the offset requirement in its contract with the Koreans. However, earlier this month he had received a "clarifying" telegram from Colonel Park Lee of the Republic of Korea Air Force (ROKAF), detailing the guidelines for gaining offset credit through procurement of electronic components.

The telegram was definite on several points. First, a specified percentage of the counterpurchase must be a direct input or component to the radar system known as a Ground Control Approach radar unit (GCA) that Raytheon was selling to Korea. Second, only companies with special clearance from the ROKAF could be suppliers to the system Raytheon was assembling for Korea. And third, prior approval was needed

Source: This case was prepared by Professor J. Alex Murray for the sole purpose of providing material for class discussion. Some slight alteration of the facts was used to disguise events. 1986, School of Business and Economics, Wilfrid Laurier University, Waterloo, Canada.

before any serious negotiations were to proceed with a supplier.

## Counteroffers

An offset program had been established by the Korean government in 1984. The guidelines called for support of high-priority industries and the offset of imports from high-technology countries with "like" products from Korea.

The Koreans were seeking electronic product offsets by Raytheon as an entry into the North American market. Six months earlier, arrangements had been made with Hyundai Canada Inc. whereby Raytheon would sponsor the entry of 4,000 automobiles to Canada over two years. (The GCA system sale was for $20 million.) Hyundai had arranged for approval from Canada's Foreign Investment Review Agency to ship the automobiles duty-free, as a developing country. The company was able to establish dealerships in the major cities across Canada and was ready to import the new automobiles by early spring of 1984. This was a test-market before Hyundai was to launch its cars into the United States in mid-1986.

The value of the cars matched the value of the purchase, satisfying the 100 percent general offset requirement. However, soon after the offset had been signed, Colonel Lee visited Raytheon and indicated that the Hyundai car named "Pony" would have succeeded without the help of Raytheon, and since sales were actually projected to be higher than the levels proposed by Raytheon, the Koreans felt that this was not a very advantageous offset and sought additional ones.

The Defense Industry Bureau (DIB), as the ministry watchdog for promoting Korean high tech, obviously wanted to negotiate the best offset contract to assist in technology transfers and employment to selected companies, particularly those firms the DIB felt had the most promise. Raytheon located and contacted Lucky-Goldstar, a supplier to Sears of branded television sets, who agreed to be part of the offset arrangement. This left only two items on the agenda — the dollar amount required to satisfy the additional offset requirement and the timetable for the offset purchase in order to satisfy the agreement.

By the fall of 1985, Stevenson was ready to go back to the Korean government with a proposal to purchase 5 percent of the contract's value (about $1 million U.S.) and take delivery over the next five years. The Koreans suggested 50 percent of the contract (about $10 million U.S.) in addition to the Hyundai offset purchases with delivery within two years of the agreement.

## Offset Arrangements

The Koreans said they would consider Lucky-Goldstar as a supplier for the offset, but to Stevenson's surprise, they insisted television sets could not be the product of the offset. He was told these were not considered "like" products under the guidelines. Raytheon would have to take electronic components (e.g., integrated cir-

cuits) from a specified supplier in order to satisfy the terms of the offset agreement. This was the major line manufactured in Korea that was "favoured" by the government.

In order to accept the "like" products as an offset, Stevenson realized that such components would have to meet extremely rigorous quality standards, whereas similar electronic components from Korea were untried and untested. For example, The U.S. Air Force audited Raytheon suppliers on a yearly basis with regard to performance quality and supply timing. And key foreign suppliers at such distances presented major problems in areas of exchange inspections and on-site quality testing (a process where U.S. authorities would accept offshore inspection by local authorities if they had been long-term suppliers). It was because of the need for quality performance that procurement management had been strategically located within the Raytheon marketing organization. Stevenson knew that all these offset arrangements were important to long-term export contracts with the Koreans, but still exports were only 15 percent of Raytheon's total business and he did not want to jeopardize the other 85 percent of the company's business.

## Questions

1. Should Raytheon give up on Lucky-Goldstar even though their initial contacts indicated that it was a promising supplier of electronic components?

2. Does Stevenson have any options to maneuver Raytheon into a better bargaining position?
3. What are the lessons that Raytheon might learn from this experience?

CHAPTER 14

# Pricing in International Marketing: I

*Learning Objectives*

We now examine price-setting in international markets. International pricing is complex, influenced by differences in consumer behavior across markets, competitive response, the firm's own cost structure and profit objectives, and government regulation. Exchange rate fluctuations add spice to this mixture. The main goals of this chapter are to

1. Establish a framework covering the broad principles governing international pricing.
2. Compare export prices to domestic prices.
3. Explain why and how prices escalate in export selling.
4. Discuss how exchange rate fluctuations challenge the export marketer.
5. Explain how export price quotations are used in export marketing.
6. Discuss the importance of export credit and financing for successful export marketing.
7. Explore the special roles and problems of transfer pricing in international marketing.

Pricing is part of the marketing mix. Pricing decisions must therefore be integrated with other aspects of the marketing mix. And since price is just one attribute of a product, along with others such as quality, reliability, service, and user satisfaction, tradeoffs are necessary. A lower-priced product may be offered with lower quality or a less comprehensive warranty policy, for example.

The most useful way to deal with the complexities of pricing internationally is to consider the kinds of pricing situations and decisions the firm faces in international marketing. Based on an analysis of company practice, we will use the following classification of international pricing problems: (1) export pricing and terms, (2) transfer pricing in international marketing, (3) foreign market pricing, and (4) coordination of prices in world markets. But first let us consider the primary decision areas in the overall picture of international pricing.

## Factors in International Pricing

Factors important in international pricing are

- Setting pricing and strategic objectives.
- Monitoring price-setting behavior by competitors and assessing their strategic objectives.
- Evaluating consumers' ability to buy in the various country markets.
- Relating price to a firm's costs and profit goals.
- Understanding the product-specific factors, including product life cycle stage, that affect pricing. Generally, prices are reduced on mature products as they become more commodity-like and face increased competition.
- Recognizing differences in the country environment governing prices in each national market — differences in the legal and regulatory environment, the volatility of foreign exchange rates, market structure (especially distribution channels), and competitive environment.

All of these differences will influence the firm's price-setting behavior in each market.[1] Figure 14–1 sets out the framework.

**Price, Competition, and Strategic Objectives**

Pricing will affect realized demand and hence is an influential tool in gaining market share. Or thinking in reverse, competitive objectives toward gaining market share will determine pricing. As market share and competitive positions differ from country to country, therefore, prices will, too.

Note that competitive objectives do not always demand a lowered price. In an oligopolistic environment with few competitors, a company may attempt to head off ruinous price-cutting by signaling its intent to keep prices steady or even raise prices. For example, an airline might file a fare increase for the following week in a computer reservation system to see if its competitors raise prices, too. Such signaling is part of the role played by prices in affecting competitive position.

**Consumer's Ability to Buy**

Incomes, cultural habits, and consumer preferences differ from country to country. Thus, for the same price in two different country markets, different amounts may be demanded.

Furthermore, extending pricing strategies from more information-saturated markets to markets where a consumerist movement is just starting might not be appropriate. Shoppers in country markets that lack cut-priced distribution channels, for example, may not have formed the habit of waiting for sales when making large purchases. Consumers may not have developed a habit of obtaining information about competing brands.

**Figure 14-1**                          **Framework for International Pricing Strategy**

**Firm-Level Factors**
Strategic Objectives
   Market Share, Profits
Marketing Mix Elements
   Product Positioning, Consumer Segments
Cost Structure
   Fixed Costs
      Product Development, Manufacturing, Marketing
   Manufacturing Costs
      Experience Curve, Scale Economies, Lowest-Cost Objective
   Marketing and Other Costs
      Inventory Levels

**Product Specific Factors**
Life-Cycle Stage
Substitutes
Other Product Attributes
   Quality, Service, Delivery
Shipping/Distance Costs
Place in Product Line
Financing
   Term of Financing, Below-Market Interest Rate

**Market-Specific Factors**
Consumers
   Ability to Buy, Information-Seeking
Government Intervention
   As Buyer, Countertrade Demands, Price Controls,
   Transfer Price Controls, Customs: Floor Price Setting
Market Specific Costs
   Product Adaptation, Marketing/Service Costs,
   Distribution Channels
      Choices/Multiple Outlets, Discounting Pressures
Barriers to Trade
   Quotas and Tariffs, Protection/Subsidies, Non-Tariff Barriers

**Environmental Factors**
Competition
   Competitive Goals, Price Signaling
Exchange Rate Effects
   Short-Term Effects, Hedging Costs, Currency of Quote,
   Long-Term Currency Trends
Product Flow between Markets
   Gray Market Appeal
Macroeconomic Factors
   Business Cycle Stage, Level of Inflation, Role of Leasing

**Export Price Setting**
Product Prices in Relation to Product Line
Responding to Gray Markets
Product Redesign and Price Implications
Outsourcing
Shift to Low-Cost Manufacturing Sites
Transfer Price Setting and Administration
Inflation Adjustments
Pricing for Multinational Clients
Client-Specific Pricing and Discounting
Price-Bundling
Initiating Countertrade Leasing

| **Price in Relation to a Firm's Costs and Profit Goals** | In the long run, prices must be set to cover full costs. But in the short run, prices may be set below that level in order to gain market share, and to accommodate economic recessionary cycles in particular markets. Also, the company may decide to accept losses from low prices in certain markets because these losses can be offset with profits from other markets. |

In a similar vein, a company may deliberately price below costs in anticipation of reducing costs through increases in manufacturing volume. It thus gambles on gaining learning- and experience-curve efficiencies[2] to produce long-run profits. The Japanese have used this method to penetrate a number of industries, such as motorcycles.[3]

Shipping and transportation are further elements of costs specific to international pricing. Such additional "distance" costs are a deterrent to gaining market share in overseas markets and a difficult problem to overcome.

| **Price and the Product Line** | Products within a product line with less competition may be priced higher to subsidize other parts of the product line. Similarly, some items in the product line may be priced very low to serve as loss-leaders and induce customers to try the product, particularly if the company and its products are recent entrants into that country market. Another variant of such strategies is *price-bundling,* where a certain price is set for customers who simultaneously buy several items within the product line (i.e., a season ticket price, or a personal computer package with software and printer). In all such cases, a key consideration is how desirous consumers in diverse country markets are to save money, to spend time searching for the "best buy," and so forth. |

## Export Pricing and Terms

In this discussion, we will assume that the firm is committing itself to exporting on a continuing basis and thus is aiming for long-run profits and market position. We will not concern ourselves with the less common short-run viewpoint, such as when a firm sees export markets as dumping places for temporary surpluses or as a chance to make a one-time killing.

The firm committed to continuing export marketing will encounter a number of questions not faced in domestic pricing concerning the relation between export prices and domestic prices, tariffs, transport costs, export packaging, insurance, and foreign taxes.

| **Export Prices in Relation to Domestic Prices** | Should export prices be greater than, equal to, or less than domestic prices? If costs associated with export sales are greater than those associated with domestic sales, perhaps prices should be higher also. For example, exports may require special packaging and handling. Extra costs may arise in translating and processing export orders. Credit and collection costs may be greater. If the company has an export department, its operating costs may be higher as a percentage of sales. |

As an example of one kind of cost, the National Committee on Trade Documentation estimates that 64 man-hours are needed to generate and process the documents for a single export shipment. These costs may be as much as 10 percent of the total value of goods shipped.

Careful accounting is needed, however, before concluding that costs are higher for exports. Some costs allocated to domestic sales do *not* apply to export sales, such as domestic promotion or marketing research. For example, Scientific Instruments charged foreign distributors 20 percent less than domestic customers because they bought in larger quantities, assumed warranty responsibility, and were not provided advertising and trade-show support. Exports should bear only those costs for which they are directly responsible plus, perhaps, a share of general overhead.

Even if export sales have higher costs, it does not follow necessarily that the export price should be higher than the domestic price. The best export price is the one that maximizes profits. If foreign markets have lower income levels or more elastic demand curves, the most profitable export price may be lower than the domestic price. The firm may even find it necessary to modify the package or simplify the product to get the lower price needed for foreign markets.

**Export Price Less Than Domestic.**    Setting the f.o.b. plant price lower on exports than on domestic products favors export sales. Some good reasons for such an approach are the following:

1.  The lower income levels in some foreign markets may require the firm to set a lower price to achieve sales.
2.  Foreign competition may dictate a lower price.
3.  The firm realizes that even with a lower f.o.b. plant price, the product still can be more expensive in the foreign market because of the transport and tariff costs and other add-ons. All these add-ons could price the product out of the market if the f.o.b. plant price were high.
4.  The firm may consider that costs of exports are actually less because research and development, overhead, and some other costs are already covered by domestic sales.

But the firm that sells abroad at less than domestic prices may be accused of *dumping,* which is the technical term for selling goods in foreign markets at prices lower than those in the producer's home market. Recipient nations may complain of such seemingly favored treatment because their producers claim that such low-price competition is unfair to them. To avoid this type of producer resentment, countries tend to penalize imports sold at dumping prices.

At a given point in time, marginal cost pricing may be the profit-maximizing strategy for the firm. A Conference Board survey showed that over half of the 80 companies used marginal cost pricing on exports, at least occasionally. Marginal cost pricing for exports may be appropriate when there is excess capacity; but if new investment is needed, company profit goals will probably indicate full cost pricing for exports. The excess capacity justification for lower export prices will no longer exist.

Another problem with export prices that are lower than domestic prices is that the producing division has less interest in export sales. In fact, it will have a bias against them as long as prices are higher domestically. Only when no domestic alternative presents itself do export sales become interesting.

One of America's largest electrical equipment manufacturers noted that its producing divisions used incremental pricing (marginal cost pricing) when domestic demand was down. The export department thus found itself in a stronger market position when domestic sales were weak. Unfortunately, its position would reverse itself when domestic sales were strong. Even in this large company, export sales had only a residual, second-class position. As this pricing practice was based on *domestic* supply and demand conditions, it is not surprising that the firm was having trouble maintaining a consistent position in *foreign* markets.

## Market-Oriented Export Pricing

A good starting point for export price analysis is the determination of conditions in foreign markets: What are the demand and competitive situations in the target markets? Within what price range could the firm's product sell? By determining the demand situation in foreign markets, the export manager can get a base price for evaluating export opportunities. Having figured out what the market will pay, the firm must see if it can sell at that price, a determination it makes by working back from the market price (base price) to the cost structure of the firm. The various intermediary margins, taxes, duties, and transport and handling costs must be subtracted from the consumer price. The resulting figure will help determine the firm's f.o.b. plant price for exports.

## Price Escalation in Exporting

Because of the additional costs and steps involved in exporting, the final price to a consumer in the importing country often increases significantly. There are incremental transportation and insurance costs, and more intermediaries such as freight forwarders involved in the channels of distribution. There are charges for export documentation, specialized packaging, and import duties. Table 14–1 illustrates this phenomenon.

The implication from Table 14–1 is that an exported product will typically be sold for a higher price than the same product sold domestically. The higher price in turn raises two questions: (1) Can foreign consumers afford to buy the product at the higher price? Will demand be lowered because of it? (2) Will the higher price make imports less competitive against domestically produced products? The incremental distance costs associated with exporting allow domestic costs to be higher while the product remains competitively priced.

In reality, shipping costs and tariffs totaling $2.04 in the table represent the true higher cost of the imported product. A manufacturer in the importing country can have higher production costs of up to $2.04 and still match the import price.

**Table 14-1**                              **Export Price Escalation**

|  | Export Price | Domestic Price |
|---|---|---|
| Manufacturer's f.o.b. price: | $ 9.60 | $ 9.60 |
| Ocean freight and insurance: | 1.08 | — |
| Landed or c.i.f. value: | 10.68 | — |
| Tariff: 9% on c.i.f. value: | .96 | — |
| C.i.f. value plus tariff: | 11.64 | — |
| 12% value-added tax (VAT): | 1.40 | — |
| Distributor cost: | 13.04 | 9.60 |
| Distributor markup @ 15%: | 1.96 | 1.44 |
| Retailer cost: | 15.00 | 11.04 |
| 40% retail margin: | 10.00 | 7.36 |
| Consumer price: | 25.00 | 18.40 |

If, in fact, the manufacturer's costs in the importing country are only $1 higher, then it can offer a price cut of about $2.20.[4] In that case, the exporter must consider several alternatives:

1.  It can forget about exporting, which may be a wise decision *if* it has plentiful opportunity for profitable growth in the domestic market.
2.  It can consider marginal cost pricing for exports if it has excess capacity that is expected to continue. This would allow exports to increase profits for as long as no more attractive domestic opportunities arose.
3.  It can try to shorten the distribution channel, for example, by selling direct to wholesalers or large retailers. Each step in the channel costs the firm something extra. Whether elimination of certain steps lowers costs for the exporting firm depends on how well it can perform the functions eliminated.
4.  It can modify the product to make it cheaper. A stripped-down model and smaller sizes or packaging are ways to achieve this. The company may also try to change the product for a lower duty classification.
5.  It can consider foreign manufacturing or assembly or licensing as ways to tap foreign markets, avoiding many of the steps that inflate export prices. Although foreign manufacturing involves greater commitment, it could be the most profitable method if markets are large enough.

**Impact of Exchange Rate Fluctuations**

As Table 14–2 shows, currencies have changed value against one another over the year November 1988 to November 1989. The U.S. dollar has recovered from a long period of weakness, gaining against every one of the six other currencies in the table. It gained the most against the Japanese yen, meaning that, on average, an export item priced in dollars had a price increase of 19.3 percent when sold to Japan, as against competing exports from other countries to Japan. This assumes that the dollar price has not changed. In the same fashion, if Japanese exporters had not changed their yen prices, this would have led to price cuts of 19.3 percent for U.S. customers, and about 16 percent for customers in France, West Germany, and

**Table 14–2**                     **Potential Effects of Currency Movements on Sales Prices: Percentage Changes on a Trade-Weighted Exchange Rate Basis, November 1988 to November 1989**

|                | France | Germany | Italy | Japan | Switzerland | United Kingdom | United States |
|----------------|--------|---------|-------|-------|-------------|----------------|---------------|
| France         | —      |         |       |       |             |                |               |
| Germany        | +0     | —       |       |       |             |                |               |
| Italy          | +.6    | +.6     | —     |       |             |                |               |
| Japan          | −16.0  | −16.0   | −16.4 | —     |             |                |               |
| Switzerland    | −5.8   | −5.7    | −6.4  | +8.6  | —           |                |               |
| United Kingdom | −12.3  | −12.3   | −13.1 | +3    | −6.2        | —              |               |
| United States  | +6.7   | +6.7    | +6    | +19.3 | +11.7       | +17.0          | —             |

Source: Derived from trade-weighted exchange rates published in *The Economist,* November 25, 1989, 120.

Italy, while price cuts to the United Kingdom would have been only around 3 percent. In other words, a world of volatile and fluctuating exchange rates results in unexpected price increases and declines, even though the producer has not changed its list price in the domestic currency.

The data from Table 14–2 present an interesting decision for exporters. The average U.S. exporter faces a 19 percent price rise for its goods when sold to Japan. It may lose some sales because of this price increase, and it might want to consider lowering its dollar prices so that the price increase in yen is not equal to the total 19 percent appreciation of the dollar. Conversely, the Japanese exporter to the United States has the option of passing on the full 19 percent reduction in the value of the yen, or allowing yen prices to rise somewhat, retaining some of the windfall gains from the appreciation of the dollar.

## Export Price Quotations

Finding the right foreign market prices is one task of export marketing. In addition to proper pricing, however, the exporting firm must be market-oriented in its price quotations and conditions of sale. The base foreign-market price calculated above was a consumer price. Here we consider the price and terms to the importer-buyer, who is usually the final buyer insofar as the exporter is concerned.

**Currency of Quotation.**   A first question concerns the currency used for the price quotation. The U.S. firm quotes in U.S. dollars domestically and would like to do the same on exports. Quoting dollar prices is easier than figuring the price in a number of foreign currencies, especially if these change in value. The arithmetic is the least important aspect, however. Two other aspects have more influence on the choice of currency for quotation. First, importers would prefer all quotations in their own currency for easier comparison of the offers of various foreign and national suppliers. Second, both exporters and importers worry about the foreign exchange risk. If the importers' currency is susceptible to devaluation or depreciation, they would prefer the price quote in their own currency so that on the due date of their invoice they will not have to pay a larger number of francs or cruzados for a given dollar amount. Similar reasoning lies behind U.S. exporters' preference for a dollar quote: Exporters do not want to receive fewer dollars when payment is finally made.

Assume, for example, a U.S. Exporter has a shipment for France worth $10,000, or 70,000 French francs, with payment due in 90 days in francs. If the French franc depreciates by 15 percent during that period, the importer will still pay 70,000 francs, but this now translates into only $8,500. In this case, the exporter has a big loss. Conversely, if the quote had been in dollars, the importer would still pay only $10,000, but this would now cost him 80,500 francs instead of 70,000. The importer would be the loser. Although each party could hedge its position in the forward exchange market, hedging has a cost.

How is the conflict resolved? The choice of currency for the price quotation depends partly on trade practice in the country and industry in question, but also partly on the bargaining position of the parties. In a buyer's market, the exporter will be anxious for sales and will tend to yield to the importer's desires. In a seller's market, the situation will be reversed. Thus, in 1984, when GM was losing exports because of the rising dollar, it continued to quote in dollars but began to guarantee the exchange rate for a period of time to protect the importer.

Since 1973, most major currencies have been floating, so exchange rate changes are a daily occurrence. Export pricing has consequently received much more management attention. Some specific company adaptations to pricing with floating exchange rates include the following:

1. Decision making becomes more centralized; headquarters exercises more control.
2. Sources of supply and prices to customers are more tightly controlled.
3. Credit terms are cut back.
4. There is more hedging and there are more renegotiation clauses in long-term contracts.
5. Price lists are reviewed more frequently.
6. More sales are on a "spot price" basis — the firm uses the exchange rate on the day of order.

An innovative response to the problem of fluctuating currencies has been tried by the French multinational Saint-Gobain. The company wanted to reduce the foreign exchange risks and the accounting complexities created by doing business in many currencies, so it decided to use the European Currency Unit (ECU) for cross-border billing purposes. The ECU is a weighted average of the European currencies, and fluctuates less than the relationship between any two currencies in the basket. Transactions are settled in the currency of the importer at its rate against the ECU.

SG finds two major advantages in ECU billing. One is the reduction of exchange losses. (Of course, it also reduces exchange gains.) Second, the system is considered more equitable because exchange gains and losses are now shared between the exporter and importer. Before, one party, the ex-

**Table 14-3**                              **Export Price Quotations**

    I.  ex (point of origin)
        ex factory, ex mine, ex warehouse, and so on
   II.  f.o.b. (free on board)
        1.  f.o.b. (named inland carrier)
        2.  f.o.b. freight allowed to (named point of exportation)
        3.  f.o.b. vessel (named port of shipment)
        4.  f.o.b. (named inland point in country of importation)
  III.  f.a.s. (free alongside)
        f.a.s. vessel (named port of shipment)
  IV.  c & f (cost and freight)
        c & f (named point of destination)
   V.  c.i.f. (cost, insurance, freight)
        c.i.f. (named point of destination)

Note: These quotations are defined in detail in the "Revised American Foreign Trade Definitions, 1941."

porter or the importer, bore all the risk. Though SG pioneered ECU billing, others have followed it in this practice.

This example is important to note because currency baskets such as the ECU or the SDR (Special Drawing Right) are a useful answer to some of the problems posed by floating exchange rates. Their usage is likely to increase. Already some banks in Europe accept deposits denominated in ECUs or SDRs and will also make loans in those denominations. Such usage of the ECU could be the first step toward a truly European currency.

**Export Price Quotations Defined.**   Export price quotations are more complex than those used in domestic selling. It is important for exporters to assure agreement on the exact meaning of the terms being used so that they and their importers both know their respective duties and liabilities. See Table 14–3 for a listing of terms.

Price quotations are important because they spell out the legal responsibilities of each party. Sellers favor a quote that gives them the least liability and responsibility, such as f.o.b. (free on board) their plant. In this case, the exporters' responsibility and liability both end when the goods are put on a carrier at their plant. Importer-buyers, on the other hand, favor a c.i.f. (cost, insurance, and freight to port of discharge) price, which means their responsibilities begin only when the goods are in their own country. Importers favor c.i.f. pricing also because it makes it easier to compare the prices of different exporting nations and those of national suppliers.

Generally, a market orientation would indicate c.i.f. (port of importation) pricing by the exporter. Note that the price quotation does *not* affect the total amount paid or received but merely indicates the division of labor in providing for various transportation, handling, and insurance arrangements. It may be that the total burden of these arrangements is lessened when exporters and importers do what they are most qualified to do. Exporters would deal with their fellow nationals in arranging transportation

**Figure 14-2**                    **Price Increases in Relation to Rising Exchange Rate and Unit Labor Costs**

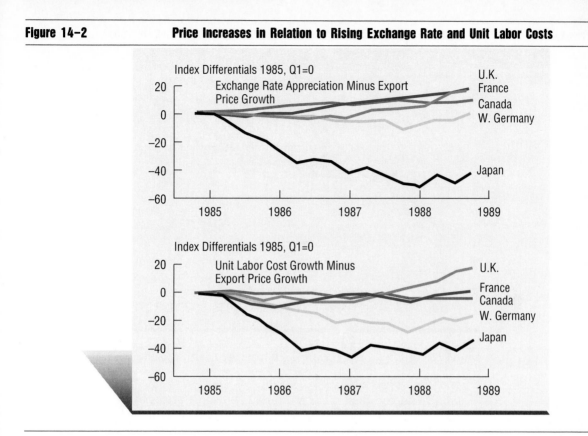

Source: Steven Strongin and Jack L. Hervey, "The Dollar Can Only Do So Much," *Chicago Fed Letter*, October 1989.

to the port, insurance, and overseas shipping, whereas importers would deal with their compatriots in the unloading and transportation in their country. Occasionally, the importer is a large international organization — one of the Japanese trading companies, for example — that is better qualified to handle insurance and transportation than the exporter. That importer can gain economies of scale by taking these tasks out of the exporters' hands.

**Raising Prices Because of Exchange Rate Changes**

Figure 14–2 shows how some of the major importing nations have dealt with appreciation of their currencies. The graph in the top portion of the figure shows the extent to which price increases have been less than or greater than exchange rate appreciation. While countries such as the United Kingdom, France, and Canada have increased their prices by more than the rate of exchange rate appreciation, Japan has passed on only about half of the appreciation of the yen in the form of a price rise. Japanese exporters have been willing to keep market share by absorbing some of the impact of yen appreciation.

The bottom graph in the figure relates price increases to increases in a country's unit labor cost, which is an important element of total costs. On

**Figure 14-3**                **Auto Prices for United States and Foreign Competitors, 1980–1987**

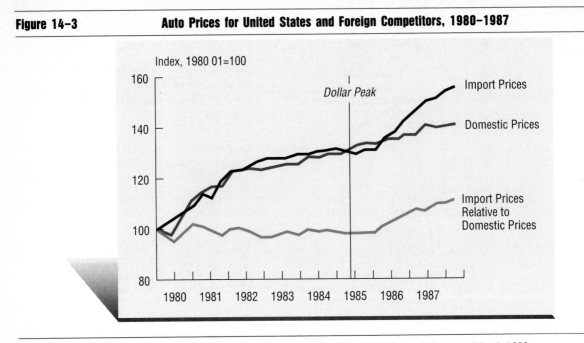

Source: Jack L. Hervey, "Dollar Drop Helps Those Who Help Themselves," *Chicago Fed Letter*, March 1988.

this basis, too, Japan has not raised its export prices by the full amount of cost increases, but only by about 60 percent, absorbing about 40 percent.

If in fact prices of imports are being raised because of exchange rate appreciation, this presents a golden opportunity for U.S. companies to regain market share by keeping their prices constant and thus gaining a price advantage. Figure 14–3 shows how U.S. car prices have evolved in relation to prices of their foreign competitors. The prices of imported autos went up over the 1980–1985 period even though the dollar was gaining strength. The voluntary quotas on Japanese autos led Japanese car manufacturers to ship more expensive models, creating the price rise. In response, U.S. auto manufacturers had two choices: keep prices steady and attempt to win back market share, or raise prices in lock-step with the Japanese. As Figure 14–3 shows, U.S. auto price increases kept step with import prices through 1985, when the dollar reached its peak. After that, import prices rose faster than domestic car prices, as the foreign currencies appreciated against the dollar, giving U.S. cars a relative price advantage. Combining the insights from Figures 14–2 and 14–3, we can surmise that Japanese price strategy is to match domestic price trends when the dollar is strengthening, but absorb some of yen price appreciation when the dollar is weak. In sum, the Japanese prefer to hold onto market share rather than try to recover the full impact of any exchange rate appreciation from their foreign customers.

**Strategies for Coping with Foreign Exchange Risk**

Subaru of America (the U.S. distributor of Subaru cars) is an example of a company that was seriously affected by exchange rate changes. It was one of the most profitable companies in the United States for over a decade. Then the yen appreciated almost 50 percent against the dollar from the end of 1985 through 1987, and the dollar price of Subaru cars had to go up because of yen appreciation. Suddenly, Subaru sales dropped by over 20 percent, and it began registering large losses.

As Subaru's example shows, even highly profitable companies can be devastated by exchange rate changes. Three areas of risk are involved: transaction risk, competitive risk, and market-portfolio risk.[5]

**Transaction Risk.**   When a firm makes a transaction denominated in a foreign currency it exposes itself to *transaction risk,* meaning that changes in the value of the foreign currency may diminish the financial results of the firm. For example, if a firm purchases supplies from West Germany totaling 100,000 deutsche marks (DM), and the exchange rate is 2 DM = $1, the dollar value of the purchase is $50,000. Further, if the period of credit granted is 90 days, and the DM appreciates so that the rate at the end of 90 days is 1.80 DM = $1, the debt is now equal to $55,556. The importer is thus required to pay more dollars, raising its costs and reducing profits. The exporter has gained by holding an asset denominated in DMs at a time when the DM has been appreciating against the dollar. Such transaction risk can be guarded against by hedging, through the use of forward markets and the purchase of futures and options contracts.

**Competitive Risk.**   The geographic pattern of a company's manufacturing and sales configuration, when compared to that of its key competitors, can cause *competitive risk* to arise. Thus, if Firm A manufactures in a country with depreciating exchange rates and sells to a country with appreciating exchange rates, it stands to gain considerable market share without raising prices. Now suppose Firm B does exactly the opposite, manufacturing in a country with appreciating exchange rates and selling to a country whose exchange rate is depreciating. In this situation, Firm A could gain market share at the expense of Firm B without having to change its prices in its own domestic currency.

Subaru's problem in 1987 stemmed from the fact that it sourced its cars from Japan and sold into the United States at a time when the dollar was weakening significantly against the yen. Thus, Subaru was influenced by the performance of two currencies, the yen and the dollar. All Japanese manufacturers importing cars from Japan for the United States had a greater competitive risk than the European car makers such as Volvo of Sweden (the kroner did not appreciate as much as the yen against the dollar).

**Market-Portfolio Risk.**   The third kind of risk, *market-portfolio risk,* arises from a firm's export markets as compared to the country-market portfolio of its global competitors. A more diversified company, one that sold to several country markets, would not be as influenced by changes in the yen/

dollar rate. Subaru of America manufactured in Japan and sold 75 percent of the cars it received into the United States, with the remainder going to Canada and Europe. In contrast, BMW manufactured in West Germany and derived only 36 percent of its sales from the United States. Since BMW manufactures in West Germany, whereas Subaru manufactures in Japan, to the extent that the mark appreciates less than the yen, BMW would be less affected by the devaluation of the dollar. This is the difference in the two companies' competitive risk.

But, in addition, Subaru concentrates most of its export output on the U.S. market. So by putting all its eggs in one basket, it is more vulnerable to changes in the value of the yen versus the dollar. In contrast, BMW exports its output to other countries beyond the United States, including Japan. Thus, its market-portfolio risk is different from Subaru's, since its foreign revenues are not affected only by the dollar's performance. BMW has a more diversified portfolio of markets, and hence faces less risk. One solution for Subaru is to similarly diversify markets, either by selling to many more countries and/or by manufacturing in major markets. Subaru's decision to begin producing its new Legacy model in a U.S. plant is an example of such a solution.

But Subaru would not be likely to lose market share if all other car manufacturers were similarly affected. Subaru's problem is that it competes against *U.S.–made subcompacts* manufactured by U.S. car companies and by Japanese firms such as Mazda. In addition, imports of subcompact cars are also increasing from countries such as Brazil, Mexico, and South Korea. These countries do not have the exchange rate disadvantage of Japanese manufacturing. In response, all of the major Japanese car companies have begun manufacturing cars in the United States. This changes both their competitive and their market-portfolio risk, with all of the manufacturers seeing a reduction in their exposure to yen appreciation; this also changes their competitive risk compared to their European competitors who do not have such U.S. manufacturing facilities.

## Export Credit and Terms

Export credit and terms constitute another complex area in pricing for the international market. What the marketer needs to know is how export credit and terms can help achieve maximum profits in exports.

The task is to choose payment terms that satisfy importers yet safeguard the interests of the exporter. On purely financial considerations, the exporter would favor very hard terms, that is, cash in advance of shipment — or even in advance of production for custom items. Because importers dislike bearing the financial burden implied in cash-in-advance terms, the exporter normally can demand prepayment only when producing merchandise to an importer's specifications.

In lieu of cash in advance, the export marketer can consider a range of terms that generally add to the convenience of the buyer while increasing the risks and financial burdens of the exporter. The common payment methods in order of increasing attractiveness to the *importer* are

1. Cash in advance.
2. Letters of credit.
3. Time or sight drafts (bills of exchange).
4. Open account.
5. Consignment.

**Letters of Credit and Drafts.**   Letters of credit and drafts are the most common forms of export financing. A *draft* is drawn by the exporter on the importer, who makes it into a trade acceptance by writing on it the word "accepted" and signing it. The signature makes payment a legal obligation. The *letter of credit* is similar, except that it is drawn on a bank and becomes a bank acceptance rather than a trade acceptance. The bank's entrance into the payment process means greater assurance of payment for the exporter.

The terms of both are relatively strict and favor the exporter in that they spell out specific responsibilities and payment times for the importer, although they do not preclude credit extension. For example, time drafts are customarily drawn for periods ranging from 30 to 180 days after sight or after date. The exporter usually feels more secure with a letter of credit than with a draft. While it is safer for the exporter, it is more costly for the importer to get a letter of credit.

**Open Account.**   In *open account* sales, terms are agreed to between buyer and seller but without documents specifying clearly the importer's payment obligations. Open account terms involve less paperwork and give more flexibility to both parties. However, the legal recourse of the exporter in case of default is less satisfactory than under the methods discussed above. Open account sales are more attractive to the importer, but because of the risks to the exporter, they tend to be limited to foreign subsidiaries, joint ventures or licensees, or foreign customers with whom the exporter has had a long and favorable experience.

As a further precaution in open account sales, the exporter must consider the availability of foreign exchange in the importing country. In countries with tight foreign exchange positions, imports covered by documentary drafts generally receive priority in foreign exchange allocation over imports on open account.

**Consignment.**   Since the exporter retains title until the importer sells the goods, *consignment* sales are not really sales. Because exporters own the goods longer in this method than in any other, their financial burdens and risks are greatest. In addition, legal recourse in case of misbehavior by importers and foreign exchange allocations are more difficult to obtain. Because of these problems, exporters tend to limit consignment arrangements to their subsidiaries abroad.

When exporters want to introduce goods to a new market, a consignment arrangement might be necessary to encourage importers to handle the new merchandise. Furthermore, if exporters wish to retain some control over the foreign market price, this is most feasible under a consignment contract.

They can set the price when they own the goods, as they do under a consignment contract.

## The Financing of International Sales:
## A Component of International Pricing

The terms of financing determine the final effective price paid by a buyer. If the cost of capital is 12 percent per year, and a buyer is allowed to pay its bill in 90 days, this 90 days free credit amounts to a 3 percent discount on the purchase price. When products from international competitors are perceived as being reasonably similar, the purchaser may choose the supplier that provides the best financing terms resulting in the greatest effective discount. Thus, when Embraer, a Brazilian manufacturer of small aircraft, wanted to introduce its 19-seat commuter plane to the United States, it offered long-term (six years or more) financing at around 8 percent. Because it was a state-owned enterprise, it could guarantee the availability of such credit. Fairchild Aircraft, a U.S. competitor, filed an "unfair trade practices" complaint with the U.S. International Trade Commission because of this low-interest-rate financing, offered at a time when U.S. interest rates were around 12 percent.[6]

Without government help, U.S. firms might find it impossible to offer the necessary financing. Ellicott Machine Corporation of Baltimore could not have sold its dredges to Yugoslavia without such help. It had bid on a project to supply a dredge to mine coal near the Danube river, but the customer needed financing. Ellicott was able to get a State of Maryland guarantee from the Maryland Industrial Development Financing Authority and was thus able to offer 100 percent financing. Further, with the help of the Maryland Office of International Trade, it was able to get a Maryland State grant to offer training to customer personnel. This led to scholarships at the University of Maryland to train Yugoslav engineers in disciplines relevant to the project. Such government help led to an initial contract awarded Ellicott of $25 million, with add-ons possible that could total nearly $100 million.[7]

To successfully use financing as a competitive weapon in international marketing, two conditions are typically necessary. The firm must have the ability to fund the long-term receivables at below-market interest rates. This condition usually favors state-owned enterprises and larger multinationals, who can borrow at lower rates and in countries where borrowing costs are low. Second, official government backing to subsidize the lower interest rates offered, as well as guarantee the loans, is necessary to match the best offers made by international competitors. Without government guarantees, private (U.S.) banks will not make the loan, and without a government subsidy, below-market rates cannot be offered. Several nations have an established policy of offering such favorable financing as part of packages designed to promote exports from their countries.

A related problem for U.S. firms is the relative lack of interest on the part of commercial banks in trade finance. Banks can make as much money on residential mortgages as they can on government-guaranteed export loans. It is also a labor-intensive business, requiring manager expertise. As a result, several large money-center banks have deliberately reduced their trade-finance activities. Firms must therefore turn to the branches of foreign banks who may be interested primarily in financing exports to countries near their home base or certain geographic areas deemed to be in their strategic interest.[8] A stunted U.S. institutional structure for trade finance is a further obstacle that U.S. firms face in the global competition for markets. And subsidized financing from other nations rubs salt in the wound.

Twenty-two industrialized countries met in the early 1980s to limit such credit subsidies, and the result was an agreement that specified minimum interest rates and maximum repayment periods for most categories of exports sold on credit terms of over two years.[9] However, a loophole is the use of *tied aid,* where foreign aid is granted with the condition that a portion of the aid be used to buy goods from the aid-granting country. Thus, an exporter seeking a sale of $1 million might be able to allow the importer to use $100,000 of aid granted by the exporter's government to pay for part of the sale. This way, the exporter is offering a price cut of $100,000, or 10 percent, which is equivalent in effect to a direct interest-rate or price subsidy. A 1989 Eximbank (Export-Import Bank of the United States) study estimated that $400 million to $800 million in potential U.S. exports were being lost because of tied aid in industries such as telecommunications, electric power systems, computers and heavy earth-moving vehicles. Countries such as Canada, France, West Germany, Italy, Britain, and Japan account for about 75 percent of all such credits.

While decrying such practices, the United States has also, in self-defense, begun providing some tied aid on a limited scale. In 1986 Eximbank offered the government of Gabon an $8.4 million loan at 2 percent interest with an 8.5-year grace period and repayment over 20 years — when coupled with a U.S. export transaction backed by an Eximbank-guaranteed commercial loan for $12.8 million at market rates.[10] Yet, the United States accounted for only about 2 percent of the world volume of tied aid. Eximbank is the main U.S. financing agency for international trade. In 1987 it supported $9.2 billion of U.S. exports through $600 million in loans, with the rest in loan guarantees and insurance.

**FCIA**

In the 1960s, the U.S. government began to address the lack of strength of U.S. companies in world markets. Eximbank asked the private insurance industry to join with it in forming a syndicate that would allow American companies to compete more vigorously overseas and thus increase U.S. exports. The result, in 1962, was the formation of the Foreign Credit Insurance Association (FCIA) to market, underwrite, and service insurance policies that protect against the inability of the foreign debtor to pay its obligations due to designated commercial and political risks.

FCIA is an association of leading property, casualty, and marine insurance companies operating under a reinsurance agreement with Eximbank that specifies Eximbank's full reinsurance of all FCIA risk.

FCIA's various programs offer two basic types of credit insurance: *Short-term coverage* is up to 180 days and can be comprehensive or political. Comprehensive coverage covers both political and commercial risks including currency inconvertibility, cancellation of import license, expropriation, loss due to war, and the commercial risks of insolvency and protracted default. *Medium-term insurance* covers sales of capital goods on terms from 181 days to five or more years. It also includes a choice of comprehensive or political-only coverage.

With the growth in world trade and the increasing demands for export credit insurance protection, FCIA policies have adjusted to the needs of American companies. Among the most important features of its many programs are discretionary credit limits, deductible provisions, coverage for international services, liberal inventory and receivables financing coverage for franchised dealers abroad, preshipment coverage, and special coverage for consignment sales.

## Transfer Pricing in International Marketing

The management of export prices and terms is the first, and often the only, international pricing task facing firms. Once the firm expands beyond exporting, however, it encounters other international pricing problems. When a company begins to establish foreign subsidiaries, joint ventures, or licensing agreements, its international pricing becomes more complex. *Transfer pricing* (intracorporate pricing) is one area that has special implications for international marketing. It refers to prices on goods sold within the corporate family, that is, from division to division or to a foreign subsidiary.

**Product Division to International Division**

The transfer price paid by the international group to the producing division should have certain characteristics if it is to optimize corporate, rather than divisional, profit. For the producing division, the price should be high enough to encourage a flow of products for export. The transfer price will do this if sales to the international division are as attractive as sales to other parties. The price to the international division may be even lower than to other parties if the services the international division renders (market research, promotion, and so on) warrant this.

For the international division, the transfer price should be low enough to enable it to be both competitive and profitable in the foreign market. Obviously, there is room for conflict here. The producing division wants a high price, and the international division wants a low price. The transfer-pricing mechanism must be such that the overall corporate interest is not ignored in the divisional conflict. Quite possibly a profit margin that is unattractive to one or the other division, or to both, might be worthwhile from the overall corporate viewpoint.

Assume that the producing division makes a product at a full cost of $50. It sells this to outside buyers for $60, but the transfer price to the international division is $58. The producing division may be unhappy because the markup is 20 percent lower to the international division ($8 versus

$10). The international division adds its various export marketing expenses of $10 for an export cost of $68. For competitive reasons, the international division cannot sell the product for more than $72, or a $4 return. Since this is less than 6 percent of sales, the international division is also unhappy. However, the return to the corporation is $12 on $72, or almost 17 percent ($8 from the producing division plus $4 from the international division). The corporation may find this attractive, even though both divisions are unhappy with it.

Different approaches can be taken to solve this problem. One solution is to eliminate one division or the other as a profit center. The producing division can be judged on the basis of costs and other performance criteria instead of profit. Then it can sell to the international division at a price enabling the latter to be competitive in foreign markets. Market pricing will not be handicapped by their internal markups of the transfer-pricing process, and the total corporate profit will be given greater attention.

On the other hand, the international division can operate as a service center rather than as a profit center, thus eliminating one source of conflict. Some question arises, however, as to whether a *selling* organization will be as efficient and as motivated when it is not operating under a profit constraint. A related possibility is to have the international division act as a commission agent for the producing divisions. Where the international division is not a profit center, its expenses can be allocated back to the product divisions.

**Transfer at Manufacturing Cost.**    Where profit centers are maintained, several alternatives are possible. At one extreme, and favoring the international division, is the transfer at direct manufacturing cost. This would be the lowest cost, probably well under what the producing division could obtain from other customers. The producing division dislikes selling at manufacturing cost because it feels it is subsidizing the international division and thereby losing out when compared with other profit centers. The firm may offset this by an accounting or memorandum profit to the producing division on its sales for export. Such memorandum profits, unfortunately, are never as satisfactory as the real thing. When the product division is unhappy, the international division may get sluggish service because the product division satisfies more attractive domestic opportunities first.

**Transfer at Arm's Length.**    The other extreme in transfer pricing is to charge the international division the same price any buyer outside the firm pays. This price favors the producing division because it does as well on internal as on external sales, or even better. The services rendered by the international division and the elimination of the credit problem can make export sales especially profitable.

If the product has no external buyers, however, a problem arises in trying to determine an arm's length price. An artificial price must be constructed. Further difficulties arise because such a price fails to take into account the services performed by the international division, and because the international division may be noncompetitive with such a price. Finally, there is no real reason that the price to foreign buyers should be determined by the domestic market.

**Transfer at Cost Plus.**    Between the transfer-pricing extremes just discussed is a range of prices that involve a profit split between the producing and international divisions. Starting from the cost floor, cost-plus pricing attempts to add on some amount or percentage that will make the resulting price acceptable to both divisions. The "plus" may be a percentage negotiated between the divisions, a percentage of product division overhead, or a percentage return on product-division investment. Further variation can be caused by using different definitions of cost. In any case, the pricing formula is less important than the results obtained. A good transfer-pricing formula should consider total corporate profit and encourage divisional cooperation. It should also minimize executive time spent on transfer-price disagreements and keep the accounting burden to a minimum.

## International Division to Foreign Subsidiary

When the international division sells goods to a foreign subsidiary of the company, the transfer-pricing problems are somewhat different. The same general criteria apply; that is, total corporate profit must be considered, interdivisional cooperation is necessary, and management must be able to control and evaluate the contributions of different divisions. Furthermore, the transfer-pricing alternatives are the same: cost, cost-plus, or arm's-length prices. When national boundaries are crossed, however, several new factors come into play, namely, the requirements of domestic and foreign tax authorities and foreign customs officials. The firm's level of involvement is another complication, because the company may want to charge a different price to each kind of buyer — wholly owned subsidiary, joint venture, licensee, and distributor. This is especially troublesome if the firm has more than one kind of involvement in a given market.

**Domestic Tax Authority's Interest.**    When countries have different levels of taxation on corporate profits, it is not a matter of indifference to the company where it accumulates its profit. The firm would like to get more profits in low-tax countries; that is, it would like to use a low transfer price to subsidiaries in low-tax countries and a high transfer price to subsidiaries in high-tax countries. (*High* or *low* is used here in reference to the tax level in the domestic country.)

U.S. companies, for example, are tempted to sell at low transfer prices to countries that have lower corporate tax rates than the United States. The U.S. Internal Revenue Service (IRS), however, is on guard against this because the IRS does not want to lose taxable income to other countries. Therefore, IRS carefully scrutinizes the transfer prices of international companies to assure that they are not too low. One specific demand of the IRS is that export prices bear a share of domestic research and development expenses. The IRS wants to be sure that an equitable portion of the income remains under U.S. tax jurisdiction.

The Eli Lilly Company was charged with seeking to avoid U.S. taxes through low transfer prices to its Western Hemisphere marketing subsidiary (which paid lower taxes). The IRS won the suit, and Eli Lilly had to pay several million dollars in back taxes and penalties, although the company claimed the lower prices were accounted for by the services the subsidiary performed for the parent company. This scrutiny is not unusual.

**Foreign Tax and Customs Authorities.**    Foreign *tax* authorities, like the IRS, wish to maximize taxable income in their jurisdiction. They watch for "unreasonably" high transfer prices. Motivations behind high transfer prices to a country could be several. One is a high tax rate on corporate profits. Another is restrictions on profit repatriation. Even if a country has a low corporate tax rate, it makes no sense to accumulate profits there if they cannot be remitted to the parent company. Fear of devaluation could be another reason for a high transfer price to a foreign subsidiary. Profits, even if remittable, are eaten away by a devaluation. The differing interests of home-country and host-country tax authorities caused one drug company executive to complain, "The Third World countries say our transfer prices are too high, while the IRS says they aren't high enough."

Customs authorities also have an interest in the transfer price. They are on guard against duty avoidance through low transfer prices. The firm wishing to aid a subsidiary by low transfer prices may be hindered by the customs authorities.

**Level of Involvement.**    We have been discussing international transfer pricing between a domestic division and a wholly owned foreign subsidiary. A new factor enters when the firm sells to other foreign companies with which it has some association. Other things being equal, a firm would want to sell at a higher price to a joint venture than to one it fully owned. It would desire an even higher price from licensees or distributors. A low price to joint ventures or licensees means, in effect, that some of the profit is being given away outside the firm rather than merely being transferred to another part of the company.

A major U.S. electronics/computer firm charges foreign distributors 10 percent more than its foreign subsidiaries. It justifies this difference because (1) subsidiaries pay for product training, while distributors get it free; (2) the company has a 50–50 cooperative advertising program with distributors, while subsidiaries pay their own; and (3) subsidiaries and distributors are not in the same countries.

**Managing International Transfer Pricing**

Many variables affect international transfer prices. Many different pricing formulas are possible. However, developing, administering, and defending all these pricing formulas can be a monumental task. Some simplification is probably desirable.

The need for simplification arises partly from efficiency considerations but partly from developments outside the firm. Foreign customs officials and foreign and domestic tax authorities limit the firm's flexibility in pricing

# Global Marketing

## Tuna Prices in Japan: Price and Value

As connoisseurs of fish, the Japanese are finicky about the quality of the raw fish used to make sashimi, a national favorite. Tuna is one of the major fish varieties commonly used in sashimi, and both yellowfin and bigeye tuna are found in quantity off the coast of Australia in the Coral Sea. Australian fishermen have been encouraged to export chilled fresh tuna to Japan for consumption raw as sashimi. Chilled tuna must be exported by air, but auction prices in Japan are attractive: about A$1 (Australian dollar) per kilogram (in 1987) in Japan, as against A$1 per kilogram in Australia. The economic incentive is clearly high. Yet, Australian exports of such tuna have been low, even while Japanese fishing boats have been active in these waters.

It seems that Australian fishermen were discouraged by the high variation in prices received at the Tokyo fish auctions, and this led them to believe that Japanese auction buyers colluded to keep Australian imported fish out of the market and hence favor the Japanese fishing fleet in the Coral Sea. Australian researchers, therefore, meticulously studied auction prices for 27 days in October 1985, attempting to relate prices (in yen per kilogram) to factors such as fish meat color, freshness, condition (degree of carcass damage, bruises, etc.), weight of the whole fish, and origin (whether the tuna was caught in the waters off Japan, Philippines, Taiwan, Australia). Since sashimi is eaten raw, consumers are willing to pay more for "good" meat color, such as the absence of a concentration of red meat pigments in the flesh of the tuna. They also want the freshest fish possible. (The degree of freshness can be measured by the presence of breakdown products such as adenosine triphosphate, which increase with length of time.)

Aside from the importance of freshness and color, the study also found that auction prices were lower for bigeye tuna caught in non-Japanese waters. However, research could not determine the reason. Bigeye tuna have high fat content, and one possibility was that the food organisms found in the particular feeding grounds off the waters of Taiwan or the Philippines may be absorbed into the fat, yielding flavors that are less acceptable to the discerning Japanese palate. The main conclusion of the study, however, was that Japanese consumers choose raw fish for their sashimi on the basis of its appearance. Hence, buyers at auctions are willing to pay more for tuna that has good color. The implication, then, is that Australian fishermen must select tuna of the requisite freshness and meat color for export to the chilled tuna auction in Tokyo, if they want to get high prices.

The researchers also found that while the Tokyo market accounted for nearly 60 percent of all chilled bigeye tuna sold in Japan, two other markets, Nagoya and Osaka, accounted for about 40 percent of all chilled yellowfin tuna, as compared to the Tokyo market's 16 percent. Thus, Australian fishermen were erroneously concentrating on the Tokyo market alone because of lack of information.

The market for tuna in Japan may be of little interest to most people. But the principle that emerges from the study is important: The price that people are willing to pay for a product depends on the value perceived. Careful market research can uncover what consumers in different countries look for in a product. The price set for a particular country market must be appropriate to the value delivered in that market if the company wishes to avoid over- or underpricing the product.

Source: Stephen C. Williams and John W. Longworth, "Factors Influencing Tuna Prices in Japan and Implications for the Development of the Coral Sea Tuna Fishery," *European Journal of Marketing* 23, no. 3 (1989).

between national markets and between levels of involvement. The IRS, for example, can compare a U.S. firm's export prices to all markets and types of buyers. It can demand justification for those differences it considers unwarranted.

An export price based on cost-plus usually can be worked out that satisfies both domestic and foreign tax authorities as well as foreign customs authorities. The more uniform the cost-plus formula is, the better it can be defended. IBM claims to apply a uniform cost-plus method: "This is a simple, above-board billing practice accepted by host country authorities and questioned only in a few developing countries."

Where an arm's-length price can be determined, it has the advantages of simplicity, uniformity, and the maximization of profit in the domestic operations. Unfortunately, it might not achieve the firm's goals abroad. The result is that the firm will probably need a variety of international transfer-pricing formulas that meet internal goals while satisfying the external constraints. A limit on the number of formulas used will be set by the costs of developing, administering, and defending them. Hans Schaffner, Chairman of Sandoz, the Swiss drug company, claims that firms cannot get away with varying transfer prices. They "are under continuous scrutiny by many different government authorities which would react immediately and forcefully to the first evidence of a 'zigzag' policy." And Caterpillar felt strongly enough about this to state in its Worldwide Code of Business Conduct that all international transfer prices are to be arm's-length prices.

Transfer pricing is an area where profit objectives, managerial motivation, and government regulation intersect. The expertise of many different people is needed: the accountant, legal counsel, tax adviser and division managers. The international marketing manager's contribution will be primarily concerned with two aspects of the problem: the supply of goods to world markets and the foreign market impact of the transfer price. *Tax considerations should not outweigh sound business practice* and corporate pricing goals — that is, motivation, control, and evaluation of performance as well as market penetration.

The income tax authorities of national governments have also begun cooperating in the area of transfer pricing. For example, the United States has entered into simultaneous examination agreements with Japan, as also with France, Germany, the United Kingdom, and Italy, and with Norway and Canada. This means that U.S. companies must be able to satisfy two sets of authorities as to why the transfer-pricing decisions taken by them are fair. Further, closer cooperation with the United States means that the local tax authorities of the countries cited above have begun treating transfer pricing with greater diligence, and the outcome will be stricter enforcement and tighter regulation over multinational attempts to transfer profits into or out of a tax jurisdiction.

## Summary

Pricing in international markets is affected by the firm's strategic objectives, competitive behavior, consumers' ability to buy, the product life cycle stage, and market-specific environmental considerations such as government regulation.

Export prices need be set such that export sales are at least as rewarding as other sales outlets.

Export sales prices may be less than domestic prices because of the additional costs involved and the need to keep the final consumer price affordable. Export prices in the short run can be set at just above marginal cost, though this could invite government accusations of dumping. Shipping and insurance costs, tariffs, market-specific taxes such as VAT, and distributor markups all add to the cost of exported products.

Exchange rate fluctuations can affect consumer prices, too. Offsetting such fluctuations may entail the sacrifice of profit margins to maintain market share.

Quoting prices in a firm's domestic currency may seem to avoid exchange rate–related problems. But whether buyers will accept such quotes depends on the relative strength of demand and supply, as well as competitive behavior.

Export price quotations specify which services, such as shipping, insurance and documentation, are included in the quoted price.

When currencies appreciate, firms often raise prices by less than the amount of appreciation. Japanese firms are prone to such pricing behavior.

Exchange rate risk can be classified into transaction risk, competitive risk, and market-portfolio risk; each of these risks suggests different strategic actions.

How sales are financed is crucial to winning export orders. Hence, financing terms and conditions form an integral part of international pricing policies.

Government help to exporters often comes in the form of subsidies that allow the firm to offer below-market rates of interest on customer receivables, thus offering a hidden price discount.

Transfer pricing becomes relevant when a product division in one country supplies another division located in a foreign market. Transfer prices must be set so that they yield a satisfactory profit but are not high enough to discourage sales.

Common transfer-pricing formulas are based on arms-length market prices, cost-plus pricing, negotiated prices, and transfers at cost with shared profits. In all cases, motivation is as important as the profit accruing to each division.

Governments often intervene in international transfer pricing to ensure that prices are not set so low as to avoid taxes. Customs authorities may set a floor on the transfer price to prevent tariff avoidance.

## Questions

14.1  What are some of the major factors affecting international pricing? In particular, how are prices influenced by the firm's strategy, its competition, consumers' ability to buy, the firm's cost and market structure, and the complete product line?

14.2  What should be the relationship between export and domestic prices?

14.3    What are the consequences of charging an export price below the domestic market price?

14.4    Are there reasons why export prices should be higher than domestic prices? What are the marketing implications of export price escalation?

14.5    How do exchange rates affect international pricing? Why might a firm with an appreciating currency not raise its export prices?

14.6    Is quoting export prices only in the firm's domestic currency a viable strategy to avoid the impact of exchange rates?

14.7    What are the different ways in which export prices can be quoted?

14.8    What are the different risks that a firm marketing its products internationally faces because of exchange rate fluctuations? How might it cope with these categories of risk?

14.9    How and why are export credit financing terms and conditions relevant to international pricing?

14.10    How can governments help in financing international sales?

14.11    What is transfer pricing? Why is it a consideration in international pricing?

14.12    What are some useful formulas in setting transfer prices?

14.13    Why do the tax authorities of both the parent country and the host country concern themselves with transfer prices? How might such intervention affect the multinational corporation?

14.14    What are the factors affecting prices received for export of tuna from Australia to Japan? What generalizations concerning pricing in foreign markets may be drawn from this illustration?

## Endnotes

[1] For reviews of pricing in the marketing mix, see: Vithala R. Rao, "Pricing Research in Marketing: The State of the Art," *Journal of Business* Vol. 57, 1984; and Gerard J. Tellis, "Beyond the Many Faces of Price: An Integration of Pricing Strategies," *Journal of Marketing* Vol. 50, Oct. 1986.

[2] Boston Consulting Group. *Perspectives on Experience.* Boston: BCG 1972, and Robert Dolan and Abel Jeuland, "Experience Curves and Dynamic Demand Models: Implications for Optimal Pricing Strategies," *Journal of Marketing*, Winter 1981.

[3] See "Note on the Motorcycle Industry," Harvard Business School Case Services, No. 578–210.

[4] That is, $10.60 local manufacturer's price plus 12 percent VAT equals $11.87; plus 15 percent distributor markup equals $13.65; plus 40 percent retail margin on price equals $22.80. Since the import price is $25, the domestic manufacturer can undercut the import price by up to $2.20, that is, $25 minus $22.80, or $2.20.

[5] Staffan Hertzell and Christian Caspar, "Coping with Unpredictable Currencies," *The McKinsey Quarterly* (Summer 1988).

[6] Ravi Sarathy, "High Technology Exports from Newly Industrializing Countries: The Brazilian Commuter Aircraft Industry." *California Management Review* 27, no. 2 (Winter 1985): 60–84.

[7] Peter Bowe, President, Dredge Division, Ellicott Machine Corporation, as reported in *Maryland Trader*, 1987.

[8] "Financing for Exports Grows Harder to Find," *The Wall Street Journal*, May 14, 1987.

[9] See *Trade Finance: Current Issues and Developments*, International Trade Administration (Washington, D.C.: U.S. Department of Commerce, November 1988), 34–43.

[10] "Eximbank Announces First Successful 'Mixed Credit' Deal, Clinching Contract in Gabon," *International Trade Reporter,* May 28, 1986.

## Further Readings

Arpan, Jeffrey. "International Intracorporate Pricing," *Journal of International Business Studies* (Spring 1972).

Dolan, Robert, and Abel Jeuland. "Experience Curves and Dynamic Demand Models: Implications for Optimal Pricing Strategies," *Journal of Marketing* (Winter 1981).

Hertzell, Staffan, and Christian Caspar. "Coping with Unpredictable Currencies," *The McKinsey Quarterly* (Summer 1988).

International Trade Administration. *Trade Finance: Current Issues and Developments.* Washington, D.C.: U.S. Department of Commerce, November 1988.

Rao, Vithala R. "Pricing Research in Marketing: The State of the Art," *Journal of Business* 57 (1984).

Sarathy, Ravi. "High Technology Exports from Newly Industrializing Countries: The Brazilian Commuter Aircraft Industry." *California Management Review* 27, no. 2 (Winter 1985): 60–84.

Tellis, Gerard J. "Beyond the Many Faces of Price: An Integration of Pricing Strategies," *Journal of Marketing* 50 (October 1986).

Walters, Peter G. P. "A Framework for Export Pricing Decisions." *Journal of Global Marketing* 2, no. 3 (1989).

# 14.1 Subaru of America

Subaru of America (SA) distributes cars manufactured in Japan by Fuji Heavy Industries, which is itself one of Japan's smallest car manufacturers. Fuji has majority control of SA. SA had been one of the most profitable companies in the United States, as the table below shows:

| Year (ended October) | Net Income (Millions of Dollars) | Return on Equity |
|---|---|---|
| 1978 | $ 7.2 | 70% |
| 1979 | 10.4 | 62 |
| 1980 | 17.7 | 68 |
| 1981 | 26.3 | 62 |
| 1982 | 39.4 | 59 |
| 1983 | 49.5 | 48 |
| 1984 | 60.0 | 41 |
| 1985 | 77.1 | 39 |
| 1986 | 94.0 | 35 |
| 1987 | −30.0 | −9 |
| 1988 | −57.9 | −22 |

Source: Subaru of America 1988 Annual Report.

market for the parent Fuji company in Japan, accounting for between 32 and 35 percent of total Fuji shipments.

Subaru's American sales peaked at 183,242 units in 1986. Since then, sales have fallen to only about 150,000 units in 1989.

Several problems contributed to the declining performance at Subaru, primarily the declining dollar. Between the latter part of 1984 and the end of 1988, the dollar declined from a peak of about 250 yen to the dollar to as low as 120 yen to the dollar in 1989 (see Table 1). Thus, dollar prices effectively doubled for a Japanese product priced in yen, unless the Japanese manufacturer chose to absorb some of the effects of a rising yen.

While Fuji wanted Subaru to be seen as an American company with American management, Fuji did have control of SA. Its agreement was that Fuji and SA would negotiate transfer prices for each model on an annual basis. How-

## Fuji Heavy Industries Auto Exports

| | 1984 | 1985 | 1986 | 1987 | 1988 |
|---|---|---|---|---|---|
| Exports as percent of total sales | 54.5 | 46.8 | 49.1 | 50.6 | 49 |
| Exports to U.S. as percent of total sales | Not available | Not available | 35.2 | 34.5 | 32.3 |

Subaru was popular for its subcompact four-wheel drive cars that were built well and priced low. It was the first auto firm to make four-wheel-drive available on a low-priced compact car. The United States was an important and profitable

Case prepared by Associate Professor Ravi Sarathy for use in classroom discussion. All rights reserved.

Source: "Counterattack," *Forbes*, November 13, 1989; Fuji Heavy Industries, Annual Reports; and Subaru of America Inc. 1988 and 1989 Annual Reports.

ever, Fuji could renegotiate the prices based on its cost structure. Within Japan, Fuji is one of the smaller auto makers, with a limited number of models in the subcompact segment of the market. Overcapacity in Japan led to price-cutting, putting pressure on profits at Fuji. Fuji was thus trapped by a series of developments:

1. Overcapacity in Japan and slowing growth in demand for cars in Japan.

2. A swiftly appreciating yen.

**Table 1**   Subaru of America Inc.: Years Ended October 31, Millions of Dollars

| | 1988 | 1987 | 1986 | 1985 | 1984 | 1983 | 1982 | 1981 | 1980 |
|---|---|---|---|---|---|---|---|---|---|
| Total sales | 1,673.2 | 1,785 | 1,939.3 | 1,502.3 | 1,174.9 | 1,057.5 | 977.6 | 916.1 | 744.2 |
| Cost of goods sold | 1,584.8 | 1,688.8 | 1,680.1 | 1,286.5 | 996.8 | 908.4 | 848.5 | 823.4 | 671.6 |
| Gross margin | 88.4 | 96.2 | 259.2 | 215.8 | 178.1 | 149.1 | 129.1 | 92.7 | 72.6 |
| Gross margin percent | 5.28% | 5.39% | 13.37% | 14.36% | 15.16% | 14.10% | 13.21% | 10.12% | 9.76% |
| Selling & general expenses | 203.9 | 170.2 | 116.1 | 98.5 | 81.3 | 67.1 | 59.9 | 43.6 | 38.7 |
| Net income | −57.9 | −30 | 94 | 77.1 | 60 | 49.5 | 39.5 | 26.3 | 17.7 |
| Cars sold (thousands) | 156 | 177.1 | 183.2 | 178.2 | 157.4 | 156.8 | 150.3 | 152.1 | 143 |
| Revenue per car | $10,726 | $10,079 | $10,586 | $8,430 | $7,464 | $6,744 | $6,504 | $6,023 | $5,204 |
| Exchange rate: yen/dollars | 125.16 | 135.54 | 160.38 | 207.03 | 237.31 | 237.37 | 248.24 | 220.11 | 225.68 |

3. Price-cutting in Japan.

4. Increasing wage costs in Japan, as the older workforce received raises based on seniority.

5. Fear of losing quotas to the United States, putting pressure on Subaru to accept cars in excess of normally sustainable demand.

Under these circumstances, Fuji chose to pass on some of the price increases forced by yen appreciation. In effect, Fuji and Subaru agreed to share the pain of a stronger yen, with each side absorbing half the price rise implied. Thus, if the yen rose by 20 percent, Fuji would raise transfer prices by 10 percent, and in turn, Subaru would not pass on the full increase in transfer prices in the form of increased U.S. car sticker prices.

Table 1 summarizes the cost of goods sold, gross margin percent, unit revenue, and total sales at Subaru, as well as the number of units sold and the changing value of the dollar against the yen. In 1986 alone, adjusting inventory values to reflect the changing value of the yen would have meant increasing the value of inventory by 97.5 percent (see Table 2).

Thus, if the FIFO (first-in first-out) method of inventory had been used, inventory values in 1986 would have been shown at $155.24 million, a 97.5 percent increase (meaning that because of yen appreciation, delivered cost in dollars had risen by that percent).

The quota system also affected Subaru's inventories. The Japanese voluntary export restraints on cars sold into the United States had limited each individual Japanese firm's unit exports to the United States; hence, most of them moved upscale, selling higher value-added and more profitable models, at higher prices. Fuji's United States quota had been steadily increasing:

It went up from 148,000 cars in 1981 to 199,000 in 1985. If Fuji did not ship the total number of cars allowed to it under the voluntary quotas assigned to Japanese car companies by MITI, it would face cuts in the quota for the ensuing year. To avoid this, Fuji shipped cars in excess of demand, with Subaru of America having to stockpile these cars in its inventory and with its dealers. By April 1988, dealer inventory had risen to 110 days, from a level of just 53 days in October 1987.

The U.S. car industry was also on the brink of a recession. Over the period of 1983 to 1987, more than 70 million cars and trucks had been sold in the United States, the most in any five-year period. It was time for a pause. The 20 percent reduction in sales (from peak-year sales) that Subaru experienced may have been partly due to this weakening of demand; in comparison, Porsche sales declined over 50 percent, Jaguar's sales by 20 percent, and Mercedes-Benz by about 10 percent. Overall, auto imports were affected by the weak dollar.

Subaru's problems were compounded by a product line reaching maturity: Its models were nearly five years old, and it had to introduce newer models. In addition, it began facing competition from models such as the Jeep Cherokee and the Ford Bronco II, both American-made, competitively priced, and also offering four-wheel drive. Further, its models were predominantly lower-priced subcompact cars. Subaru had been advertised as "inexpensive and built to stay that way." Therefore, SA experienced much consumer resistance to price rises and the adding on of extra (and profitable) options.

Another problem was rising labor costs in Japan while countries such as South Korea were

### Table 2  Impact of Yen Appreciation on Inventory Values: Subaru of America

|  | 1988 | 1987 | 1986 |
|---|---|---|---|
| Inventory Values, LIFO, Millions of Dollars | 210 | 133.4 | 78.6 |
| Percent Increase in Value to Reflect Yen Appreciation (FIFO Value Increase) | 40% | 57.2% | 97.5% |

challenging Subaru with their own subcompacts manufactured with lower-priced labor. The Hyundai Excel was introduced to the United States in early 1986, and sales had reached 250,000 units by 1987. In response, the other Japanese car companies had moved upscale, selling compact sedans averaging $15,000 in price. But Subaru as a sales subsidiary was limited by its parent company Fuji's focus on producing subcompact cars.

As did most car companies, Subaru was forced to use incentives to sell cars. It began offering rebates to buyers of its cars, averaging about $500 per car sold. Such incentives temporarily increased sales. In August 1987, the first month that incentives were in effect and heavily advertised, 17,745 cars were sold, as compared to 14,436 the previous month. But these incentives also decreased gross margins and reduced profits. Subaru also had to advertise heavily to move inventory and maintain market share. The total scale of additional selling effort can be seen in the trend for selling expenses in Table 1.

Fuji initially responded by supplying Subaru in 1988 with four-wheel-drive Justy models (its most popular compact car) from Fuji's Taiwan factory. Lower Taiwanese wages meant lower prices and cars imported from Taiwan also fell outside the Japanese quota granted Fuji. In theory, Fuji could continue to ship its full quota from Japan in addition to the Taiwanese shipments. The goal was to bring in 30,000 to 40,000 cars a year from Taiwan. However, the dollar had been depreciating significantly against the Taiwanese currency, which tended to undercut the benefits of importing from Taiwan.

Fuji also initiated a joint venture with Isuzu Motors to open a car factory in the United States—Subaru/Isuzu Automotive Inc. (SIA)—to produce 120,000 cars annually, including 60,000 new Subaru Legacy model cars. Plant construction was begun in May 1987, with production scheduled to begin in October 1989. A total of $550 million was invested, employing 1,700 workers. Fuji provided the investment funds and hence bore all of the risk. Thus, Subaru could get U.S.–made cars and overcome the yen disadvantage, with its parent company bearing the financial risk.

The Legacy model was part of Subaru's response: a new entry in the compact sedan and station wagon segment to compete against cars such as the Honda Accord, the Toyota Camry, and the Mazda 626. This allowed Subaru to move into the higher-priced and less price-sensitive market segment. The Legacy was to feature antilock braking systems, a 2.2 liter 130 HP engine, European styling, and four-wheel drive. It would be priced between $11,000 and $19,000. It would carry a "Made in America" label, in a factory incorporating the latest technology provided by the Fuji factories in Japan. Harvey Lamm, SA CEO, contended, "We have a car in technology that the Germans can't match at twice the price."[1]

SA saw several benefits coming from starting U.S. production: shelter from the ravages of a strong yen, freedom to operate without the constraints set by the voluntary export quotas agreed to by the Japanese car manufacturers, lower costs and more efficient distribution from the central U.S. factory location, larger gross margins, quicker reactions to changing market conditions, and the ability to add the "Made in America" label to the new Legacy product.

However, the U.S. car industry was on the verge of a recession in 1989. Sales were declining even as an additional capacity to manufacture 2 million cars was promised for 1990 by new factories owned by the Japanese. It was an open question when Subaru might achieve a turnaround in sales and profits, even if the yen weakened. Yet, at the end of 1989, Fuji decided to convert Subaru of America into a wholly owned subsidiary. It offered to buy up all the shares held by the public, thus making the U.S. sales operation an integrated part of Fuji's operations.

## Questions

1. Explain how the yen appreciation hurt Subaru.

2. How did Fuji's transfer pricing policies affect Subaru's U.S. prices?

3. What other factors may have contributed to Subaru's declining sales in the United States?
4. How did Subaru respond to the problems created by the yen price rise? And how did the Fuji parent company respond?
5. Were Fuji's other Japanese auto industry competitors similarly affected by the yen appreciation? And how might the dollar devaluation have affected other auto importers from areas such as Mexico, Brazil, South Korea, and Europe?
6. What is your assessment of Subaru's future? How might the future outlook have affected Fuji's decision to convert Subaru into a wholly owned subsidiary?

### Endnote

[1]"Counterattack," *Forbes,* November 13, 1989.

CASE

# 14.2 Federal Cash Registers: Price Competition Overseas

Supermercados Mundiales, S.A.
1, Avenida Bolivar,
Caracas, Venezuela,
May 17

Señor Donald Fraser,
Presidente,
Federal Cash Registers de Venezuela, S.A.
247 Calle Libertad,
Caracas, Venezuela

Dear Donald:

It is with great regret that I have to inform you of our decision to equip our new supermarket with cash registers from the Japanese firm Nippon Business Machines. As I told you over the telephone yesterday, I cannot wait until you make another trip to Chicago to see if your head office will give a lower price; I have given my word to the Nippon sales manager, and there is no likelihood, if you will forgive my saying so, that you could ever come close enough to their prices to secure our business in future stores.

Source: This case was prepared by John S. Ewing, Department of Marketing, California Polytechnic State University, Chico, California. Used by permission.

At least not as matters now stand. I am, however, concerned about your inability to compete, for, as you know, I have friendly feelings toward Federal and personally I and my brothers have benefited greatly from our attendance at your seminars in Chicago. We have also found the training you offer here to our checkers to be most useful and I think you will admit that in our earlier stores we showed our gratitude tangibly by installing your machines. However, that was before Nippon began to market here and during a time when you had things pretty much your own way.

But, not only am I disturbed about your apparent inability to compete but also about the way in which other American firms are being underpriced. We here have good feelings toward the United States, except for some foolish ones, and we know that you buy most of our oil, so we should buy from you in return. But, leaving apart any difficulties over oil quotas and restrictions, how can we buy from you when other countries, with whom we are also friendly, can outsell you and, I conclude, still make profits? I have certainly not rushed into this purchase of Nippon registers, as you must admit, for I have waited a long time for your counteroffers. It is only now that your offers are still above Nippon's by a substantial margin that I have decided I must act.

Let me review the history of the situation with you, and perhaps you can draw from it some help for the future. I assure you that we will always give you the chance to offer for the business, and I hope you will be able to persuade Chicago to support you.

As you know, when I called for the bid on the registers, your original price was well above the other price, by an outlandish figure. You took it up with Chicago and succeeded in getting the difference reduced, but not sufficiently to be interesting. You went back again for help, and this time the suggestion was that you send in Italian registers from your factory there (which I must say I found a curious thing). But even then, though the difference was reduced from $30,000 for the American machines to $19,000 for the Italian ones, you were still way over the other price.

You asked me yesterday what the competitor's edge was. I can tell you now that his price is better than yours by $9,000, and I think you must agree that that amount is too much to be sacrificed to sentiment. How he does it, I don't know, nor do I much care. So we have gone ahead and placed the order.

You brought up the question of parts and service, particularly in wartime. To the first, I must in all logic point out that the kind of war which seems likely will make the problem of parts an academic one, but in any event, the chances of our getting parts from Japan are as good as they are of getting them from a U.S. firm, which is sure to be at war.

As to service, I have this to say. We keep open on Saturdays and Sundays in many departments, as you know. We have had occasion, in other stores, to call your company on Friday afternoons for service and to be told that you don't work the "American weekend" and nobody will be available until Monday. You explain this as being because of labor restrictions and the like. About this I don't care. I do care that Nippon, called on Friday, or any time, will come on Saturday, Sunday or in the middle of the night. The general sales manager himself will come and work on the register, and it is this that we want, no excuses about "American weekends." If you want our business, you must be prepared to work for it.

So this is the story. If you want to discuss it with me further, I shall be happy at any time to see you. I hope we can remain friends, but I am not sure that we can remain in the position of doing business with each other.

My warm regards to your esteemed señora.

With great cordiality,


Jaime Aragon, Presidente

## Questions

1. What action should Donald Fraser take with regard to this letter: (a) Should he take the matter up with Jaime Aragon again? (b) Should he send the letter on to his Chicago headquarters?

2. What bases for action with regard to new business are suggested by the letter?

3. What is the significance of this letter in terms of U.S. business operating abroad?

CASE
# 14.3 Alimentaires de Barria S.A.: Operating in an Inflationary Economy*

Alimentaires de Barria is the Barrian subsidiary of a large multinational food processor based in Europe, Produits Alimentaires. Barria is a Latin American nation of 19 million people. The Produits Alimentaires subsidiary has been in Barria for over 35 years, but Mr. Bruno Piperno, the manager of Alimentaires de Barria, was concerned about the future prosperity and survival of the subsidiary because of the great increase in inflationary pressures in the mid-1980s. He was wondering what pricing and other operating policies he should follow to ensure the continued success of his company.

Alimentaires de Barria is a leading food processor in the Barrian market. Its primary products are canned fruits and juices, vegetables, and meats. Through an acquisition a few years ago, it is now also a factor in processed dairy foods. Mr. Piperno has been considering diversifying into frozen foods as well, because the nature of the raw materials would be much the same as the present product line. Most of the food products canned came from Barrian sources. Some things were imported, however: sugar for the syrups, tin plate for the cans, and some subtropical vegetables and fruits, like papaya and pineapple. Furthermore, most of the specialized production equipment was imported from Europe or the United States.

Although it was a subsidiary of a European multinational firm, Alimentaires de Barria was largely autonomous and responsible for its own operations. Normally Mr. Piperno enjoyed this independence, but occasionally he felt they could use some help. The spring of 1986 was one of those times. Mr. Piperno had been in Barria for eight years and had faced many problems with

reasonable success. In addition to the "usual" problems he had to deal with the chronic inflation that characterized so many Latin American countries including Barria (see Table 1). Compounding the problem of inflation was the government policy of imposing price controls on some of the company's products. Inflation was driving up costs while the government was putting price controls on most of the company's products.

Inflation had a mixed impact on the firm's operations. On the one hand it raised costs, and on the other hand it raised company sales. On the cost side, the impact of inflation fell differently on different ingredients. This was partly because these ingredients had differing rates of inflation and partly because some ingredients had their price controlled at times by the government (see Table 2).

As Mr. Piperno considered the inflationary cost picture, he knew he faced a complex problem, as each ingredient had different determinants and constraints. In the case of wages, for example, a strong government had kept wage increases below the inflation rate in his early years in Barria. In recent years, however, wage increases surpassed the rate of inflation as the new government felt less secure in office. As an important dietary item, sugar was price-controlled, so its cost lagged behind other items in the general cost of living. The price of tin depended on (1) the price of tin on the world market and (2) the Barrian exchange rate, since all tin was imported. Both of these factors were subject to rather abrupt fluctuations.

The price indexes for vegetables, fruits, and meats were averages, because there were many different kinds of vegetables and fruits as well as three different kinds of meats canned by Alimentaires. The inflation rate between different

*This case may also be used with Chapter 15, which further discusses the impact of inflation on pricing.

**Table 1    Cost of Living Index in Barria**

| Year | Index |
|------|-------|
| 1976 | 100 |
| 1977 | 123 |
| 1978 | 148 |
| 1979 | 179 |
| 1980 | 211 |
| 1981 | 255 |
| 1982 | 312 |
| 1983 | 398 |
| 1984 | 675 |
| 1985 | 1,220 |

**Table 2    Price Indexes of Various Ingredients**

| Year | Wages | Sugar | Tin | Vegetables | Fruits | Meats |
|------|-------|-------|-----|------------|--------|-------|
| 1976 | 100 | 100 | 100 | 100 | 100 | 100 |
| 1977 | 110 | 100 | 114 | 109 | 134 | 140 |
| 1978 | 130 | 128 | 122 | 120 | 158 | 176 |
| 1979 | 155 | 128 | 141 | 135 | 187 | 168 |
| 1980 | 210 | 128 | 241 | 182 | 216 | 251 |
| 1981 | 243 | 190 | 313 | 212 | 269 | 245 |
| 1982 | 328 | 227 | 462 | 351 | 327 | 349 |
| 1983 | 435 | 285 | 614 | 377 | 409 | 418 |
| 1984 | 750 | 401 | 889 | 474 | 695 | 462 |
| 1985 | 1,318 | 752 | 1,602 | 768 | 1,229 | 891 |

vegetable products did not vary as much as that for fruits and meats. Some of the fruits were imported, and their prices varied according to the Barrian exchange rate in addition to regular supply conditions. The various meat products had a more irregular supply. Suppliers would produce a lot when the prices were high. This would tend to make for an excess supply and a decline in prices. This led in turn to a decline in supply in a later year.

The bright side of Mr. Piperno's experience in Barria was that he had expanded the sales and market share of Alimentaires' products. Unit sales of all three of the firm's product categories had more than kept up with the growth in population and real income in Barria. Even in competition with other food processors, local and foreign, Alimentaires' market share had gradually increased over the years. This was a source of satisfaction to Mr. Piperno, and it was appropriately noted back at corporate headquarters.

While Mr. Piperno felt he had done a good job in Barria with those things he could control, he was disturbed by the many things beyond his control. One of these "uncontrollables" was the availability of foreign exchange. Certain fruits and tin had to be imported. Also, any new equipment had to come from abroad. Because of its international debts, Barria had tight exchange controls. Every year Mr. Piperno had to battle with the Central Bank to get the foreign exchange he needed. Companies that exported received more favorable treatment in getting foreign exchange, but Alimentaires had no exports.

Another "uncontrollable" that bothered Mr. Piperno even more than the foreign exchange problem was the existence of government price controls on most of Alimentaires' products. Not all products in Barria were price-controlled, but a great many were, especially so-called necessities, the items that entered into the cost-of-living calculation by the Central Bank. Since Alimentaires' products were food items, they were subject to price controls of varying rigidity. Some items, such as pineapple slices and the fancier meat products, were considered more like luxuries and therefore less tightly price-controlled than the more prosaic products of everyday consumption. Also, the older the product, the tighter the price controls generally were. For Alimentaires this meant that its original canned vegetable line had generally more rigid price controls than its fruit products which were a more recent part of the product line, especially certain new varieties and the juices that had been added only in 1980.

Mr. Piperno had been intrigued by the patterns of government price control and had ordered an internal study of its effects on Alimentaires. He found strong correlation between the degree of price control and unit sales growth of a product—the products most tightly controlled in price experienced the fastest unit sales growth. He wondered if this sales pattern meant that Alimentaires was subsidizing the consumption by Barrian consumers of these products.

Inventories were another aspect of operations only partly subject to management's control. There was a seasonal aspect to the supplies of some of the vegetables, fruits, and meats processed by Alimentaires. The people would tend to buy fresh products when they came on the market and buy canned products during the other seasons. Alimentaires had to schedule its procurement and production according to these patterns of supply and demand. Another inventory problem arose because of the uncertainty of foreign exchange allocations. Imported items had to be purchased when foreign exchange was available even if they were not needed at that time.

The net effect of all these conflicting forces was not positive for Alimentaires or Mr. Piperno. Even though unit sales had grown steadily and market share had increased, Alimentaires' total sales had not kept pace with the rate of inflation. In other words, government price controls had kept Alimentaires' selling-price increases below the increases in its costs. This meant a steady erosion of profit margins that had become especially worrisome in the past few years of more rapid inflation.

Mr. Piperno was very aware that a U.S. producer of baby food had left the Barrian market in 1985 after ten years of struggling with these problems. The U.S. firm faced particularly tough price controls because of the sensitivity of its product line. Mr. Piperno didn't feel that Alimentaires was in the same situation as the U.S. firm, but he felt that it might be if inflation continued at its present frantic pace. Therefore, he was trying to think of possible adjustments he could make in Alimentaires' operations to meet these challenges.

## Questions

1. What problem does Mr. Piperno face?
2. Identify and evaluate various courses of action Mr. Piperno might consider in attacking his problem.
3. What generalizations can you make about operating in an inflationary economy such as Barria?

CHAPTER 15

# Pricing in International Marketing: II

*Learning Objectives*

Going beyond export pricing and transfer pricing, this chapter considers other aspects of pricing in international marketing. The main goals of this chapter are to

1. Determine the influence of foreign-market variables such as government, inflation, local demand, and costs on pricing.
2. Discuss how a firm deals with international competition—the pressure to cut costs and prices and the role of manufacturing decisions and product design in meeting low-cost competition.
3. Define gray markets, and explain how to deal with them.
4. Explore the dimensions and implications of countertrade, a sizable segment of world trade.
5. Discuss the role of leasing in international marketing.
6. Explain when and why coordinating prices is necessary in international marketing, and describe how it is done.

## Foreign-Market Pricing

Management concern in both export pricing and international transfer pricing is with getting goods *into* foreign markets at some appropriate price. In both cases, the problem is one of *international* pricing. Foreign-market pricing is concerned with pricing *within* foreign markets; as such, it is a matter of *domestic* pricing. However, it is a concern of the international marketer for two reasons: (1) the firm's prices in any market are usually related to supply and demand factors beyond that market, and (2) an important part of international marketing is the coordination of domestic marketing in each of the firm's markets, which includes pricing policy.

Because foreign-market pricing is pricing for a national market, all the pricing considerations that are discussed in domestic marketing texts are relevant. These include pricing over the product life cycle, product-line pricing, original equipment versus replacement sales, pricing to intermediaries,

| Table 15–1 | **Determinants of Foreign-Market Pricing** |
|---|---|

Company Goals
Costs:
   Manufacturing
   Transportation
   Marketing
Demand
Competition
Government
Taxes and Tariffs
Inflation
Product Line
Distribution Channels
Marketing Mix

and skimming versus penetration strategies. The determinants of a firm's prices in a market are indicated in Table 15–1.

## Foreign-Market Variables: Company Goals

A firm's objectives generally vary from country to country. In growth markets the firm will probably stress market share and may have a penetration pricing strategy. In stagnant markets, the firm may try a holding pattern with pricing strategy appropriate to that goal. A joint venture puts a special constraint on pricing because the firm must consider the desires of its national partner as well as its own.

When a firm first enters foreign markets it sets goals appropriate for the situation at that time. As the environments in these markets evolve (e.g., political changes as in Lebanon, South Africa, or the Philippines, or economic development as in China or South Korea) the firm's goals for these markets will also change. This leads to modifications in pricing strategy over time.

## Foreign-Market Variables: Costs

The costs relevant to foreign-market pricing include everything necessary to get the product to the ultimate buyer. When a firm operates in just one market, the relevant costs are easy to determine. In the international firm, it is not easy to determine the relevant costs for a particular market. A subsidiary in one country is usually part of an international network on both the supply and the demand sides. Allocating indirect costs *among countries* is similar to the problem of allocating them among different product lines. In addition, the international firm has a different cost structure in each of its markets.

**Manufacturing Costs.**   Of the costs that must be covered by the price, one, of course, is manufacturing. When the products sold in a market are produced there, determination of manufacturing costs is no problem. But questions arise when a market is served by other production sources: If a firm has several plants, which plant's costs should be used? Should variable or full cost be used? What does "full cost" mean for a product coming from a plant in another country; that is, what constitutes R&D, overhead, and so on? Obviously, some costs, such as local advertising or marketing research, do not apply to products sold in another country.

The general guideline is that in the long run, a market price should cover *those costs for which it is responsible.* This then becomes a problem of cost accounting.

**Marketing Costs.**   Distribution and marketing costs also must be covered in the foreign-market price. Because tariffs can be an important part of delivered cost, the subsidiary will tend to prefer a source from a country having favorable tariff relations with its own. Thus a subsidiary in the EC will usually choose another EC subsidiary, because no tariff barriers exist.

Marketing costs in the foreign-market price are primarily those generated within that market by the national subsidiary. Occasionally, however, the firm incurs cost for marketing research or other services rendered by a regional division (or international division) for the subsidiary. Local marketing costs will vary from one country to another. This variation derives in part from differing product lines and company goals in each market.

**Inflation.**   In many markets, one cannot discuss costs without considering a special determinant of costs, that is, inflation. Almost all countries face some gradual increase in prices over time. However, continuing strong inflation characterizes a limited number of countries. In those markets where price levels rise by 20 percent or more every year, pricing is a different problem.

Selling in an inflationary market might well appear to be a marketer's dream. People are anxious to exchange their money for something that does not depreciate so fast. Indeed, it would be a good situation for sellers if it were not for other factors that usually accompany high rates of inflation. First, costs may go up faster than prices. Second, countries with high rates of inflation are usually those with strong price controls. Third, countries with rampant inflation usually have strict controls over foreign exchange. Profits earned in those countries may not be remittable, at least not until they have been eroded by the devaluations that usually accompany inflation.

Pricing for inflationary markets requires accounting for changing values over time. Material and other costs of a product must be recovered (plus a margin for profit) at the time of sale—or at the time of payment, if credit is extended. If prices are stable, pricing can be a simple process of addition. If prices are rising rapidly, addition of the various cost elements at the time they were incurred will not assure that the *current* value of these costs is recovered.

The following examples illustrate these contrasting situations. The currency unit is the peso, a currency of a country that has experienced rapid inflation for many years.

## Stable Currency Situation

| | |
|---|---|
| Raw materials | 250 pesos |
| Overhead | 100 |
| Labor | 100 |
| Packaging | 50 |
| Total costs | 500 pesos |
| Gross profit (20%) | 100 |
| Selling price (cash sale) | 600 pesos |

## Inflation Rate of 84 Percent Per Year

Assume that raw materials were purchased four months before being used in the product; labor costs were incurred one month before product sale; overhead was charged for a one-month period; and packaging materials were purchased three months before sale.

| | | |
|---|---|---|
| Raw Materials | 250 + 70 (28% inflation—4 months) | 320 pesos |
| Labor | 100 + 7 (7% inflation—1 month) | 107 |
| Overhead | 100 + 7 (7% inflation—1 month) | 107 |
| Packaging | 50 + 10.5 (21% inflation—3 months) | 61 |
| Total costs | | 595 |
| Gross profit (20%) | | 119 |
| Selling price (cash sale) | | 714 pesos |

Although both examples are simple, the second is a gross oversimplification. In reality, many more cost elements go into a product than the four general headings given here; for example, marketing costs are not mentioned. In addition, each of the cost elements will have a rate of inflation different from the average (here 84 percent a year increase in the *general* price level). Finally, time may elapse between production and sale—as well as between sale and payment. This additional time is a further inflation cost to be considered in the price.

Another problem arises if government price controls prevent raising the price. Where the firm does have freedom to raise prices, it often fares better by making frequent small price increases than occasional large increases that jolt the consumer. Such was the experience of companies in Brazil. During one period, companies raised their prices 7 percent on the first of every month. At one time, General Foods' Brazilian subsidiary, Kibon, had to raise prices on popsicles from 10 cruzeiros to 60 cruzeiros in just two years. The buyers were mainly children whose income had not risen anywhere near six times its original amount. Kibon tried to raise prices by small steps and undertook special promotions each time to minimize the shock. In one such promotional program, those who got a marked popsicle stick won a free bike.

Pricing in inflation will never be easy, especially if there are price controls. However, there are certain guidelines that can help.

1. Good cost accounting is critical, especially *forecasting* of costs for pricing.
2. It may be possible to source materials or components from lower-cost suppliers in other countries.
3. Long-term contracts may need *escalator* or *reopener* clauses.
4. Credit terms can perhaps be shortened.
5. Product ingredients and/or the product line can perhaps be changed to items less subject either to inflation or government price control.

## Foreign-Market Variables: Demand

Price is determined by supply and demand. The supply or cost side we have looked at briefly in preceding paragraphs. A market-oriented manager knows, however, that the "right" price is one that also suits the market or demand side.

The international firm faces a different demand curve in each of its markets. Demand for the firm's products is a function of the number of consumers, their ability to pay, their tastes, habits, and attitudes relating to the product, and the existence of competing products. It is improbable that these will be identical in any two markets. A U.S. firm will find another variable affecting demand is the attitude toward the United States and products made there. The implication of differing demand is that the firm must charge different prices in each market.

## Foreign-Market Variables: Competition

In a purely competitive market, all producers would sell at identical prices. In the imperfectly competitive real world, the firm must take note of *competitors' prices*. However, it has some freedom to sell above or below these prices. U.S. firms abroad generally prefer to compete on a non-price basis. A study by Lecraw found that U.S. firms tended to set their prices in relation to an industry leader in the foreign market.[1]

The Singer Company was facing strong price competition in sewing machines in a Far Eastern market. It was able, however, to maintain a strong market position even though its prices were significantly higher than prices of the Japanese machines. The company emphasized product quality, liberal credit terms, and sewing classes for buyers in its successful attempt to maintain market position.

The *nature of competition* is another variable. The number of competitors and the way they compete will differ between Belgium and Brazil, or between Italy and India. Even in neighboring countries the situation differs. Thus, a drug firm charged 25 percent more for an identical dosage in Belgium than in neighboring France. The firm had a strong position in the Belgian market, where it also had a plant. It was relatively weak in the French market, and the government health service was threatening to buy from Italian drug "pirates." (These "pirates" made the drugs without royalty payments to the originating firm and thus had no R&D expense to cover.)

An example of differing *competitive behavior* comes from the automobile industry: An executive with a U.S. automobile producer complained about

Renault "dumping" cars outside the French market, that is, selling them at less than full cost. According to him, Renault (owned by the French government) was more interested in maintaining employment in France than in making profits. Therefore, it was willing to sell cars at a loss for the political benefits of employment. He felt it was much easier to compete against more "rational" profit-oriented companies than against a government-owned firm.

In 1985, when the Japanese yen rose about 19 percent against the dollar, Nissan and Toyota raised their prices in the United States by only about 5 percent. They were concerned not only about U.S. competition, but especially about impending Korean competition.

Competition in a foreign market depends further on *business and government attitudes.* In the United States, both business and government are in favor of competition; in fact, no other country puts such emphasis on competition. The Rome Treaty contains a competition policy for the EC in Articles 85 and 86. The implementation of this policy varies among EC member countries, however.

The U.S. firm will often find that its chief competitors in a market are multinationals from Europe or Japan, which exhibit differing competitive behavior. Lecraw found, for example, that Japanese multinationals "tended to set prices to achieve market penetration," that is, set low prices.[2] Third World multinationals are also coming on the scene.

## Foreign-Market Variables: Government

Governments influence the firm's pricing in a variety of ways. Some influence is exerted via tariffs, taxes, and competition policy. Some governments have specific legislation, such as the U.S. Robinson-Patman Act. Most commonly, however, governments have the power to control prices directly if they so choose, and they use their power in varying degrees. In the United States, public utility pricing has been regulated, and price freezes have been occasionally employed. Other governments also regulate specific prices, or occasionally all prices, in their country.

The purpose of price controls is generally to limit price increases. The control technique is usually as follows: The manufacturer must apply for a price increase with data to support the request (increased costs of energy or materials, higher wages, etc.); then there will be a waiting period before the price can be raised, *if* the request is approved. There is also usually a limit to how frequently the firm can apply for a price increase.

Government controls obviously limit the firm's freedom in setting prices. They raise the cost of price administration by requiring more record keeping and management time. They also probably result in lower and less frequent price increases. The government limit to approved price increases may be quite arbitrary. The greatest challenge to the firm, however, arises when its request for a price increase is denied, an outcome more common in Latin America than in Europe. Inability to raise prices in an inflationary environment threatens the very survival of the firm.

Gerber Products Co. had been operating in Venezuela since 1960 when it sold its Venezuelan operation in 1979, claiming inability to make a profit, primarily because of government price controls. Some of the company's products were still being sold at prices set in 1968. Gerber's requests for price increases had been frequently denied. Because of the price squeeze, its product line had been reduced from 88 varieties to only 12 items. The company reportedly lost $500,000 in the first six months of 1979.

Government price controls may be universal, but frequently they are limited to selected product groups. Some products are perceived as being more strategic or sensitive and are more susceptible to government regulation. Pharmaceuticals have the unenviable position of being the most frequently subject to price controls. Even countries that don't control other prices usually control pharmaceutical prices. It is interesting to note, however, that drug firms manage to show consistently good profits. In spite of the Gerber example then, price controls do not *necessarily* preclude survival or even profits.

France had economy-wide price controls in the early 1980s to fight inflation. By 1986, 90 percent of the restrictions had been removed. Controls remained on pharmaceuticals, auto parts, some food and clothing. In Japan, a country with limited price controls, the government *cut* the reimbursement price of drugs by 16 percent in 1984. However, unique new drugs were granted price increases.

Firms can handle government-imposed price controls in a variety of ways. Usually, the price controls apply to the basic product. Hence, firms can charge an additional amount for extras such as delivery, warranty, on-site service, and installation. A similar approach is *unbundling,* where the product is broken down into separate components and a separate price charged for each component such as add-on tools and peripherals. Another technique is the *matched-sales* technique, where sales of the price-controlled product are coupled with purchases of another, perhaps complementary product not subject to price controls.

Firms may also deliberately change their product line to move away from items that are price-controlled, and then continue featuring "phantom" products on which price controls are exercised. Another technique is defining orders as "special orders," by adding product features and customization. Prices can generally be negotiated free of price controls on such custom products. Finally, companies can try to increase transfer prices on imported products so as to raise the base price, since price controls generally allow increases in product costs to be passed along to the consumer.[3]

**Foreign-Market Variables: Distribution Channels**

A final determinant of the firm's price to consumers in a foreign market is its distribution channels there. Although different channels obviously may have different costs, using the same channel in two countries does not necessarily indicate costs will be similar. The costs and margins of a given channel are not the same from country to country. This suggests that a channel decision may also be a pricing decision. The firm may be forced to choose a particular channel in a market to get the consumer price it needs. Table 15–2 illustrates the intercountry variability of channel costs.

**Table 15-2**              **Cost Variability of the Same Channel in Different Countries: Medicines**

| Country | Manufacturer's Price | Wholesaler's Mark-up | Retailer's Mark-up | VAT | Total |
|---|---|---|---|---|---|
| Germany | 100 | 25 | 92 | 24 | 241 |
| Switzerland | 100 | 21 | 99 | none | 220 |
| France | 100 | 12 | 56 | 34 | 202 |
| United Kingdom | 100 | 18 | 59 | 14 | 191 |
| Italy | 100 | 10 | 38 | 9 | 157 |

Source: Member country data.

# International Competition and Price-Cutting Pressures

Comparative-advantage concepts indicate that developing nations with their lower labor costs are likely to have an advantage in world competition in labor-intensive products. Such advantages also arise when foreign companies gain a technological advantage or obtain higher productivity. The resultant lower prices allowed can give the foreign firm a toehold in the market. For example, a Russian-made Belarus 85-horsepower tractor sells for about $15,000, compared to about $30,000 for a comparable John Deere machine. Raw-material costs are subsidized in the Russian factory, and Soviet labor is about $2.25 an hour. The machines are simple, of older design. While the Deere tractor is "quiet, smooth-shifting, with a short turning radius, a steering wheel that responds to one finger and pushbutton four-wheel drive," the Belarus is "loud, smoky and cantankerous." The tractors are shipped from Russia, unloaded, inspected, and repainted orange, with English-language instruction decals. The marketing is price-based, with ads in local farm papers such as *Focus on Farming* and *Country Folks*. The ads say: "Get a new $30,000 to $40,000 tractor and pay only $13,900 for it."[4]

Regardless of the source of comparative advantage, the end result is that foreign firms may have lower prices. The dilemma then facing the domestic (U.S) firm is whether it should respond by also cutting prices. Suppose a U.S. manufacturer of machine tools bids on an order. The salesman calls the purchasing agent to check on the status of the bid and is told that a Japanese company has submitted a lower bid, and the American firm must cut its prices by a certain amount to get the order. But the salesman's boss is adamant that company policy is not to compete on prices, and that the salesman must convey other advantages of the American firm, such as its position as long-term supplier to the client, its greater experience, its location closer to the client, its reputation for better service and so forth.[5]

The problem here is in judging how the role of price as an attribute of the product has changed. That is, as the technology inherent in a product is diffused, there are fewer differences in the product itself as between the U.S. firm and its foreign competitors. As the product becomes less differentiated, price-cutting is more likely. Then, if the foreign firms can also match the U.S. firm on other attributes of the product such as service, quality, and delivery terms, price becomes more influential in the decision to buy.

To generalize, U.S. firms must constantly monitor the prices charged by their foreign competitors and understand the reasons why foreign firm prices are lower. Are the price cuts of a temporary nature, designed to aid in initial market penetration? Or do they represent the net cost advantage enjoyed by the foreign competitors? In other words, price-cutting is the symptom. The correct response to such price cuts requires understanding the cause.

## Price Pressure and the Need to Cut Costs

If the U.S. firm must lower its prices, it will be able to do so only after cutting its costs—either by redesigning the product to cut component and direct labor costs or by moving manufacturing overseas to a location with lower labor costs. However, this last, and seemingly obvious, choice can backfire on the company. Quality may be lower, and delivery may be delayed. The cost savings on the labor side may be eaten up by the need to maintain larger U.S. inventories; otherwise, the company may lose sales because its inventory is inadequate to meet orders on a timely basis. Manufacturing in a distant overseas location also makes it harder to respond to changing client needs.

Consider the garment industry, where low labor costs have led many U.S. firms to manufacture clothes in plants in the Far East. But designs must be sent over to Far Eastern plants in the spring for clothes meant to be sold in the fall in the United States. Then, in September, when the company finds out that certain designs are selling well, it is too late to attempt to increase production, and potential sales are lost. Similarly, if some items are poor sellers, the company is stuck with excess inventory that must be sold off through sales at price discounts; the reduced profits caused by such discounting offset the gains from manufacturing overseas with lower labor costs.

A halfway house between using overseas manufacturing and staying at home is the development of *maquiladora plants,* which are set up along the Mexican border by U.S. firms using Mexican labor that averages less than one dollar an hour. These workers perform assembly operations on parts and components imported from the United States; tariffs are paid when the completed product is brought back into the United States, but only on the value added by Mexican labor in Mexico. Such factories allow U.S. firms to become more competitive with imports from low-wage countries in the Far East.

The idea that prices must be set in relation to foreign competition applies to all products, whether they are consumer goods or industrial products such as machine tools. How Jaguar prices its cars is an illustration of this concept. Traditionally, Jaguar has always priced its cars in relation to Cadillac prices.

As Mike Dale, senior vice-president of marketing, explains it, "Cadillac has always been Jaguar's major source of growth." The goal was to let the Cadillac owner take his two-year-old car and $23,000 and step into a Jaguar. Thus, in 1986, the Jaguar was priced at $12,610 over a Cadillac. But as the dollar weakened in subsequent years, the price differential increased to almost $20,000. Jaguar had to cut prices so as to bring the price differential back to about $12,000. It achieved this by introducing a modified 1990 model version of the Jaguar XJ6 priced at $37,900, as compared to a 1989 model price of $44,000. To get such a price reduction, it had to redesign the car. Price had become even more important with the introduction of two new Japanese luxury cars, the Nissan Infiniti and the Toyota Lexus both priced between $35,000 and $40,000.[6]

High domestic prices relative to world market prices invite foreign competition. An interesting example of this issue is Japan. At a 135-yen exchange rate to the dollar, nearly all goods and services are more expensive in Japan than in the United States: housing, office space, cab fares, cars, VCRs, food and beverages, shoes, and so on. A survey by Japan's Economic Planning Agency for a broad sample of 306 goods and services showed Tokyo prices to be between 26 and 48 percent higher than in New York.[7] This price disparity may be due to the Japanese deliberately charging higher prices at home, and it may also be partly due to the less efficient Japanese distribution system. But Japanese consumers seem less sensitive to prices, showing loyalty to high-quality products, especially if they are of Japanese origin.[8]

Clearly, the complex distribution system acts as a barrier to foreign competition. Despite this, Japanese consumers are beginning to pay attention to the lure of lower prices. This is particularly true of low-priced electronic product imports from South Korea, Taiwan, and Hong Kong. Such imported products are simpler, with fewer features, and are attractively priced. For example, in 1987, 1.8 million compact cameras were imported into Japan, a 50 percent increase over the previous year. They cost half as much as Japanese products. Similarly, in 1987 imports of VCRs were nine times as high as the year before, and sixteen times as many color television sets were imported. One of the hardest hit industries was the electric fan industry, with 2 million imported units out of a total market of 3.8 million units. Imported fans were selling at 7,000 to 8,000 yen, compared to prices on Japanese fans of around 20,000 yen. Even Japan is not immune to overseas competition. The major conclusion to draw is that the Japanese market presents an opportunity due to its domestic high prices.[9]

## Pricing Implications of International Manufacturing Decisions

Switching manufacturing locations to take advantage of lower labor costs or other factor costs is a long-run solution. It is costly and irreversible, but it is becoming increasingly common. Bosch G.m.b.H. is the world leader in automotive electronics, with over 50 percent world market share in fuel injectors and anti-skid brakes. But two-thirds of its output is manufactured

**Table 15–3**      **Cost Structure of Irons Manufactured at Various Locations**

| | Unit Cost | Materials | Labor | Mfg. Overhead | Number of Parts | Number of Screws Needed |
|---|---|---|---|---|---|---|
| Sunbeam (Old Model) | 9.5 | 4.32 | 1.06 | 4.12 | 73 | 13 |
| Sunbeam (Redesigned Model) | 6.66 | 4.10 | .48 | 2.08 | 68 | 13 |
| Black & Decker (Singapore) | 5.98[a] | 3.40 | .53 | 1.25 | 74 | 19 |
| Sunbeam (Global Model) | 5.33 | 3.40 | .35 | 1.58 | 52 | 3 |

[a]Includes .80/unit of transportation costs.

Source: M. Therese Flaherty, "Emerging Global Business Environment and Managerial Reaction to It," Paper COF-8, presented at the Ministry of International Trade and Industry Conference, Tokyo, 1988.

in West Germany, where wages are high and unions strong. Hence, in April 1989 Bosch selected Wales as the site for a new 320-million-mark factory. Car-manufacturing capacity will exceed demand worldwide in the 1990s, which means that price competition will be strong, and cost-efficiency will be rewarded.[10]

As noted earlier, price-setting is partly determined by the company's cost structure. In competing in global markets, the firm must contend with the cost structure of its international competitors. Factor endowments and factor prices affect the cost structure of all companies, so an international competitor with lower-cost labor or capital can have a comparative advantage because its overall total costs are lowered to whatever extent its labor and capital costs affect its total cost of production.

However, while low-cost labor is an important factor affecting total costs, so are technology, the experience curve, and the capital intensity of manufacturing. As lower-cost direct labor is substituted for by technology and capital equipment, therefore, the paradoxical situation emerges that the country with the lowest-cost labor does not necessarily have the lowest total costs of production. A case in point is the example of the global iron.[11] Table 15–3 gives the statistics, which show how innovative manufacturing can overcome higher labor costs.

**Product Redesign and Pricing Implications**

Table 15–3 compares cost structure for irons manufactured by different companies in various locations. The irons are (1) Sunbeam's traditional product, the old iron; (2) a redesigned iron; (3) the Black & Decker iron, designed to be manufactured in Singapore; and (4) Sunbeam's latest product, the "global" iron, designed to be manufactured at low cost and sold around the world.

Sunbeam's old iron had an enormous cost disadvantage based on both the design (using more materials) as well as the higher labor costs and manufacturing overhead. Black & Decker's approach was to manufacture an iron in Singapore using almost the same design (the high number of parts needed and assembly operations indicated by the number of screws needed), but with lower-cost materials, overhead savings, and lower-cost labor. The unit cost advantage seems insurmountable. But Sunbeam was able to respond to the competitive challenge with a strategy that included

- Redesign of the product to lessen the number of parts and assembly operations needed, thus reducing the use of direct labor.
- Reduction in the cost of materials.
- Reduction in the cost of direct labor, although overhead is higher than in the case of Black & Decker in Singapore, reflecting the more capital-intensive nature of the manufacturing process used.

Overall, the table underlines the importance of cost structure in competing in product areas that are mature and subject to global competition where low-cost labor is significant. In such circumstances, pricing strategy becomes relevant only after the cost disadvantage can be overcome, which means paying attention to reducing labor cost, manufacturing overhead, materials cost, and redesigning the product so that it can be manufactured at a lower cost. Pricing strategy thus becomes closely linked to the firm's overall manufacturing strategy.

Switching manufacturing locations is therefore not the only way to cut costs. Product redesign and more capital-intensive manufacturing are also options. Baldor Electric, a manufacturer of industrial electric motors, faced severe competition from Taiwan, South Korea, and Japan, but was unwilling to move to an overseas low-wage location. It feared that quality of its product would go down, and that a weakening dollar would diminish the gains from manufacturing overseas. Hence, Baldor tripled its rate of capital investment, using an adaptation of just-in-time manufacturing. Each worker assembles a complete motor from the full set of parts on a tray, with a computer printout giving him or her information on the motor and how to assemble and test it. Four of five workers attended in-house quality control seminars. The capital spending, new manufacturing methods, and focus on quality all helped Baldor innovate and stay in business while continuing to manufacture in the United States.[12]

Remember, *pricing problems are symptoms*. In the short run, price-cutting and adjustment might be the answer to them, but over the longer term, solutions lie in analyzing their causes. As shown, exchange rates may be the initial cause of pricing problems, but a fundamental solution to these problems will require comparing the firm's cost structure with that of the competition and then taking actions to reduce or nullify the effects of a cost disadvantage.

## Gray Markets

An additional pricing problem in international marketing is the incentive that the consumer price differential between countries creates to shop for a given product in a country with lower prices. For example, it has become common for planeloads of Japanese tourists to take weekend shopping trips to Taiwan and Hong Kong to buy goods such as consumer electronics, perfumes, and clothes to take advantage of price differentials.

In international marketing, where a product may be manufactured in more than one location, currency fluctuations can make *gray marketing* profitable. Gray marketing is the unauthorized import and sale of products intended for one market in another, higher-priced market. When the dollar was appreciating in the early 1980s, it was profitable for dealers to bring in unauthorized imports of Caterpillar tractors from Europe because of the weak European currency. In such cases, even after shipping and tariffs, the landed cost in the United States of such imported Caterpillar tractors was less than the price charged for U.S.–made Caterpillar tractors.[13]

The major problem with gray marketing is that established distributors lose motivation to sell the product as they see their margins eroded by low-overhead gray marketers. (Consider, for example, the mail-order PC resellers, whose main expense is telemarketing.) Meanwhile, the gray marketer is primarily interested in quick immediate sales and short-run profits. Over time, the manufacturer could lose markets, as the gray marketer competes only on price and will drive away customers who seek after-sales service and other forms of support. This issue is particularly serious for industrial products. On the other hand, gray markets provide an outlet for excess production and, indeed, allow a firm to gain economies of scale by deliberately increasing production, some of which will go into the gray market. And where product life cycles are short, gray markets allow a firm to gain market share and not be stuck with obsolete inventories.

Ultimately, gray marketing arises because of unsustainable price differences between two markets. When a perfume manufacturer charges U.S. wholesale prices that are 25 percent higher than similar prices in Europe, it is not surprising that some of the product sold to European wholesalers leaks into the United States. And such importing is legal under U.S. law. Companies must carefully examine their pricing policies in different markets and attempt to maintain a price differential. Otherwise, gray marketing is merely an efficient market response to ill-thought-out attempts to charge higher prices in certain markets.

## Strategies for Foreign-Market Pricing

We will review pricing strategies that follow from the preceding discussion. First, in dealing with *costs* in a foreign market, international marketers have options not available to national firms. They may control costs through a choice of supply sources with differing production costs, tariffs, and transportation charges. They may further affect costs by changing the firm's level of involvement in a market. Changing from exports to some form of local production will change not only tariff and transportation charges but production costs as well.

In dealing with *inflation,* a replacement cost formula was suggested along with careful cost accounting, escalator clauses in contracts, and a shortening of credit terms. Changing the input mix should also be considered, because not all the firm's inputs will have the same rate of inflation. If the firm can use inputs with lower than average inflation rates, it will have an advantage in its pricing. Changing the product mix is another possible approach, because not all of the firm's products are equally buffeted by inflation or price controls. In India, for example, multinational drug companies expanded into areas of the pharmaceutical business, where price controls were less stringent. In Mexico, under price controls, appliance manufacturers were offered very attractive prices if they would concentrate production on a limited number of basic models of eight kinds of appliances.

In facing *demand* in a market, the firm has less flexibility than in facing costs. The marketer must adapt the price to the local demand. Of course, demand occasionally can be influenced through promotional activities, or there may be a price-quality association concerning the firm's product, enabling it to sell above competitors' prices.

In regard to *competition,* the marketing firm must determine the appropriate relation between its own and competitors' prices. It may have some flexibility in meeting national competitors' pricing through the logistics arrangements possible in the international company. There should be economies of scale through multinational production sources and markets. Using nonprice competition may offer further pricing flexibility.

*Government* is a powerful constraint on pricing, but the firm does have some freedom. It can, of course, avoid those markets where government price controls are too rigid. If it is already in such markets, the extreme alternative is to withdraw, as the foreign-owned public utilities effectively did in South America. A more common and generally more desirable alternative is to cooperate with the government, presenting the company's arguments and working toward a compromise. Companies in Brazil provide an example. They finally gained some relief from stringent price controls by acting through their professional association, Abrifarma. The government was suspicious of drug company pricing and profits and was refusing requests for price increases. Abrifarma hired an independent firm (Price Waterhouse) to audit the pricing of 33 major drug firms. When this analysis was presented to government price controllers, they approved some drug price increases greater than the amount of inflation for the first time in four years.

**Pricing and the Marketing Mix.**  Although we have discussed pricing in partial isolation from the rest of the marketing mix, the kind of price a firm can have in any market will be connected with the rest of its marketing program. We provide the following illustration.

In the early and mid-1960s, the major oil companies in Britain saw discounters take 10 percent of the market by emphasizing lower prices. The major companies were slow to react till Esso finally took the lead. In 1967, Esso cut prices by as much as 6½ cents on an imperial gallon to meet the discounters head on. The visible and necessary price cut, however, was combined with, and made possible by, a complex series of moves. The following steps were among those which permitted a significant pricing change.

1.  Reduction in number of gasoline grades from four to three.
2.  A shuffling of octane ratings.
3.  Pulling out of marginal stations.
4.  Reduction of dealer margins by ½ cent a gallon.
5.  Dredging to allow supertankers to reach the Esso refinery at Frawley.

6.  Building of Britain's longest pipeline.
7.  Bargaining hard for new, lower freight rates.

Items 5 through 7 served to reduce costs of *physical distribution*. Items 1 and 2 represented *product changes*. Items 3 and 4 were changes in *distribution strategy*. All were necessary to permit a price cut that would not mean an equivalent loss of profits.

## Countertrade

Countertrade is a form of financing international trade wherein price-setting and financing are tied together in one transaction. It is essentially *barter,* the exchange of goods for goods, but with some flexibility. In barter, the exact item to be exchanged is specified, such as oil for machinery. In countertrade, a range of goods is specified that can be taken in exchange for exports from a Western supplier. For example, Catalyst Research of Maryland had begun selling specialized batteries for pacemakers to Tesla, the Czech electronics collective. In 1986 Tesla bought the rights to manufacture the pacemaker battery, with Catalyst selling the equipment, supplies, and raw materials needed. As part of the agreement, Catalyst Research started buying product inventions from the Czech Academy of Sciences to fulfill its countertrade obligations.

A typical transaction might be as follows: A Polish apple juice factory may need new equipment but be unable to buy from a U.S. supplier because no U.S. bank will lend it money. However, an Austrian bank is willing to guarantee its debt, hence the order goes to an Austrian manufacturer. The Austrian bank undertakes to buy a large portion of the apple juice produced for resale on Western markets. It is able to do this because most Austrian banks have their own in-house trading companies; Austria's proximity to the Eastern European countries has led to a concentration of countertrade expertise in Vienna. Through this convoluted chain, the Polish factory gets the equipment, the Austrian manufacturer an order, while the bank makes fees from the loan guarantee and commissions on sale of the apple juice.[14]

The role of countertrade in world trade is increasing, accounting for about 10 percent of all world trade in 1986. A U.S. International Trade Commission study showed that $7.1 billion of U.S. trade in 1984 was through countertrade, though 80 percent of such countertrade was for defense goods and armaments. Still, countertrade is becoming increasingly common in nonmilitary trade.[15]

Much of the growth in countertrade arises because of the domination of the Communist bloc economies by state trading. Such government monopolies use countertrade to make up for economic inefficiencies while using their ability to control access to their domestic markets as a way to convince Western suppliers to agree to countertrade.

There are several forms of countertrade:

1.  *Barter,* the simplest, is the direct exchange of goods for goods. It is cumbersome, since each party must have goods that the other party wants, in the exact quantities. It is the least attractive form of countertrade.

2.   *Counterpurchase* is reciprocal buying, to be fulfilled over some time period in the future, with flexibility as to the actual goods to be purchased. In such transactions, a majority of the purchase price is paid in cash. An example of this is the way in which Lurgi, a European construction and engineering firm, built a methanol plant for East Germany. In return for the 400 million DM contract to build the plant, Lurgi took back 408,000 tons a year of methanol, out of its total capacity of 800,000 tons. At the time the contract was signed, there was excess supply, which eased only gradually as older, environmentally unacceptable plants were closed in Western Europe. But Heinz Schimmelbusch, chairman of Metallgesellschaft A.G., sees such deals as the major growth path for his Lurgi subsidiary, since Eastern Europe is more willing to accept polluting plants if Western companies can solve their foreign exchange shortages.[16]

3.   *Offset* is similar to counterpurchase and is more likely at the government level. In dealing with government buyers, there is a generalized commitment to buy a certain percentage of the initial export transaction from the country. Thus, when Boeing sold AWACS to the British defense department, it agreed to buy 130 percent of the value of the transaction in British goods.

4.   *Buyback* occurs when capital equipment sales are sold with a counterpurchase clause that can be fulfilled by buying some of the output of the plant that is set up with the imported capital equipment.

5.   *Switch trading* involves a third party, usually a specialized trading house with expertise in certain industrial sectors and with certain countries, usually centrally planned economies. Austria and Switzerland are two sources of expertise, with several such switch trading firms located in these two countries.[17]

Countertrade involves forced sourcing, often from centrally planned economies and newly industrializing nations. Such sources of product may not have advanced technology and high-quality products. By default, then, countertrade forces the exporter to develop a strategic purchasing policy towards countertrade opportunities.

Before the firm begins countertrade, it should scout firms in the targeted country to decide whether reliable suppliers (of raw materials or components) can be developed. Before deciding to enter into countertrade, the firm should be willing to help upgrade the manufacturing capability of potential suppliers, so that the countertrade opportunity results in obtaining useful raw materials and components at reasonable prices; otherwise, the firm is likely to be stuck with poor-quality goods that are difficult to trade.

Countertrade, then, should be viewed as the initiation of a long-term relationship with a country and its firms. This in turn will satisfy the needs of the countries that resort to countertrade. Typically, such developing nations use countertrade because

1.   They lack foreign exchange.
2.   Just as important, they want multinationals as partners, who will help sell their goods overseas.

**Figure 15-1**                    **Countertrade Implementation**

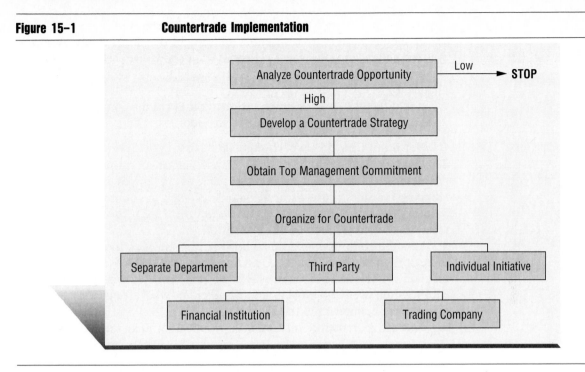

3.  They hope that successful technology transfer will take place as multinationals work with domestic firms to transform them into reliable suppliers of quality raw materials and components.
4.  All of which, they hope, will increase domestic employment, incomes and lead to economic development.

    In order to be successful in countertrade, a company must develop a strategic plan to implement it. Figure 15-1 outlines the major steps in implementing countertrade. They are

1.  Ensure that the benefits outweigh the costs of carrying out countertrade.
2.  Develop a countertrade strategy, including the development of foreign countertrade suppliers.
3.  Get top management support by explaining to them the task involved and why countertrade will benefit the company.
4.  Develop an organization structure for countertrade; this will include deciding whether to rely on outside help or to keep the entire effort in-house. Outside help is particularly useful when goods obtained in countertrade are not needed by the exporting firm.

Separate contracts for the sale of goods and for the receipt of goods in countertrade can help make the operation successful. The contract should specify the quality and the nature of goods to be received in countertrade; and it should clarify any restrictions that might be sought on the resale of Western goods, and into what territories such goods may be resold. Penalty clauses and bank guarantees may be necessary to protect against noncompliance.[18]

It is difficult to ascertain the ultimate profit from a countertrade transaction. The relevant payment streams include

1.  Net profit from the export of goods.
2.  Plus/minus the profit or loss on disposition of goods received in countertrade; in the case of commodities such as oil, prices can fall rapidly, reducing the sales proceeds of the goods received in countertrade.
3.  Less the imputed interest on the capital tied up in inventory of goods received in countertrade until disposed of.
4.  Less the commissions paid to third parties, such as trading companies to help in disposing of goods received in countertrade. A World Bank study on countertrade deals in Indonesia found that about 85 percent of the total commissions went to brokers and middlemen who arranged the various steps in the countertrade transaction.[19]
5.  Less the incremental marketing expenses associated with countertrade.

The above factors help determine the short-term profit associated with a countertrade transaction. Generally, this will be lower than a straightforward market-based transaction, reflecting the second-best and inefficient nature of the countertrade approach. However, countertrade does have a strategic aspect—as a long-term source of materials and components and as a way of breaking into new markets. Hence, the opportunity costs of a countertrade transaction can be viewed as a strategic investment in gaining long-term market position. Countertrade as an isolated transaction makes little business sense.

## Leasing in International Markets

Leasing—an alternative to outright purchase—is an important pricing-financing-marketing device for expensive equipment. Offering competitive leasing terms can be crucial to winning orders in international markets.

For example, GPA Group Ltd., an aircraft leasing firm, placed a $16.8 billion order in 1989 for over 300 jet aircraft, one of the largest orders ever. Its order accounted for 10 percent of all aircraft to be built through 1995. Leased aircraft accounted for about 14 percent of all aircraft world-wide in 1989, compared to 6 percent in 1985. Leased aircraft will account for about 20 percent of the world aircraft fleet by 1991.[20] In 1988, 24 percent of McDonnell Douglas sales was to leasing firms. Jet aircraft are expensive, at about $35 million for a modern Airbus A320, and climbing up to $125 million for a long-range Boeing 747. Given their high capital cost, leased aircraft appeal to small startup airlines and to large carriers. In both cases, precious capital can be conserved for other areas, such as ground support, acquisition of aircraft gates, and building up of a worldwide airline reservation system.

In effect, airlines are deciding that it is not necessary to own an aircraft in order to provide an airline service. But the separation of ownership of aircraft from the airlines that operate them raises questions. Will an adequate inventory of spares be kept? And will the lessee provide the same quality of maintenance service to leased aircraft? If leased planes are quickly available, will there be enough time for training of flight crew? Aircraft manufacturers have traditionally relied on the airlines to give them information about their needs and market trends, which are used in designing new aircraft. If manufacturers cannot get direct market information from the airlines deciding on the correct passenger capacity and flying range for a new model aircraft may be more difficult. Also, the emergence of a few large buyers such as GPA, ILFC (International Lease Finance Corporation) and Ansett, who then lease the purchased aircraft, means that we have an oligopoly on the buy side. Such clout can help drive down prices and reduce margins for aircraft manufacturers.

As can be seen from the aircraft example, leasing is most likely with expensive capital equipment and undercapitalized purchasers in an environment where credit is tight. But leasing can also be seen as an opportunity. It is less risky to the purchaser, and firms can use this lessened risk to convince would-be buyers to try new equipment. In new markets, leasing can be the avenue to obtaining the first few sales, thus providing an installed base. Then subsequent sales prospects can be referred to these initial lease sales, from whom they can get data on machine performance. In industrial selling, demonstrations of equipment in a practical real-life environment can be a powerful motivator to closing a sale.

Leasing can also help cope with downturns in an economy, when corporations might find it easier to take on moderate-sized lease payments, whereas obtaining approval of large capital investments might not be possible. A number of such leases also lead to a predictable and recurring revenue stream in the form of lease payments. Another advantage to the lessee is the better maintenance available under the lease contract. In countries with shortages of trained service personnel, service facilities, and spare parts, such a maintenance service can be important. Finally, when product life cycles are short, customers may be unwilling to purchase high-priced equipment that might become obsolete. Leasing allows the sale to be made, with the manufacturer sharing a portion of the risk from obsolescence.

A complicating factor in international leases is the currency in which the lease is denominated. If local currency leases are allowed, issues such as the expected pace of local inflation and expected future devaluations are relevant. Clauses allowing for adjustment to such anticipated or expected inflation and devaluation are a must. Also the company must obtain the necessary permissions to ensure conversion into a foreign (hard) currency, and repatriation of the lease payments to the parent company headquarters, if desired. Again, competitive behavior should be a reference point. If competition does not press the local government to allow repatriation, and instead permits lease payments in local currency to be accumulated in the economy for latter local investment, then the company may have no choice but to do the same thing. Then long-run strategic intent becomes important: Why are we in this particular country market? Why are we permitting leasing in this market? And what are our long-range strategic market share goals for this market? Needless to say, short-term leasing objectives should fit into the overall long-term market strategy.

## Coordinating Pricing in International Marketing

The final pricing question is the degree to which the international marketer must coordinate prices in different markets. For most marketing functions, the firm faces the issue of international standardization versus local adaptation. The same issue arises in pricing.

**Final Consumer Prices**

We noted that the international firm faces a different supply and demand situation in each market. This indicates different optimum prices for each country. If the firm has national subsidiaries operating as profit centers, this also suggests the use of national rather than international prices. Profit-center operation would lead to different subsidiaries having different prices.

In addition to the situation of the individual firm, there are external factors causing price variations between markets. For example, the EC is called a common market, but studies have shown repeatedly that there is no common market in pricing. Even with tariffs eliminated and value-added taxes subtracted, there remain great disparities in the prices of widely traded goods. These disparities arise from variations in competition, distribution efficiency, and national tastes, as well as manufacturers' pricing policies.

The food sector in Germany and Italy illustrates differences in distribution efficiency. Eighty-five percent of German retailers are cooperatively organized versus 10 percent in Italy. Germany has 350 inhabitants per food store—Italy 105. Germany has a self-service food store for every 700 citizens—Italy one for every 68,000. Not surprisingly, the highest food prices of all EC countries are to be found in Italy. In automobiles, Britain is a high-cost market. A Jaguar XJ6 costs about $8,000 more in Britain than in Belgium. A major reason is the difference in the dealer margins, 30 percent in Britain versus 10 percent in Belgium.

Where consumer prices on a product vary significantly, consumers may undertake some price arbitrage on their own by resorting to the gray market.

Where the markets can be kept separate, differential pricing is usually successful. Where the markets cannot be kept separate, it may not be successful. It is frequently employed in Western European countries but is often unsuccessful there because of the growing integration of these markets in the EC. An example of how firms can run into trouble trying to have different prices in differing EC countries is provided by Kawasaki. Prices on its motorbikes varied by from $500 to $1,300 in different EC markets, with the United Kingdom market being the cheapest. Kawasaki enforced these differences by a contract with its dealers prohibiting them from exporting.

When a Belgian consumer tried to buy a bike in Britain to take back to Belgium, the dealer refused to sell. The consumer complained to the EC, which found this practice illegal and fined Kawasaki, $130,000.

The difficulty of maintaining uniform consumer prices in different markets does not mean that pricing *strategies* cannot be consistent. A company can maintain a uniform policy of pricing at the market level, above it, or below it. Even though final consumer prices differ, the firm can be consistent in being at the same particular part of the price spectrum in each country.

## Control Techniques

Apart from external pressures toward or away from uniform international prices, the firm itself must play a conscious role. To obtain optimum performance, some central coordination is necessary. Various methods are available to control pricing in international operations. Consumer prices are least susceptible to control, except where the firm has *direct distribution* to consumers. Singer, Avon, and Tupperware are examples in this category, as well as many firms selling to the industrial market. Similarly, the firm has greater control over pricing where it has its own *sales subsidiary* than where it sells through distributors.

Few countries allow *resale price maintenance* as a form of control. Where this is not available, the firm is concerned both about distributors that price too high—and limit the market—and those that price too low—and cause an erosion of prices and margins. Use of *recommended, listed, or advertised prices* may help to restrain distributors' pricing independence. Use of *consignment selling* is an effective, though costly, way to control prices. Extension of *credit* to the buyer may be another way of maintaining greater control over prices. In general, anything that ties the seller to the producer gives the producer some control.

## Subsidiary Pricing of Exports

Where subsidiaries are profit centers, they need reasonable pricing freedom on sales within their own market. In this case, the annual budget and product margin agreed upon by parent and subsidiary may provide sufficient control. Where several subsidiaries *export* the same product, central control over export prices is needed to avoid suboptimization. If each subsidiary tries to maximize its own sales and profits, the total company may suffer as the subsidiaries compete against each other.

Coordination of export prices is essential when the firm has different production sources for a product. In the absence of coordination, each subsidiary producing the good would set its own price, and buyers would choose the plant offering the lowest delivered cost. The result would be that buyers would determine the logistics of the producing company, that is, which plant would be the supplier. This may result in suboptimization. To avoid this, firms sometimes set uniform f.o.b. plant prices on exports for each producing subsidiary. The customer still chooses the source offering the lowest delivered cost, but the parent firm has greater control. The subsidiary also has an incentive to reduce costs because with a fixed export price, any cost reduction is added to its profits.

Another way of controlling export prices is to require all exports to be handled through one export organization, regardless of source or destination. This is occasionally applied to licensee and joint venture exports, as well as to wholly owned operations. Such an organization may be located in Switzerland or Panama, but also in New York City or Midland, Michigan (as with Dow Chemical Company). The centralized export operation can set prices and determine logistics to get the most efficient source, lowest landed cost, and greatest total company profit. Such a centralized operation can offer economies of scale in logistics administration and optimization of global supply and demand.

## Summary

Inflation is a major influence on prices within a foreign market. Rapid inflation, coupled with government controls on price increases, erodes profits and is a major problem.

International competition creates worldwide pressure to cut prices. Firms must rethink the role of price as a product attribute. Alternatives to matching price cuts are competing with differentiated products and relying on a technological or marketing edge.

If competitive price cuts must be matched, firms need to cut their costs of production. A common solution is to shift production to low-cost overseas locations. Such cost reductions may be achieved, however, at the expense of new problems with quality and timely delivery.

Price differentials between country markets lead to arbitrage attempts. Gray marketing, the unauthorized import of cheaper goods from other foreign markets, can create problems with distributor channels and affect product image.

Product redesign is another avenue to providing customer value and cutting costs without necessarily competing with cheap labor manufacturing solutions.

Countertrade is a form of pricing, since the sale is tied to accepting other goods in exchange. It is rapidly growing in importance and should be viewed as an opportunity to nurture a long-term source of quality raw materials and components.

International leasing is an alternative to outright sale and is important in the international capital goods market. Firms must be able to offer leasing alternatives as part of their international pricing policies to compete effectively in such cases.

Finally, careful coordination is necessary to manage the conflicting demands of export pricing, foreign-market pricing, and global pricing policies to respond to competition.

## Questions

15.1 How can the level of inflation affect the setting of prices in different country markets?

15.2 How should a firm cope with government price controls in foreign markets?

15.3  Why might international competition force a firm to consider price cuts? What are other alternatives open to a firm facing such price pressures in international markets?

15.4  What are the advantages and disadvantages of moving production offshore to a low-cost production site?

15.5  What is gray marketing? How does it affect international marketing and price setting?

15.6  How is product redesign relevant to international pricing?

15.7  What is countertrade? Why should firms be willing to consider countertrade arrangements in their international marketing efforts?

15.8  Why do countries seek countertrade? How can the firm assess the profitability of a proposed countertrade transaction?

15.9  How should a firm organize itself to deal in countertrade?

15.10  How does international leasing form part of the global pricing decision?

15.11  What are some organizational issues relevant to international pricing?

## Endnotes

[1] Donald J. Lecraw, "Pricing Strategies of Transnational Corporations," *Asia Pacific Journal of Management* (January 1984): 112–119.

[2] Ibid., 117.

[3] "Price Control Strategies," *Business Latin America,* September 12, 1988.

[4] "It Was a Matter of Economics," *Forbes,* February 22, 1988.

[5] Mary Karr, "The Case of the Pricing Predicament," *Harvard Business Review* (March–April 1988).

[6] See "Jaguar Is Taking the Aggressive Tack to Claw Its Way Out of Sales Sag," *The Wall Street Journal,* September 12, 1989; and "Jaguar Has a New Pride of Cats on the Prowl for Cadillac, Lexus," *The Boston Globe,* September 17, 1989.

[7] Charles Wolf, "The Weaknesses Amid Japan's Economic Strengths," *The Wall Street Journal,* May 19, 1989.

[8] Robert Weigand, "So You Think Our Retailing Laws Are Tough," *The Wall Street Journal,* September 13, 1989.

[9] Takahiro Takesue, "Cheap Imports That Signal a Quiet Revolution," *Journal of Japanese Trade and Industry* (July–August 1988).

[10] "A Booming Bosch Frets About the Future," *The Wall Street Journal,* April 19, 1989.

[11] M. Therese Flaherty, "Emerging Global Business Environment and Managerial Reaction to It," Paper COF-8, presented at the Ministry of International Trade and Industry Conference, Tokyo, 1988.

[12] "Baldor's Success: Made in the U.S.A.," *Fortune,* July 17, 1989.

[13] F. V. Cespedes, E. Raymond Corey, and V. Kasturi Rangan, "Gray Markets: Causes and Cures," *Harvard Business Review* (July–August 1988).

[14] Stephen S. Cohen with John Zysman, "Countertrade, Offsets, Barter and Buybacks," *California Management Review* 28, no. 2 (Winter 1986): 43.

[15] Joseph R. Carter and James Gagne, "The Dos and Don'ts of International Countertrade," *Sloan Management Review* (Spring 1988).

[16] George Melloan, "Countertrade Suits Metallgesellschaft Fine," *The Wall Street Journal,* August 2, 1988.

[17] Countertrade has become sufficiently important that De-Bard, a Swiss company operating in Britain, has published *The Oxford International Countertrade Directory,* listing participants in the business worldwide.

[18] Sarkis Khoury, "Countertrade: Forms, Motives, Pitfalls and Negotiation Requisites," *Journal of Business Research* 12 (1984).

[19] "Too Much Barter is Bad for You," *The Economist,* May 9, 1987.

[20] "GPA Group Becomes Leader in Plane Leasing," *The Wall Street Journal,* May 1, 1989.

## Further Readings

Carter, Joseph R., and James Gagne. "The Dos and Don'ts of International Countertrade." *Sloan Management Review* (Spring 1988).

Cespedes, V., E. Raymond Corey and V. Kasturi Rangan. "Gray Markets: Causes and Cures." *Harvard Business Review* (July–August 1988).

Cohen, Stephen S., with John Zysman. "Countertrade, Offsets, Barter and Buybacks." *California Management Review* 28, no. 2 (Winter 1986): 43.

Khoury, Sarkis. "Countertrade: Forms, Motives, Pitfalls, and Negotiation Requisites." *Journal of Business Research* 12 (1984).

Rabino, Samuel, and Kirit Shah. "Countertrade and Penetration of LDC's Markets." *Columbia Journal of World Business* (Winter 1987).

CHAPTER 16

# International Marketing of Services

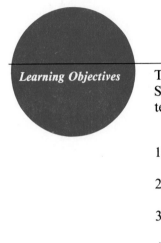

*Learning Objectives*   Trade in services is growing faster than the international trade in goods. Services have special characteristics that pose special problems in international marketing.

The main goals of this chapter are to

1. Identify the characteristics that distinguish services from goods and influence the way they are marketed internationally.
2. Determine the basis of comparative advantage in service industries.
3. Define the roles played by governments and GATT in the service trade.
4. Discuss the following industry examples:
   • Media and entertainment.
   • Airlines.
   • Professional services.
   • Retailing.
   • Hotel industry.
   • Financial services.

What are services? Industries such as wholesaling and retailing, communications, transportation, utilities, banking and insurance, tourism, and business and personal services are all service industries. Services account for the largest portion of output and employment in the advanced industrialized countries. If we exclude the government sector (which is also considered a service "industry"), services were 53 percent of GDP (gross domestic product) over the period 1980–1984 in the United States, 47 percent in Japan, 41 percent in West Germany, and 42 percent each in Canada and Britain.[1] Services typically become more important as an economy becomes more developed. Thus, U.S. employment in service industries was 24 percent of total employment in 1870, 31 percent in 1900, 55 percent in 1950, and 72 percent in 1985.[2] Similar increases were recorded in Japan, in Germany, in France, and in Britain. The service industry as a whole has been increasing

**Table 16–1**

### Services in the U.S. Economy, 1985 Percentage Share in Total Employment and Output by Selected Service Sectors

|                                         | Employment | Output |
|-----------------------------------------|:----------:|:------:|
| All Services                            | 71.9%      | 67.6%  |
| Transportation                          | 3.1        | 3.5    |
| Communications                          | 1.2        | 2.6    |
| Utilities                               | 0.9        | 2.9    |
| Wholesale Trade                         | 5.6        | 7.4    |
| Retail Trade                            | 15.5       | 9.5    |
| Finance, Insurance, and Real Estate     | 6.2        | 14.6   |
| Government                              | 16.3       | 11.1   |
| Other Services, comprising:             | 23.2       | 15.0   |
| Personal Services                       | 1.5        | .6     |
| Business Services                       | 4.5        | 3.3    |
| Auto Repair                             | 1.1        | .8     |
| Health                                  | 6.0        | 4.3    |
| Legal                                   | .9         | 1.0    |
| Misc. Professional                      | 1.6        | 1.5    |
| Other                                   | 7.7        | 3.3    |

Source: Mack Ott, "The Growing Share of Services in the U.S. Economy—Degeneration or Evolution," *Federal Reserve Bank of St. Louis Review* (June–July 1987): 7, 9.

in importance for almost a century in the advanced industrialized nations. Table 16–1 provides a summary of the role of services in the U.S. economy in 1985.

Given the importance of services in the national economies, it is not surprising that they are becoming increasingly important in world trade. Trade in services accounts for between 20 to 25 percent of all world trade, having grown at about 16 percent a year for the past decade, as against a 7 percent growth rate for merchandise trade.

In Table 16–2, note that all of the ten major exporters of services are developed nations. This is in keeping with our observation that services play an increasingly important role in advanced economies, thus giving them a comparative advantage in world markets. In 1987 South Korea was the developing country with the highest level of services exports, at $8 billion, making it the fifteenth largest exporter of services. Services exports in total were about $500 billion in 1987.

However, a growing proportion of services is being provided within a nation by foreign companies through the vehicles of foreign direct investment, franchising, and joint ventures. Hence, the $500 billion estimate for services exports worldwide underestimates the total size of the international market for services.[3] U.S. services that have been exported successfully include

**Table 16–2**                 **The Top Ten Exporters of Services, 1984 and 1987**

|  | Billions of Dollars | |
| --- | --- | --- |
|  | 1984 | 1987 |
| United States | $45.4 | $56 |
| France | 39.2 | 53 |
| United Kingdom | 28.9 | 43 |
| West Germany | 26.9 | 41 |
| Italy | 19.4 | 33 |
| Japan | 24.6 | 28 |
| Netherlands | 18.3 | 23 |
| Spain | 14.0 | 22 |
| Belgium/Luxembourg | 11.9 | 19 |
| Austria | 9.1 | 15 |

Source: *IMF; Balance of Payments Statistics;* and *The Economist,* September 30, 1989.

- Construction, design and engineering services.
- Banking and financial services.
- Insurance services.
- Legal and accounting services.
- Computer software and data services.
- Training and education.
- Entertainment, music, film and sports.
- Management consulting.
- Franchising.
- Hotel and lodging services.
- Transportation services, including airline and maritime services, and both passenger and cargo.

As can be seen from this list, the United States exports a wide variety of services. It is interesting to note the major service sectors within the United States that are not represented in the list. For example, Table 16–1 shows the utility sector, auto repair services and personal services (laundry, barber shops, home-cleaning services) in the service sector. Yet these are not well represented in U.S. service exports. In the next section, we review some service industry characteristics that make international trade difficult.

## Services: How Are They Different from Products?

Services have been defined as "those fruits of economic activity which you cannot drop on your toe: banking to butchery, acting to accountancy."[4] Indeed, services are mostly intangible. The distinguishing characteristics of services include intangibility, heterogeneity, perishability, and, often, simultaneous production and consumption.[5] Because of these characteristics, services are more difficult to price and measure than products.

## Global Marketing
### McDonald's in Hungary

McDonald's began operations in Budapest, Hungary, on April 30, 1988. On its first day of operation, it broke a McDonald's record for the most transactions. Today it is one of the busiest McDonald's in the world, with 9,000 transactions daily.

Plans to establish a McDonald's in Hungary began with a joint-venture agreement in November 1986, although negotiations began back in 1985. McDonald's is a 50 percent owner, its partner being Hungary's Babolna Agricultural Cooperative.

McDonald's supplied all of the restaurant equipment, including equipment to establish sources of supply such as a bakery to make hamburger buns. McDonald's also contributed something intangible: a standard of quality for the fast-food industry. It had to develop a supplier infrastructure by introducing new food-processing techniques and forcing development of new products in Hungary, as well as insisting on the improvement of existing products to meet world standards of quality. Products such as hamburger buns, the kind of cheese used in its cheeseburgers, and orange-juice concentrate were unavailable in Hungary. While ketchup was available, it did not meet McDonald's quality standards. It took over a year to develop supply sources. McDonald's experts in purchasing and quality control then worked with suppliers on a monthly basis to get the desired product and quality.

Locally produced food products are used, except for McCormick spices, which are used exclusively by McDonald's around the world, and sesame seeds, which cannot be grown in Hungary. Paper products such as paper cups are imported.

McDonald's opened with 7 partially trained managers and with another 20 employees loaned from stores in other countries. Most of the loaned employees returned home after a month, with the exception of an American manager who stayed on as an adviser and trainer. New employees did have training, but little experience, and had to learn on the job in the middle of huge crowds. During the first few days, there was always a line outside the store. Some of the training focused on inculcating attitudes of customer service. In a country of shortages where people are accustomed to waiting, customer service was to some degree an unfamiliar concept. Also, McDonald's found it impossible to get part-time help, which it relies on in most countries. However, with a successful opening behind it, McDonald's plans to open another five outlets in the next five years in Budapest. Real estate is difficult to buy at any price, so the company must build its restaurants in existing buildings. As yet, McDonald's has not chosen franchisees, but plans to do so for perhaps three of the proposed five restaurants.

Source: Joint Ventures in Hungary, *CW Informatika Ltd.* (Budapest) 2, no. 1 (1989): 9–10.

---

**Intangibility**

Services are often performances, as in performing an audit, designing a building, fixing a car. In this sense they are *intangible*. Questions pertinent to the international marketing of services would include (1) whether actions are being performed on people (e.g., education) or things (e.g., air freight),[6] (2) whether the customer needed to be physically present during the service or only at initiation and termination of the service, and (3) whether it is enough that the customer be mentally present—that is, can the service be performed at a distance?

**Heterogeneity**

Different customers going to the same service company may not receive exactly the same service. This quality of *heterogeneity* occurs because different people perform the service. It is therefore impossible to make sure that the service is performed in exactly the same way each time. One sales clerk may be less polite or amiable than another, resulting in consumer dissatisfaction. The implication of heterogeneity is that *quality is difficult to control.*

A logical response is to attempt to standardize the service. One way is to develop a detailed blueprint of the steps in providing the service and then analyze results as these steps are taken to ensure that quality standards are maintained. This may mean changing the way the service is performed so as to reduce complexity and the possibilities for divergence among different service providers.[7] But it is exceedingly difficult to standardize services where the personnel providing them must exercise a high degree of judgment. Where a firm's advantage is based on customizing the service, any attempt at standardization means that the fundamental strategy of the business is being changed.

When extending the service to international markets, there is also the question whether the service standardized for one national market will satisfy customers in other markets. For example, one way to standardize a service is to personalize the interaction between customer and service provider by training retail salespersons to greet customers by name and use certain standard conversational gambits. When such "scripts" are to be followed,[8] though, cultural factors will likely demand a somewhat different "script" for each country market.

Also, it is possible that the training of customer-contact personnel should be conducted differently in different cultures. For example, the two-week training given to Kentucky Fried Chicken workers in Japan would be uneconomical in the context of high labor turnover in the United States; but it is appropriate for Japan, given the greater job loyalty among workers and, more important, Japanese customers' expectations of high levels of politeness and courtesy from Japanese service workers.

## Perishability

Services are *perishable* in that they cannot be inventoried, saved, or stored; thus, a plane seat that is not sold when the flight takes off is lost forever. This makes it harder to adjust the supply of a service to fluctuating demand, especially at times of peak demand. Service companies therefore seek innovations that allow the service to be "inventoried" in some fashion, or that allow demand to be managed so that the supply of services is adequate and can be economically provided. An example would be providing a restricted number of reduced-fare, advance-purchase seats on flights, with the number of such seats being increased if seats on the flight do not appear to be selling as forecasted.

Marketing services internationally makes the task of forecasting demand for services more complex, since the vagaries of individual national markets will affect demand in unique ways. Further, service must match demand in many different markets. It is likely that idle capacity will exist in some markets while excess demand is encountered in other markets.

**Simultaneous Production and Consumption**

In services, production and consumption of the service often take place at the same time; that is, the producer and the seller of the service are often the same person. Moreover, the customer must often be present for the service to take place. Unlike products, services usually cannot be exported, so international marketing means that the service must be performed by the firm itself in the country market, whether through franchising, licensing, a direct investment, or an acquisition. The fundamental question is, can the service be performed at a distance? And if not, how should the firm position itself in a distant market in order to offer the service?

**Pricing Services**

Services are difficult to price, because it is difficult to calculate the cost of producing them.[9] Price can be set in relation to full costs, or based on what competition charges, or simply be set at whatever the customer is willing to pay. Service businesses have a high fixed-cost ratio. Hence, if the service can be offered without much modification in many national markets, prices can be lower, since the fixed costs have presumably been recovered in the home market. Some advantages of scale therefore accrue to the company that is first to market with a new service. For example, in the case of a banking innovation such as a credit card, American firms have already recovered much of their fixed costs of developing the credit-card concept through sales in the U.S. market. Hence, their foreign credit-card service prices can be lower, since they do not have to incur the fixed costs of product development a second time.

**Measuring Services Quality**

Service quality is difficult to measure, since it is often unclear what the consumer expects, yet quality is a matter of meeting customer expectations. In other words, it depends on consumer perception, which in turn is determined by the following:[10]

1. Person doing the service.
2. Technical outcome of the service.
3. Overall image of the company whose employee is carrying out the service.

Technical quality may be amenable to traditional quality-control approaches borrowed from a manufacturing setting, but only if the service process is standardized. If corporate image affects the perception of quality, the firm must decide if the same corporate image is needed in all countries. Should all employees wear the same uniforms? Should the physical facilities look the same in all national markets?

Consumer dissatisfaction may arise from unrealistic expectations. Other reasons for the gap between desired quality and perceived quality include not understanding what consumers expect in a service, inability or unwillingness to meet customer expectations, problems with service delivery, and communications gaps where the firm fails to communicate realistic expectations about what service quality will be offered.[11]

**Importance of Customer Loyalty to Services**

Since services cannot be stored, a basic marketing strategy is to ensure repeat business by generating loyalty in existing customers. Devices such as frequent-flyer plans may be used to reward customer loyalty. But given that consumers have different characteristics in different countries, are such plans necessary for all national markets, or should they be shaped mainly by competitive variations in each market? Loyalty can also be maintained and rewarded through pricing, and the question for each national market is whether volume discounts and membership strategies work equally well in all markets.

## Additional Decision Areas in International Services Marketing

**Advertising**

How are services best advertised? By word-of-mouth, direct mail, satisfied customer referrals, or ads in newspapers and television? Are there national differences in the relative appeal of these different forms of advertising of services? These questions will have to be answered for each country market.

**Organization**

A decentralized organization seems more apt for service industries given the inherent heterogeneity of the product and the customer base. But if a firm moves to standardize the service performance, can it do so without considerable centralization? This is a key decision for the firm that chooses to market its services internationally.

**Cultural Variables**

Since services generally involve close interaction between the service provider and the customer, cultural variables affect user satisfaction; they also affect product design and the nature of interaction with the customer. An interesting illustration involves a book-contract signing in Russia.

Little, Brown, a U.S. publishing house, wanted to obtain the rights to Anatoli Ryabakov's *Children of the Arbat,* a novel about life in Stalinist Russia. As is the norm in Russia, Little, Brown had to negotiate with the state-owned copyright agency, VAAP, represented by a team of eight officials, two translators, and the author. Settling on the amount of advance was easy, but royalties created some difficulties. U.S. royalties are tied to the mode of selling; thus, they may be lower on discounted sales to book clubs, direct-mail sales, and to large wholesalers. But VAAP would accept a reduction only for paperback and book-club sales. VAAP also wanted to have the right of approval over the translation, book jacket, flap copy, and promotional material.

VAAP also wanted a clause that the publisher would do no harm to "VAAP, the author, or the book." When Roger Donald of Little, Brown responded to this demand by discussing the acceptable amount of monetary damages, VAAP countered that this was not the meaning of injury to reputation. When Mr. Donald asked how the clause was enforceable without a monetary provision, he was told that this would be based on honorable behavior. The difficulty was solved by inserting a clause vowing never to inflict "intentional harm." And when at the end of successful negotiations, Mr. Donald invited the VAAP team to a fancy dinner, he found that they all spoke English.[12]

## Comparative Advantage and the Service Industries

Why do the advanced industrialized nations dominate services exports? What factors lead to a nation and its firms having a comparative advantage in services? Clearly, each service industry is distinct, with a different production function; that is, each service industry uses technology, labor, capital, and management in different proportions to deliver the service. Still, we can examine the role that factors of production play in service industries.

**Labor**

Service industries are generally labor-intensive, with both highly skilled and unskilled labor being used. In services such as retailing, barber shops, and florists, labor may not need much training and is likely to be low-paid. In such cases, countries with low labor costs would have an advantage. At the other extreme are legal and accounting services that require highly educated and highly paid personnel such as lawyers and accountants. It is likely that advanced countries would have an advantage in such services. However, such high-level skills may be country-specific, and not easily transferable to other countries. Expertise in U.S. tax law may not be meaningful to tax practice in Europe; however, the *methodologies* used by American law firms to research and argue tax issues may be pertinent to tax law practice in advanced nations.

**Capital**

Traditionally, services have low capital-to-labor ratios. Lower amounts of capital are used per worker than in manufacturing industries. Service productivity has been lower than in manufacturing, and the future growth of service industries will require larger amounts of capital per worker to raise productivity and quality. In banking, for example, greater use of computers results in more productive workers, faster transactions, and more satisfied customers. If this trend continues, countries and firms with lower costs of capital will gain an advantage in international markets.

**Technology**

Services vary in their use of technology (although it is an increasingly pervasive influence in all industries). Services such as airlines and shipping, custom computer software, and banking can be termed high-technology services compared to, say, interior decorating, which uses less sophisticated technology.

A case in point is the use of ISDN (Integrated Services Digital Network) networks by a French maintenance company to provide maintenance services at a distance. ISDN networks integrate voice, data, and graphic images in communication networks, allowing pictures to be sent with text and numbers. *Service SA* has developed a Service Expert System to provide technical assistance to dealers for the maintenance of compact disc (CD) players sold to customers throughout France under terms of a customer warranty.[13]

Service staff affiliated with dealers needed help in repairing the CD players, and a previously established interactive computer network handled only data. A videotape would have had to be shipped to handle visual images. But with the new Service Expert System, pictures are stored with reference numbers as part of the maintenance manual. Then, as the mechanics need help, they can call up both the relevant portions of the manual and the pictures by a call to the central database maintained by Service SA. This allows Service SA to update both the manual and the pictures at will.

The major saving is the reduction in the direct labor cost of the repair, since diagnostic time is cut in half. Also, not only is the latest information sent quickly to dealers, but statistical information on product defects and repairs is fed back to quality control at the factory. This immediate feedback of problems and repairs enhances the manufacturer's ability to redesign the product.

Clearly, the capital investment in R&D that allowed the creation of this technology application led to a comparative advantage for the company—and for the country, since it can use the technology to enter the global maintenance industry in a new fashion, bypassing former barriers.

**Transfer of Information, Technology, Capital, and People**

Very important in the export of services is a global communications network. In essence, such trans-border data flows have created a whole new category of industries, enabling previously nontradable goods to enter international trade. The provision of custom software programming services by *teleports* is an example of this phenomenon. Companies such as Hewlett-Packard and Texas Instruments have set up software development labs in India using Indian programmers, who provide maintenance and upgrading of mainframe software from India to the parent company and other clients in the United States by means of remote terminals and computers and telecommunications links.

Of course, services need not be provided solely through information transfer. Foreign direct investment involves the transfer of capital and ideas, often technology through which the service is provided. The Service Expert System described earlier is one example of the role of technology in deriving competitive advantage in services. Another is the use of laser scanners and bar codes, with which checkout at grocery stores and other retail outlets is speeded up. Going a step further, companies such as Information Resources have developed proprietary databases of the information gleaned from laser scanning the entire sales volume of a store. This data is analyzed and sold to companies seeking more information about their consumers. As such companies begin selling such services outside the United States, they must first ensure that the technology of bar codes and laser scanning is available in that country, as well as the computer software used to analyze the raw data and prepare reports.

Thus, for services to be provided overseas, there must also be a transfer of information (or other intangible assets), technology, capital, and people—the service providers who interact with customers.[14]

**Other Bases for Comparative Advantage**

Other bases for comparative advantage include (1) management skills specific to service industries, (2) size, (3) experience in a particular service sector, and (4) the firm's global reputation. Thus, U.S. firms have been able to dominate the world software industry because of their long experience and skilled management developed through years of being in business. Specific skills that U.S. firms have developed include transforming custom software into packages that have the widest customer-base appeal; supervising the development of complicated software within large teams of programmers; and marketing software to an end-user base that is technologically unsophisticated through indirect channels of distribution such as computer industry retailers and department stores.[15]

In short, services can be more or less capital-intensive and technology-intensive, along with greater or lesser reliance on skilled labor. Advanced nations such as the United States and France are likely to have a comparative advantage in the more capital-intensive, skilled labor–intensive, and technology-intensive service industry sectors.

## Government Intervention in the Trade in Services

As is true for goods, international trade in services is also subject to government interference and protection. U.S. manufacturers in a survey noted several government barriers:[16]

- Rights of establishment (meaning the right to establish a branch or subsidiary in a foreign country; for example, many nations ban ownership of television stations by foreigners).
- Trade barriers, including limitations on the proportion of a market that can be served by a foreign company, and discriminatory taxation of services provided by a foreign company.
- Foreign exchange controls; limits on remitting profits from service businesses.
- Government procurement barriers, where government buys services only from "national" companies.
- Technical issues that may serve to keep out foreign firms, such as through the use of standards and certification conditions.
- Government subsidies, countervailing duties, and high customs valuation of foreign services, leading to higher total tariffs.
- Licensing regulations that impose unreasonable terms of entry or insist on licensing as the only mode of entry.
- Restrictions on professional qualifications, including ban on entry of qualified service company personnel.
- Tolerance of commercial counterfeiting.

Further, U.S. managers of service industries indicated that while the key reasons for the success of other countries' service firms in world markets were factors such as experience, technology expertise, and superior quality, some of their success was also attributable to lower price, government support, preferential financing, political or regional bias, and U.S. government restrictions (particularly in reference to selling to Comecon countries).

Telecommunications is an industry where government intervention is particularly important. U.S. deregulation and the breakup of the AT&T Bell system has created many opportunities for foreign firms to participate in the U.S. market for telecommunications services. A major growth segment is VANs (value-added networks), where private firms provide services and information over public telecommunication networks. An example would be an on-line credit-reporting and credit-verification service for credit-card customers. The problem here is that European and Japanese markets have been slower to deregulate, creating inequality of opportunity for American firms.[17]

**Fair Trade in Services: The Uruguay Round**

As services grow in importance in world trade, nations have begun seeking a consensus on fair trade practices with regard to services. The latest round of GATT talks, the "Uruguay" round, has given special attention to protecting *intellectual property rights,* referring to the ideas that form the basis for many high-technology services, such as custom software. Such a protocol might address the issues of barriers to trade in services, national treatment of foreign firms, allowance of FDI in services without undue restrictions, temporary admission of foreign-service workers, international agreement on the extent of regulation of international data flows and ownership rights in international databases, and the importation of materials and equipment necessary for provision of services. Other thorny issues are the need for a framework to control restrictive licensing practices, and the right of "non-establishment," which is growing increasingly important as service firms deliver their service electronically or through the mail without being physically present in a country. This governs the conditions under which a foreign firm can be said to have established a presence in a foreign market, which may determine whether the foreign firm qualifies for treatment as a domestic firm; similarly, establishing a domestic presence is often necessary to qualify for protection under the laws of intellectual property rights in that country.[18]

The U.S. government does offer some specialized help to service industries. Within the Department of Commerce, an Office of Service Industries has divisions covering specific industry sectors such as the information industries, transportation and tourism, and finance and management.

In the remainder of this chapter, we examine the global marketing of a variety of service industry sectors.

## Global Media and Entertainment Industry

Entertainment has always been one of the United States' largest exports. In 1988 the United States earned $5.5 billion in entertainment industry exports, second only to its aerospace industry.[19] The private-enterprise system governing U.S. television and the burgeoning of alternative channels, first on pay-TV, then on cable television, and now satellite television, has led to fierce competition. Each station seeks larger audiences so as to sell more commercials and charge higher prices for commercial time; this means showing the programs that attract the largest audiences. Over time, U.S. firms have become very adept in producing such mass audience – pleasing programs. This is their comparative advantage in world markets.

Deregulation of U.S. television, the large U.S. population, the large number of available programming hours, and the multiplicity of TV channels and theaters all combine to make it worthwhile for U.S. companies to invest additional resources in TV and film production since the potential audience for any hit program is enormous. These investments also become a comparative advantage, as the U.S. industry enjoys economies of scale arising from a multiplicity of "customers," both in the number of TV channels and movie theaters, and in the large English-speaking audience.

**European Media Environment**

In sharp contrast to the United States, European television was at one time largely government-controlled. Basically, government ownership of stations meant noncommercial television except for rare and restricted instances. In West Germany, for example, television advertising was restricted to 40 minutes a day; in Switzerland, 20 minutes a day.

Deregulation of European television has changed the competitive environment. The use of new technologies (satellite broadcasting, cable and pay-TV) has increased the number of channels. For example, in Japan, after 1990, 24-hour satellite TV broadcasting will increase the number of channels available from 7 to 12 or 13.

Now that there are more TV stations in Europe and Japan, and more air time to fill, there will be a greater demand for TV programming. Also, deregulated TV stations and channels will show more commercials, so there will be more advertising by firms seeking a European market. This, in turn, means more business for advertising agencies and their suppliers. The market for exports from U.S. producers of films and TV shows will grow; and, in response, government attempts at protection are likely, to stay the onslaught of American companies and allow the emergence of a "European" TV industry.

Such changes broaden the scope of the media industry, which now encompasses broadcasting and production of TV and motion picture films, while also including books and newspapers, printing services, and alternative modes of information delivery such as the creation and sale of proprietary databases. Information and entertainment can be delivered in so many ways: by record and cassette, by television and movie theater, in book form, and as data that can be down-loaded from on-line databases.

All over Europe, commercial interests are attempting to gain a share of the new TV stations. One estimate is that Europe will require about 300,000 hours of new programming in 1990. But in 1987 an hour of "Dallas," the popular American TV show, could be licensed for a fee of $32,000, as compared to the $400,000 cost of producing one episode of the "Chateuvallon" series on France's A2 station. By 1989 the rights to an American TV movie could be purchased for about $70,000, as against an estimate of $1 million to produce an original French production.[20] As TV channels proliferate in Japan and Europe, the competition for American films and TV programs pushes their price up.

Technology has played a key role in changing the nature of the industry. The Europeans are creating new TV channels by using high-power *direct-broadcast satellite* (DBS) systems that can beam programs from satellites directly into the home via a small (18-inch) backyard dish receiver. In England, British Satellite Broadcasting received the British franchise. West Germany and France have similar satellite systems, with four channels each. And Luxembourg has launched Astra, a medium-power system with sixteen channels. The obstacle to the spread of this form of TV is that households must buy the small dish receivers. If they are unwilling to do so, traditional terrestrial TV stations will take the lion's share of the European TV market. The other problem is that satellite TV is an alternative to cable, and if it does not win market share quickly, homes that become wired with cable will be less interested in satellite TV. However, satellite TV has been successful in Japan, with almost half a million dishes being sold within a year of launch of NHK's first two noncommercial TV channels via satellite.[21]

## Satellite TV and a Pan-European Audience

Satellite TV promises the possibility of creating a pan-European cross-cultural audience. The satellite channels create overlapping signals. Britain's satellite channel signals can be picked up in Ireland, Belgium, Holland, and large parts of France. France's TF-1 will reach to Spain, central Europe, and nearly all of Italy and the United Kingdom; while Germany's TV Sat will cover all of central Europe, half of France, nearly all of Italy, the eastern United Kingdom, and southern Norway and Sweden. Sweden and Ireland also have similar plans. (The hidden benefit of these cross-national TV channels is that their programming can escape government regulation. Governments can regulate the content of only those programs whose signals emanate from within their own countries' borders.[22])

What decisions are involved in reaching a pan-European audience? First, the firm must try to predict which programs are likely to appeal to viewers from different European countries. Second, it must determine the appropriate forms of advertising for those viewers. For example, Coke sponsors the Coca-Cola Eurochart Top 100 show on the Sky channel using images and tunes calculated to be effective with a young audience all over Europe.

Companies must also develop one brand name to push in their pan-European commercials. Thus, Unilever cannot easily advertise its cleaning fluid branded as Vif in Switzerland, Viss in Germany, Jif in the United Kingdom and Greece, and Cif in France. And nationalistic country managers must be persuaded to use standardized brand names and advertising channels.

Before the advent of television deregulation in Europe, European companies spent about $5 billion a year on advertising, compared to the U.S. level of nearly $20 billion with a quarter less population.[23] Obviously, European companies must advertise more heavily if they wish to compete effectively with their Japanese and U.S. counterparts. Philips of the Netherlands aims to do so: It ran the same ad in 44 countries reminding listeners and viewers of its sponsorship of the 1986 World Cup soccer tournament. Its sign on the fence surrounding the playing field was seen for 38 minutes of a 60-minute game watched by an estimated 500 million people.

Cable TV is not as widespread in Europe as in the United States and may never become as strong because of competition from DBS (satellite) television. One of the more successful cable TV stations in Europe is MTV Europe, itself a joint venture of American and European partners. Understanding why MTV has been successful is the key to understanding the potentials and pitfalls of a pan-European television network. So let's examine its history.

MTV President Tom Freston has said, "Music crosses borders very easily, and the lingua franca of rock n' roll is English. Rock is an Anglo-American form; German rock bands sing in English; Swedish rock bands sing in English." Not surprisingly, MTV is now available in 24 countries. It is particularly interested in Europe because of the proliferation of TV channels there. MTV's mission? "We want to be the global rock n' roll village where we can talk to youth worldwide." MTV Europe, in a joint venture with Mirror Newspapers and British Telecom, is a 24-hour-a-day, 7-day-a-week service. In Japan it is restricted to a few hours in the early morning. But its goal is to establish a "brand name" against the day when more TV air time on newer channels will be available in Japan.

*The key to cross-national TV networks is language.* People seeking entertainment are not likely to choose a foreign-language show. In contrast to MTV's success, SuperChannel, an English-based satellite and cable station, lost nearly $100 million in two years for this reason. It then changed ownership and format, emphasizing sporting events, where language is less important.

As *The Economist* puts it, entertainment in a foreign language is seldom "light." The Germans were glad to watch Sky and SuperChannel for a while, until the two German satellite stations RTL Plus and SAT1 were available. Rock-music videos on MTV succeed mainly because language is irrelevant. But even here, cultural preferences are important: Teenagers in different countries may prefer different kinds of rock music.[24] To overcome the language problem, cross-national TV channels must focus on special-interest programs, such as sports, business news, and first-run movies.

An interesting response to the need for home-grown "European" programs is the decision to produce a pan-European soap opera, "Monte Carlo," by the New York–based EC Television subsidiary of the Interpub advertising agency. The plan is to produce 260 episodes a year in English, to be dubbed later in French, German, Italian, and Spanish. The estimated cost of production of $40 million is almost completely bankrolled by TV stations in the four largest European markets: Granada in England, TF1 in France, Berlusconi in Italy and Studio Hamburg in West Germany. Furthermore, many of the TV stations will pay for the show by bartering air time, which the agency will then sell to clients desiring time on these stations. The growing demand in Europe for programs (285,000 hours a year in 1989) is not only fostering a European TV production industry, but is also providing a diversification opportunity for advertising agencies who can presumably offer some people-pleasing skills.[25]

## Entertainment Industry Economics

The media industry has some significant cost-structure characteristics that interact with the environmental changes discussed thus far to create the need for new global strategies.[26]

First, this is an industry with a high fixed-cost structure. Most costs are incurred in the production of programs and in the establishment of the distribution system, that is, the TV network, be it via satellite, on-air, cable, or pay channels. These high fixed costs place a premium on obtaining a large subscriber base, and create high leverage, with handsome profits occurring once breakeven levels are reached.

The media industry is also cyclical, at least in the United States, with sudden jumps in revenue being derived from hit films, TV programs, books, and records. Thus, the industry has a high level of risk, and requires abundant capital to survive long periods of negative cash flow. In turn, this creates a bias within the industry to control distribution channels, that is, media outlets, be it book publishers, TV channels, or record clubs.

The maturation of the U.S. market has brought lower growth rates and an abundant supply of TV channels as compared to markets in Europe or Japan and the Far East, where fewer channels are available and growth rates are higher since market saturation is low. This situation, together with the cyclical nature of the industry and its high fixed costs, results in a bias toward larger companies and produces a strategic advantage for those able to control distribution channels as well as produce programs for them. That is, companies that own both TV stations and TV film production companies tend to enjoy higher profits, less risk, and faster rates of growth.

## Global Mergers in the Media Industry

A conjunction of environmental change and industry characteristics has led to the globalization of the media industry, with a concentration of acquisitions by foreign companies of major U.S. media companies. Table 16–3 summarizes some of the major acquisitions that have taken place since 1988 in the media industry.

As the table shows, the bulk of activity has been concentrated in the United States. There are several reasons for this U.S. focus:

1.  The United States has had long experience in developing films and TV programs, and Hollywood and U.S. productions have enjoyed worldwide success. Owning these facilities would deliver a stream of films and TV programs, books, records and magazines to be then marketed around the world.
2.  The U.S. market is huge, offering high potential profits. It is also a lead market, so programs successful here can be easily sold to Europe.
3.  U.S. film and TV production technology is to be desired, as well as the talent and experience of U.S.–based film and TV production crews. Rather than try to transport talent to European markets, companies may prefer to acquire it through acquiring a U.S. company.

**Table 16–3**                    **Global Media Empire Building: Acquisitions Since 1988**

| Acquirer | Acquisitions Made |
| --- | --- |
| Sony Corp. | CBS Records, Columbia Pictures, and Gubers-Peters Productions. |
| Time-Warner | Merger combining books and magazines, pay and cable TV, film production, records, and movies. |
| Bertelsmann | RCA Records, Bantam books, and Doubleday books. |
| News Corp. | Twentieth Century Fox films and several TV stations: the Fox network, Sky TV in Europe, *TV Guide,* and *Premiere* magazine. |
| Hachette | Diamandis (magazines) and Grolier (encyclopedias). |
| Maxwell | Macmillan Publishing, Official Airline Guide. |
| Cap Cities | Through ESPN, 40 percent ownership of Japan Sports Channel, 25 percent of British-based pan-European cable network, Screensport. |
| U.S. West | Joint-venture cable TV franchise for all of Hong Kong and cable TV properties in the United Kingdom and France. |
| Television South Plc | MTM (Mary Tyler Moore) Productions. |

The best example of this globalization phenomenon is News Corp., controlled by Australian entrepreneur Rupert Murdoch. He first expanded from Australia to the United Kingdom, primarily in TV and newspapers. He built up Sky Channel as a pan-European service using both cable and satellite delivery; next, he developed a U.S. base, buying several independent TV stations and the Twentieth Century Fox film production company, along with its library of films, as the nucleus for creating a fourth U.S.–wide, on-air TV network. The network would distribute (i.e., show) films produced by Twentieth Century Fox, and the same material could appear in England and Europe on Sky Channel. Then he acquired *TV Guide* and created *Premiere* magazine, both vehicles to appeal to the U.S. national TV audience and further publicize his network. Murdoch's News Corp. is an example of the implementation of a globalization strategy in a global services industry. The principal points of his strategy include a physical presence in two major markets, Europe and the United States, and combining of both distribution channels, the TV stations and channels themselves, together with production facilities and "software" (the actual programs) in the form of a backlist of films and TV programs to be continually resold.

The same trend affects other segments of the media industry, such as the news segment and cable television. For example, Cable News Network (CNN), which is an all-news format now, sells condensed versions of its news production to 83 countries (in 1989).[27] The news is somewhat customized, including local weather and some local news. It is available in hotel rooms around the world through cable feed by satellites. As CNN goes global, it needs to internationalize its product by supplying more international news, and it is therefore opening more international news bureaus, 18 in total by the end of 1989.

**Cable TV**

Cable TV is another area where major U.S. companies are looking for growth overseas, although foreign government regulations limit its profitability. In many countries, cable TV is viewed as a public utility and controlled by a utility company. In others, cable fees are set by the government. Still, the U.S. cable companies' greater experience gives them an edge in countries where regulation has not reduced cable's attractiveness. The real issue is competition in the form of satellite DBS systems that can be picked up with dish antennas. Nevertheless, as Table 16–3 shows, U.S. West, one of the Baby Bell companies, is willing to invest $500 million in building an advanced cable network in Hong Kong that would handle fax, videotext, and TV.[28]

**Sports**

Sports is an area of the entertainment industry that is rapidly becoming globalized, principally because of the media industry itself. ESPN, for example, took on a 40 percent share in Japan Sports Channel, in a joint venture with C. Itoh corporation, the Japanese trading company. It plans to derive additional revenues from overseas by broadcasting American sports for which it has already obtained rights, such as National Football League games. At the same time, it hopes to get rights to foreign sporting events and show them to U.S. viewers as well as worldwide.

It is interesting to consider how the U.S. sports industry itself has been changed by the globalization of the media industry. A sporting event would generally be considered a nontradable good, perishable and evanescent, yet TV media have made it commonplace for sporting events to be seen around the world, so now the sports industry has begun to reason, why not move players and the game itself to overseas locations?

In soccer, it has been customary for the world's best players to play for teams in other countries depending on who pays the highest amounts. Thus, Brazilian and Argentinian soccer stars routinely play for high salaries in Italy, Spain, and Germany. But it was a bit of a surprise for the NBA (the U.S. National Basketball Association) when Danny Ferry, a first-round draft pick, signed to play with an Italian team, Messagero Roma; so did Brian Shaw, a second-year player originally with the Boston Celtics. Basketball is Italy's number two spectator sport, after soccer, and over 50 countries regularly broadcast NBA games. The NBA projects foreign revenues to grow at 30 percent a year, and sales of all U.S. sports programming overseas are estimated to reach 50 percent of total U.S. revenues by 1992. Stars such as Michael Jordan are known around the world, so Nike uses Jordan endorsements to sell sneakers not just in the United States, but in Germany, Greece, Japan, and elsewhere.[29]

It is appropriate, then, that the National Football League plans a new spring league with American-style football teams located in Europe as well as in the United States; there will be 12 teams in the league, of which 6 will be based in London, Frankfurt, Barcelona, Milan, Montreal, and Mexico City. The NFL's decision was based on the fact that the large number of new TV channels in Europe would need something to fill the hours, and previous exhibition games played in Europe attracted as many as 70,000 fans. There is some question as to whether the league should wait till the 1990 soccer World Cup ends, and there will be some adaptation issues to be resolved since Europeans are used to soccer games lasting about two hours on TV as opposed to the usual three-hour format of American football.[30]

## Music

The music industry is also rapidly becoming global; the worldwide popularity of rock and roll owes much to MTV. Bertelsmann, a music conglomerate, has tried to sell pop music around the world, acquiring RCA records, because it saw the U.S. music industry as the primary source of innovation in the international music business. Upon acquiring RCA, this German company, Bertelsmann, moved its music division headquarters to New York. Michael Dornemann, its CEO, follows a policy of "breaking" an artist into a country's market by launching the act on TV and on stage, and through publicity in newspapers and magazines. Only then will he begin to bring in records and tapes. In effect, he designs a separate marketing program for each artist for each country.[31]

## European Trade Barriers in Entertainment

However, even while foreign companies buy United States companies and get market share as well as production capabilities, there is alarm in Europe over the domination of TV channels and air waves by United States product and, by extension, United States culture. As European governments respond to the opportunity they have created for new television programming, they have begun to favor home-grown shows. Smaller countries fear that their culture will be overrun by programs from countries with large internal markets such as the United States; the French fear that English will become even more accepted as a world language. In May 1989 the European Community adopted a directive requiring that a majority of the shows on European television be European "where practicable." The French consider television to be Europe's cultural cement and see the issue as one of cultural imperialism.[32] But the effect of possible quotas and subsidies for production in Europe is that United States production companies, such as MTV Europe, which produces a non-MTV series youth program in London called "Buzz," will now set up shop in Europe.[33]

## Future Outlook for Globalization of Media and Entertainment Industry

In sum, the globalization of the media industry, together with the proliferation of TV channels and other media overseas, presents enormous and growing markets for U.S.–made entertainment, sports, and news programming. The opportunities are there for U.S. firms to reap profits from their comparative advantage in this industry. So far, foreign companies have been aggressive in obtaining ownership in U.S. media properties, however, U.S. firms have been more lackadaisical about overseas opportunities.

## International Airline Industry

What does international marketing in the airline business consist of? Mainly, offering air transportation services on foreign routes. However, foreign governments have traditionally regulated access to domestic routes by

**Table 16–4**                  **Growth of Airline Passenger Traffic by Region (Percent Growth Rate)**

|           | North America | East Asia/ Pacific | Europe | Latin America | Middle East | Africa |
|-----------|---------------|--------------------|--------|---------------|-------------|--------|
| 1976–1986 | 7.3           | 9.5                | 6.5    | 8.1           | 11.5        | 8.0    |
| 1986–1996 | 5.1           | 6.8                | 5.8    | 6.4           | 5.0         | 5.5    |
| 1996–2006 | 4.6           | 6.5                | 5.5    | 6.3           | 5.4         | 5.5    |

foreign competitors. They have also regulated the right of foreign airlines to offer service to their own international passengers. Such traffic rights have generally been subject to bilateral negotiation between governments.

Governments have also regulated the fares charged, the routes airlines may fly, and which airlines will be allowed to compete in the market. In many countries, there are one or two dominant airlines, either owned by the government, or having quasi-public status; such "flagship" carriers are given preference in allocation of new routes, finances, and fare increases. Examples of such flagships are Lufthansa, Air France, Japan Air Lines, Royal Jordanian, and Air India. Thus, if a U.S. airline wishes to compete for foreign passenger traffic, it has had to wait for the U.S. government to negotiate a bilateral agreement.

Deregulation of the U.S. airline industry facilitated entry by foreign airlines and led many to seek a portion of U.S. air traffic, such as through SAS acquiring a stake in Continental Airlines, and a joint-marketing agreement between British Airways and United Airlines. In the latter agreement, each airline agreed to use the other airline for ongoing service on complementary routes and to list each other's flights in the *computer reservation system,* which is the heart of competitive advantage in the industry (airlines that own such systems can more easily fill seats on a flight).

The major industry trend is faster growth outside the United States. In such a regulated industry, the dilemma for U.S. airlines is how to obtain and increase market share in these fast-growing overseas markets, when host governments seek to favor their domestic flagship carriers.

Table 16–4 summarizes global airline traffic growth trends. Note that though the North American market is growing, it will register the lowest estimated rates of growth over the next 15 years, while the Asia/Pacific region will have some of the highest growth rates. Hence, airlines around the world will be seeking route authority to permit them to fly passengers on Pacific routes and will seek government help so that greater competition is introduced. Of course, factors such as airspace congestion and airport-capacity limitations also hinder efforts at route expansion by airlines.[34] Yet, government regulation will not disappear overnight. U.S. and other airlines must therefore seek alliances with carriers from the Far East, while also requesting U.S. government help in obtaining fairer access to these burgeoning markets.

Air transportation also includes cargo traffic. The international express-delivery market was estimated at about $6.5 billion in 1988, with growth at 20 percent per year through the 1990s. And the top 15 companies together only accounted for about 50 percent of the total international market. An example of global thinking in this industry is Federal Express's acquisition of the Flying Tiger line in order to get access to its worldwide delivery route system built over 40 years. Tiger was the world's biggest heavy-cargo airline, flying from the west coast of the United States to all of the Far East and Australia, and from the east coast to Brazil and Argentina and Europe and the Persian Gulf. It plans to use the acquired routes to offer global delivery of small packages, its major strength.[35]

In response to competition from Federal Express, Japan Air Lines began negotiating with Lufthansa and Air France to establish an international airfreight company, integrating their ground cargo and aircargo systems. This combination would result in a company that carried 1.8 million tons of freight in 1988, as compared to the Federal Express/Tiger combination's volume of 2.6 million tons in 1988.[36] Further, the combined company would have global reach and be able to deliver a package to anywhere in the world.

Such joint ventures are the preferred path for the Soviet Union as it expands its presence in the international airline industry. Since Aeroflot flies fuel-guzzling Ilyushin aircraft, it has been using Shannon Airport in Ireland as a transit airport. Aeroflot imports fuel from Russia in tankers to the airport, with excess fuel being bartered as payment for landing fees, ground handling, and catering. In a joint venture with Aer Rianta, the Irish airport authority, Aeroflot opened hard currency duty-free shops, with Aer Rianta also managing duty-free sales on all international flights out of Moscow.[37] In a similar fashion, Aeroflot formed a joint venture with Marriott Corp. to provide in-flight catering. One goal is to improve the quality of in-flight catering and attract more international passengers in a competitive environment. Marriott will renovate the Moscow flight kitchen near the terminal, with an initial planned volume of 10,000 meals a day.[38]

## International Professional Services

Professional services such as accounting and management consulting, legal offices, advertising, and public relations are driven by growth among their business clients. Their international expansion is therefore driven by the overseas growth of their clients. As their clients open offices and factories and set up joint ventures abroad, they will demand legal help, advertising help, accounting help, and so forth. At the same time, as the foreign economies grow, and begin adopting professional management habits, they, too, will seek professional services with global networks. Again, the market growth will be higher and more attractive outside the United States. The question is, how to market overseas?

As an example, how does one export legal services? Jones, Day, Reavis & Pogue provides a model. Initially a regional law firm, it began by acquiring a New York law firm with a primarily international practice. Since then, it has opened offices in Geneva, Hong Kong, London, Paris, and Riyadh, with new offices opening in Tokyo and Brussels. The firm's "product" strategy is interesting: "We are an American firm using American methodology for solving legal problems." Foreign offices are staffed with U.S. citizens and

## Global Marketing

### Manpower in Japan

Manpower Japan was established by its U.S. parent, Manpower, in Japan in 1966. By 1988 it had grown to 26 offices throughout Japan with 12,000 part-time workers on its roster, 98 percent of whom were women. The company had 7,500 clients and ranked fifth in sales among 32 country subsidiaries, behind the U.S., British, Canadian, and French companies.

Anthony Finnerty, the man who convinced headquarters to set up this subsidiary, realized that the Japanese employment system forced large numbers of women clerical workers to quit when they married or when they became regarded as too old. A pool of temporary help personnel was thus available. The question was, would Japanese companies agree to use temporary help? Traditionally, Japanese companies had believed that everything should be done in-house. Hence, Manpower's initial clients were foreign companies who responded to ads in the English-language newspapers.

The first Japanese companies to take on temporary help were the *sogo shosha,* the trading companies, who needed temporary help until the recruitment drive in the spring of each year. Next came engineering companies, who had projects lasting three to four years and an unsteady revenue stream, so were reluctant to take on permanent help. With the 1973 oil crisis, however, demand dried up, as Japan went into an economic recession. But as the recession continued, many Japanese companies decided to reduce their permanent pool of workers; thus, the prejudice in favor of using only in-house workers began to disappear.

While Japanese companies gave on-the-job training to their own workers, they expected that personnel provided by Manpower would be able to perform their jobs right away. Hence, Manpower implemented a quality-control system consisting of two components: rigorous training in office automation and careful monitoring and grading of workers based on their performance. Manpower used its parent company's training program with modifications to ensure that workers received training in both English-language and Japanese-language word processors. The training was free at the Tokyo head office, with remuneration going up as additional technical skills were learned. Manpower also gathered data on how the workers did on their assignments and on the working environment at client firms. This computerized database connects all Manpower offices in Japan and helps the company match workers to assignments.

About a third of Manpower's temporary help are between the ages of 25 and 29, and 87 percent are under 40. Most have worked previously in offices for between three to six years and choose to work for Manpower so that they can choose their working days.

Source: Toshio Iwasaki, "Manpower: Talents in Reserve," *Journal of Japanese Trade and Industry,* September–October 1988.

---

foreign nationals with long U.S. education and experience. For example, the company does not attempt to practice Japanese law for Japanese clients, since local firms could do this more effectively. Instead, its goal is to provide a world view, helping Japanese clients in Europe, and U.S. and European clients in Japan. A key aid is an in-house computerized communication system to allow the lawyers in the firm almost instantaneous contact with one another around the world.

## International Retailing

Retailing, one of the major sectors of any economy, typically requires contact between retailer and seller. It is generally a labor-intensive and geographically diffused activity, with considerable national and regional variation in business practices. And it is an industry subject to considerable government regulation. Finally, to wind up our profile, it is a major generator of jobs and requires considerable management time and attention. Now let us consider how internationalization of retailing services can proceed.

There are two major avenues that can be pursued. One is to obtain control of retailing channels through direct investment, with joint ventures and franchising being modified approaches to the overseas retailing industry. The key objective here is to have a degree of control over the retailing channel and also receive as much market information as possible from retailers about the ultimate consumer. Such control is often linked to a vertical-integration strategy. But retailing offers attractive returns in its own right, as a means of participating in the growth of an economy. From this angle, the foreign retailer hopes to bring a competitive edge to the domestic industry in the form of more efficient management, greater worldwide purchasing clout, and superior retailing technology and information systems.

The second avenue for internationalization of retailing services lies in using technology to diminish the need for direct contact between retailer and customer and thus allow for long-distance retailing. Computerized electronic shopping and direct mail are two instances of such an approach. Foreign retailers can service domestic customers in another country market this way without physically entering the domestic retail industry. Some examples of international retailing will illustrate the range of possibilities in this industry.

**Entering the Japanese Retail Industry**

We have discussed the rapid growth of Japanese incomes and the willingness of Japanese consumers to step up consumption. This may be the reason why Aeon Corp., a Japanese retail conglomerate, decided to buy the U.S.–based *Talbots* chain consisting of about 150 clothing stores in the United States. Aeon Corp. planned to expand the number of U.S. Talbots clothing stores. But more important, international sales were planned to be about half of a targeted 1994 global sales of $1 billion. The internationalization plan encompassed opening 50 to 75 stores in Japan by 1994. The first store was scheduled for a Tokyo opening in 1990.

Talbots has a specific image — preppy clothes, the classic New England look. The Talbots stores in Japan were to feature the same clothing, trademark red storefront, and maplewood floors as in the United States, hoping to appeal to working women and housewives. (Aeon has had much success with Laura Ashley boutiques in the best Japanese department stores, and Talbots is positioned as more middle market than Laura Ashley.) But, as Michael Golding of Access Japan Inc. notes, Japanese women in their late twenties who are not married and still live at home have the most money to spend, and this group, with perhaps $25,000 in the bank, are more sophisticated in their tastes than American women. Furthermore, Japanese women are reputed to be label-conscious and willing to pay premium prices for quality and snob appeal.

Bearing this in mind, Japanese managers will select garments from Talbots line that they think will sell in Japan. They plan to establish the Talbots brand name in Japan, perhaps by sponsoring a classical music radio show in Tokyo in much the same way that Talbots sponsors the Morning Pro Musica show on WGBH in Boston. They also plan to borrow direct-marketing techniques from Talbots USA in selling from catalogs. Rosy Clarke of ASI Market Research (Japan) noted that catalog sales have become a hip way to shop in Japan. Stores close by 7:00 p.m., and catalogs might appeal to working married women who have less time to shop.[39]

A similar initiative is the joint venture between Toys "R" Us and McDonald's Co. of Japan. This joint venture would allow McDonald's to operate restaurants at toy stores. Toys "R" Us plans to rely on McDonald's expertise in picking Japanese retailing sites. (McDonald's had 675 stores in Japan by 1989, and this is Toys' first move into Japan.) Although Japanese stores were forecast to do twice as much business as the average U.S. store, margins were expected to be lower because of high real estate costs. Toys "R" Us was basing its Japanese expansion on the long-term potential of the Japanese market, banking on a competitive edge derived from offering low prices and a large selection of toys. The company has had success with its toy stores in Europe, having opened 41 stores in Europe through 1989, and obtaining about 9 percent of 1988 sales from overseas.[40]

While Japan is a large and growing market, the United States is always an attractive retail environment for foreign companies. Thorn EMI, a British electronics and entertainment company, has rented TV sets and VCRs for a long time in the United Kingdom. It wanted to enter the similar "rent-to-own" retailing segment in the United States. About a third of United States households cannot get credit, and hence have little alternative to renting if they want to obtain a TV or other appliance. The business may sound pedestrian, but it has strong cash flow, and Thorn estimates that the United States rental industry will double by 1992 from about $2.5 billion in 1987. Given the fragmented nature of the industry, Thorn decided to enter the United States market by buying out Rent-a-Center Inc. of the United States, a company that rented video equipment, appliances, and furniture to middle- and lower-income households. The stream of weekly rental payments added up to 2–3.5 times the retail price. Speed of entry and an established market share were the motivations behind Thorn's acquisition mode of entry into the rental retailing environment in the United States.[41]

## International Hotel Industry

The hotel industry is another one whose growth is fueled by the growth of international business. As more business people travel internationally, they demand lodging on a scale comparable to that experienced at home. Similarly, increasing international tourism leads to greater demands for hotel beds, again with amenities comparable to home. Plus, there is a need for more hotels in the towns of fast-growing countries in the Third World, in Eastern Europe, and in the smaller cities of Europe and Southeast Asia. Here the demand is domestic, which can be satisfied by international hotel chains. Thus, business and leisure travel represent two major segments, as do foreign and domestic guests.

Hotels have a tangible side to them: their construction and ownership. Then there is the management of hotels, including the marketing of hotel rooms worldwide, the provision of the hotel service itself, and related services such as ongoing maintenance. The internationalization of the hotel industry means a separation of these two aspects, with domestic investors often building and owning the hotel, while foreign hotel conglomerates provide hotel management services on a commission fee and profit-sharing basis.

As in the case of airlines, a key element in marketing hotel services worldwide is the use of computerized reservation services. This is a way of capitalizing on brand image. With such systems, a business person can book rooms in any city in the world where the hotel chain has a presence, all with one local phone call. This ease of use leads travelers to favor such hotel chains as the Hyatt or Westin, giving them a competitive edge over more isolated hotels.

The other major variable is service. Top-notch service is labor-intensive and requires considerable training. Thus, Tokyo's Hotel Okura has 1,600 workers for 880 rooms, compared to about 1,000 workers for 1,008 rooms at the Helmsley Palace in Manhattan, both among the world's most prestigious hotels. Offering room service around the clock, and a business center for sending international messages and translating documents are examples of the expected levels of service, even though these operations lose money themselves.[42]

## International Financial Services

International financial services are also growing rapidly. In this segment, availability of low-cost capital is a critical advantage. Following clients as they go overseas becomes a major influence on international expansion. Two other critical variables are innovation—coming up with ideas for new financial services—and technology—being able to deliver innovative new services at arm's length, at low cost, and with high quality.[43] Twenty-four-hour trading, international bank lending, global foreign exchange trading, and hedging products to manage interest and currency exposure are services demanded by multinationals as they spread around the world. Japan, the United States, and the United Kingdom account for over 50 percent of all international bank lending and are the major financial centers of the world. Any company wanting to operate in the international financial services market needs to have a presence in each of these markets.

As Table 16–5 shows, 12 of the world's 15 largest banks are Japanese. Not only do Japanese banks dominate the list of the largest banks in the world, but they are also increasing their overseas position. In turn, this enhances their ability to serve multinational corporations, whether of Japanese, European, or American origin. Yet, American banks are often the first to develop new products such as commodity swaps and securitization

**Table 16-5**                              **World's Largest Banks, December 1988**

| Bank | Country | Assets (Billions of Dollars) |
|------|---------|------------------------------|
| Dai-Ichi Kangyo | Japan | $386.9 |
| Sumitomo | Japan | 376.1 |
| Fuji Bank | Japan | 364.0 |
| Sanwa | Japan | 348.4 |
| Mitsubishi | Japan | 343.6 |
| Industrial Bank of Japan | Japan | 257.6 |
| Norinchukin | Japan | 242.0 |
| Tokai | Japan | 225.1 |
| Mitsui | Japan | 219.7 |
| Mitsubishi Trust | Japan | 210.5 |
| Credit Agricole | France | 208.0 |
| Citicorp | U.S. | 203.8 |
| Sumitomo Trust | Japan | 196.6 |
| Banque Nationale de Paris | France | 194.5 |
| Barclays | U.K. | 189.2 |

of loans. This suggests that over the next few years, Japanese banks will form partnerships with smaller and more innovative U.S. and other banks to further strengthen themselves in the global market.

Another aspect of banking is *private banking,* where banks tailor their banking services for very rich individuals. And for banks looking for rich people, there is no place like Japan. It was estimated that there were over 333,000 people in Japan in 1988 owning land worth $2 million or more. Foreign banks such as Citicorp are in the forefront of competing for rich Japanese clients. Again, this is a labor-intensive business, with highly qualified and specialized staff needed who can develop customized financial packages for each client. American banks are aggressively pursuing this opportunity in Japan, using their global networks to win clients by offering opportunities for global investment and tax minimization. Of course, the Japanese banks have extensive branch networks in Japan and a reputation for service. So they will make every effort to provide similar quality banking services, and the competition will be keen, both in Japan and in other countries.[44]

## The International Credit Card Market

U.S. banks are similarly targeting the Japanese credit-card market. Penetration of credit cards in Japan is only about one-third of U.S. levels, even though the two countries are comparable in terms of per capita incomes and purchasing power. The Japanese, on average, had less than one credit card per capita in 1988. Segments are important, with American Express and Diners Club dominating the upscale market. Since credit-card companies get their income from the commission received on purchases with credit cards, companies such as Diners benefit from the fact that their cardholders spend about three times as much as holders of the average bank card.

In the lower-spending segments, the issue is market penetration. About one-third of all individual savings in Japan is held by the post office savings system. When Visa wanted to increase its penetration of the Japanese market, it struck an agreement allowing it to market Visa cards to the 70 million savings account holders. Since Japanese banks compete with the post office system, this made them less willing to offer Visa cards through their branch networks. In contrast, Mastercard uses an indirect entry method, with Japanese banks acting as franchisees, issuing bank cards under their own names, as part of the international Mastercard network.

All of the international entrants must compete with Japan Credit Bank, which is Japan's top-selling card and the chief domestic competitor. JCB is also planning to expand into international markets, with the idea of protecting and even increasing market share when its JCB cardholders begin to travel and spend money overseas. Another source of competition is retailers who issue their own store cards. An anomaly in Japan is that holders of store credit cards can pay off their outstanding balances in installments while owners of bank credit cards must pay their balances in full.

## International Investment Banking

Investment banking and brokerage services are another attractive international services industry. It is generally accepted that investment portfolios must be diversified internationally for superior performance, which means that there is a need for information about and access to investing in foreign stock markets. Further, stock markets around the world have been growing faster than the U.S. market. For example, the value of all companies on the Tokyo Stock Exchange was about three times the value of companies on the New York Stock Exchange (as of August 1989). The question for American brokerage houses is how they might go about selling brokerage services in Japan in the face of intense competition from giant Japanese brokerage houses with extensive retail networks. It is expensive to do business in Japan: Salaries, rents, and overhead costs are all high, and large volumes of business are needed to break even and make profits.

Foreign firms can either concentrate on a specialty or, if they are large, offer the breadth of global investment opportunities. Accordingly, some large firms offer Japanese institutional clients the options of investing in U.S. Treasury securities, trading in futures and options, hedging currencies, and investing in the major stock markets of the world. Smaller companies usually specialize. Thus, Britain's Baring Securities offers trading in more warrant issues than the large Japanese brokerages. Japanese companies routinely issue warrants with their bonds, and Baring has decided to become expert in this narrow niche in the market.

Along similar lines, a U.S. company such as Wasserstein Perella, which specializes in mergers and acquisitions, has formed alliances with large Japanese companies that are weak in that area. Here, the two sides bring complementary skills: Wasserstein, its detailed knowledge of merger opportunities and contacts in the United States, and the Japanese partner, its clients and capital.

But aside from the product, patience and cultural sensitivity are crucial to success, since personal relations with individual clients determine the volume of business. Salomon Brothers in Tokyo has been successful because of its autonomy and Japanese orientation. It is run largely by Japanese managers, including three of Japan's top securities experts from major Japanese firms. Salomon benefits from the personal contacts built up by these employees through the years in the profession and through college ties. Their colleagues manage the portfolios at Japan's life insurance and trust companies and thus determine how much institutional funds are invested through Salomon. Also, Japanese managers make Salomon more Japanese and therefore more successful in recruiting qualified young Japanese analysts and managers.[45]

**International Insurance Markets**

Insurance is another segment of the financial services industry where international markets are growing much faster than the U.S. market. The United States accounted for about 40 percent of the nearly $900 billion in premiums collected worldwide in 1986, but it is a saturated market, especially in life insurance. The potential for future growth lies primarily overseas, in markets where incomes are rising and individuals and heads of families are beginning to purchase insurance products. Yet U.S. insurance companies have little penetration overseas. Only about 2 percent of sales come from overseas and consist mainly of business from U.S. clients who have multinational operations.

The integration of Europe will present an opportunity for U.S. companies to offer lower prices and take advantage of inefficient local competition; for example, insurance products in Italy are priced at between 77 percent and 245 percent higher than the average of the four European countries with lowest prices, in areas such as life insurance, home insurance, automobile, commercial fire and theft and public liability insurance.[46]

But competition from European companies will be strong, and greater opportunities might be found in the Far East. Aetna, for example, has had success selling U.S. dollar–denominated insurance to Hong Kong natives worried about the Chinese takeover, while Japan is even more attractive due to its high rate of savings. Insurance is generally sold in Japan by women. One U.S. company, Equitable, plans to approach the Japanese market by selling investment-based insurance products such as annuities to wealthy Japanese using a salesforce that is 85 percent male, and trained in financial planning. While American insurance companies may face a fight for market share in advanced economies that have their own entrenched domestic insurance firms, this might be the opportune time to position themselves in the newly industrializing countries. See Case 4.3.

## Other Opportunities in International Services

There are many more opportunities available in international services than those discussed thus far. Century 21, the U.S. real estate franchise chain, has been growing steadily in France. Once again, the chain found the U.S.

real estate market saturated. Hence, it began looking overseas, first selling a master Japanese franchise to C. Itoh, the trading company. But cultural differences made it difficult to sell real estate the Century 21 way. M. Evans, senior vice-president of foreign operations for Century 21, noted that selling property is sometimes considered a disgrace among Japanese families and so must be done secretly and with confidentiality. Century 21's banners, open houses, and lawn signs are embarrassing in this Japanese context.

The company next expanded to England and France. The French market was fragmented, with many small "mom-and-pop" shops surviving on low volume. The U.S. parent felt that conditions were right to introduce modern real estate selling techniques, such as blanket mailing to all the homeowners in a neighborhood, and notices of recent house sales and the price at which the sale took place, both techniques geared to "farming" an area to drum up new business. The goal is to generate larger volumes per broker and thus raise profits from economies of scale.

In another unusual venture, Mobile Fidelity Sound Lab, a manufacturer of high-quality recordings and tapes for audiophiles, was able to initiate a joint venture with Soviet musicians to produce and sell their music in Western countries. Originally, the company wanted to distribute Soviet recordings available only from Melodiya, the Soviet music recording monopoly. Problems with Melodiya led Mobile to form a joint venture with the Union of Composers (which represents Soviet musicians), Soyuzconcert (the domestic concert agency) and Eletronica (an electronic equipment manufacturer). The ensuing venture, Art & Electronics, began competing with Melodiya, with Mobile arranging to distribute the resulting records and tapes through MCA in the United States, in order to diminish the financial risks which were being borne entirely by Mobile.[47]

A similar joint venture formed the basis for bringing Soviet circus artists to the United States. Mr. Steven Leber had gained experience with U.S. tours of rock n' roll groups, and with marketing musicals such as "Jesus Christ Superstar" and "Beatlemania." He visited Russia to consider importing Soviet rock groups, but ended up being impressed with the huge Russian circus industry. He negotiated with Soyuzgoscirk, the national circus authority, to obtain the rights to promote the Moscow Circus in the United States. Then he obtained corporate sponsorship, initially from Unilever and American Express. The result has been a growing U.S. interest in Soviet circuses. But putting the package together required considerable flexibility and sensitivity to Russian ways of doing business.[48]

Finally, one of the more arcane examples of international services is the Swiss company, Societe Generale de Surveillance (SGS), which inspects goods shipped between countries. It checks measures, quality, invoices, and prices of imported and exported goods, typically on behalf of governments. Such inspection is necessary to allow proper application of tariffs, since tariff rates often vary with the exact category into which the traded goods fall. But the most important reason for inspection is to prevent underinvoicing, where the price is set below what the exported goods are worth, with the difference being credited to the exporter's overseas bank accounts. Underinvoicing thus becomes a means of smuggling capital out of a country, and SGS has contracts with governments to prevent such practices. Inspection also helps governments prevent transfer pricing from being used to avoid or reduce duties and taxes on profits.[49]

## Marketing Services Overseas: What Have We Learned?

Experience has taught that since services are intangible, exporting them is often unfeasible without also exporting the personnel to provide the service. Hence, foreign direct investment, licensing and franchising, and joint ventures are common vehicles for providing services in international markets.

Intangibility makes selling services overseas harder, as the buyer must take on faith the quality of service. A corporate brand name and reputation sometimes help.

Financing the overseas expansion of services can be difficult, with the cost structure leaning toward fixed costs. While heavy capital investments may not be necessary, working capital needs may be high initially, especially in regard to the personnel required to provide the service. This is another reason why joint ventures and strategic alliances are common when a firm seeks to sell services overseas.

Clearly, since direct interaction between buyer and service provider is essential to marketing services, cultural differences must be accounted for in seeking buyer satisfaction. Establishing a local presence and using local personnel are usually recommended for this reason. And if the service must be adapted to the foreign market, the interaction between buyer and foreign provider takes on additional importance, since direct contact can facilitate cooperation and result in more appropriate adaptation.

Service markets are largest in the advanced industrial countries. The U.S. market is generally saturated for a variety of services, making overseas expansion attractive. Even with stiff competition in the advanced industrial nations, service markets as a whole offer greater unrealized potential than goods markets, especially for U.S. firms, with their accumulated experience in service industry sectors.

However, service exports or foreign sales do not take place in a vacuum. They often accompany goods sales. Thus, if exports of goods are faltering, service sales will be affected. For example, the billings of U.S.–based advertising agencies overseas are somewhat dependent on the success of their U.S. clients overseas. To the extent that a client such as IBM or Coca-Cola generates overseas sales growth, there are more likely to be opportunities for U.S. advertising agencies to increase their overseas billings.

This last point also suggests a path of least resistance for overseas growth: follow the client! Such a strategy has been successful for Japanese auto parts companies in the United States, and for Japanese banks providing Japanese-language, yen-based financial software and services to their Japanese clients. But concepts from the international marketing of goods can be carried over to services. For example, gap analysis (see Chapter 7) can be used to determine whether the actual market for a particular service (say, the use of overnight parcel and small package delivery) is below the forecast potential. Similarly, the international product life cycle model can be used to predict, say, when a developing nation will begin accelerating its consumption of long-distance phone and facsimile services based on the experiences of the more developed nations.

In conclusion, the ways in which the international marketing of services differs from that of goods create closer links to an overall strategy, with issues such as acquisitions and joint ventures being as important as pure marketing issues.[50]

## Summary

Services cover a number of industries, including wholesaling and retailing, communications, transportation, utilities, banking and insurance, tourism, and business and personal services. Services account for an increasing portion of output and employment in all of the industrialized nations and, consequently, are becoming increasingly important in international trade.

In the United States, nearly three out of four jobs outside agriculture come from the service industries. The most important service sectors in the United States (other than government) are the retail and wholesale trade, finance and insurance, health-care and business services.

All of the major service exporters are developed, industrialized nations. But service exports do not tell the whole story, since many services can be provided only from within a foreign market.

Services are difficult to market because of their special characteristics: intangibility, heterogeneity, variability in service quality, perishability, simultaneity of production and consumption, and the predominance of fixed costs.

Challenges in international services marketing include how to standardize services and how to manage demand so as to match supply and generate repeat business. Cultural variables are an important factor in user satisfaction.

Comparative advantage in services marketing can arise from labor, capital, technology, or management skills. Technology, in the form of computer hardware and software, and communication networks are useful in providing services at a distance. Services are information-intensive.

Government intervention in trade serves to keep out foreign competition from domestic markets. Restrictions are placed on the right of foreign firms to do business, sell to the government, repatriate profits, and transfer personnel. Trade barriers, licensing regulations, and divergent technical standards are also used to limit competition from foreign firms.

The "Uruguay" round of talks on trade has focused on removing barriers to trade in services, with emphasis on protecting intellectual property rights and on setting parameters for government intervention in trade in services.

Entertainment is one of the United States' largest exports. Deregulation of TV in Europe is increasing the demand for U.S. programs. However,

European "local content" laws applied to TV programs may diminish the market opportunities.

The emergence of a global entertainment industry has also led to mergers, with multinationals jockeying to obtain global competitive advantage and representation in the key triad markets. All of the major firms seek to control both production and distribution of entertainment programs, whether it be films, TV programs, sports events, or news and variety shows.

Foreign airline markets are growing faster than the U.S. market, with highest growth occurring in the Pacific Rim area because of economic growth in Japan and in its neighboring countries. Joint marketing and strategic alliances are being used to obtain market share.

Professional services are a growth market overseas, particularly as multinationals expand operations around the world, placing domestic professional service providers in various foreign markets. Retailing offers considerable growth opportunities overseas as incomes rise around the world. Technological innovations allow retailers to offer their services at a distance. Acquisitions are the major mode of participating in retailing in foreign markets.

The international hotel industry is expanding because of growth in business and tourist travel internationally. Management skills and computerized global reservation systems provide U.S. hotel chains with a competitive edge.

The globalization of industry leads to growing demand for international banking services, such as global foreign exchange trading and international lending and hedging services to manage interest rate and currency exposure. Innovative new services, as well as having a low-cost source of funds, are both critical to competitive advantage in overseas markets.

Firms can profit from targeting niches within financial services, such as private banking, credit cards, investment banking and brokerage services, and insurance. Since client contacts are important in finance, cultural sensitivity is as important as financial know-how.

Considerable untapped market potential exists for insurance products in the newly industrializing countries of Asia, in the nascent single Europe, and in Japan. These foreign markets are characterized by high prices and have fewer innovative products available. Experienced U.S. insurance companies may have a competitive edge, though they have not been active in seeking foreign markets.

A few generalizations can be made about the service sector overall: (1) foreign markets offer attractive growth prospects, (2) following domestic clients overseas is one avenue to gaining foreign sales, and (3) some form of direct involvement in the foreign market is necessary to gain significant market share.

## Questions

15.1   What are services? Why are they important in industrialized nations?

15.2   Which service-industry sectors are important in the U.S. economy? Can these sectors easily enter into U.S. trade?

15.3 Who are the major service-exporting nations? What might explain the number of advanced industrialized nations that appear on this list?

15.4 Explain the steps by which McDonald's was able to initiate operations in Hungary. What difficulties did it face, and how did it solve them? What generalizations can you make from the McDonald's example?

15.5 What are some distinguishing characteristics of services? Explain why these characteristics make it difficult to sell services in foreign markets.

15.6 Discuss how culture can affect the sale of services overseas. Use the Little, Brown–Russian negotiation as an illustration.

15.7 What are the bases of comparative advantage in services? Explain how capital and technology have transformed global competition in services.

15.8 Why and how do governments intervene in services? How is GATT attempting to create freer trade in services?

15.9 What is intellectual property? Why is it the focus of GATT negotiations in the services area?

15.10 Why are U.S. firms dominant in the world entertainment industry?

15.11 How is environmental change in the television industry in Europe creating opportunities for American firms?

15.12 How does the spread of satellite TV affect pan-European advertising by multinational firms?

15.13 Why has MTV been successful in Europe?

15.14 Explain the reasons behind the rise in global mergers in the media industry. How do such mergers help the firms sell more entertainment services around the world?

15.15 Where is airline traffic growing the fastest? How should U.S. airlines respond in order to obtain a share of passenger traffic growth overseas?

15.16 What are the problems of expanding professional service operations overseas? Illustrate your answer using Manpower's experience in Japan.

15.17 How can retailing services be expanded overseas? Why is acquisition a popular approach?

15.18 What are the forces creating greater demand for hotel services in foreign markets? How can multinational hotel chains profit from such growth?

15.19 How is banking becoming a global business?

15.20 Analyze multinational competition within the credit-card industry in Japan. What are the respective competitive advantages of foreign and Japanese banks? How do these advantages affect the marketing of credit-card services?

15.21 Comment on how foreign brokerage and investment banking firms have marketed in Japan. Why is culture important in selling financial services?

15.22 What are the prospects for the international marketing of insurance products?

15.23 Can any generalizations be made about the international marketing of services?

# Endnotes

[1] D. Blades, "Goods and Services in OECD Economies," *OECD Economic Studies* (Spring 1987).

[2] Mack Ott, "The Growing Share of Services in the U.S. Economy—Degeneration or Evolution?" *Federal Reserve Bank of St. Louis Review* (June–July 1987).

[3] Irving Kravis and Robert Lipsey, *Production and Trade in Services by U.S. Multinational Firms,* National Bureau of Economic Research Working Paper No. 2615.

[4] "Service Area in a Fog," *The Economist,* May 23, 1987.

[5] V. Zeithaml, A. Parasuraman, and Leonard L. Berry, "Problems and Strategies in Services Marketing," *Journal of Marketing* 49 (Spring 1985).

[6] Christopher Lovelock, "Classifying Services to Gain Strategic Marketing Insights," *Journal of Marketing,* 47 (Summer 1983).

[7] G. Lyn Shostack, "Service Positioning through Structural Change," *Journal of Marketing* 51 (January 1987).

[8] Carol F. Suprenant and Michael R. Solomon, "Predictability and Personalization in the Service Encounter," *Journal of Marketing* 51 (April 1987).

[9] Joseph P. Guiltinan, "The Price Bundling of Services: A Normative Framework," *Journal of Marketing,* 51 (April 1987).

[10] See C. Groonroos, "A Service Quality Model and Its Marketing Implications," *European Journal of Marketing* 18, no. 4 (1984).

[11] A. Parasuraman, V. Zeithaml and Leonard Berry, "A Conceptual Model of Service Quality and Its Implications for Future Research," *Journal of Marketing,* 49 (Fall 1985).

[12] Helen Dudar, "Moscow Rights: Doing a Book Deal with the Soviets," *The Wall Street Journal,* February 23, 1988.

[13]"ISDN Executive Report: Snapshot of the French Scene," *Computerworld,* December 12, 1988, 80.

[14]Geza Feketekuty, *International Trade in Services: An Overview and Blueprint for Negotiation* (Cambridge, MA.: Ballinger Books, 1988).

[15]Ravi Sarathy, "The Export Expansion Process in the Computer Software Industry," in *Managing Export Entry and Expansion,* ed. Philip Rosson and Stan Reid (New York: Praeger Press, 1987).

[16]U.S. International Trade Commission, *The Relationship of Exports in Selected Service Industries to U.S. Merchandise Exports,* USITC Publication, No. 1290, Washington, D.C., September 1982.

[17]J. Aronson and P. Cowhey, *When Countries Talk: International Trade in Telecommunications Services* (Cambridge, MA: Ballinger Publishing, 1988).

[18]Geza Feketekuty, *International Trade in Services: An Overview and Blueprint for Negotiation* (Cambridge, MA.: Ballinger Books, 1988).

[19]"Fancy Free: A Survey of the Entertainment Industry," *The Economist,* December 23, 1989.

[20]"Europe May Slap a Quota on General Hospital," *Business Week,* March 27, 1989; "The Media Barons Battle to Dominate Europe," *Business Week,* May 25, 1987.

[21]"European Satellite TV: Just so much Pie in the Sky?," *Business Week,* October 24, 1988.

[22]See "All the World's a Dish," *The Economist,* August 27, 1988.

[23]"Cable and Satellites are Opening Europe to TV Commercials," *The Wall Street Journal,* December 22, 1987 and "The Media Barons Battle to Dominate Europe," *Business Week,* May 25, 1987.

[24]"Beaming Soap to Babel," *The Economist,* October 22, 1988.

[25]"Monte Carlo or Bust," *The Economist,* September 2, 1989.

[26]"Meet the New Media Monsters," *The Economist,* March 11, 1989.

[27]"Keeping Up with the Murdochs," *Business Week,* March 20, 1989.

[28]"American Cable is Lassoing Foreign Markets," *Business Week,* August 14, 1989.

[29]"How Do You Say Slam-Dunk in Italian?" *Business Week,* August 28, 1989.

[30]"Global NFL Game Plan: Springtime Play Overseas," *New York Times,* July 20, 1989.

[31]"Going Global with Rock and Roll," *The Wall Street Journal,* December 20, 1988.

[32]"The Battle for Europe's TV Future," *The Wall Street Journal,* October 6, 1989.

[33]"Empty Threat," *Forbes,* November 13, 1989.

[34]See Daniel Kasper, *Deregulation and Globalization: Liberalizing International Trade in Air Services.* (Cambridge, MA.: Ballinger Publishing, 1988).

[35]"Mr. Smith Goes Global," *Business Week,* February 13, 1989 and "Federal Express Corp. Agrees to Acquire Tiger International in $800 Million Deal," *The Wall Street Journal,* December 19, 1988; also "Battle Heats Up Over Global Air Delivery," *The Wall Street Journal,* December 19, 1988.

[36]"JAL, Lufthansa and Air France Discuss Venture," *The Wall Street Journal,* October 19, 1989.

[37]"Soviet-Irish Joint Ventures are Taking Wing at Shannon Airport," *The Wall Street Journal,* October 17, 1989.

[38]"Aeroflot, Marriott Cooperate on In-Flight Catering Service," *Aviation Week & Space Technology,* January 23, 1989.

[39]"Dressed for Success in Japan," *Boston Globe,* November 3, 1989.

[40]"Toys "R" Us Sets Venture in Japan with Food Chain," *The Wall Street Journal,* September 27, 1989.

[41]"Thorn Purchase Would Mark End of Retreat," *The Wall Street Journal,* July 30, 1987.

[42]"How Hotels in Japan and the U.S. Compare in the Services Game," *The Wall Street Journal,* September 21, 1988.

[43]See Olivier Bertrand and T. Noyelle, *Human Resources and Corporate Strategy: Technological Change in Banks and Insurance Companies.* Paris: Organization for Economic Cooperation and Development, 1988.

[44]"In Japan, Banks Get Personal to Get Rich," *Business Week,* November 28, 1988; and "U.S. Banks Are Losing Business to Japanese at Home and Abroad," *The Wall Street Journal,* October 12, 1989.

[45]"Trading in Tokyo: U.S. Brokerage Firms Operating in Japan Have Mixed Results," *The Wall Street Journal,* August 16, 1989.

[46]P. Cecchini, *The European Challenge: 1992, The Benefits of a Single Market* (Brookfield, Ver.: Gower Publishing, 1989), table 6.1.

[47]"U.S. Firm's Music Pact with Soviets Is Demo for Others," *The Wall Street Journal,* May 8, 1989.

[48]"Entrepreneur is Ringmaster of U.S.–Soviet Promotions," *The Wall Street Journal,* October 4, 1989.

[49]"SGS: Inspectors General," *The Economist,* May 16, 1987.

[50]For more on the subject, see Office of Technology Assessment, *International Competition in Services.* Washington, D.C.: Govt. Printing Office, 1987.

## Further Readings

Bertrand, Olivier, and T. Noyelle. *Human Resources and Corporate Strategy: Technological Change in Banks and Insurance Companies.* Paris: Organization for Economic Cooperation and Development, 1988.

"Fancy Free: A Survey of the Entertainment Industry." *The Economist,* December 23, 1989.

Feketekuty, Geza. *International Trade in Services: An Overview and Blueprint for Negotiation.* Cambridge, MA.: Ballinger Books, 1988.

Groonroos, C. "A Service Quality Model and Its Marketing Implications," *European Journal of Marketing* 18, no. 4 (1984).

Lovelock, Christopher. "Classifying Services to Gain Strategic Marketing Insights," *Journal of Marketing* 47 (Summer 1983).

Office of Technology Assessment, *International Competition in Services.* Washington, D.C.: Government Printing Office, 1987.

Parasuraman, A., V. Zeithaml and Leonard Berry. "A Conceptual Model of Service Quality and Its Implications for Future Research," *Journal of Marketing* 49 (Fall 1985).

Sarathy, Ravi. "The Export Expansion Process in the Computer Software Industry" in *Managing Export Entry and Expansion,* ed. Philip Rosson and Stan Reid. New York: Praeger Press, 1987.

Shelp, R. *Service Industries and Economic Development.* New York: Praeger Press, 1984.

Shostack, G. Lyn. "Service Postioning through Structural Change." *Journal of Marketing* 51 (January 1987).

Zeithaml, V., A. Parasuraman and Leonard L. Berry. "Problems and Strategies in Services Marketing." *Journal of Marketing* 49 (Spring 1985).

# 16.1 Baseball: The Japanese Game

Babe Ruth toured Japan with an All-Star team in 1931. Pro baseball resumed in Japan in 1950, for the first time since the war. On average, Japanese baseball players are of smaller size, and the teams play each other all the time. There are twelve professional teams, divided into two leagues, the Pacific and the Central. The champions from each league play each other in an end-of-season playoff, a Japanese "World" series. The teams are

| Central League | Pacific League |
| --- | --- |
| Yomiuri Giants | Nippon Ham Fighters |
| Yakult Swallows | Lotte Orions |
| Taiyo Whales | Seibu Lions |
| Chunichi Dragons | Nankai Hawks |
| Hanshin Tigers | Kintetsu Buffaloes |
| Hiroshima Carp | Hankyu Braves |

Four of these teams are located in Tokyo and four in Osaka. The teams are all owned by corporations. The Yomiuri Giants are owned and run by Japan's leading newspaper chain, the Yomiuri. The Chunichi Dragons are owned by another newspaper chain, and five of the teams are owned by railroads: Seibu, Hankyu Braves, Kintetsu and Nankai, all in the Pacific League, and the Hanshin Tigers in the Central. Other team owners include Taiyo, a fish producer, Nippon Ham, a meat producer, Lotte, a chewing-gum manufacturer, Yakult, a soft-drink company, and Mazda, which owns the Hiroshima Carp. The Central League is stronger, with an attendance of 12 million compared with 7 million for the Pacific League in 1987. The Yomiuri

Case prepared by Associate Professor Ravi Sarathy for use in classroom discussion. All rights reserved. Based on a three-part series by Larry Whiteside, *Boston Globe*, July 17, 18, and 19, 1988.

Giants alone are on TV five or six nights a week, and all 65 of their home games and most of their away games are covered. Similarly, Taiyo and Yakult both have separate TV contracts and hence strong fan loyalty, and home attendance is high.

As in the United States, TV is a strong influence on baseball. The Yomiuri Giants have a national following because of TV, and with Sadaharu Oh (who has 868 home runs to his name), won nine straight national championships between 1965 and 1973. They play in the new Tokyo Dome, modeled after the Metrodome in Minnesota, and they share it with the Nippon Ham Fighters.

Built by the Korokuen Corp. for about $280 million, the new Tokyo Dome produced first-year revenues of over $325 million. It can draw on a population of nearly 30 million in a 100-square-mile radius (due to Japan's excellent and fast public transportation system). The 56,000-seat arena also hosts track meets, bicycle races (on which big bets are placed in Japan), rugby matches, and events as diverse as Michael Jackson concerts and Mike Tyson boxing matches.

To combat the greater financial strength of the Central League, the Pacific League began importing American players. This practice is now standard in both leagues. Each team can have two active foreign players, with an additional "imported" player in the minor leagues who can be called up in case of injury. Japanese baseball now offers an opportunity for the younger U.S. ballplayer who almost makes the U.S. major-league teams. An example is Jim Paciorek, who worked in the Milwaukee Brewer farm club organization for five years. Unable to make the Brewer team, he moved to Japan to work for the Taiyo Whales in Yokohama.

The foreign players, *gaijin senshu,* are well paid, with the appreciating yen making Japanese salaries look even better. Randy Bass had a contract of $1.25 million with the Hanshin Tigers, and Mike Easler signed with the Ham Fighters in May 1988 for $975,000 for one year. He had been cut by the Yankees and, at age 37, saw Japan as his only chance to continue playing in the majors. Others signing the same year were Doug DeCinces, Bill Madlock, and Bill Gullickson. The transition was made easier by playing in the Tokyo Dome, the only real major-league facility in Japan. It may have helped that Easler played ten seasons of winter ball in Mexico and Venezuela, thus becoming more comfortable with foreign cultures. Salaries for U.S. baseball players are high when compared with the following average 1988 salaries for Japanese players: $93,680 for pitchers, $76,160 for catchers, and between $112,000 and $113,000 for infielders and outfielders in the Central League.

The Japanese players come up the traditional way: through high school baseball and then into Japan's only minor league, or through four years of college. Once in college, though, they cannot be drafted for four years. Japanese players know that the Americans are better paid, and accept that the current generation of American players are bigger, stronger, faster, and hit with more power than most Japanese players. Mike Lum, a hitting coach with Kansas City who played in Japan noted, however, that Japanese pitching was good. It helps that the Japanese strike zone is wider and deeper, from below the belt to the armpits. But for the Japanese player, the pay difference is not a major bone of contention: the player is ultimately a company employee, and he knows that the company that owns his team will absorb him into the company culture and find him a position should he quit baseball.

While the pay is good, life is not easy for the American ballplayer in Japan. For one thing, the entire team relies heavily on him. For another, although teams hire interpreters who work with the player nonstop, he and his family must cope with the culture, the scarce housing, and the expensive way of life. Then there are the playing fields themselves. The Tokyo Dome is fine, as are three other stadiums that have artificial turf.

But the remaining clubs have all-dirt infields and grass outfields, or even all-dirt fields. When it rains, the field can be a swamp, and in the hot season, it has been compared to playing on a basketball court. The work ethic, quintessentially Japanese, often is the undoing of the aging American baseball player who comes over expecting some easy money. It is not surprising that, faced with the demand to believe that the company or team is what matters and that the manager must be listened to, many American players quit after a year.

Randy Bass's story is an example of the culture gap. Randy Bass became Japan's leading slugger, winning the Triple Crown in both 1985 and 1986. He became the highest paid player in Japan. But he left the Hanshin Tigers for San Francisco in May 1988, as his son had been hospitalized with excess fluid in the brain. He was contravening the Japanese cultural code that puts loyalty to the company above personal considerations. When he did not return by June 17, as he had agreed, he was released.

A major difference between U.S. and Japanese baseball is that since there are only six teams in each league, teams play each other all the time. Pitchers watch and learn about batters. The pitcher's chief weapons are the curve, the slider, and the forkball—in other words, control. After facing a hitter so many more times during the Japanese season (and studying him like a hawk), the better pitcher has a distinct advantage. As Easler puts it, "They know everything about you — what you can hit, what you can't; before the game, you have a video of each team that you play. We go over everything in great detail. The practice habits and work habits here are just exceptional . . . It's like spring training every day."[1] One other difference is the stress on pitching complete games. Easler thinks that this builds confidence, since the pitcher learns to bail himself out. "Patience is the key to hitting in Japan. You are definitely going to have to hit the ball the other way. If you don't you'll die here." Easler, who used to be a dead pull hitter, has returned to the spray hitting style that he learned under Walter Hriniak with the Boston Red Sox.

As a result, he was hitting .312 after 39 games by mid-July 1988.

## Will There Be a World Series Some Day?

What of the future? A major influence is the Japanese yen, which is strong, and allows Japanese clubs to bid more dollars for better American players if they so choose. The concentration of teams in Tokyo and Osaka may hinder attempts to expand baseball in Japan by adding new teams in other cities. On the other hand, the success of the Tokyo Dome points to the possibility of moving franchises and creating expansion teams linked to new major-league-quality stadiums. And now that baseball is an Olympic sport, on the horizon is the possibility of a Japan–U.S. world series, with the Japanese champions challenging the U.S. World Series winners. This means raising the quality of Japanese baseball, increasing the size of the roster from the present 25 men, and perhaps importing additional foreign players beyond the current three-man ceiling.

Selling U.S. baseball to Japan is an "export" possibility. Growing TV revenues in the United States (the Yankees' $200 million deal over the next 15 years is a straw in the wind) may indicate that a similar high-paying market might exist in Japan. TV rights for baseball games to be shown on Japanese TV might bring yen-based revenues for U.S. entrepreneurs. Promotional opportunities for ballplayers in Japan are underexploited, being currently under control of the company owning the team. There are no Japanese baseball cards. And if baseball can be exported, can ownership rights be far behind? Would Sony buy up a U.S. baseball team? After all, the owner of the Seibu Lions was willing to buy the Seattle Mariners when they were for sale. If the two richest markets in the world are baseball-crazy, there are surely opportunities for further trade in baseball between these nations.

## Questions

1. How is Japanese baseball marketed? In what ways does it differ from the selling of American baseball?
2. How would an aging U.S. baseball player market himself to a Japanese team?
3. How is the growing popularity of baseball in Japan likely to affect U.S. baseball?
4. Does U.S.–Japan collaboration change the market for U.S. baseball players? How should the Major League Players Association (the union) react so as to protect its member interests?
5. Why would U.S. enterpreneurs and agents be interested in Japanese baseball players?
6. Why would someone in Japan want to buy a U.S. baseball team? What are the implications of an internationalization of the baseball scene?
7. How can trade in baseball be seen as an example of trade in services?

## Endnote

[1]Larry Whiteside, "He's Still a Big Hit," *Boston Globe,* July 18, 1988, 45.

CASE
# 16.2 Sony Corp.

Sony has long been known for its innovative consumer electronics products, such as the pioneering Walkman. It is an international corporation, with 70 percent of its sales coming from outside Japan, and non-Japanese owners owning 23 percent of its stock. Sony also manufactures about 20 percent of its output outside Japan. As of 1986 its sales mix was video equipment (VCRs) 33 percent, audio equipment (compact disk players) 22 percent, TVs (the Trinitron) 22 percent, and other products (records, floppy disk drives, and semiconductors) 17 percent. Sony has always emphasized R&D, spending about 9 percent of sales on it.

## The Betamax Experience

Sony has been facing increasing competition from other Japanese companies and from countries with lower labor costs, such as Taiwan and South Korea. Its strategy of inventing new, advanced-technology products and then waiting for the market to buy seemed to be faltering. Sony's biggest failure was the Betamax. Having invented the Betamax format for VCRs, it refused to license the technology to other manufacturers. It was higher-priced, and recording times were somewhat shorter than with the competing VHS format, although quality of the images was better.

Sony's competitors, such as Matsushita (Panasonic), Hitachi, and Toshiba, all banded together around the VHS format. They licensed the format to any manufacturer who wanted it. Con-

Case prepared by Associate Professor Ravi Sarathy for use in classroom discussion. All rights reserved.
Source: "Sony Sees More Than Michael Jackson in CBS," *The Economist*, November 28, 1987; "A Changing Sony Aims to Own the Software That Its Products Need," *The Wall Street Journal*, December 30, 1988; "Sony Sets Pact with Coca-Cola for Columbia," *The Wall Street Journal*, September 28, 1989; "Dynamic Duo: Producers of 'Batman' Stir Whammo Battle over Future Services," *The Wall Street Journal*, October 20, 1989.

sequently, the total number of VHS sets produced and sold was far higher than the Betamax format VCRs, which meant lower retail prices because of accumulated volume and resulting economies of scale. Also, far more "software" was available for the VHS format; that is, movie producers were more likely to make home video copies of their films available for purchase and rental on VHS tapes. This further increased demand for VHS-format VCRs. The net result was that Betamax gradually faded, and Sony stopped its production in 1988.

## Rethinking Basic Strategy

The difficulty of selling advanced technology coupled with the speed of imitation and the impact of low-wage-country competitors led Sony to change its basic corporate strategy. The CBS/Sony Group Inc., a 50–50 joint venture between Sony and CBS, Inc., has grown dramatically over a 20-year period to become an industry leader in the multibillion-yen Japanese music industry. It releases recordings in Japan, Hong Kong, and Macau, on compact disk and other formats, by popular Japanese artists such as Seiko Matsuda and Rebecca, as well as foreign artists.

## Sony's Diversification into the Entertainment Industry

Sony's diversification into the global music industry is therefore not unexpected. In January 1988 it agreed to buy CBS Records worldwide for $2 billion. But subsequent moves have dramatically transformed Sony, as it moves to become more of a service company. Table 1 summarizes the major entertainment industry acquisitions made by Sony since 1988.

The acquisitions themselves are large, totaling over $5 billion, or about half of Sony's total assets. More interesting is the reasoning behind

**Table 1  From Electronics to Entertainment: Sony's Acquisitions since 1988**

| Date | Company Acquired | Price |
|---|---|---|
| October 1989 | Guber-Peters Productions | $200 million |
| September 1989 | Columbia Pictures | $3.4 billion |
| January 1989 | Tree International country music publishers | $30 million |
| January 1988 | CBS Records | $2 billion |

Sony's decision to acquire a slew of entertainment companies. A summary follows:

**CBS Records.**  For $2 billion, Sony was able to acquire control of the world's largest record company, CBS Records. Sony had traditionally sold music hardware, being one of the world's largest producers of compact disk players (CDs), tape recorders (including the phenomenally successful Walkman), and stereo television. But all of these products were subject to competition, as innovative ideas could be imitated and prices cut. Sony realized that being in the music business allowed it to take advantage of the entire installed base of compact disk players around the world, not just those manufactured by itself. Imitation was impossible, as each music act was unique; however, the music business was a creative one, consisting of managing personal relations with relatively young pop stars with large egos. Managing such a creative business required far greater cultural sensitivity and required the use of local managers rather than predominantly Japanese management.

The music industry is also a fast-growing business. In 1988 over 150 million CDs were sold in the United States alone, and there were over 11 million CD players in households. CBS Records, Inc. consists of CBS Records (Domestic), CBS Masterworks, CBS Records International, CBS/Sony, Columbia House, and CBS Musicvideo. The acquisition gave Sony an immediate international presence in the music industry.

**Columbia Pictures.**  The major attraction here of Columbia Pictures was a large library of movies that continue to earn revenues every time they are shown at cinemas and on video around the world. Columbia also has a profitable TV production and syndication business. Thus, the acquisition gives Sony products to sell to owners of TV sets and VCRs in a manner analogous to providing music on record and tape for owners of CD players and tape recorders.

There are two other reasons why Sony might have found Columbia Pictures attractive. One, TV in Japan is being liberalized, with a doubling in the number of TV stations and on-air time because of the launch of satellite television. There will be a sudden increase in demand for product, such as films and TV shows, to fill air time on Japan's satellite stations. Sony will be in a position to supply such product at a time when demand will be increasing, thus being able to charge premium prices in yen.

The other reason is hardware-related. Sony has been trying to establish its 8 mm camcorder format, again in competition with a VHS-C based format from competing Japanese producers. This standards battle brings to mind Sony's previous experience with Betamax. But this time Sony realizes the need to build up the installed base. Hence, it has licensed the 8 mm technology to other producers and is willing to manufacture the camcorders for sale by others under their own brand names. Sony is thus making sure that volume sales of the 8 mm camcorder will be achieved, resulting in economies of scale and lower prices. The next step is to stimulate demand by making available a variety of movies in this format. Sony can do this by putting the entire Columbia Pictures catalog on 8 mm video, thus giving consumers a reason to buy the camcorder.

This availability will be crucial to the success of Sony's newly introduced 8 mm video Walkman, a pocket-sized portable color TV set that will appeal to the extent that videos are available for use with the video Walkman.

Thus, with the CBS Records and Columbia Pictures acquisition, Sony becomes one of the world's major producers of entertainment hardware and software: record producer and CD player producer; a leading manufacturer of TV sets and an owner of a library of classic films.

**Guber-Peters Productions.** When Sony purchased Columbia Pictures, it obtained a film library as well as film production facilities such as a film studio. But Columbia had gone through four producers in five years and needed more capable film production management. The logical step was to take over one of Hollywood's most successful film production companies, Guber-Peters (G-P) (formerly Barris Productions), which had been responsible for *Batman,* one of Warner Communications' all-time best selling films. In fact, G-P had signed a five-year exclusive agreement with Warner, to produce movies on its behalf. G-P's expertise lay in spotting hot properties, signing them up, and then convincing major studios to bankroll and distribute the resulting films. What G-P had was a unique culture-specific talent for working in and with Hollywood, producing successful films for the huge U.S. TV and film audience. Sony acquired G-P for over $200 million, or about five times G-P's latest-year revenues. The two key producers, Peter Guber and Jon Peters, received about $50 million for their stock in G-P, a 10 percent stake in future profits at Columbia Pictures, 8 percent of the future appreciation of Columbia Pictures' market value, and about $50 million in total deferred compensation.

Warner immediately sued Sony for acquiring G-P. Warner refused to release Peter Guber from the long-term contract. Of course, Sony and Warner ultimately settled out of court, exchanging valuable assets such as a share of the movie studio, video rights, and so on. Clearly, Sony wanted the management talent, Americans who knew Hollywood and could hire the right people, had the appropriate financial and creative contacts, and, most important, knew how to make hit films.

**Tree International.** Sony also acquired, through CBS Records, the ownership of Tree, the premier country music publishing company. Once again, the ownership of rights to several generations of hit country songs guarantees a steady stream of revenues, especially as the catalog is further popularized around the world and in Japan through Sony's music and video production divisions. While this is a minor acquisition, it may point to a trend toward acquiring other music publishing companies as a means to further controlling the software end of the entertainment business.

## Future Outlook for Sony

Looking to the future, Sony is heavily involved in new hardware technologies such as advanced high-definition TV, computer workstations, and compact disk interactive technology. These hardware advances will require further research and development; but their acceptance by consumers will depend equally on the availability of software products that showcase the new hardware products. Long term, Sony is becoming more of a services and entertainment company; and paradoxically, this will also help it become a stronger hardware company, while reducing risk by smoothing revenue fluctuations and providing the stability of recurring earnings from sales of music, film, and videotapes.

## Questions

1. What were the threats facing Sony?

2. Trace the various entertainment industry acquisitions made by Sony. Why did Sony make these acquisitions? Have they helped the com-

pany compete more effectively in international markets?

3. What are the risks of Sony's strategy of buying U.S. entertainment companies?

4. What would you recommend that Sony do next? And how do you think Sony's Japanese competitors might respond?

5. Is Sony becoming a global company, or is it becoming a company with products adapted for each specific country market?

6. What generalizations can you make about the global service industry from Sony's experience?

PART

3

# Coordinating International Marketing

In Part 1 we looked at the world environment that shapes international marketing. In Part 2 we looked at how managers perform the functional tasks that constitute international marketing — that is, marketing intelligence, pricing, and so forth. In Part 3 we are concerned with how the separate functional tasks of organization, planning, and control are blended together into an effective international marketing mix. Part 3 also includes a chapter on the future of international marketing.

# CHAPTER 17

# Planning, Organization, and Control of International Marketing

In previous chapters, we have discussed global strategy and its marketing implications. We have dwelt at length on specifics of marketing internationally. However, the proof of the pudding is in the eating; a recipe alone does not yield a feast. It is the implementation of plans and strategies that decides how well the firm functions in the global marketplace. Therefore, this chapter is concerned with implementation — which entails planning, organization, and control.

The main goals of this chapter are to

1. Identify the elements of the planning process.
2. Describe how firms develop plans for national markets and coordinate those plans.
3. Describe the nature and role of long-range planning.
4. Identify the variables that affect organization design.
5. Describe the alternative designs available for international organization.
6. Examine how companies really organize internationally and what roles headquarters can play.
7. List the steps in the control process.
8. Discuss how standards are established for international control.
9. Describe the control devices available.
10. Explain the role of the information system in international control.

## Planning for Global Marketing

Planning consists of systematic steps that help the company formulate detailed actions to implement broad strategies. Thus, the stages of planning should mirror the steps used in formulating strategy as set out in Figure 6–1 in Chapter 6. Planning can be for the short or long term. Typically, firms plan for three to five years ahead, with the long-term plan being revised annually. Then the year immediately ahead becomes the short-term plan, with more detailed estimates.

There is an advantage in having the annual plan be part of a longer planning horizon. It keeps planners from being shortsighted by forcing them to consider the future impact of each year's operating plan. The short-range plan for international marketing can be composed of several elements, including, for example, a marketing plan for each foreign market, plans for individual product lines, and a plan for international product development.

Elements of the marketing plan are as follows:

1. *Situation analysis: Where are we now?* The company must analyze its current environment in each of its markets: What are the important characteristics of demand, competition, distribution, law, and so on? What problems and opportunities are evident in the current situation?

2. *Objectives: Where do we want to be?* Given an understanding of the firm's current situation in markets around the world, management can propose objectives that are appropriate for each market. These objectives should be challenging, but they should also be reachable. And they must be specific if they are to be operational.

3. *Strategy and tactics: How can we best reach our goals?* Once the firm has identified concrete objectives for foreign markets, it must prepare a plan of action to reach these objectives. The approach will include assigning specific responsibilities to marketing personnel and to the marketing functions.

These three basic elements — situation analysis, objectives, and strategy and tactics — provide an adequate framework for discussing the planning problems of the international marketing manager. The short-range planning task of the international marketer has two basic parts: (1) developing the plan for each foreign market and (2) integrating the national plans into a coherent international plan.

## Developing Plans for Individual Markets

The amount of planning for each of the firm's markets will depend on the firm's volume of business in the particular market. Where the firm does a small volume of business, the amount of planning will be small also, unless the firm has a goal of expanding its business in that area. Another variable is the firm's product line, which may vary from market to market. A third constraint on national market planning is the firm's level of involvement in the market. We will examine this constraint before discussing the planning process itself.

**Exporting.**   When the firm sells to an importer or distributor in a market, it is not physically present to do a situation analysis or to design strategy. Although it can partially compensate for this limitation by visiting export markets, planning is hindered if the firm does not have a continuing personal presence in the market. In export markets, the firm must rely on its local representative for most of the data for the plan. We noted some methods for encouraging distributor cooperation in Chapter 10.

Perhaps because of their reliance on exports, Japanese firms traditionally had internationalized their planning process less than Western firms. By

1985 a study by Noritake Kobayashi showed that they had become much closer to Western firms in internationalizing their planning.[1] Toyota, for example, operates primarily as an exporter to world markets. It conducts both *top-down* and *bottom-up* market planning. The bottom-up side of this planning originates with sales agents in foreign markets. It then goes to regional departments, and finally to headquarters in Japan, where it is compared with the top-down plan. Cooperation is good, partly because Toyota's line is important to agents.

**Licensing.**   In licensee markets, the firm has no personal presence in the market, and its licensees will cooperate in planning only to the degree that it is to their own interest. One factor, however, probably places the licensors in a stronger position than the exporters. The licensors' business is usually more important to the licensees than the exporters' is to the importers. This may be reflected in stronger contracts and reporting requirements in licensing agreements.

**Joint Ventures.**   Joint ventures are more favorable for planning, since the firm does have personal representation in the market. The joint venture can present difficulties, however. Local partners may have objectives and strategies different from those of the international firm. They also will want the situation analysis conducted from the viewpoint of the joint venture rather than from that of the international corporation. Therefore, even the joint venture cannot be integrated easily into international planning.

**Wholly Owned Subsidiaries.**   A wholly owned subsidiary eliminates the problems encountered in the other kinds of involvement. The planner can count on company personnel to participate in planning. The international planner and those in the national subsidiaries will probably have a line relationship. The focus of our discussion will be the planning process when wholly owned subsidiaries are involved. Then the appropriate modifications can be noted for those countries where the firm has a lesser involvement.

**Situation Analysis**

The firm will be in a different situation in each market. It will use one basic method to examine these situations, however, and, by doing so, give its subsidiaries an advantage over their national competitors. The international firm's planning expertise can be made available to all its subsidiaries, saving them the cost of developing it on their own. In each market the firm examines the same variables — for example, demand, competition, law, and so on — using a standard format. This aids the international planner in evaluating them.

In addition to the current situation, the national analysis should identify the problems and opportunities expected to arise during the period of the plan. These problems and opportunities will guide the strategic planning. The situation-analysis format used is probably derived from that employed in the firm's domestic market. The more carry-over from domestic to foreign planning, the better comparisons the firm can make of opportunities in the two areas. Such comparisons are necessary for a firm to optimize its performance on an international basis.

The techniques used for national planning will probably also derive from domestic practice. A study of 80 foreign subsidiaries in Brazil found that their planning systems were typically modeled after that of the parent.[2] Planning is usually most highly developed in the firm's domestic operations. The firm should assure that the best planning tools and models are used in each of its markets.

## Setting Objectives

Having determined its current situation, each subsidiary must set objectives to be attained during the period of the plan. The objectives should be spelled out for major products and marketing functions. The subsidiary should help set its own targets. Its participation will keep the targets related to the market and assure the subsidiary's cooperation in reaching them.

The actual objectives in the national plan should be quite detailed. Some items that could be included are

1. Target sales of each product, in units and dollars.
2. Target market share by product.
3. Target number of new distribution outlets.
4. Target percentage of brand awareness.
5. A new-product introduction with a specified sales or distribution level.
6. Local market test of new product by target date.
7. Export target of some dollar or percent-of-sales level.
8. Specific marketing research activities to be completed.

## Strategy and Tactics

Deciding on objectives is one aspect of strategy. A second aspect is the determination of the approach for achieving these objectives. The specific tools and programs used to implement the strategy constitute the tactics. For example, a firm might have an objective of reaching a certain market share in a country. Its strategy might be to compete on a non-price basis by emphasizing product quality, by introducing new products, and by making a strong promotional effort. Its operating plan would spell out in detail the particular tools and techniques to implement the strategy, including an appropriate budget. For instance, the plan would identify the product-development activities for the year; the new product to be introduced, its timing and marketing program; the advertising program, including appeals and media schedules; and so on.

The operating plan that spells out the firm's tactics is the most comprehensive part of the short-range plan. It includes a calendar of events; the assignment of responsibility to the marketing people in the firm and to those working with the firm, such as distributors, advertising agencies, and marketing research groups; and the budget allocations necessary for these responsibilities. International managers must oversee the development of operating plans for each market. To keep this task manageable, however, they must realize some synergy in the planning effort. Efficiency can be improved by the proper division of labor in the organization and by the use of comparative analysis.

**Stages in the Planning Calendar**

Thus, a series of typical planning steps might include

1. *Communication of company-wide goals,* subsequently broken down into global, regional, and country-specific goals, and goals for product lines.
2. *Detailed country and product-manager plans* showing how goals such as market share, competition containment and return on investment will be achieved.
3. *Aggregation of detailed country and product-line plans* to determine whether the overall result is compatible with corporate headquarters' goals.
4. *Translation of plans into budgets,* setting out quantitative and qualitative targets in terms of market share, unit volume growth, prices, target-market segments, distribution channels, advertising budgets, new product introductions, and personnel and training needs.
5. *Actions by product-line and country managers* based on plans and budgets, which also form the criterion used to judge performance.

**Adapting Plans to Individual Countries**

A centralized coordination of programs is necessary so that, for example, global products can be introduced into different markets on a staggered basis. The experience of lead markets may be used to tailor product-introduction programs for other markets. In addition to country and product-manager initiatives, some programs may be initiated at headquarters and communicated to subsidiaries.

When broad plans must be adapted to specific country markets, additional information may be needed from those markets regarding segment positioning, competitor actions, and government regulations. Analysis of such data may be a joint effort of headquarters and subsidiary managers. As we shall see, the extent of centralization of such tasks is influenced by the nature of the business and by the management style adopted by the parent headquarters.

Consider the example of Avon's planning process for Latin America.[3] Local executives gather information and develop preliminary country business strategies. Scrutiny of the operating environment is given precedence, focusing on the political, economic, and regulatory environment in each market, as well as making forecasts for the next five years. Next, competitors are identified, their products, market share, strengths and weaknesses assessed. Avon seeks to learn the sources of its competitors' competitive advantages and compare them with Avon's own competitive advantage. Out of such analysis emerges a plan designed to capitalize on opportunities and competitive weaknesses. Contingency planning is emphasized, the question being, what actions are necessary to achieve planned results in the face of unforeseen events?

The Avon planning process is initiated by Avon's top management, which visits each of Avon's key country subsidiaries over a period of two months. While each country subsidiary's general manager prepares the plan, headquarters planning staff, including the planning director, help key markets with their plans. Once all the plans are completed, they are forwarded to headquarters for review and integration. Country proposals are reviewed and prioritized, and through comparison, headquarters can detect unexploited opportunities and suggest imitation or adaptation of plans currently scheduled for implementation in one country.

## Division of Labor in International Planning

Avon's approach highlights the importance of organizational arrangements in international marketing planning. How the company is organized will affect the quality of the plan, and whether it can be implemented. *Who* contributes *what* to national operating plans? What are the respective roles of corporate headquarters and the national subsidiaries?

Usually corporate headquarters can contribute planning know-how based on its domestic and international experience. This would include planning guidelines, a planning schedule, and training of subsidiary personnel.

If the national subsidiary is not self-contained, headquarters can provide information for the situation analysis as to how the subsidiary is related on the supply or demand side to the rest of the firm's operations. The international marketer will also have ideas as to appropriate objectives for each market and effective strategies and tactics, based on the firm's experience.

Thus international marketers contribute to all three aspects of the national operating plan: (1) they give guidance and information to the situation analysis; (2) they provide a corporate viewpoint as to the appropriateness of subsidiary objectives; and (3) they transfer corporate know-how about strategies and tactics.

The national subsidiary must do most of the actual planning, but it has an advantage over its national competitors. Because of help received from its corporate parent, the subsidiary should be a more effective planner. The major contributions of the subsidiary are (1) the actual work of preparing the plan and (2) local knowledge. Whereas the international parent has planning expertise, only the subsidiary has the intimate local knowledge needed. Most of the data for the plan, therefore, must be supplied locally. The resulting plan is more effective because of the complementary contributions of the two parties.

Nestlé provides an example of interactive planning, but with a bias toward decentralization. Some guidance comes from headquarters, but each national company essentially prepares the annual marketing plan and budget. Once a year each affiliate comes to Vevey, Switzerland, to review the plan with headquarters specialists. Compromises and adjustments are made at that time.

## International Coordination of National Plans

The final role of the international planner is to coordinate the national plans into an international plan. This coordination is not done *after* the national plans have been completed; rather, *it must start at the beginning* of the planning process. Otherwise, national plans will make conflicting claims on company resources and require time-consuming revision. Therefore, coordination begins with guidelines sent to each national operation at the beginning of the planning period. National plans may be modified during the planning process, but good communications will assure that these changes can be coordinated within the overall international plan.

A good example of the coordination process is found at Burroughs. It begins its planning cycle in August. Each country prepares its plan, which goes to its regional headquarters and then to international headquarters in the United States. Between September and November there is continuing exchange of information among these three levels. The final coordination takes place at area-wide meetings in December, where country managers, regional managers, and headquarters people meet for one or two weeks. These meetings are sometimes held in the area — Europe, Latin America, and so forth, and sometimes in the United States.

## Comparative Analysis for International Planning

The ability of the international manager to contribute to the subsidiary's planning derives from two sources, the firm's domestic experience and its international experience. If the manager has analyzed the company's operations in all of its markets, certain insights will have emerged.

The international manager may then raise subsidiary targets and ask for greater performance if analysis has shown that this is a reasonable request based on comparisons with subsidiaries and markets with similar characteristics. International comparisons are unpopular with subsidiary management, which always claims its situation is different. A well-done analysis, however, compares the subsidiary only with others in a similar situation.

Comparative analysis is also useful in determining strategies and tactics for particular markets. If markets have been appropriately grouped, the international marketer can help plan strategy for one market based on the firm's experience in similar markets.

A pharmaceutical firm used an A, B, C, D rating or classification system to guide its detail people in scheduling call frequencies for doctors. The doctors who had the greatest influence on adoption and use of an ethical drug had an A rating, and so on. This system was used in the firm's domestic operations. The international division of the company adopted a similar rating system for foreign markets. It was used to prepare the promotional strategies and budgets for these markets.

In another situation, an electronics company was studying sales data of one of its major product lines in foreign markets. The various analyses showed clearly three distinct market groupings for this product line. This led to a change in the firm's international planning. Instead of preparing individual guidance for each of the foreign markets, planners began preparing guidance for three groups of countries. They added just one page of individual material for each country to handle anything that was peculiar to it.

AM International provides an illustration of an analytical approach to international markets planning. It is a leader in the world graphics industry, with divisions including offset presses and printing equipment, engineering and architectural market graphics equipment, and duplicating equipment. International sales are 42 percent of total sales, and AM's strength is its worldwide sales and service infrastructure, with 180 sales branches in 102 countries on 6 continents, and a worldwide base of installed equipment that is a continuing market for supplies and service. To manage this global busi-

| Table 17-1 | **AM International's Global Markets Analysis** |

| Market Segment | Market Growth Rate | AM Growth Rate | International Division Presence |
|---|---|---|---|
| *Traditional* | | | |
| Offset Printing | 5% | 4% | X |
| Engineering/Graphics | 0 | 0 | X |
| *Growth* | | | |
| Bindery | 9% | 13% | X |
| Imagesetting | 7 | 13 | X |
| Forms Press | 6 | 3 | X |
| Newspaper Inserts | 14 | 19 | X |
| Computer Graphics | 9 | 18 | |
| Copiers | 9 | None | X |

Source: AM International Stockholders Meeting Presentation, December 1, 1988.

ness, it operates 150 warehouses, has a worldwide logistics system, and offers worldwide service capabilities, including training. A large portion of the costs of this infrastructure is fixed, and hence its primary goal is to maximize sales from the worldwide infrastructure already in place. In practical terms, this means selling more products through the sales and service organization. To accomplish this, AM analyzes the outlook for international markets for each of its market segments as shown in Table 17–1.

As can be seen in the table, AM has been developing a new international presence in copiers, an area in which it had not been active previously. The AM International division agreed to market the entire line of Konica copiers in Europe under the AM label. This is part of the plan to leverage the existing distribution channel by taking on worldwide distribution rights to market "contiguous" products under the AM brand name. Copiers are considered contiguous to duplicators, and AM expects considerable overlap with its current customer base.

AM further analyzes markets by geographic area, with a recognition that growth rates of over 30 percent per year registered in the Asia/Pacific region will continue and should be exploited aggressively. At the same time, the above analysis, extended to include current market share and future potential, discloses areas for further attention. Such comparative information gathering is the cornerstone of successful planning for international markets.

## Long-Range Planning

Long-range planning deals with the future of the company over a period of five to ten years. Uncertainty is high, and the level of detail that can be forecast is low. The major concern is with determining the shape of future markets and competition. How will the environment change, how will competition change, how will our customer base change, and what will their needs be in the future? The firm seeks to learn enough about the future so as to prevent unpleasant surprises that can cut the firm's competitive advantage.

The flavor of long-range planning can be seen in TRW's approach, which extends its planning to the year 2000. It addresses questions such as the following: What markets should we be in at that time? What products should we be making then? What business and operations methods will be valid then?

In TRW's Automotive Worldwide Group, the plan is prepared at group headquarters in Cleveland by a four-person Planning and Development Department. It draws on data assembled by the group's product divisions and foreign subsidiaries. The plan's coverage includes

1.   Historical trends in the automotive industry.
2.   Forecasts of demand for cars, trucks, and off-road vehicles.
3.   Forecasts of the economies of the countries where the group has operations.
4.   The competitive situation in those countries.
5.   Possible future modes of transportation.
6.   Possible future energy problems.

Both short-range and long-range plans reflect the automotive supplier's dependence on the plans of the major auto companies. The planners rely heavily on contacts within these companies for inputs to the plan.

## Responding to Competition

A central aspect of planning is responding to competition. In a global context this may involve actions in more than one market, making integration of activities across markets essential. Response may be defensive or aggressive, and may involve waiting for a competitor to act, or it may be preemptive, seeking to ward off or warn competitors against certain actions such as price cuts, competitive product introductions, and expansion of dealer networks.

Being ready to respond to competition is partly a matter of contingency planning. While a firm does not know what a competitor will do, it can make reasonable guesses as to that competitor's options over the planning horizon. Planning should therefore include appropriate responses to those options. Models such as DEFENDER[4] allow the firm to play out these scenarios.

Strategic response may sometimes entail cooperating with the competition — termed *strategic alliance.* This action is becoming increasingly popular as companies realize the importance of having a global strategy. The problem for many companies is that their global ambitions exceed their resources, and if they move too slowly in developing global markets, they may be swallowed up by stronger and already established global competition. Strategic alliances sometimes solve this problem. We will review a variety of recently formed strategic alliances, with examples from the pharmaceutical, tire, and auto industries.

**Competitive Response in Pharmaceuticals Industry.**   The pharmaceutical industry presents an interesting arena for competitive response. It is stable, with an aging population in the rich countries, boding well for growing demand. Major markets include the triad economies of Japan, Europe, and the United States. However, developing a new drug is costly, perhaps exceeding $100 million, and taking several years. Drug companies must be able to sell the drug quickly in all three triad economies, so may need partners to help them market a drug or to help defray the cost of developing a new drug. And they may want partners who also have something of their own to offer: ideally, a new drug of their own, marketing rights for which can be swapped for the firm's own new drugs.

There is also pressure on drug companies to reduce costs, since governments pay for much of health-care costs and want to keep drug prices low. Hence, drug companies have to increase sales volume to make up for lower margins. Price pressures are also a threat from generic drug companies, which make drugs no longer protected by patents. As these generic drug companies do not have to spend on R&D, they can charge lower prices.

The merger of SmithKline Beckman with Beecham PLC of the United Kingdom is an example of such thinking.[5] The combination created the world's second-largest drug company with sales of $6.7 billion, 6,000 sales-people in the United States, Japan, and Europe, and an R&D budget of over $500 million per year.

Sales of SmithKline's major drug, Tagamet, an anti-ulcer drug, were falling off, and no new drug was ready for introduction; worse, patents on Tagamet were to expire in 1994. Beecham had some promising new drugs, including Eminase, for treating heart-attack victims, and Reliflex, an anti-arthritis medicine. It needed more marketing power, which SmithKline could provide. Also, Beecham is strong in the over-the-counter drug market (Sucrets and Geritol, for instance), especially in Europe (and its Tums antacid has 27 percent of the U.S. market). It could help sell an over-the-counter version of Tagamet that SmithKline was developing. Thus, each party had something to offer.

Of course, mergers are not necessary to form strategic alliances. Glaxo, another British drug firm, contracted with Hoffman La Roche, a Swiss pharmaceutical company, to sell Zantac, an anti-ulcer drug and a competitor for Tagamet, in the United States. Glaxo used La Roche's 800 U.S. salespeople to augment its own salesforce of 400, and within three years it had captured the lead from Tagamet.[6] Glaxo has done much the same in Japan, using a partner to sell in Japan (Glaxo would otherwise need its own salesforce of over 1,000 to affect the Japanese medical establishment) while focusing its scarce resources on European marketing. Similarly, Du Pont has been the leader in developing new drugs to combat high blood pressure and heart disease. Du Pont will use Merck, the world's largest prescription drug company, to market these new drugs; it expects that the alliance will save it about two years in bringing the drugs to market.[7]

**Competitive Response in Tire Industry.**   The tire industry has seen similar global strategic responses. The United States accounts for almost 45 percent of the $45 billion world tire market, excluding the Eastern bloc countries. Of the seven major U.S. tire manufacturers, four have recently forged international alliances. Table 17–2 illustrates the results of this wave of merg-

**Table 17-2**          **Major U.S. Tire Manufacturers and Their International Ties**

| U.S. Company | Foreign Partner | Share of U.S. OEM Market | Capacity, 1988 (U.S., Thousands of Tires/Day) |
|---|---|---|---|
| Goodyear | None | 35.5% | 225 |
| Uniroyal | Michelin | 36.6 | 172 |
| Firestone | Bridgestone | 13.1 | 82 |
| General Tire | Continental | 12.8 | 61 |
| Cooper | None | — | 57 |
| Armstrong | Pirelli | — | 40 |
| Dunlop | Dunlop | 2.0 | 32 |

ers. Note the somewhat domino effect. When one foreign manufacturer acquired a U.S. tire company and seemed to dominate the market, the other global tire manufacturers immediately set about making similar acquisitions, preserving competitive balance.

In every case, the foreign tire manufacturers have acquired U.S. tire companies to obtain a U.S. market presence. Bridgestone began this trend by acquiring a 75 percent interest in a venture that eventually took over all of Firestone's tire lines of business. Bridgestone dominates Japan with a 50 percent market share and also installs tires on Japanese cars imported into the United States. In 1983 it purchased a radial tire plant in Tennessee from Firestone. A strong yen and the danger of U.S. protectionism led Bridgestone to begin manufacturing in the United States. It needed more plants there as the auto manufacturers will buy only from local plants with whom they can coordinate operations closely. Another motivating factor was that Japanese auto manufacturers (Bridgestone clients in Japan) were setting up plants in the United States and would be manufacturing over 2 million cars a year. Again, these Japanese manufacturers would be looking for a U.S. source.

The Firestone acquisition immediately gave Bridgestone five additional factories in the United States and six in Europe. It also acquired distribution: Firestone's U.S. network of 1,500 tire, auto parts, and repair stores. Such a network helps persuade auto manufacturers to install Bridgestone tires on new cars, as they can be assured of buyers easily obtaining service. Issues to be decided in the future include upgrading existing Firestone plants, and deciding whether to support both the Firestone and Bridgestone brands in the United States.[8]

Pirelli of Italy had earlier tried to acquire Firestone but lost to Bridgestone's $2.6 billion offer. Pirelli was in the same position, exporting 1 million tires to North America, but without a single plant in the United States; hence, it could not get OEM orders from U.S. auto manufacturers. Therefore, it decided to buy Armstrong Tire, giving it three U.S. plants. Armstrong had been distributing tires through Sears since the 1930's. This gave Pirelli a 7 percent share of the replacement-tire market (compared to 8.5 percent each for Firestone and Michelin, and 16 percent for Goodyear). Profits are higher on replacement tires; a reasonable share of that market indicates a desire to maintain a continuous presence in the market and is essential to win OEM business from the auto manufacturers.[9] OEM sales are important because car buyers tend to replace tires with the same brand; therefore, getting your tire on a car in the form of an OEM sale, even at low margins, guarantees a certain share of the replacement-tire market.

The latest foreign acquisition of a U.S. tire company is by Michelin. In buying Uniroyal Goodrich in 1989, it became the world's largest tire maker. It, too, had sought to buy Firestone earlier. The merger gives Michelin/Uniroyal worldwide sales of $10.3 billion (compared to Goodyear's $8 billion). The Uniroyal acquisition gives Michelin about 25 percent of the U.S. tire market, doubling its previous share. Earlier, Michelin had formed a joint venture to manufacture tires with Okamoto Industries of Japan, and it had formed similar operations through joint ventures with Siam Cement Co. of Thailand and Wuon Poong International of South Korea.[10]

The Uniroyal purchase also gives Michelin entry into the private-label market, in which it had not participated earlier. Thus, Michelin, with a reputation for high-priced tires for luxury cars, is entering a different market segment. The acquisition should also give Michelin/Uniroyal almost 45 percent of GM's tire business. GM might seek to reduce this so as not to become too dependent on one supplier. At the same time, Michelin might use its added U.S. presence to gain share with Chrysler, where Goodyear supplies most of Chrysler's needs. As concentration increases among global tire manufacturers, price wars are likely, and margins will fall as the large global companies seek market share to keep their extensive factories running at capacity.

**Competitive Response in Auto Industry.**   In the automobile industry, Ford Motor Co. has been avidly seeking a luxury-car line to complement its existing brands. It attempted to buy Alfa-Romeo but lost out to Fiat. Then it began negotiating an alliance with Saab of Sweden. Saab has low volume and high costs but represents a distinct brand. However, losses at Saab made Ford decide to turn its attentions to Jaguar. After a short bidding battle, it acquired control of Jaguar. This gave it the upscale brand it needed to complement the lower-priced Lincoln line.

Ford needs such separate brands to compete against the Japanese as they introduce their luxury brands, such as Lexus and Infiniti. Ford may be able to offer its engineering expertise and thus help in reducing production costs, while using its extensive dealer network to increase market penetration of Jaguar cars. Jaguar represents a market more upscale than Saab. Jaguar has also been losing U.S. sales and has limited funds to launch a new car project. What Ford offers is the cash to fund a new car project, seeking in return a position in the upscale market segment consisting of brands such as BMW and Mercedes-Benz.[11]

**Why Form Strategic Alliances?**   In a strategic alliance, firms join together in some area of their business to reduce risk, obtain economies of scale, and obtain complementary assets, often intangible ones such as market access, brand names, and access to government procurement. The allure of acquiring technology and the pressures of government are also reasons for such alliances. They are typically formed in one of three broad areas: technology, manufacturing, and marketing.

Another reason for alliances is that consumers are becoming alike in the developed nations. They tend to receive the same information, and their discretionary incomes are roughly equal. As a result, tastes are becoming homogenized. As Kenichi Ohmae puts it, "Everyone in a sense wants to live and shop in California."[12] But no one company can expect to dominate all technologies and create entire product lines for the developing global market. A likely solution, therefore, is to swap products.

Another factor is that fixed costs account for a larger proportion of total costs. Global sales help recover these higher fixed costs even when lower prices are charged. (Volume compensates for a smaller contribution per unit.) The reason to lower prices and sell globally is that product life cycles are becoming short, and fixed costs are more likely to be covered by resorting to global markets. But it is difficult to exploit worldwide markets without global alliances. Short product life cycles mean that firms must move quickly to exploit their technological lead, which is actually a disappearing asset, diminishing in value with the passage of time. Strategic alliances allow a firm to simultaneously penetrate several key markets.

Alliances, however, require that each party has something to swap. In the tire industry, General Tire supplies Japanese auto companies in the United States on behalf of Japanese companies, which in turn supply companies in Japan on behalf of General Tire and Continental. Several alliances can be formed within the same country. IBM, for example, works in Japan with Ricoh to distribute its low-end copiers, with Nippon Steel to sell systems integration services, with Fuji Bank to sell financial systems, with OMRON to penetrate the computer-integrated manufacturing market, and with NTT (Nippon Telephone) to sell value-added networks.

Technology sharing, joint marketing, and supply arrangements are the main foci of such alliances. What is interesting is that such alliances often occur between companies that also compete with each other in other markets. In choosing such partners, the following criteria are useful:[13]

- The competitor should have a competitive advantage — economies of scale, technology, or market access — and these areas should be critical in the value-added chain.
- The contributions of each partner should be complementary or balanced.
- The two partners should agree on the global strategy to be followed.
- The risk that the partner will become a future competitor should be low.
- There should be a preemptive value in having the firm as a partner rather than as a rival.
- There should be compatibility of organizations, as well as of top management of the two firms.

# Organizing for Global Marketing

All the planning in the world will be in vain unless the company is organized to implement these plans. Organization structure determines who does what, including which employees exercise gatekeeping power in supporting or undermining decisions made by others. Organization structure also sets up the rewards that motivate performance and determines the degree to which activities can be integrated, which is particularly important in global strategy, since implementation must be carried out by subsidiaries in different countries, without many opportunities for face-to-face communication. Indeed, some of the worst problems facing international marketing result from the friction between headquarters and foreign subsidiaries.

The basic issue for all organization structure in global corporations revolves around centralization versus decentralization. Global corporations need strong coordination at headquarters to provide and supervise implementation of global strategy. But local subsidiary managers may have different opinions and pull away from that strategy. Or local government pressures may require greater local responsiveness, even if it means diverging from global strategy. Thus, the major task for organization structure is to mediate between the opposing needs for centralization and local responsiveness.[14]

Recent research suggests that in some industries where consumers around the world buy essentially the same product, as in consumer electronics, centralization and large-scale manufacturing are the key to success. In industries where national consumers have distinct product preferences and much product adaptation is necessary, as in branded packaged goods such as detergents, a large degree of national subsidiary autonomy is needed. Then there are industries where scale economies demand centralized large-scale manufacturing, yet monopolistic consumers have distinct product preferences, as in the telecommunications industry. Here, both centralization and local responsiveness are needed.[15]

**Variables Affecting Organizational Structure**

A major question is whether the global firm should structure itself along geographic areas, product lines, or functional lines (production, R&D, marketing). The goal is to avoid duplication and achieve synergy in integrating its separate national operations into a coordinated unit. The organizational form that is appropriate for a company is a function of many variables, and an individual case solution is necessary. Some of the variables are the following:

1. Size of its business — overall volume and foreign volume.
2. Number of markets in which it is operating.
3. Level of involvement in its foreign markets.
4. Company goals for international business.
5. Company's international experience.
6. Nature of its products — technical complexity, service needs.
7. Width and diversity of its product line.
8. Nature of its marketing task.

## Separation or Integration?

Two basic approaches are possible: A company can either handle its international business in a separate and specialized way, or it can integrate it with the domestic business. Separate treatment can range from selling abroad through an export management company (EMC), to an in-house export manager, to a full-fledged international division. Integrated treatment, or the *world company* approach, can take varied forms also, as we will see.

**Organizational Separation.**  When companies begin international marketing, they usually make some special arrangement for it because it is so different from their regular business. As international business grows, the special arrangement may change from export manager to export department to international division. The last usually is accompanied by overseas production (licensees, joint ventures and subsidiaries). Whereas the export department is primarily a sales department, the international division is concerned with all the functions of business abroad, for example, production, finance, personnel and so on.

Some kind of separate organizational provision is very common, partly because it is most appropriate for smaller companies whose principal international business is through exporting. Even many large companies have a separate international division. This is especially true for U.S. companies wherever international sales are one-third or less of the total corporate volume.

*Advantages.*  Handling international business separately offers several advantages. It is possible, for instance, to centralize all the specialized skills and international expertise in one place. Another advantage of separation is that international business is less likely to be lost in the press of a large domestic business. For most American firms, the U.S. market is more important than other markets. If international business were not separated, many international opportunities might be overlooked.

Yet another advantage of separating international business lies in the potential contribution to corporate management. The international division can take a company-wide look at international markets better than individual product divisions with their parochial interests.

*Disadvantages.*  Although it is advantageous to handle international business separately when it is small, problems may arise as international business grows. The international division may be separate — but not equal. It may receive less top management attention than its potential warrants. Producing divisions often place servicing of the international division low on their list of priorities. This subordinate position can be reinforced by transfer-pricing policies.

Another danger in the international division approach is suboptimization. Treating international business separately may segment corporate resources, preventing their optimal use in the firm's global interest. Especially in U.S. companies where the domestic market is so large, expertise available from domestic operations may not be fully transferred to the international division, making it less successful than it could be.

**Figure 17–1**                    **International Division Approach**

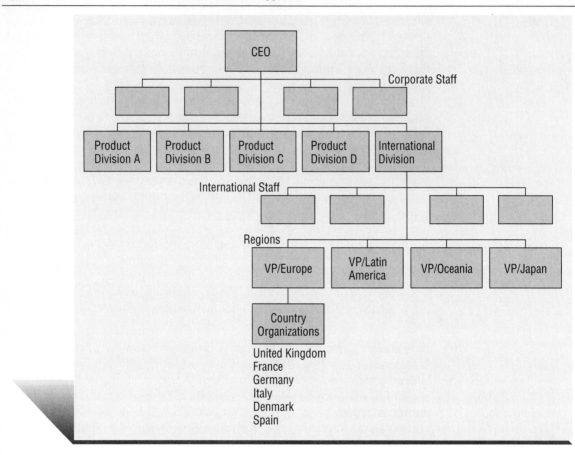

A further problem relates to company politics. When the international division is small, it usually has less power to influence company decisions than its potential would indicate. When the international division becomes important, other divisions usually want to control their own international business. In this situation, the international division has developed from being insignificant to rivaling other divisions. Figure 17–1 illustrates the international division structure.

**The Global Company.**   The global corporation is an organizational form that makes no distinction between domestic and international business. This global outlook would apply not only to investment decisions, but also to sourcing, staffing, research, and other company activities. Operational and staff groups would have global responsibilities, handling both domestic and international business.

## Area, Product, or Functional Orientation?

Whether a firm takes an international division or a global company approach to organization, it still must decide whether this organization should be structured along geographic, product, or functional lines. International business decisions usually require these three kinds of expertise. For example, the question of whether to introduce a new product in Brazil obviously requires area knowledge. However, product knowledge and marketing expertise are also necessary.

**Structuring by Area.**   When the company is structured by area, the primary basis for organization is by divisions for major regions of the world. For example, when CPC International reorganized from an international division to a world company approach, it set up five operating companies — one for Europe, one for Latin America, one for the Far East, and two for North America (consumer products and industrial products). Although this is primarily a regional form of organization, the North American area is divided on the basis of product. Union Carbide has a similar structure: product divisions for domestic business and regional companies for business outside the United States. The regional organization form is used primarily by companies that are highly oriented to marketing with relatively stable technology, such as those in consumer nondurables, pharmaceuticals, and automotive and farm equipment.

Several factors favor a regional approach to organization. The growth of regional groupings is one. As nations within a region integrate economically, it makes more sense to treat them as a unit. The proximity of countries provides one logical basis for organization. Certain kinds of expertise can be grouped within the region for the benefit of individual country operations. Communications are easy, and there can be coordination of product and functional know-how in the region. A narrow product line and similarity in technology and methods of operation also favor regional organization. The greater the international similarity of the firm's products, the greater the importance of area knowledge.

In spite of its popularity, the regional organization has drawbacks. It assures the best use of the firm's regional expertise, but it means less than optimal allocation of product and functional expertise. If each region needs its own staff of product and functional specialists, duplication may result — and also inefficiency — if less than the best staff is available for each region. This inefficiency is most likely if the regional management is located away from corporate headquarters. If regional management is at corporate headquarters, centralized staff can serve all regional units, providing some economies of scale. One U.S. firm brought back its regional management to corporate headquarters for this reason. Of course, then regional headquarters is not in intimate contact with its region. To keep in closer touch with Asia, IBM in 1985 moved 200 of its Asia Pacific people to Tokyo. Finally, regional organization may optimize performance within the region, but there is danger of global suboptimization if there is no coordination among the regions.

**Figure 17-2**                    **Worldwide Regional Organization Structure**

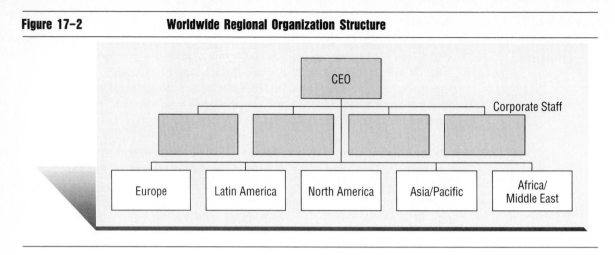

Each region must blend into a global operation. Figure 17-2 illustrates a regional organization structure.

**Structuring by Product.**   Organizing by product line means that product groups have global responsibilities for marketing; thus it is a global company approach by product division. An international division can be organized along product lines too, but by its very nature it also includes area expertise. Structuring by product line is most common for companies with several unrelated product lines, because their marketing task varies more by product line than by region. Diversified companies such as Rockwell International and Eaton have variations of the product structure. Firms that have expanded by merger and acquisition into unrelated fields — for example, Litton Industries — also favor a product approach to organization. As Figure 17-3 shows, the global product structure gives each product group what amounts to its own international division.

Structuring an organization along product lines has the merit of flexibility, in that the firm can add a new product division if it enters another business unrelated to its current lines. However, the product division approach has several potential limitations. Where the domestic market is more important to a product division, international opportunities are likely to be missed. Shortage of area knowledge is a common weakness of product-structured organizations. Each product division cannot afford to maintain its own complete international staff.

Another problem in a product-structured approach is the difficulty of achieving company-wide coordination in international markets. If each product division goes its own way, the firm's international development will encounter conflicts and inefficiencies. The organization must provide for global coordination to offset the sometimes contradictory international plans of individual product divisions. For example, it is probably unnecessary for each producing division to have its own advertising agency, service organization, and government relations staff in every market. Where foreign

**Figure 17-3**                    **Worldwide Product Organization Structure**

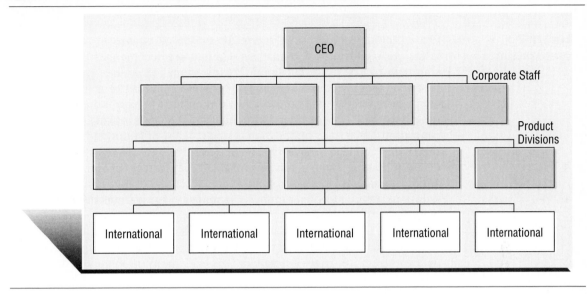

plants manufacture products of different divisions, coordination among these divisions is usually a problem also for a product organization.

Eaton provides an illustration of how companies with global product organization try to overcome some of its weaknesses: Eaton is highly diversified in the capital goods and automotive industries. It has five worldwide product groups and each has a managing director for European operations. To get a better overall *corporate* understanding and response to European problems in such areas as legislation, labor, and taxes, Eaton formed a European Coordinating Committee (ECC), composed of the five product division managing directors, several European staff, and one executive from world headquarters.

The chairing of ECC rotates among the managing directors, and meetings are at different European facilities. Eaton was satisfied enough with ECC to set up Country Coordinating Committees to coordinate the product groups within each European country. Eaton also formed a Latin American Coordinating Committee to achieve the same integration in Latin America.

**Structuring by Function.**  A functional structure, whereby top executives in marketing, finance, production, and so on, all have global responsibilities, is most suitable for firms with narrow, homogeneous product lines, where product expertise is not a variable. It is also helpful if regional variations in operations are not great, thus lessening the need for regional expertise. Because these conditions are not usually met, the functional form of organization for international operations is not common among U.S. firms except in extractive industries. It is more common for European companies. Although functional executives in American firms do have international responsibilities, these are usually in conjunction with a product or regional form of organization.

## The Matrix Organization

One of the more interesting organizational developments in recent decades is the *matrix* form of organization. Companies became frustrated with the shortcomings of unidimensional organizational structures (product, area, function) that we noted above. They therefore moved to a more complex organizational form that allowed two dimensions to have more or less equal weight in their organizational structure and decision making. A matrix organization has a dual rather than a single chain of command. That means that many managers have two bosses. Matrix also involves lateral (dual) decision making and a chain of command that fosters conflict management and a balance of power. Product and market (geography) are the two dimensions receiving equal emphasis in matrix organizations in international business.

Matrix became the popular way to organize for international business in the 1970s. While it helped to answer some problems of the simple product or area structure, matrix organizations had many problems of their own arising from inherent conflicts and complexity. One study of 93 multinationals found that unitary reporting structures still prevailed because dual reporting was perceived as too problematic. Also unitary structures could be altered to obtain the benefits espoused for matrix organizations.[16]

## Examples of Global Organization

It is difficult to appreciate arguments about organization structure in the abstract. The subtleties of structure are more easily grasped in the context of a product and a market. Hence, in this section, we discuss specific examples of organization structure evolution, to show how market realities are incorporated in the process of organizational change.

**Reynolds: European Regional Autonomy.**   The planned single European market for 1992 has led many global corporations to reexamine how they structure their European operations. Reynolds Metal used to have 25 European subsidiaries report to the International Division located at headquarters in Richmond, Virginia. This meant that each European country manager dealt directly with the United States and rarely attempted to coordinate operations with the other European countries. Thus salespeople from different national units would compete against one another for the same multinational client. There was duplication of manufacturing operations and differences in cost and quality. The pending changes in Europe meant that Reynolds had to integrate European operations, as it would be facing intense competition from pan-European companies such as Pechiney and Alusuisse.

Consequently, Reynolds created a European headquarters in Lausanne, Switzerland, to oversee all European operations, so that they would have a "single voice."[17] Lausanne was headed by a top management team consisting of a president, a chief financial officer, an executive vice-president in charge of manufacturing, and several vice-presidents with responsibilities in areas such as marketing. Lausanne was chosen as a neutral site, unlikely to create regional tensions that a country with a strong national unit, such as France or Germany, might. Reynolds (Europe) Ltd. had direct responsibility for manufacturing facilities.

Reynolds plans to focus on downstream, household-oriented products, as well as the aluminum can market: Europe consumes only 6 billion cans, compared to about 74 billion sold in the United States. Reynolds expects many benefits to flow from the organization change, including

- Rationalized manufacturing, lowering costs.
- Faster decision-making.
- A pan-European thrust in production, marketing and advertising.
- Greater influence in Brussels, which is fast becoming the seat of European government.

**Unilever: Worldwide Product Divisions.**   Unilever also reorganized itself to better implement global strategy. Formerly, its product divisions based in Europe set policy only for Europe, which accounts for 60 percent of Unilever's total sales. As part of the reorganization, Unilever created three worldwide product divisions: detergents, personal products, and food products. The change means that major U.S. subsidiaries such as Lipton and Ragu Foods will report to the food products division, rather than to the regional headquarters of Unilever U.S.; that is, rather than the United States being treated as a separate division, major U.S. subs are being integrated into a worldwide product organization. The former head of Unilever U.S. was appointed head of the worldwide food products division.

Unilever seems to be going in a direction opposite to that of Reynolds Metal. While Reynolds Metal was creating a special regional headquarters organization in Europe, Unilever was reducing the autonomy of its U.S. subsidiary and integrating key U.S. product groups into a global product organization. Unilever plans to use local management to monitor local consumer trends, while the global product divisions will ensure better centralized control. The global product divisions will develop high-quality, nutritional, convenient foods, targeting areas such as microwave cooking, chilled foods, and polyunsaturated high-fiber, low-calorie foods.

**General Motors: Reducing U.S. Control.**   General Motors is another company that for the first time in its history is decentralizing authority from Detroit, and setting up European headquarters in Zurich (to be known as GM European Passenger Cars: GMEPC).[18] The head of GMEPC is from Opel (West Germany), GM's largest subsidiary, with other top management coming from Vauxhall (the British sub), GM-Canada, and the Saginaw, Michigan plant. GMEPC will coordinate European planning and operations, with a strict division between national and European HQ tasks. Thus, Zurich will focus on Europe-wide planning and strategy, environmental matters, personnel, and relations with the EEC in Brussels and other European capitals.

# Global Marketing

## Reorganization at Square D Company

Square D Company is another example of the role of organization structure in mediating headquarters and regional interests. Square D manufactures electrical products in over 100 factories, including 31 outside the United States. Until recently, international responsibility was based at U.S. headquarters. The work was divided between vice presidents for international marketing and international manufacturing. U.S. products were sold overseas,

foreign subsidiaries had little authority, and communication with the United States was infrequent.

To implement a global strategy, the electrical group was divided into three business units: distribution equipment, power equipment and controls. At the same time, five regional divisions were created: U.S., Asia Pacific, Canada, Europe, and Latin America. The result was a product/region matrix. The structure is as follows:

## Reorganization at Square D Company

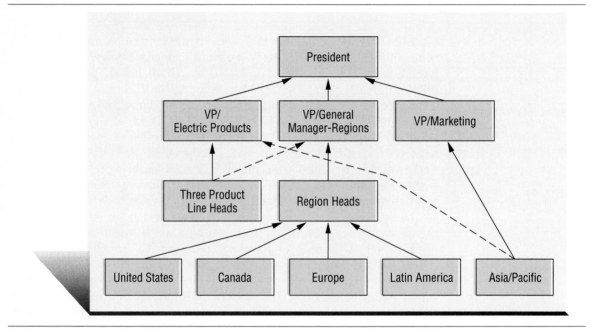

The matrix consists of product-line heads and regional managers, except for Asia Pacific, which reports directly to a vice-president of marketing, as Square D's manufacturing presence in Asia is limited. Quarterly meetings are held in the United States with the product-line and regional heads as well as domestic marketing managers. Communications are emphasized through a quarterly videotape and an in-house magazine distributed worldwide.

The benefits from this reorganization include

• Greater regional autonomy with profit and loss responsibility.

• Timely relaying of market information about electrical standards, priorities for each market, and feedback on demand trends and competition, to benefit manufacturing worldwide.
• Ability to design a global product effectively and at low cost; the smooth flow of information from around the world helps determine global product requirements and allows pooling of manufacturing and engineering capabilities.
• An emphasis on cooperation and global line responsibilities, fostering a global corporate culture.

Source: "Square D Unites Managers to Compete Globally," *Business International*, September 21, 1987.

**Shell: Relying on Matrix Organization.**    The Royal Dutch/Shell Group of companies has also adopted a matrix structure, with the additional innovation that the matrix involves three dimensions:[19] regions, industry sectors, and functions. Shell's several hundred operating companies, which are autonomous, can then draw on global resources of the "service" companies, including regional, sectoral, and functional management.

Shell has nine service companies providing specialized advice and services and consisting of executives that have considerable operating experience in the field. Thus, an operating company could call on experts in petroleum-exploration techniques, in financial management, or in managing a chemical plant. The service companies include trading companies dealing in oil, chemicals, and coal.

The three dimensions of the service companies include five regional coordinators who monitor the profits of the operating companies and approve investments and six business sectors, consisting of upstream oil and gas and downstream oil, including marketing, natural gas, chemicals, coal, and metals. There are sectoral panels that supervise strategy for country, region, and worldwide lines of business. Further, there are nine specialized functional departments, including finance, legal affairs, materials, planning, public affairs, research, safety and environment, information systems, and, human resources and organization. But it is the CEO of each operating company that must draw up the annual plan, calling on any of the service companies for assistance if desired. The quality and experience of the service companies are what make the system work; a drawback is the vast quantity of information that flows to headquarters. But Shell feels that the gains from giving autonomy to operating companies provide a compensatory quick-response capability.

**Philips: Global Product Divisions.**    Philips, the Dutch electronics multinational, also stresses quick local responses and a marketing orientation as it reorganizes for global operations.[20] Philips has been reducing local subsidiary autonomy to focus on three core global-product divisions: consumer electronics, electronic components, and information technology/communications. National subsidiary autonomy was reduced to allow a global manufacturing and marketing strategy to be formulated for each product division. The importance of the product line is stressed by bringing product division directors on the board. At the same time, central control allows for rationalized manufacturing on a global scale, *for each product line,* to gain economies of scale.

How can such a system not stifle local subsidiaries? Philips wants to be creative in creating new products, and wants input from key markets for this decision. At the same time, central control is needed to prevent inventing different national products for each market. Philips has located "competence centers" in crucial markets — such as car electronics in Germany and domestic appliances in Italy. Also, it uses multidisciplinary teams with expertise in development, design, manufacturing, and marketing, thus keeping in mind technical and manufacturing as well as marketing considerations.

As Dr. van Hamersveld, marketing manager at Philips, puts it, "The international product axis underlies corporate policy, but the contribution of national organizations is vital for local marketing and distribution and in dealing with national regulations and handling relationships with governments."

Philips takes care to balance the opposing demands of centralization and local responsiveness over the stages of the product life cycle. In the early stage, product launch is centrally coordinated in Europe, the United States, and Japan, while centralized manufacturing and standardization reduce costs. In the maturity phase, local subs play a larger role, tailoring local marketing, including possibly some product modifications. In the decline phase, emphasis shifts to centralized manufacturing and cost saving. Local subsidiaries make the greatest contribution and have the greatest autonomy in choosing distribution channels, which Philips feels must be adapted most to local conditions. The powerful distribution and dealer networks built up by local subs become a key competitive advantage in Philips' global strategy.

## What Role Should Headquarters Play?

A constant theme running through the various attempts at creating an organizational structure appropriate for global strategy and marketing is the role that the parent company headquarters should take. There are three roles that corporate headquarters can play in its dealings with subsidiaries scattered around the world: controller, coach, or orchestrator.[21]

A controller gives considerable autonomy to subsidiaries and uses measurements such as profits by a small business unit to determine when to intervene. This is classic management by exception.

The coach also decentralizes authority to subsidiaries, but is available to provide support and advice, somewhat along the lines of the Shell example described above. This means that the coach will intervene when it appears necessary, attempting to strike the right balance between decentralization and central control.

The orchestrator is an interventionist with central control and responsibility for activities such as manufacturing, R&D and finance. Subsidiary managers, therefore, have less autonomy. Such a style may be appropriate for industries where global integration is important and investment needs are large, as in oil, steel, mining and financial services.

In addition, headquarters can also play two other temporary roles: surgeon and architect. When major upheavals threaten the firm and its industry, the company may have to be restructured with many units divested, product lines dropped, and workers laid off. Responses to corporate raiders at companies such as Gillette are typical of such a stance. The other extreme is restructuring through acquisitions, as in the current case of Sony, which reacted to the failure of the Betamax video format by deciding to emphasize "software," i.e., music and film production. This has led it to acquire United States record companies and film studios. This phase also requires strong central direction, from the architect who reshapes the company according to a global vision before returning to the mode of coach or orchestrator.

**Table 17–3**                    **Headquarters Roles and Line of Business Characteristics**

|  | Controller | Coach | Orchestrator |
|---|---|---|---|
| *Synergy* | Little/None | Medium | High |
| *Risk* | Low | Medium | High |
| *Competition* | Stable | Open | Intense |

Source: Goold & Campbell, *Strategies and Styles.* Ashridge Management Centre, United Kingdom, 1989.

Company roles should be consistent with the nature of businesses within the global firm. The degree of synergy between the various lines of business in a firm, the level of risk facing the firm, and the intensity of competition determine which headquarters style is appropriate for a specific firm (see Table 17–3).

If a company's lines of business are such that both high and low risk are present the headquarters' task becomes blurred, since for the high risk business it may have to play the role of orchestrator while for a low risk business a controller role is more appropriate. Unless the company then restructures so that only one kind of business line profile prevails across the firm, it must live with multiple roles. This implies that there is no one organizational structure that is appropriate for a global firm with many lines of business. This is the reason why large global firms seem to be constantly changing their organizational structure. As the profiles of the various lines of business change, new organization structures are necessary.

## Implementation and Organization

A global strategy makes it inevitable that some headquarters intervention will be necessary, ranging from informing, to persuading, then coordinating, to approving, and culminating in directing.[22] As headquarters moves from informing to directing, it is taking greater control and lessening autonomy at the subsidiary.

Headquarters involvement may vary from country to country, with greater intervention occurring in regions experiencing troubles. However, greater autonomy may be given to some subsidiaries for certain elements of the marketing mix. Table 17–4 sets out a hypothetical example of how a company might arrange headquarters' role in implementing strategy.

The five modes of involvement are

1. *Informing.* Headquarters management informs subsidiaries of news, statistics, market research findings, corporate goals and objectives, competitive developments. Successful experiences in a country or product line are disseminated throughout the organization, with top management relying on the business judgment of subsidiary managers to pick up relevant ideas for adaptation into their own lines of business. An example would be the use of a quarterly videotape by Square D to communicate developments in the electrical products group worldwide.

## Table 17–4          Global Marketing Strategy Implementation: Headquarters' Role

|  | Informing | Persuading | Coordinating | Approving | Directing |
|---|:---:|:---:|:---:|:---:|:---:|
| New-Product Development |  |  |  |  | X |
| Product Line |  |  |  |  |  |
| *Marketing Mix:* |  |  |  |  | X |
|   Product Characteristics |  |  | X |  |  |
|   Product Segmentation |  |  | X |  |  |
|   Brand Policy |  |  | X |  |  |
|   Packaging |  |  |  | X |  |
|   Advertising |  |  | X |  |  |
|   Promotion |  | X |  |  |  |
|   Distribution Channels |  | X |  |  |  |
|   Pricing |  |  |  | X |  |
|   Customer Service |  |  | X |  |  |
| *Country Markets:* |  |  |  |  |  |
|   Market 1 |  | X |  |  |  |
|   Market 2 |  |  | X |  |  |
|   • |  |  |  |  |  |
|   • |  |  |  |  |  |
|   • |  |  |  |  |  |
|   Market *n* |  |  |  |  | X |

Source: Adapted from John Quelch and E. Hoff, "Customizing Global Marketing," *Harvard Business Review* (May–June 1986).

2. *Persuading.* The three-dimensional service groups used at Shell are an example of this approach, with autonomy still resting at the subsidiary level. Much of matrix management involves persuasion and can be a slow process, though long-term results are more likely, since the subsidiary managers will have been convinced of the merit of the actions taken.

3. *Coordinating.* This is the approach used by Avon, where subsidiary managers in Latin America develop their own plans, but headquarters coordinates the various country plans. Notably, Avon uses a bottom-up approach, preferring that plans originate with the national managers; this allows good managers to develop at subsidiaries and heightens the chances of their retention.

4. *Approving.* Headquarters must approve plans drawn up by subsidiaries. This allows for global strategy, influenced by competitor response, to take precedence over plans tailored to the needs of a specific subsidiary.

5. *Directing.* Subsidiary managers do as they are told by headquarters. This approach may be necessitated by a critical situation, or because of a lack of seasoned managers, or because the issue must be standardized on a global basis. The effect on manager motivation can be damaging. Those who are competent may chafe at the restraint and move on to other companies. It is also unlikely that top management's decisions will always be right. What is lost in this approach is the sensitivity of local managers to the adaptation needs of the local market.

A global company needs strong local managers, but managers need experience to become strong. As Table 17–3 makes clear, some products, functions, and marketing activities can safely be left to subsidiary managers. Indeed, companies should seek to create some areas where such autonomy is fostered.

**Regional Headquarters: A Halfway House**

We have considered decentralization in terms of the division of labor between corporate headquarters and the units in foreign markets. Frequently, however, as the firm's business in a region such as Europe or Latin America grows larger, it becomes important enough to warrant separate attention. This could lead to the establishment of a new level in the organization between corporate headquarters and the foreign markets, that is, a regional headquarters. A regional headquarters is not necessarily located within the region, although usually it is for the larger regions, such as Europe. Many U.S. companies, for example, have their Latin American headquarters in Coral Gables, Florida, truly a halfway location between corporate headquarters and country operations. Regardless of location, however, regional headquarters gives undivided attention to the affairs of the region.

Almost all the world's major computer companies find it necessary to have a regional headquarters *within* Asia for the important Asia-Pacific market. Based in Hong Kong are such firms as Apple, Burroughs, DEC, Hewlett-Packard and Wang. ATT is in Singapore, IBM is in Tokyo, while ICL is in Australia.

**Conclusions on Organizational Structure**

From the above discussion, three generalizations can be made about organizational structure. One is that structure must be tailored to the situation and needs of the individual firm. There is no standard model. Another conclusion is that changing conditions require adaptation by the firm so organization structures are in almost continual evolution. Perhaps the most important conclusion, though, is that firms are now recognizing that organizational structure can never be a complete and satisfactory means of coordinating their international operations. Accordingly, they are now trying to incorporate the product, geographic, and functional dimensions into their decision making *without changing their organizational structure.* In other words, there are other things besides organization structure that can be used in coordinating international business.

Stopford studied structural changes but noted that "management skills" were more important than the formal organization structure.[23] In a more recent study, Bartlett found that many successful firms did not worry about structural change but focused attention on the individual tasks facing their companies. "Instead of joining the quest for the ideal structure, they looked at the connection between environment, strategy, and the 'way of managing.' "[24] Hedlund found the same story for Swedish multinationals. Instead of introducing matrix structures, they complemented their simple organization forms by changes in information systems, budgeting, rotation of personnel, and so forth.[25] These changes and what Bartlett calls the "way of managing" include a variety of things that can best be considered under the heading of control devices, a topic to which we now turn.

## Controlling International Marketing

Companies market internationally to attain certain corporate goals. The purpose of control is the direction of operations to achieve the desired objectives. Considered in this way, control is the essence of management. According to Koontz and O'Donnell, the basic control process involves the following steps:[26]

1. Establishing standards.
2. Measuring performance against the standards.
3. Correcting deviations from standards and plans.

Control is inextricably related to the previous topics, planning and organization. Indeed, Koontz and O'Donnell call planning and organization prerequisites of control systems. Planning involves the setting of standards and goals, the first step in the control process. The organization of the firm establishes the hierarchy, division of labor, and the communications channels for management control. Furthermore, the degree of decentralization affects the control task. General control principles are as valid internationally as domestically. The special problems arise from the different environments in which these operations occur. The communications gaps are the major causes of difficulty — the distance between the firm's different markets and the differences in language, nationality, and culture. Problems also arise from differences in financial and monetary environments. For example, government supervision, exchange controls, and differing rates of inflation limit the firm's ability to control transfer prices, remittances, and logistics, that is, where it will buy and sell internationally.

The following discussion is organized around the three steps of the control process: (1) establishing standards, (2) measuring performance against the standards, and (3) correcting deviations from standards and plans. Within this framework, we will note the various techniques available to facilitate the control of international marketing.

What we refer to here as the control process, some have referred to as coordination, or integration, of international marketing. A *Business International* study mentions a number of methods for "integrating" international marketing:[27]

1. Standard planning systems.

    2.  International product management.
    3.  Marketing committees.
    4.  International marketing meetings.
    5.  Task forces.
    6.  Marketing support services.
    7.  Internal marketing publications.
    8.  Rotation of marketing personnel.

## Establishment of Standards

The establishment of standards determines the pattern of the control process. The way standards are used will influence human relations and the effectiveness of corporate control. To be effective, standards must be clearly defined and understood and accepted by those whose activities are being controlled.

**What Standards?**  The concern of the international manager is with the firm's marketing performance in all markets. If corporate goals are growth and profits, the standards should relate to the achievement of these goals. Overall growth and profits, however, are too general to be operational standards. Therefore, intermediate standards must be established that further the attainment of the larger goals.

Control standards should cover all aspects of marketing that are controllable, that is, those in which subsidiary management can affect results. Standards can be set for all marketing functions performed locally. For example, marketing research standards can be set as to the number and kinds of studies. Targets can be established for sales volume by product line and perhaps by month or quarter; market-share targets are another possibility. In the product area, quality standards can govern local production, targets can be set for product development, and service standards set where products require them.

In distribution, standards can be set for market coverage, dealer support, and performance of the channel. In pricing, standards can be established for price levels and margins on different products and for price flexibility or stability — including regular increases in markets with high rates of inflation. In promotion, standards can be set concerning the volume and nature of local advertising, the media used, and some measure made of the effectiveness of advertising. Salesforce development and performance would be included under promotional standards.

Management is concerned with meeting targets but also with efficiency. Therefore, the standards will include efficiency measures such as marketing cost ratios or return on sales or investment. In calculating profits, a special problem arises in international operations. Should they be calculated in the local currency where earned or in the currency of remittance, that is, after devaluation? Although an American parent company may want dollar profits, that places a burden on local management different from accountability for local currency earnings. This problem arises primarily where inflation and currency depreciation are common.

**How Are Standards Determined?**  The issue is corporate control of marketing within foreign markets. The standards set, therefore, must be appropriate to the situation within each market. Headquarters cannot impose standards arbitrarily but must use local input to establish local standards. Nationals know the local situation better, and will work harder to achieve goals they helped to determine.

Although local management plays an important role in determining local standards, the international manager must help in establishing local marketing standards. Headquarters must see that local standards are challenging enough to demand the best performance from the subsidiary. The standards finally incorporated into the operating plan will be some compromise between subsidiary and corporate management.

The actual methods of setting standards are several. Establishment of standards normally is done in the annual planning process. As the operating plan is finalized, many of the standards will be indicated in the budget. Although much of the communication between subsidiary and headquarters will be impersonal, personal contact during the year is highly desirable. Such contact may be through the travel of executives or through regional or corporate-wide meetings of the relevant managers. Personal meetings can help to minimize the misunderstandings that arise from impersonal communications. Subsidiary resentment of corporate control can be offset partially by such face-to-face encounters.

## Measurement and Evaluation of Performance

Once management has appropriate standards of marketing performance in the subsidiaries, it must monitor actual performance against those standards. Standards are not self-enforcing. They are adhered to only through the control process.

**Reports.**  Critical factors in feedback are the nature and frequency of reports from subsidiaries. The reports should cover all factors over which corporate headquarters wants control. They should be regular enough so that management has time to react in controlling or redirecting operations. Some items or deviations may need to be reported immediately, others on a weekly, monthly, or quarterly basis.

From the headquarters side, a frequent problem in international reporting is that too much information unnecessary for decision purposes is coming in at the same time that insufficient information is received on variables that trigger decisions. Many companies could make their information system more efficient by concentrating on relevant decision variables, thereby saving executive time as well as data transmission and storage costs. Another problem is that information comes in too late for management to take effective action. A streamlined, relevant reporting system can be a way of improving management's control of international operations.

The subsidiary also has problems with the reporting system. Subsidiary management often feels that corporate reporting requirements are too numerous, represent undue interference and inadequate delegation of authority, and show a lack of understanding of the local situation. The reports often breed resentment between subsidiary and parent. These problems suggest the need for streamlining the reporting requirements to just those *items on which corporate action is necessary*. Also, Brandt and Hulbert found much less dissatisfaction by subsidiary management when they received feedback on the reports sent to headquarters, when they felt the reports were being used.[28]

**Meetings.**   In contrast to written reporting is the personal approach to obtaining information through meetings of subsidiary management with corporate executives. These gatherings permit more intensive interchange. The major limitation on such meetings is the executive time and travel involved, but it is minimized if regional rather than headquarters executives attend. A further benefit of this approach is that misunderstandings are reduced. Of course, meetings must be frequent enough to allow management to retain control of current operations.

The most famous example of the meeting method of control is provided by International Telephone and Telegraph (ITT). President Harold Geneen instituted a monthly review of ITT's European operations. It was held in Brussels and was based on the company's "business plan," a two-year operating plan, rewritten annually and reviewed monthly. Subsidiary managements met monthly with top ITT executives.

In contrast to these pre-electronic meetings of ITT is an example of teleconferencing by Hewlett-Packard (H-P). H-P engineers held a one-hour meeting to review a project: Twelve managers were in a room in the United States and nine in a room in Britain. Each room had 52-inch TV screens and microphones. "To keep both halves of the project running smoothly, we teleconference on a regular basis."

**Special Measurement Techniques.**   In addition to regular reporting, specialized techniques exist for evaluating marketing performance. Two of the most noteworthy are distribution cost analysis and the marketing audit.

*Distribution cost analysis* is a technique for analyzing the profitability of different parts of the marketing program. It can be used to study product lines, distribution channels, customers, or territories. Through comparative *distribution cost studies* of markets, international marketers can recognize weaknesses in marketing programs and find solutions to recommend for markets having problems.

The *marketing audit* is a methodical examination of the total marketing effort, often by some outside expert.[29] Such an audit perhaps could be done by international marketing managers for each market every few years. Certainly the audit would add to management's understanding of the firm's foreign marketing and aid in improving it.

A marketing audit would be especially useful when the firm is changing its involvement in a country. At a higher level, an audit could be made of the total international marketing of the firm.

**Evaluation.**   The purpose of measuring subsidiary performance is to be able to take action (control) when things get out of line (deviate from standards). Therefore, performance not only must be measured but also must be evaluated. Management has to know what deviations from standards are un-acceptable and require action. For evaluation of subsidiaries, comparative analysis can again be useful. As Yoshino notes:

> There are two ways corporate headquarters can evaluate the performance of each foreign affiliate. One is to examine each unit against its own standards and goals, and the other is to assess each affiliate against the others. Of course, the two methods are complementary in nature. Comparability can also be achieved in two different ways. One is to reduce the data submitted by various affiliates to common denominators. The other method is to limit comparison to those operations with similar operating characteristics.[30]

## Correcting Deviations

To attain corporate goals, management must correct performance that deviates from standards; that is, management must control operations, and the control process culminates in actually making the necessary adjustments. In international business, control and adjustment are often difficult because of the distance and communication gaps. However, both are necessary if the country operations are to be an integrated international operation.

## Means of Maintaining Control

The various aspects of maintaining control include planning, organization, the budget, using subsidiaries as profit centers, providing positive and negative incentives, and maintaining an information center.

**Planning.**   Planning is not usually considered part of the control process but actually it is. Goals are established in the planning process, but more important is the commitment by subsidiaries to meeting the standards spelled out in the plan. The use of a uniform international planning process is what Wiechmann calls integration through *systems transfer*. One executive explained its value thus:

> Everyone must understand and use the annual planning format, which is our Bible. It's the cornerstone of our activity. This has helped me educate our men and make them fit for competition more than anything else.

**Organization.**   The purpose of organization is to facilitate management control. The organization structure shows the lines of authority, the hierarchy of control. Going beyond organization structure, a study by Doz and Prahalad emphasizes *organizational context* as a means of maintaining strategic control.[31] By organizational context they mean that there are administrative mechanisms (apart from changing the organization structure) that allow headquarters to maintain control in changing environments and circumstances. Table 17–5 gives an overview of these administrative mechanisms. Their argument is that headquarters must maintain strategic control if international operations are to be optimized, and to achieve this, organizational context (these administrative mechanisms) is more effective than structural change. Dow, for example, refuses to create a written organization chart because this would deemphasize the nonstructural methods Dow uses to deal with competing strategic imperatives.

**Table 17-5**                 **Administrative Mechanisms for Strategic Control**

| Data Management Mechanisms | Managers' Management Mechanisms | Conflict Resolution Mechanisms |
|---|---|---|
| 1. Information systems | 1. Choice of key managers | 1. Decision responsibility assignments |
| 2. Measurement systems | 2. Career paths | 2. Integrators |
| 3. Resource allocation procedures | 3. Reward and punishment systems | 3. Business teams |
| 4. Strategic planning | 4. Management development | 4. Coordination committees |
| 5. Budgeting process | 5. Patterns of socialization | 5. Task forces |
| | | 6. Issue resolution process |

Source: Yves L. Doz and C. K. Prahalad, "Headquarter's Influence and Strategic Control in MNCs," *Sloan Management Review* (Fall 1981): 16. Copyright 1981 by the Sloan Management Review Association. All rights reserved.

We can give only a brief illustration of how some of these administrative mechanisms might work.

In executive placement it may be necessary to consider the propensity of individual managers to take a headquarters/business perspective versus a subsidiary/market perspective. Reporting relationships may be made to encourage greater or lesser local autonomy. Management accounting and reward systems may be used to enforce a strong national profit center mentality, or create an international perspective. Membership in critical committees may be adjusted to recognize either global or foreign national concerns. Critical functional staff groups may be centralized at headquarters or attached to local operating units.[32]

**Budget.**   The budget is the basic control technique used by most multinationals. The control offered by the budget is essentially negative; it may prevent excessive expenditure, but it does not assure that goals are reached. Furthermore, if the foreign subsidiary is substantially independent financially, control from headquarters can be difficult. In this case, the administrative mechanisms mentioned by Doz and Prahalad become especially important.

**Subsidiaries as Profit Centers.**   One way of minimizing the control burden on corporate headquarters is to have each subsidiary operate as a profit center. Profit centers can take on varying degrees of responsibility. Where there is a high degree of delegation, the subsidiary handles most control problems. Headquarters may enter the scene only if profits are unsatisfactory. Most U.S. companies operate their foreign subsidiaries as profit centers, but with differing degrees of decentralization.

The profit-center approach to controlling subsidiaries has several advantages. It maximizes the use of local knowledge and on-the-spot decision making and minimizes the frictions of absentee management. It is good for subsidiary morale because local management likes to "run its own shop."

On the negative side, local management, evaluated on short-run profitability, may act in ways that endanger long-run profits. Very autonomous subsidiaries are difficult to integrate into a coherent international operation. Therefore, a high degree of decentralization is most feasible when the subsidiaries are most self-contained in buying and selling and have minimal reliance on the corporation for other inputs.

**Interdependence and Common Interest.**  Control may take on aspects of both the carrot and the stick. It usually will employ both positive and negative incentives. The negative approach, which includes legal pressures and the threat of firing, is probably reasonably effective in getting minimum performance. Obtaining outstanding performance, however, is more likely with a positive approach. Some of the positive motivations in subsidiary performance are the benefits it receives from its interdependence with the international company. In contrast to the self-sufficiency of autonomous subsidiaries, interdependent subsidiaries are more or less reliant on the parent corporation. Some of the benefits a subsidiary may receive from the parent include the following:

1. Product inputs, from raw materials to finished products.
2. An export marketing network for its production.
3. Financial resources.
4. Technological assistance in engineering and production.
5. Marketing know-how, as discussed in Part 2.
6. Management development programs, which may lead to promotions.

**Controlling Licensee and Distributor Markets.**  Most of the control techniques do not apply to licensees and distributors. In these markets, the corporation has no ownership control. The principal legal tie is the agreement, but, as we have seen, legal pressures can only assure minimum performance at best. At worst, they can lead to a severing of relationships and, possibly, loss of the market. Therefore, the best "control" is to motivate licensees and distributors by making the relationship valuable so that they also benefit from doing what the company wants done. We examined several advantages they may obtain from the relationship, including good products, well promoted, and marketing, technical, and management support. The task is to make the nonfamily member feel a part of the family.

**Information Systems for Control.**  Information is needed to plan, to assess performance against plans, and to monitor changes in the competitive and client environment. The company's planning and organization structure will determine what information is gathered and how it will be channeled through the organization. The amount of information collected can be enormous. Table 17–6 outlines some categories of useful information.

Without information, global corporations cannot be integrated efficiently. Mattel, a U.S. toy company, is a good example of this. Toy sales

| Table 17–6 | Categories for a Global Marketing Information System |
| --- | --- |
| Market Information | Market potential, consumer behavior and attitudes, channels of distribution, communications media, market information sources, and new products launched. |
| Competitive Information | Competitors' objectives, goals and strategies in the areas of technology, manufacturing, and marketing; and details of competitor operations (logistics, human resources, etc.). |
| Environmental Information | Foreign exchange perspectives, foreign government regulation, taxes and attitudes to foreign firms, U.S. government regulations. |
| The Firm's Resources | Available human and financial resources, technology, raw materials, strategic partners. |
| General Information | Macroeconomic trends, social structure, political climate and risk, technological advances, management trends. |

Source: Adapted from Warren J. Keegan, *Multinational Marketing Management* (Englewood Cliffs, N.J.: Prentice-Hall, 1984).

are concentrated around the Christmas season, with 60 percent of sales between late-September and mid-December, and toy makers must be able to stock sufficient quantities of the best-selling toys in order to do well. Mattel produces most of its toys in plants in the Far East, and needs to be able to change production plans so as to take advantage of new sales forecasts, which in turn are based on sales figures. That is, if a certain toy is sold out by early November, Mattel needs this information, and must be able to change production in Hong Kong to produce more of the best-selling toy and then ship it where demand is greatest. Dakin, another toy company and maker of stuffed animals, faced such a situation when it introduced its Garfield "Stuck on You," a stuffed animal with suction cups on the paws. Dakin had an initial inventory of about 12,000 units, but initial orders exceeded 40,000.

Equally important, if a toy is not selling well, the company needs to know so that production can be stopped. Mattel had increased production of its "Masters of the Universe" toy line because of excellent 1983 sales. Then 1984 sales dropped to $40 million, from $300 million in 1983; as a result, Mattel had to write off inventory.

Mattel also needs updated figures on toy inventory at its warehouses around the world so that it can shift excess inventory from slow-selling areas to markets where demand is high. All this requires a global computer and communication system that can track production of several thousand individual toy items and inventories at warehouses in various countries, plus retail stocks, again, for each of several thousand individual toys. Hence, Mattel built a global information system linking headquarters with distribution centers and the Far East plants. Now the company knows what finished goods are due from which plant on a daily basis, and where inventory is located.[33] This allows for "better alignment of the production schedule, market forecast, and real orders." Another benefit is that engineers can quickly exchange product specifications with plants, reducing the time it takes for a toy idea to become a product. The global information system allows Mattel to update inventory, production schedules, and engineering specifications on a one-day turnaround basis, as opposed to between 7 and 30 days formerly. In addition, the system allows Mattel to reduce inventories significantly. Without such systems, global strategy and its implementation would remain a dream.

Once such networks are in place, they can be used for other purposes. Conversational interaction through electronic mail facilities allows for closer coordination of international marketing, making local autonomy and centralized coordination simultaneously achievable. Such systems also allow for close monitoring and exchange of information about competition from around the world, which can be invaluable in determining competitive response.

## Summary

Planning for international marketing follows the steps by which strategy is formulated as outlined in Figure 6–1 in Chapter 6. The basic elements of the marketing plan include the environment and the company situation in each market, the firm's objectives, strategy, and tactics that will help it achieve its objectives.

Plans have a short-range and a long-range component. They should be developed for each foreign market and within the context of a global plan integrating country markets and other areas of activity, such as manufacturing, technology planning, and R&D.

A comprehensive operating plan is necessary to help achieve the firm's objectives in the short term. It should include elements such as detailed sales and market-share targets, planned new distribution outlets, brand-awareness goals, new-product introduction plans, test-marketing plans, and other market research activities.

A planning calendar will typically require reconciliation of national plans with headquarters' goals. Once headquarters accepts the plan, budgetary targets are derived and become the basis for managerial action and evaluation.

Broad company-wide plans will have to be adapted to individual markets. Local participation is necessary, and additional information gathering and analysis will ensure a plan better adapted to individual market realities.

Long-range planning deals with uncertainty. The focus is on developing scenarios in basic areas such as technology, market growth, competitive change, and the firm's resources. The goal is to be prepared for contingencies and be alert to major opportunities.

Responding to competitive moves is another essential aspect of planning. This is in the nature of contingency planning, with the firm deciding how it will react if competition cuts prices, launches a new product, or strikes up a strategic alliance.

Paradoxically, the best way to counter competition might be through a strategic alliance with other competitors. Such alliances reduce risk, save time, provide access to technology and markets, and even secure sources of supply. The main question is whether it is better to have a competitor as a partner. Generally, the competitor must possess a complementary asset for a strategic alliance to work well.

Planning cannot work without a well-designed organization structure to implement plans. The basic choice is between centralization and decentralization; in some cases, manufacturing may be centralized and technology development, product adaptation, and marketing decentralized.

Multinational organizations can be structured along geographic, product, or functional lines. The chosen structure may then evolve to a matrix organization. As the environment changes, organization structure will also have to change.

Examples of companies such as Reynolds Metal, Unilever, General Motors, Square D Co., Royal Dutch/Shell and Philips show that there is no one way to structure an international organization. The examples also show that firms do change their structure over time.

A central issue is the role that headquarters should play. One approach is to view headquarters' roles as controller, coach, or orchestrator. In addition, when major changes are occurring in the environment, headquarters may play the role of surgeon or architect.

Further, headquarters' styles must be consistent with the nature of the firm. Firms may be grouped on three criteria: synergy between lines of business, level of risk, and intensity of competition facing the firm.

Headquarters can affect the quality of implementation, taking a stance ranging from informing, to persuading, coordinating, approving, and directing subsidiary actions. It must decide how much autonomy to grant subsidiaries. In some cases, it may want to direct new-product development while using persuasion in the area of pricing.

Control is necessary to monitor progress against plans and budgets. The chief control tasks are establishing performance standards, measuring performance against standards, and taking corrective action in the case of deviations. Marketing audits are useful in looking at foreign-market performance.

Global information systems are a necessary component of international planning. A wide variety of information can be gathered, and if usefully organized, can help increase sales, manage global factories and inventories, and ultimately give the firm a competitive edge.

# Questions

17.1   What basic elements should be included in a company's international marketing planning?

17.2   What distinguishes a short-range plan from a long-range plan? What sort of activities are appropriate for inclusion in a short-range plan?

17.3 How should the marketing plan be integrated with other aspects of the firm such as technology and manufacturing?

17.4 What elements would you include in a firm's operating plans for international markets?

17.5 What is the appropriate relationship between a national subsidiary's marketing plans and headquarters' broad goals?

17.6 Why should headquarters' broad plans be adapted to individual country markets?

17.7 Why should future scenarios be incorporated in a firm's long-range marketing plan?

17.8 How does competition affect international marketing planning?

17.9 Why would a firm consider forming partnerships with competitors?

17.10 Analyze the tire, pharmaceutical, and auto industries as examples of strategic-alliance formation. What general principles emerge from your analysis?

17.11 How is a firm's organization structure relevant to international market planning?

17.12 "Organization structure is essentially a choice between headquarters centralization and local autonomy." Discuss.

17.13 What are the merits of choosing functions, products, and geographic areas as the basis for organizational structure?

17.14 Compare the organization structures chosen by Reynolds Metal, Unilever, General Motors, Square D Co., and Royal Dutch/Shell and Philips. Explain why each organization has chosen a different path for its organizational structure. Is there an ideal structure?

17.15 How can headquarters influence the implementation of plans? Under what conditions will it be more or less directive?

17.16 What is control? How is control related to multinational planning?

17.17 What are some measurements that could be useful in controlling a multinational marketing subsidiary?

17.18 What is a marketing audit? How might such an audit be useful in international markets?

17.19 What are the components of a global information system? How do such systems fit in with international market planning?

17.20 Explain how Mattel's global information system gives it a competitive edge in the global toy industry.

# Endnotes

[1] *The Economist,* December 7, 1985, 30.

[2] James M. Hulbert, William K. Brandt, and Raimer Richers, "Marketing Planning in the Multinational Subsidiary," *Journal of Marketing* (Summer 1980): 7–15.

[3] "How Avon Tackles Strategic Planning for Latin America," *Business International,* December 5, 1988.

[4] J. P. Hauser and S. M. Shugan, "Defensive Marketing Strategies," *Marketing Science* (Fall 1983).

[5] "Global Drug Industry Appears to be Headed for Big Consolidation," *The Wall Street Journal,* April 13, 1989.

[6] "Never Mind the Analysts," *Forbes,* June 13, 1988; and "SmithKline's Case of Ulcers," *Business Week,* October 10, 1988.

[7] "Du Pont Signs Agreement with Merck In Effort to Speed Up Drug Marketing," *The Wall Street Journal,* September 2, 1989.

[8] "Firestone Tire to Receive $1.25 Billion in Venture with Bridgestone of Japan," *The Wall Street Journal,* February 17, 1988; and "Firestone Venture May Help Bridgestone Sell Tires to Japanese Companies in U.S."; and "Firestone Chief Sees Bridgestone Deal as Grand Chance for Transformation," *The Wall Street Journal,* February 18, 1988; and "Can Bridgestone Make the Climb," *Business Week,* February 27, 1989.

[9] "Market Hungry Pirelli Pumps Up its U.S. Tire Unit," *The Wall Street Journal,* March 14, 1989.

[10] "Michelin to Acquire Uniroyal Goodrich, Becoming World's Largest Tire Maker," *The Wall Street Journal,* September 25, 1989; and "Could Uniroyal Let Air Out of Michelin," *The Wall Street Journal,* September 27, 1989.

[11] "Europe's Luxury Cars Face Pressure to Join with Big U.S. Makers," *The Wall Street Journal,* September 20, 1989.

[12] Kenichi Ohmae, "The Global Logic of Strategic Alliances," *Harvard Business Review* (March–April) 1989.

[13] M. E. Porter and Mark Fuller, "Coalitions and Global Strategy" in *Competition in Global Industries,* ed. M. Porter (Boston: Harvard Business School Press, 1986).

[14] See C. K. Prahalad and Yves Doz, *The Multinational Mission* (New York: The Free Press, 1988).

[15] Chris Bartlett and Sumantra Ghoshal, "Managing Across Borders: New Strategic Requirements," *Sloan Management Review* (Summer 1987).

[16] R. A. Pitts and John D. Daniels, "Aftermath of the Matrix Mania," *Columbia Journal of World Business* (Summer 1984): 48–54.

[17] "Reynolds Metals Selects Lausanne as Nerve Center for its European Operations," *Business International,* March 20, 1989; "Reynolds Metals Plans Unit to Better Tap Hard-to-Reach Can Market in Europe," *The Wall Street Journal,* January 27, 1988.

[18]"General Motors Sets Up First European Regional HQ," *Business International,* October 20, 1986.

[19]"Shell: A Global Management Model," *Management Europe,* March 13, 1989.

[20]"Philips: Thinking Global, Acting Local," *Management Europe,* April 10, 1989.

[21]M. Goold and A. Campbell, *Strategies and Styles.* Ashridge Management Centre, United Kingdom, 1989.

[22]John Quelch and Edward Hoff, "Customizing Global Marketing," *Harvard Business Review* (May–June 1986).

[23]Stopford and Wells, *Managing the Multinational Enterprise* (New York: Basic Books, 1972).

[24]Christopher A. Bartlett, "Multinational Organization: Where to After the Structural Stages?" (Cambridge, Mass.: Harvard Business School, 1981), unpublished.

[25]Gunnar Hedlund, "The Evolution of the Mother-Daughter Structure in Swedish Multinationals," *Journal of International Business Studies* (Fall 1984): 109–123.

[26]Harold Koontz and Cyril O'Donnell, *Management,* 6th ed. (New York: McGraw-Hill, 1976), 640–642.

[27]*Business International, Managing Global Marketing* (New York, 1976), 103.

[28]William K. Brandt and James M. Hulbert, "Patterns of Communication in the Multinational Corporation," *Journal of International Business Studies:* 57–65.

[29]Philip Kotler, W. T. Gregor and W. H. Rodgers III, "The Marketing Audit Comes of Age," *Sloan Management Review* (Winter 1989).

[30]Bertil Liander, Vern Terpstra, M. Y. Yoshino, and A. A. Sherbini, *Comparative Analysis for International Marketing,* Marketing Science Institute (Boston: Allyn and Bacon, 1967), 32.

[31]Yves L. Doz and C. K. Prahalad, "Headquarter's Influence and Strategic Control in MNCs," *Sloan Management Review* (Fall 1981): 15–29.

[32]Gary Hamel and C. K. Prahalad, "Managing Strategic Responsibility in the MNC," *Sloan Management Journal* 4 (1983): 348.

[33]See "Mattel Net Chases Xmas Blues" and "The New On-Line World of Santa's Helpers," *Computerworld,* December 19, 1988.

## Further Readings

Bartlett, Chris, and Sumantra Ghoshal. "Managing Across Borders: New Strategic Requirements." *Sloan Management Review* (Summer 1987).

Calantone, Roger, and C. A. di Benedetto, "Defensive Marketing in Globally Competitive Industrial Markets," *Columbia Journal of World Business* (Fall 1988).

Daniels, John D. "Bridging National and Global Marketing Strategies through Regional Operations," *International Marketing Review* (Autumn 1987).

Diamantopoulos, A. and B. Schlegelmilch. "Comparing Marketing Operations of Autonomous Subsidiaries." *International Marketing Review* (Winter 1987).

Goold, M., and A. Campbell, *Strategies and Styles.* Ashridge Management Centre, United Kingdom, 1989.

Hulbert, James M., William K. Brandt, and Raimar Richers. "Marketing Planning in the Multinational Subsidiary." *Journal of Marketing* (Summer 1980).

Kotler, Philip, W. T. Gregor, and W. H. Rodgers III. "The Marketing Audit Comes of Age." *Sloan Management Review* (Winter 1989).

Ohmae, Kenichi. "The Global Logic of Strategic Alliances," *Harvard Business Review* (March–April 1989).

Porter, M. E. and Mark Fuller. "Coalitions and Global Strategy" in *Competition in Global Industries,* ed. M. Porter. Boston: Harvard Business School Press, 1986.

Prahalad, C. K., and Yves Doz. *The Multinational Mission.* New York: The Free Press, 1988.

Quelch, John, and Edward Hoff, "Customizing Global Marketing," *Harvard Business Review* (May–June 1986).

Verhage, Bronislaw and Eric Waarts. "Marketing Planning for Improved Performance." *International Marketing Review* (Spring 1988).

# 17.1 Pall Corporation

Pall Corporation makes filters to purify liquids and gases. Its customers are global and come from a variety of industries. Pall's foreign sales were 40, 45, and 51 percent of total sales of $332 million, $385 million, and $429 million for the years 1986, 1987, and 1988. Foreign sales nearly doubled, from $131.8 to $220.2 million, from 1986 to 1988. In 1988 three-quarters of its overseas sales came from Europe and the rest from its Asia/Pacific region.

## Filters for All Occasions

Pall's products have numerous applications. It sells filters to remove contaminants from hydraulic fluid used in aircraft engines. (The hydraulic fluid allows the pilot to control the plane.) Its filters are also sold to the wine and beer industries to remove bacteria, yeast, and other contaminants, often replacing cumbersome older-generation, low-technology, sheet filters. Makers of "Blue Nun" white wine at Sichel Winery prefilter and cold-sterilize wine with Pall filter systems. Coty, a perfume maker, uses Pall filters to clarify perfumes at its Montreal operations before bottling. Beecham pharmaceuticals uses Pall filters in producing penicillin.

Hospitals and blood banks use its filters to remove leukocytes (white blood corpuscles) so as to prevent rejection during blood transfusions. Its filters are used to prevent bubbles in blood from reaching the brain during open heart surgery. Auto and truck manufacturers such as Volvo in Sweden and Honda in Suzuka, Japan, use Pall filters to remove contaminants and provide a better paint job and clear coat finishes on auto and truck bodies. Manufacturers of photographic film, floppy and hard disks, compact disks and videotapes, pharmaceutical manufacturers, even household water purifiers, all use Pall filters. Industrial uses include paint and chemical processing, nuclear power plants, natural gas and oil-well operations.

## Finding and Keeping Customers

Pall's customers are global, and the company develops new filters based on information gained by close interaction with leading-edge customers around the world, be it IBM, Siemens, or Hitachi. Much of the electronic industry is concentrated in countries such as Japan, South Korea, and Taiwan, and Pall has set out to provide enhanced distribution and service, as well as product breadth in this region. It has a Japanese subsidiary, Nihon Pall, to supply the Japanese market. Its products are used by Japanese breweries, including Asahi's new dry beer manufacturing plant. Other clients include Japanese photographic film, lithographic plate, and automotive companies, which use Pall products in Japan. As Japanese auto companies begin manufacturing automobiles in the United States, they have continued to specify Pall equipment for their new factories.

Drawing on such experiences, Pall plans to increase OEM sales by convincing industrial equipment firms in Japan and elsewhere to incorporate Pall filters into their products. By thus making indirect sales, Pall can grow even when more of the market share for industrial equipment sold worldwide goes to foreign equipment manufacturers.

Government clients include hydraulic fluid filter sales to Taiwan for its Defense Aircraft Fighter program, to Argentina for its new jet trainer IA63, and to the Brazilian aircraft com-

Case prepared by Associate Professor Ravi Sarathy for use in classroom discussion. All rights reserved. Source: Pall Corporation Annual Report 1987, 1988, and 1989; Presentation to the New York Society of Security Analysts, January 5, 1989; and First Quarter Report to Shareholders, October 28, 1989.

pany, Embraer, for its new 19-seat turboprop CBA123. Pall supplies filters for all of Aerospatiale's Airbus planes, which are gaining market share worldwide against Boeing.

## Global Vision

Pall Corp.'s 1988 annual report is titled "Focusing on Global Opportunities." When Pall was formed in 1961, its point of view was that (1) it was a technology company, (2) technology is used worldwide and (3) the world outside the United States is larger than in the United States. Hence, right from the beginning, Pall has been aware of the importance of international markets and has focused on global opportunities. Pall forecasts high growth likely in Asia and Eastern Europe now that countries such as China, India, and Russia have each announced a move to "quasi-democratic, semi-capitalistic" systems.

Pall's competitors are global, including firms such as Sartorius, Hydac, and Mann & Hummel in Germany; Koito, Taisei, Shoketsu, and Teijin in Japan; SoFrance in France; and Fairey-Vokes, Fairey-Arlon, and Normalair-Garrett in the United Kingdom. Pall's goal is to meet the competition on their turf, investing heavily to build manufacturing, marketing, sales, and scientific capability in key markets. It plans to establish a physical presence wherever there are budding competitors.

## The Challenges of a Global Market

However, being a global company means changing its ways of doing business to accommodate foreign governments. Pall gets nearly 40 percent of its sales from Europe and sees the integration of the European countries in 1992 as being achieved at the expense of outside interests. With Europe growing more protectionist, it plans to adapt by increasing its manufacturing within Europe so that nearly all products sold there are also manufactured there.

At present, Pall divides its manufacturing equally between Europe and the United States and ships components from the United States to Britain, producing in Britain for the European market. Its goal is to be equally represented in the United States and in Europe, being capable of making everything it sells in each market separately. This course of action may be less efficient than others, in that capacity is duplicated and smaller-scale multiple plants have to be built, reducing gross profit and leading to unnecessary capacity, since politics rather than immediate demand dictates the plant-expansion decision.

Pall's future growth and new-product development is highly dependent on customer relations. It has put in place a scientific and laboratory services unit (SLS) that calls on customers only to solve technical problems and never to make a sale. These globetrotters are used by Pall solely to gather information from customers and feed it back to research and production personnel. There are about 300 scientists helping connect clients to Pall's leading-edge R&D. The company believes it is important to work with its leading-edge customers all over the world — not only IBM, but also Hitachi and Siemens, for example.

**Selling to Japan.** Pall is a leading supplier in Japan to the biotechnology industry. It sells to multinational biotechnology firms such as Sumitomo, Takeda, Hoechst, and Wellcome. Selling into the Japanese market is a challenge. A. Krasnoff, Pall's CEO, resignedly jokes about delays in certification in Japan that typically add six months to a year before market entry into Japan is possible. Government procedures and regulations for receiving certification in health-related products differ from country to country, and Pall must be patient in winning government approval to sell its filters for the pharmaceutical and healthcare markets. In Europe, Pall has allied itself with major vendors of intravenous set and solution suppliers to speed up the certification process. The alliance also helps to obtain greater sales of its intravenous (IV) filters that remove pyrogens (fever causers) for up to 96 hours before they have to be changed. IV filter use is not as widespread in Europe, and Pall hopes that such an alliance will increase market penetration.

Exchange rate fluctuations also affect profitability at Pall, since over half of its sales are realized overseas; thus, changes in the dollar versus other foreign currencies affect the translated dollar value of total sales, with a dollar that is getting weaker magnifying the sales and profit impact of foreign sales. Given the importance of its manufacturing facilities in Britain and its function as a source of products for the European market, Pall also benefits from a lower sterling against continental currencies.

## Organizing for Global Markets

Going global involves considerable coordination. Pall must meet the need of diverse customer segments in different industries in each country; for example, it has developed transmission fluid filters for use with General Motors Detroit Diesel Allison engines used in large off-highway vehicles. To capitalize on this opportunity, Pall must put in place a worldwide distribution network, distinct from that used to market, say, its cabin air-purification filters used on commercial aircraft, or its blood and IV filters. In many cases,

this will mean forming parallel organizations in the same country pushing distinct product lines from different divisions within Pall.

Thus, within the market region denoted "the Americas and Pacific Basin," Pall has group vice-presidents in charge of aerospace, industrial, and biomedical segments; subordinate to them are senior vice-presidents for marketing and for Pacific Basin operations, and at the next level, vice-presidents in charge of fluid process manufacturing, fluid power manufacturing, biomedical, and scientific and engineering services. Nine senior executives have responsibility for the Americas and Pacific Basin region. Coordination and communication of information can be difficult, especially when a client company buys filters from more than one division of Pall. Pall has launched a worldwide information system to link itself to customers (to permit payment of invoices, place orders and access inventory and engineering data). The same system will link Pall to suppliers and distributors, as well as provide an internal network for exchange of management and scientific information.

## Questions

1. How should Pall be organized in light of its international goals?
2. For the organizational structure that you recommend, note the impact on new-product development, client relations, government relations, regional emphasis on Europe and Asia/Pacific regions, and in countering competition.
3. Several aspects are critical to Pall's functioning, such as catering to different end-user industrial markets, managing an international manufacturing network, and monitoring international financial flows. How would your proposed organizational structure affect these areas?
4. What are the broad information needs of Pall's senior management?
5. Are Pall's organizational structure needs typical of a medium-sized technology corporation? What generalizations can you draw from the Pall experience about organizational structure issues over the next decade?

# 17.2 Catalina Lighting: "Quality Lighting at *Very* Affordable Prices"

Catalina Lighting began importing and distributing lighting fixtures into the United States in 1985, and has grown rapidly, from $3 million in sales in 1985 to $27 million in sales in fiscal 1988. It has concentrated on carving out a niche as an intermediary, handling design and distribution, while leaving manufacturing to subcontracting factories in the Far East.

The overall U.S. market for lighting fixtures in 1987 totaled $7.3 billion, of which residential lighting accounted for the largest portion at $2.7 billion. There are over 150 domestic manufacturers and about 200 importers, making for a competitive market. New entry is easy, as capital requirements are not high, and technology is not a barrier. Design is all-important, with new styles sweeping the market, particularly in the United States; but individual product life cycles are short, because designs are fairly easily copied and retailers and customers continually move on to new ideas. Delivery times become crucial when new models have short lives; the first manufacturers to ship new models to retail stores can garner larger market shares. Innovative new designs tend to achieve the greatest portion of total sales during the first year that they are on the market.

Manufacture of lights is labor-intensive, and imports have been taking an increasing share of the U.S. market, to the point that 10 percent of lighting fixtures sold in the United States in 1987 were imported. Most imports come from Asia, about half from Taiwan. There are about 350 reg-istered lighting manufacturers and at least as many unregistered ones. When a new design appears to be successful, it is quickly copied, with the result that Taiwanese firms cut prices to gain sales of essentially similar products: The cost of producing a Taiwanese lamp is estimated to be one-third of that of a similar U.S. product. Further, most of the Taiwanese industry's output (about 75 percent) is sold to trading companies.

Annual wages in Taiwan and South Korea were about $3,800 and $2,600, respectively, in 1985, and the lack of regulation of the labor market means that overall wage costs are not increased by the costs of compliance with government standards on matters such as fringe benefits, job safety, and EPA regulations. Europe is another major source of imports, accounting for 24 percent of total U.S. imports, principally from Italy (10 percent) and Spain (7 percent).

Having rapidly grown as a purveyor of fashionable lighting at low prices, Catalina's ways of doing business are worth examining.

## Design/New Product Ideas

David Moss, chairman of Catalina, has said, "A pioneer is a guy who walks around with arrows in his back. I might try to make it better, but I only offer to the mass market what I know will sell." Catalina's designers visit lighting trade shows in the United States and Europe to identify new styles most likely to appeal to fashion-conscious consumers. Catalina then designs similar fixtures based on ideas derived from the shows. It provides these designs, shipping drawings and pictures taken from catalogs to factories in the Far East. Catalina does not pretend to be original, seeing its ability to market proven designs that sell well as a reason for its success. Thus, a European chandelier that retails for $350 in a traditional lighting store can be found in a Catalina clone version for about $125 retail.

Case prepared by Associate Professor Ravi Sarathy for use in classroom discussion. All rights reserved. Source: Ed Cabrera, "Catalina Lighting: Detailed Study," Raymond James & Associates, St. Petersburg, Fla., December 16, 1988; R. Jerry Falkner, "Catalina Lighting, Investment Opinion," Gulfstream Financial Associates, Boca Raton, Fla., January 17, 1989; *Catalina Lighting Prospectus,* May 9, 1989; *Catalina Lighting Annual and 10 K Report,* year ended September 30, 1988.; Larry Birger, "Catalina Lighting on Orient Express," *Miami Herald,* February 13, 1989.

Catalina devotes development efforts to ensure a constant stream of new products. Over 100 new products are introduced annually, with current emphasis on outdoor lighting products, such as a motion-sensing infrared model, as well as solar-powered lighting products. It has over 850 different models in its current product line, including chandeliers, recessed lighting, track lighting, security lighting, and table and floor lamps, pole lamps, and torchieres ranging in price from $1.50 to $400.

| Catalina Product Categories June 1987 to June 1988 | |
| --- | --- |
| Outdoor Lighting | 40 |
| Ceiling Fans | 20 |
| Bathroom Fixtures | 15 |
| Table Lamp | 10 |
| Others | 15 |

However, sales within product categories can change considerably from year to year. For example, as homeowners spend more on remodeling bathrooms, Catalina has added new bathroom fixture products to expand sales and take advantage of this fad.

In the outdoor lighting area, both lighting and security are being sold. Catalina introduced a product retailing for under $30 in which passive infrared motion-sensor switches go on when there is motion within range of an infrared sensing field. Such products had been selling for over $100 a unit, and Catalina's launch of a fashionable product at low prices was an immediate success, garnering sales of over $2 million.

A similar strategy of introducing a lower-priced version of a successful new idea can be seen in Catalina's solar-powered outdoor light, which uses photoelectric cells, turning on automatically at dusk and off at dawn.

## Safety/UL Seal of Approval

Catalina has worked with Underwriters Laboratories (UL) to make sure that its products get speedy UL approval (within two to three months), which is important in marketing electrical products. Catalina assigns engineers solely to this assignment. Two of Catalina's employees worked previously at UL.

## Manufacturing: Subcontracting in the Far East

*Catalina does not manufacture anything that it sells.* After lamps are designed in Miami, the design is submitted for UL testing, while, concurrently, manufacturing planning begins with manufacturers in the Far East, overlapping with the UL process and thus reducing manufacturing lead time to about one to two months. Catalina can get a new product from initial design to display at retailers in *three to six months*. As noted earlier, being first to market can generate additional sales. Quotations from the manufacturers are priced in dollars, as are customers' orders, to avoid exposure to exchange rate fluctuations.

## Manufacturing Control/ Independent Agents

Fourteen independent agents based in Taiwan and Hong Kong work with Catalina to supervise manufacturing; they frequently visit plants to ensure that they meet the company's and UL specifications and expedite orders so that delivery times can be met. Most important, they inspect the finished product before shipping. When UL certification is obtained, UL issues a listing report that provides a technical description of the fixture. It provides manufacturers selected by the company with procedures to follow in producing the products, and periodically requires inspections of products at such manufacturers. Catalina uses over 70 independent plants in Taiwan, South Korea, Hong Kong, and the People's Republic of China. To lower risk, Catalina always uses at least two factories in different countries to manufacture fixtures under contract. However, its upper management is directly involved in major buying decisions (signing subcontracting manufacturing contracts), and buying decisions can be made quickly to take advantage of opportunities.

## Direct Sales to Large Clients (Home-Improvement Stores)

Catalina uses a direct sales method whereby large clients buy container lots, shipped directly from the Far East manufacturers to the clients. The goods become the responsibility of the retailer once they leave the foreign port, with the retailer responsible for all freight costs, insurance, customs clearance, and payment of customs duties.

Catalina pays manufacturers after receiving payment itself. That is, upon receipt of a customer's letter of credit, Catalina establishes a separate letter of credit payable to the manufacturer. But a key proviso is that draws may not be made by the manufacturer until Catalina is entitled to be paid under the terms of the customer's letter of credit. Catalina draws on its customers' letter of credit once the goods have been inspected by its agents and accepted, delivered to the overseas ports, and the appropriate documentation, (title to goods) presented to the bank that issued the letter of credit within the established time period.

This system developed because Catalina at startup had little working capital. It therefore attempted to work with clients who were willing to finance the entire shipment. These large clients are home-improvement stores catering to the Do It Yourself (DIY) market; Catalina's first such customer was Pay'n Pak, a chain store based in Seattle. Such clients accounted for 65 percent of revenues in the year ending September 30, 1988.

## Innovation in Distribution Channels and Packaging

Selling through home-improvement chains is itself an innovation. Light fixtures were traditionally sold through lighting showrooms, which provided advice and information about the product, delivery, and installation service. Catalina pioneered in selling lighting fixtures through home-improvement stores. Its largest clients are Payless Cashways, Lowe's, Wickes, Home Depot, Gross-

man's, Hechinger, Channel Home Center, Builder's Square, Rickel, and Home Club. DIY chains have themselves been growing as more homeowners have taken up remodeling. Products sold through such stores must then be designed for easy assembly.

When sold through lighting showrooms, the fixtures were packaged in plain cardboard boxes, with salespeople describing product features and charging for installation. With the move to home-improvement stores, clerks had to educate customers about the product as well as provide instructions on installation. This proved burdensome, and the stores needed a way to stress self-service and convenience. This change in the channels of distribution for lighting fixtures led Catalina to repackage the goods in full-color litho boxes, enabling retailers to develop self-service lighting departments for their stores. Assembly instructions were printed directly on the colorful and attractive boxes designed to stand out on crowded shelves.

Catalina has achieved considerable penetration in the large home-improvement segment, selling to 16 of the 20 largest chains, but only having 14 of the next 80 retailers as clients. Future growth could thus come from greater penetration of the small retailer segment. Catalina has begun targeting mass merchandisers and department stores as outlets for its products.

## Warehouse Sales to Smaller Clients

Catalina also sells from warehouses in California, Florida, New Jersey, and Dallas, to smaller companies that cannot afford to buy in container lots and do not want to provide letters of credit. They are willing to pay a higher price for the privilege of not having to place orders many months in advance and being able to buy a larger assortment but in smaller quantities. In this case, Catalina is responsible for all shipping and customs costs, and risk is higher, since Catalina carries the full inventory necessary to speedily ship orders from stock. Catalina must also issue letters of credit and banker's acceptances to get inventory for its warehouses, since it is now buying for

### Distribution Channels for Lighting Products (Based on Units)

| Distribution Channel | 1970 Percent | 1987 Percent |
| --- | --- | --- |
| Lighting showrooms | 61% | 28% |
| Home-improvement stores | 10 | 35 |
| General merchandise | 12 | 17 |
| Other | 17 | 20 |

Source: Quoted in Ed Cabrera, "Catalina Lighting: Detailed Study," *Home Lighting & Accessories,* Raymond James & Associates, St. Petersburg, Fla., December 16, 1988.

its own account. It went public in May 1988, selling 920,000 shares for $2.6 million net, and it used $2 million of the proceeds to buy inventory in order to expand its warehouse operations.

Such warehouses also allow Catalina to provide emergency shipments of items in demand that retailers have run out of. In return, it gets a higher margin on such sales. It has been trying to increase the portion of its total sales made to smaller clients from its warehouses as a way of increasing profit margins. In the year ending September 1988, warehouse sales were over $9 million, 136 percent greater than in 1987.

These sales to smaller clients are handled through 15 manufacturer's representatives, who are nonexclusive and sell from the company's catalog, being compensated on a commission basis. Catalina also carries out some private-brand sales.

## Low Prices: Economies of Scale in Outsourcing

Initially, Catalina bought from a few factories in Taiwan. Over time, it became the largest buyer of lighting fixtures in Taiwan, and it currently subcontracts manufacturing with over 70 factories in four countries. As the largest buyer, it has gained considerable negotiating clout, and negotiating low prices from the manufacturers translates into lower purchasing costs. Thus, a fixture that might sell for $200 in a lighting showroom would retail for around $79.95 at Home Depot, courtesy of Catalina's economy-minded approach to design and manufacture.

However, as Mike Gaines, a merchandising manager for Grossman's, points out: "We use Catalina because it offers a quality product at an excellent price." And Mr. Kirchner, merchandising manager with the midwest Handy Andy chain, notes, "There are plenty of low-cost importers who offer lighting out of the Orient. But none except Catalina offers a complete program, and if we run out of a product, they can deliver extra product in a hurry" (from its large and complete line of inventory maintained in warehouses).

A characteristic of its outsourcing is a no-return policy on direct sales once the manufacturing agent has inspected and approved a shipment. Under the retailer agreement, a "defective" allowance is netted from the invoice for any unsalable product. Retailers cannot return a product once it is delivered unless they can prove that the lot had an unusually large number of unacceptable products. It is notable that Catalina manufacturing agents reject nearly one-third of all products inspected prior to shipment.

## Cooperative Marketing with Windmere

As Catalina relies heavily on low-cost imports to compete in U.S. markets, efficient outsourcing becomes critical. Windmere, with its long experience in the People's Republic of China, where it employs 10,000 people in its factory in southern China, has agreed to produce quality products for Catalina in its mainland China factories. As wages there are even lower than in South Korea and Taiwan, this could help Catalina cut labor costs by about a third over that of Taiwan, which will be important as competition increases. Windmere has also provided advice in establishing a subsidiary in Hong Kong so as to cut taxes paid by 20 to 30 percent.

Catalina recently arranged to let Windmere buy a 19 percent ownership share, and has signed a cross-selling agreement. Windmere, which sells low-price hair-care appliances, will introduce Catalina products into its channels of distribution, mainly drug stores and catalog showrooms; it will also help market Catalina products in Canada, while Catalina will attempt to persuade its clients, the home-improvement chains, to carry Windmere hair dryers, fans, and air cleaners. This agreement has led to Catalina products being sold through the catalog retailers who currently handle Windmere products.

## Customer Service

Manufacturer's representatives service about 150 accounts, while David Moss, CEO, and Robert Hersh, executive vice-president, personally service the top 25 accounts. Customers are naturally concerned about importing large quantities of product manufactured in distant Asia. Hence, Catalina schedules customer trips to Asia to permit first-hand observation of manufacturing facilities and products prior to shipping.

## Geographic Expansion by Acquisition

With a supply pipeline in place, Catalina began focusing on expanding its distribution. In this effort, it purchased Unitex sales, a Dallas-based firm that sells light fixtures and ceiling fans under the Christina brand name. The acquisition would add about $18 million to sales in fiscal 1989, with some seasonal diversification in that ceiling fans are mostly sold in the April-to-June period. Further, Christina products were sold in some home-improvement chains not yet penetrated by Catalina; thus, Christina was strong in sales to Payless Cashways, Lowe's Co., Channel Home Center, Builder's Square, and Rickel.

Much of Catalina's success is due to its chairman and president, David Moss, who is the largest shareholder in the firm, with about a one-third ownership. Moss worked as senior vice-president at Keller Industries, an aluminum processor, where he managed sales growth from $85 to $130 million in three years. He then went on his own, importing wooden doors, lock sets, and electric heaters. Moss Manufacturing was established in 1980, doing $70 million in sales of ceiling fans within three years. Moss then turned to light fixtures, in part because he would be selling to the same buyers he had dealt with when selling ceiling fans. Moss humorously observes that when he was in the ceiling fan business, he was always praying for hot weather. And when he used to sell heaters, he wanted cold weather. But in the lighting business, he does not have to worry, because it always gets dark.

Margins were high in the lighting industry, and Moss felt that he could break into the industry by shaving margins, grabbing chain-store buyers' attention (and getting initial orders) with prices half that of competition. Low prices and a quality product, bright and colorful packaging, understandable assembly instructions, and a large variety of products (over 500 styles of lighting accessories) all helped Catalina obtain shelf space.

Catalina's planning of sourcing and marketing have enabled it to capture about 2 percent of the U.S. market. Tables 1 and 2 provide income statements and balance sheets for Catalina showing that it doubled its profit from 1987 to 1988, with return on equity of 27 percent in fiscal 1988.

Looking to the future, Catalina plans to expand into Canada with Windmere's help. Windmere already has experience and a distribution system in place in Canada. Catalina has also begun exporting to the European market, with orders for $2 million from British and Belgian customers. This includes orders from G.B. Inno, Belgium's largest retailer and owner of major interests in Scotty's and Handy Andy, themselves among the major home-improvement chains in the United States, and established Catalina customers. In Britain, direct sales are made to an

**Table 1   Catalina Lighting, Inc. Income Statement: Year Ended September 30, 1986, 1987, 1988, and First Half of 1989 (Millions of Dollars)**

|  | 1989 (6 Months) | 1988 | 1987 | 1986 |
|---|---|---|---|---|
| Net sales | 22.1 | 26.9 | 19.8 | 11.8 |
| Cost of sales | 18.3 | 22.3 | 16.9 | 10.2 |
| Gross profit | 3.8 | 4.6 | 2.8 | 1.6 |
| SGA expense | 1.9 | 2.9 | 2.0 | 1.3 |
| Operating income | 1.9 | 1.7 | .8 | .3 |
| Other expenses | .3 | .1 | .1 | .1 |
| Profit before tax | 1.6 | 1.6 | .7 | .2 |
| Net income | 1.1 | 1.0 | .4 | .2 |

**Table 2   Catalina Lighting, Inc. Balance Sheet: Year Ended September 30, 1986, 1987, 1988 and First Half of 1989 (Millions of Dollars)**

|  | 1989 (6 Months) | 1988 | 1987 | 1986 |
|---|---|---|---|---|
| Current assets: |  |  |  |  |
|   Cash | 1.2 | .2 | .7 | — |
|   Accounts receivable | 7.0 | 3.7 | 1.4 | 1.8 |
|   Inventory | 12.3 | 6.7 | 1.2 | .4 |
|   Other | .4 | .2 | — | — |
|   Total current assets | 20.9 | 10.8 | 3.3 | 2.5 |
| Plant and equipment | .7 | .3 | .2 | .1 |
| Other | .6 | .5 | .1 | — |
| Total assets | 22.2 | 11.6 | 3.6 | 2.6 |
| Current liabilities: |  |  |  |  |
|   Notes payable | 11.3 | 4.2 | 1.0 |  |
|   Accounts payable | 2.2 | 2.0 | 1.2 |  |
|   Other | .2 | .5 | .4 |  |
|   Total current liabilities | 13.7 | 6.7 | 2.6 | 2.0 |
| Long-term debt | .1 | — | — | .2 |
| Convertible debentures |  | — | .1 | .2 |
| Stockholders equity | 8.4 | 4.8 | .8 | .4 |
| Total liabilities | 22.2 | 11.6 | 3.6 | 2.6 |

independent distributor. The Catalina trademark is registered in the United States, West Germany, France, and the Benelux countries, with trademark applications pending in other countries in Europe and the Far East. Catalina has established European offices in Germany and Belgium. Beyond that, warehouses are planned for Perth, Scotland; Sydney, Australia; and Tokyo, to aid in developing sales in these market regions. It has also begun factoring receivables to reduce risks of exposure to a few large clients (the major home-improvement chains) while also conserving working capital.

## Questions

1. Discuss the comparative advantage and the competitive advantage possible in the lighting fixture industry.
2. How has Catalina Lighting taken advantage of the comparative and competitive advantage features noted in your answer to Question 1 to configure and coordinate its value-added chain?
3. What are some of the major strategic choices at Catalina that help make a success of its basic philosophy of sourcing overseas?
4. What are some of the weaknesses of Catalina Lighting?
5. What are the sources of potential competition for Catalina?
6. Could Catalina's customers bypass Catalina and buy direct from Taiwan, South Korea, and other countries?
7. What do you see as problems facing Catalina? How should Catalina plan to change in the future?
8. Are you optimistic about Catalina's prospects for the future? What would you recommend?

# CHAPTER 18

# The Future of International Marketing

*Learning Objectives*    International marketing is about identifying the needs of customers around the world and then satisfying these needs better than one's competitors. Consequently, the future of international marketing will be shaped by how global customer needs are changing and how global competition is evolving to satisfy those needs.

The main goals of this chapter are to

1.  Describe what is happening in global markets and how global customers are changing.
2.  Describe how the global competitive system is evolving.
3.  Discuss the ways in which a firm can respond in order to gain a competitive edge in global markets.

## Global Customers and Global Markets

The phrase *global markets* points to a major evolution of the global economy. The world is truly composed of many markets. It used to be that firms could prosper by selling mainly to the American market. But the triad economy is now a fact of life. Japan and its neighboring countries constitute a bloc of fast-growing economies with considerable discretionary incomes. A second major bloc is Europe, poised for further growth and prosperity with the coming of a "single Europe" in 1992. The third bloc is United States–Canada and its neighbors, also a pool of wealth and purchasing power. Table 18–1 summarizes the size and wealth of the three major developed economies.

**The Japanese Opportunity**    Japan offers one of the most attractive and difficult markets of the world. It ostensibly has one of the highest per capita incomes in the world, but standards of living are not as commensurately high. A study by the Union Bank of Switzerland (UBS) found that net domestic purchasing power in 1987 was twice as high in the United States as in Japan,[1] even though the yen had been appreciating against the dollar for the previous two years. By adjusting for what the Japanese could buy with their yen, UBS found that high prices in Japan canceled out the effect of high incomes.

**Table 18–1**                               **The Triad Economy, 1987**

| | GNP in Trillions of Dollars | Population in Millions |
|---|---|---|
| United States | $4.5 | 244 |
| European Community | 4.1 | 324 |
| Japan | 2.8 | 121 |

This represents a major opportunity for foreign companies. While Japanese savings rates are still high, domestic consumption and spending have been growing rapidly. A booming stock market, a rapid rise in Tokyo property prices, and an economy growing at over 6 percent a year have created Japanese prosperity. Finding themselves wealthy, the Japanese have begun to spend heavily on housing, on consumer durables, on luxury goods. If foreign companies can penetrate the Japanese market and can match Japanese products in quality, high domestic prices will provide a wedge with which to gain market share from Japanese firms.

Domestic prices are high in Japan because of its internal distribution system, with far too many small retailers tied to specific suppliers, and granted liberal credit and offered liberal sales-return policies. The system is inefficient, and there is little pressure to discount prices.[2] Thus, if foreign companies can penetrate the Japanese market, and if they can cut prices while matching quality, they stand to gain significant market share. This is the Japanese challenge and opportunity.

**Japan's Neighbors**

While Japan is important in itself as one of the wealthy nations of the world, its neighboring countries are growing even faster. South Korea, Taiwan, Hong Kong, Singapore, Malaysia, and Thailand are among the fastest-growing countries of the world, with Taiwan's per capita income exceeding $7,000, and Taiwan now becoming actively involved in providing foreign aid to the developing countries.

Simply put, the growth in discretionary incomes in these areas make them attractive to companies, whether they be from the United States or elsewhere. The net result of economic growth around the world is that in nearly every industry sector over half the potential world demand is outside the United States; this is why global markets and global marketing are important.

**The Opportunities of a Single Europe**

Europe has always been an important market for U.S. companies because of geographic and cultural proximity. The passage of the Single Europe Act and the forecasted impact of a single Europe in 1992 has raised worldwide interest in European markets. Barriers that are physical, technical, and fiscal in nature are expected to disappear, including

• Border controls.

- Divergent product standards.
- Different technical regulations.
- Conflicting business laws.
- Protected public procurement.
- Differences in taxation (value-added taxes, or VAT, and excise taxes).

The real gains of 1992 may lie in the removal of these barriers, which together have served to stop entrepreneurs in one European country from entering the same business in other European countries. But the removal of barriers can also benefit non-European companies provided they receive the same treatment as European firms. From a marketing perspective, the gains are great from not having to adapt a product to the divergent standards of 12 different countries. Similarly, companies will benefit from being able to compete for government orders with a superior product; this was a market segment formerly closed to all but national companies.

The reasoning behind creating a single Europe is that the enlarged single market will lead to more competition; at the same time, the larger market created through merging the various national markets will allow larger-volume production, leading to economies of scale and thus bringing down costs. Enhanced competition, economies of scale, and the drive to greater efficiency should all lead to lower consumer prices, more jobs, higher profits, and ultimately, a more prosperous Europe.[3] Not surprisingly, companies from the United States and Japan, as well as from other countries, have been busy establishing themselves in Europe awaiting the coming of 1992. The concern here is that they be treated as insiders, and not discriminated against in case a fortress-Europe mentality sets in. Table 2A-1 (in the Appendix to Chapter 2) summarized the scale of the European markets and suggested why they represent enormous potential.

## Liberalization in Eastern Europe

Another interesting market trend is the liberalization movement in eastern Europe and in Russia itself. After decades of stagnation and dead-end economic philosophies, these nations have suddenly decided on a free-market orientation. While the eastern European nations are relatively small in size and population, they all possess a relatively well-educated workforce; in addition, Russia has the attraction of a large domestic population and significant technological capabilities in some areas. Participating in their economic growth will mean getting direct access to a market with increasing purchasing power and long-repressed consumption desires.

While these internal markets may be slow to develop, they represent an intriguing challenge. The eastern European countries and their firms are not accustomed to working with Western-style profit-oriented enterprises, and this could be an obstacle to growth initially. But helping these economies to develop through participating in their export-oriented industries, and supplying them much-needed hard currency, will prove to be an advantage at a later stage when their domestic market begins to grow. Table 18–2 summarizes the promise of eastern European markets. Incidentally, developing countries present much the same opportunity profiles as eastern Eu-

**Table 18-2**                          **Marketing Implications of Change in Eastern Europe**

1. Eastern Europe is backward and will want to develop. It will be a market for capital goods and technology.
2. It lacks a private sector. A market for consumer goods may be slow to develop, though there is much repressed demand.
3. Wages are low, hence they can be a source of low-cost production. For example, GM produces autos in Hungary for this reason.
4. Health-care and food products are likely to be growth markets.
5. The main mode of entry is likely to be joint ventures and countertrade. Eastern Europe lacks capital with which to buy foreign goods, hence the importance of countertrade. And export-oriented ventures will receive high priority.

ropean countries. They are also similarly beset with the need to grow and raise domestic standards of living, while suffering from shortages of capital, outmoded ideologies, and wasteful anti-business bureaucracies. Less developed countries also offer immense market potential, particularly for basic products and consumer durables, as they strive for economic growth.

**Global Markets, but Distinct Markets.**   There are significant differences among the growing markets in Europe and the Far East. Even within the United States, there is a large and growing Hispanic market for which distinct marketing and advertising themes are needed. Hence, a continuing basic issue for companies will be that of standardization versus differentiation. While homogenization of tastes and moves such as the creation of a single Europe encourage product standardization, cultural and historical differences are sufficiently strong that some adaptation will be beneficial in increasing market share. The marketing challenge lies in knowing how much standardization is appropriate, and in deciding which elements of the product mix should be adapted to individual country and regional markets.

**More Customers for New Products.**   The rise of global markets means that the total market size for new products is expanding. In looking over new-product introductions of the past decade, we find several new products that have been successful in all of the triad economies. For example:

- The personal stereo popularly known as the Walkman.
- The "fax" machine.
- Express mail and overnight small-package delivery services.
- The entire packaged software industry (as opposed to developing custom software for individual clients).
- Compact disk players and compact disk records.
- Mountain bikes.

The list above includes consumer products, business products, and services. Clearly, there will always be a market for well-thought-out new products. The difference is that these new products can now be sold in several middle- and upper-income countries in the Far East, Europe, and North

America. A successful product can yield even higher profits, and the larger total market justifies taking more risk and spending larger amounts on R&D.

**The Newly Rich: A Growing Global Market Segment.**   A striking aspect of new products is the entire category of "luxury goods".[4] By this we mean products such as Chanel perfumes and scarves, Gucci shoes and handbags, Lalique crystal, Vuitton luggage, haute couture in Paris, and Patek Phillipe watches. Common to these products is the idea that price is irrelevant. These products are as likely to be purchased in Japan, Taiwan, and Hong Kong as in Europe or the United States. Their market has expanded enormously. We can talk of a homogenization of taste for luxury products. More to the point, however, is the spread of a profitable consumer market segment across countries, a spread from the Old World to the New, and then to the newly rich Orient. The rise of global markets is also giving rise to new and larger market segments across countries, which may have been ignored previously as too narrow to be profitable. Firms need to be attentive to these emergent phenomena of the global marketplace.

**Services.**   As noted in Chapter 16, services are becoming increasingly important in world trade. Just as in the goods sector, foreign multinationals are beginning to challenge U.S. dominance in services. In some sectors, such as banking, European and Japanese banks have already caught up with U.S. firms. In others, such as international airlines, foreign airlines are moving fast to establish international networks as they seek market share in the growing Pacific Rim markets. Marketing services internationally is a major growth and profit opportunity, and a sector that will become intensely competitive.

## How Is Global Competition Evolving?

What makes a firm competitive in world markets? Table 18–3 summarizes the key factors. Global competition is intense and likely to become more so. As firms become larger in size, they seek to sell to all major markets in order to spread their growing fixed costs over a larger sales volume. But global competition is not limited to competing for sales and market share. It is also a competition for knowledge and scarce resources. In any industry, multinationals avidly seek to nullify their competitor's technological edge.

**Technology in the Global Marketplace**

The search for information by multinationals leads to rapid spread of scientific knowledge and reduces the long-term competitive edge of having proprietary knowledge.[5] This fact of life in the global arena has two implications: One, a firm with proprietary knowledge had better constantly innovate and produce new technology; and two, if a technology advantage will be short-lived, the firm should earn rents from it by rapidly marketing it in the global marketplace. This can be accomplished by manufacture and worldwide sale of products embodying the technology, perhaps with joint-venture partners, or by licensing the technology. What matters is that the technology be marketed in a timely enough manner to reap its benefits.

**Table 18–3**                          **Factors Affecting Competitiveness**

1. *Wage rates.* If a product is labor-intensive, a low-wage country has an advantage.
2. *Productivity.* If workers work harder, produce better-quality products, using more up-to-date machines, the company/country is more efficient.
3. *Cost of capital.* If it costs less to borrow money or raise equity capital, a company can invest more and accept lower returns.
4. *Technology.* A country or company that is the first with an advanced-technology product, which can be protected by patents, has an advantage.
5. *Management.* This covers a variety of skills, including manufacturing and marketing skills, as well as ability to organize for worldwide operations. This is primarily a firm-specific issue, arising out of the quality and experience of its human resources.
6. *Government.* Domestic companies can be helped by their government's industrial policy providing subsidized funds for new-product research, development, and marketing. Government can also be a negative factor by over-regulation, high taxes, and controls on industry. In particular, the U.S. government, by running a budget deficit, drives up interest rates and hence the cost of capital.
7. *Exchange rates.* Prices charged in world markets are affected by exchange rates. As a currency gets stronger, it is harder to sell overseas; at the same time, the strong currency makes imports cheaper, driving up demand for imports.
8. *Country-specific factors.* A better-educated population, with a culture that stresses hard work, savings, and a concern for society at large is more likely to be competitive in world markets.

## Environmental Factors Affecting Global Competition

Some environmental forces that affect the firm's success in global markets are

- Government intervention, protection and subsidies.
- Fluctuating exchange rates.
- High uncertainty, caused by rapid unforeseeable change.

These environmental forces will either undercut or enhance the firm's marketing and managerial efforts, in the same way that a headwind or a tailwind can slow down or speed up an aircraft. Their impact will be even greater in the future, so marketing managers must be ever more alert to incorporating environmental effects in formulating their marketing plans and tactics.

For example, government intervention may result in more managed trade. In such cases, the firm's own government must be enlisted as a player in order to obtain support and win market share overseas. Government intervention may also be defensive, providing subsidies to enable the firm to recover from overwhelming foreign competition. If a system of tailored trade gains dominance, firms might be best off deciding to locate manufacturing and marketing facilities in each of the three triad economy blocs — Japan, the United States, and Europe. This may be suboptimal, yet pragmatic.

Firms also need a long-range strategy to cope with exchange rate fluctuations, paying heed to short-term transaction effects and also to longer-term competitive and market portfolio exposure. An environment with increased uncertainty places a premium on cautious management, one that avoids leverage, shares risk, and aims for steady long-term results rather than attempting to buy short-term market share and manage short-term earnings.

## How Can the Firm Gain an Edge in Global Markets?

A firm's competitive advantage derives from four sources:

- Labor productivity and labor costs.
- The cost of capital.
- Technology, both product and process.
- Management and marketing skills, including speed of response, process manufacturing skills, and design skills.

We have just seen that the technology is not long-lasting and by itself is a precarious basis for long-term competitive advantage. Both cost of capital and labor cost are comparative advantages accruing to an entire economy rather than to one particular firm in a specific country. This leaves labor productivity and management skills, including marketing, as the central source of firm-specific and firm-controllable competitive advantage. *In other words, the company that markets the best will win out.*

**The Strategic Challenge of 1992 and a Single Europe**

One of the notable examples of government intervention affecting corporate strategy is the movement to create a single European market in 1992. Table 18–4 summarizes some of the strategic implications of this event for U.S. corporations.

As can be seen from Table 18–4, 1992 will require responses in all areas, not just marketing. Firms can best exploit the market potential of a single Europe by being aware of all strategic ramifications.

**Beyond 1992: Strategic Areas of Prime Importance**

Going beyond 1992, global marketing strategy will be affected by certain strategy areas:

- Technology, and the related areas of incremental innovation and time-based competition.
- Marketing itself, principally the question of global brands, and their relation to other product attributes.
- Organization, and adaptation to strategic alliances, as well as the role of personal contacts in international markets.
- Control issues, including the role of global information systems.

**Technology.**    We begin with technology since it is a fundamental source of new products. The pressing need is for applied technology that can be used to develop consumer and industrial products, rather than one-of-a-kind custom military products. Ideally, technology should be produced to serve customer needs, rather than technological advances determining what products

| Table 18–4 | 1992: Strategic Issues for U.S. Corporations |
|---|---|

*Competition:*

> Stronger European companies.
> Less allowance for inefficiency.
> Europe-wide, not national, competition.

*Entry Strategies:*

> Expansion and acquisition.
> Foreign direct investment.
> Joint ventures and alliances: "twinning."
> Shakeouts and restructuring.

*Government Relations:*

> Government and industry associations to counter protectionism.
> Lobbying in Brussels.

*Manufacturing:*

> Rationalization; larger, flexible plants.
> Plant location; "greenfield" (starting from scratch) versus acquisition.
> Logistics and JIT (just-in-time) implications.

*Marketing:*

> Sheer size: Europe will be as large as the U.S. market.
> Aim at European rather than discrete national markets.
> Europe-wide coordination and planning, restructuring of existing
>   organization.
> Europe-wide brands, distribution, pricing and servicing.
> But national cultures will not disappear.

*R&D:*

> The effects of European government programs and subsidies.
> "Local content" applied to R&D activities.
> Cross-licensing.
> The standards issue: global versus European versus U.S. standards.

are developed. Furthermore, with consumer products, it is incremental innovation that matters rather than being the first to market with a new product. Companies must monitor new-product introductions by competition and then not only match them but improve on them.

If a new product is protected by patents,[6] competitors might try engineering around the innovation or perhaps mount a challenge to the patent — a viable strategy only for large companies competing against minnows. The real solution is to buy the needed technology, deliberately developing a strategy of cross-licensing. We earlier made reference to the quick spread of knowledge. One result is that no one company can expect to dominate all technologies. Even IBM has begun forging strategic alliances to obtain crucial technologies not available in-house. Developing new semiconductor chips is becoming so risky that IBM is teaming up with Siemens to develop 64 megabit DRAMS for sale in the mid-1990s.[7] Thus, cross-licensing and strategic alliances, together with incremental innovation, will become the backbone of new-product development efforts in the future.[8] Strategic alliances are particularly important to small firms, where resource scarcity and a lack of capital may hinder attempts to penetrate overseas markets. Such alliances also allow the smaller firm to share the risk of global market entry and allow it to enter several country markets in a timely, nearly simultaneous manner.

*Incremental innovation* is about making things better than the competition: better quality, more features, at lower cost, providing better service and for longer periods. Manufacturing is involved here. Engineers working with salespeople and product designers increases the probability of creating new products that appeal to customers yet can be produced at high quality and reasonable cost. As suggested earlier in this text, marketing has linkages with other areas of the enterprise, notably technology and manufacturing.

Another emerging basis for competition is time. Being able to respond quickly to the marketplace and to competitive moves gives a firm a competitive edge. Such a quick-response capability depends heavily on design engineers and process technology. For example, new developments in flexible manufacturing allow companies to manufacture small batches of products quickly and economically. This reduces the importance of economies of scale and gives an advantage to the firm that can satisfy customers with a large variety of products.

**Marketing.**   What about marketing itself? Are there crucial aspects of international marketing strategy that can help firms in the global marketplace? *Global brand* development is certainly one such concept.[9] There are few truly global brands, perhaps only one — Coca-Cola. A Landor Associates study showed Coke to have the number one brand-awareness and esteem position in the United States, number two in Japan, and number six in Europe. No other brand comes even close to being in the top ten in all three market areas. The only other global "brands" are media stars, such as Mick Jagger. Why is it so desirable to have a global brand?

A brand name allows a firm to charge more. Brands also ensure a certain degree of repeat purchases from loyal customers. Thus, a global brand could yield handsome returns on the investment necessary — through advertising and establishing a reputation for quality — to create it. Having a global brand means additional volume sales overseas, which in turn justifies additional expenditures to create new global brands and defend the established one.

There are many aspects to pursuing a global-brand policy. Acquiring brands is one way to establish market position quickly. Creating new brands is another, as Toyota seems to be doing with Lexus in the United States, and as Honda has accomplished with immense success with the Acura car line. (These brands seem to be approaching global status.) Once created, brands must be defended; they can wither away unless continually tended to. Brand families are important, as shown by American cereal companies who have been creating new cereals in response to such fads as the oat-bran obsession. And global brands can be applied to services as well as brands;

Singapore Airlines is an example of an attempt to create a global service brand.

Aside from branding, global marketing must pay attention to all of a product's attributes. Global firms are increasingly competing on the basis of quality, design, and service, more than on the basis of low prices. These attributes are what a brand often stands for: dependable, reliable, safe, with an implied warranty as to performance. It is not surprising that global firms seek to make explicit their product's merits in these areas.

**Organization.**   Global marketing requires people to implement plans, and coordinating their activities is of paramount concern. Companies have to balance the desire to centralize activities at headquarters and at regional centers against the demand for local autonomy and the desire of governments that the company be responsive to local concerns. Companies therefore have to determine which activities need centralized direction, and which would benefit from scale economies. Sensitivity to local concerns will shape the extent of decentralization.

An organization that can respond quickly must necessarily have few layers of management and be less hierarchical. The use of teams, greater autonomy for lower levels of the organization, and widespread dissemination of information and in-house expertise throughout the organization can speed up the response capability of the global organization.

Companies also need an organization conducive to managing strategic alliances, where the interests of two or more separate companies must be meshed and reconciled. When two major multinationals such as Siemens and IBM become partners in a major venture to produce 64 megabit DRAMS, both parties will want control. In practice, control will be shared. How should such shared-control structures be designed? What does centralization mean in such a context? Trust, shared goals, and informal communications are at least as important in such instances as the formal organization that is imposed.

Similarly, as the organization becomes global, a global network of personal contacts becomes important. An illustration of this fact comes from Chrysler's recent reentry into Europe. Chrysler had to leave Europe in the mid-1970s because of financial problems. In 1986, when Chrysler decided to sell in Europe again, it first called on an ex-Chrysler employee who was heading up Ford's operations in Europe. Next, it contacted all the auto distributors who had been selling Chrysler products in the 1970s. Through this network, it was able to find qualified people and in some cases, finance their entry into business as Chrysler distributors in Europe. It was personal contacts that allowed Chrysler to put in place a distributor organization spanning West Germany, France, Switzerland, Holland, and Belgium within a short period of time, ready for the launch of the Plymouth Voyager wagon and the Cherokee Jeep.[10]

**Control.**   Going global will require greater attention to performance evaluation, so as not to fritter away scarce resources in unpromising markets and on failing products. The major issue here is to allow for long-term thinking rather than being swayed by short-term results and setbacks. U.S. publicly held firms have the unfortunate problem of being in the grip of pension-fund managers' obsession with quarterly earnings progression. Yet, they cannot compete against long-term oriented German and Japanese companies unless budgets and reward systems focus on long-term results. One proposal, put forth by Peter Drucker, is the use of a *futures budget,* amounting to about 10 percent of total expenses, that aims to build and preserve a company's long-term competitiveness. Such a futures budget would never be cut in bad times nor raised because results are good.[11] The concept is one that exemplifies the innovation in control systems that will be required to ensure that global marketing plans are not crippled by unrealistic budget expectations.

Innovation is also needed in the area of marketing measurements, such as in the development of product-profitability analysis. Here the goal is to derive a product's contribution after adjusting for factors such as margins, amount of time product is in inventory, the shelf space that it takes up, its share of direct advertising costs, direct service and warranty costs, and so forth. Modeling in domestic marketing is fairly advanced, and similar efforts will be of great help in the global arena.

**Global Information Systems.**   Without constantly updated information from global markets, the company is driving in the dark without lights. The technological advances in point-of-sale systems, the use of scanners, and the availability of global computer networks that link factories, warehouses, salespeople, and retail establishments all allow a firm to get timely information on the evolution of demand and customer tastes. Such systems allow responsive pricing, facilitate just-in-time purchasing systems with suppliers, and guide the product-development process. The use of EDI (electronic data interchange) with suppliers dispenses with paperwork and speeds up order transmission direct from the factory floor as production progresses. Such EDI systems are beginning to be used at ports and by customs authorities in countries such as Singapore to speed up product flow into and out of the country, and to reduce bureaucracy. These systems also allow error-free application of tariffs and checks for compliance with documentation requirements.

When tied to the service network, an analysis of recurring product problems allows for better design and manufacturing. Such systems are needed to allow a firm to customize its production for individual customers, and to compete on the basis of variety rather than mass production. Information systems can build up customer histories and these databases can be accessed to develop relationship marketing, with directed marketing appeals to narrow segments of customers. Without detailed customer histories, such advances are not possible. Information is a strategic weapon, and in global marketing, it can give a firm the competitive edge.

In sum, companies must compete globally. They must strive to be different from their competitors, and a focus on marketing and its linkages to the rest of the firm is essential to global marketing success.

# Endnotes

[1] "Pity Those Poor Japanese," *The Economist,* December 24, 1988.

[2] "Japan's Consumer Boom: The Pricey Society," *The Economist,* September 9, 1989.

[3] P. Cecchini, *The European Challenge: 1992, the Benefits of a Single Market* (Brookfield, Ver.: Gower Publishing, 1989).

[4] See, for example, "Lace at $300 a yard," *Forbes,* October 23, 1989; and "French Luxury Firms are Merging, Turning into Big Multinationals," *The Wall Street Journal,* December 28, 1987.

[5] Kim B. Clark, "What Strategy Can Do for Technology," *Harvard Business Review* (November–December 1989).

[6] The fact that technology cannot be the basis of long-run competitive advantage does not mean that patent protection is not a strategic weapon. See Robert J. Thomas, "Patent Infringement of Innovations by Foreign Competitors," *Journal of Marketing* (October 1989).

[7] "IBM Joins with Siemens AG to Develop Advanced Chips, Hoping to Share Risk," *The Wall Street Journal,* January 25, 1990.

[8] Ralph E. Gomory, "From the 'Ladder of Science' to the Product Development Cycle," *Harvard Business Review* (November–December 1989).

[9] "The Year of the Brand," *The Economist,* December 24, 1988.

[10] Michael Hammes, "Chrysler Kommt! Reestablishing a Brand in Europe," *The Journal of European Business* (January–February 1990).

[11] Peter Drucker, "The Futures That Have Already Happened," *The Economist,* October 21, 1989.

# Name and Company Index

# Subject Index